HARRY BRELSFORD'S SMB SERIES

MICROSOFT SMALL BUSINESS SPECIALIST PRIMER

Beatrice Mulzer
MCSE, MCT, USA SBS Hands-On Lab Instructor

Mei Ying Lim
MOSS MVP

SMB Nation Press

SMB Nation Press

P.O. Box 10179

Bainbridge Island, WA 98110-0179

360-779-1140

ISBN10: 0-9770949-6-0

ISBN13: 978-9770949-6-7

Cover Design: Michael Young

Editors: Barbara Wallace

Interior Layout: Stephanie Martindale

Proofreader: SaraLiz Klinedinst

Contents

Section I ❧ Small Business Specialist Community

Section II ✂ Exam 70-282

CHAPTER 3

Microsoft Small Business Specialist Primer
& 70-282 Exam Preparation Guide!

X

Visit www.microsoft.com/technet for the latest updates for any Microsoft product.

Section III ❧ Exam 70-631

Section IV ❧ Additional Exams and Assessments

Appendices

About The Authors

This book was thoughtfully written by two long-time Small Business Server users (affectionately known as SBSers) with significant international experience:

Beatrice Mulzer, Cocoa, Florida USA

Beatrice Mulzer is a Small Business Specialist and USA Small Business Server (SBS) Hands-on Lab instructor and a real world experienced SBS consultant. She hold the MCT and MCSE titles and develops and delivers Hands-on-Lab training on Microsoft products globally, conducts live training web casts and develops technical training courses on DVD. Beatrice is the executive editor of SMB Partner Community magazine, has written columns for Reseller Advocate Magazine and CERTIFICATION Magazine and MCP magazine. Beatrice is a contributing author in the *Advanced Windows Small Business Server 2003 Best Practices* book, ISBN 0-974858-03, Co-author of the *Microsoft Small Business Specialist Primer & 70-282 Exam Preparation Guide* ISBN 0-974858-03 and author of *Making IT Big in Small Business 2006*, ISBN 0-9770949-2-8. In her spare time she plays with the latest Microsoft software releases and cycles for miles on end. Beatrice currently lives in the Florida sunshine state.

Mei Ying Lim, Singapore

Mei Ying Lim, MOSS MVP, is a Senior Consultant at Avanade, a global technology integrator specializing in the Microsoft platform. Mei Ying has extensive experience in designing, implementing and supporting enterprise web applications as well as setting up Microsoft Content Management Server (MCMS) systems across the enterprise. An active contributor to the Microsoft newsgroup community, she has spent many hours figuring out the dos and don'ts of MCMS technologies, and thrives on the challenge of finding new ways to solve MCMS-related problems. Mei Ying, who has earned the prestigious title of Microsoft's Most Valuable Professional award for Content Management Server. Mei Ying has co-authored *Building Websites with Microsoft Content Management Server*, *Advanced Microsoft Content Management Server Development* and *Enhancing Microsoft Content Management Server* with ASP.NET 2.0. Mei Ying lives on the sunny island of Singapore.

Dedication

To all eager small-business technology consultants around the globe seeking professional fulfillment and prosperity!

Acknowledgements

No writer is an island, although many writers live on islands. It takes a team to produce a book including the following kind souls who made good things happen to get this book to market!

Cyndi Moody– tireless operations manager at SMB Nation who continues to impress her peers daily with new feats of accomplishment.

Stephanie Martindale – Proved to the team daily that hard working honest people still get up at the crack of dawn, work two jobs, and deliver service with a smile. Great page layout work, Stephanie!

Barbara Wallace – our long-time magazine and book editor does it again.

Arlin Sorensen– a long-time SBSer who contributed Chapter 15.

SaraLiz Klinedinst – a super proof reader and new friend of SMB Nation!

Jennifer Hall – our events manager

Jonathan Hassell and **Jack Westbrooks** who each made significant contributions to this book.

Andy Goodman and **David Anderson** contributed the insightful Appendix C

FOREWORD
Are You Ready for the New SMB Revolution?

Humanity's advancement can be charted along a timeline of exploration and innovation. From the advent of fire to the age of the microchip, mankind has steadfastly charted new paths, set new directions, headed for new horizons.

It's in this spirit that we celebrate the beginning of another great journey. It may not seem to be the simple genius of sliced bread or the noble sacrifice of a mission to Mars, but Microsoft's entrance into the small/medium business (SMB) partner space is certainly worthy of notice.

Some would say it's about time the software giant more aggressively played in the important, growing market beyond the Fortune 1000. Others would counter Microsoft has already reached all markets, if only through trickle-down theories. Either way, a more formal strategy is emerging, and the book you're holding here is a good guide for those ready to blaze an expanded trail.

Kudos and congratulations to Beatrice Mulzer, emerging SBS guru, for writing this helpful volume. *Microsoft Small Business Specialist Primer* sets out to help IT professionals prepare and certify themselves for careers as Small Business Specialists. In an industry beset by outsourcing, automation, and general malaise, IT professionals could do much worse for themselves by coming to the same conclusion Microsoft obviously has: Working with businesses of *all* sizes drives continued commerce and offers new avenues for growth and development.

That's a message we at *Certification Magazine* can certainly get behind. Since our first issue in the days before the burst of the IT bubble, we've been preaching the message of continued growth, ongoing learning and creative solutions to problems of all types, from technology trials to careers stuck in neutral. Even with recession worries seemingly less pressing, the new opportunity for expansion Microsoft is offering couldn't be timelier. We can certainly hope *Microsoft Small Business Specialist Primer* and the Small Business Specialist certification it supports are just the first salvo in a barrage of books, certifications and opportunities for Microsoft to interact with its channel and channel members to take advantage of the certified skills of a loyal army of IT experts.

At *Certification Magazine,* we support the three-sided partnership that can breathe new life into the careers of individuals and into businesses small, medium and super-sized. In Harry and Beatrice's thorough work, you'll find a roadmap to a new specialty, a guidebook to new challenges and directions to sustainable success.

It's a new era for the certified IT professional. Are you ready to take the one giant step into small-medium businesses?

Tim Sosbe
Editorial Director
Certification Magazine
www.certmag.com

Preface

Welcome aboard and congratulations on your first steps toward becoming a Microsoft Small Business Specialist! This is an exciting new partner opportunity that was introduced worldwide by Microsoft in July 2005. Read on!

What This Book Is About

First and foremost, this book is really about how to become a Microsoft Small Business Specialist. Microsoft has set some VERY AGGRESSIVE worldwide recruitment goals for this new program and we're delighted to provide this "How To..." resource to help you become a successful Microsoft Small Business Specialist. We're happy knowing you're using our guide to better your station in life and improve your standard of living. Last time we checked, you only go around once in life, and we want to help you make the most of it.

This book fulfils its goal of supporting the new Small Business Specialist Community by emphasizing preparation for the Microsoft 70-2 82 certification exam: Designing, Deploying, and Managing a Network Solution for a Small- and Medium-Sized Business, which is one of the ways you can fulfill the Small Business Specialist certification exam prerequisites. We detected a distinct lack of study materials for the 70-2 82 exam.

A welcome addition to this book is the 70-631 Configuring Windows SharePoint Services 3.0 materials to fortify your efforts to pass this entry point into the Small Business Specialist Community program.

xxviii

Microsoft Small Business Specialist Primer
& 70-282 Exam Preparation Guide!

The alternative 74-134 certification exam: Preinstalling Microsoft Products using the Preinstallation Kit can be used to satisfy the certification exam requirement, so we allocate Chapter 14 in this book to that exam. Microsoft also has a business development/sales assessment that is required to become part of the Small Business Specialist Community (Chapter 15). Participants must successfully complete this assessment, and we provide guidance on how to do so in this book!

Something you've come to expect from SMB Nation books—balanced discussions of significant business issues and deep dives into technology areas—continue in this book. Our half-and-half approach is especially germane in the context of the Small Business Specialist Community. Why? Because the Small Business Specialist Community is really about business and technology. The materials speak to both camps and Microsoft is demonstrating a new appreciation that the small business technology consultant is really a business person and a tech-head!

This book wears a lot of hats: business, technical, preparation for different certification exams (with emphasis on the 70-282 exam), and preparatory discussion for a business-related assessment. Step back and reread that last sentence and think for a moment—doesn't that sound a lot like the multifaceted and joyfully fragmented day of a thriving small business consultant? Sure does, and this book captures that flavor from cover to cover.

And finally—this book is global. Beatrice started her life in Germany and is now an American citizen, so she brings a Euro-American perspective to the small business technology community. An American by birth, Harry is an experienced world traveler and he delivers SBS workshops in over 25 countries globally each year. Harry's international niche is developing countries, so you'll see appropriate discussion on opportunities that the "rest of us" can relate to!

How This Book Is Organized

This book is organized into three sections.

- **Section I** introduces you to the Small Business Specialist Community.

- **Section II** helps you prepare for passing the 70-282 certification exam.
- **Section III** prepares you for the 70-631 exam.
- **Section IV** considers the 74-134 certification exam and offers valuable insights on successfully completing the Small Business Sales and Marketing Skills Assessment.

Section I: Small Business Specialist Community

The discussion in this section is necessarily "business speak" to properly introduce the book and the Small Business Specialist Community. It sets the tone for this book and gets you jazzed about being a small business technology consultant. You'll see that your greatest wishes surrounding Microsoft and the small business community have been answered in spades. But you'll find the discussion balanced from a critical third-party perspective with "SMB Nation speak" and not "Microsoft speak." That's what you're paying for in this section.

Section II: Exam 70-282

This is the "red meat" of this book and clearly the topic area we're emphasizing. This cut-to-the-chase series of chapters map directly to the 70-282 exam topics. The content is presented at a sufficient level of depth to prepare the newbie, intermediate, and even advanced professional to PASS the 70-282 exam. We stay very focused on passing the exam, so when a discussion topic begins to stray beyond that scope, we point you to our other books where you can dive into deeper discussions. For example, for richer SBS setup and deployment information, who could forget the *Windows Small Business Server 2003 Best Practices* book, where over 100 pages are devoted to describing every nuance of SBS 2003 setup (to the point of being annoying!)? Want to know much more about SBS 2003 migrations beyond what you'll read in this book to pass the exam (and understand Microsoft's migration paradigm)? We refer you to Jeff Middleton's excellent Chapter 15 in the *Advanced Windows Small Business Server 2003 Best Practices* book. You get the point. Read this section, stay focused, and pass the 70-282 exam.

Section III: 70-631 Exam

The third section presents a popular certification exam surrounding Windows SharePoint Services 3.0. It is a new way of thinking for Small Business Specialists and clearly beyond the "server box" and elevates you past mere infrastructure. This is one of the few books in print that addresses this exam.

Section IV: Additional Exam and Assessment

The third and final section presents a certification exam alternative (74-134), which is applicable if you are a system builder seeking to use the Original Equipment Manufacturer (OEM) Preinstallation Kit. The book concludes with a chapter we can all rally around, which is guidance for successfully completing the Small Business Sales and Marketing Skills Assessment. You will receive some rich business discussion in that chapter. Those with a strong technical background but a weaker business skill set will truly appreciate this chapter.

Who Should Read This Book

Readers of this book fall into a few identifiable categories:

- **Newbies.** You're the apple of our eyes and much of the reason we wrote this book. Eat it up! We are salivating over the fact that there are thousands of newbies out there trying to improve their lives using Microsoft small business solutions and looking into becoming Small Business Specialists!

- **Experienced consultants.** The underlying paradigm woven in, around, and out of these pages is that more capable SBSers—those serving small business as trusted advisors and consultants—are aggressively seeking a leg up on their professional peer group and hoping to better serve their customers. Passing the 70-282 exam and becoming a Small Business Specialist are positive steps in this direction! And better yet – looking at the 70-631 exam could be a new career path!

- **Other channel members.** In addition to consultants, there are system builders, independent software vendors (ISVs), and distributors who also constitute part of the channel. A surprisingly strong readership group, these channel partners are seeking to learn more about the SMB space and deliver much-needed services and solutions to starving small business customers. Engaging in educational endeavors like passing the 70-282 exam and the Small Business Sales and Marketing Skills Assessment is all good.

- **Curious cats.** We can't fault someone for simply having a deep interest in SBS 2003 and other Microsoft SMB product stack components! These readers want a book that expands their horizons. Good enough, mate! Enjoy the read and find ways to make the certification exam(s) and the Small Business Specialist Community work for you!

- **Gurus.** There are currently 50 SBS gurus in the world, known as SBS Most Valuable Professionals (SBS-MVPs). Of course, these guys and gals are welcome to read this book. In fact, a few helped in the review process (thank you!). But to be honest, no author or publisher can profitably write and print a book for only 34 readers, so if you're a guru, kindly understand that this book is written for the common man and woman and we're takin' it to the small business streets around the world!

Who Shouldn't Read This Book

- **Negative people.** SMB Nation Press books are positive. A lesson learned by many and emphasized in all our publications is you get a lot more in life with sugar, not hot chilies!

- **Enterprise technology professionals.** The technology field is huge, and there are many specialists who improve businesses and entire civilizations each and every day with technology! In this book we're committed to staying focused on the small business technology sector; a committed enterprise technology professional might not get much value from it. There are many excellent MCSE books on the market oriented more toward our enterprise brethren!

- **End user customers.** As many readers know, SMB Nation Press books typically speak to the consultants, resellers, and channel partners who serve the loyal end-user customer. That's our publishing paradigm and we're sticking to it! That is, we want end-user customers to **hire and**

engage our core readership group who used this book to become fat and happy Microsoft Small Business Specialists!

Who Wrote What?

This book had two authors but occasionally we use the first person writing style to better tell our story. So just for the record, here is who wrote what! Harry Brelsford wrote the front matter and Chapters 1,2 and 14. Beatrice Mulzer wrote Chapters 3-10, Mei Ying Lim wrote Chapters 11-13. Arlin Sorensen wrote Chapter 15. Andy Goodman and David Anderson wrote Appendix C. Whew!

March Forward!

Microsoft heard y'all loud and clear that it didn't "get it" when it comes to the small business technology space. Be careful what you ask for! With the introduction of the Small Business Specialist Community, it's time to get an umbrella over your head when you walk outside, as small business technology content, technology solutions, and CUSTOMERS will be falling from the sky. It's a nice problem to have!

We sincerely hope you enjoy this book. Feedback is always welcome!

Beatrice Mulzer
(beatricem@smbnation.com)
MCSE, MCT, USA SBS Hands-On Lab Instructor
Melbourne, Florida USA

Section I ❧ Small Business Specialist Community

Chapter 1
Introduction

Chapter 2
Small Business Specialist Community

CHAPTER 1
Introduction

A few years ago in the middle part of the decade, Microsoft turned its attention to the small business space in a meaningful way, something you no doubt ascertained by picking up this book and thumbing through a few of its pages. This chapter introduces some key elements of the book, including certification exams and the Small Business Specialist Community program (now in its third year as of this writing). But from this paragraph forward, this book first and foremost remains loyal to its core mission: helping you pass the 70-282 certification exam: Designing, Deploying, and Managing a Network Solution for a Small- and Medium-Sized Business. However, this book goes beyond being a simple "cram" for the 70-282 certification exam because it provides the broader context of the new Small Business Specialist partnership program. The relationship is that the 70-282 exam can be used to complete your certification exam requirement to join the Small Business Specialist partnership program.

But wait as there is even more. This book also rocks when it comes to helping you pass the 70-631 certification exam: Configuring Windows SharePoint Services 3.0. This is a new entry point into the Small Business Specialist Community as of January 2007 and really speaks to a different audience from the traditional network infrastructure crowd.

Let's get started!

Certification Exam 70-282

First things first. What is the 70-282 exam: Designing, Deploying, and Managing a Network Solution for a Small- and Medium-Sized Business certification? It is Microsoft's attempt to establish a certification program baseline whereby technology professionals can prove their skills related to small businesses and the deployment of Windows Small Business Server 2003 (SBS 2003) and the traditional Windows Server 2003 products. It's the newly created bar people must jump over if they want acknowledgement from Microsoft in this area. The 70-282 certification exam is broken into several major categories, as shown in Table 1-1. This exam flow is essentially the major outline for this book (although we've added additional value by discussing the new Small Business Specialist partnership program and other examinations).

BEST PRACTICE: The 70-282 certification exam has been updated at least once since December 2003 and now reflects more Windows 2003 Server questions.

Table 1-1
70-282 Certification Exam Categories and Flow

Category	Comment
Analyzing the Existing Environment	This is a traditional business systems analysis designed to build appreciation for using business tools in the deployment engagement.
Designing a Business Technology Solution for a Small- or Medium-Sized Business	The intent here is to honor the architectural planning role in the small and medium business technology deployment scenario.
Installing and Configuring Windows Small Business Server 2003	This is the testing category for the down and dirty details for installing SBS 2003.
Supporting and Maintaining Windows Small Business Server 2003	This is an appropriate exam area for the downstream support function after the SBS 2003 deployment concludes.

Category	Comment
Expanding the Windows Small Business Server 2003 Network	This section addresses a key Product Support Services (PSS) issue of adding more servers to the SBS network.
Installing and Configuring Windows Server 2003	This section was added so that the 70-282 certification exam wasn't strictly SBS-focused and allowed for two other forms of competency testing: medium-sized organizations running Windows Server 2003 and those small businesses that might opt for Windows Server 2003 over SBS!

To be honest, the 70-282 certification exam has had a slow start over the past couple of years. Microsoft's traditional certification path is very enterprise-oriented, so the 70-282 exam has been something of an outcast in the context of the "get certified" message. Combine that with the lack of "butts in chairs" at training centers learning about SBS in the early part of this century, and you have historically low levels of excitement for the 70-282 certification exam. But hope is on the way!

Microsoft has given new life to the 70-282 certification exam by:

- Turning the bow of the Microsoft ship to focus on the small business segment.

- Creating a new partnership opportunity, the Small Business Specialist, which treats the 70-282 certification exam as one of two options for fulfilling the certification exam prerequisite (more certification exams are expected to qualify at a later date).

- Promoting the value of Microsoft Certified Professional (MCP)-level certification in numerous public no- or low-cost outreach efforts like hands-on labs and USA TS2 seminars, where you can interact with a Microsoft technology professional. Note that passing the 70-282 certification exam qualifies you to become a Microsoft Certified Professional and it also counts as elective credit towards higher-level certifications such as the Microsoft Certified System Engineer title.

- Periodically offering reduced-cost testing vouchers and other inducements to complete this examination.

- Encouraging attendance at the Microsoft Official Curriculum course 2395a: Designing, Deploying, and Managing a Network Solution for a Small- and Medium-Sized Business, which is associated with the 70-282 certification exam.

You will learn much more about the 70-282 certification exam in Chapters 3 through 10 of this book. To review the Preparation Guide for Exam 70-282, go to the Microsoft Learning site: http://www.microsoft.com/learning/exams/70-282.asp.

Certification Exam 70-631

The authors all believe the Windows SharePoint Services 3.0 (WSS) application is really cool and brings nothing short of a paradigm shift to how technology can be used in small and medium-sized businesses. For example, SMB Nation uses WSS to manage the documents associated with book and magazine publishing.

The good news is that the WSS product is readily available and easily implemented at customer sites. It can be used immediately and result in instant IT return on investment (ROI) because it's impact is instant. Documents can be checked-in and checked-out on day one. Version control can be automatically implemented. Schedules, policies and procedures better managed.

More importantly, the WSS "crowd" is a welcome addition to the Small Business Specialist Community because it complements the traditional network infrastructure "crowd." That is, WSSers can work side-by-side with SBSers satisfying a customer. Or perhaps one person will develop multiple skill sets and be both a WSSer and a SBSer.

Some would argue that WSS is a niche and you will see WSS specialists, such as members of the Microsoft Office Specialist (MOS) join our "community." Hopefully you get the point so let's move on to the exam specifics shown in Table 1-2.

Table 1-2

Skills measured by exam 70-631

Deploy Windows SharePoint Services 3.0 (WSS)
Configure WSS server roles.
Configure WSS topology.
Create WSS namespace.
Upgrade WSS 3.0 from WSS 2.0.
Install WSS.
Monitor Windows SharePoint Services
Maintain storage performance.
Configure centralized monitoring for WSS.
Configuring performance monitor.
Identify WSS problems using the Web Event Viewer.
Monitor logs.
Configure Security for Windows SharePoint Services
Configure Web application authentication.
Configure a Web application for SSL.
Configure NTLM or Kerberos authentication.
Configure roles and site permissions.
Implement access policies.
Manage database permissions.
Configure Information Rights Management (IRM).
Administer Windows SharePoint Services
Configure site settings.
Manage Central admin.
Administer Windows SharePoint Services by using STSADM.
Configure backup and restore (disaster/recovery).
Manage Customization
Configure master page.
Customize pages by using SharePoint Designer.
Customize pages using browser.
Configure code access security.
Configure Network Infrastructure for Windows SharePoint Services
Configure names resolution.

Configuring Network Load Balancing (NLB).
Configure WSS to support perimeter network.
Configure Internet Security and Acceleration Server (ISA).

Learn more about the 70-631 certification exam, including an updates, by visiting http://www.microsoft.com/learning/exams/70-631.mspx.

Certification Exam 74-134

Chapter 14 of this book is devoted to the 74-134 certification exam: Preinstalling Microsoft Products using the Preinstallation Kit. Why? Because it is the alternative certification exam you can take to fulfill your examination requirement to become a Small Business Specialist. That is, you could take exam 74-134 instead of 70-282 as your required certification exam. But few people will take this exam because it really is focused on two types of individuals: original equipment manufacturers (OEMs), like HP, and system builders heavily into the white box clone market. Historically, these haven't been the "doers" serving customers as consultants in the SBS and small business communities. But, as a courtesy, this examination is discussed here in Chapter 11.

A little bit of firsthand history on Microsoft's interest in exposing its partner channel to the OEM Preinstallation Kit (OPK): At the turn of the century, I was a USA hands-on lab instructor for a vendor who delivered the hands-on labs for numerous Microsoft products. (I toured upwards of 50 U.S. cities per year and very much enjoyed meeting many readers along the journey!) For about a two-year period, it seemed like any hands-on lab delivery included a section on the OPK. SBS hands-on labs weren't immune, and I often found myself lecturing on and demonstrating the SBS OPK during the final hour of the day. (Scheduling our OPK discussion late in the day allowed folks to leave early if the topic wasn't of interest.) Why was the OPK included in these training forums? It's not that Microsoft was necessarily trying to make deeper inroads with partners such as HP, Dell, IBM, and others. Rather, Microsoft was trying to get the local small-town computer builder to embrace the OPK approach to implementing its operating systems. While the motive is pure, I can state that my audience was underwhelmed by the OPK message. That's why we'll honor the 74-134 exam in this book, but not emphasize it.

The 74-134 certification exam contains the following components, as shown in Table 1-3.

Table 1-3

74-134 Certification Exam Categories and Flow

Category	Comment
Use OPK tools to preinstall operating system	This is the OPK hands-on lab and content being put to the test.
Create and apply preinstallation images	This is a technical deep-dive section on imaging, using remote installation services and other approaches.
Preinstall applications, drivers, and updates	Covers the deployment of Microsoft and third-party applications, etc.
Comply with the licensing requirements	Obligatory licensing content that centers on the preinstallation environment. Microsoft is seeking to test your licensing knowledge here.
Troubleshoot the preinstallation environment	Delves into common maladies and associated troubleshooting approaches and resolution.
Preinstall SBS	Condition for an SBS 2003 deployment, creating the domain controller, and configuring the installation of Exchange and other applications.

You can learn more about the 74-134 exam in Chapter 14 of this book and at the Microsoft Learning site: http://www.microsoft.com/learning/exams/74-134.asp.

IMPORTANT: Passing either the 70-282 or 74-134 exam will qualify you to become an MCP. Either exam satisfies the Small Business Specialist technical examination certification requirement.

Small Business Sales and Marketing Skills Assessment

This book also addresses the online Small Business Sales and Marketing Skills Assessment, a required component of the Small Business Specialist program (see Chapter 15). Microsoft recognizes that its Small Business Specialists are indeed wearing multiple hats as technicians, business people, sales people, managers, and so on. This requirement—passing a business-focused quiz to demonstrate your basic sales and marketing comprehension—is a welcome addition. Why? Because I and other long-time small business technology consultants will attest to the importance of business acumen in the world of technology consulting and service delivery. The inclusion of a business-related assessment as a requirement in the Small Business Specialist partnership program speaks to the following small business consulting trends:

- **Backroom and Boardroom.** Microsoft is a technology company, and many of its past assessments and exams were technology and product focused. The inclusion of the Small Business Sales and Marketing Skills Assessment signals that the business boardroom is just as important as the technical backroom for the small business consultant.

- **Cultural Revolution.** Blue collar meets white collar. Let's face it; many customers still view the "computer guy" or "computer gal" as a tech-head and a business lightweight. Consider the Small Business Sales and Marketing Skills Assessment as one step toward turning the blue collar mentality a bit more white collar!

- **Analytical Advancement.** MBAs and MCPs getting along. As you ascend the small business consulting food chain, you'll need to have part of your brain thinking BUSINESS. So, consider this Small Business Sales and Marketing Skills Assessment your "mini-MBA." Upon passing this assessment and joining the Microsoft Small Business Specialist partnership program, you're a card-carrying business person. Welcome to the club!

- **Communication Skills.** Sales people like to talk. It's as simple as that. With your legitimate exposure to the world of sales and marketing, you're going to also find your communication skills improving. Watch out, as you might go from gruff technical guru to optimistic super-salesperson without even realizing it!

- **Higher Pay!** Last and certainly not least, there is the economic advancement issue. Knowing all the "bits" surrounding the Microsoft small business product stack is dandy. But bringing home more BUCKS is even better! Hopefully the technical and business mix of the new Small Business Specialist partnership program will let you have more "Bits" and "Bucks." The Small Business Sales and Marketing Skills Assessment exam is one path to greater financial success because many of us know that after a certain point along your career path, your sales skills will contribute more to your net worth than your technical thinking. You read it here first.

The Small Business Sales and Marketing Skills Assessment is discussed further in Chapter 15 of this book. Note that the Small Business Sales and Marketing Assessment has been updated once and Chapter 15 reflects the updates as of our publication date.

Tips for Getting Certified

I write this section from a place of passion because I feel many other Microsoft Certified System Engineer (MCSE)-type certification books speak to the "secrets" for getting certified rapidly, in your sleep, with little or no effort. I want to emphasize some practical paradigms for you to pass the 70-282 exam (in particular) and become a Microsoft Small Business Specialist.

Experience

Old hands in small business technology consulting will appreciate that I've listed "experience" first and foremost. While we're an inclusive community and we welcome new small business technology consultants into our profession, don't underestimate the role experience plays in your dealings. It can also be a great asset in passing the 70-282 exam (and becoming a SUCCESSFUL Microsoft Small Business Specialist). Granted, saying experience is important to a newbie creates the chicken-and egg construct. That is, while everyone acknowledges experience is essential, how do you get experience when you're new and can't get work until you have applicable experience? It's a problem all professionals face at some point; the time-honored path of doing good work, paying your dues, and just plain showing up are key success factors in becoming a well-respected, experienced professional. More practically speaking, experience will help you pass the 70-282 exam as much as any late-night study session will! So consider the following approaches for gaining experience:

- **Install SBS 2003 for yourself and use it.** Even for a home-based business like Amway or managing the madness of raising a family, use SBS 2003 each and every day. BE your own best customer and think through the installation. It is a little-known fact that many Microsoft employees in Redmond run SBS 2003 at home so they can use and learn SBS 2003 in the "real world." Repeat this behavior and you are well on your way to success.

- **Volunteer.** Nothing like working for free to get experience. Talk to schools (deploy SBS at a small, private school), political campaigns, and even unprofitable small businesses and see if you can become a small business savior with SBS 2003!

- **Life experience.** Don't understate the life experience you've gained from going around the block a few times. Heck, even a stay-at-home parent has bona fide business experience: raising kids, scheduling activities, budgeting the family funds, balancing the checkbook, provisioning the pantry, and keeping the facilities sanitary all qualify as work experience in this book. Likewise, unrelated jobs you've had along the highways and byways of life have all contributed to your awareness and allow you to critically analyze situations. It's this core set of skills based on life experience that'll prove helpful when taking a certification exam or serving a small business customer. Trust me.

- **Get a mentor.** Attend your local technology user group, identify a successful professional in your chosen field, and HANG OUT WITH THAT

PERSON! It's really the shortest path to business success and will allow you to gain experience rapidly. By being selective in the business friendships you make, you'll find yourself "invited" into business transactions, consulting opportunities, and the like. Hey—if you want to win the Tour de France bike race, start training with Lance Armstrong, a seven-time winner of that race. Hanging out with mentors typically creates interesting opportunities, such as customer engagements, which translate into obtaining valuable experience very quickly.

- **Maturity.** The simple passing of time, no matter what your station in life, results in experience. Heck, at a minimum, you've got finely tuned survival skills that'll allow you to hunt down customers as a certified small business technology consultant!

Enthusiasm

Honest enthusiasm and a positive attitude may not show up on your résumé, but they are real forces nonetheless, and they play a powerful role in helping you achieve what you want in life! Use your SBS-related PASSION to PASS that 70-282 exam, fulfill other requirements, and become a super Small Business Specialist. So how do you switch from being negative and reorient yourself in a more proactive and positive way? Here are three thoughts to build enthusiasm:

- **Simple steps.** When people with an addiction seek to fundamentally change their situation and improve their life, they often use one of the step-by-step recovery programs. Similarly, for today, discover something you LIKE about SBS 2003 and want to tell the world. Treat your local technology user group meetings as your recovery movement meeting. Attend and participate.

- **Smell the roses of financial success.** I don't know about you, but my attitude improves dramatically when I'm making a lot of money. Funny how everyone started to really like SBS once they started making money with the product. So, if you're new to small business consulting, have the maturity and wisdom to know that your enthusiasm will build exponentially as your wealth increases. There is no stronger direct correlation in business.

- **Be young again.** Remember how exciting people, places, and events where when you were a child? Some of us who are now older, seasoned small business consultants remember how excited we were when we met SBS for the first time. Personally, seeing the excitement of life in my two young boys has been a source of strength to keep me positive and excited about small business technology. So perhaps drawing from the fountain of youth will allow you to tap into the positive energy you'll need to prepare for and pass the 70-282 exam and succeed in your quest to become a Microsoft Small Business Specialist!

Education

Hopefully, you're interested in knowing more about things in both your professional and personal life. Not only does such an attitude serve you well socially and make you more interesting, it also allows you to better serve your small business customers as a technology consultant. As a consultant, almost by definition, you need to know more than your customer. That's why the consultant gets paid by the customer. It's really a simple business model.

A commitment to being a lifelong learner and continually nurturing a desire to know *more* is a bona fide success factor in preparing to pass the 70-282 exam and ultimately becoming a Microsoft Small Business Specialist. Thus, being a lifelong learner and a seeker of knowledge keeps you relevant as a small business consultant. When you made the decision to serve small businesses as a technology consultant (and soon to be Microsoft Small Business Specialist), you hopefully accounted for the fact that you'd need to stay current or suffer the consequences of being put out to pasture at a tender age. Staying current is an important cornerstone to being a successful small business technology consultant, and continuous learning will always be important!

So, just how do you become educated with respect to the 70-282 exam and other aspects of the Microsoft Small Business Specialist partnership program? You've got to become educated the old-fashioned way—with a lot of elbow grease and other forms of hard work! Consider the following educational opportunities to increase your small business technology-related know-how.

Microsoft Official Curriculum

Microsoft historically releases a Microsoft Official Curriculum (MOC) course that is casually related to a certification exam. These courses are delivered at certified training centers that are Microsoft partners and are taught by Microsoft Certified Trainers (MCTs). The strength of the relationship between the course and exam varies, but historically the correlation, while positive, hasn't been high.

In the case of the 70-282 exam, the path is clear. You would take MOC Course 2395a: "Designing, Deploying, and Managing a Network Solution for a Small- and Medium-Sized Business," available from the Microsoft Learning site: http://www.microsoft.com/learning/exams/70-282.asp. Learning opportunities for the 70-631 certification exam are found at http://www.microsoft.com/learning/exams/70-631.mspx and include Course 5060. For the 74-134 exam, there isn't as strong a MOC study path. As shown in Figure 1-1, the Microsoft Learning page lists multiple courses (not all MOC approaches) that are tied to the 74-134 exam (http://www.microsoft.com/learning/exams/74-134.asp).

Figure 1-1

> To prepare for the 74-134 exam using Microsoft-based educational resources, you need to select parts of several different learning curriculum offerings, as shown here.

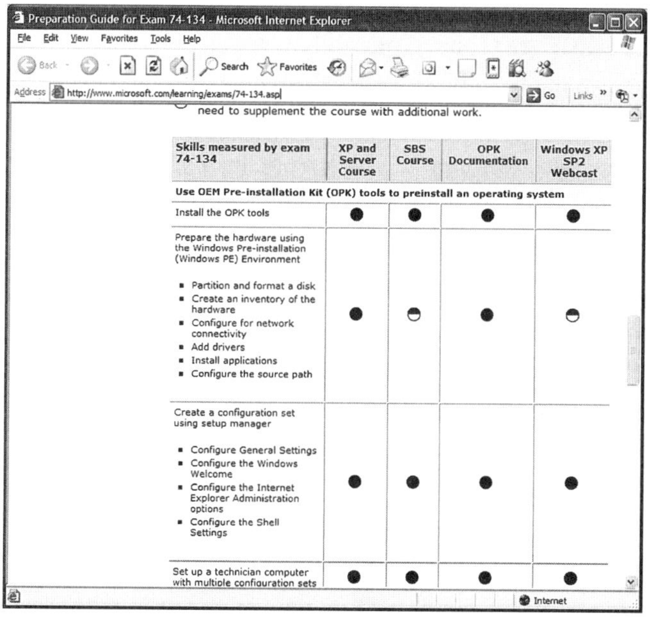

Visit www.microsoft.com/technet for the latest updates for any Microsoft product.

Self-Study/Online Study

We're delighted to report that this third-party book is one of your best resources for passing the 70-282 certification exam and completing the other steps needed to become a Microsoft Small Business Specialist! Microsoft also has many online and self-study resources available to make you successful on this journey:

- **70-282 certification exam:** A self-study version of the MOC course 2395a, developed by the authors of this book for Microsoft, was released in the summer of 2007.

- **70-631 certification exam**. Complete online collection 5403. Visit https://www.microsoftelearning.com/eLearning/offerDetail.aspx?offerPriceId=127428 to learn more.

- **74-134 certification exam:** The Microsoft Learning page (http://www.microsoft.com/ learning/exams/74-134.asp) offers several gold nuggets, including suggestions that you study the SBS 2003, Windows XP, and Office 2003 OPK document set.

- **The Small Business Sales and Marketing Skills Assessment:** Chapter 12 lists a boatload of free self-study/online training resources.

Workshops

At SMB Nation, we are proud of our global one-day workshops targeted toward boosting the technical and business performance of small business consultants. These workshops are one-day professional development or continuing education programs where attendees can step back from the madness of building a thriving small business consulting practice and think strategically. I liken it to a retreat where peer-to-peer interaction is just as important as receiving the technical and business content being served up. Visit http://www.smbnation.com for more details.

IMPORTANT: Rumor has it that starting in late 2005 or early 2006, Microsoft will offer, on a global basis, invitation-only training for Small Business Specialists. Chalk that up as another reason to get certified on the 70-282 exam and complete the other requirements to become a Small Business Specialist!

Annual SMB Nation Conference

Another sign of success and true professionalism is to attend at least one industry conference per year. The annual SMB Nation Conference, held each fall in Seattle, Washington, is submitted for your consideration and approval. This event brings together over 650+ small business technology consultants from around the world to talk the talk about walking the walk!

> IMPORTANT: See Appendix A for additional resources that will assist you in preparing for the 70-282 certification examination and becoming a successful Microsoft Small Business Specialist. You'll find references to blogs, newsgroups, and much more.

Economics

Mind if I act like your beloved parents for a moment? Have you created a budget for getting certified and becoming a Small Business Specialist? While Microsoft has taken great strides to minimize the hard costs and direct financial outlay associated with passing the 70-282 exam and becoming a Small Business Specialist, there are hidden costs I want you to consider:

- **Courses/Courseware.** Either attending courses (expensive) or obtaining courseware (less expensive) is a bona fide cost you incur. Account for it.

- **Study time.** There is a "true opportunity" cost associated with studying for the 70-282 exam and completing the other requirements for hurdling the bar to become a Small Business Specialist.

- **Retakes.** Certification exam retakes have a real cost. As a general rule, you must pay $125 USD each time you want to take the 70-282 exam.

- **Return on investment (ROI).** Imagine this scenario wherein you've worked very hard and reached your goal of passing the 70-282 exam and becoming a Small Business Specialist (congratulations are in order). But, what if you've burned out along the way? What happens if you get to the finish line only to decide you want to hang up your running shoes!?!? You've just incurred massive sunk costs and definitively encountered negative ROI. They say economics is the dismal science, and this has certainly emerged as the most dismal paragraph of the book, but I want you to be "scared straight" as you move along so you are focused on making this entire process work for you in a most positive way! Make your ROI the highest possible, because you're incurring costs in the journey whether you know it or not.

- **This book.** You've made a huge step by purchasing a book that focuses on the 70-282 exam and the mechanics of becoming a Microsoft Small Business Specialist. I'd like to think the cover price of the book will pay for itself many times over. Nonetheless, you've "bought the book," as they say in business. It's a real cost.

Envy

My final tip for you in passing the 70-282 certification exam and becoming a Microsoft Small Business Specialist is this: GET JEALOUS! When you attend your SBS user group meeting, scan the horizon and observe your brethren who appear more well-heeled (in the self-made sense, not the inherited wealth variety). Sit next to this person, buddy up, and get JEALOUS! When he or she drives away in a Volvo or Lexus and you're in a low-end car, let that burning feeling of envy MOTIVATE you to do better tomorrow, pass the 70-282 exam, become a Microsoft Small Business Specialist, and go out and KICK BUTT!

Summary

The purpose of this chapter is to get you excited about this book and motivate you to not only get certified on the 70-282 exam, but to run out and become a Microsoft Small Business Specialist! Microsoft is increasingly going to tie its interaction opportunities with small business technology consultants to those who are bona fide Small Business Specialists. It just makes sense. Wouldn't Ford or General Motors, the USA automobile companies, restrict sales opportunities to its network of car dealers? Yes!

This chapter painted the overall picture of the book with its focus on the 70-282 exam and my unbridled excitement about Microsoft's new Small Business

Specialist Community program. Hopefully, I've done my job and you'll now move along to Chapter 2 to learn much more about the Small Business Specialist Community!

CHAPTER 2
Small Business Specialist Community

When we published the original edition of this book, myself and Beatrice were delighted that Microsoft had finally provided a partnership opportunity for the little fella. As you will learn in this chapter, Microsoft's turn toward focusing on small businesses has coalesced into the new Small Business Specialist Community after much evolution. This is a community with three winners:

- You. Benefit from positive affinity and affiliation with the Microsoft Partner Program at a meaningful level.

- Customers. Enjoy the assurance that a small business technology consultant has met certain qualifications to hold the Small Business Specialist community title.

- Microsoft. The big "M" gains a legion of community-minded partners dedicated to the small business space. Microsoft also learns more about the "S" small business space.

Note in this chapter, I'll use the word "consultant" to generically include true technology consultants, value-added resellers, value-added providers, technology resellers, and even system builders! I will also refer to title holders as Small Business Specialists and the program as the Small Business Specialist Community.

> IMPORTANT: For those readers who like to skip the wedding and go straight to the reception (naughty-naughty) you can drop to the end of the chapter and read the Elevator Ride Version section to get a quick overview of the Small Business Specialist community. Then look at the links in the Community Resources section that follows.

The Case for Partnering With Microsoft

One of the big reasons to read this book and follow our advice is to partner with Microsoft. Some readers go back a few light years in the SMB technology community and remember in the late 1980s and early 1990s when Novell's certification and partner program ruled the land (circa NetWare 2.x and 3.x). People loved the Novell partnering opportunity and Microsoft was a partner program no-show.

That all changed in the early to mid-1990s when Dwayne Walker (who worked for Microsoft between 1989 and 1996) fathered the modern Microsoft Partner Program with Steve Ballmer's executive endorsement. Walker later went on the run a "dot-com" called Network Commerce and ultimately sued Microsoft for patent infringement (2002-2003), but that's a whole different story (you can read about Dwayne at http://www.windowsitpro.com/Windows/Article/ ArticleID/2249/2249.html).

Fast forward to modern times and here's how Microsoft's Partner Program is defined and where the program is at, as seen in Figure 2-1.

Definition

Microsoft's own Partner Program definition is:

> *The worldwide Microsoft Partner Program is for technology companies that use Microsoft software for building and distributing software or hardware solutions or as the building blocks for value-added services.*

> IMPORTANT: You can read an updated overview of the Microsoft Partner Program in the July edition of Redmond Channel Partner magazine at http://rcpmag.com/news/article.aspx?editorialsid=8734. It reveals who's who in the zoo in Redmond.

What's interesting about the definition is how it sets expectations and boundaries. Clearly the Microsoft Partner Program is focused on the consulting and reseller community. Redmond Channel Partner magazine had a great article in August 2007 that dug deep into the "numbers" with respect to how much revenue the partners generate (somewhere around 96 percent of MS revenue, which now exceeds $50 BILLION USD! You can read this excellent article at www.rcpmag.com).

Microsoft's community outreach to its partners is best defined by its annual Worldwide Partner Conference (WWPC), recently held in Minneapolis (July 2005), Boston (July 2006) and Denver (July 2007). (Visit: https://partner.microsoft.com/global/events/ wwpartnerconference/). Contrast this major Microsoft conference with other Microsoft conferences. The developers that support the Microsoft ecosystem possibly haven't even heard of the Microsoft Partner Program and would attend very different Microsoft soirées, such as TechEd. In short, Microsoft interacts with different stakeholder groups in different ways. One partner told me that the owner and sales people attend the WWPC and the technical staff attend TechEd. There's your boundary definition for you!

> IMPORTANT: In designing the SMB Nation annual conference, we attempted to cater to both crowds in the small business technology consulting space by having both a business and technical track. This multi-track approach allows multiple people from the same Small Business Specialist Community firm to attend the same conference. For more information on this annual event, held each fall in the Seattle area, visit www.smbnation.com. There is also an east coast (USA) version held each spring.

Starting with WPC Boston in July 2006, Microsoft's Partner Program has supported a Small Business Symposium day. Beatrice and I feature this event in the August 2006 and the August\September 2007 editions of our SMB Partner Community magazine.

Partner Pyramid

Figure 2-1 presents a graphic view of the Microsoft Partner Program (nothing like a simple graphic drawn on a napkin to convey a concept!).

Figure 2-1
Microsoft's Partner Program can be viewed as a pyramid.

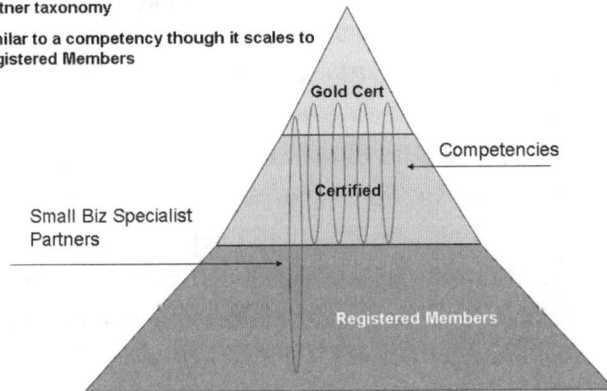

How does Small Business Specialist fit into
the MS Channel Taxonomy?

- A vertical "flavor" cutting across the partner taxonomy
- Similar to a competency though it scales to Registered Members

Gold Cert

Competencies

Certified

Small Biz Specialist Partners

Registered Members

Starting at the bottom of the Microsoft Partner pyramid, you might be interested to know that the organizational and financial commitment increases as you climb upwards. For example, a Registered Partner simply registers at a Microsoft Partner site. I spell out the requirements to become a Small Business Specialist in great detail in the next section. A Certified Partner needs to have two Microsoft Certified Professionals on staff, earn 50 Partner Points and pay an annual fee to join the Microsoft Partner Program. A Gold Certified Partner pays the same fee but has to achieve additional milestones, such as more Partner Points and competency requirements.

There are other requirements to become a Certified Partner and Gold Certified Partner that I won't explore here (the above discussion is a sampling to provide context). Visit https://partner.microsoft.com/global/30000104 for complete Microsoft Partner Program details. Kindly note that Microsoft Partner Program requirements often change and I do not attempt with this book to present the most current information. Just like the "cyber professor" likes to remark: check the Web for the latest updates.

Partner Points

Partner Points are part of the Partner Program and a scorecard Microsoft uses to reward its most committed top performers. The official definition is touted on the Partner Point web site:

> *Partner Points are designed to create a level playing field for solutions partners of all sizes. As a solutions partner you can qualify as a Certified Partner or Gold Certified Partner in the Microsoft Partner Program based on the number of Partner Points earned. This qualification method recognizes your success in the marketplace, gives you a great deal of flexibility, and helps open up the highest program levels to partners of all sizes and types.* (https://partner.microsoft.com/global/program/partnerpoints)

As you will read later, when you become a Small Business Specialist, you are awarded up to 25 Partner Points!

Small Business Specialist Strategy

This section describes the strategies surrounding the Small Business Specialist Community.

Five-Step Initial Strategy

How can you make a difference today as you read this early chapter in this book and ride the FAST PATH to becoming a Small Business Specialist Community member? When the clock strikes midnight tonight, is there any single task you could have completed to inch closer to the finish line? YES! Follow these initial strategy steps. Note this section assumes you are starting as a Registered Partner.

- **Step One.** Sign up as a Registered Partner at: https://partner.microsoft.com/global/program/levels/registeredmember. This gets you in the door and establishes a business relationship with Microsoft. Go do it RIGHT NOW; I'll wait for you to return.

- **Step Two.** Welcome back! The next step you can immediately undertake is to PURCHASE THE ACTION PACK! Read about the Action Pack before consummating your transaction, but understand that this is a requirement of the Small Business Specialist Community program. After reading this chapter, go to https://partner.microsoft.com/global/40009735 and purchase the Action Pack! Note that there have recently been "updates" to the Microsoft Action Pack Subscription (MAPS) program and you are encouraged to check online how these changes impact you. For example, you need to complete a quiz in order to be eligible for a subscription.

- **Step Three.** Complete the Small Business Sales and Marketing Assessment. This is the "business quiz" which the authors strongly endorse to get you to engage in "BusinessThink."

- **Step Four.** Sign up for a qualifying technical certification exam. See the IMPORTANT note that follows! We endorse the 70-282 exam as our favorite (and the focus of this book). You can sign up to take your certification exam by starting at this Microsoft Learning site: http://http://www.microsoft.com/learning/mcpexams/register/default.asp. Then completely read this book, join our 70-282 online study group (detailed in Appendix A) and TAKE AND PASS THE CERTIFICATION EXAM!

IMPORTANT: Please set your certification examination date at least 14 days from today (30 days may be even better). This gives you time to read this book and completely prepare for your certification exam. The key point is to set a testing date so you have a DEADLINE and are motivated to complete your examination preparations!

- **Step Five.** Fulfill the other requirements. Here there is good news to report. Microsoft updates its enrollment process in the spring of 2007 to automatically enroll you as a Small Business Specialist if you met the core requirements. This chapter and the remainder of the book spell out the "gives" that you must extend to Microsoft to become a Small Business Specialist. It's really easy and soon you'll be a member of the club! And we haven't forgotten the "gets" which speak towards "what's in it for me" crowd.

Growth Strategy

Both authors are acutely aware that some readers will simply use the Small Business Specialist Community as a stepping stone on the way up the partner ladder. Some readers don't intend to remain Small Business Specialists for long. For those, this is merely their starting point to building a relationship with Microsoft, acquiring some customers who are "referencable and referable," and becoming a Certified Partner or Gold Certified Partner going after upper/mid-market or enterprise-level work.

For what it is worth, here's our one-word reply: COOL! You are welcome to stay in the Small Business Specialist Community as long as you like. Just because you get big doesn't mean you can't remain small!

IMPORTANT: It's a well-known and appreciated growth strategy to start small and become big. That's how the game is played and it's how the likes of Microsoft and HP and other great companies launched! Who knows? It's entirely possible that someone reading this chapter will ascend to stardom and be the next billionaire!

Along the same line, some people use opportunities like the Small Business Specialist program as a "station in life." Realistically, the opportunities available in the small business space allow you to make a good six-figure living. However, the small business opportunity probably isn't a seven-figure opportunity (to make you a millionaire just from installing SBS at customer sites). But, you can use your small business consulting income to leverage into other opportunities, such as commercial real estate, where you then go on to make millions. That's the power of leverage.

Notes:

Get Involved—Partner Community Building

There is another interesting way to interact with the Microsoft Partner ecosystem beyond just the official way. I cite a very successful SBS consultant in Houston, Texas—Tim Loney and his company SOLUTIONS Information Systems (www.solutionsis.com)—as a perfect example of this. Ever the businessman with a deep technical skill set, Tim understands the value of business relationships and the need to meet and greet regularly. It's what impressed me most about him: his Texas business moxie! Tim has been very active in a third-party trade association, the International Association of Microsoft Certified Partners (IAMCP, www.iamcp.org), to improve his business and the small business partner community. If imitation is the sincerest form of flattery, then you might want to mimic Tim's success and become a player in the Microsoft Partner community. Another prominent SBS partner, Michael Cocanower, from IT Synergy in Phoenix, AZ, has used this same IAMCP strategy with great success.

Gives and Gets

Every relationship is about giving and getting. This holds true in both business and personal settings, and the Small Business Specialist Community is no different. Frankly speaking, it should be that way, as relationships that last long term require both parties to have skin in the game and remain motivated.

Gives

Before you can "get" the Small Business Specialist benefits, you have to first "give" to get into the partnership program. Here are the gives.

Get the Edge and Get The Call

In other professions, one might say they received their calling to become a minister, barrister or candle stick maker. We sincerely hope that becoming a Small Business Specialist is your calling. And we can make it happen! Microsoft USA launched a "Get The Edge" site where you START the entire journey and you receive a telephone call from a Microsoftie advising you of the next steps. So click over to http://www.smbizspecialist.com/ and complete the form. Then wait for your calling!

> IMPORTANT: We recommend the above step because the Microsoft Small Business Specialist Community program details are subject to change (sometimes after we've published our book). More Small Business Specialist Community web site URLs are given at the end of this chapter. This is especially applicable for worldwide readers seeking to proper program entry point.

Honor System Experience

The Small Business Specialist Community program is recommended for experienced small business technology consultants with at least six months of experience installing, configuring, and supporting SBS 2003 and future releases, Office 2003\2007, and Windows XP\Vista in small business environments. Clearly there is little Microsoft can do to enforce this requirement, but it is noble that Microsoft is trying to improve the quality of its program membership.

Purchase the Action Pack

The Action Pack is hardly a "give" because what you get clearly outweighs the $299 USD annual investment (note that pricing and subscription requirements are expected to change as of November 2007 after this book is published). Historically, Action Pack was a quarterly subscription service for Microsoft Registered Partners (the very lowest partnership level, also known as site-registered partners). If you were a Registered Partner, you could acquire Action Pack. Learn more about Action Pack at https://partner.microsoft.com/40016455.

Action Pack currently contains popular Microsoft front office and back office business applications that are particularly well-suited for use in small- and medium-sized businesses. Action Pack, updated quarterly, is how SMB-class consultants and partners acquire their learning bits. With Action Pack, Registered Members of the Microsoft Partner Program have fully licensed, popular SMB-focused Microsoft applications that you can use in your own consultant practice to LEARN the products. Its generous licensing program allows you to climb the learning curve before delivering services to your customers.

> IMPORTANT: Action Pack doesn't have strong "goodness of fit" for enterprise-class consultants and partners because its focus is on components that are better suited for the SMB space. And to be honest, Microsoft Certified Partners and Gold Certified Partners who are better equipped to serve the enterprise space would acquire their learning bits from the monthly mailer (a box of application software and partner-related materials), which is a separate deliverable for partners at these levels with the Microsoft Partner Program (MSPP).

Action Pack components easily exceed $25,000 USD in value, if valued when compared to perpetual licensing! And the Action Pack subscription isn't just about software. It also includes professionally designed marketing collateral and self-paced training curricula (e.g., CD-based courses) that you can engage with.

> IMPORTANT: Action Pack is updated quarterly so application content offerings can be refreshed with updated versions, new releases, new partner guides, and even service packs and other fixes. To receive quarterly update kits, Partners must be Registered Members in the MSPP (which occurs when you purchase Action Pack) and have an active Action Pack subscription.

Financial Commitment

The Action Pack is a worldwide program that currently has an annual subscription fee of $299 USD annually (subject to change as of November 2007). Prices vary by country and according to monetary currency fluctuations, but one thing is clear worldwide: YOU MUST RENEW your Action Pack subscription to continue using the learning bits in your consulting business! Action Pack subscription prices are subject to change, so please check the Microsoft partner site for the most current pricing!

So, why would you renew your Action Pack subscription in the second and later years if the learning bits are running just fine? Will the software police raid your domicile? (Action Pack Licensing Terms and Conditions violations are always subject to enforcement.) Will the bits burn up on the 366th day of use after your one-year licensing period expires? To answer these questions, check the Microsoft Action Pack program site as this team is always looking to update its enforcement effectiveness. So, why would you renew your subscription to Action Pack? I can think of two reasons:

- **Moral compass.** I believe that people are basically good and act in a positive, altruistic manner. (That is a time-tested political science theorem from some Greek philosopher whose name escapes me.) I believe you'll renew your Action Pack subscription simply because it's the right thing to do.

- **Staying Current.** In the body politic, there is a competing viewpoint that people act only in their best interest, and I'll accommodate that line of thinking, too. As actor Michael Douglas uttered while walking on a beach in the popular late-1980s movie *Wall Street,* "Greed is good." Greed will motivate you to renew your Action Pack subscription. Far be it from you to be seen using legacy Microsoft SMB product stack applications in your own consultant practice. Most embarrassing! More important, letting your Action Pack subscription lapse sets in motion the economic obsolescence of your knowledge-based technical professional skill set. You are no longer the most current SBSer and your days as a leader of the pack are numbered if you let yourself become an SMB technology dinosaur. Off with your head!

Your drive to stay current necessitates your Action Pack renewal!

You'll receive communication from Microsoft approximately 30 days before your subscription is set to expire. If for some reason you become disenchanted with Action Pack after one year or any subsequent annual renewal period, and/or you become otherwise disenfranchised from Microsoft and your Action Pack subscription lapses, then you must remove the learning bits provided by Action Pack from your technology infrastructure! Case closed.

Licensing

Another "heavy" comment that must be conveyed concerns the use of your Action Pack learning bits. The fact of the matter is that your Action Pack learning bits may not be utilized for your customers; they are for your private and specific use to enjoy these Microsoft front office and back office applications. While I'm using simple Texas talk to convey a serious message, if somehow I am not getting through to you, kindly read the licensing agreement that accompanies your Action Pack subscription. I'll meet you back right here in a few minutes!

Worldwide Program

Another sage observation I want to share with you concerns Action Pack content and its positioning as a worldwide product offering from Microsoft. In some ways, Microsoft could potentially offer you more for less with Action Pack if it were only a USA product SKU. What, how, and why, you ask? Let me explain. In working closely with the USA and worldwide Action Pack teams at Microsoft in Redmond (two different and distinct groups), I've often suggested the inclusion of certain interesting business applications, such as Small Business Financials, in the quarterly distributions. I was then made privy to some international relations insights that explain why some products don't fit the Action Pack worldwide model. For example, the accounting applications offered via the Microsoft Business Solutions (MBS) organization—while very desirable for

SMB consultants seeking to elevate their SMB consulting practices above and beyond mere infrastructure—must be tailored for each country. That is, the Generally Accepted Accounting Principles (GAAP) used in the USA don't transfer easily or readily to foreign lands. Other countries have different accounting treatments, and Microsoft's MBS products in the accounting realm can't simply be dropped in a box and shipped out as part of a quarterly mailer. I completely understand this and can appreciate how such global dynamics affect the contents of Action Pack! And now you know the rest of the story on how, in part, applications are selected for inclusion in Action Pack.

Affinity and Adoption

I close this section with a discussion about Action Pack adoption rates and affinity-based acceptance based on geographic locations. A couple of years ago, when delivering my worldwide SMB Nation Summit one-day workshops in over 40 cities and 25 countries annually, I surveyed attendees about Action Pack and also gave away Action Pack as a door prize. Needless to say, this workshop format provided impressive data about Action Pack.

- **High positive affinity.** Worldwide Action Pack subscribers who attended my workshop LOVE ACTION PACK. It's all about value. For example, in the USA, Microsoft delivers the SMB application space library as the Action Pack subscription, valued in excess of $25,000 USD, for just under $300 USD annually (you must renew annually to continue to use that software library and this price is subject to change). What's not to love about that! Try this analogy on for size. In the U.S. Congress, an elected member who easily wins reelection is said to have a safe seat. The same could be said about Action Pack in the SMB consulting community—it has a safe seat.

- **USA traction, global need for action.** Over 80 percent of USA SMB Nation Summit attendees happily subscribe to Action Pack. However, in the worldwide community, I found that, at best, only 20 percent of attendees subscribe to Action Pack. This is ironic because Microsoft's SMB product stack, including Windows Small Business Server 2003, does so well worldwide and lags in the domestic USA market. Life sometimes delivers cruel punishment and unusual fates, and clearly this inverse performance relationship between Action Pack and the Microsoft SMB product stack is one of the paranormal phenomena I can't explain.

IMPORTANT: Bottom line? An Action Pack subscription is a prerequisite for membership in the Small Business Specialist Community. Learn more about the Microsoft Action Pack at https:/ /partner. microsoft.com/global/40009735.

Successfully Pass One Certification Exam

Time to get serious after that lengthy Action Pack discussion! To become a Small Business Specialist, you must successfully pass a Microsoft Certified Professional (MCP) exam.

IMPORTANT: NOTE: This exam requirement is waived if your company is an active partner in the Microsoft Business Solutions (MBS) competency. This is IMPORTANT because it essentially gives Dynamics partners (CRM, etc.) a short-cut into the Microsoft Small Business Specialist Community. I'm fine with the "grandfathering" clause because Lord knows the partners paid their dues on the way up. However – this shorter path hasn't been very messaged and perhaps you can benefit from knowing this factoid.

Currently, you can select from two MCP certification exams:

- **70-282: Designing, Deploying, and Managing a Network Solution for a Small- and Medium-Sized Business.** Discussed in detail in Chapters 3 through 10, this is clearly the major certification exam we focus on in this book. Both authors feel strongly that this will be the watershed examination event in the Small Business Specialist Community program with its focus on SMB consultants and value added reseller (VAR) partners. Ergo—we give you eight chapters to prepare for that specific examination. What about the examination itself? It's very SBS 2003-centric, but it acknowledges the proper role of a Windows Server 2003 standard edition in an SMB organization.

- **70-631 - Configuring Windows SharePoint Services 3.0.** This credential is designed for IT professionals who can administer, deploy, customize, implement, or support Windows SharePoint Services 3.0. Read Chapters 11-13 in this book for more information.

- **74-134: Preinstalling Microsoft Products using the OEM Preinstallation Kit** (covered in Chapter 14). Including this niche examination is Microsoft's way of signaling its intention to be system-builder inclusive in the Small Business Specialist program. Microsoft would love to engage more with the system builder community in the SMB space; including the 74-134 exam in the Small Business Specialist Community certification testing requirements is part of that outreach.

- **Future exams.** The Microsoft program team behind the Small Business Specialist Community program is madly working to add more MCP exam options to satisfy the certification exam requirement. Look for this as a major area of growth in the Small Business Specialist Community program: more exams to select from!

IMPORTANT: Exam 70-282 qualifies the successful candidate to be a Microsoft Certified Professional and hold that title. Exam 74-134 does NOT qualify the successful candidate to be an MCP. Both authors recommend the 70-282 exam.

Applause extended to the Small Business Specialist Community team at Microsoft for demanding a certification exam requirement. Not only has it given new life to the above exams, but I really like how incumbent Small Business Specialists have to demonstrate basic technical competency. That is, not just anyone can become a member of this club—you have to earn this privilege!

IMPORTANT: Need motivation to complete and return the book registration form at the back of this book? By being a registered book owner, you'll receive notification of new eligible MCP exams in the Small Business Specialist Community program!

Microsoft currently has the following exam retake policy shown below. Kindly note that there has been some confusion as a few folks believed that you could only take an exam three times in total. Such is not the case. You are welcome to take the exam as many times are you desire. But, if you can't pass within three tries, we would like to suggest you revisit your overall decision to become a Small Business Specialist (perhaps you should keep your day job kid!). The retake policy is:

Microsoft has revised its policy for retaking exams to increase security. If you do not pass an exam the first time, you may retake it at any time. If you do not achieve a passing score a second time, you must wait at least 14 days to retake the exam a third time. A 14-day waiting period will be imposed for all subsequent exam retakes. If you have passed an exam, you cannot take it again. Beta exams may be taken only once.

Successfully Pass the Online Small Business Sales and Marketing Skills Assessment

This is clearly one of my favorite components of the Small Business Specialist Community program and reflects the world we live in as small business technology consultants and VARs. The prototypical small business technology consultant is a sole proprietor businessperson serving other small businesses. As such, you must wear many hats including technician, business owner, and sales person.

So, Microsoft has correctly determined that a successful Small Business Specialist must be sales and marketing savvy. Three cheers! Speaking only for myself, I can say that I've made more money with the sales and marketing skill set (namely, business development) than I have carrying the tools as a technician. But don't misinterpret that last comment, as it takes the "full package" to be a well-rounded and well-respected Small Business Specialist. The main point is this: embrace, don't fight, sales and marketing.

Time to get geographic and look at the online sales and marketing assessment from a popular sociology vantage point of global "haves" and "have nots." Sociologists in the research and academic communities are deeply concerned about a widening socioeconomic gap between developed and emerging countries. Study after study suggests that the rich get richer and the poor get poorer. That is, the "haves" get more and the "have nots" get less. I can offer casual support for the sociologists' empirical work from my own travels to over 25 countries to promote SBS and the SMB consulting opportunity.

Enter the Small Business Sales and Marketing Skills Assessment as one small step in trying to save the world. Hear me out on this theory. Whereas, wealthy American small business technology consultants have grown up around a developed business community and probably have benefited from "table talk," where they overhear successful sales and marketing techniques and approaches, my friends in India, the Dominican Republic, and other emerging markets didn't enjoy the same competitive advantage growing up. Truth be told, I can think of some American small business technology consultants who might get lucky and be able to pass the Small Business Sales and Marketing Skills Assessment without studying (an approach I don't endorse, but I do acknowledge). But, my friends in developing countries can truly benefit from studying for and passing the Small Business Sales and Marketing Skills Assessment. These "have nots" can take pride in passing this online assessment and quickly elevate and assimilate into the "haves" community. In sum, I see the preparation required for and the successful completion of the Small Business Sales and Marketing Skills Assessment being of the greatest benefit to the eager and earnest small business technology consultant in developing countries!

Chapter 15 is devoted to the Small Business Sales and Marketing Skills Assessment. After our technical deep dive into the certification exams, I elected to end the book by bringing you back to business reality and prepare you to pass this REQUIRED online assessment!

> IMPORTANT: To further build credibility regarding my "pocket MBA" preaching, I direct you to a legacy article I wrote many years ago about the value of testing business drivers in the Microsoft Certified Systems Engineer (MCSE) certification program, submitted as evidence for your review at: http://mcpmag.com/features/article.asp?EditorialsID=1 7.

Optional Learning Opportunities

To become a Small Business Specialist Community member, you should engage in appropriate educational opportunities. I like this requirement because it supports a "life learner" approach to the Small Business Specialist Community program and encourages ongoing professional development.

First and foremost, you are strongly encouraged to join the 70-282 online study group hosted by Beatrice and Harry (that's me) at MSN. Click over to http://groups.msn.com/70-282examcram and, after you apply and your admission is accepted, you should see a screen similar to Figure 2-2.

Notes:

Figure 2-2

Be part of the community! Join the 70-282 newsgroup and accelerate your journey to completing your requirements to be a Small Business Specialist. As of this writing, the group has over 1,000 members.

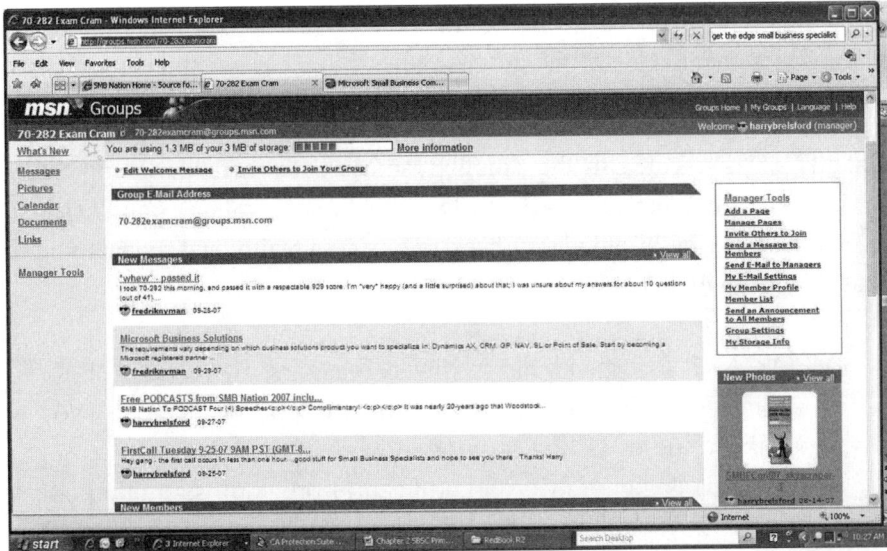

Note there is also a study group for the 70-631 certification exam at http://groups.msn.com/70-631ExamCram. As of this writing, the group has over 100 members and is growing rapidly!

There are some online learning opportunities which are updated frequently. For example, during 2007, there are 50 Webcasts relating to both technical and business topics. Known as 5W/50 webcasts, these session are found at www.mssmallbz.com/sbstraining.

You are strongly encouraged to complete 10.5 hours of online training as listed in Table 2-2. Two highly recommended courses, "Selling the Microsoft Solution to Small Business" and "Small Business Solutions Accelerators," are described in further detail on the following pages.

Notes:

Table 2-2

Strongly recommended but optional training and readiness curriculum.

Sales and Marketing (3 hours)	Technical (7.5 hours)
Selling the Microsoft Solution to Small Business (1 hour)*	Designing, Deploying, and Managing a Network Solution of the Small- and Medium-Size Business (1.5 hours)
Volume Licensing Essentials (1 hour)	Windows XP and Office Small Business Edition (1 hour)
Competitive Selling With Respect to Open Source (1 hour)	Supporting Microsoft Windows Small Business Server 2003 Parts 1-4 (4 hours). See Chapter 12, Table 12-2 for a list of URLs.
	Small Business Solutions Accelerators (1 hour)

* Highly recommended by both authors and Microsoft's Small Business Specialist Community team!

Selling the Microsoft Solution to Small Business

Lesson 1: Selling to the Small Business Market

- Define the small business market.
- Describe the small business decision maker.
- Outline the keys for selling to the small business market.

Lesson 2: Identify and Reach Your Target Market

- Describe Microsoft Small Business segments.
- Outline the process for creating a marketing plan.

Lesson 3: Determining Customer Needs and Creating a Winning Message

- Describe the needs of small business segments.
- Identify which products to sell to which segment.
- Create a value proposition.

Lesson 4: Case Study Practice

- Define value and cost for customers' solutions.
- Describe how to keep customers

IMPORTANT: Guess what's missing from this course, which is a crying shame? A learning module on overcoming objections! That's what a superior salesperson does best. You try to get a customer to articulate one or two key objections and then you find creative ways to overcome them. I discuss overcoming objections at length in Chapter 6 of SMB Consulting Best Practices (ISBN: 0-974858-06-4, SMB Nation Press).

Small Business Solution Accelerators

Small Business Solution Accelerators

- Introduce the Solution Accelerator Model.
- Provide prescriptive guidance on how to get the most value from the accelerators for your business.
- Help make your solution implementations more predictable and repeatable.

Solutions Training

- Delivers prescriptive training on solutions for small business based on a SBS network.
- Helps make your solution implementations more predictable and repeatable.

Both authors can speak *ad nauseam* about the Small Business Solution Accelerators, found at: https://partner.microsoft.com/global/productssolutions/smbsolutions. Harry wrote the *Peer-to-Peer Networking With Windows XP* solution accelerator and assisted with the technical and editorial review of the *Small IT Solution* document (and he maintains a close relationship with the Microsoft segment team to this day!). Beatrice holds a seat on the Small Business Solutions Accelerator advisory board. But self-promoting accolades aside, the real context is this: These excellent solutions accelerators are the basis of the current "SBS FRANCHISE" curriculum theme on the SMB Nation Summit global workshop tour in 2005. (Learn more about the SBS FRANCHISE at http://www.smbnation.com.) It is a good investment of your time to investigate these solution accelerators!

Last and not least, be sure to read Eric Ligman's blog (he is in the Microsoft USA small business area). You'll find it at http://blogs.msdn.com/mssmallbiz/ and tell him Harry sent ya!

Direct and Indirect Costs

In the mid-1990s, I wrote a popular *MCP Magazine* article (http://www.mcp mag.com) on the true costs of obtaining the MCSE title. This article, which was widely distributed to budding MCSE candidates, provided an MBA overview of both the hard and soft costs associated with the tremendous commitment necessary to obtain the MCSE title. The MCSE title resulted in a positive return on investment (ROI), and readers felt reassured about committing the resources necessary to get their MCSEs. I encapsulate that same thinking in this section as the direct and indirect costs associated with becoming a member of the Small Business Specialist Community.

> IMPORTANT: There is no specific entry fee, cover charge, or other required membership fee to join the Small Business Specialist Community. Contrast that with a membership fee for Microsoft Certified Partners and Microsoft Certified Gold Partners. This is good news for us! But please read the next section for two financial outlays (I like to call "investments") you will be required to make.

Direct Costs

Here are the direct costs associated with becoming a member of the Small Business Specialist Community:

- **Action Pack subscription:** $299 USD (subject to change)
- **Certification examination fees:** $125 (see Figure 2-3). Microsoft periodically has certification exam promotions to encourage people to take exams. One current promotion involves discounted fees for

initial testing and retakes. Read about it at: http://www.mcpmag.com/news/article.asp?EditorialsID=804 and monitor *Certification Magazine* (http://www.certmag.com) and *MCP Magazine* (http://www.mcpmag.com) for current promotions.

Figure 2-3

A popular test provider's site shows the fees associated with test taking. If you must take the test multiple times to achieve a passing score, your certification examination fee component will necessarily increase.

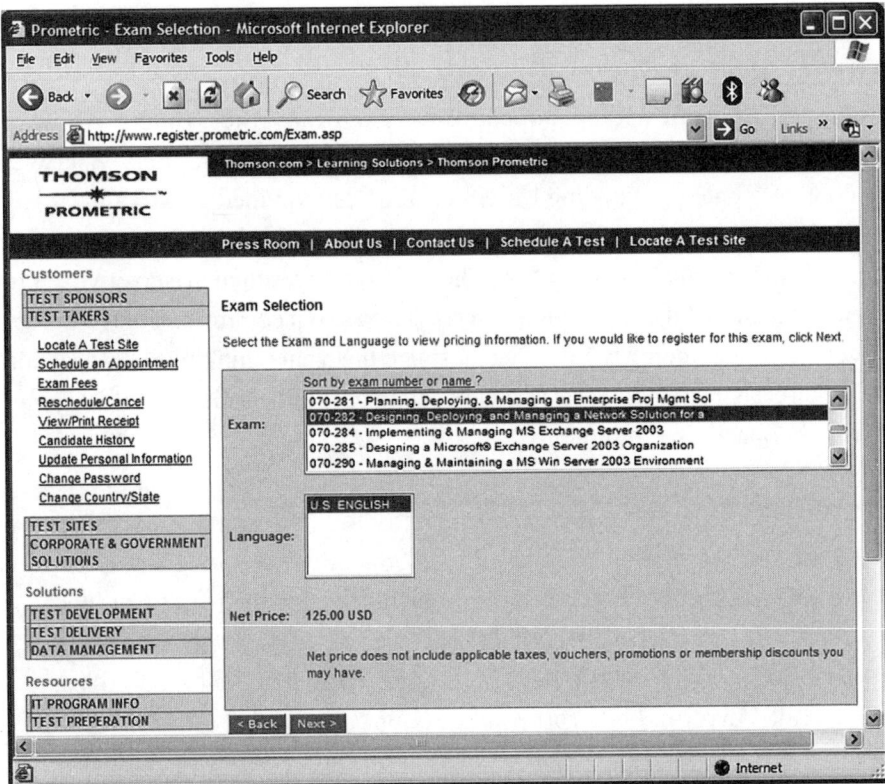

Note that as of mid-2007, Thomson Prometric is the only vendor allowed to administer the Microsoft certification exams. PearsonVue has been terminated by Microsoft.

Indirect Costs

It's easy to overlook the hours spent on any endeavor that don't show up on an accounting report. These are the "lost hours" we should somehow recognize if we're true to ourselves about the time and effort expended to reach an achievement. Gaining membership in the Small Business Specialist Community is no different. You'll put in some off-the-clock hours en route to earning this designation performing the following types of activities:

- **Installing the Action Pack applications.** I know that when my Action Pack arrived, I was mesmerized by all the cool stuff inside. I spent many hours installing the software and perusing the Partner Guides. No doubt you'll engage in this same obsessive-compulsive behavior and need to recognize those hours spent along the way, albeit wisely, playing with the bits.

- **Preparing for the Certification examination.** I honestly believe you need to schedule 20+ hours preparation time regardless of your expertise and background. Some readers might burn over 100 hours preparing for a single exam. .

- **Completing the online Small Business Sales and Marketing Skills Assessment.** While this online assessment doesn't impose a test-taking fee, you are committing time to prepare for and complete this excellent assessment. Budget a few hours here.

- **Reading this book.** Both authors are delighted you've elected to purchase, read, and review this book on your road to becoming a Small Business Specialist Community member. Allocate more than a few hours here.

- **Opportunity costs.** This financial concept concerns the cost of lost opportunities. Hey—if you spent all this time getting your membership into the Small Business Specialist Community, that took time away from becoming a realtor or other type of professional in another sector. Did you forgo another lucrative opportunity with the time commitment you made to this Microsoft Partner path? Perhaps, but both authors would hold up the Small Business Specialist Community as having high ROI and being something you'll enjoy. The opportunity-cost concept doesn't measure pleasure, so take this reasoning with a pinch of salt, as readers in the UK would say!

Gone

One thing you no longer have to "give" is a customer essay-writing exercise. One early rendition of the Small Business Specialist Community program had incumbents writing a few customer success story essays per year and submitting them to Microsoft. This was a non-cost way for Microsoft to receive another "give" from the incumbents and collect a significant amount of small business sector research at little or no cost. This requirement was later dropped. Too bad. Both authors feel writing skills contribute mightily to being successful in business! Plus, Microsoft was planning to use these customer reference submissions for future case studies and public relations for the Small Business Specialist.

Gets

Enough deferred gratification. Time for the good stuff: the GETS! This section outlines what you get as a Small Business Specialist Community member. Without further delay, check this out!

Amazing Customer Referrals!

At some level, we're all motivated economically, and the Small Business Specialist Community program recognizes that! When you become a Small Business Specialist, you are listed in the Small Business Partner Finder at http://www.microsoft.com/smallbusiness/partner/vendorsearch.mspx and as shown in Figure 2-4.

Notes:

Figure 2-4

Small Business Specialist Community partners will be listed above Registered Partners, showing a higher partnership status and level of expertise and commitment. All good!

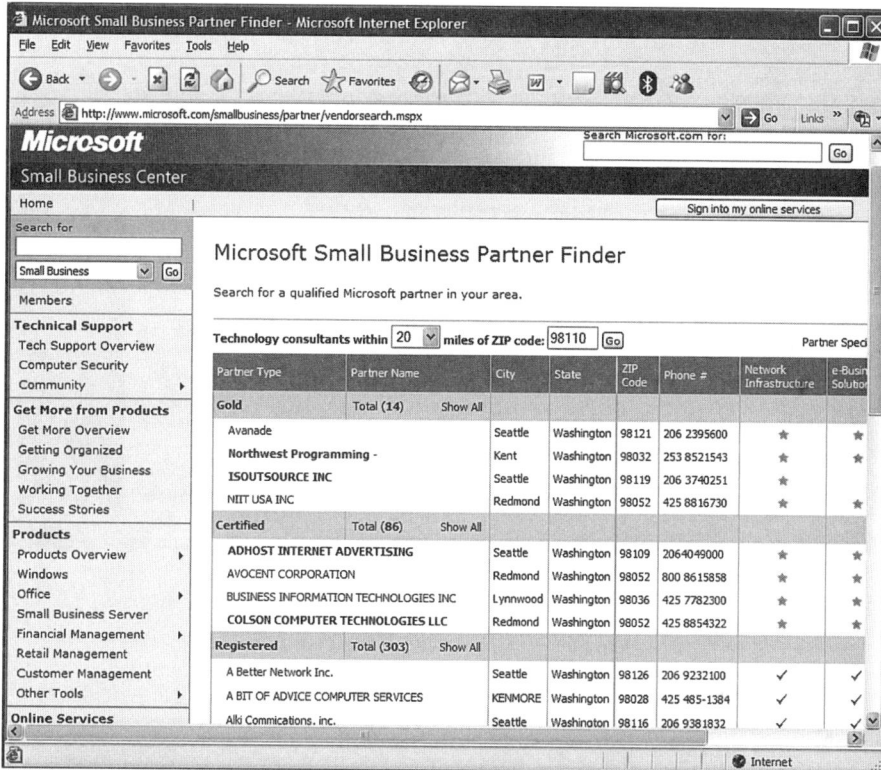

Receiving referrals from this Microsoft search site will likely emerge as one of the primary reasons many people jump on board the Small Business Specialist Community opportunity!

Demand Generation Updates

In late September 2007, Microsoft USA sought to add more "gets" or value to Small Business Specialists. This capable effort resulted in three specific "gets" that I personally applaud. These are shown in Figures 2-5, 2-6 and 2-7.

Figure 2-5
  "We Got The Guy" is a simple message to drive more customer business to existing Small Business Specialists. Visit http://www.wevegottaguy.com/ to learn more.

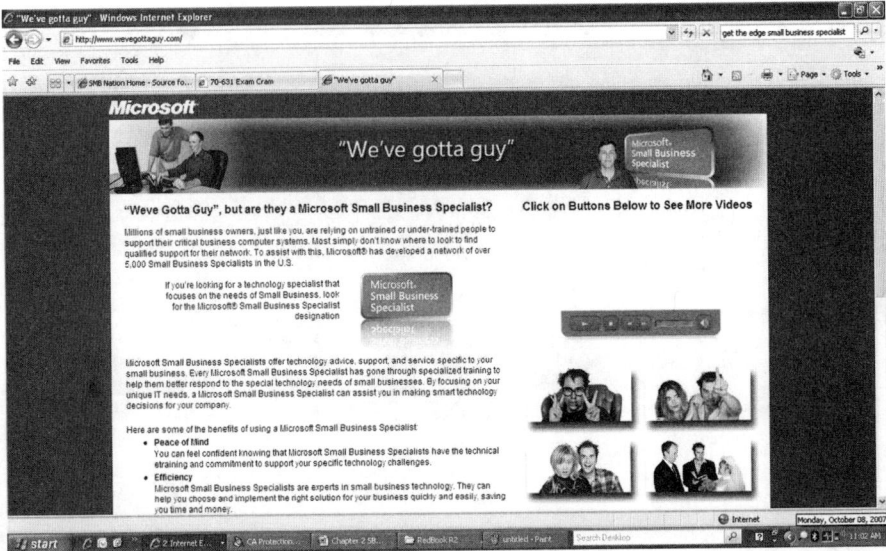

Figure 2-6
  Existing Small Business Specialists are eligible to participate in contests and WIN great prizes such as this Colorado rafting vacation.

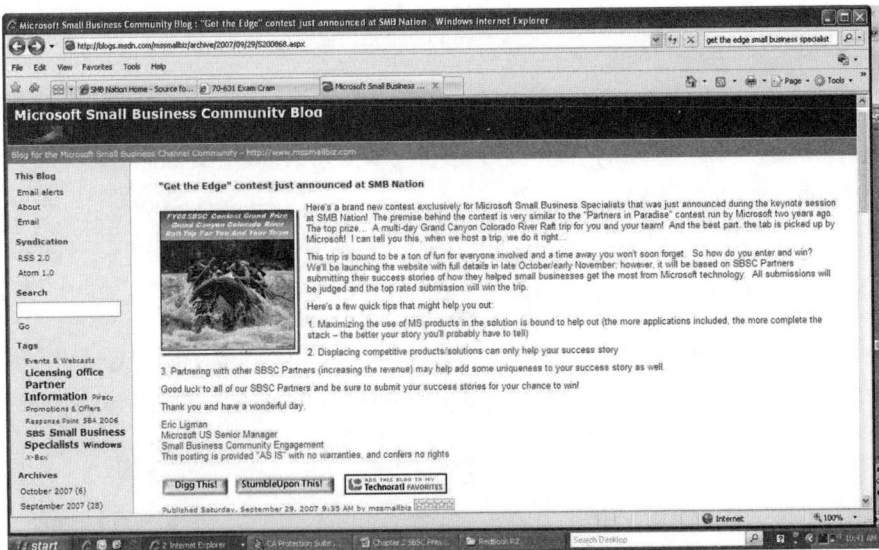

Figure 2-7

Another exclusive benefit for Small Business Specialists is the opportunity to re-broadcast customer-facing content on Web sites. This allows you to leverage existing messaging to tell the technology story to potential customers!

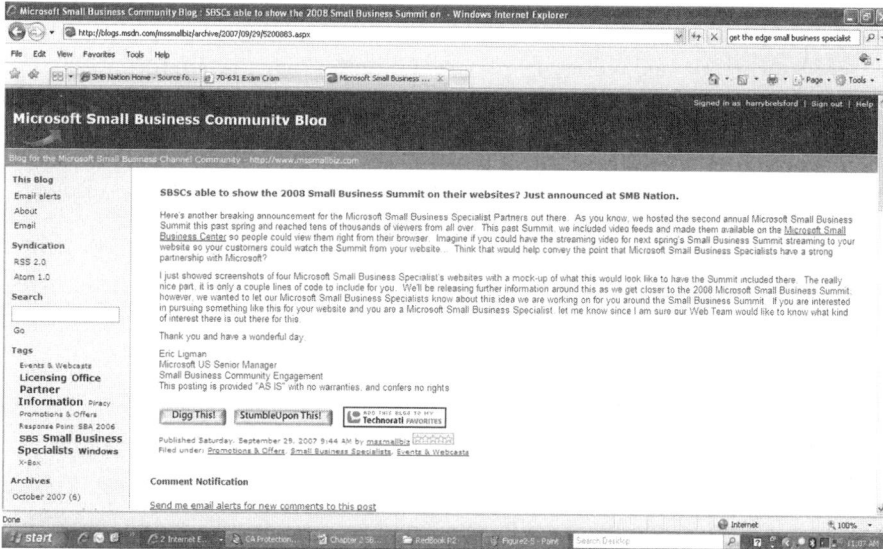

Affirmation and Affiliation

Membership has its privileges, and being a Small Business Specialist Community member is no exception. First, you have Microsoft's affirmation that you've achieved a significant accomplishment. It's an honor, not a right, to be a Small Business Specialist Community member. It wasn't handed to you on a silver platter—you earned it. Take a bow!

Second, the affiliation with Microsoft is invaluable. Whereas the "red meat" media often likes to focus on negative news about the big "M," this is a case where the media's version of the truth is inconsistent with the real world. On a global basis, I can attest that people in the SMB space overwhelmingly like Microsoft. It's not lost on folks that Microsoft started out as a home business with two eager entrepreneurs trying to create opportunity and improve their lots in life. Microsoft went on to be the richest corporation in the history of the world, with worth exceeding other great institutions like organized crime and the Roman Catholic Church! It's been the authors' experience that, rather than being green with envy about Microsoft, people really respect the software giant. Sounds like someone you'd want to partner with!

> IMPORTANT: Thankfully, the Small Business Specialist Community program is available worldwide. Why? Because the affirmation and affiliation message will really play much better overseas on the streets of Mumbai, India, than in the streets of Peoria, Illinois. Wealthy American small business technology consultants stand to gain less than their brethren in developing countries.

Some might view the affirmation discussion in terms of validation. Small business technology consultants who provide services to small businesses need the validation of the Small Business Specialist Community.

Affinity Group

Trade associations, fraternities, and social clubs all know one thing: People like to work together because human beings need social interaction. This "birds of a feather" benefit is clearly present in the Small Business Specialist Community, and it's not lost on Microsoft that it is providing real value to program incumbents by simply organizing such a community and providing opportunities for social interaction.

Submitted for further evidence is some of the interaction that occurs with the SBS Most Valuable Professionals (MVP). SBS-MVPs are technical gurus who volunteer support for a product such as SBS. One year, around the holidays, as the SBS-MVPs exchanged obligatory niceties, it occurred to me that being an SBS-MVP involves more than supporting a product. For these technical gurus from around the world, many of whom work alone, this was about participating in an affinity group. That was the value-add. I fondly remember one SBS-MVP subsequently posting a message saying, "...you are my family" in a highly complementary manner.

So, for many readers, the Small Business Specialist Community is their new affinity group that allows these globe-wandering small business technology marauders to come in from the cold. Welcome to your new home!

IMPORTANT: One way to shorten your path to becoming a Small Business Specialist is to utilize a great free technical resource: SBS MVPs! Meet and greet the S BS-MVPs at http//www.microsoft.com/windowsserver2003/sbs/community/default.mspx. Use 'em to meet your needs!

Access and Attention

During my Fall 2004 worldwide SMB Nation Summit workshop tour, I was allowed to show a sneak preview of the Small Business Specialist Community program to attendees to solicit feedback and conduct a follow-up survey. One of the overwhelming themes, something I discuss later in the chapter, related to small business technology partners feeling left out, ignored, and bereft of meaningful or productive relationships with live people at Microsoft.

This will change under the Small Business Specialist Community program. Microsoft is staffing positions that will serve the Small Business Specialist hand-and-foot! As an example, at Microsoft USA, there are Telephone Partner Account Managers (TPAMs) who make a monthly "buddy call" to every Small Business Specialist just to "check-in." Impressive!

Exclusive Premium Content!

Access to the PRIVATE Small Business Specialist premium content is another benefit. There's only one thing better then belonging to a community-based affinity group, and that's being a member of an EXCLUSIVE community-based affinity group! Microsoft addresses this need for exclusivity for Small Business Specialist Community members via a private forum and premium content.

Appealing Logo Usage

I can't comment on the exhibitionist tendencies of Small Business Specialist Community members, but folks in general like to publicly proclaim their accomplishments with logo usage. This can take several forms, such as logo wear clothing and logo usage rights. Both are discussed here.

Logo Wear and Trinkets!

An enduring memory from a MCSE-era book from the late 1990s was a photo in which incumbents proudly wore logo clothing. There will be a provision for logo wear and trinkets for the Small Business Specialist Community. What is not yet known is how the logo wear will be acquired: free or fee. That is, will Microsoft give you an attractive shirt to wear to show customers your Small Business Specialist Community status, or will you have to buy it?

> IMPORTANT: Be sure to subscribe to the free SMB Technology Watch newsletter at http://www.smbnation.com so you can stay current with Small Business Specialist Community updates.

Logo Usage Rights

Microsoft has a well-established operational tradition of allowing its partners to use program and product logos subject to certain rules and regulations. (As you would expect, Microsoft wants to ensure appropriate use.) Small Business Specialist Community members are granted logo usage rights. When qualified, the logo will be available for download from the Partner Program website by clicking the Sales and Marketing link and using the Partner Logo Builder.

> IMPORTANT: Time for a global moment. I have witnessed the greatest up-tick in logo usage in the worldwide community, not the USA. In my travels, I've found that global communities tend to display a higher need to communicate achievement, success, and credibility by dress and logo use. This is especially acute in the Latino cultures. I think a small part of this cultural difference between the USA and the global communities relates to education. In the USA, many small business technology professionals are university-level degreed. In emerging markets, fewer people have access to university-level education and must display their accomplishments differently, such as manner of dress and achievement-based logos. I shared with the Small Business Specialist Community team at Microsoft that the logo will play out very positively overseas!

Figure 2-8

At the Small Business Symposium day at the Microsoft Worldwide Partner Conference (Denver, Colorado July 2007), this "yellow shirt" was created for attendees and it displayed global variations of the Small Business Specialist logo!

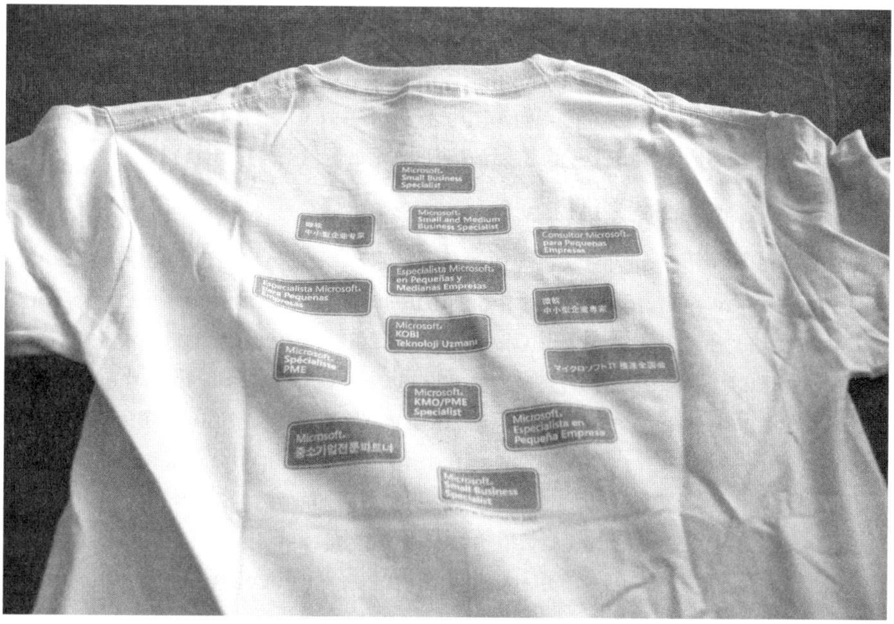

Exclusive Academic Education

Small business technology consultants in the Microsoft community have long been jealous of Microsoft Certified Partners and Gold Certified Partners who received invitation-only technical and business training. The perception was that this gave those elitists a leg up on the competition (true!). That has changed with the Small Business Specialist Community program, where incumbents now get to attend by-invitation, partner-only training. The playing field with the big guys has effectively been leveled!

Action Pack Content

The Action Pack is a "blended beast" that was best presented earlier in this chapter rather than later. Clearly, you "gave at the office" to purchase the Action

Pack subscription. But as you've concluded by now, you get SO MUCH STUFF from Action Pack that clearly the "gets" outweigh the "gives."

Accrue Partner Points and Aspire for More!

The Microsoft Partner Program correctly rewards achievers. That's just good free market behavior, where competition results in rewards for the winners! Small Business Specialist Community members receive up to 25 Microsoft Partner Points (this model was described earlier in the chapter).

I want to emphasize one item about the Partner Points system and aspiration. Around the world, fair-minded folks will use the Small Business Specialist Community program to improve their professional standing and their personal net worth. In short, the Small Business Specialist Community has opened a door for thousands to pull themselves up and do better economically than their parents did! This is a classic free market aspiration model that is honored globally. The Partner Points program provides a structure to move up the Microsoft Partner ladder. Perhaps you want to start out as a Small Business Specialist but you're really only biding time until you have enough customers to build up your references and go after mid-market and enterprise-level work. Hey—you're welcome to stay at the small business segment level as long as you like and free to leave for happier hunting grounds when the time is right. The Partner Points model supports such aspirations and you'll start out with 25 such points once you become a Small Business Specialist. Good on ya!

Additional Gets

A few other cool gets in the Small Business Specialist Community program are:

- **Marketing offers.** Small Business Specialists receive exclusive marketing offers and opportunities.

- **Additions.** The only thing constant with the Small Business Specialist program is change, and you can reasonably expect that more gets will be added to the benefits of membership.

Historical Context

The old adage that Microsoft gets it right on the third try is very true when it comes to how Microsoft has entered the small business space. Let's face it—it wasn't until SBS 2000, the third major release of this application, that Microsoft got it right! In this section, I'll provide some historical context about how Microsoft has finally gotten it right with the introduction of the Small Business Specialist Community.

> IMPORTANT: The good news is that Microsoft hangs in there until it gets it right! Heck, with over $53 billion in corporate treasury cash (Seattle PI, April 2005,http://seattlepi.nwsource. com/business/169588_msftnotebook19.html), it's got some deep pockets to develop and refine programs and products until traction is achieved. Seems like a compelling reason right there to partner with Microsoft— it's in it for the long haul!

Attempt #1: Sweet Success

Upon the launch of SBS 2003 in October 2003, the Microsoft Partner Program launched a "Sweet Success" small business partner campaign where participants submitted SBS 2003 customer success essays in a context format. Monthly winners received a shopping spree at Best Buy (a retail store that later went on to buy the small business consulting firm Geek Squad), an Action Pack subscription, and cookie deliveries (the kind of cookies you eat, not those that infest your web browser!). The grand prize winners received cash, travel, and hardware. This was documented in my November 2003 *SMB Technology Watch* newsletter at http://www.smbnation.com/newsletter/Issue3-2.htm. This essay-writing campaign, where Microsoft gained heaps of valuable small business customer data, was the genesis for the inclusion of the three-customer essay submission requirement in the first draft of the Small Business Specialist Community (circa November 2004). As you read above, this essay-writing requirement was unfortunately dropped in later Small Business Specialist Community drafts.

Attempt #2: Small Business Partner Engagement Program

To pump up the small business technology community and refine its final versions of the Small Business Specialist program, Microsoft launched the Small Business Partner Engagement Program (PEP) in the USA for a sixth-month period starting January 2005 and terminating just before the launch of the Small Business Specialist Community in July 2005. In Figure 2-9, you can see the gives and gets of the channel-facing community-building outreach effort by Microsoft to boost the number of Registered Partners.

Figure 2-9
Small Business PEP Gives and Gets

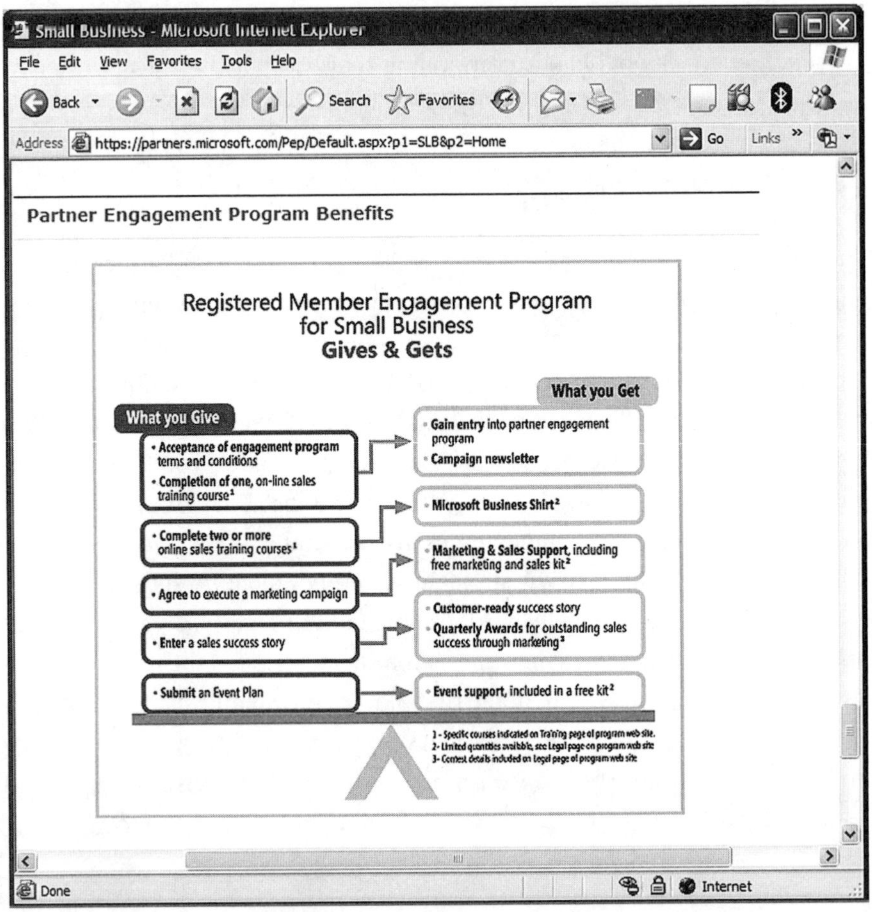

If you look closely at Figure 2-9, you can clearly see that Microsoft was testing the waters and softening the small business technology community defenses as it rolled out some gives and gets that are very similar to those incorporated into the Small Business Specialist Community. The Small Business PEP is discussed in detail in the January through April 2005 editions of the *SMB Technology Watch* newsletter at http://www.smbnation.com.

> IMPORTANT: Time to share a mild partner program resentment. Microsoft has no provision to grandfather or "fast track" existing Small Business PEP participants into the Small Business Specialist Community program. That is unfortunate, because there is precedent in the technology industry for doing exactly that. How do I know? I was there! My Novell Certified NetWare Engineer (CNE) title (circa late 1980s/early 1990s) provided me an exemption into IBM's Certified LanServer Engineer (CLSE) program. Instead of having to complete six IBM CLSE-related exams, I was only required to take one "step-up" exam that I easily passed. No such step-up or fast track exists for expedited entry into the Small Business Specialist Community. But I'd be delighted to take a wager on the following: If for some reason Microsoft misses its aggressive Small Business Specialist Community recruitment goals (trust me—it is a very large worldwide number that I won't repeat here), you will probably see some grandfathering clauses introduced.

Attempt #3: Small Business Specialist Community

Believe it not, the Small Business Specialist Community has long been in the making. Microsoft conducted extensive research with its small business partners and found that small business partners:

- Want to provide more consultancy and business solutions.
- Want being a "partner" to differentiate them from non-partners.
- Want more from simply being a partner:
  - Services,

- Personal Contacts/Services.
- Have issues with Microsoft:
  - It is impersonal,
  - It is a very big corporation, and
  - They feel they are too small to be noticed.
- Want great dialogue with Microsoft

These findings, combined with other factors like the recent history outlined above, resulted in the first draft of the Small Business Specialist Community that was beta tested in the UK in the fall of 2004 and early 2005. Additional feedback from that beta period was used to refine the program you see in place today!

Summary

This chapter provided a deep dive into the Small Business Specialist Community program. You started with an insightful overview of the entire Microsoft Partner Program. We then dove right into the GOOD STUFF of gives and gets! That was followed by a historical view of how the Small Business Specialist Community came into existence. It was a lot of reading, and throughout this chapter heaps of context was woven in to provide maximum value. That's what a good book should do best!

Hopefully you're now super-psyched and jazzed about the Small Business Specialist Community. Remember that it all starts at http://www.smbizspecialist. com. Now, turn the page and start preparing for the 70-282 certification exam. See you there!

Authors Beatrice Mulzer and Harry Brelsford launch the new book at the Microsoft Worldwide Partner Conference in Minneapolis with Allison Watson, vice president of worldwide partner sales and marketing at Microsoft

Section II ❧ Exam 70-282

Chapter 3
Analyzing the Existing Environment

Chapter 4
Designing a Business Technology Solution for a
Small- or Medium-sized Business

Chapter 5
Installing Windows Small Business
Server 2003

Chapter 6
Securing Windows Small Business
Server 2003

Chapter 7
Configuring Windows Small Business Server 2003

Chapter 8
Supporting and Maintaining Windows Small
Business 2003

Chapter 9
Expanding the Windows Small business Server
2003 Network

Chapter 10
Installing and Configuring Windows
Server 2003

CHAPTER 3
Analyzing the Existing Environment

Perform a Needs Assessment

At one point in your career, whether you are a technician working for a larger firm that provides Information Technology support or the small- and medium-business (SMB) consultant in business for yourself, you will have to assess parts of (or even the entire business environment of) your customers.

Technicians generally like to think of hardware and software when the word "assessment" is used and know just the tool to investigate the network. But, in reality, business hardware needs cannot be properly assessed unless they are aligned with the business goals and objectives. What point is there in installing a new server that works at lightning speed when the business-critical application does all its processing on the workstations?

To properly assess a business need, conduct a two-part assessment - a business assessment and a technology assessment. Microsoft offers a great tool called the *Microsoft Business and Technology Assessment Toolkit* that will aid you in your studies for the 70-282 exam. This is shown in Figure 3-1 and can be found at http://www.assessmentframework.com. It also provides a great follow-through methodology in real-world situations.

Figure 3-1

The Microsoft Business and Technology Assessment Toolkit is an excellent study tool.

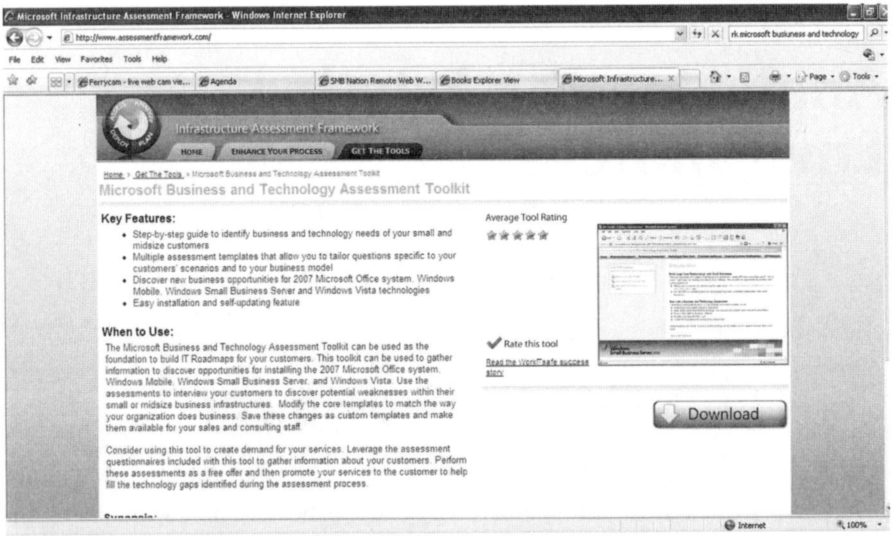

Business Assessment

The business assessment should be conducted with the business owner or a managing partner. The purpose of this assessment is to find out how executive management or the owner sees the future business. In some cases, you will find that the business owner is very content at ten employees and has no future plans to grow the business but would rather maintain the current size or revenue. In other cases you will find that the owner plans on adding ten additional employees over the next six months or is thinking about purchasing another business soon – all affecting the decisions to be made for managing the infrastructure, selecting hardware and software licensing. Using a tool like the templates contained in the *Microsoft Business and Technology Assessment Toolkit* will enable consistent and thorough research from the business point of view. Areas covered from the business side include:

- Business Demographics

- SWOT (Strenghts, Weeknesses, Opportunities and Threats), Vision and Strategy
- Pain Points
- Regulatory Compliance Issues
- Technology Budget
- Major Projects
- Business Functions and Applications
- Business Intelligence, Process and Workflow
- Business Continuity and Disaster Recovery
- Communication and Telephony

To point out the importance of the business assessment, just look at business functions and applications. It is good to know how the business makes its money, who the customers are, how they are sold to, communicated to, invoiced, etc. This is important information to have for a basic understanding how the business operates. Business intelligence, process and workflow will provide a picture of how the business uses technology. Is the Internet used for research? How is customer data kept and managed?

The need for business continuation and recovery provides the best example yet of how important this step is. Automatically one's thinking jumps to hardware like RAID drives, backup drives, tapes and software. The tough question to ask during the business assessment would be how long will it take your business to be operational again if someone were to break in and steal the server and several workstations, or if a fire destroyed the office? How many hours or days will you be out of business, un able to resume normal operations?

As you can see, getting these questions answered will affect the technology assessment a great deal. If these critical questions are asked beforehand, many potential issues can be snuffed right from the get-go and you can ensure the right considerations going into the technology assessment.

Notes:

Technology Assessment

After you have done your homework with the business assessment, you are now ready to dive into the nuts and bolts of the technology assessment. You will have to evaluate technical tasks, functions, and capabilities currently in place. Assessing technology needs requires a complete review of the current state and is best established in a Technology Plan. Using one of the templates in the *Microsoft Business and Technology Assessment Toolkit* will again offer a methodology and guarantee consistency. The technology assessment includes:

- Business Demographics
- Hardware – Servers, Clients and Thin Clients
- Printers and Fax Machines
- Software Versions and Licenses
- Network Infrastructure
- Business Functions and Applications
- Connectivity
- Messaging
- Internet Use
- Back-up
- System Management
- Technology Management
- Security
- Wireless
- Communication and Telephony
- Remote Access
- Power
- Storage
- Training and Usability

As an example of what kinds of questions should be asked in the business functions and applications area (during the technology assessment) compared to the same question in the business assessment, it is important to find out what primary business applications and software tools are being used. What functionality does the line-of-business (LOB) application provide? Are there maintenance contracts in place and is it possible to connect the LOB to another application or feed into another database? Discussing the back-up, all the technology points including the actual back-up tools, hardware, and tape rotation schedule are now the focus.

It's a good idea to draw up a network diagram and document configuration based on the information gathered and review recurring costs associated with each component. Everything should get documented in the Technology Plan. This will be the basis for the overall business picture.

Identifying and Analyzing Business Problems

Once the business and technology assessment information has been gathered, it is easy to determine the "current state" and compare those to the "preferred state" the business owner or executive management envisions (regardless of whether it is realistic or affordable). The difference between the current state and the preferred state is then considered a "need."

At this point, the gaps between the current state and the preferred state are easily identified and can be analyzed further. The business problem analysis starts with stating the business goals of the preferred state and the steps that must be undertaken to achieve these goals can now be outlined.

Look for inefficiencies in the current state—processes that consume an excessive amount of resources, such as employee effort and time, equipment, or money. Take into consideration what is critical to the business, its objectives, and its long-term goals.

Real-World Examples

Here are two examples of small business situations you could encounter in the real world.

Example 1. An attorney's office has a receptionist, three paralegals, a bookkeeper, and three attorneys. The business started out small with just two partners, with each of them keeping their data on their own laptops, and there was little need to share information. Eventually, more staff was hired and a peer-to-peer network was implemented to support the initial business needs. The business continued to grow, more customers, more staff and temporary staff was brought on board. Despite being on a peer-to-peer network with a master share, staff members still keep some of their projects and data files on their local machines, which are not being backed up. Staff members share their drives with other staff members and vice versa. There is a color laser printer connected to the receptionist's computer, which everyone prints to, and the receptionist keeps a ring binder appointment book at her desk. Everyone has to walk to her office to add their individual appointments to the master schedule. Once a week, a staff meeting is held to bring everyone up to speed on the status of current court cases. Staff members express that they would like to be able to access both their e-mail and their data at the office while working from home or the court house.

Example 2. A construction company has 25 office staff, 40 on-site managers out at construction sites and a list of over 3,000 contractors (plumbers, electricians, roofers, etc) who work with the construction company on different projects. The 40 construction site managers have to come to the office at the end of each day to update the job site progress documents or call in and communicate this over the phone. There are errors in the communication and important information gets omitted or not updated in a timely manner. Every couple of days, staff has to send out a RFP (request for proposal) to either plumbers or roofers for a particular project, but it is a time-consuming task because all the contractor contacts are being e-mailed the RFP one at a time. The site managers would like to be able to access their work documents over the web and share documents with general contractors. The staff would like to find a way to bundle all contractors into categories instead of having to send the RFPs out individually.

Both examples outline the bottlenecks and business problems which are easily identified. Once a business problem has been analyzed it can be placed into one of these different categories:

• Functionality

- Efficiency
- Total cost of ownership
- Availability
- Reliability
- Security
- Flexibility
- Ease of manageability

At this point in the real world, recommendations should be added to the Technology Plan under a heading called "Business Requirements." The recommendations should demonstrate how implementing each recommendation would answer the business needs. The Technology Plan is basically a business problem statement—a platform on which you build your case for implementing the project.

> Important: During the Microsoft exam you may encounter a simulated version of a real world business problem and you will be given a list of technology solutions to choose from. In these cases, make sure to read the question at the end of the story very careful. At times it could be as simple as the answer that covers the "least expensive" or "most secure" solution. Many test takers fail because they compare exam questions with real life and start creating their own solutions. Do not fall into this trap – read the question twice – and stick to the exam objective.

Critical Considerations

In real life there are always *business constraints* that could limit the ability to achieve the preferred state and business goals. Business constraints can play a significant role, and meeting the business requirements within those constraints are key to a successful implementation. These critical considerations should always be factored into the Technology Plan.

Time Frame: The time frame or schedule could affect decisions. If the schedule is too aggressive, you may have to scale back goals, change priorities, or change your approach.

Budget: The budget should always be considered in the design phase, starting with the cost of completing the project and including continuing costs for the resources required to maintain the project over a certain lifetime.

Resources: Besides capital expenditures, you must consider all necessary resources for the implementation. This would include considering the existing hardware and network infrastructure as well as maintenance, administration, training, and support.

TCO (total cost of ownership): On top of the resource expenditure, don't forget about hardware and software upgrades, unexpected out-of-pocket expenses, and other factors that affect TCO, like the cost of telecommunications or equipment leases.

Company Policy: Knowing and understanding the company's standards or policies are important factors that could play into the technical aspect of the design, method of implementation, and product selection.

These critical considerations will be unearthed by following the methodology of the *Microsoft Business and Technology Assessment Toolkit*. When you combine the business and technology assessments all the necessary information will be covered:

- Business success factors.
- Size, type, and scope of the business.
- Required software applications.
- Current applications and required access to them.
- Required number of computers, printers, and other devices.
- Current hardware.
- Amount of anticipated network traffic.
- Network security level.
- Critical constraints.

- Anticipated change in business process or structure.
- Plans for growth.

This is the blueprint for designing a business network solution. The next step is identifying and selecting the appropriate hardware and software for the implementation.

> Important: We recommend downloading the *Microsoft Business and Technology Assessment Toolkit* at https://partner.microsoft.com/40025740 (must have access to the Microsoft Partner site) and using it as a study aid for this chapter.

Identify and Select Appropriate Hardware and Software for the Environment

The right computer hardware will enable a business network to run efficiently and function effortlessly. Windows Small Business Server 2003 requires a server and network components equipped to meet the unique requirements of the business and preferred state.

Equally important is the business having the right software tools to resolve those issues that have been identified. You must ensure that the software applications are compatible and were designed and tested on Windows Server 2003 and the respective client operating systems.

There are also considerations about the client hardware, the network cabling, routers, switches, mobile devices, and type of Internet connection. To get the best performance out of the entire network, all components must play together like a well-rehearsed orchestra. Having one component out of tune will affect the performance of the entire opera.

> Important: System requirements for Small Business Server 2003 are covered in chapter 5. System requirements for Windows Server 2003 are covered in Chapter 10.

Hardware Functionality and Effectiveness

Regardless of what brand computer you buy, with all the different models, options, and components available, some key components will have a fundamental performance impact. These components are the motherboard, processor, memory, and hard disks. To ensure that these components work with Small Business Server 2003, you should check the Windows catalog at www.microsoft.com/windows/catalog before you buy.

Motherboard: Even though you could run SBS 2003 on a workstation-class motherboard, since no explicit specification exists, it is not recommended. The motherboard ties together all computer components, including the processor, memory, hard drives, and other peripherals. You should get a server-class motherboard to achieve the best performance base for Windows Small Business Server 2003.

Processor: The main processor consideration is the clock speed at which it operates, measured in MHz (megahertz) or GHz (gigahertz). The clock speed determines how fast the server can perform computing tasks. Windows Small Business Server 2003 supports up to two physical processors and can support up to four logical processors using hyper-threading technology. If you will be putting a large load on the server and using it for line-of-business (LOB) applications or communication or collaboration, we recommend using two physical processors at the highest clock speed your budget will allow.

Memory: Memory measured in MB (megabytes) or GB (gigabytes) can have a dramatic impact on server performance. Physical memory, also referred to as RAM (random access memory), determines the amount of data the server can manage simultaneously. Installing additional memory is easy; if you have budget constraints, we recommend putting your money into other server components first and purchasing additional RAM later.

Hard Drives: Several options and configurations are available that allow you to match the disk storage to the small business needs. You can choose from three interfaces: IDE, SATA, and SCSI. All drives come in ranges from 36 GB to 300 GB, and a server can hold multiple hard drives that can be used to create fault tolerance. We'll discuss this in more depth later in Chapter 8, "Supporting and Maintaining Windows Small Business Server."

Network Adapter: NICs come in different speeds of 10 Mbps, 100 Mbps, and 1 Gbps. Even though there are different types of networks, Small Business Server 2003 is designed to work on an Ethernet network and I always recommend using two NICs for NAT-ing functionality.

Hubs: Don't buy a hub; buy a switch. Switches are able to operate in duplex mode, meaning they allow a client to send and receive at the same time. Hubs operate only in half-duplex mode, which means they can allow either sending OR receiving data at the same time, but not both.

Switches: Switches can be considered faster than hubs. They route traffic directly between ports instead of broadcasting traffic across all ports, meaning that each port on a switch gets dedicated bandwidth. This can make a big difference when transferring large files between multiple computers.

Routers: A router performs additional logical functions over a switch, enabling Internet access to the network. Often routers are configured to also act as a hardware firewall and help secure the network.

Firewall: Windows Small Business Server 2003 Premium Edition comes with ISA (Internet Security and Acceleration) Server which is an enterprise-level firewall product. Windows Small Business Server 2003 Standard Edition comes with basic firewall software using RRAS (Routing and Remote Access) and NAT (Network Address Translation). You could also purchase a hardware firewall appliance. Most DSL modems and broadband modems come with an integrated firewall as well. More on firewalls in Chapter 6, "Securing Windows Small Business Server 2003."

Modem: You will need a modem, either a DSL or a broadband modem, to connect to the Internet. Windows Small Business Server 2003 allows users to "dial in" to the network using a secure VPN (virtual private network) connection. This lets users connect directly to the network. You can also use a conventional dial-up modem for Internet connectivity, but with the difference in speed and price, it wouldn't make sense unless you don't have any other choice—like if your business is located near the North Pole. See the chart below for Internet connection types and average speed.

Table 3-1
Internet connection types and associated speed

Type of Connection	Download Speed	Upload Speed
Dial-Up	28.8 – 53 Kbps	28.8 – 40 Kbps
ISDN	64 -128 Kbps (one channel or two)	64 – 128 Kbps (one channel or two)
ADSL	256 Kbps – 8 Mbps	128 Kbps – 1 Mbps
IDSL	128 – 144 Kbps	128 – 144 Kbps
SDSL	128 Kbps – 2.3 Mbps	128 Kbps – 2.3 Mbps
Cable	128 Kbps – 8 Mbps	128 Kbps – 1 Mbps
Frame-Relay/T1	56 Kbps – 1.54 Mbps	56 Kbps – 1.54 Mbps
Microwave Wireless	256 Kbps – 10+ Mbps	256 Kpbs – 10+ Mbps
Geosynchronous Satellite	150 Kbps – 3 Mbps	33.6 Kbps – 128 Kbps

Fax Modems: Besides providing an Internet connection, a fax modem will allow you to send or receive faxes from the Windows Small Business Server 2003. This will require a separate phone line, but is so much cooler than receiving faxes on the old standalone fax machine. With the built-in fax module in SBS, you can receive a fax in a central folder on the network or in a fax folder in Share Point services, or route a fax into the Outlook 2003 e-mail client of specific users. Users can also fax directly from their desktop. More on configuring the fax service in Chapter 7, "Configuring Windows Small Business Server 2003."

Wireless Access Points: Currently you can choose from three different wireless standards: 802.11b, 802.11g, and 802.11a.

- 802.11b: Very inexpensive now, but also the slowest of the three with a speed limit of 11 Mbps (5 Mbps real-world). Supports a maximum of 32 connections per access point and up to three non-overlapping channels, allowing for three separate wireless networks. Operating at the 2.4 GHz band, it is very susceptible to RF interference from cordless phones.

- 802.11g: Slightly more expensive, but backward-compatible with 802.11b. Throughput is 56 Mbps (11 Mbps real-world) and supports a maximum of 32 connections per Access Point and three non-overlapping channels. Operating at 2.4 GHz, it is prone to the same interference issues as 802.11b.

- 802.11a: Most expensive, but also the fastest standard at 54 Mbps (19 Mbps real-world). Operating at 5 GHz, with twelve separate non-overlapping channels, allowing twelve access points set to different channels in the same area without interfering with each other. This is a great solution for a dense user area that requires a high throughput. Beware: Due to the higher frequency, the distance is limited to about 80 feet.

Printers: It makes sense to purchase one $300 network printer instead of three individual $100 printers. SBS 2003 makes sharing printers easy. However, before purchasing a printer you want to share on the network, make sure it is designed for network use. All network printers today have their own NIC that supplies the Ethernet connection. Make sure the printer you choose will work with the Windows 2003 operating system and supports the TCP/IP protocol. A nice feature is a web-based management interface so you can check the status from a remote location. See Chapter 7, "Configuring Windows Small Business Server 2003," for configuring printers.

Client Computers: You want a client system whose hardware supports fast connectivity and performs well on the Small Business Server 2003 network. Consider the key components: processor, memory, hard drive and CD-ROM/ DVD-ROM, and NIC card; and get the best money can buy. The 70-282 exam is based on Windows XP Professional as the recommended choice for the client operating system. Minimum hardware requirements are as follows:

Table 3-2
Minimum Windows XP hardware requirements

Requirement	Minimum	Recommended
Processor	233 MHz	1 GHz or faster
RAM	128 MB	256 MB or higher
Hard Drive	4 GB	40 GB
NIC	10/100 Mbps	x10/100 Mbps

Laptops: Most laptops come with built-in wireless cards. You want to make sure they are equipped with a card that is compatible with the wireless access point you plan to use.

Mobile Devices: SBS 2003 has special features included to ensure that mobile devices—like smart phones and pocket PCs—can take advantage of the remote access features such as accessing your e-mail and schedule. For more information on mobile devices, see Chapter 7, "Configuring Windows Small Business Server 2003."

Second Servers: Depending upon the purpose of your second server, you will need to consider the type of hardware it will require, as it represents a completely separate undertaking from your Windows Small Business Server 2003 server. Also, your second server will need to use a Windows Server 2003 operating system edition other than Windows Small Business Server 2003, such as Windows Server 2003, Standard Edition, since **you can only have one Windows Small Business Server 2003 server running in a network**. The second server will require one CAL (Client Access License) to access the Small Business Server.

Software Efficiency

It is possible to run client operating systems such as Windows 98, Mac OS X, and Linux on a Small Business Server 2003 network, but you will lose out on support for automatic application and service pack installations as well as shared fax and modem services and Outlook 2003. Windows XP Home is not supported on the SBS network because it is designed to be a Home user system and cannot be joined to a domain. Windows 2000 will take advantage of the

SBS 2003 features, but the preferred choice is Windows XP Professional, which is designed to work with the Windows Small Business Server 2003 network environment. It adds security, reliability, performance, and functionality to the local network for all users.

Practice Questions

Question #1

You have received a call from a potential customer asking for help. They want to improve the response times of their applications and network, but despite having upgraded the memory on their server, applications are still running slow. What is the proper way to engage this customer? (Choose the best answer.)

a.   Send the customer a time and materials quote with an estimated cost to find and resolve their problems.

b.   Schedule a Technology Assessment engagement with the customer to determine which software/hardware components need to be replaced or upgraded to resolve their problems.

c.   Call the customer back and ask which applications are having an issue. Then send the customer a time and materials quote with an estimated cost to find and resolve their problems.

d.   Schedule a meeting with the customer and perform a Business and Technology Assessment to get a better understanding of their business goals and technology requirements. Utilize the findings to make recommendations designed to resolve current issues and meet long term business and performance goals.

Question #2

Which of the following areas are considered important in both the Business Assessment and the Technology Assessment phases of the information gathering process?

a.   Technology Budget, Technology Management.

b.   Business Functions and Applications, Business Demographics.

   c. Business Continuity and Data Recovery, SWOT (Strengths, Weaknesses, Opportunities, and Threats).

   d. System Management, Technology Budget.

Question #3

Your prospective customer's critical line-of-business application's latest revision will only support clients running Windows XP Professional. The Business and Technology Assessment you performed for the customer has revealed the following information about the current client desktop and laptop configurations:

- 20 desktops, each running Windows 98, 10 MB NIC, 128 MB RAM, 3.2 GB hard disk drives.

- 5 laptops each running Windows 98, 802.11b wireless network cards, 256 MB RAM, 40 GB hard disk drives.

The customer also intends to purchase an 802.11g wireless access point to give network access to the laptops from the conference room.

Which components will need to be upgraded to meet Microsoft's minimum requirements for Windows XP Professional and provide the required wireless connectivity? (Choose all that apply.)

   a. Desktop disk drives must be upgraded.

   b. 802.11b wireless network cards will have to be replaced with 802.11g wireless network cards.

   c. Desktop memory must be increased to 256 MB or greater.

   d. Desktop NIC must be upgraded to 10/100 NIC.

Question #4

Your Business Technology and Technology Assessment has been completed for a local small manufacturing firm. Among your findings are the following:

- The customer has 25 desktops each running Windows XP Professional. They each meet or exceed the Microsoft recommended HW standards.

- Each desktop computer has a color inkjet printer connected to it via a parallel printer cable. The cost of printer ink is a major expense, especially since very few users need to print in color.

- There are 4 to 8 port hubs that provide office connectivity. One of the hubs is plugged directly into the DSL modem for access to the Internet. The Internet link is slow and security is an issue.

- The desktops are connected as a peer-to-peer network, but needed shared files could be on any of the 25 computers.

- The inventory Access database needs to be ported to SQL server.

Which of the following would most likely be listed in your recommendations to the customer? (Choose the best answers.)

a. Install a network-enabled (TCP) color printer for access by all users and remove all of the connected inkjet printers.

b. Install and implement Small Business Server 2003 Standard.

c. Upgrade the Internet link to a T1.

d. Replace all hubs with switches.

e. Install and implement Small Business Server 2003 Premium.

Question #5

The customer's stated goals are to decrease costs, increase Internet security, provide secure remote access, and have better and faster internal connectivity.

Which of the following would most likely be listed in your recommendations to the customer? (Choose the best answers.)

a. Exchange is too hard to set up for non-IT people; SBS makes it simple!

b. SBS Premium comes standard with not only Exchange but also ISA Server which provides enterprise level firewall security. SBS also allows remote access to files/folders and local and external e-mail as well as supporting e-mail and scheduling access on Smartphones and PDAs.

c. Since you can only have one SBS server on a network you don't have to worry about setting up multiple servers.

d. POP3 e-mail can be easily and automatically pulled down using the SBS POP3 connector. This means that users don't have to log in twice, even on the road.

e. SBS comes with a menu-driven management interface and wizards which makes everyday system management, such as adding users and reporting, simple, even for the novice systems manager.

Question # 6

Your customer is a sales firm with a growing need to provide remote connectivity for their sales people on the road who have laptops and/or Smartphones/PDAs. The CEO, who is new to the company, used Microsoft Outlook and Microsoft Exchange in his previous job and is anxious to implement it at this company, even though he knows that initially the staff will have to continue to use their externally-hosted POP3 e-mail. He is also concerned that the company does not have an effective firewall and the IT staff does not have the capability or expertise to install or maintain either. Because there are less than 75 users in the company, you have determined that Small Business Server 2003 Premium Edition would be the best fit for their needs. Which of the following statements would more concisely describe this solution to the CEO? (Choose the two best answers.)

a. Exchange is too hard to setup for non IT people, SBS makes it simple!

b. SBS Premium comes standard with not only Exchange but also ISA Server which provides enterprise level firewall security. SBS also allows remote access to files/folders and local and external email as well supporting e-mail and scheduling access on Smartphone's and PDA's.

c. Since you can only have one SBS server on a network you don't have to worry about setting up multiple servers.

d. POP3 e-mail can be easily and automatically pulled down using the SBS POP3 connector. This means that users don't have to log in twice, even on the road.

e. SBS comes with a menu driven management interface and wizards which makes everyday system management such as adding users and reporting simple, even for the novice systems manager.

Question#7

A potential customer has called and is interested in having a better understanding and control of their computing environment. They have about 50 users running mainly Microsoft Office applications, though there are some custom line-of-business applications used mostly by mangers and selected users. It has become obvious to the CEO that the IT person is not 100% confident in the functionality of their current backup application or what to do in case of a major disruption to their site or equipment. The CEO is also concerned that, although they seem to have printers everywhere, none of them produce output with enough quality to actually give to a customer. In fact they spend way too much on printer supplies and having to send items out to be printed when they should be able to do much of it in-house. Which of the following steps would be especially appropriate in a Needs Assessment engagement for this particular customer?

a.   Technology Assessment

b.   Effective Backup Strategy

c.   Business Continuity and Disaster Recovery

d.   Business Assessment

e.   All of the above

Question #8

Your customer has a server running Small Business Server 2003 and 10 users running Windows XP Professional with Microsoft Office 2003 and 2007 applications. Though e-mail is used a great deal for customer communications, documents are also frequently exchanged via fax. The single fax machine in the office is subject to breakdowns and paper jams so often it is keeping the receptionist away from answering important customer calls while she is constantly fixing it. What would be the best recommendation for this customer? (Choose the best answer.)

a.   Install fax modems and telephone lines at each desktop to remove the burden from the receptionist. This will allow her to go back to answering phones instead of fixing the fax machine.

b. Implement Shared Fax service on SBS. Faxes can be sent to a printer, sent to an e-mail recipient, or placed on the SharePoint website for easy access.

c. Install a back-up fax machine in the office. Configure it to notify the Key Operator (KO) by e-mail if a breakdown or paper jam should occur.

d. Install a second fax machine at the receptionist's desk. She would then be able to hand carry the received fax to the recipient should the main fax machine fail.

Question #9

A law office is looking to upgrade to a domain environment. There are currently 20 Windows XP Professional PCs configured in a peer-to-peer network. The customer would like to implement Exchange, remote connectivity, and file sharing but has spent so much money on the standalone Windows 2003 server for the special line-of-business SQL application and a hardware firewall that their budget is somewhat strained. The LOB server will operate as a member server in a domain. They do not know how to set one up but would like to put one in place for management purposes. What would you most likely recommend based on the findings of your Business Technology Assessment? (Choose the best answer.)

a. Make the existing server a domain controller and install Exchange on it.

b. Install a second server with SBS Standard and make the SQL server a member of the domain. Implement remote connectivity using Remote Web Workplace.

c. Install a second server with Windows Server 2003 and make the SQL server a member of the domain. Install and configure Exchange to support the customer's e-mail requirements. Install and implement VPNs and/or Remote Web Workplace.

d. Install a second server with SBS Premium and make the SQL server a member of the domain. Implement remote connectivity using Remote Web Workplace.

Answers:

Question #1: Answer: d

a. This is the traditional way that break/fix shops work but it is probably a one-problem, one-fix engagement. If you are interested in building a relationship and ongoing business with a customer, it is important that you understand their needs as well as how to possibly fix a problem.

b. This is only half the answer. The customer's immediate issue will be resolved but a truly successful engagement involves truly knowing the customer's current and future business and related technology requirements.

c. A little more refined than answer a, but still a break/fix solution, not a true consultative engagement.

d. Correct. The key here of course is that the customer is operating slower than they would like, they are not down and unable to conduct business. A Business Technology Assessment is not the correct answer if the server is on fire! If the ongoing problem is causing production issues, you may have to resort to break/fix mode to at least get them working. But once you do, taking the time to learn the business and the customer's processes will pay off in the long run, both in your ability to propose the proper solution and the customer's confidence in your professionalism and technical abilities.

Question #2: Answer: b

a. Technology Budget, Technology Management.

b. Correct. Business Functions and Applications, Business Demographics.

c. Business Continuity and Data Recovery, SWOT (Strengths, Weaknesses, Opportunities, and Threats).

d. System Management, Technology Budget.

Question #3: Answer: a, d

a. Correct. Minimum requirement for XP Professional is 4 GB.

b. The Wireless NICs do not have to be replaced because 802.11g is backwards compatible with 802.11b

c. Trick question-remember we are looking for the minimum requirement for XP Professional. No one in their right mind would run XP with 128 Mb, but remember sometimes reality just doesn't apply! Read the questions carefully

d. Correct. The minimum requirement is a 10/100 NIC not 10Mb

Question #4: Answer: d, e

a. Though a network printer should be installed in this instance to eliminate the expense associated with all of the inkjet printers, the requirement states that very few users need to print in color. So based on the stated requirements, this answer would be incorrect.

b. Since increased Internet security is a requirement, Small Business Server Premium Edition with ISA Server would be the correct solution.

c. Though Internet speed was cited as an issue, so was internal connectivity and performance. Because the hubs are common to both the internal network and the Internet there is a good chance that they are the issue. A T1 would be overkill for this network anyway, especially in a tight budget situation. A properly provisioned DSL link, at a higher data rate (several rates are usually offered by the provider), should be sufficient.

d. Correct. Hubs are very slow and are prone to congestion. All ports receive all traffic, and as a result all NICs have to at least inspect each packet to see if it contains its address. Switches know which node (by MAC address) is on which port. Nodes on other ports do not see non-broadcast traffic.

e. Correct. SBS 2003 Premium will provide the domain services and remote connectivity requirements. The Internet security requirement is also met with ISA server acting as the corporate firewall. SBS 2003 Premium also includes SQL, though it is not required in this instance for use by the customer's LOB application because of the separate SQL server already installed. There is no

problem having additional application servers in an SBS domain. SharePoint can be configured to utilize SQL on the SBS Premium server for superior search capabilities.

Question #5: Answer: b, e

a. Though this is not the correct answer it is a valid point. Installing and configuring Exchange from scratch is not a point-and-click operation. It can be a daunting undertaking to do it correctly. SBS takes the complexity out of the install. Answer a few questions and it's finished and working.

b. Correct. SBS Premium meets all of the customer's stated requirements and security concerns at a very low cost with excellent ROI. A win-win for the customer (and you)!

c. True, but a very small advantage in this case.

d. The POP3 e-mail requirement is a lower level requirement and should be considered, but not as a main priority.

e. Correct. Systems management is an issue with many small companies who cannot afford to properly train their "IT Guy." The SBS server management GUI allows customers to perform everyday tasks such as adding a user very easily with just a minimum of training.

Question #6: Answer: e

a. Technology Assessment

b. Effective Backup Strategy

c. Business Continuity and Disaster Recovery

d. Business Assessment

e. All of the above

Qustion #7: Answer: b

a. A costly and the least efficient option.

b. Correct. The easiest solution, especially since the customer already has SBS installed. Requires only a fax modem installed in the server.

c. Again very costly and inefficient.

d. The problem is the receptionist is already too busy fixing the fax to answer the phone. Now she is also doing deliveries.

Question 8: Answer b:

a. The software vendor has already stated it was supported as a member server and not a domain controller. As a general rule it is a good idea to not install additional services on an application server. It will probably affect its performance if not break it entirely.

b. Correct. This solution meets all the customer requirements without affecting the existing network. Since the customer has installed a HW firewall SBS Premium is not required.

c. The amount of time and expense involved in installing Windows Server 2003 and Exchange would certainly not be possible within the customer's budgetary constraints. It also does not make sense for an environment of this size.

d. SBS Premium is overkill. The customer has an HW firewall and has an SQL server already on the network. His functionality can easily be met with SBS standard.

Summary

In this chapter we covered analyzing the existing environment and took a closer look at how to perform a needs assessment by identifying and analyzing business problems. We pointed out critical consideration that can not be ignored when designing a Technology Plan. You learned about selecting the appropriate hardware and software for an SBS 2003 server and its functionality and effectiveness.

Chapter 4
Designing a Business Technology Solution for a Small- or Medium-Sized Business

Howdy! Welcome to follow-on tasks from the previous chapter, where you established the technology plan using the Business and Technology assessment. You are now ready to fill the gaps (needs) and start designing solutions. In Windows Small Business Server 2003, several Windows Server 2003 technologies have been leveraged and packaged to respond to small business needs.

Design a Messaging and Collaboration Specification

A couple years back, just when SBS 2000 had made its debut, I met with a client to discuss small business technology solutions. This client—an accountant who shall remain unnamed to protect the innocent—had done his own business analysis and figured out that he was in desperate need of communication solutions.

This Old House

The client's office is located in an older building that is two stories tall (see Figure 4.1), and the way the staff communicated was by either picking up the intercom or yelling up the stairs. Needless to say, clients did find his bellowing, "Hey you!" very unprofessional.

Figure 4-1

The real-world client used in this example. Be sure to treasure your real-world experiences as one study method to pass the 70-282 exams.

We installed server hardware, a real Internet connection (abandoning dial-up), and immediately started using the simple messenger application. The client and staff loved the company folder on everyone's desktop and proceeded to stick every thinkable document, application, picture, and who knows what in it. Even though we had the fax module, the client didn't trust it and continued to use the old fax machine. Such was life for that customer in the SBS 2000 days. But stand by, as things change for the better.

IMPORTANT: Let's talk about modularity. Microsoft Learning uses some time-tested education models that are very sound. Modularity is a key methodology used by Microsoft Learning. It means:

a. A student could take a MOC course, assuming all prerequisites have been met.

b. The student would be able to complete the exercises.

c. The exercises would be self-contained (e.g., all keystroke procedures start with a logon command and end with a logoff command).

So, in the spirit of modularity, you do not need to have working knowledge of SBS 2000 (the prior SBS release) to pass the 70-282 exam. The 70-282 exam uses SBS 2003 as its baseline and makes no assumptions and has no expectations about your SBS 2000 legacy wisdom. This is an important tip to help keep you focused on passing 70-282. Please see the other IMPORTANT item at the end of the chapter (right before the questions).

SBS 2003 to the Rescue

With the introduction of SBS 2003, we finally made the big step and fully integrated all the features available in SBS. The client was ready to elevate and better exploit the technology prowess of the SBS 2003 bundle. The following sections show how the client utilized the communication capabilities of SBS 2003.

Fax

Faxes are now being delivered to two employees' Outlook clients as well as a shared folder on the network. With the ability to remote in to the desktop via Remote Web Workplace and check e-mail through Outlook Web Access when needed (and view the faxes), the owner finally understood the value of the integrated fax module and gave up the old fax machine, which is now seldom used. To fax out material, we are discussing the addition of a high-speed scanner, which could be used to also route documents to fax, but that is another discussion. Note you can also store inbound faxes in Windows SharePoint Services.

Real-Time Communications

Messenger is still the number one inter-office communication tool and the way you instant message in SBS 2003. The receptionist now quietly IMs the owner and two other employees from the first to the second floor and there is no longer a need to yell up the stairs in front of the customers. It's worth mentioning that some customers in the real world are questioning whether instant messaging is used strictly for business purposes.

IMPORTANT: SBS 2003 removed Exchange-based instant messaging functionality.

Exchange Server 2003

Exchange-based e-mail and other services have been implemented and we finally got rid of the POP3 accounts at the ISP. The customer was so amazed at how fast his e-mail was working—we could almost consider it real-time communication. I won't forget the big smile on his face when he told me that he was conversing with another accountant on the other side of the USA and it was just as fast as using IM. I guess the best part, with them being tax people and all, and having to work very hard during the first four months of the year, was implementing RPC over HTTP where they could receive their e-mail at home without having to use a VPN connection. Almost all communications with their clients takes place via e-mail now, and Exchange has become a pivotal point in productivity.

Windows SharePoint Services

And what do you think happened to the Company Shared Folder? It went away. Why? Because Windows SharePoint Services (WSS) is being positioned, whether it likes it or not, as the document and data store of choice. Back at the customer site, we finally got things organized and set up document libraries in WSS. We very much have a business focus and restrict uploading to business documents. Even though the client is using a proprietary accounting solution for the bulk of the transactions, WSS has taken on the important role of catchall for everything that doesn't fit into the accounting software. It also serves as a discussion and transaction history tool, keeping track of goings-on with client files that need to be documented and retained for future use. One of the great productivity features is the ability to set "Alerts"—an advisory to a user that there has been a change made to a document without anybody needing to pick up the phone or send an e-mail. Everyone is on the same page on all projects, and all information is kept neatly in one place. WSS is discussed further in Chapter 7 of this book.

Shared Resources

The default shared folder on an SBS 2003 network is called "Users Shared Folders" with the share name USERS. The company folder no longer exists, because the SBS development team received feedback that customers were confused in the SBS 2000 time frame when there were both Users and Company Shared Folders. There are no shared folders on any of the workstations by default, and all data is kept on the server. (In Chapter 7 you will learn there is a My Document redirection setting that moves all of the workstation data to the Users Shared Folders on the network—an administrator's dream!)

Recently a high-speed color laser printer was purchased, which is shared on the network and available for everyone to print to. This addition is already saving money for the company by eliminating the need for individual color printers, ink, and maintenance.

> IMPORTANT: For this part of the 70-282 exam, you need to have your design thinking intact and view yourself as an architect. In that paradigm, kindly consider the following bit of history. In the earliest days of the local area network (LAN), when disciples kissed the Token Ring and surfed ArcNet (two legacy networking standards), traction was gained because a LAN offered great cost efficiencies in a business via shared resources. The early printers cost a great deal of money, so clearly a small business couldn't afford to place a dot matrix or a laser printer on each worker's desk. However, a LAN allowed a small business to have everyone share one printer. Brilliant! So when designing a small business network and taking the 70-282 exam, you'll never go wrong by returning to your roots: shared resources being the driver for many small business network implementations.

Notes:

Design a Connectivity Specification for Networking and Remote Connections

One of the reasons this particular client had a dial-up connection when I first started working with him was really to save a penny. It took me a while to convince him that he would be able to use high-speed Internet access and still come out better on the cost/benefit equation.

Broadband

SBS 2003 is easily implemented on a broadband connection, using either a dynamic or a static IP address. I always recommend using the static IP, especially if you are running the Exchange server as your primary e-mail solution and want to make good use of the Remote Web Workplace. While configuring the E-mail and Internet Connection Wizard (CEICW) "for a direct broadband connection," you will be given the choice of either using a dynamically assigned IP address or entering a static IP as your broadband connection option. This will be performed for the network adapter on the server that will oversee the external connection. Note that once a small business person uses a high-speed broadband connection, it is unlikely she will return to a modem connection (or anything slower). This is a design consideration: Speed is addicting!

There are two traditional methods of broadband connectivity: DSL and cable. DSL is preferred by many small businesses, as it's a service typically provided by the telephone company and oriented toward business use. DSL is usually offered with a static IP address (but you'll see the exception to this in a moment). Cable is more consumer-oriented and typically uses a dynamic IP address, but in some cases can be much faster than DSL. So, there are truly two choices here. Back at the customer site, we ended up purchasing a DSL line, because we were only 300 feet from the CO (central office). DSL can be easily set up with the CEICW since it includes the option to set up "a connection that requires a user name and password" (PPPoE—Point-to-Point Protocol over Ethernet). This is the "exception" referred to earlier. Thereby we were obtaining a dynamically assigned IP address. This scenario required two network adapters— one for the local network and one for the Internet, and the server would provide routing and network address translation (NAT) services. But I'm starting to jump the gun on a few technologies that will be detailed later in this book. However, the design phase must necessarily incorporate some technical considerations at this early stage.

Local Router with Static IP

At another customer site, we ordered a static IP address and therefore used the static setup option in the CEICW titled "a local router device with an IP address." This is the SBS way for connecting a static IP DSL router, dial-on-demand router, or ISDN router. The static IP address is supplied by the ISP on the external network adapter card or interface. If the connection requires authentication information, you must configure the router with a user name and password, even if your router supports Universal Plug and Play (UPnP). UPnP is a standard that allows SBS 2003 to easily configure the router device.

Remote Web Workplace (RWW)

Bingo! Going back to the cost/benefit equation, here is where the client can definitely see the benefits, which are usually hard to establish in IT. In our case, we had a pregnant mother who had difficulty climbing the stairs in the office. We set her up with a workstation at home and registered a .com name in DNS for Remote Web Workplace (RWW), which I showed her how to use. She then was able to use RWW, connecting from the comfort of her own home to her XP client workstation at the office. She continued managing her daily tasks without a dip in productivity. That is what I call a win/win situation.

> IMPORTANT: Be sure to build in training time for the customer to learn how to use the SBS 2003 network. Customers gladly pay for training time to learn features such as RWW, which is an SBS 2003 portal for supporting the mobile worker.

Design the Application Specification

Unfortunately, clients rarely give you much choice on this, as they usually have already purchased the software with little thought about the hardware or operating system it will be running on and expect you to make it all work. One of the most overlooked issues concerns application compatibility.

Application Compatibility

Occasionally you will have the client who will have purchased SBS 2003 and new server hardware only to find out that his old proprietary application—for which he refused to pay the upgrade five years ago—will not be supported by the system. In this case you can always use virtual PC for the legacy application and still bring the rest of the network up to SBS 2003 and Windows XP SP2.

SQL Server 2000

When installing SQL Server 2000, you will be offered a chance to add a password for the system administrator logon. This is presented for backwards compatibility of earlier SQL versions and disabled while Windows authentication mode is used. Make sure to set a very strong SA logon password if SQL is configured for mixed-mode authentication. Mixed-mode authentication enables the SA logon, which uses a blank password by default.

> IMPORTANT: Review the premium technologies setup documentation found on Disc 5 of the SBS 2003 premium product. Print it out and spend 10 minutes reviewing it at a high level so you have an appreciation for the design issues surrounding SQL Server 2000 and ISA Server 2000/2004.

Backup

SBS 2003 contains a much improved backup solution (which is featured in Chapter 8 of this book). However, if you decide to purchase a third-party backup program, make sure that it supports VSS (volume shadow copy service) so it can take advantage of VSS and use it to back up open files. Veritas Backup Exec 10 robustly supports SBS 2003 and addresses VSS and other features.

Utilities

Make sure to examine existing technologies before acquiring and deploying workstation and server utilities, base applications, infrastructure services, network connectivity components, and platforms. To be honest, you can find this out by joining some of the public newsgroups and posting a question about utility compatibility. See Appendix A for a list of these types of SBS resources.

Third-Party Applications

SBS 2003 provides a stable and secure infrastructure to run small business applications, such as an accounting system or industry-vertical specific application. Before purchasing a third-party application, ensure that you have enough disk space and check for application compatibility and any application dependencies. If you have a specialized third-party line-of-business application (LOB), you may opt for getting a second server and using Terminal Services in application sharing mode, which will then be solely dedicated to the LOB application.

> IMPORTANT: One thing you WILL NOT find on the 70-282 exam is direct references to specific third-party backup solutions, utilities, and applications. Back in Redmond, Microsoft Legal would never allow it (trust us on this one). So with our third-party mentions above, we've gone further than the scope of the 70-282 exam, which we are trying really hard to stay focused on in this book. But for the 70-282 exam, you'd need to have on your "radar screen" the conceptual and planning issues surrounding third-party applications and utilities.

Design a Management and Operations Specification

Another client I work with also came from a peer-to-peer environment. Users had different e-mail accounts and shared resources, which were scattered amongst several workstations. Things were difficult to locate and access. Some PCs with Internet connectivity had shared resources accessible by "Everyone," allowing full access and no password protection. Calendars and schedules were kept individually. After an SBS 2003 installation, many clients wonder now how they used to manage this way. So, before proceeding any further, let me tell you the first thing we did for the client. We implemented centralized storage on the server, which has made it easy to locate and access resources. This early win allowed the client to gain confidence in SBS 2003. It's always good to have an early win when introducing technology in the small business.

> IMPORTANT: Expectation management. Once SBS 2003 technology is introduced into a small business that previously lived in the Dark Ages, you can anticipate a gusher of requests as the business and its culture seek to "leap frog" and exploit more of SBS 2003 sooner rather than later. So you should consider a deployment schedule that appropriately introduces increased SBS 2003 functionality over time at a rate that allows the client to digest all this cool stuff! If you throw too much technology at customers too fast, they become overwhelmed and build up resentment! So, be disciplined in your plan and introduce technology to the small business in phases.

E-mail, Networking, and Internet Connectivity

Exchange Server 2003 allows for centralizing e-mail services, calendar, and resource scheduling at the customer site. The above-mentioned client is now using the same e-mail address for both internal and external e-mail communications. And even though this office already had a hardware firewall/Internet router, having the built-in firewall in SBS 2003 adds an extra level of protection.

Active Directory

Using Active Directory allowed the client to centralize security and authentication. Now users have to remember only one username and password for the entire network instead of using multiple usernames and passwords for different resources (e-mail, file shares, etc.). What we're really talking about here is the single sign-on experience on the computer network. Even though you will never really have to touch Active Directory in SBS, this exam speaks also towards mid-size businesses, and therefore we will have to dig a little deeper into this later in this chapter.

Server Administration and Management

With the preconfigured management consoles in SBS, you have a set of
management tools for network management, allowing the delegation of basic
tasks to power-users. They can add additional users and groups and perform basic
tasks such as managing printers, shared folders, and faxes. Central to managing
SBS 2003 is the Server Management console, shown in Figure 4-2.

Figure 4-2

*The Server Management console should be completely explored on a live
server prior to taking the 70-282 exam. Drill down into each component and
"look and see."*

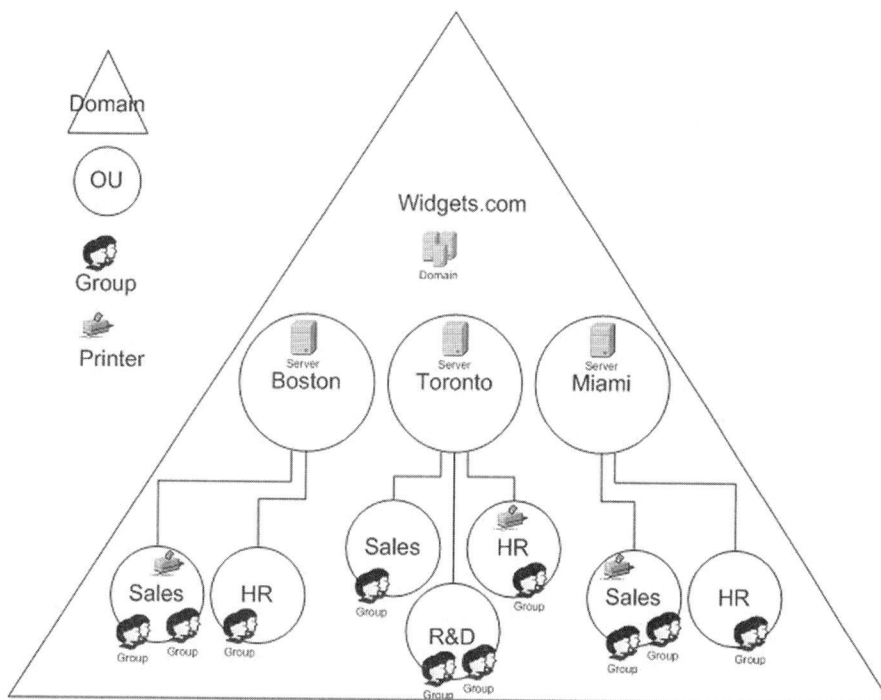

Easy Setup of Client Computers

You can anticipate positive leverage in the deployment and administration
phase of the SBS 2003 life cycle because of wizards. Deploying applications
and adding client computers to the network is easy when using the integrated
wizards. By doing so, you are able to configure settings for an entire group of
computers and push out applications to all computers instead of installing them

one at a time. So you're really talking about "doing more with less," which could be less time, less money spent on consultants performing routine tasks, etc. Consultants are now freed to work on more meaningful tasks. And don't forget that major Microsoft branding themes, like "doing more with less," have a way of weaving themselves into Microsoft certification exams. Microsoft will, in crafty ways, assure itself you're on board with its corporate messaging and ways of thinking. So, when in doubt, think the "Microsoft way," on an exam.

> IMPORTANT: Consoles and wizards are central to the SBS experience and you can expect to be held accountable for having sufficient knowledge of these two features. Don't you think that Microsoft, rightfully proud of its SBS consoles and wizards, would want to test you on these? You betcha.

Monitoring and Reporting

SBS 2003 has rich monitoring and reporting capabilities you can see from the Monitoring and Reporting link under Standard Management in the Server Management console. In the real world, being able to receive performance and usage reports has really made my clients feel more comfortable knowing what is going on with the network. Usually I forward a copy of the user usage report with comments as well as an occasional performance report so my clients know they are under watch 24/7. Proactively monitoring a customer's SBS 2003 site and communicating about potential issues sooner rather than later reflects the maturity of a successful small-medium business consultant, the type who would be welcomed into the Small Business Specialist program! Chapter 8 of this book explores the monitoring and reporting area in greater depth.

Design a Disaster Prevention and Recovery Specification

Having a business in Florida makes you think twice about disaster prevention and recovery. Why? Because the winds are known to blow hard in Florida during the "mean season." Well, we already know that disasters like the occasional hurricane cannot be prevented, but you can definitely prepare for them, undertake risk mitigation, and plan for business continuity. Disaster prevention must take many possibilities into consideration, from natural (hurricanes, fire, and flood) to manmade (power grid brownouts, worms, and hackers) to personal (vindictive employees and unscrupulous competitors) to political (terrorist acts and government interference). The point is not only to fully recover from a disaster, but to be able to continue business operations despite a disaster.

Integrated Backup

SBS 2003 allows you to fully recover from a disaster with its integrated Backup Solution. It is easy to schedule and implement daily full server backups using the Backup Configuration Wizard. The Backup Configuration Wizard is a reliable way to back up your entire system including the system state, registry, data files, and Exchange store. Backups are explored in much more detail in Chapter 8.

Storage Devices and Media

Your small business client is going to tell you that he doesn't have the money to purchase a tape drive, tapes, or other media solutions for the data backup. When you run into this type of situation, you may want to ask the customer how much money he will lose if the business suffers X amount of inoperable hours due to the loss of its infrastructure. Storage technology is rapidly changing, and in addition to tape drives there are so many other options, like using USB external hard drives, backing up to workstations across the network, burning data to a DVD, or performing a nightly backup across the Internet. These are all viable solutions, and you must take into consideration the cost of the media, extensibility, speed, and reliability.

Checking Backup Status

There are two ways to check the backup status in Small Business Server 2003.

- Have the report e-mailed to you, with the backup log files attached.
- Check the last 10 backups for success or failure in the Manage Backup task pad in Server Management.

To receive the status reports by e-mail, you must first run the Monitoring Configuration Wizard from the Server Management console. I highly recommend that you do keep an eye on the backups and log files and do periodic test restore of individual files. (That means once a month!)

Landing on Your Feet

If you plan for a disaster and adhere to a rigid backup schedule and test restores, you will be prepared, when disaster strikes, and land on your feet. It is a good best practice to document the recovery steps, including information on server hardware, such as disk size, controllers, and motherboard chipsets, as well as partition or volume information and drive letters. Document, label, and plan. Then review your recovery plan every three months and perform a test restore at least once a month.

Design a Hardware Specification

Hardware specifications will depend on the load that will be placed on the Small Business Server 2003. If you are currently running on an existing server and have to design a specification for a migration to a new server, you could sample performance on the existing server. For 70-282 examination purposes, remember the following mantra, which will be reiterated in the next couple of chapters:

Go with Microsoft's hardware specifications for SBS 2003. What Microsoft posts on its public-facing SBS 2003 website is gospel on the 70-282 exam regardless of how you personally feel.

With your architect hat on, think about the best time to baseline the current performance so you get a data point to track the SBS 2003 network over time. A baseline would be performed during times of heavy usage—for instance, when everyone logs in first thing in the morning and checks their e-mail and the morning news and launches their applications that connect to the database on the server. That's when the network is most heavily taxed and stresses will be revealed.

The next three sections view hardware by usage classification.

Database Server

If your SBS server will mainly be used as a database server, you want to take a close look at the storage and memory subsystem. Take into consideration the amount of hard drives you should use to get the best performance. You may want to consider placing the database log files on a separate hard drive from the data files if you plan on running SQL server, doing so not only for performance, but also for recovery reasons.

File Server

If your SBS server will be used as a departmental file server—for instance for a company that works with larger files like AutoCAD (Architects) files or multimedia files (Photo Studio) that easily average 30 MB and more—consider faster disk drives and a gigabit network card. Remember that the file server function is historically one of the reasons folks implemented local area networks.

E-mail Server

Running Exchange on the SBS server will use storage, memory, and some CPU cycles. Just as we recommended for the database server, placing the log and data files on physically separate hard drives is a good idea. So consider the following test-taking tip in the design context: Knowing the role of the server will help you determine the appropriate hardware requirements.

Fault Tolerance Considerations

Having covered disaster prevention and recovery using the Backup Configuration Wizard and available media options, let's not forget additional hardware options available to us based on the Windows Server 2003 operating system. If you are able to purchase more than one hard disk, you can implement a RAID (redundant array of independent disks) solution to the point where you could continue operating despite a single hard drive failure.

Mirrored Drives (RAID 1)

This is a simple solution requiring at least two hard drives. As the name states, one disk drive is the exact mirror of your currently working disk. If the working disk should fail, you have fault tolerance with the second disk and the system will continue to operate using the unaffected disk. You can create a mirrored drive set in the Disk Management console. Usually the write-performance takes a hit with RAID 1, due to the controller having to write the data to two disks simultaneously. RAID drives are discussed in Chapter 10.

RAID 5

This requires at least three disks and uses intermittently striped data and parity for fault tolerance. Parity is the information that allows you to re-create a single failed disk based on the data information of the remaining two intact disks. If two disks fail simultaneously, you will not be able to recover. RAID 5 volumes are created on dynamic disks and can not be extended or mirrored. If you use hot-swappable drives, you will be able to remove the failed disk while operations continue (at a somewhat decreased speed, since the remaining two disks have to create the data of the third missing disk), and then swap out the failed disk with a healthy disk, and the RAID array can rebuild the data without interruptions to your operation. RAID drives are discussed in Chapter 10.

If They Let You...

If you have a client who sees the value of continued business, and she follows your advice and lets you implement the best solution, I recommend a system with a minimum of five drives: two for the system partition, which should be mirrored, and the remaining three as the data partition in a RAID 5 array. It is possible to partition a RAID5 array. This can be beneficial, as you can separate your mission-critical data files from the users' shared folders and also separate application files. You could run a separate additional backup on just the mission-critical data to make sure you have additional redundancy on top of your regular full SBS backup. The above solutions can be implemented by using built-in tools in the Windows Server 2003 operating system, meaning that these are software solutions. These solutions, since they are software-driven, will impact the performance on the server. You could choose to use a hardware solution, using a hardware drive controller. That would cause a higher initial outlay, but would not use system resources since the read/write operations would be performed by the hardware controller and not the system.

> IMPORTANT: I promised another important tip and here it is. DO NOT OUTSMART YOURSELF on the 70-282 exam. If you are an SBS 2000 and SBS 2003 guru, it might be easy to become confused about which version of SBS contained which feature. It's kinda like taking classes in college. When you have a full schedule of classes, you might use a word differently in one course versus another. For example, the word "risk" can have different meanings in your real estate class than your finance class. And when you have to define risk on the respective exams for each course, you might get confused and transfer the definitions inappropriately. Ergo—while honoring your SBS expertise, keep an eye out for questions that call for a Windows Server 2003 solution! Case closed.

Designing in the "M" space

This may seem early in the game, but since this is the chapter on "designing," it seems like a good way to bring your attention away from SBS and start talking a little "medium enterprise."

No doubt Microsoft loves talking about Active Directory design, just venture out to www.microsoft.com/reskit and click on the Windows Server Deployment Kit link and you will find a bucketful of stuff you can design around! For instance you will find a lot of reading material on Designing a Managed Environment (that means designing Group Policy infrastructure) or Designing and Deploying Directory and Security Services, which leads you into designing site topology, designing a resource authorization strategy, designing a Public Key infrastructure and more fun bits and pieces like that.

I do not expect you to read volumes on this, but please don't expect us to write volumes about it here either. Fact is, that you should probably stick your nose into some of those (maybe in a dark and stormy night when there is nothing else to do?) and see what it will be like expanding into the "M" space. Expect the exam to sport some medium enterprise level questions, and since SBS is built on top of Windows Server 2003 and Active Directory, it makes sense to expect questions in these areas. In Chapter 9 we'll cover the technical portions of migration and expansion of the SBS network, and Chapter 10 will be all about Windows Server 2003. We will have other items weaved throughout the chapters of this book as needed. And in case you wondered what the "M" space is, that would be medium businesses with less than 1000 network devices. Cheers!

Designing in Active Directory

Before we even start talking about designing scalable, secure and manageable infrastructure we need to establish that there are two types of structures in Active Directory:

- Active Directory Logical Structure
- **Physical** Network Structure

Logical Structure

Active Directory uses domains and forests to represent the logical structure of the directory hierarchy. Forests represent the security boundary for Active Directory and domains are used to manage users, computers and network resources. Domains contain Organizational Units, helping subdivide administration. Each object in Active Directory stores not only its own name, but also the name of its superior container all the way up to the root container. This is referred to as a hierarchical naming system, where the objects in the tree seem to be nested inside other objects. The basic logical components of Active Directory are:

- **Organizational Unit** – Provides the logical grouping of users, groups and computers and other objects in a domain which often mirrors the functional structure of the company.

- **Domain** – One or more Windows Server 2000 or Windows Server 2003 Domain Controller (DC) containing users and groups that share a contiguous namespace and the Active Directory database for authentication and server resources.

- **Domain Tree** – One or more Active Directory domains that share a hierarchical Domain Name Space (DNS), i.e. europe.smbnation.com. (Could be the smbnation child domain in Europe. More on DNS in Chapter 9.)

- **Domain Forest** – One or more Active Directory domain trees (a domain tree has its own DNS namespace) sharing the same Active Directory database.

The logical structure helps organize the directory objects, managing network accounts and shared resources.

Physical Structure

The physical structure serves to facilitate network communication and the setting of physical boundaries around network resources. Physical structures consist of:

- **Subnets** – A network group with a specific IP range and subnet mask.
- **Sites** – One or more subnets. Used to configure Active Directory access and replication.

Active Directory Management and Operations

A well-designed Active Directory logical structure facilitates the efficient integration of features such as Group Policy, enabling desktop lockdown, software distribution, and user, group, computer, and server administration, into your system. We will cover more on this in Chapters 8, 9 and 10, providing more information on administering Active Directory Services on Windows Server 2003. Part of administering Active Directory includes working with applications (resources) like Exchange Server and SQL.

So why are we putting such an emphasis on the difference between logical and physical structures? Let's do the 10,000 foot level overview to give you a glimpse of what is so cool about Active Directory.

Figure 4.2
The Widget Company logical layout

Figure 4.2 depicts the logical layout of the Widget Company which has offices in Boston, Toronto and Miami. Toronto is the home office, with control over its Research and Development (R&D), Sales and HR divisions. This company grew organically. When additional offices in Boston and Miami were opened, it was decided it would be better to handle sales and Human Resources locally. In this case, the Active Directory structure allowed the company to manage administration basically following the company functional chart. Boston has a Sales and Human Resources OU which it manages locally, and so does Miami. Lo and behold, the Widget company, due to its poor management, is soon bought up by the Uber-widget Company, which has a totally different organizational/ functional layout. But, since the resources (employees, workstations, servers) are already in place at the old Widget Company, and the Uber-widget Company wants to keep these offices where they are for strategic reasons, the Uber-widget Company absorbs the Widget Company as is. Since the Widget Company is running on Windows Server 2003 and Active Directory, it just joins it to Uber-widget Company's forest and redesigns its logical structure!

Figure 4-3
The Uber-Widget Active Directory Forest

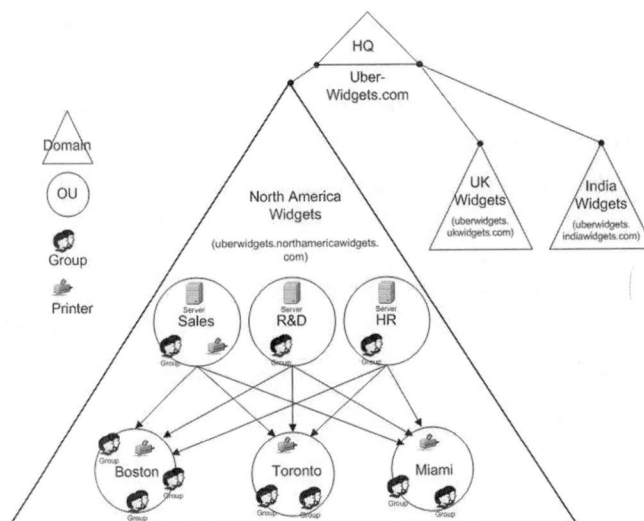

Now the Uber-widget Company, despite having its HQ overseas, is managing its subsidiaries through an Active Directory Domain Forest. (See Figure 4-3) The Uber-widget Company now is sure to apply its company policy across all domains, including the UK Widgets, India Widgets and North America Widgets companies. The offices in Boston, Miami and Toronto are still there, but no longer autonomous. The Sales, R&D and HR OUs ensure that there is consistent application of company policy throughout the three different sites. Since this is a logical structure, it can be virtually managed from anywhere. The domain admin could be living in Hawaii (fat chance of that) and guarantee that everyone has the same desktop environment regardless of which city or department users sign on from.

This is a very basic example showing you the flexibility of being able to manage by logical structure. Mergers and acquisitions are commonplace; think about the nightmare larger companies would have to endure if they had to re-deploy their entire infrastructure because the organizational chart changed! With Active Directory you can rename domains (one thing you cannot do in SBS), move users and groups logically to where they belong on the functional chart, and manage by group policy, so you're able to deploy software and enforce consistency across the entire domain.

Practice Questions

Question #1

One of your customers has decided to finally be hooked up to the Internet. They would like speed but also the ability to easily publish a web site directly. They are also concerned that their site be easy to find by just typing in a simple URL, without customers having to type in a complicated one. It is also important that they not have to worry about the connection. They should be able to send and receive data transparently without having to worry about configuration files or addresses that may change. Since they are a small company with less than 30 PCs and one server, the cost of the link is a concern and should be taken into consideration. What would be the best solution for their high-speed link? (Choose the best answer.)

a.   A DSL or Cable connection with a static IP address. Their external DNS should be hosted by the ISP or other third party.

b.   A DSL or Cable connection with a dynamic IP address. DNS is not an issue because the address is not guaranteed to be the same every time it's renewed.

c.   An ISDN link directly to the ISP; DNS and external look-ups can be facilitated by e-mailing a host's file to strategic customers.

d.   A satellite link, which is less expensive in the long run because its geosynchronous orbit keeps it in an area that is visible to anyone in the world. The local router will hold the external address whether it is dynamic or static.

Question # 2:

Your customer has a server with 10 hot swappable disks. They are configured as follows:

Volume 1 - 2 x 36 GB RAID 1

Volume 2 - 3 x 36 GB RAID 5

Volume 3 - 2 x 36 GB Mirrored

Volume 4 - 3 x 36 GB RAID 0

Which of the following statements are true? (Choose all that apply.)

a.   Volume 4 is equal in size to Volume 2.

b.   Volume 1 is the same configuration as Volume 3.

c.   Volume 2 is the same size as Volume 3.

d.   Volume 3 is the same size as Volume 1.

Question #3:

Your customer has a server with 10 hot swappable disks. They are configured as follows:

Volume 1 - 2 x 72 GB RAID 1

Volume 2 - 3 x 36 GB RAID 5

Volume 3 - 2 x 36 GB RAID 1

Volume 4 - 3 x 36 GB RAID 0

Which of the following statements are true? (Choose all that apply.)

a. It takes twice as many failed disks on Volume 2 to cause complete data loss as it does on Volume 4.

b. Volume 4 is more cost effective than Volume 2 and more resilient than Volume 3.

c. Volume 1 is more cost effective than Volume 2,

d. Volume 2 is more resilient than Volume 4 and more cost effective than Volume 3.

Question #4:

Which items below should be an integral part of an effective recovery plan? (Choose all that apply.)

a. Test and verify the restore process often.

b. Check backup logs often.

c. Document all backup/restore procedures, passwords, and hardware, volume and RAID configuration options thoroughly.

d. Review procedures and documentation quarterly.

e. All the above.

Question #5:

In your conversations with an accounting firm, the customer has expressed interest in the new Microsoft Active Directory infrastructure that you have proposed. They are, however, anxious to understand the advantages it will provide, specifically in the areas of resource access and security. Which of the following statements would most accurately describe these advantages to the customer? (Choose the best answer.)

a. Active Directory provides centralized authentication and authorization services for windows based clients and resources. Its main function is to provide a fully searchable catalog of available users and the resources available to them.

b. Active Directory provides the mechanism necessary for Exchange to equate a POP3 username with a Microsoft Windows user ID without having to recreate the mail storage folder or modify the X.400 descriptor.

c. Active Directory provides centralized authentication and authorization services for Windows-based clients and resources. Its main function is to provide the mechanisms and security necessary to grant access tokens to users and provide single-sign-on secure/auditable access to resources across the enterprise.

d. Active Directory provides centralized authentication and remote access capabilities to users of all types, including LINUX, MAC (OS 10 or better), TACACS+, or RADIUS to those resources not usually available to them. With a minimum of management configuration and involvement.

Question #6:

Your customer has a server with 10 hot swappable disks. They are not yet configured and you want to build multiple RAID volumes to provide the best data protection and performance. You want to provide volume sizes as follows:

OS Volume – 36 GB

Data – 288 GB

SQL log – 72 GB

You have:

6 – 72 GB drives

4 – 36 GB drives

Choose the proper, most cost-effective RAID setting for each volume. Include sparing when available:

a. RAID Setting A

- OS = 3x36 GB drives RAID 5 w/36 GB HS

- SQL Log = 1x72 GB drive RAID 0 w/72 GB HS

- Data = 4x72 GB drives RAID 5

b. RAID Setting B

- OS = 2x36 GB drives RAID 5 w/36 GB HS

- SQL Log=1x72 GB drive RAID 0 w/72 GB HS

- Data= 4x72 GB drives RAID 5 w/36 GB HS in DBL Mode

c. RAID Setting C

- OS = 4 x36GB drives RAID 5

- SQL Log =2x72GB drive RAID 0

- Data= 4x72GB drives RAID 5

d. RAID Setting D

- OS = 36 GB RAID 1 ((2x36 GB) – 36 GB)

- SQL Log= 72 GB RAID 0 (2x36 GB)

- DATA = 288 GB RAID 5 ((5*72 GB) – 72 GB), w/72 GB HS

Question #7:

Which of the following are Small Business Server 2003 features that are not found in any of the other Wndows Server products? (Choose all that apply.)

a. Integrated Backup.

b. Active Directory.

c. Volume Shadowing Service (VSS).

d. Server Management Console.

e. SharePoint Services

Question #8:

Which statements are true about the Exchange implementation on Small Business Server 2003? (Choose all that apply.)

a. The implementation of Exchange on SBS 2003 is fully functional and is not "crippled" in any way.

b. Small Business Server 2003 can support multiple e-mail domains within the Exchange implementation.

c. The Exchange data store cannot be backed up using the integrated backup utility. A third party utility must be used.

d. Outlook Web Access (OWA) is installed by default during the installation of Small Business Server 2003.

Answers

Question #1: Answer: a

a. Correct – If you want your customers to find you via your website URL then you should stay in the same place. A static address does exactly that. The address you are known as, and DNS resolves the name against, never changes. If the address of the site keeps changing (i.e. is dynamic) then it is much harder (though not impossible) for DNS to associate the URL with the proper IP address. Cable or DSL are both inexpensive high-speed links and would be the best choices here. Cable can be much faster, but also tends to be more expensive for "business" level service –a static IP. DSL on the other hand is more business oriented and receiving a static address is a common feature.

b. This is incorrect because it misses the basic customer requirement of allowing his customers to easily get to his web site without having to type in a complicated address – inferring name resolution, i.e. DNS. A dynamic address is one that is assigned each time the device connected to the provider (usually the router), is powered up. The address will expire after some period of time, forcing the device to ask for a renewal. The kicker is that there is no guarantee that the renewed address will be the same as the one that expired. If the address has changed, then the DNS record will be incorrect and thus the connection will fail. There are utilities that will keep track of the potentially ever-changing address, but those are beyond the scope of this book and are not covered (or an acceptable answer choice) on the exam.

c. This is incorrect. An Integrated Services Digital Network (ISDN) connection is probably not the best choice here. Though once the only technology available, they have been for the most part replaced by less expensive, faster, and more readily available options such as cable, ISDN, and even satellite. Combining multiple channels traditionally allows up to 144 kbps which pales in comparison to other technologies available. A host file is a text file which lists each system's name and associated address. They were a common way to do name lookups before DNS was prevalent or easily available in small organizations. Today they are only used in special circumstances and sending a host's file is not a solution for a number of reasons.

d. Incorrect. The physical location or visibility has nothing to do with a site's visibility on a network or the Internet. It's all about IP addressing and DNS.

Question #2: Answer: b,d

a. Incorrect. Incorrect – Volume 2 is a RAID 5 array. RAID 5 eats up the size of 1 physical disk in parity information. The size of the volume in this case would be (3*36) – 36 = 72 GB. Volume 4 on the other hand is RAID 0, meaning all the disks are available to the volume 3*36 = 108 GB.

b. Correct RAID 1 is by definition mirrored drives.

c. Incorrect - Volume 2 is a RAID 5 array. RAID 5 eats up the size of 1 physical disk in parity information. The size of the volume in this case would be (3*36) – 36 = 72 GB. Volume 3 on the other hand is mirrored (RAID 1), meaning that the second disk is an exact copy of the first. Therefore only ½ of the total disk volume is available (2*36) - 36 = 36 GB.

d. Correct – Both volumes are RAID 1 by different names. Both are (2*36) – 36 = 36 GB in size.

Qestion #3: Answer: a,d

a. Correct – A single disk failure on a RAID 0 volume will result in loss of all the data on the volume. Losing two disks on a RAID 5 volume will result in total data loss. Hint: don't use RAID 0 for important data if you have a choice!

b. Incorrect - Volume 4 is more cost effective than Volume 2 or Volume 3 because the total size of each disk purchased is available for use (3 x 36 = 108). However, Volume 4 is RAID 0, which offers no protection. Therefore Volume 4 has NO resiliency and both Volume 2 and Volume 3 are better choices for important data storage.

c. Incorrect – Volume 2 is a RAID 5 array. Though RAID 5 eats up the size of one physical disk in parity information, in this case it is still only 1/3 of total disk capacity. 2/3 of the total disk size is still available for use. Volume 1 is mirrored and therefore only 50% of the total drive capacity will ever be available.

d. Correct – Volume 2 is a RAID 5 array and is very resilient. A loss of a single drive in Volume 2 will slow down the system because data has to be recreated using the other disks and the parity information stored on them. But the system is still operable. In addition because this particular server has hot swappable disks the bad drive can be replaced without taking the system down. The new disk will be rebuilt automatically and when completed the system performance will return to normal. Volume 4, on the other hand has no resiliency; a loss of any disk is a loss of all data on the volume. Though RAID 5 eats up the size of one physical disk in parity information, in this case it is still only 1/3 of Volume 2's total disk capacity. 2/3 of the total disk size is still available for use. Volume 3 is mirrored and therefore only 50% of the total drive capacity will ever be available.

Question #4: Answer: a,b,c,d,e

a. Correct – Surprisingly, it is not unusual for customers to learn how to restore their data while attempting to recover from a system failure. Needless to say, this is no time to learn. I have had more than one frantic call from customers who discovered during a restore that their backup media was defective and they had no data to restore!

b. Correct – Every day in fact. This is a great service you can provide for your customers (for a fee, of course) that will protect you both.

c Correct – Volume 2 is a RAID 5 array. Though RAID 5 eats up the size of one physical disk in parity information, in this case it is still only 1/3 of total disk capacity. 2/3 of the total disk size is still available for use. Volume 1 is mirrored and therefore only 50% of the total drive capacity will ever be available.

d. Correct – Recovery is much less of a problem if procedures are fresh in your mind and you know they are current. One successful recovery will fully justify all the preparations and work performed. Of course, a failure gets the point across as well but – well, you get the idea!

Question #5: Answer: c

a. Incorrect – Though Active Directory does provide the ability to search for available resources and users. It is not its primary function.

b. Incorrect – Active Directory does provide single-sign-on services that can be extended across external resources such as POP3 e-mail, but its primary function is authentication and access control. The X.400 descriptor and mail storage folder are not involved in any way.

c. Correct – **Active Directory is not only the authentication provider but it is also a true directory. It is a hierarchical structure that contains information about objects on the network including user accounts, computer accounts, shared printers, volumes and much more.**

d. Incorrect – Not the correct answer, but admittedly a lot of impressive acronyms.

Question #6: Answer: d

a. Incorrect – OS volume is the wrong size (72 GB),SQL Log is correct size but spare unnecessary, Data RAID 5 volume is the wrong size (216 GB).

b. Incorrect – OS volume only has two drives and can't be RAID 5. Move spare to array the volume is the wrong size (72 GB),SQL Log is correct size but spare unnecessary., Data RAID 5 volume is the wrong size (216 GB), HS wrong size, no such thing as DBL mode.

c. Incorrect – OS RAID 5 volume is the wrong size(108GB),SQL Log RAID 0 volume is wrong size(144GB), Data RAID 5 volume is the wrong size(216GB,)

d. Correct – The OS is protected by RAID 1 (mirrored drives). SQL log is a RAID 0 volume which does not need protection. Data is protected by a RAID 5 volume with a hot spare.

Question #7: Answer: a,d,e

a. Correct – The Small Business Server 2003 integrated backup utility is unique to the Small Business Server product. Accessed through the Server Management Console, it allows manual and scheduled backups to be easily performed to tape or disk.

b. Incorrect - Active Directory is the central component of the Microsoft Windows platform. All Windows server products have Active Directory functionality integrated as a key component.

c. Incorrect – The Volume Shadow Copy Service allows the backing up of files or databases that might be open by other applications. It is standard on the Windows 2003 Server products.

d. Correct – The Server Management Console only comes with SBS 2003 and takes much of the complexity out of day-to-day management functions. With very little training even non-technical customers can add users, add shares, and connect to the Internet.

e. Correct - Windows SharePoint Services (WSS) is available as a free add-on to all Windows Server 2003 products. But SBS 2003 has WSS loaded and positioned as the document and data store of choice. It allows users within the SBS environment to share documents and files and more easily collaborate and automate business processes.

Question #8: Answer: a,b,d

a. Correct – The Exchange implementation has the same functionality as the standard version of the product. It has just been integrated within the SBS server platform to make installation cleaner and less complicated.

b. Correct – Because the SBS Exchange Implementation is a standard implementation, multiple e-mail domains and user e-mail aliases are possible.

c. Incorrect – The integrated backup utility will fully backup the SBS 2003 Exchange messages store.

d. Correct – OWA is installed but is not operable until Remote Access has been configured using the "To Do List."

Summary

So you thought this chapter was pretty easy? Mind you that planning is 80% of the job, and if that is done right, the implementation will take only 20% of your time because you planned it right and didn't run into any unsuspected surprises!

In real life, designing a business technology solution for a small- or medium-sized business depends on budget, available resources, and all sorts of sometimes unexpected factors. Good thing you are taking an exam, because in the exam world, designing a technology solution will be straightforward. You already know which tools you would recommend. (Hint: they are developed by a big company in Redmond, Washington whose name starts with an "M" and ends with a "t.") The question will tell you the objective; least expensive, easiest to manage, most secure etc., and you will just have to pick up on that fact. It's almost like listening to a customer!

This chapter explored the upstream design function associated with planning for and deploying SBS 2003 networks. Context is king in understanding that. On the 70-282 exam, there is clearly a design section that has you thinking like an architect. This chapter touched on the major design areas and incorporated the "specifications" as the end product for the designing and planning tasks. Areas covered included:

- Messaging and collaboration.
- Connectivity.
- Applications.
- Management and operations.
- Disaster prevention and recovery.
- Hardware.

And all this was presented to you in the context of the REAL WORLD with client war stories, and then topped off with a 10,000 foot level view of Active Directory logical and physical structures. Good stuff!

CHAPTER 5
Installing Windows Small Business Server 2003

This chapter discusses the installation of a Windows Small Business Server: first-time installation, upgrading from Small Business Server 2000, and migrating from Small Business Server 4.5 or an NT 4.0 Server.

Deployment Planning

Preparing for an operating system installation requires many steps and a lot of in-depth planning. You need a fundamental understanding of Windows Small Business Server 2003 and its features, and you must decide which of those features to deploy to make an appropriate fit for the business. Knowing how to take advantage of technology is the key to increasing productivity, reducing total cost of ownership (TCO), and improving workflow processes. Deployment planning works from the ground up, so let's get started with the basics.

> IMPORTANT: Microsoft's product documentation, which ships with the SBS 2003 product (Quick Start Guide) and numerous other goodies, can assist you in understanding the Microsoft view of the world with respect to deployment planning. Part of passing an exam, as you may well recall from grammar school, is to appreciate the intent of the teacher. In this case, the teacher is Microsoft.

System Requirements

First we need to ensure that we have a sufficient hardware-level to support the Windows Small Business Server minimum requirements as shown in the Tables 5-1 and 5-2. (Remember that the exam is based on Windows Server 2003 and has not been updated to reflect Windows Server 2003 R2.)

Table 5-1
SBS 2003 Standard Edition system requirements

Requirement	Minimum	Recommended
CPU speed	300 MHz	550 MHz or faster
RAM	256 MB	384 MB or higher (4 GB max)
Hard disk	4 GB of available hard disk space*	8 GB of available hard disk space*
Drive	CD-ROM	CD-ROM or DVD-ROM
Display	Super VGA, 256-color monitor and video adapter (800x600 or higher resolution)	Super VGA (800 × 600) or higher-resolution monitor
Other devices	• Hardware that supports console redirection • Ethernet network interface card	• Keyboard and Microsoft Mouse or compatible pointing device • Two Ethernet network interface cards
Additional items and services required for Internet access	• Some server functionality requires Internet access and payment of a separate fee to a service provider; local and/or long distance telephone charges may apply. • Broadband or high-speed modem Internet connection	• Some server functionality requires Internet access and payment of a separate fee to a service provider; local and/or long distance telephone charges may apply. • Broadband or high-speed modem Internet connection

Requirement	Minimum	Recommended
Additional items required for networking	• Dedicated Class 1 fax modem to use fax service	• Dedicated Class 1 fax modem to use fax service • Pocket PC Phone Edition 2003 or Smartphone2003 for Outlook Mobile Access • Windows XP Professional or Windows 2000 Professional for client operating systems

* Actual requirements will vary based on your system configuration and the applications and features you choose to install.

Table 5-2

SBS 2003 Premium Edition system requirements

Requirement	Minimum	Recommended
CPU speed	300 MHz	550 MHz or faster
RAM	256 MB	512 MB or higher (4 GB max)
Hard disk	5 GB of available hard disk space* (only 2 GB required if upgrading from Small Business Server 2000)	8 GB of available hard disk space* (only 2 GB required if upgrading from Small Business Server 2000)
Drive	CD-ROM	CD-ROM or DVD-ROM
Display	VGA or hardware that supports console redirection	Super VGA (800 × 600) or higher-resolution monitor
Other devices	• Hardware that supports console redirection • Ethernet network interface card	• Keyboard and Microsoft Mouse or compatible pointing device • Two Ethernet network interface cards

Requirement	Minimum	Recommended
Additional items and services required for Internet access	• Some server functionality may require Internet access, a Microsoft Passport account, and payment of a separate fee to a service provider; local and/or long-distance telephone toll charges may apply. • Broadband or high-speed modem Internet connection	• Some server functionality may require Internet access, a Microsoft Passport account, and payment of a separate fee to a service provider; local and/or long-distance telephone toll charges may apply. • Broadband or high-speed modem Internet connection
Additional items required for networking	• Dedicated Class 1 fax modem to use fax service	• Dedicated Class 1 fax modem to use fax service • Pocket PC Phone Edition 2003 or Smartphone 2003 for Outlook Mobile Access • Windows XP Professional or Windows 2000 Professional for client operating systems

*Actual requirements will vary based on your system configuration and the applications and features you choose to install. Additional available hard-disk space may be required if you are installing over a network.

IMPORTANT: Clearly the above tables have been obtained from Microsoft and reproduced here. There is an important reason for this apparent copy-and-paste operation (and not just to spare the author from typing it out!). When you take the 70-282 examination, it's essential to recite "chapter and verse" the system requirements AS UNDERSTOOD AND STATED BY MICROSOFT.

You likely have formulated your own opinion as to what makes an optimal system baseline for running either Standard or Premium Edition SBS 2003. Right on! However, your own opinion, while reflecting your own personality and professional experience, might not make for a proper answer on the 70-282 exam. Avoid being the test taker who is "too smart" for the exam and views potential correct exam answers with, "I don't do it that way." Such an attitude results in retakes!

Real world SBS hardware discussions may be found in the Small Business-related solution accelerators from Microsoft (written by a segment team, which has more editorial freedom than a product team). Visit www.microsoft.com/partner, click Product and Solutions, and then select Solutions for Small and Medium Business.

Network Interface Cards

At least one NIC (network interface card) is required for the Small Business Server to function. We recommend installing two network cards so the server can take advantage of the basic firewall included in SBS (NAT firewall). If you will be installing the Premium Edition and plan on using ISA Server 2004, you will have to install two NICs.

Disk Partitions

A single disk partition is required. There is no requirement to create multiple disk partitions, but if you choose to do so, there are several ways this can be done. When you partition a disk, each section functions as a physically separate disk. It is a good idea to decide where you would want to place Windows Small Business Server 2003 components prior to the server installation. Dividing up the storage makes sense even if you are using RAID hardware. By dividing the disk space into logical partitions, you can distribute the data, such as operating system files, continuously changing data files, and static storage —i.e. program files—onto different logical disks which will allow for backup segregation and easier disaster recovery.

- You can create partitions during the text-mode setup of the server installation. Minimum recommendation is at least 4 GB, but real-world experience recommends at least 10 GB or more if you have enough drive space available.

- To setup software RAID, create the set after the setup process has completed.

- For a **mass storage controller**, such as SCSI, hardware RAID, or a Fibre Channel adapter, you might need to hit the F6 key at the beginning of the text-mode setup and then insert the manufacturer's floppy with the driver files when prompted, or setup will not see any mass storage controllers and the install will be halted. You will know this when your first setup pass fails because the storage was not detected.

Due to NTFS file system dependencies, Active Directory and Exchange 2003 components will only function on Windows Small Business Server 2003, if the system partitions, as well as the partitions holding transaction logs, the database and binary files are formatted with the NTFS file system.

> IMPORTANT: You should always choose NTFS as the file system for all partitions to receive the benefits of Shadow Copies, disk quotas, and encryptions in addition to NTFS permissions.

> Also, beware of tricks on exams where blatantly false answers are provided to mislead you. For example, if you were to see a file system answer referring to HPFS (high performance file system), you would know this was a false answer on the 70-282 exam because HPFS is an OS\2 concept (IBM's legacy operating system from the 1990s) and hasn't been available on Microsoft network operating systems since the Windows NT Server 3.51 era.

First-Time System Installation

A first-time system installation is the best scenario you can wish for. After you have gathered all the information on the business and conducted the needs analysis and finished your technology plan, you can plan and design the server to exactly the specifications that will best support the preferred state of the business.

To prepare the server for a first-time installation, ensure that you have:

- Adequate hardware for the load you are going to place on it. (See minimum system requirement above.)
- The latest system BIOS.
- Set the boot order in the BIOS to boot from the CD-ROM first.
- All driver files for SCSI, Fibre Channel, RAID (if needed).
- HAL (Hardware Abstraction Layer) drivers for custom hardware.
- Disconnected UPS devices (may cause setup to fail).

Now you are ready to begin the installation and boot the server with the Small Business Server 2003 Disc 1 CD-ROM. Upon boot, you will be prompted to press any key to start the installation and enter into the first phase of the setup mode.

IMPORTANT: For security reasons, it is recommended that you disconnect the server from the Internet during installation. This prevents slippery worms like BLASTER from sneaking in!

Setup Modes

There are two parts to setup. The first phase is completed in text-mode setup and the second phase in GUI (graphical User Interface) mode setup.

Text-Mode Setup

- Loads the Windows Small Business Server operating system.
- Starts the Setup Wizard.
- Loads drivers and detects storage devices.
- Enables creation of new partitions.

Text-mode setup starts the program for Windows Small Business Server operating system and prepares the computer for the rest of the installation process. At the end of the text-mode setup, the server will reboot into GUI mode setup.

GUI Mode Setup

In GUI mode, the wizard:

- Detects and installs devices found on the computer.
- Configures each device.
- Installs and configures networking components.
- Copies installation files that were not copied during text-mode setup.
- Installs any additional components.
- Writes the setup log files to the installation directory.

In the GUI-mode setup, the wizard completes the installation of the Windows Small Business Server 2003 operating system. Here you will specify license information, computer name, server components and network settings.

IMPORTANT: If the server does not support booting of the CD-ROM (like a non el-torito compatible CD drive), insert a start-up floppy disk with CD-ROM drivers and navigate to the CD-ROM drive letter, run i386\winnt.ext to start copying the installation files.

Small Business Server Component Installation (Standard Edition)

After the GUI-mode setup is completed, the server will reboot and the Windows Small Business Server Setup Wizard will launch the first time you log in. Before proceeding with the Small Business Server Setup, make sure you:

- Check that NIC are installed and functioning properly.
- Plug in the UPS.
- Plug one cable into the NIC for the internal network.

Do not customize your server until you are done with the entire Windows Small Business Server 2003 installation.

IMPORTANT: When adding the domain name, accept the default of .local or choose another extension like .prv or .internal to keep your internal domain as secure as possible. This way you are ensuring that your internal network will stay isolated from the Internet. (NOTE: Do not use .local if you are using Mac OS X clients on the network.)

At this point you can proceed with the SBS Setup Wizard. If setup requirements are not met at any time, a Setup Requirements page will launch, advising you of the issue so you can correct it before proceeding with the installation.

The Setup Wizard will now install the Server tools and application which are listed on the Components screen. These are applications typically used by small businesses and selected by default. They are:

- Intranet.
- Monitoring.
- Networking.
- Administration.
- Client Deployment.
- Exchange Server.
- Fax Services.

Components are installed to the default location at **C:\Program Files\Microsoft Windows Small Business Server**.

Notes:

Figure 5-1

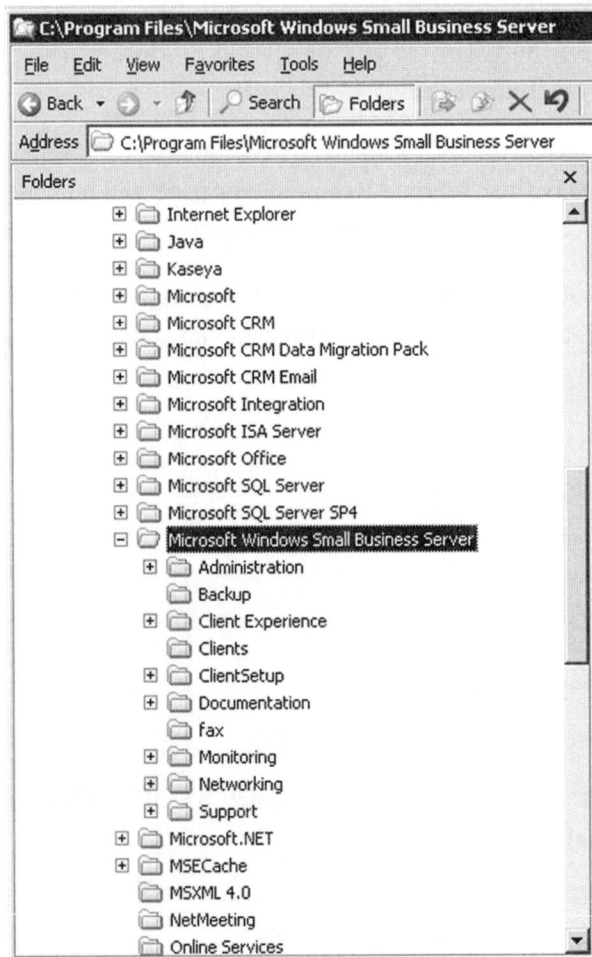

You can also allocate the location of various data folders at this point, like users, shared folder, Exchange database, SharePoint, and fax folders. If you have several drives in your server, I recommended you choose different partitions for data, applications, and users' shared folders.

The complete install at this point can take anywhere from one hour (unlikely) to several hours (most common) depending on your hardware. If you are installing SBS from the CD set, you will be prompted several times to insert different CDs. If you are installing from a DVD, you may as well go get a big cup of coffee or take a nap for a while.

After the Small Business Server 2003 installation is completed, the server will reboot and come up with the "To Do List" when you log in.

> IMPORTANT: Once Windows Small Business Server Setup has run, you are not able to change the computer name. The SBS tools and applications are configured to work with the full DNS name for the internal domain and the NetBIOS name. To change the server name, you would have to reinstall Windows Small Business Server 2003.

Small Business Server Component Installation (Premium Edition)

ISA Server 2000 and SQL Server 2000 and Microsoft FrontPage are included in the Premium Edition of Windows Small Business Server 2003, but do not get installed as part of the core SBS setup. In effect, you install the premium components after completing the SBS 2003 Standard Edition deployment steps. First, follow the install steps for the SBS 2003 Standard Edition. After having a successful SBS install, you can then insert the Windows Small Business Server Disc 5 CD-ROM (Premium Disc) and a new install splash screen will launch, prompting you to install the premium components.

> IMPORTANT: The exam is based on Small Business Server 2003 prior to Service Pack 1 (SP1). Service Pack 1 included:
>
> - SP1 for Windows Server 2003.
> - SP1 for Exchange Server 2003.
> - SP1 for Windows SharePoint Services 2.0.
> - SP 4 for WMSDE.
> - SP 4 for MSDE.
> - SP4 for SQL 2000.
> - ISA Server 2004 with SP1.
> - Stop! You don't need to know any of this stuff!
>
> This is the part that lends itself to much confusion about which parts are covered on the exam and which are not. Having said that, you will **NOT** be tested on service pack levels or version details and if

SQL server or ISA server are mentioned on the exam, it will be part of a generic narrative story, and you are not being tested on reporting services or proxy clients!

Installing SQL Server 2005 WorkGroup Edition/ SQL 2000 with SP3a

Now, having said that you will not be tested on SQL components directly - when the exam team re-crafted the exam in late 2006, (they did go through the trouble of updating certain items and you may encounter a question on SQL 2005) - be aware; when you see such a question I can tell you that **the solution will be indifferent to the version** of the application mentioned. Microsoft exam questions in this case are built to be version-neutral. You can worry about version next time when you are taking an exam on SQL, CRM or Exchange straightforwardly.

This has led to several discussions among the authors on how this subject should be approached. After reviewing the installation steps of SQL 2000 with SP3a and SQL 2005 WorkGroup Edition, we find that the installation part is initiated the same in both instances, using the setup bootstrapper presented on the Small Business Server Premium Technologies Setup screen. From there you continue through the default screens, adding company information and license code (if requested). On the Setup screen, select your preference if you want to install the:

- Default Instance (created a new instance of a database).
- Named Instance (updates named instance to SQL 2005).

You would choose **Default Instance**, because you are installing a new instance of a database. By selecting a Named Instance you would end up upgrading, for example, an existing MSDE database, like MSSQL$SBSMONITORING, which is not supported. The setup screens do differ in both versions but basically you still get to make choices on whether to use the:

- Built-in system account:

- Domain user account:

This will determine the account to be used as the log in for the Service account, which launches the SQL Server service. A rule of thumb here is to have a previously created Service account that doesn't belong to a domain user at all, but is set up just for the purpose of launching different services; this way a service doesn't stop working unexpectedly if a domain user changes his or her password.

The Authentication Mode specifies the security used when connecting to SQL Server, you can select:

- Windows Authentication Mode.
- Mixed Mode (SQL Server Authentication and Windows Authentication).

A rule of thumb here is that using a separate SQL administrator account is more secure. After a couple more screens, SQL will start to copy files. Then click Finish. For SQL 2000 you would go back to the Premium Technologies CD install screen and install Service Pack 3a for SQL.

After the installation (regardless of the version#) there are certain points to consider:

- Do not upgrade the instance of MSDE that is installed for Monitoring (MSSQL$SBSMONITORING), because it is not supported.

In the case of SQL 2005 you would also have the MSDE instance for Windows Server Update Services (WSUS). (Attention: this would occur in SBS R2 only.)

- Do not upgrade the instance of MSDE that is installed for Update Services (MSSQL$WSUS), because it is not supported.

Now, hear me out. The oddity is that the exam does not feature the latest version of WSUS, hence the confusion, because if you see SQL 2005 on an "SBS" exam you would automatically **assume** this exam is based on the SBS R2 version. (You know what the word "assume" really makes of you and me if you break it apart, don't you?)

So having bewildered and befuddled you at this point (at least I have done my job!), let me reiterate that **the solution will be indifferent to the version** of the application of the exam question. You will be tested on your general knowledge and your wits, because if you don't pay attention to detail and let a word like SQL 2005, CRM 3.0 or ISA 2008 throw you off, the exam writers got the best of you!

> IMPORTANT: I'm not proud of having to break it to you in this way. At least you will now be familiar with the "bewildered and befuddled" feeling you may encounter during the exam. If this is the case and you encounter an oddity such as this (where you mistakenly peg real world against exam question), remember what was said here. This is not new. Thinking back to the very first NT exam, which had replication questions (remember those PDCs and BDCs?) on it, there was an odd "reality check" moment, because replication didn't work in real life until Service Pack 1 was released!

Upgrading SharePoint

SharePoint comes included with SBS (standard and premium editions) using the MSDE (Microsoft SQL Desktop Engine). Even though the 2 GB size limit and maximum user restriction of five have been removed from the MSDE, you should upgrade SharePoint to use a full instance of SQL server to take advantage of its indexing and search capabilities. Here again, if we were true to version# you know that you can't really upgrade to SharePoint 3.0 in SBS. Microsoft has a document (Installing Windows SharePoint Services 3.0 on a Server Running Windows Small Business Server 2003 – just use your favorite search engine to find it) explaining that an in-place upgrade from WSS2.0 is currently not supported and a side-by-side installation is strongly recommended.

So, there is real life and then there is the Microsoft exam. Reverting back to doing an upgrade from the MSDE to SharePoint on SQL2000, SQL the Microsoft recommended steps are as follows:

When installing SQL server to upgrade SharePoint, make sure you:

• Stop the http://companweb website (in Internet Information Services).

- Stop the MSSQL$SHAREPOINT Service.

- Select UPGRADE when prompted (do not install a new instance).

- Choose SHAREPOINT from the upgrade box.

- Install SQL SP3a after the SQL upgrade.

- Check that the MSSQL$SHAREPOINT Service started.

- Start http://companyweb.

IMPORTANT: SQL Service Pack 3a must be installed on every single instance of an SQL new install or upgrade. If you install a new instance and upgrade SharePoint to use an SQL instance, you must install SQL SP3a for each individual instance.

Before you undergo this procedure it is recommended that you back up the SharePoint database files which are located at:

%SystemDrive%\Program Files\Microsoft SQL Server\MSSQL$ SHAREPOINT\data

and back up the following files:

- STS_ServerName_1.mdf

- STS_Config.mdf

- STS_ServerName_1.mdf_log.LDF

- STS_Config_log.LDF

Installing ISA Server 2000/2004

Just like installing SQL, installing ISA Server 2000/2004 is an easy task to complete. To properly perform the installation, you must use the setup bootstrapper by clicking on the Install ISA Server icon presented after the premium technologies disk is launched.

IMPORTANT: SBS originally came with ISA Server 2000, ISA Server 2004 was introduced with SBS SP1. Again questions will reflect the words ISA Server 2004, but **the solution will be indifferent to the**

version of the application and tie into the narrative story line of the exam question.

We will cover both installations of ISA Server, because quite frankly there isn't much difference at all. The main difference in the 2000 version that it asked you to make a decision of the role ISA Server 2000 was to play, either be a:

- Caching Server.
- Firewall Server.
- Caching & Firewall Server.

At this point the ISA installation would run on autopilot until you click Finish. Then you had to re-run the CEICW to configure ISA Server.

ISA Server 2004 installs even more silently, but with one difference (well, two): it doesn't ask what type of server role to install and it launches the CEICW automatically during the ISA Server 2004 install. After you finish the CEICW, the ISA installation wizard will be on the last screen, prompting you to click Finish.

After installation is completed, ISA (version X) will not appear in the Server Management console, but will be available under **All** Programs of the Start Menu.

1. Log on to the SBS 2003 server machine as **Administrator**.

2. Click **Start**, click **All Programs.**

3. Click **Microsoft ISA Server** followed by **ISA Management**.

Now you have covered all bases of installing Small Business Server 2003 Standard and Premium Edition. Chapters 6 and 7 will cover the server side configuration of SharePoint and ISA Server.

Notes:

Completing Post-Installation Tasks (To Do List)

The To Do List is a great tool containing a collection of tasks that must be undertaken to finalize the Windows Small Business Server Setup. Here you can connect your server to the Internet, create user accounts, connect printers and workstations, and perform all tasks that will allow a small business to have a fully functional network.

The To Do List is broken up into two sections:

1. Network Tasks

   - View Security Best Practices.
   - Connect to the Internet with the EICW (E-mail and Internet Configuration Wizard).
   - Configure Remote Access.
   - Activate your Server.
   - Add Client Licenses.

2. Management Tasks

   - Add a Printer.
   - Add Users and Computers.
   - Configure Fax.
   - Configure Backup.
   - Configure Monitoring.

Notes:

The To Do List is shown in Figure 5-1 below.

Figure 5-2
The To Do List is central to the SBS experience and is representative of the SBS culture about using the GUI to complete tasks.

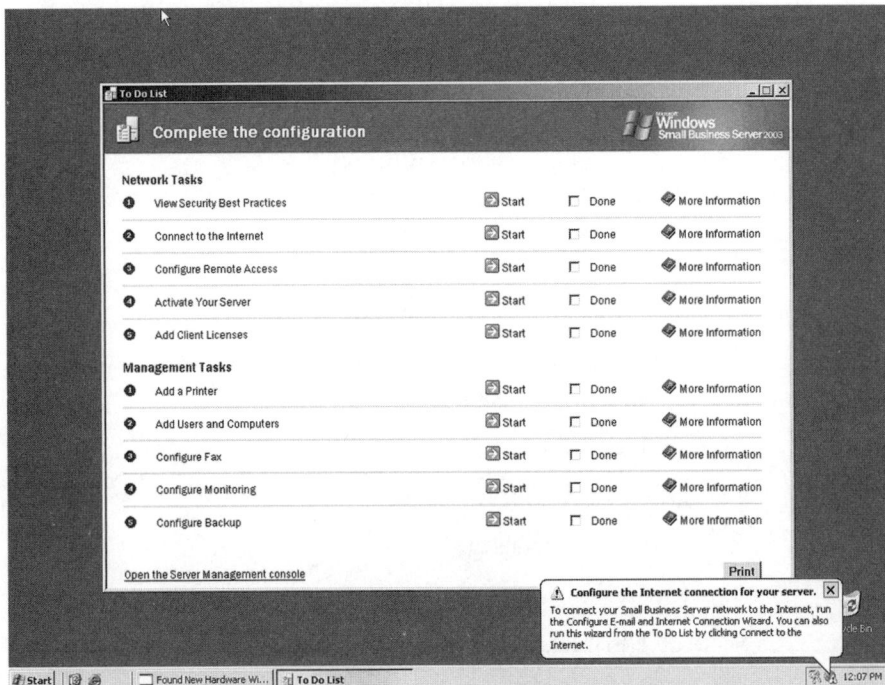

These are the choices the To Do List tasks will offer after a successful clean installation. If you did an upgrade, there will be other tasks listed depending on the setup variation.

The benefits in the real world for the task lists are multiple. If you are an administrator or consultant for a small business, you can set up the server offsite (adding user accounts, configuring group policies, etc.) and install the required applications. Then you can bring the server online onsite and migrate data and connect to the Internet, in short order. This really cuts down the time spent in another cramped closet all weekend.

We will be covering the To Do List in more detail in Chapter 7, "Configuring Windows Small Business Server 2003."

IMPORTANT: Even though it is recommended that you complete the To Do List in order, it can be completed in any order. The list can be accessed from the Server Management console.

Upgrade and Migrations

This section discusses upgrade and migration approaches applicable to the 70-282 exam. It is recommended that you read this carefully!

In-Place Upgrade from Small Business Server 2000 to Small Business Server 2003

An in-place upgrade to Small Business Server 2003 can be done from:

1. Windows Small Business Server 2000

2. Windows 2000 Server

3. Windows Server 2003

Coming from Windows Small Business Server 4.5, NT4.0 or another operating system would be considered a migration and not an upgrade.

Upgrading a server is much less complex than performing a migration, less disruptive, and less expensive. On the other hand, when you perform an upgrade, you will retain junk data, forgotten accounts, incorrect settings and the pictures of someone's grandchildren who quit the company three years ago.

Performing an in-place upgrade to Small Business Server 2003 is easy and will take little time if planned and implemented properly. Microsoft has "official" upgrade information on its public-facing Upgrading page at http://www. microsoft.com/sbs. Select the *Technical Documentation* link.

Preparing the Server

To ensure a smooth and painless upgrade, there are several items to be considered and steps to be taken. Prior to the upgrade you must:

1. Meet or exceed the minimum system requirements.

2. Have an additional 2 GB hard drive space for temporary setup files.

3. Install all necessary Service Packs and updates.

4. Clear all fax and e-mail message queues.

5. Run Disk Clean-up (cleanmgr.exe).

6. Run Disk Defragmenter (Dfrg.msc).

7. Log on as the administrator using the built-in Administrator account.

8. Ensure you have SBS 2000 Service Pack 1 installed.

9. Check for updated and compatible drivers.

10. Check the latest BIOS.

11. Disable the external NIC.

It is imperative that you plan and document the steps prior to the upgrade. Skipping steps and not taking the time to prepare the server properly can result in a fatal outcome. It will be helpful to prepare a disaster recovery plan ahead of time. Choose a time for the upgrade where downtime will create minimal disruption to the business.

> IMPORTANT: It is recommended that you anti-virus scan all files and drives, except for the M:\ drive (Exchange) and perform a full, complete backup of the System State, data, and Exchange and verify the backup integrity. (Test restore.)

I'll have more information about backup and restore in Chapter 8. When checking for compatibility issues, consider:

- Third-Party Applications – check with the manufacturer.
- Device Drivers – replace aging devices that are not supported by SBS 2003.
- Client Computers – Windows 95 clients and older should be axed.

You must also remove discontinued Exchange components like:

1. Microsoft Exchange MSMail Connector.

2. Microsoft Exchange Connector for Lotus cc:Mail.

3. Microsoft Exchange Instant Messaging Service.

4. Microsoft Exchange Chat Service.

5. Microsoft Exchange Key Management Service.

Removing Exchange components can be done in the Add/Remove Program panel by selecting Microsoft Small Business Server 2000, then choosing Change/Remove and running the SBS Setup Wizard to remove the Exchange components.

Now that you have prepped the server, let's take a look at the clients.

> IMPORTANT: Since Small Business Server 2000 does not have Shadow Copy, boot into safe mode to run the backup. Fewer files will be in use and there is a greater chance of a successful backup.

Preparing the Client for an In-Place Upgrade

In an in-place upgrade scenario, Windows XP Professional and Windows 2000 Professional clients will not require any preparation. If you have a Windows 95 or an NT 4.0 workstation and your boss just can't live without them, you could tell him that these operating systems just don't communicate well with the Windows Small Business Server 2003. If that doesn't work, you could:

- Quit,

- Install the Active Directory Extensions (dsclient.exe) located on the SBS 2003 Disc 1 on the Windows 95 client, or

- Install Windows NT 4.0 Service Pack 6a, IE6 and dsclient.exe on the NT 4.0 workstation. The Windows NT 4.0 Service Pack 6a essentially supports legacy workstations.

> IMPORTANT: Besides preparing the server and clients, it is a good idea to prepare the end users as well. Advise them of the network upgrade and how they will benefit from it.

Notes:

Performing the Upgrade

Now that you have prepped the server and client workstations, you are ready to proceed with the actual upgrade. Windows Small Business Server 2003 upgrades the system by first upgrading the operating system, then configuring the operating system for Windows Small Business Server 2003, and performing the actual upgrade last.

Once the system has been upgraded to Windows Small Business Server 2003, you will have to rerun the To Do List and fulfill several other tasks.

Before we get to this point, there are some final steps to take prior to the upgrade:

1. Disconnect UPS.
2. Disable third-party disk utilities.
3. Disconnect from the Internet.
4. Disable anti-virus programs.

Log on as the built-in administrator and launch the Small Business Server 2003 Disc 1. Follow the on-screen instructions, which will appear very much like the first-time install.

Once the upgrade has been completed and the system rebooted, you should complete the tasks in the To Do List in the order represented. Make sure to run the Change User Permissions Wizard, of all things, to ensure that users get their permissions migrated and are able to properly access all resources on the domain.

Migrating from Small Business Server 2000, Small Business Server 4.5, or NT 4.0 Server to Windows Small Business Server 2003

Migrating (versus upgrading) will involve moving the entire SBS installation from the source (old) server to the destination (new) server. A migration, generally referred to as a painful process, exposes large amounts of useless and irrelevant data that has been hanging around for eons. If you already have an existing network infrastructure in place, don't want to interrupt the flow of business or upset end-users, but still continue with identical operations after moving to new hardware, a migration is the only way to go.

There are slight differences between migrating from an SBS 2000 domain (already has Active Directory) and migrating from SBS 4.5 or an NT 4.0 server (no Active Directory). The procedures follow the same logical steps, and we will point out the differences on the way.

Preparing for the Migration

To have a successful migration from Windows Small Business Server 2000 to SBS 2003, Small Business Server 4.5 or an NT 4.0 Server, on the **source server** you should first:

- Record all information on the source and destination servers.
- Record the location of any shared folders.
- Record the line-of-business (LOB) data location.
- Record general user data that is not located in a shared folder.
- Record POP3 mailbox account information – has to be reconfigured on the destination server.
- Ensure SBS 4.5 and NT 4.0 servers run SP6a.

    1. If running Exchange 5.5. or 2000:

        - Record distribution lists.
        - Record Custom recipients.
        - Record Public folder custom permissions.
        - Export public folders to .pst files.
        - Export the administrator account mailbox and rules.

    2. If running SQL 7.0, check the SQL version number 7.00.1063 and make sure SP4 is installed.

    3. Record custom server setting for:

        - SMTP connector.
        - DHCP scope options.
        - DNS records.

- RRAS service settings.

- GPOs.

- ISA settings.

- Custom IIS websites.

4. Verify that hardware drivers and software are supported.

5. Ensure the source server is running the latest service packs.

6. Do a full system backup on the source server including system state and Exchange

7. Back up and create an ERD (Emergency Repair Disk) for SBS 4.5 and NT 4.0 Server.

Carefully heed the following section and its words of wisdom. You should be aware that the migration has a high probability rate for failure if you don't follow the rules listed below, starting with:

- **The source and destination servers must have different internal DNS and NetBIOS names.** This does not affect your external DNS name.

- **The source and destination server computer name must be different.** Beware of client PCs using UNC paths; ensure you remove any references to the source server on the client machines.

- **The DHCP service on the source server must be disabled.** The DHCP service must be running on the destination server, so therefore you must disable the source server's DHCP service to avoid contention between them.

- **Use the Active Directory Migration Tool (ADMT) to migrate user, group, and computer accounts**. This will preserve the SIDs (Security Identifiers).

- **Use the Exchange Migration Wizard.** The Exchange Migration Wizard is the successor to ExMerge and a more simplified and reliable method of moving mailboxes. Beware it does not export mailbox rules or migrate the administrator account mailbox or rules on public folders. (You could use ExMerge to export public folders and the administrator account.)

- **Custom server settings must be configured manually on the destination server:**
  - ○ SMTP connector
  - ○ DHCP scope options
  - ○ DNS records
  - ○ RRAS service settings
  - ○ GPOs
  - ○ ISA settings
  - ○ Custom IIS website settings
- **Create DNS forwarders on the source and destination server.** ADMT requires those to work with the source and destination servers.

Okay, so the good news is that desktop profiles on Windows 2000 and Windows XP machines are preserved during the migration. Yeah!

> IMPORTANT: Ensure that user folders to not exceed 1 GB. Disk quotas are enabled by default on the partition where the users' shared folder is located. While in the real world you might know of ways to work around this disk quota matter, accept this as GOSPEL on the 70-282 exam.

Configure the Destination Server

First you must install SBS 2003 on the destination server. (See the above section, "First-Time System Installation," in this chapter.) While filling out information for server setup, make sure you:

- Enter a different DNS and NetBIOS name than the source server.
- Have DHCP disabled on the source server.
- Enter an IP address on the same subnet as the source server.
- Install ADMT on the destination server—the ADMT is located on Disc 1 on the SBS 2003 disk set at *D:***I386\Admt\Admigration.msi (where *D* represents the drive letter).**
- To configure ADMT, you must run this in the command prompt:

```
Net Localgroup "Pre-Windows 2000 Compatible Access" Everyone /Add
Net Localgroup "Pre-Windows 2000 Compatible Access" "Anonymous Logon" /Add
```

- To migrate user accounts you must also run:

```
Runas /Netonly /user:SourceDomainName\Administrator "Mmc\"%Program Files%\
Active Directory Migration Tool\Migrator.msc\""
-replace SourceDomainName with the source domain name
```

This will cover Windows 2000, as well as SBS 4.5 and NT 4.0 servers.

IMPORTANT: Account names are automatically truncated if they are longer then 20 characters and will cause migration errors.

Prepare Clients for Account Migration

There are a few steps that need to be performed on the client machines to prepare them for the account migration:

- Ensure that the Domain Administrator group from the source server is a member of the local built-in Administrators group.

- Disable any personal firewalls.

- Disable Internet Connection Firewall in IE.

- Do NOT disable the ISA 2000 firewall client.

- NT 4.0 workstation and NT 4.0 member servers must have SP 6a installed.

- Users should export their mailbox rules.

- Delete desktop shortcuts to the company folder and users' shared folder.

- Delete printers and faxes that point to the source server

- Delete all Favorites that reference the source server:

   o   Microsoft Small Business Internet Services

   o   Microsoft Small Business Server website

   o   My E-mail

     o   SBS User Guide

     o   Small Business Server Administration

- Disable real-time virus protection on each client and run a virus scan.

- If migrating from an SBS 4.5 or NT 4.0 server, remove the following applications:

     o   WinSock Proxy Client

     o   Fax Server Client

     o   Modem Sharing Client

- If migrating from SBS 2000, remove the Modem sharing client.

- Release and renew the IP address.

When performing the account migration, be aware that the ADMT has a differential treatment depending on the OS. Table 5-3 speaks to the migration treatment of different client operating systems.

Table 5-3
  ADMT and client operating systems

OS	Tool
Windows XP Professional Windows 2000 Professional Windows 2000 Server Windows 2003 Server NT 4.0 Workstation	Can be migrated by using the ADMT.
Windows 98 Windows 95 Windows Me	Must be configured manually for the destination server.

Ensure that you have a CAL (client access license) for each client machine and member server on the destination server.

> IMPORTANT: If you have a second Domain Controller that is a Windows 2000 Server, you must run **dcpromo** to remove AD and then migrate the computer account to the destination server.

Performing the Migration

Ensure that the Domain Administrator group is a member of the built-in administrator group on the local client machines. Also, double-check that you are not running anti-virus software on the source or destination server.

You will first launch ADMT and then migrate the following accounts:

- User accounts
- Group accounts
    - To migrate group accounts, you will have to run the ADMT Group Account Migration Wizard twice. You will separately migrate:
        - Security Groups
        - Distribution Groups
- Computer accounts
    - Before migrating computer accounts, be sure to wait about 15 minutes after the source server reboots so that the DNS records can be updated or the client configuration for the destination domain will fail.
- Change mailbox quotas on Exchange if client mailboxes exceed 200,000 KB (default limit) or clients will not be able to send or receive e-mail.
- Move the users Exchange mailboxes.
- Move users shared folders.
- Move the Company folder to the SharePoint Site.
    - Files larger than 50 MB will be blocked.
    - Files with extensions like .exe and .vbs will be blocked.
- Move SQL server databases.
- Move LOB data.
- Move any other data folders.
- Remove the DNS forwarder used for the migration.
- Remove any permissions used for the migration.

Net Localgroup "Pre-Windows 2000 Compatible Access" Everyone /Delete
Net Localgroup "Pre-Windows 2000 Compatible Access" "Anonymous Logon" /Delete

- Uninstall ADMT.

- Connect to the Internet and create the DNS forwarder.

  o Having migrated all the user, group, and computer accounts, you must still perform some final configuration on the destination server to ensure that users have the appropriate permission to access the new SBS 2003 network.

- Assign new permissions to migrated accounts (run the Change User Permissions Wizard on all the SBS 2003 templates on each user account migrated from the source server.)

- Complete all steps of the Management tasks on the To Do List (covered extensively in Chapter 7) in the order presented, including:

- Assigning applications.

- Adding printers.

- Configure fax.

- Configure monitoring.

- Configure backup.

- Re-create custom settings from the source server on the destination server.

- Configure distribution lists.

- Configure custom recipient policies.

- Configure POP3 e-mail accounts (if used).

- Copy any custom logon scripts you used on the source server.

IMPORTANT: Log on to a client machine (after it has been configured to work with the destination server) as the administrator and import the mailbox and rules to the destination server.

You are almost done! At this point you can disconnect the source server from the network and focus on some final tasks to be completed on the client side:

- Disconnect the source server.

- Install DSclient.exe (Active Directory Client Extension) for Windows 9x, Me, or NT 4.0 Workstation. (These are two different clients, one for NT 4.0 and the other for Win9x and Me, available for download from the Microsoft site.)

- Ensure clients can log on to the domain.

- Remove the ISA Server 2000 firewall client if you previously used ISA Server 2000 and migrated to the SBS 2003 Standard Edition.

- Install the ISA Server 2000 firewall client if you are using the Premium Edition.

- Ensure all proxy settings are configured properly.

- Install applications if needed.

- Install Outlook 2003 (it will auto-configure for the profile).

Now that you have finished the migration, it is recommended that you be on-site the first day users will be working on the newly migrated network—or be very, very far away, without a cell phone and having forgotten to let anyone know your whereabouts. (Just kidding on that last point.)

> IMPORTANT: Don't forget that you should actually install SBS 2003 a few times before you take the 70-282 exam. It's one thing to read this chapter and answer the questions that follow. But there is nothing like the active learning experience gained from deploying and using the SBS 2003 product in the real world. Don't kid yourself! It's not wise to "read" yourself into successfully passing the 70-282 exam — use our words of wisdom to supplement your real-world experience.

There are two ways to get a free 180-day copy of SBS 2003 Standard Edition:

- SMB Nation Press starter kits and resource kits: www.smbnation.com

- Microsoft trial software: http://www.microsoft.com/windowsserver 2003/sbs/evaluation/trial/default.mspx

Practice Questions

Question #1:

There are two parts to Windows Small Business Server setup, the Text Mode phase and the GUI phase. Which of the following occur during the GUI phase? (Choose all that apply.)

a. System partition is created.

b. HW devices are detected and installed.

c. Networking components are installed and configured.

d. Loads drivers and detects storage devices.

e. Boots CD.

Question #2:

You have installed Small Business Server 2003 and are just beginning to go through the To Do list to complete the installation. The customer contact comes into the "Server Room" (OK, closet) and informs you that the CEO has decided that the server should be named after his cat "AppliCATion" instead of the third planet in the Trixtem galaxy (Smegdorf). How do you rename the SBS server (Standard Edition) to meet the new requirement? (Choose the best answer.)

a. Remove the DNS A record for node Smegdorf from the Forward Lookup Zone; remove the ptr record for node Smegdorf from the Reverse Lookup Zone; modify the _ldap SRV record in the _ldap._pdc. _mscds.*domain.local* node with the new server name; right click **My Computer>Change Name;** reboot the server; restart SBS.

b. Reinstall Small Business Server.

c. Open the Server Management console; browse to Advanced Mangement; open the **Migrate Server Settings** icon; choose **Import Templates;** browse to the **\Windows\Settings_Local** sudirectory; choose the **Local for NameChange (SBS Standard)** template and click **OK** to import the settings; when complete, select **Export Templates;** click **Next** at the **Welcome to the Export Templates** screen; select "**New _LocalServer Name (SBS Standard) into local hive** from the templates listed; when complete exit the wizard, restart DNS and then reboot the server.

d. Right click **My Computer > Properties >Computer Name>Change** and type the new name in the name field. DO NOT CHANGE THE DOMAIN NAME!

Question #3:

Which of the following can be accomplished using the To Do list? (Choose all that apply.)

a. Add a Printer.

b. Add a Disk Volume.

c. Configure the Internet connection.

d. Add a backup Domain Controller.

Question #4:

When installing SBS 2003 which of the following are true when creating and/or defining disk partitions. (Choose all that apply.)

a. You can create all partitions during the text-mode setup or only the system partition. Additional partitions can be created during the GUI portion, preferably before Exchange is installed.

b. Active Directory and Exchange require an HPFS Volume to function properly.

c. Whenever possible create a single RAID 5 partition. Having all files in one place makes it easier to restore in case of a failure.

d. The system partition must be 8 GB.

Question #5:

You have just upgraded your customer from SBS 4.5 to SBS 2003 Standard Edition. Even though everything seemed to go properly, users complain they are unable to get to disk shares and other resources. What are the steps you need to take to complete the upgrade and resolve the user issues? (Choose the best answer.)

a. Open the **Server Management Console;** open **Advanced Management;** open **Migrate Server Settings;** select **To Do List;** and run the **Change User Permissions** wizard.

b. Click **Start;** select **Administrative Tools;** click **Active Directory Users And Computers;** right-click the **domain object**; click **Properties;** on the **Group Policy** tab, ensure that **Default Domain Policy** is selected and then click **Edit;** navigate to **Computer Configuration\Windows Settings\Security Settings\Account Policies\Migrate 4.5,** double click then set the **Permissions** policy to **True.**

c. Rerun Setup at the command line with the **\Migrate_Permissions** option.

d. All of the above.

Question #6:

Disk Quotas (Choose all that apply.)

a) Disk quotas are managed on a per-user basic and enabled at a per-folder level.

b. Disk quotas are managed at the group level and enabled at the volume level.

c. Disk quotas are only supported on volumes defined within a RAID array.

d. Disk quotas are managed on a per user level and enabled at a volume level.

Question #7:

Your customer is currently running SBS 4.5 on a Pentium 4 2.8 Ghz server with 512 MB of memory and 450 MB of free disk space. He wants to simply be upgraded to an SBS 2003 environment on the same server because he has heard it is a much less disruptive process. Why is migration a better solution in this case? (Choose the best answer.)

a. Upgrades are not "clean" installs and always include junk data, forgotten accounts, and other "leftovers" from the previous version.

b. There is not enough disk space to upgrade (a minimum of 500 GB is required).

c. An upgrade from SBS 4.5 to SBS 2003 is not supported. The server must be migrated.

d. ExMerge must be used to upgrade the SBS 4.5 Exchange environment. It requires 500 MB of temporary disk space in addition to that required by the OS.

Question #8:

Which of the following statements are true about the Microsoft Active Directory Migration Tool (ADMT)? (Choose the best answer.)

a) ADMT will migrate Printer and fax shares from the source server to the destination server.

b) ADMT requires a CAL from the destination server, but a separate "Source" license must be purchased directly from Microsoft.

c) If ADMT is used to migrate user accounts, security groups, and computer accounts, their SIDS will be preserved.

d) ADMT must be purchased separately from Microsoft.

Answers

Question #1: Answer: a, d, e

a. Correct! The reason Setup starts in text mode is because a fully functional operating system has not yet been built. The operating system that has been created by Setup is only temporary and is running totally in memory. It has just enough functionality to begin building the environment that the operating system will live in. One of the first steps is to create the partition that will hold all of the needed files that make up the OS.

b. Not quite! As mentioned above, in text-mode we are running a limited operating system that is temporary in nature. Only those drivers that help us access the storage and display hardware we need to begin building the system partition are *loaded,* nothing is *installed* - a not-so-subtle difference. Loading drivers is temporary, installing devices infers permanence which is not possible until the OS is built and at least partially functional.

c. No, again the key word "installed" is used and until we get into GUI mode with a created system partition there is nothing to install to!

d. Correct! The drivers needed by the Setup operating system to begin talking to the hardware are loaded including drivers for common storage devices. And a "brute force" storage device detection takes place. (Hmmm, I'll try a SCSI disk, no - how about IDE, no wait ATPI!) If the right type of device (or devices) happen to respond, then Windows Setup will present them as possible locations for the OS to be installed. If not, then a message is displayed to let the installer know a suitable storage device could not be found. Pressing F6 at the beginning of the text-mode process alerts Windows Setup that the driver needed to support the RAID or other storage HW is not one of those loaded by default and a diskette with the proper driver will be inserted when prompted. The installation process will use the provided driver and will also remember to copy it to a location on the system partition for installation in the operating system.

e. Correct! Booting the OS CD starts the entire installation process so it must be part of text-mode!

Question #2: Answer: b

a. Though this procedure sounds impressive – I just made it up! Even though all of these various references are incorrectly named, changing them will do nothing for you other than mess everything up so you will have to re-install SBS – which is where you should have started.

b. Correct! A simple name change is not simple! So make sure everyone has agreed to the name before installation and is aware of the fact that a reinstall can be costly.

c. Incorrect! Another exercise in creative writing!

d. Incorrect! This is where most people would expect to be able to change the name. But all you get here is a reminder that a Domain Controller's name cannot be changed here.

Question #3: Answer: a, c

    a. Correct! Choosing this option will take you directly to the add printer wizard – those SBS folks think of everything!

    b. Incorrect! A disk volume cannot be added via the To Do List.

    c. Correct! Choosing "Connect to the Internet" will invoke the Configure E-mail and Internet Connection Wizard, aka CEICW. Now repeat after me "THE CEICW IS MY FRIEND, I REALLY LOVE THE CEICW!!!, IF I COULD, I WOULD BUY THE CEICW A CAR!!!". Ok, forget the last part, but don't forget the Configure E-mail and Internet Connection Wizard! The CEICW will not only help you setup the initial connection to the Internet, configure the firewall, web server certificate, and Internet e-mail configuration, but will also let you reconfigure those items when they quit working – the ultimate "save yer bacon" utility. I cannot accurately tell you how many flaky issues have been resolved for me just by just rerunning the CEICW. Either because something changed or I accidently shot myself in the foot - not that that has ever happened…

    d. Incorrect! A DC cannot be added via the To Do list. The easiest way to add a new domain controller is to just run DCPROMO on the Windows Server you want to make a DC in the domain.

Question #4: Answer: a

    a. Correct! Setup gives you the opportunity to create as many partitions as you need when the system partition is created and before continuing the installation process. Most of the time you will find it easier to just create the system partition and then wait until the first part of the GUI is completed – before it actually begins the SBS added value install (CD 2) - and use the easier disk management interface to define and format additional partitions.

    b. Incorrect! HPFS (High Performance File System) s and IBM standard supported on earlier versions of Windows and Windows NT. It is no longer supported and was never required.

c. Incorrect! Though there are reasons to consider RAID 5 partitions, this is not one of them.

d. Incorrect! Microsoft recommends a minimum of 16GB of available disk for SBS 2003.

Question #5: Answer: a

a. Correct! The Change User Permissions Wizard, enables you to update one or more user accounts and to change group memberships and Windows SharePoint Services site group memberships by applying a user template. All previous group memberships, Windows SharePoint Services site group memberships, and the permissions defined by these memberships are removed and replaced by those defined in the template you specify. Users are assigned a home folder and an Exchange mailbox, if they do not have them already. If specific permissions were previously applied directly to the user accounts, those permissions are not changed.

b. Incorrect! There is not a Group Policy that will migrate user permissions.

c. Incorrect! There is not a Setup command line switch that will migrate user permissions.

d. Incorrect!

Question #6: Answer: d

a. Incorrect! Disk Quotas can only be enabled for the entire volume – not a single folder.

b. Incorrect! Disk Quotas are managed per user. Not on a group basis. That may sound incorrect but it is not. Files and folders are owned by individuals, not groups (the only exception to this rule is the Administrator Group which owns any file created by a member of the administrator group). If you wish to control quotas for a group of users, define a template for the group and modify the quotas for the template. Reapply the template to the existing users who are a member of the group. New users that have the template applied will automatically get the quota settings.

c. Incorrect! As long as the volume is an NTFS volume, Disk Quotas can be enabled. It does not matter if the volume is part of a RAID set.

d. Correct! Disk quotas make it easy for the system administrator to control the amount of disk space consumed by individuals. Quotas are enabled for the entire volume.

Question #7: Answer: c

a. Incorrect! Though the statements about upgrades are true, the points are not valid here because SBS 4.5 cannot be upgraded to SBS 2003.

b. Incorrect! The amount of disk space is irrelevant because SBS 4.5 cannot be upgraded to SBS 2003.

c. Correct!

d. Incorrect! SBS 4.5 cannot be upgraded to SBS 2003; it must be migrated.

Question #8: Answer: c

a. Incorrect! ADMT will only move computer, user, and group accounts. Print shares must be recreated.

b. Incorrect! Additional licenses are not required to use ADMT.

c. Correct! SIDs, or Security Identifiers, uniquely identify users, groups, and computers within a domain. Being able to associate a migrated user with the SID they had in the previous environment will also keep the resource access and previous security relationships intact. So now the new Joe can still get to the stuff the old Joe created!

d. Incorrect! ADMT is free and is located on Disk 1 of the CD set as \I386\Admt\Admigration.msi. Microsoft is constantly updating this tool so the best bet is to go to www.microsoft.com/downloads and search for ADMT.

Notes:

Summary

This important chapter covers the fundamental SBS 2003 deployment and setup discussion as it relates to the 70-282 examination. You were schooled in matters surrounding the underlying system requirements, first-time installations, and upgrades and migrations. The "wrapper" around this chapter was to keep you focused on the 70-282 examination. Migrating and Expanding the SBS network is covered at length in Chapter 9. Grab a cup of Java and take five or do some Yoga stretches before moving on to the next chapter!

Chapter 6
Securing Windows Small Business Server 2003

There is so much to say about security for Small Business Server 2003 (SBS), we could have started this chapter and written all the way to Timbuktu about it. The topic of security presents a particular challenge because the body of security knowledge changes daily. Bad guys and gals are constantly seeking to impart evil on computer networks and thwart the effective, efficient, and honorable use of technology for peaceful and profitable businesses. It's a dark side of an otherwise sunny SBS 2003 disposition! Many small businesses today are using IT and rely heavily on the Internet for all aspects of communication—from simple e-mail to e-commerce transactions to VoIP—and sensitive information is constantly crossing networks. Most small businesses keep their data on a single server (or workstation) and don't recognize the value of their data until it has been compromised. Vulnerabilities are numerous, from viruses and drive-by browser jackers to full-blown security breaches, and it's beginning to feel like a Mad Max movie out there.

But, let's not forget that you are reading this book for the purpose of mastering the 70-282 exam, and focus on the Microsoft way of securing SBS. So let's keep this simple. What components does Microsoft offer to secure a Windows Server-based environment right out of the box? We can start with Authentication Protocols, Access Control Entries (ACEs), user and group accounts, group policies and security certificates, and work our way up all the way to ISA Server 2004.

Windows Server 2003 Security

When we talk about Windows Server 2003 Security we are also talking about SBS 2003 Security. For instance, when you manage resources through the SBS wizards for network users, you are effectively using Windows Server 2003 components to assign permissions and privileges to user and group accounts, determining which actions can be performed by users and which resources they can access. So please follow me for a little stroll into the Windows Server 2003 Security Model.

Authentication Protocols

Several network authentication protocols are supported by Windows Server 2003 that support a key feature, the **Single Sign-On**. The Single Sign-On allows a domain user to log on to the domain by using the user account credentials (username and password), or by swiping a smart card through the reader. The credentials are then authenticated in Active Directory (on a Domain Controller), and the user has access to network resources. At this point the user can authenticate on any resources (computers, shares) without having to authenticate again. The Single Sign-On authentication process is now automatic. The primary authentication protocols used by Windows Server 2003 are:

- **Kerberos v5** – This is the primary authentication mechanism in Windows Server 2003 and a standard Internet protocol used for authenticating users and systems.

- **NT LAN Manager (NTLM)** – Used to authenticate computers on a Windows NT domain.

- **Secure Sockets Layer/Transport Layer Security (SSL/TLS)** – An authentication mechanism primarily used to access secure web servers.

- **.Net Passport Authentication** – Used to enable Active Directory information to authenticate Internet, intranet and external users and is enabled through Internet Information Services (IIS)

Access Controls

Every time an administrator creates a new user account, group account or a shared resource, Active Directory defines this as an **Object**. Each object in Active Directory receives **Access Control Entries (ACEs)** by way of **security descriptors.** A security descriptor:

- Specifies permission that have been assigned to a user or a group.
- Defines ownership of an object.
- Lists users and groups that are granted access to objects.
- Tracks events for auditing of objects.

Then there are the **Access Control Lists (ACLs) which are made up of ACEs**. All objects in Active Directory are protected by an ACL; the ACL determines what objects a user or group is allowed to see, and what actions can be performed on the object. And while we are at it, let's throw the **Security Identifier (SID)** into the mix to make this story whole. The SID is a unique identifier that is also generated when the user or group account is created, containing a unique domain security ID prefix and a unique relative ID. (Discussing these further is beyond the scope of this book and should be researched at http:\\www.microsoft.com\reskit.) This means that even if the name is changed on a user account, the SID will still be able to track the user account and apply the ACE to it.

The way this plays out in terms of security on the Windows Server (or SBS), is that at the time a user logs on to the domain, the server will create a security token that specifies the SID and ACE for the particular account for this session (until logoff). When the user tries to access another Active Directory object (computer, share, printer, etc.), the ACEs in the token will be compared to the ACL of the object which will then determine if the user has access to it and what functions the user can perform with the object.

> IMPORTANT: ACEs can be inherited from their parent objects in Active Directory meaning that child objects have the same permissions as their parent. Hence, if a user account is made a member of the Domain Admin group, the user account inherits all the permissions granted to the Domain Admin group.

Configure User Accounts and Permissions

Now that we have covered ACEs and ACLs, we can move on to configuring user accounts and permissions. Small Business Server 2003 uses the *Add Security Group* wizard and *Default User Templates* to create distribution and security groups and create user accounts. You can control what users can and cannot do on the SBS network by simply placing or removing the user accounts to and from specific security groups.

User Rights and Permissions

Managing users and groups can appear to be a daunting task, but as an administrator you have two friends called:

- User Rights.
- User Permissions.

User Rights

User rights are defined by the capabilities, like performing a task. In general, user rights apply to the entire system. There are two types of user rights:

- Privileges.
- Allow a user to perform actions like running a backup or a security audit.
- Logon Rights.
- Allow a user to access the computer in a certain way.

User Permissions

Permissions dictate access to a particular object (files, printers) allowing the user to interact with the object in a certain way (read, write, print). As shown in Figure 6.1, you can view NTFS permission settings. Looking at the folder name, of course, should teach you to never let new techs have default permissions. But besides that, notice that the Domain Users Group here has Read and Execute, List Folder Contents, and Read Permissions inherited by default.

Figure 6-1
NTFS permission settings on the WorldofWarcraft folder.

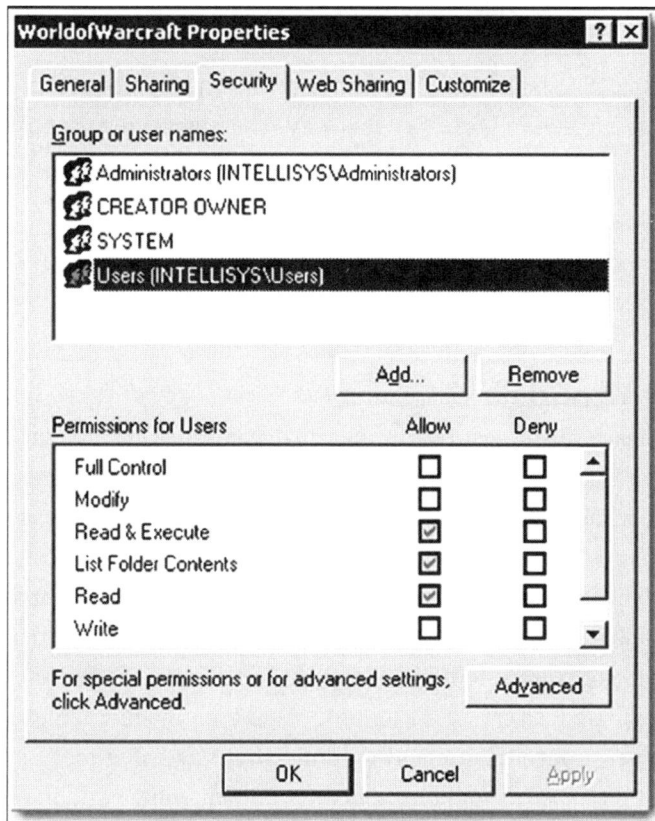

Create and Configure User Groups

Configuring user groups? Now that is a trick question in SBS, the reason being that groups have already been preconfigured for you! Depending on what user template you use, permissions will then be assigned based on the template settings. You can create and configure domain groups by the use of two links on the Server Standard Management console, the **Security Group** link and the **Distribution Group** link. There is no need to venture into Active Directory Users and Groups; again, wizards are available to make this an effortless experience.

What should be pointed out here is that the SBS Security and Distribution Groups are located in Active Directory under yourdomainname.com, **MyBusiness** organizational unit **(OU)**, **Distribution OU**, and **Security OU**. It is important that you use the Standard Management console links to create your new Security or Distribution groups, because the newly created accounts will be placed into the proper OU in Active Directory this way. There are three group types:

Local Groups

Local groups are created on **local computers only**. They can be created with the Local Users and Groups utility.

Security Groups

SBS 2003 has built-in security groups that have already assigned rights to facilitate simplified administration. You can place a user into the Fax Operators group (which has specific fax-related rights assigned), and the user will be able to manage fax queues and cover pages. This is a time-tested network administrative practice of using security groups to manage permissions. A security group is exactly what the name states, a group that has certain rights and permissions assigned to it that dictate how different objects on the domain can be manipulated. Creating a user group and then placing the user accounts into the security group streamlines the administrative burden and simplifies user management. Even in a small business environment where you may only have five user accounts, it is good practice to use security groups instead of assigning user accounts individually to resources. More on this embedded security stuff in a moment under the Group Scopes section. When creating new groups in SBS, you should always use the **Server Management Console** and use the **Distribution Group** and **Security Group** links.

> IMPORTANT: Security groups may have an e-mail address (techni-
> cally an SMTP e-mail address). The members of the security group
> would receive the e-mail that is sent to said security group (sounds
> a lot like a distribution group, eh?). So sometimes, a security group
> can act like a bucket that holds permissions plus assume the behavior
> of a distribution group.

Distribution Groups

Distribution groups are used as e-mail distribution lists only and do not have security descriptors associated with them. Accounts added to distribution groups can be e-mailed to, but cannot be used to log on to the domain. (Due to missing ACEs, no token will be generated!). You can add a Distribution group with the *Add Distribution Group* wizard. Distribution groups facilitate communication by making it easy for you to reach all the recipients in a specific group using only one e-mail address—say, for example, everyone in the accounting department could be reached via a distribution group titled ACCOUNTING (Humor Zone: Kindly ignore the fact that this isn't the type of group you would want to spend a rollicking New Year's Eve with, as accountants are known for being somber). Distribution groups can include mail-enabled contacts, which are user accounts created to be available in the contacts list and receive e-mail at an external mail account. Mail-enabled users are not domain members, like a vendor with whom your company works. They should be included in all e-mail communications with a particular department or group and should show up in your GAL (Global Address List).

> IMPORTANT: You can set up mail-enabled contacts with or without an Exchange mailbox. A mail-enabled contact is usually a member of a distribution group and cannot log on to the domain.

> IMPORTANT: You can change a security group to a distribution group or vise versa in a Windows Server 2003 domain set at a functional level or in a Windows Server 2000 domain in native mode. This cannot be done in a Windows Server 2000 domain in mixed mode.

Creating the security or distribution group in **SBS**:

- Create and configure domain groups by going to Start, Server Management and, in the **Server Standard Management** console, the **Security Group** and **Distribution Group** link.

Creating the security or distribution group in Active Directory (only perform this on Windows Servers, not SBS):

- Create and configure domain groups by going to Start, All Programs, Administrative Tools **Active Directory Users and Computers.** Right-click on domain, e.g. *DomainName.local* name, click **New**, click **Group** and enter the information into the **New Object – Group** windows.

Group Scopes

At this point we are going to add to the mix by defining the scopes of each group and how they can interact with each other. This is an important part of securing Windows Server 2003:

- Domain local.
- Built-in local.
- Global.
- Universal.

The **Domain local** group can be used for assigning permissions within the local domain only. A domain local group can contain user accounts and global and universal groups from any domain and other domain local groups from the same domain. A domain local group:

- Can be changed to a universal group only if it does not have other domain local groups as its members.
- Is listed in the global catalog, but the memberships are not.

Built-in local groups have domain local permissions. They cannot be created or deleted, just modified. Often they are included in the domain local groups.

Global groups can contain accounts and other global groups from the same domain in Windows 2003 server and Windows 2000 server in native mode. The global group can be used for assigning permissions throughout the entire forest. A global group can only contain user accounts and global groups from the same domain the global group is in.

- A global group can be changed to a universal group if it is not a member of another global group.
- Is listed in the global catalog, but the memberships are not.

A **Universal** group in Windows 2003 server and Windows 2000 server in native mode can be used for assigning permissions throughout the entire forest. A universal group can contain user accounts, computer accounts, and global and universal groups from any domain in the forest. Opposite to domain local and global groups, universal groups are replicated to every global catalog in the entire forest.

- A universal group can be changed to a domain local group at any time.

- A universal group can be changed to a global group only if it does not have other universal groups as its members.

- A universal group can be listed in all global catalogs in all domains across the forest.

The underlying idea is to place a user account into the proper group so you have to manage the user account only once, and by association of group membership, inherits the proper permissions assigned to all resources on the domain.

All security groups in SBS have universal group membership by default when they are created, which means they can be placed into any domain local group. In reality, we only need domain local groups and global groups, because SBS will never be replicating to another domain. The day may come when you transition into a Windows Server 2003 solution. (See Chapter 9 on expanding networks). Placing users into appropriate groups and applying proper group strategies allows the administration of a domain with the least amount of effort.

Built-in Groups

The Built-In container (located in Active Directory Users and Computers) houses the following groups, which are all domain local groups and cannot be moved to another container or OU. They are created by default in Windows Server 2003 with the following rights:

Account Operators - Members of this group can administer domain user and group accounts, log on locally, and can shut down domain controllers. Account Operators cannot modify the Administrators or Domain Admins groups and accounts.

Administrators - Members of this group have full access to the domain or computer. By default, this group contains the Domain Admins and Enterprise Admins groups and the Administrator user account.

Backup Operators - Members of this group can back up or restore files without being limited by file permissions. Back-Up Operators can also log on locally and shut down domain systems.

Guests - Members of this group have the same permissions and rights as the Users group by default. The Guests user account is disabled by default. This Guests group contains the Domain Guests group as a member.

Incoming Forest Trust Builders - Members of this group can create incoming, one-way trust relationships to this forest. This group appears only in the root domain of the forest.

Network Configuration Operators - Members of this group can change the TCP/IP settings on domain controllers in the domain.

Performance Monitor Users - Members of this group can monitor performance counters on domain controllers in the domain.

Performance Log Users - Members of this group can manage performance counters, logs, and alerts on domain controllers in the domain.

Pre-Windows 2000 Compatible Access - Members of this group have read access to all users and groups in the domain. This group provides backward compatibility for computers running Windows version pre-Windows 2000, such as Windows NT 4. The Everyone group is a member of this group by default.

Print Operators - Members of this group have the appropriate rights to administer printers connected to domain controllers and shared printer objects in the Active Directory. Print Operators can also log on locally and shutdown domain systems.

Remote Desktop Users - Members in this group are granted the right to log on remotely using a terminal session.

Replicator – A system group account used for file replication in a domain, this group has no members—and you should not add them, either.

Server Operators - Members of this group can administer shared resources on domain servers, start and stop certain services, and format hard disks. Additionally, members of this group have the same rights Backup Operators have.

Users – Members of this group have sufficient permissions and rights to run certified Windows applications, but cannot run most legacy applications. This prevents regular users from making system-wide changes. The Users container includes domain local, global, and universal groups that can be moved to other OUs if needed. A list of the groups and their rights follows:

Cert Publishers - Members of this group can publish digital certificates for users and computers.

Dns Admins - Members of this group have permission to administer DNS.

DnsUpdateProxy - Members of this group can act as a DNS proxy for clients. A DHCP server that handles dynamic updates for DCHP clients should be a member of this group.

Domain Admins - Members of this group have full control of the domain.

This group is a member of the Administrators group on all domain members including domain controller. The Administrator user account is a member of this group by default.

Domain Computers - This group contains all the computer accounts of the client and servers joined to the domain.

Domain Controllers - This group contains all domain controllers in the domain.

Domain Guests - This group contains all domain guests.

Domain Users - This group contains all domain users. When you create a new user account in the domain, it will automatically become a member of the Domain Users group.

Enterprise Admins - Members of this group have full control of all domains in the forest. This group is a member of the Administrators group on all domain controllers in the forest. The Administrator user account is a member of this group by default.

Group Policy Creator Owners – Members of this group can modify Group Policy settings in the domain. The Administrator user account is a member of this group by default.

IIS_WPG – A system group account used by Internet Information Services (IIS) 6.0.

RAS and IAS Servers - Servers in this group have access to the remote access properties of users. This group is used for IAS servers that perform authentication for a collection of RRAS servers.

Schema Admins - Members of this group can modify the Active Directory schema. The Administrator user account is a member of this group by default. Then there are some special groups that do not belong to either container but allow you to assign permissions to users, which are:

Everyone – Includes everyone with a user account.

Anonymous Logon – Includes everyone without a user account.

Network – Includes users who are currently logged on to a computer over the network. This is the opposite of the Interactive group.

Interactive – Includes users who are currently logged on to the local computer. This is the opposite of the Network group. Domain groups are only created on domain controller. They enable centralized administration within a domain and are used to grant users permissions to resources and rights for system tasks on any computer in the domain.

Group Strategies

There is one acronym that you should remember —AGDLP— that is the user and group management strategy model recommended for single domains. Let me explain this more in detail:

- Put user accounts (A) into global groups (G).
- Put global groups (G) into domain local groups (DL).
- Grant permissions (P) to the domain local group (DL).

All right, I know this looks somewhat confusing at first, so let me elaborate. Say you have a client site with 40 users, 10 users work in a call-center processing orders over the phone, five users are in charge of creating marketing material, and the other 25 users are down in the warehouse packing and shipping orders. All users must have access to the order/processing application and be able to print reports. There are several printers in the business: two high-speed color laser printers, two black-and-white laser printers, and the rest are older inkjet printers.

The owners want only the marketing team to use the high-speed color printers. The call-center is to use the black-and-white laser printers and the shop floor to use the older printers.

In this case, you should create three separate security groups, and call them Marketing, CallCenter, and ShopDudes.

1. On the high-speed color laser printer, select **Properties,** then **Security.** Add the **Marketing** security group and assign **Print and Manage Printers** and **Manage Documents** permission.

2. Remove the **Everyone** group from the group names dialog box.

3. Follow the same procedure for the black-and-white laser printer, adding the **CallCenter** group and removing the **Everyone** group.

4. Follow the same procedure for the older printers on the shop floor, adding the **ShopDudes** group and removing the **Everyone** group.

5. For the order/processing application, create an **OrderProcessingGroup,** then add all three **Marketing, CallCenter,** and **ShopDudes** groups into this group. Configure the NTFS permission on the folder where the application is housed for access by the **OrderProcessingGroup**.

Now you have ensured that everyone can print only to the printers they should have access to and all users have access permission to the order/processing application. You may think creating the security groups is a lot of work. However, you just organized the permission structure in a way where you have only to place people in one group and they will automatically get all appropriate permissions assigned. Then when someone switches departments, leaves the company, or comes on board, you just have to add their user account to the appropriate security group, instead of assigning the user account to each individual resource, which will make life as an administrator just that much easier.

> IMPORTANT: Having a simple acronym such as "AGDLP" committed to memory will help you recall a complex study topic during the heat of the battle when taking the 70-282 exam. It's a time-tested trick for passing exams.

No wizard exists in SBS to place one security group into another. Therefore the following steps apply to SBS and Windows Server 2000/2003 domains.

- To nest one group into another, go to Start, All Programs, Administrative Tools Active Directory Users and Computers. Expand DomainName. local and select the group you want to place into another group or place another group into. Click Properties and click either the Members or Members Of tab (depending on the action you want to take), click Add and in the Select Users, Contacts, Computers, or Groups, enter the name of the group (or browse to it) and click OK.

Creating and Configuring User and Computer Accounts

SBS makes life easy, especially when it comes to adding user and computer accounts. Let us restate at this point that for the purpose of getting your feet wet for this exam, we highly recommend that you install SBS and Windows Server 2003 (use virtual PC – no excuses!) and click through the interfaces we discuss in the other chapters of this book. Looking at the consoles and wizards in both systems and comparing them side by side will help tremendously when you take the exam.

Small Business Server User Templates

The "SBS experience" is kinda like a popular USA beer commercial: "Tastes great and is less filling." SBS has been maligned in a marketing sense in the haughty enterprise community because it looks like a toy and it's too easy. However, don't let the pretty SBS interface fool you. Some very sophisticated concepts (that's the "tastes great" part of the beer commercial) are being applied via simple-to-use (and we state MUST USE) SBS-specific tools. One such tool set is the SBS User Templates, which contribute favorably to the SBS experience (and make it easier to use).

> IMPORTANT: There is really no need to go into Active Directory via the Active Directory Users and Computers snap-in to create users and apply settings. There is nothing to stop you from using the Active Directory Users and Computers console. However, we're here to discourage you from such under-the-hood shenanigans unless specifically called for by a guru or Microsoft Product Support Service (PSS). Take a look at figure 6.2, which is a screen cutout of Active Directory on an SBS server. Note the *MyBusiness* OU and its sub-OUs, *Computers, Distribution Groups, Security Groups,* and *Users,* which has another OU *SBS Users* nested below it. The SB team set up these OUs on purpose and all objects (users, computers, etc.) created using SBS wizards will be placed in these OUs, which have Group Policies applied to them. Hence, if you were to create a user using the Active Directory Users and Computers console and not an SBS wizard, that user account would end up in the Users container on the bottom of the cutout, and none of the pre-configured SBS Group Policies would apply to this container.

Default User Templates

User Templates, selected from the Template Selection screen of the Add User Wizard (Figure 6.2), specify many account properties and permissions when selected for the user you are creating. There are four user templates by default in SBS 2003 and these are defined in Table 6.1. With the default four user templates, all properties like group membership, SharePoint site groups, and disk quotas have already been set. Remember that the Add User Wizard is launched from the Add Users and Computers link from the To Do List (accessed via the Server Management console).

Figure 6-2
Observing user templates.

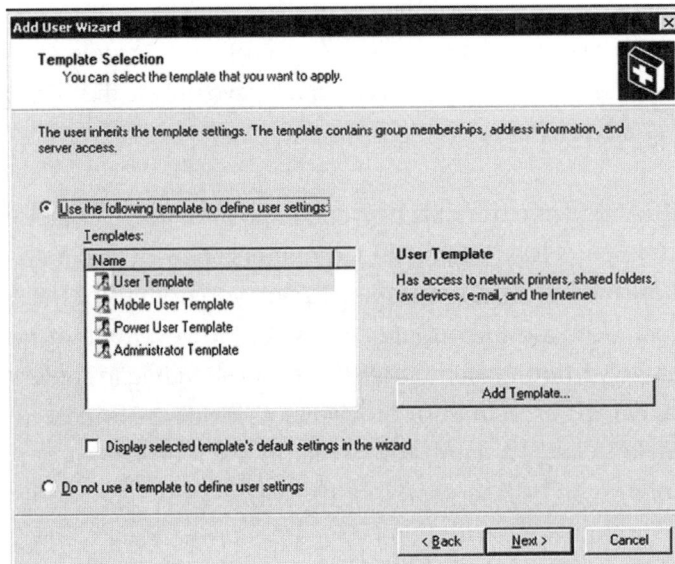

User Templates

I can't imagine things getting any easier than this. SBS comes with four preconfigured user templates that determine the user rights and permissions. Just in case they do not work for you, they can be easily modified or you can create a new user template by using the User Template Wizard to fit your organization's needs. But let's take a look at the four basic templates first:

- **User Template** allows access to:
  - Internet.
  - E-mail.
  - Shared Folders.
  - Printers and faxes.
  - Remote Desktop (to a Windows XP client, not a server).

- **Mobile User Template** has all the permissions from the user template plus:

    o VPN and dial- up access permissions.

- **Power User Template** has all the permissions from the mobile template, plus:

    o Perform delegated tasks such as manage users, groups, printers, shared folders, and faxes.

    o Log on remotely to the server, but cannot log on locally.

- **Administrator Template**:

    o Unrestricted system access.

User Templates can be migrated by using the Export Templates link and then imported at another site with the Import Template Wizard. Users should be managed by use of the **Change User Permission Wizard**, which changes permissions by assigning a new user template to a user. When assigning permissions with this wizard, you remove all previously assigned permissions from the user account and grant the new permission settings, which encompass changes to the security group membership, distribution group membership, access to WSS, and disk quotas.

> IMPORTANT: Only a domain administrator can create and modify User Templates. However, when creating user accounts, you can assign Power Users the right to use a custom template.

Take another look at figure 6.2. You may select the **Display selected template's default settings** in the wizard checkbox to show how all of the above settings are applied. Very cool. You may also select the **Do not use a template to define user settings** radio button to effectively add a user the non-SBS way. Very uncool! Another thing that is very uncoool is that if you add a user directly to Active Directory, you do not participate in the SBS user template concept.

Custom User Templates

You can create your own custom user templates by clicking the **Add template** link while completing the Add User Wizard or by going to User templates and clicking the **Add template** link, which will launch the Add Template Wizard. The use of custom templates is very exciting and very powerful. Why? Let's answer this question with a tad of Texas story-telling by the campfire. Back when knights were bold and Microsoft blue badges owned ALL the gold, there was a redhead (NetWare) on the block that was a huge threat. There were more Certified NetWare Engineers (CNEs) than Microsoft Certified Professionals (MCPs). What all CNEs knew to do was create the "perfectly" configured account (e.g., ACCT) for a department (e.g., Accounting) and then disable the account. When the customer hired a new employee in the accounting department, the ACCT account was copied over for the new user and renamed (e.g., Brisker Brelsford). This was the user template concept in its early format. Today, with SBS, you have a pretty interface to accomplish the same result. And guess what? The user templates in SBS 2003 are nothing more than disabled user accounts.

It makes sense to create custom templates that meet your needs like the accounting example. You might have a template designed for each department. You can even export templates between customer sites by selecting the Export Templates link in the Server Management console. (Server Management, Advanced Management, Migrate Server Settings) This would be really cool if you were the reseller of a line-of-business application (e.g., Microsoft Small Business Financials) and your directory permissions were the same at each client and the "accounting" template could be used at any client site. You get the point!

Use templates to make changes to a user's permissions. This is good for updating a user as needed or updating a user account that was migrated over from SBS 2000 and doesn't have the full SBS 2003 experience going for it yet! That is, if you followed the migration approaches discussed in Chapter 5, the user account brought forward would not have an SBS 2003 user template applied to it (and that is part of why you have to go over the "To Do List" again after an upgrade) and when launching the Change User Permissions Wizard, you can apply a template to already existing user accounts.

IMPORTANT: Once again. Use User templates at all times if possible. This way you will have consistent permissions assigned across all user accounts, whereas assigning them manually leaves great room for error.

Computer Accounts

You can create and manage the client computers on the SBS network using the **Client Computers** link in the Server Management console. You can also configure application deployment and other advanced tasks from here. (Assigning Applications to client computers will be covered in Chapter 8.) The Manage Client Computers contains the **Set Up Computer Wizard** that will set up SBS client computers that are running Windows 2000 operating systems or later. The Set Up Computer Wizard:

- Creates client computer accounts.
- Assigns applications to client computers.

Again, we encourage you to use the SBS wizard to create and manage computer clients for the same reasons as stated above on user accounts. You could create the computer account directly in the Active Directory Users and Computers console, but again it would be placed in the general *Computer* container and not in the computers container located under the *MyBusiness* OU.

Securing File, Folder, and Printer Objects

Now that we have worked our way through user accounts, groups and rights and permissions, let's take a look at how these are tied into securing objects on the network.

Share Permissions

In terms of "Microsoft think" on the 70-282 exam, you should always secure objects that are shared on the network. That could be folders, printers, and other devices and applications. For other users to gain access to the shared resource, it must be shared out. By default, shares allow access to Everyone (yes, there is an "Everyone" group) and assign read permissions. Once the resource is shared, you could remove the Everyone group and just add the security groups that should have Read, Change, or Full Control permissions. Share permissions apply to folders not files and will be inherited from subfolders. They are displayed in Table 6-1.

Table 6-1

Read	View the folder, subfolders, and all files contained in them; allows running programs.
Change	Allows Read access; allows changing data in files, adding and deleting files; allows creating documents and subfolders.
Full Control	Allows Change permissions access; allows changing permission settings on the folder.

IMPORTANT: What Microsoft doesn't offer (but NetWare did) is the hidden share permission attribute as a permission selection. But have no fear. It can be re-created by appending a share name with a dollar sign. (Granted—this is a very American way to hide something and probably is culturally offensive to the international readers of this book.) So a share named HARRYB$ would not be visible from the network. Hidden share questions have been known to appear on Microsoft certification exams.

IMPORTANT: Share permissions are only effective across the network. If a user logs on locally or via terminal services, share permissions will not be effective. On the other hand, Windows Server 2003 (and SBS 2003) now has all default share permissions set to READ only for the Everyone Group as shown in Figure 6-3. You should change permission settings to be more generous (in many cases), otherwise a user will encounter a "read-only" condition when working with a document. Another example is a line-of-business application. If you set up a database for sharing, users will encounter errors when trying to work with the database application.

Notes:

Figure 6-3

Default share permissions set to READ only for the Everyone Group! In prior SBS releases (SBS 2000), this was Full Control.

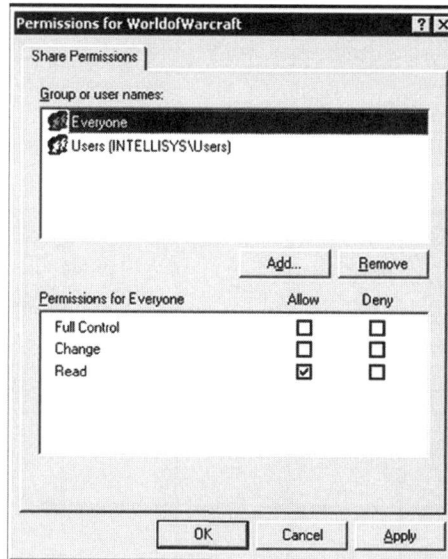

NTFS Permissions

NTFS permissions use ACLs (Access Control Lists) that are checked against the access token assigned to the user when logging into the domain.

NTFS can be configured on files AND folders and allows for greater control than share permissions. If share and NTFS permissions are applied to the same folder, the more restrictive rule will apply. NTFS permissions are effective across the network and locally.

At a minimum, you need to memorize the following NTFS permissions:

- Read,
- Write,
- List Folder Contents,
- Read and Execute,
- Modify, and
- Full Control.

You should seek to understand how the core NTFS permissions are made up of a set of special permissions as shown in the following table. Depending on what object you assign permissions to, certain permission may not be available due to the type of object. (Take a look at folder permissions compared to printer permissions.) Let's take a quick dive into table 6-2 before continuing.

Table 6-2
Deep dive into NTFS permissions In prior SBS releases (SBS 2000), this was Full Control.

Special Permissions	Full Control	Modify	Read & Execute	List Folder Contents	Read	Write
Travers Folder/ Execute File	X	X	X	X	-	-
List Folder/ Read Data	X	X		X	X	-
Read Attributes	X	X	X	X	X	-
Read Extended Attributes	X	X	X	X	X	-
Create Files/ Write Data	X	X	-	-	-	X
Create Folders/ Append Data	X	X	-	-	-	X
Write Attributes	X	X	-	-	-	X

Special Permissions	Full Control	Modify	Read & Execute	List Folder Contents	Read	Write
Write Extended Attributes	X	X	-	-	-	X
Delete Subfolder and Files	X	-	-	-	-	-
Delete	X	X	-	-	-	-
Read Permissions	X	X	X	X	X	X
Change Permissions	X	-	-	-	-	-
Take Ownership	X	-	-	-	-	-

Note that the Modify permission in the above table only has three less permissions than the Full permissions (see gray boxes). This is a MAJOR HINT!

> IMPORTANT: An interesting question that has emerged in the SBS community concerns NTFS folders versus Windows SharePoint Services (WSS). In a sense, NTFS and WSS compete with each other because they are used to store information like files inside folders. As you seek to understand the SBS product en route to becoming certified on the 70-282 exam, you'll appreciate this cultural debate. NTFS, being based on ACLs, has a very rich set of permissions. WSS, being based on four roles, has a limited set of permissions it can apply to objects like files and folders. However, WSS has version control

and alerts, something missing from NTFS. So both approaches, NTFS and WSS, have strengths and weaknesses and are present on the 70-282 exam.

Here is another test tip factoid you'll want to memorize. NTFS permissions are either explicit or inherited. When you see a permission box grayed out in on the security tab under file or folder properties, you know this is an inherited permission, whereas explicit permissions are set when you create a new folder.

Permissions and Volumes

Another testing area to pop up here and there on a Microsoft exam involves moving or copying files and folders on and in between NTFS volumes. Be aware how copying and moving files or folders can affect the original permissions, as seen in Table 6-3:

Table 6-3
Actions affect permissions.

Action	Within NTFS volume	Between NTFS volume
Copy	Inherits permission of the destination folder	Inherits permissions of the destination folder
Move	Retains original permissions	Inherits permissions of the of the destination folder
Users who copy files or folders become owners of the new copies		

It's easy to remember if you think of that a copy is just like a cut & paste operation. It physically moves the location of the files to the new destination, regardless if it is on the same volume or another volume. Whereas a move on the same volume will only *repoint* the file location, but not physically move the file. If moving to another volume, it will.

Rules for the Road

There will be times when you will have both, shared permissions and NTFS permissions assigned to a folder. In this case, remember these rules of the road:

- When using both NTFS and shared permissions, the most restrictive permission will rule

- Shared folders provide less security then NTFS security configured folders

- You can apply different NTFS permissions to subfolders of shared folders as well as files within them

Configuring NTFS Permissions to Files and Folders

To configure permissions on a folder, you would go to the folder in Windows Explorer and right-click the folder. Click **Sharing and Security** and then click on the **Security** tab in the **Properties** box. Here you can add users and groups from the SBS domain as well as set their permissions.

Configuring NTFS Permissions for Printers

Setting NTFS permissions for printers is essentially the same as for files and folders. You right-click the printer, go to **Properties,** and then select the **Security** tab. You can add users and groups here as well as set printing permissions. Table 6-4 outlines the level of access associated with print permissions.

Table 6-4
Printer permissions.

	Print	Manage Documents	Manage Printers
Print	X		X
Manage Printers			X
Manage Documents		X	
Read Permissions	X	X	X
Change Permissions		X	X
Take ownership		X	X

Note that Manage Printers has all permissions but one (see gray box).

It is easy to adopt a pious attitude toward printer devices when studying for a certification exam, believing you already know all about printers. But, Microsoft has historically asked printer questions on its certification exams. We believe printer questions are asked not because you'd truly be concerned about intense printer configuration questions on an SBS network, but rather this testing content area is a way to fail and disqualify unworthy SBSers from obtaining their passing mark on the 70-282 exam. So, take printer matters seriously even if you believe printers a "baby simple."

> IMPORTANT: Just remember, to keep it easy and not get into a permission mess, use only NTFS permissions and assign groups instead of users to files, folders, and printer objects. The Microsoft TechNet discs, part of an annual subscription, has excellent NTFS resources down to the developer level. Visit TechNet at www.micro-soft.com/technet.

Auditing File and Folder Access

Auditing Files and Folders, or Object Access is a good way of finding out who is accessing files and folders. Anytime an object configured for auditing and an action occurs with the object, the action will be written to the security log (accessible through the Event Viewer). Group Policy allows auditing of not only files and folders but also system resources, system logons and system configuration changes. Auditing requires a lot of system resources itself, therefore it is recommended to configure auditing for specific objects only. Auditing policies can be set for an entire site, domain, organizational unit or individual workstations or servers.

To enable auditing on files and folders you must first access the Group Policy container and configure the **Audit Object Access** node as shown in Figure 6-4. Once the Audit Object Access has been enabled you are ready to audit individual files and folders.

N otes:

Figure 6-4 Click through the console tree until you get to the Audit Policy node.

Figure 6-4
Group Policy Object Editor

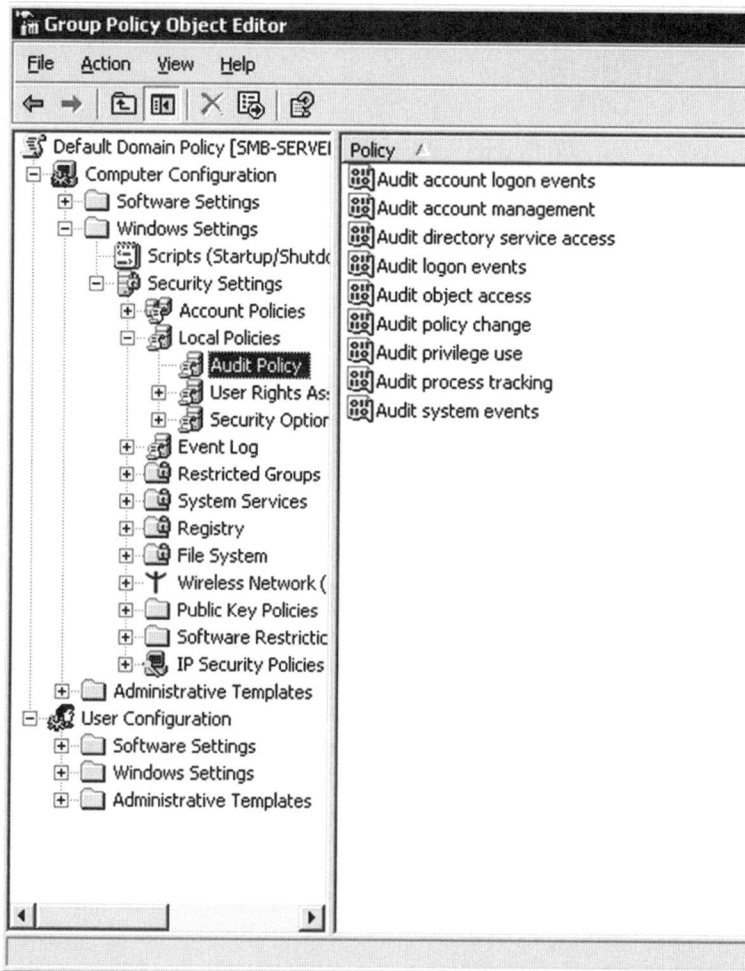

Auditing can only be performed on files and folders located on NTFS volumes. To configure auditing on an individual object, go to the file or folder to be audited through Windows Explorer, click on the file or folder properties and select the **Security** tab, then click **Advanced.**

The Access Control Settings box will open. Select the **Auditing** tab. Here you can choose to **Allow inheritable auditing entries from the parent to propagate** to this object or **Replace auditing entries on all child objects**. By clicking **Add** and **Edit** you can also use the Auditing Entries list box to select whose actions are audited (users, groups or computers), and select specific actions to be audited (create files/delete files).

Security Guidelines

If you take a look at the first step in the To Do List—the "View Security and Best Practices" task—you will find it is comprised of a security best practices covering topics from protecting your server from external AND internal vulnerabilities to security issues monitoring.

General guidelines for securing your SBS server include: Want a hint? Read the To Do List!

- Keeping your antivirus application up-to-date.
- Keep the AV signatures updated as frequently as possible, as the virus epidemic has gotten out of hand.
- Using a firewall (covered later in this chapter).
- Not downloading and running programs from untrustworthy sources.
- Malicious programs resemble trustworthy software and could initiate identity theft, data destruction, and DoS attacks. Software should only be obtained from legitimate sources.
- The principle of least privilege. A beautiful thing for administrators to use on end-users, but this should also apply to themselves. Use an account with limited permissions to handle nonadministrative tasks and use the "runas" command for administrative tasks.
- Enforce strong passwords.
- Use complexity rules and enforce a minimum of seven characters using special symbols and mixed case.
- Apply the latest software patches.
- Use SUS with GPOs (explained below).
- Use group accounts to manage users. This will be much easier than managing individual permissions.

- Do regular backups.

- Use the Small Business Server Backup Configuration Wizard or use the Automated System Recovery feature (ASR). Hang on to your hats until Chapter 8 when you'll have the opportunity to read expanded backup discussion that compares the SBS backup and ASR methods. We even throw in a few real-world war stories for giggles.

- Restrict physical access to the domain controller.

- This is a high-level risk. Secure your server and network hardware; you never know when an employee will get disgruntled.

For more security information check out http://www.microsoft.com/mscorp/twc/default.mspx.

Configure Resource Sharing

Ah, the heart of the matter. Let's embrace the SBS-ology of sharing and controlling resources on our network. Resources can easily be viewed and configured, either in the Server Management console or Server Management for Power Users console. Network users can share printer and fax resources. Administrators can add, remove, and configure network printers directly from the preconfigured management consoles. It is easy to access and modify printer settings like port assignments, security, sharing, and other printing options, such as page separators. You can also use the Server Management console to view pending jobs, change the order of print jobs, pause, resume, or cancel print jobs currently in the print queue.

> IMPORTANT: Microsoft products, especially Windows operating system-based products, offer about seven different ways to do a task. In fact, I recall a Windows 95 assessment exam that actually tested on the different ways to perform a simple task (command line, GUI, control panel, etc.). So it's an established Microsoft testing paradigm to test your recall of keystrokes and mouse movements. Don't fret too much over this observation, but do ask yourself, "Are there other ways to accomplish this task?" More importantly, ask yourself, "What is the SBS way to accomplish this task?"

Configure Print Servers

When you connect a printer to the SBS server with a USB or IEEE1394 (Firewire) cable, Windows automatically detects and installs the necessary drivers. You can also attach printers with built-in NICs to the SBS network. SBS supports TCP/IP network printers using LPD, JetDirect, and Intel NetPort. To set up a network printer:

1. Attach the printer to the network and assign it an IP address (any available address from 192.168.16.3 to 192.168.16.9 found on the exception DHCP scope).

2. In the **Server Management** console, click on **Printers**.

3. Click Add a Printer, click Next, and on the Local or Network Printer page, select the Local Printer attached to this computer option, then uncheck the Automatically Detect and Install My Plug and Play Printer checkbox. Click Next.

4. Select **Create a New Port** on the **Printer Port** page and choose **Standard TCP/IP Port** from the drop-down list. Click **Next**.

5. On the **Add Standard TCP/IP Printer Port Wizard**, click **Next** and enter the **Printer Name or IP Address** and **Port Name**. Click **Next**.

6. The wizard will try to connect to the printer, and if it fails, display the **Additional Port Information Required** page. Select the printer from the standard list and click **Next** followed by **Finish.** Alternatively, you could select **Custom** and then choose the protocol for the printer, either **RAW** or **LPR**.

7. Leave the port number at 9100 if using RAW unless specified otherwise in the printer manual.

8. Select the SNMP protocol if the printer supports SNMP and type the community name.

9. Click **OK** and then **Finish.**

Configure File and Folder Objects Sharing

Files and folders can be shared over the network by granting users access to shared folders. Before these are shared, however, make sure to set the proper

NTFS permissions on the folder. (NTFS permissions are discussed in Chapter 6 in the section "User Rights and Permissions.") You can manage shared folders in the Server Management console from the Manage Shared Folders taskpad. You can:

- Add a shared folder.
- Change shared folder properties.
- Configure MyDocuments Redirection.
- Stop Sharing folders.
- View Connected Users.
- View Open files.

You can use a command line tools to view information on shared folders:

- Net share – Displays information about all shared resources on the local computer.
- Net session – Displays information about all open sessions between the local computer and other computers on the network.
- Net file – Displays information about all open files on shared resources.

SBS also has the ability to create shadow copies of shared folders, a function that acts like an automatic backup. More about shadow copies in Chapter 8 in the section, "Volume Shadow Service."

IMPORTANT: Files cannot be directly shared over the network.

Rather, folders containing files are shared.

Configure Software Update Service

One of the most important steps you can take in securing your SBS 2003 network is downloading Windows updates. Patches and fixes can be downloaded as soon as they are made available. Of course, you could set each client machine to download Windows updates automatically, but that would create a lot of traffic at once. You can centralize updates by using SUS (Software Update Services).

Working with SUS

SUS is a free download from http://www.microsoft.com/sus and provides patch, scanning, and installation services. Once installed it will scan the network, advise which patches are needed, and apply them based on your policy settings. When installing SUS, you can choose whether you want the SUS server to download the required patches from Windows update or host all patches on the SUS server. If you decide on the latter, ensure you have at least 6 GB of space on the host machine.

> IMPORTANT: For SBS 2003 Premium Edition, ISA Server 2000 users: For clients to update successfully, you must host updates locally or configure ISA Server 2000 not to require authentication.

Approving Updates

Before patches are rolled out to clients, they must first be approved by the SUS administrator. You can access SUS over a web interface at http://servername/ SUSAdmin, where you click on the **Approve Updates** link. Select one of the update choices and then click the **Approve** button.

Configure SUS Using GPO

There are two policies you can configure for SUS, the Basic SUS Config Group Policy object and the Scheduled Install SUS Config GPO. The steps outlined below show how to configure both GPOs which will apply to computer accounts located in the **MyBusiness** organizational unit.

The **Basic SUS Config** GPO configures updates to be automatically downloaded and the user can choose when to install them. This GPO typically applies to servers on a network, but can be used to let the user of a client computer choose when to install updates.

1. Log on to the Small Business Server (as an admin or an account that has admin rights and permissions), and go to the **Server Management** console.

2. Double-click **Advanced Management** in the console tree.

3. Double-click **Group Policy Management**, double-click **Forest:** *your domain name.*

4. Double-click **Domains**, right-click *your domain name,* click **Create and Link a GPO Here.**

5. Type **Basic SUS Config** in the text box and click **OK.**

6. The GPO will show now in the details pane, right-click the **Basic SUS Config** and click **Edit.**

7. The GPO editor will open, go to **Computer Configuration.**

8. Double-click **Administrative Templates**, double-click **Windows Components** and select **Windows Update.**

9. Double-click **Configure Automatic Updates** in the details pane and select **Enabled.**

10. Leave the default setting (3-Auto download and notify for install) and click **OK.**

11. Double-click **Specify intranet Microsoft update service location** and click **Enabled.**

12. Type **http://your server name** in both text boxes. (Set the intranet update service for detecting updates, Set the intranet statistics server.) Click **OK**, and close the GPO editor.

The **Scheduled Install SUS Config GPO** is an optional GPO that configures updates to automatically download and install updates to client computers on a network based on a defined schedule.

1. Log on to the Small Business Server (as an admin or an account that has admin rights and permissions), and go to the **Server Management** console.

2. Double-click **Advanced Management** in the console tree.

3. Double-click **Group Policy Management**, double-click **Forest: your domain name.**

4. Double-click **Domains,** double-click **your domain name**, **My Business** and **then Computers.**

5. Right-click **SBSComputers** (as shown in Figure 6-5) and click **Create and Link GPO Here.**

6. Type **Scheduled Install SUS Config** and click **OK,** it will now show under **SBSComputers** in the console tree.

7. Right-click **Scheduled Install SUS Config** and click **Edit,** the GPO Editor will open.

8. Under **Computer Configuration** click on **Administrative Templates** and double-click **Windows Components** and select **Windows Update.**

9. Double-click **Configure Automatic Updates** and select **Enabled.**

10. Under **Configure automatic updating,** select **4 - Auto download and schedule the install** from the drop down and leave the default **0 – Every day** as the **Scheduled install day.**

11. In the **Scheduled install time** the default time of 3:00 will show, click **OK.**

12. Double-click **Specify intranet Microsoft update service location** and click **Enabled.**

13. Type **http://your server name** in both text boxes. (Set the intranet update service for detecting updates, Set the intranet statistics server.) Click **OK,** and close the GPO editor.

14. Double-click **Reschedule Automatic Updates scheduled installations.** The **Reschedule Automatic Updates scheduled installations** properties will open, click **Enabled.**

15. The default value **5** for **Wait after system startup (minutes)** will show, click **OK.**

16. Double-click **No auto-restart for scheduled Automatic Updates installations.** The **No auto-restart for scheduled Automatic Updates installations** properties will open, click **Disabled** and click **OK.**

17. Close the GPO editor.

Notes:

Figure 6-5

Create and Link a GPO

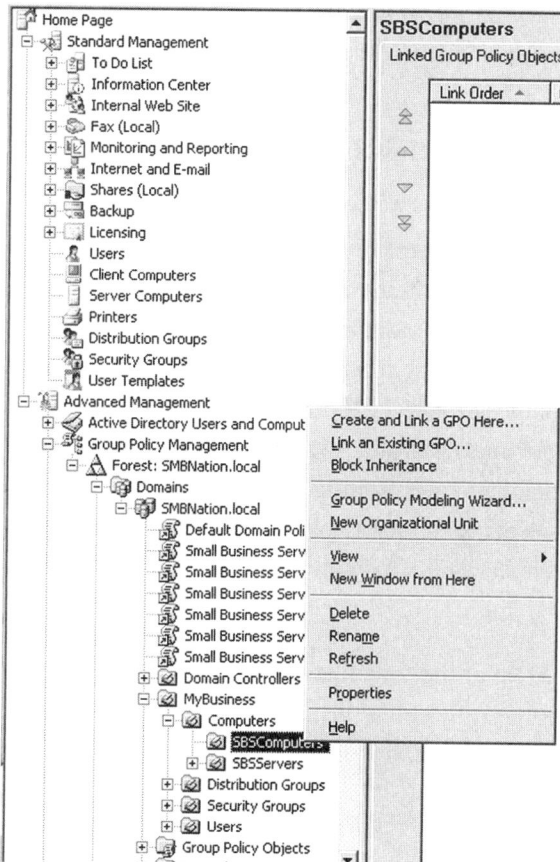

At times the Group policy may not seem to take effect (by default it should push updates from the server to clients every 90 minutes), or you want to force the Group Policy update immediately. In that case, log on as the administrator to the client machine:

1. On a computer running **Windows XP**, click **Start**, click **Run**.

2. In the Open box, type **cmd**, and click OK. The command prompt will open.

3. Type **gpupdate/force**, and press ENTER.

IMPORTANT: It is a good measure to actually click through these exercises as you read them to get the full effect of combining text with visual images. This will be your valid hands-on tool and help you recall your memory during the exam.

Configure ISA Server 2000 and Firewalls

When delving deep into ISA Server 2000 and the firewall discussion, step back and consider one approach used in assessment testing. Vendors love to test their stakeholders on the new delta features or the changes since the last release. That is a major paradigm that many exam writers adhere to: "…let's make sure our partners know about these new features!" So, if you agree, you'd want to approach the ISA Server 2000 and firewall discussion with that thinking, including it in your analytical attack strategy. You can control the flow of Internet Protocol (IP) packets to and from ISA Server with the packet filtering feature in ISA Server. When you enable packet filtering, all packets on the external interface are dropped unless they are explicitly allowed, either statically by IP packet filters or dynamically by access policy or publishing rules.

Packet filters. Most of the time it is recommended to open ports dynamically. Create access policy rules allowing internal clients to access the Internet and publishing rules allowing external clients access to internal servers.

- IP packet filters open ports statically.
- Access policy and publishing rules open ports dynamically.

For instance, if you want users to have access to all HTTP sites you would create a site and content rule and protocol rule for this access, and *not* an IP packet filter that opens port 80.

Get secure, stay secure. In the SBS 2003 release time frame, Microsoft's shift to emphasizing security in its software was at full throttle! If you understand where Microsoft was coming from when it was developing the 70-282 exam and SBS 2003, that'll yield tremendous dividends when you are flat-out stuck on a security question on the 70-282 exam and must guess at an answer. If you must guess, remember that Microsoft was just starting to enter a very conservative era relating to its security practices when the 70-282 exam was created, so you'd want to answer the Microsoft way. In that case, any answer you guess at would be the most restrictive and conservative, all things being equal.

> IMPORTANT: Again, remember that the 70-282 exam was written with ISA Server 2000 in mind, not the newly released ISA Server 2004 product. So you might actually need to build a test SBS 2003 network with legacy ISA Server 2000 installed so you THINK like the 70-282 exam!

So let's dive into ISA Server 2000 and firewalls at an appropriate level for a 70-282 exam-cram book. There are many ways to configure individual settings in ISA Server 2000 and its firewalls. ISA controls the firewall by way of access rules, the firewall clients that use them, and policy elements. The policy elements cover bandwidth, destination sets, client address sets, schedules, protocol definitions, content groups, and dial-up entries. Policy elements allow values to be set on rule properties that are defined beyond the scope of the rule itself.

Regardless whether you install ISA Server 2000 in firewall mode or in integrated mode, you must specify the local address table. The LAT is a table of all internal IP address ranges used by the internal network behind the ISA Server 2000. ISA Server 2000 uses the LAT to control how machines on the internal network communicate with external networks. All of these elements—the LAT, access rules, client types, and policy elements—play into configuring ISA Server 2000.

Configure Access Using NAT

Small businesses use private networking as a tool for sharing resources, such as an Internet connection. SBS 2003 has built-in NAT functionality called a "Basic Firewall" that is enabled through the Routing and Remote Access Service and requires two NICs to make NAT functional. The Premium Edition comes with ISA Server 2000, which uses a Secure NAT client.

How NAT Works

A user on the network requests information from the Internet. The computer will send TCP/IP or UDP datagram packets that contain information about the computer (source) to the destination server, so the destination server knows where to send back the requested information. Before the datagram packet leaves the network, the SBS server will change the outgoing packet header and change the address of the source to point to the SBS server. This way, SBS hides the real source, and by using only its own IP address appears to be the only computer at that location. When the destination server returns the requested data packets, the SBS server receives the packet and remaps it back to the client. The server running (RRAS) acts as a network address translator and allows for all client commuters to share a single IP connection, shielding their true identity from the Internet.

Configuring NAT

NAT comes with both SBS 2003 Standard and Premium Edition (in Premium you would use ISA Server 2000). Even though NAT is configured by RRS, in SBS 2003, you enable NAT by running the EICW (Configure E-mail and Internet Connection Wizard). When configuring the CEICW, you will get to the Firewall Settings screen. By checking the **Enable Firewall** radio button, you will enable NAT. At this point, a pop-up window will appear and advise you that it is stopping services to configure ISA Server 2000 before you continue with the CEICW.

> IMPORTANT: For NAT to create the Basic Firewall, you must have at least two NIC cards installed.

ISA Firewall Clients

Firewall clients redirect outbound Internet traffic through the firewall. An ISA Server 2000 machine can support three firewall clients, each of which are discussed in this section:

- SecureNAT
- Web Proxy
- Firewall

Client computers that do not have firewall client software are Secure NAT (secure network address translation) clients. Secure NAT clients benefit from many features of ISA Server , including most access control features, except for high-level protocol support and user-level authentication. Secure NAT clients do not require special software, but should configure the default gateway to point to the ISA Server. ISA Server client functionality is dependent on the proper configuration of the ISA Server itself. If the server has difficulty resolving hostnames or reaching the Internet, so will the clients. Since ISA operates in conjunction with Windows 2003, the internal and external DNS server names should be provided. The proxy service is enabled on all of the ISA Server machine's internal IPs by default at port 8080, including 127.0.0.1, the localhost IP.

Secure NAT

SecureNAT clients, which are essentially handled by the firewall service, benefit from:

- Application filters that can modify the protocol stream to allow handling of complex protocols.

- Site and content rules that can be applied by way of the firewall service that passes all HTTP requests to the Web Proxy Service.

Despite the fact that Windows 2000 NAT does not have an inherent authentication mechanism, ISA Server 2000 rules can still be applied to Secure NAT clients, including protocol usage policies, destination, and content type.

Web Proxy

Web Proxy clients are computers that have a Web browser application, which complies with HTTP1.1 and is configured to use the Web proxy service of ISA Server 2000.

Web browser settings on the client can be configured manually on the client or automatically by installing the firewall client and configuring the Web browser through the ISA Server 2000 Management console. There you can configure:

- The ISA Server 2000 and port to which the client should connect.

- Automatic discovery.

- Computers that the web browser should access directly.

- A backup route if the ISA Server 2000 machine is unavailable.

Firewall Clients

Firewall clients are computers with the firewall client software installed and enabled. Firewall clients use Winsock applications that use the ISA firewall service. When a firewall client requests an object from a computer, it uses a Winsock application and checks its copy of the local address table (LAT) to see if the specified computer is in the LAT. If the computer is not found in the LAT, the request is sent on to the firewall service. The request will then be handled by the firewall service, forwarding it to the right destination if permitted.

Firewall client software can be installed on Windows ME, Windows 95, Windows 98, Windows NT 4.0, or Windows 2000. Sixteen-bit Winsock applications are supported, but only on Windows 2000 and Windows NT 4.0. Unlike SecureNAT, the firewall client service can send user information required for authentication to ISA.

Table 6-5 compares and contrasts all firewall client methods.

Table 6-5
  Firewall client details.

Feature	SecureNAT client	Firewall client	Web Proxy client
Installation required	Some network configuration changes are required	Yes	No, requires Web browser configuration
Operating system support	Any operating system that supports Transmission Control Protocol/ Internet Protocol (TCP/IP)	Only Windows platforms	All platforms, but by way of Web application

Feature	SecureNAT client	Firewall client	Web Proxy client
Protocol support	Requires application filters for multi-connection protocols	All Winsock applications	Hypertext Transfer Protocol (HTTP), Secure HTTP (HTTPS), File Transfer Protocol (FTP), and Gopher
User-level authentication	Some network configuration changes are required	Yes	Yes
Server applications	No configuration or installation required	Requires configuration file	N/A

IMPORTANT: A favorite test-writing technique is to invoke the compare-and-contrast method used by stern composition teachers in grammar school assigning essay homework! So make the table above your test-taking buddy and understand that a compare-and contrast viewpoint, as expressed above specific to firewalls, is a popular exam question construct and can rear its ugly head on any 70-282 testing subject!

ISA Server 2000 Firewall Access Rules

As you will read in this section, you can configure access policies in ISA Server 2000 that consist of protocol rules and content rules.

Protocol Rules

Protocol rules define the protocols that can be used for communication between the local network and the Internet. Protocol rules are processed at the application level, allowing clients to use protocols like HTTP, HTTPS, and FTP. You can configure protocol rules to apply to all IP traffic, a specific set of protocols definitions, or to all IP traffic except for selected protocols.

When clients request objects using a specific protocol, ISA Server 2000 checks the protocol rules. If there is a protocol rule specifically denying use of the protocol, the request is denied.

Site and Content Rules

Site and content rules define what content clients can be accessed on what Internet sites. Site and content rules are processed at the application level, allowing or denying clients based on the content of a website and specific protocols used to access that website. When clients request objects, ISA Server 2000 checks the site and content rules. If a site and content rule specifically deny the request, access is denied.

> IMPORTANT: So how can you truly commit to memory what protocol rules and site and content rules are and how you might use them? Try this on for size. These rules prevent good girls from behaving badly (kinda sounds like an Internet web-cam site, eh?). Many faiths believe that humans are basically good, not evil. But there are temptations out there in the world that challenge the angelic behaviors of the best of us! So sometime we need a roadblock to prevent us from driving on the road to ruin. These site and content rules, when applied, can serve as that roadblock and prevent kind souls from becoming evil by visiting naughty Internet locations. Consider this akin to your buddy throwing a body block so you can't hurt yourself!

In all seriousness, one SBS site at a sheriff's department for a small county outside Denver, Colorado, uses the rules discussed in this section. Because of the nature of law enforcement work, it's essential that all employees operate and conduct their affairs in a manner above reproach. So the protocol, site, and content rules prevent employees from engaging in potentially embarrassing acts. Anything less would be criminal.

Notes:

Practice Questions

Question #1:

Which statement best describes the purpose of Domain Local Groups? (Choose the best answer.)

a. Domain local groups are used to group users within a single domain. Only users from the parent domain can be included in a domain local group.

b. Domain local groups are used to assign permissions throughout an entire forest. The primary function of domain local groups is to facilitate the use of transitive trusts to form the secure communications within domain-forest relationships.

c. Domain local groups are used to assign permissions to resources within the local domain. Universal groups, global groups, or user accounts from any domain can be placed into a domain local group.

d. Domain local groups provide the backward capability needed to facilitate upgrades from SBS 2000 and earlier versions. Local group functionality has since been replaced with the introduction of universal groups.

Question #2:

Acme Marketing recently moved their corporate HQ to a new location on the opposite side of town. Their new broadband connection is with the same ISP but now requires authentication directly at the server and not the modem. What has to be done to successfully get them working in the new environment? Their server is a 2.4 GHz P4, with 2 GB RAM, 36 GB RAID 1 OS Volume, 60 GB RAID 5 data volume, and dual 10/100/1000 NICs?. (Choose the best answer.)

a. Run CEICW and in the Firewall section choose "**Authenticate with ISP (WAN).**" Answer the questions, ensuring that the proper NIC is selected for the external connection.

b. Run CEICW and in the Network section choose "**Broadband connection requiring a username and password (PPOE).**" Answer the questions with the information provided by the ISP, ensuring the proper NIC is selected for the external connection.

c. Create a user using the details provided by the ISP. Set the user login type to "Automatic," and assign it to the local resource NIC 1 (External). Modify the DNS server properties to not attempt name resolution until after successful authentication (DNS_ON_AUTH=TRUE).

d. Reinstall SBS 2003 and choose the correct broadband connection type.

Question #3:

The specifications you are handed for the new SBS 2003 Premium edition installation are as follows:

- Internal name resolution is to occur transparent to the external network.

- Local PC's are not to have references to external name servers, but Internet name resolution should operate transparently.

- IP Addresses for local pc's are to be assigned automatically and include transparent updating of name server records.

Which of the following would meet these requirements? (Choose the best answer)

a. Disable DNS on the local SBS server, point to the ISP's DNS at the SBS server, create an internal alias referencing the external DNS server and push to local PC's with DHCP.

b. Provide proper information during the installation wizard to enable DNS and DHCP on the Server. After installation has completed, go to **All Programs >Administrative Tools** >double click the DNS icon, Right click on the server icon and choose "properties". Select the "Forwarders" tab. Enter the IP addresses of the ISP's primary and secondary DNS servers in the domain forwarders IP address list.

c. This operation cannot be completed on SBS 2003.It requires an upgrade to Windows Server 2003 Standard Edition.

d. Go to **All Programs >Administrative Tools** >double click the DHCP icon, Highlight and authorize the server node and then expand it. Right click on "Server Options", choose "Configure Options", enable option 134 "External Client Name Resolution Forwarded (transparent)", and option 128 "Local Client Lookup (local)".

Question #4:

You want to provide Internet name resolution, management, Internet mail, automatic addressing, and plug and play functionality. Which of the following are accurate acronyms for the technologies required? (In the proper order.)

a. ARP, SNMP, UPS, SMTP, UDP

b. DNS,SMTP,SNMP,DHCP, UPnP

c. LAPD, UPMC, DNS, RDP, POP3

d. DNS, SNMP, SMTP, DHCP, UPnP

Question # 5:

You would like to provide terminal services for some of the users in an SBS 2003 environment. What has to be done to enable this functionality?

a. Install SBS 2003 Premium Edition, enable **Terminal Services Applictions Sharing Mode** in the To Do list.

b. Install SBS 2003, enable **Terminal Services Applictions Sharing Mode** in the To Do list. Apply the **Power** User template to all users requiring access.

c. Terminal services are only available in **Remote Administration mode** on SBS 2003. In order to provide Terminal Services in Application Sharing mode, a separate server must be installed.

d. Install SBS 2003 with the **/app_mode** switch which unfortunately removes much of the functionality of the product.

Question #6:

Which of the following options are available when implementing Disk Quotas (Choose all that apply)

a. Limit the total disk space which can be consumed by a user on a volume.

b. Limit the total disk space that can be consumed by a user on all volumes.

c. Send the user a warning that they are approaching their maximum allocated value.

d. Limit total space that can be consumed within selected folders by a user.

e. Deny disk space to users who have exceeded the quota limit.

Question #7:

SBS 2003 comes with Microsoft Exchange preconfigured to operate in the small business environment. Which of the following statements are true about Exchange and SBS? (Choose all that apply.)

a. The implementation of additional message stores within an SBS environment requires an upgrade to another version of Exchange.

b. SBS 2003 comes with "Exchange Lite," which is not fully functional.

c. Outlook Web Access is by far the most popular e-mail software, principally because of the high purchase price for the full Outlook 2003 client.

d. Multiple licensed Exchange servers are supported on an SBS network.

Question #8

Which of the following are true statements concerning the POP3 connector implementation in SBS 2003? (Choose all that apply.)

a. The POP3 connector can connect to multiple POP3 servers to retrieve e-mail messages for multiple users but must save them in a single global POP3 mailbox.

b. The POP3 connector can be configured to deliver e-mail to multiple SMTP recipients, including Public Folders, as long as its e-mail address has been properly defined.

c. The POP3 connector can connect to multiple POP3 servers to retrieve e-mail messages for multiple users. The e-mail can then be saved in a single global POP3 mailbox, or distributed to the appropriate users' Exchange mailboxes.

d. The POP3 connector is disabled by default but the service will automatically start once the first POP3 user is added.

Answers:

Question #1: Answer: c

a. Incorrect! Domain local groups are not used to group users, but rather to provide a convenient mechanism to assign permissions to resources within a single domain.

b. Incorrect! Never pass up an opportunity to use "transitive trusts" in a sentence. There's certain poetry in the phrase – or is it just me? Domain local groups have nothing to do with trusts, only permissions within the local domain.

c. Correct! The idea being that resources are local to the machine and the starting point collection of objects within a forest is of course a domain. Domain local groups can contain users, other local groups (from the same domain), global groups, or universal groups. Remember AGDLP - Accounts into Global into Domain Local and then grant Permissions. Or All-Guys-Definitely-Love-Pizza! OK, maybe the food thing just works for me.

d. Incorrect! Domain local groups are used to assign permissions to resources within the domain. Earlier versions of NT and Windows also had the concept of local groups (though not necessarily *Domain* local groups) that backwards compatibility is certainly an added benefit.

Question #2: Answer: b

a. Incorrect! Though CEICW is the correct tool, *Firewall* is the wrong section.

b. Correct! Did I mention that CEICW is your friend? Never underestimate its usefulness. Changes like this one which may seem

complicated are usually resolved by simply rerunning CEICW and providing the new information – in this case the network section. I'm not sure what all has to happen under the hood to convert from direct connect to PPOE, but I am reasonably sure there is a long list of "gotchas" if attemped manually. Thank you SBS wizard Wizards! (Hmmm, wuz that redundant?)

c. Incorrect! Nothing near as complicated as this - just run CEICW and choose PPOE!

d. Incorrect! With a hearty and soul-felt *Thank You!* Just visit our friend CEICW and choose PPOE. Then have a nice day!

Question #3: Answer: b

a. Incorrect! The SBS 2003 server can handle local resolution and forward lookups to external DNS servers as required.

b. Correct! DHCP will provide the clients with their IP addresses and will point them to the SBS server for DNS. The SBS server will provide DNS resolution for all of the local nodes because it is authoritive for the domain. Any resolution requests received for non local nodes will be sent to the defined "forwarders" for resolution. The SBS DNS server will cache the results to minimize internet traffic for subsequent lookups.

3C: Incorrect! SBS 2003 IS Windows Server 2003 Standard Edition at the core.

3D: Incorrect!. There are no DNS forwarding server options under DHCP.

Question #4: Answer: d

a. Incorrect!

b. Incorrect. Many people confuse SNMP and SMTP

c. Incorrect!

d. Correct! Domain Name Services, Simple Network Management Protocol, Simple Mail Transport Protocol, Dynamic Host Control Protocol, Universal Plug and Play.

Question #5: Answer: c

a. Incorrect! Unlike previous versions of SBS, terminal services cannot be run in application mode on SBS 2003 – period. If Application Sharing mode is required, a separate Terminal Server server must be installed. The SBS 2003 server can be configured act as the license server, however.

b. Incorrect! Doesn't matter what template is applied. The users Application Mode terminal services cannot be enabled on an SBS 2003 server.

c. Correct! SBS 2003 only support Terminal Services in remote administration mode. The SBS 2003 server can be configured to act as the license server for another server running Terminal Services in application sharing mode.

d. Incorrect! Application Mode terminal services cannot be enabled or installed on an SBS 2003 server.

Question #6: Answer: a,c,e

a. Correct! Disk Quotas are implemented at the volume level for each user.

b. Incorrect! Disk Quotas are implemented at the volume level for each user. You cannot control disk quotas across multiple volumes.

c. Correct! Users can be sent a warning message when a preset amount of disk space has been consumed.

d. Incorrect! Disk quotas can only be implemented on a volume, not at the folder level.

e. Correct! When a user has consumed the assigned amount of disk space on a volume they are prevented from using more by the disk quota process. This is obviously the basic reason for implementing disk quotas to begin with - to make sure users don't consume all of the disk space on a volume.

Question #7: Answer: a,d

a. Correct! Microsoft Exchange (Standard Edition) which supports only a single message store, is implemented on the SBS 2003 server.

Microsoft Exchange (Enterprise) would have to be installed to support multiple message stores.

b. Incorrect! The fully functional version of Microsoft Exchange (Standard Edition) is implemented on SBS 2003. In fact the only thing removed is the complex installation procedures!

c. Incorrect! The Outlook 2003 client is provided free and its use is included in the client license purchased with the SBS 2003 server.

d. Correct! Multiple licensed Exchange servers can be present on an SBS network.

Question #8: Answer: c,d

a. Incorrect! Delivering messages to a single global mailbox is an option but it is not required.

b. Incorrect! The POP3 connector cannot be configured to deliver to a public folder.

c. Correct! This makes the POP3 connector very powerful, allowing for the immediate integration of the current mail environment into Exchange. It also makes the process of migrating from a POP3 environment a much less stressful task. With a greater likelihood of success.

d. Correct! The first user can be added either by CEICW or via the POP3 Connector Manager.

Notes:

Summary

This chapter should not be taken lightly! Obviously, you were presented with appropriate 70-282 exam discussion that focused on security in the context of permissions, ISA Server 2000, and firewalls. Equally important, we pulled the drapes back on several occasions to allow you to "think" like Microsoft about security in the SBS 2003 world. If you somehow missed that, stop and reread this chapter prior to proceeding to Chapter 7 (or going out for a beer or café latté)! This topic area is also one on which you should conduct some outside research before you take the 70-282 exam, because there are several other books focused strictly on some of the security technologies (but without our 70-282 test-taking thinking). So consider this: Your journey toward understanding security in the world of computing and SBS 2003 has now gotten off to a good start, but it is by no means over!

CHAPTER 7
Configuring Windows Small Business Server 2003

Congratulations! You have just been given the Key to Life. Other administrators have to spend their entire weekend configuring remote access, e-mail, and web services, adding users, setting permissions, creating security groups, and contending with other odds and ends, while the SBS consultant can accomplish the same tasks with the same outcome and still be able to spend the weekend with the kids. And that is the Key to Life! I have gotten so comfortable doing SBS installs that I schedule some installs during the week after working hours, knowing that I can still get home at a decent time and long before daybreak.

Configure Windows Small Business Server 2003 for Networking and Remote Connectivity.

Configuring a server for secure remote access sounds like a gargantuan task—and it could be if it were not for the smart wizards included in SBS.

Using the To Do List

What would SBS be without the To Do List? The To Do List, first shown to you in Chapter 5 as Figure 5.2, is the epitome of simplicity and I like it! The first thing that will pop up on the server after a new installation will be the To

Do List. Basically this list is a collection of tasks to be performed to finalize the SBS setup. Funny enough, the To Do List has checkboxes so you can mark what "To Do" tasks you have already performed. I always use the checkboxes when I am at the client site setting up a server, as there are always interruptions. Checking off the tasks completed means I have one less thing to remember when I come back to the server.

Connecting to the Internet

And which is the baddest wizard of all? Of course, the CEICW (Configure E-mail and Internet Connection Wizard). This is the kitchen-with-the-sink type wizard, and you will find that this wizard is the one that will save you hours of time when configuring your Small Business Server for Internet connectivity, setting up e-mail and many other items. So take a minute to click slowly through the CEICW, click on the "more information" buttons on the individual screens and really pay attention to all its available options.

The following four components are configured by the CEICW:

- Networking
- Firewall
- Secure Web Site
- E-mail

and let's take a dive to see what they encompass.

IMPORTANT: At any time you need to reconfigure a setting, you can rerun the CEICW to make changes. Settings that shouldn't be changed can be bypassed, and there is no need to reboot the server after making configuration changes.

Networking

First you will be asked to choose your connection type, which could be:

- Direct Broadband connection—Requires a DSL or cable modem that does not have an IP assigned to the modem. Requires two NICs on the server.

- Local Router—Requires a router, typically hardware-based (not anther computer) with an IP address assigned by the ISP. Can be configured with one or two NICs on the server. This is Microsoft's support for having SBS 2003 use a single NIC and using a hardware-based firewall to provide Internet security and firewall protection.

- IMPORTANT: So the cat is out of the bag here. Microsoft indeed supports hardware-based firewalls in the SBS 2003 product. It's not readily emphasized in Microsoft marketing messaging because Microsoft would rather have you use two NIC cards with its built-in SBS 2003 firewall components. So, for 70-282 exam purposes, it's important to honor the local router selection, but not dwell on it.

- Broadband connection requiring a username and password, also called PPoE, requires authentication information and uses a DSL or cable modem which does not have an IP assigned to the actual modem. Requires two NICs on the server.

The next screen is the Network Connection screen where the NIC properties will be configured. Depending on whether you have one or two NICs installed in the server, you well get a choice of either a single or, as shown in Figure 7-1, a dual NIC configuration option.

Figure 7-1

Configuration options for SBS in a dual-NIC configuration (in this case the external NIC connects to the ISPs router).

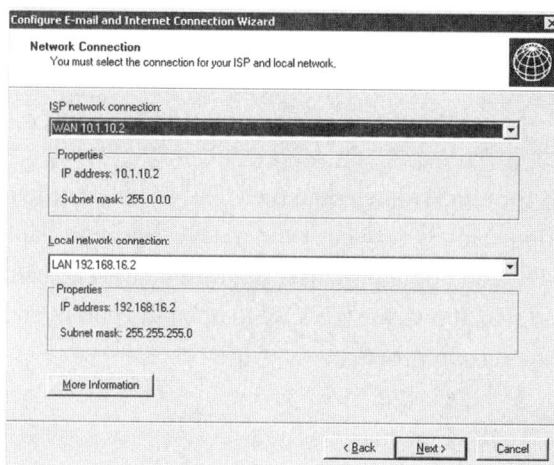

Make sure you have the IP address information from your ISP ready when starting the CEICW. Depending on your Internet connection device, you will be prompted to fill out information on an IP address, a subnet mask, and preferred DNS servers before you can continue on to configure the firewall. This will actually configure the DNS settings without the SBS admin having to touch the DNS console. Figure 7-2 shows this configuration using the CEICW.

Figure 7-2
DNS settings configuration in the CEICW

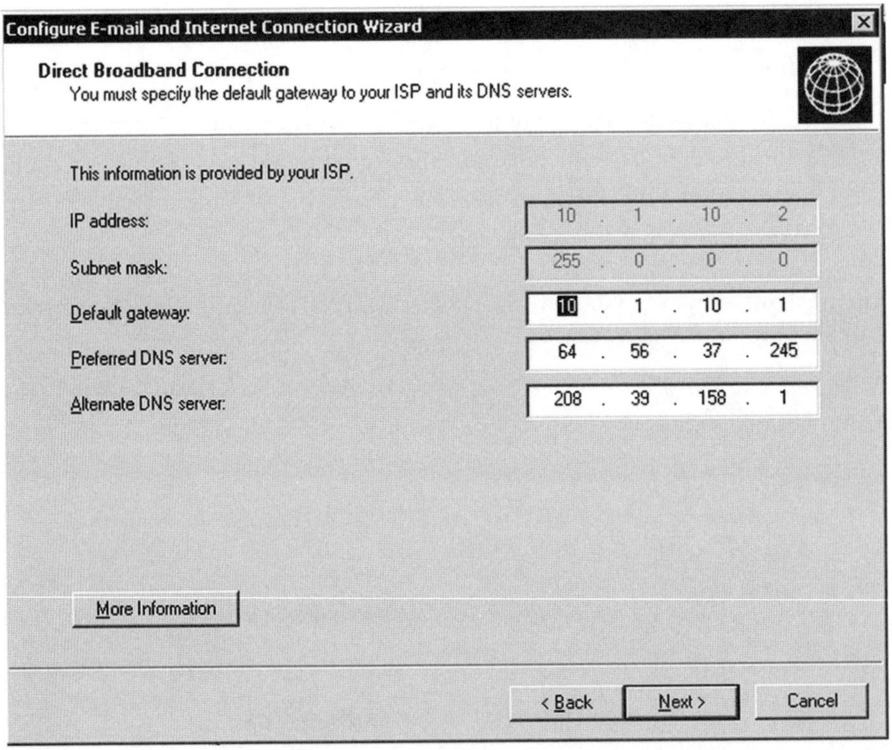

SBS has support for UPnP routers and the CEICW will configure the ports for you upon detection. This is very cool and a new feature in the SBS 2003 time frame. UPnP routers do not require user name and password authentication on the LAN port and that allows the CEICW to open the ports you have elected to open as part of the wizard process.

Firewall

In the Standard Edition of SBS, the CEICW will configure a stateful firewall that monitors all communication transactions and therefore provides a security system preventing unauthorized access. This will be done by using RRAS under the hood and configuring NAT if you have two NICs on the server. If you do not have two NICs, make sure to use a hardware firewall device or you will be completely vulnerable on the Internet.

In the Premium Edition of SBS, you are using ISA 2000 Server. The CEICW will configure ISA for you at this point. A warning message will appear stating that services are being stopped and then restarted in order to configure ISA. Figure 7-3 shows the Services Configuration screen, which opens the ports in the firewall without having to go into the ISA Server management console, or RRAS.

Figure 7-3
Opening ports SBS-style by use of the CEICW Services Configuration screen.

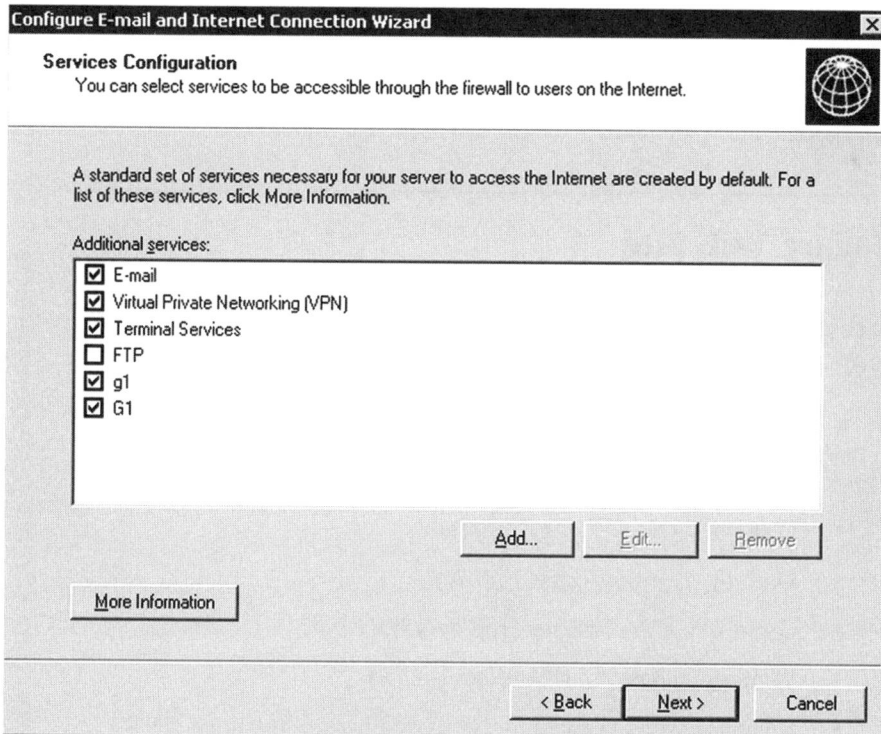

IMPORTANT: If you use the Premium edition of SBS and decide to configure ports directly through the ISA server management console, be aware that every time you run the CEICW, the settings will be re-set to default. The CEICW acts upon a set of pre-defined scripts. Therefore it is recommended that you use the services configuration options in the CEICW to open ports. Settings entered into the CEICW will be applied automatically every time the CEICW is used.

Here are some examples of commonly used ports that can be configured:

Service	Port
SMTP	25/TCP
POP3	110/TCP
VPN	1723/TCP
Terminal Services	3389/TCP
FTP	20/TCP & 21/TCP
TelNet	23/TCP
HTTP	80/TCP
HTTPS	443/TCP

Secure Web Site

The CEICW can also configure Secure Web Site services allowing or denying access to users coming from the Internet through the firewall. Web Site services include:

- Outlook Web Access (OWA)
- Remote Web Workplace (RWW)
- Performance and Usage reports
- Outlook Mobile Access (OMA)
- Outlook via the Internet (rpc over https)
- Windows SharePoint Services (WSS)
- Business Website (open only if you plan on hosting a site)

You could also choose to allow access to the entire web site from the Internet, which exposes the entire default web site on the Internet, including all services listed above as well as any additional web sites you created in the default web site. Figure 7-4 shows the Web Service Configuration screen. Just think if you had to configure these items manually!

Figure 7-4
The Web Service Configuration screen is your friend.

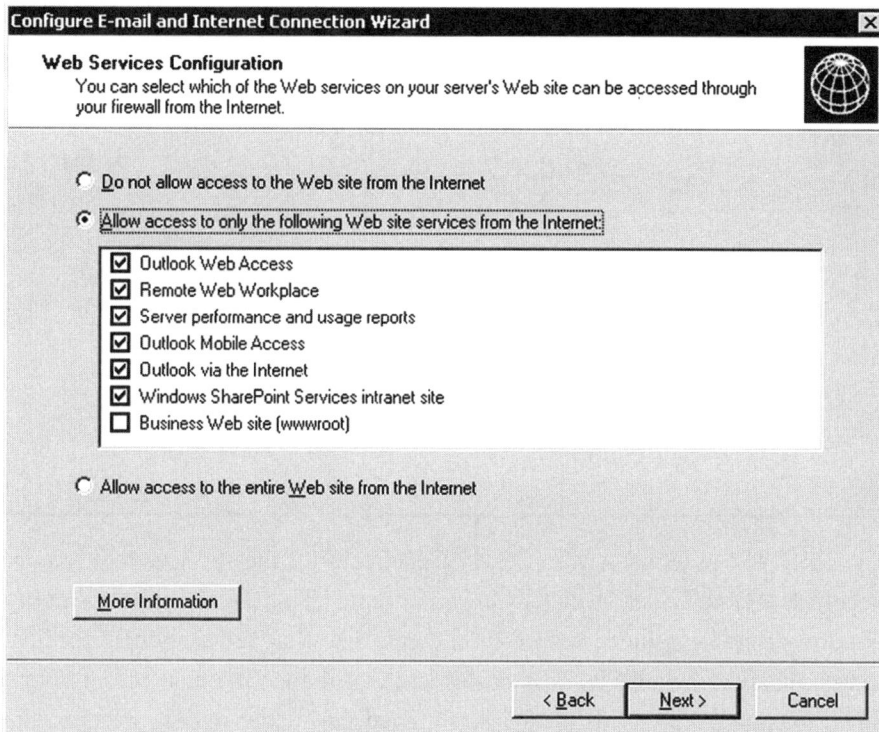

When you select to enable Windows SharePoint Services, SBS will install a fully-functional companyweb with preconfigured folders, including a fax folder, specially designed by the SBS team for small business use as shown in Figure 7-5.

Figure 7-5
Windows SharePoint Services companyweb installed by enabling one check-box in the CEICW.

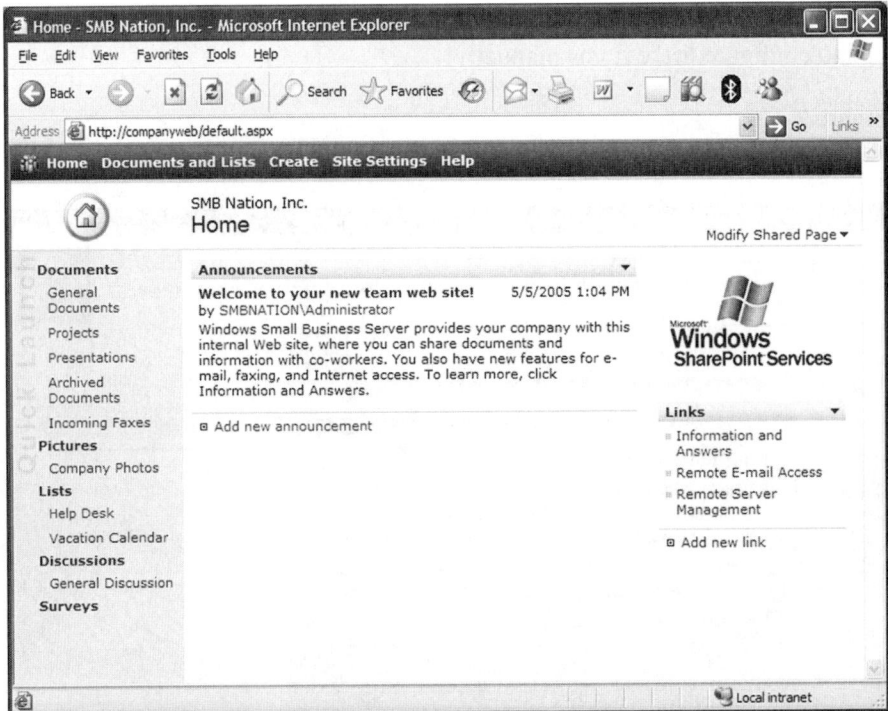

The CEICW can create a Web Server Certificate for the services that require Secure Sockets Layer (SSL) to communicate. This is effectively having Windows Small Business Server 2003 create a self-signed certificate for SSL communication. Small business customers can reduce the cost of deploying Small Business Server, using the self-signed certificate option, because the customer does not need to buy a certificate from a public certification authority (CA). You could also choose to use a certificate signed by a CA and browse to the location of the certificate file. Verisign is one such third-party CA provider.

> IMPORTANT: The self-signed security certificate discussion is new for many SBSers as it's a new capability in SBS 2003. And if Microsoft is pretty proud of this capability, don't you think it's a distinct possibility it could appear on the 70-282 exam? You bet.

E-mail

If you installed Exchange on your server, the CEICW can configure the SMTP connector required for Exchange and specify how to send and receive e-mail. Here you would choose the DNS delivery method, either **Use DNS to send e-mail** or **Forward all e-mail to an ISP**. Either way will work. There is an added benefit to using a smarthost (e-mail server at the ISP) to filter outgoing mail in case you have a virus running lose on your network. If you select this option, Exchange will forward all e-mail using SMTP to the smarthost as shown in Figure 7-6.

Figure 7-6

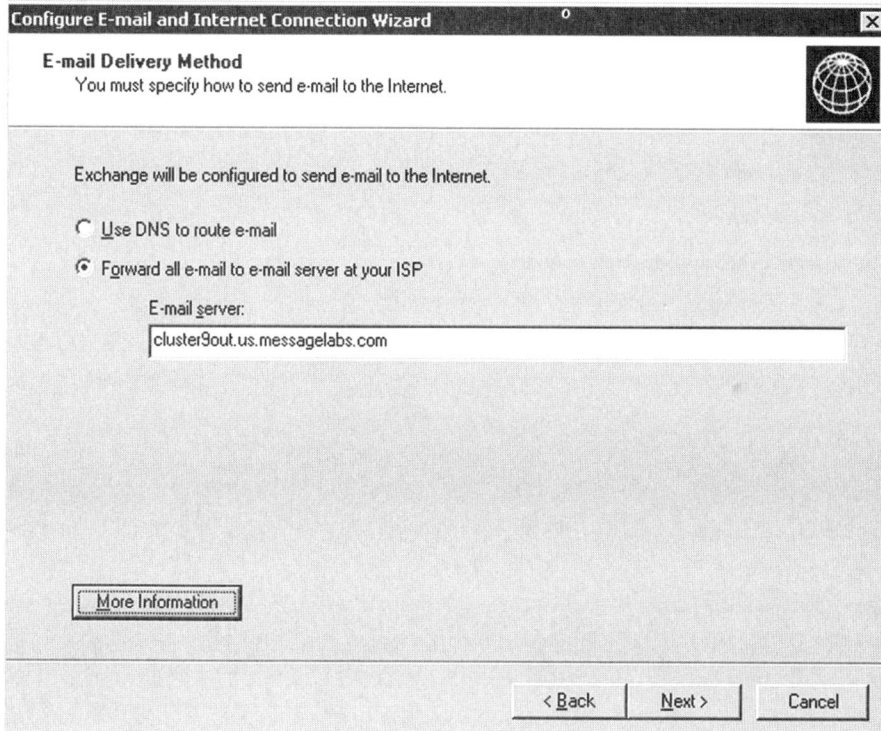

If you use POP3 mail at the ISP, you can configure the POP3 connector to route the e-mail to individual mailboxes and select whether to **E-mail from the Internet is delivered directly to my server** or **E-mail from the Internet is held at my ISP until my server sends a signal**. If you choose the latter—holding the messages at the ISP—you have to decide to then either use **TURN**

after Authentication (requires user name and password) or ETRN (requires a static IP). You still have to have Exchange installed for the POP3 connector to work, and this gives you the added benefit of using all the Exchange features and being able to access your e-mail via OWA or through RWW. Figure 7-7 shows where you would select to use Exchange, or by checking the box *Use the Microsoft Connector for POP3 Mailboxes,* enable mail retrieval from the POP3 mailbox.

Figure 7-7
Select to use Exchange only or POP3 mailbox retrieval to then route e-mail into selected Exchange mailboxes.

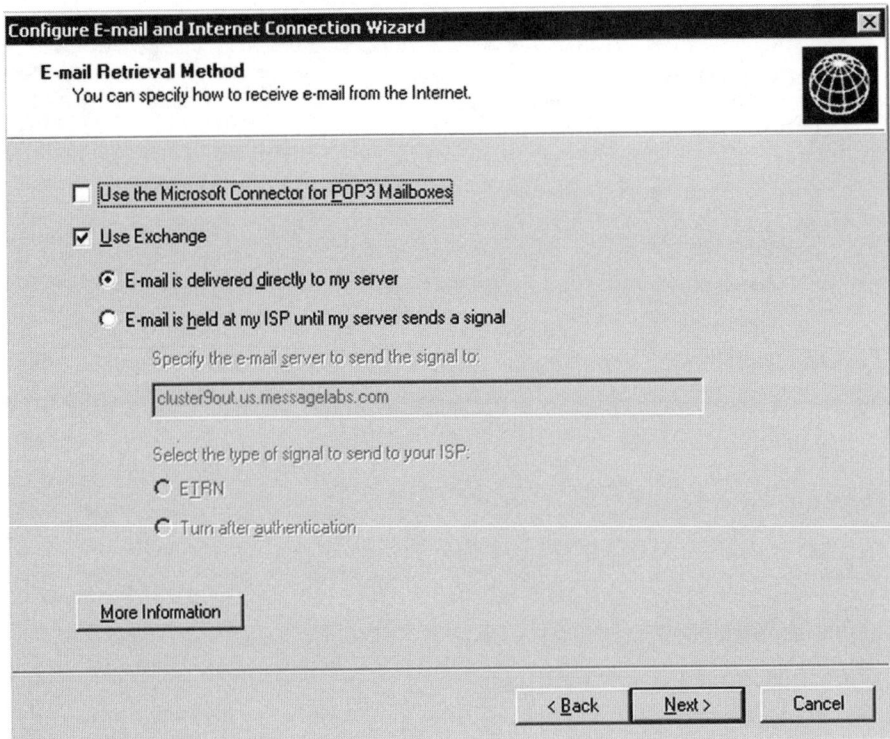

Moving clients away from POP3 accounts to use only the Exchange server is easy. Just re-run the CEICW and uncheck the POP3 box!

More information on configuring the POP3 connector is located further down this chapter under Recommend and Implement an E-mail Solution.

Removing E-mail Attachments

Not to be confused with anti-virus software, the last configuration screen in the CEICW allows you to remove unwanted attachments before they go into users' mailboxes. Our example in Figure 7-8 shows the removal of files with the .avi extension – a simple and cost effective way of keeping silly movies out of the office environment, or any other file types you would not want to circulate on your network. This is an SBS-only value-add only to be found in the CEICW!

Figure 7-8
Remove unwanted files using the file extension before they hit users' inboxes.

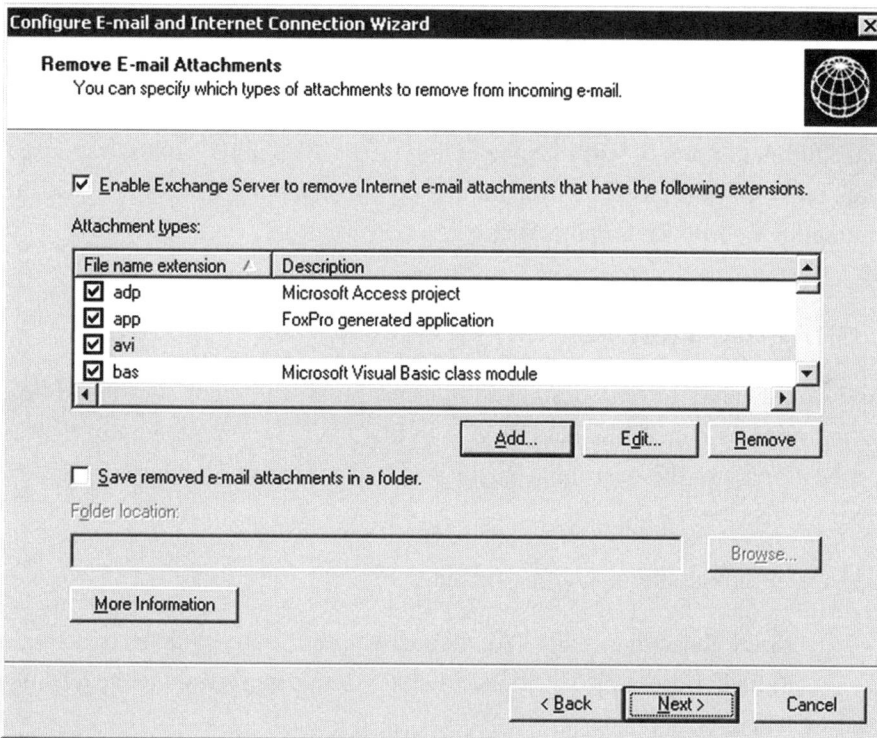

Configuring Remote Access

Another favorite of mine is the Remote Access Wizard. I call it the "three-click wizard," even though it really takes five clicks, but who's counting? The Remote Access Wizard configures:

- Dial-in access

- VPN Connectivity

Dial-in access requires a modem and phone line and is seldom used anymore in my neighborhood. VPN allows access through a secure Internet connection. To take advantage of the Download Connection Manager (available in RWW), you must configure the server name for the VPN using the FQDN (fully qualified domain name). This way, users can just connect to RWW and click on the Download Connection Manager link, installing a shortcut icon on their desktop from which they can launch the VPN connection. Voila! No more client-side configuration needed.

There are five PPTP ports configured for VPN and you could also enable support for L2TP/IPsec, which would require manual configuration steps in RRAS. If you find that you are in need of more than five VPN ports, you can add additional ports in RRAS by selecting the PORTS node. Go to Properties, click on WAN Miniport (PPTP), and then click on Configure and increase the amount in the Maximum ports box.

Configure Faxing

And would you believe it, despite all Internet e-mail and scanning capabilities, faxing remains a core business service to this day. The fax module in SBS is a robust one and the best thing about it is that you have so many choices of where to receive the faxes.

Options on Inbound Fax Routing include:

- Route through e-mail—You have the option to route faxes to a single e-mail address or distribution list by simply typing someone@some-where.com.

- Store in a folder—Simply browse or type in a shared folder location on the network.

- Store in a document library—This routes the fax to a document library in Windows SharePoint Services (WSS). By default, the document library is located at http://servername/companyweb/%20faxes.

- Print—Print faxes to any network attached printer.

IMPORTANT: A really cool new feature in SBS 2003 is the ability to store faxes in WSS. And because it's new and groovy, it's likely to appear on a product-based exam such as 70-282.

Adding Users and Computers

Another goody on the To Do List is the Add User Wizard. Here you walk step by step through setting up users. Not only can you set up one, but you have the option to bulk-add users, which makes setting up a new server—one with, say, 20 clients—very easy.

The Add User Wizard will create a:

- Mailbox.
- Home folder.
- Group membership.
- Access to SharePoint services.
- Computer account.

All this will be based on the User Template (see Chapter 6) you choose which contains group membership, address information, disk quotas, and the level of server access. Once you have chosen the user template, you will have the option to add the computer account to the domain as well. You can bulk add the client machines or just add one, and then select the applications you would like to deploy to the client machines. By default, the Client Operating System Service Packs, Internet Explorer 6.0, Microsoft Office Outlook SP1, and the Shared Fax Client are selected. You are able to add/remove and edit applications through the Add User Wizard as well, which makes it a snap to set up user accounts and their corresponding client computers and required software.

Activate the Server and Add Licenses

As you are cruising through the To Do List, you will encounter the Activate License Wizard. This wizard enables you to activate the SBS client access licenses (CALs) online. During the activation process, the product key is combined with a coded number to create the Installation ID. This ID represents the hardware components in your computer. Once activated, you cannot use the key to activate other computers.

Internet Activation

The SBS 2003 server can be activated over the Internet, where a confirmation ID is sent back to your computer, or you can call Microsoft and activate over the phone. There is a 30-day grace period; once it expires, however, you will no longer have access to core functionality of the server until it is activated. SBS 2003 comes with five CALs, which are digitally signed certificates each client stores locally.

CAL Types

Every device or user that connects to the server requires a CAL. CALs can be added as per-user or per-device CALs. The first five CALs are generic and can be either/or. When you select the per-user option, every user will have to have a CAL to access the server.

> IMPORTANT: Here is a trick for understanding SBS 2003 CAL types. These CAL types are exactly the same as the underlying Windows Server 2003 licensing! This is the first SBS release where the underlying licensing has been exactly the same. It's true and it's money in the bank when you take the 70-282 exam and encounter a question on CAL types.

Add License Wizard

You can use the Add License Wizard to add or reactivate CALs either over the Internet or over the phone. CALs can be purchased in five and 20 packs and then be activated over the Internet using the Add License Wizard.

Transfer License Wizard

With the Transfer License Wizard, you can reactivate CALs after you've made significant changes to system hardware or reinstalled the server software on another computer. You will have to telephone Microsoft to get the license reactivated. The Transfer License Wizard cannot be used to transfer ownership of CALs, as resale is not permitted, per license agreement.

License Backup/Restore

You can back up your CALs with the License Backup Wizard and, in case the license files get corrupted or lost, you will be able to easily recover the licenses with the License Restore Wizard.

> IMPORTANT: Licensing is an exceedingly popular topic during the worldwide one-day SMB Nation Summit workshops. There are two free resources for you to improve your understanding of SBS 2003 licensing for both the real world and the 70-282 preparation:
>
> - Chapter 3 in *Advanced Windows Small Business Server 2003 Best Practices*. The good news is that this is the free chapter and can be downloaded from www.smbnation.com.
>
> - Microsoft's SBS licensing page: http://www.microsoft.com/windowsserver2003/sbs/howtobuy/CALs.mspx.

Configure DHCP and IP Addressing

SBS 2003 automatically installs the DHCP server service during setup at mid-point when a screen titled Windows Components is displayed. DHCP simplifies the administration of IP address assignments to client computers on the local network. If an existing DHCP service is detected, you are prompted to choose whether you want to use the existing service (say on your hardware-based router) or disable the service and use the DHCP Server service provided with SBS. It is recommended that you disable the existing DHCP service (again—on your hardware-based router as an example) and utilize the DHCP service in SBS. This way you ensure that the DHCP settings for your local network are properly configured. During setup, if you click **NEXT, NEXT, NEXT** in the SBS Setup Wizard, SBS creates an IP Address scope of 192.168.16.1 to 192.168.16.254. Addresses from 192.168.16.1 to 192.168.16.9 are excluded from DHCP assignment.

IMPORTANT: The default private IP address range is 192.168.16. x in SBS 2003. However, you could use another private IP address range such as 10.0.0.x without any major drama on your SBS 2003 network. You would make this type of private IP address range decision when you encounter the Local Network Adapter Configuration screen (technically Step 29) during the SBS 2003 setup process. It is important for 70-282 testing purposes to understand that different private address ranges are allowed.

To view the DHCP scope:

1. Go to **Start**.

2. Click **Run**.

3. Type **dhcpmgmt.msc** and hit **Enter**.

Don't despair, the DHCP fun-wagon is not over yet. You will find much more detailed information under the heading *DHCP* in Chapter 10, *Installing and Configuring Windows Server 2003*.

Configuring an Existing DHCP Service or Firewall Device

Time to get manual, baby! If you have an existing device on the local network that assigns IP addresses to client computers using DHCP, it must be configured with the necessary settings for your local network. If the device supports Universal Plug and Play (UPnP), Setup will prompt you to configure the device automatically. If the device is not a UPnP device, you will have to configure it manually. In this case, settings have to be configured as follows:

Default Gateway

If the SBS 2003 Server has two NICs, enter the internal NIC IP address as the default gateway.

IMPORTANT: Now is as good a time as any to slip in this SBS_DHCP factoid! This is fair game on the 70-282 exam, so please read and heed. The external NIC card on an SBS server machine in a two

NIC card scenario may receive its external address from an external source, namely being assigned a dynamic IP.

Try this on for size. Imagine your client doesn't want to pay for a static IP address. In that situation you can have a dynamically assigned IP address on the external NIC card. This would bring some challenges with it, especially if you want to use Exchange or require an assigned IP for hosting a website. In this case you could revert to a third party like www.dyndns.com (which you would not find questions like this on the 70-282 exam and is provided here as a mere factoid!).

If the SBS 2003 Server has one NIC and you are using the router device to connect to the Internet, use the IP address of the router's internal interface as the default gateway.

Domain Naming Service (DNS) and Small Business Server 2003

The Domain Name System (DNS) server included in Windows Server 2003 provides name resolution for TCP/IP-based networks. SBS configures DNS automatically during setup and configures it to listen to the local network only. The DNS server is not bound to the external NIC, and in the CEICW you will configure it to use forwarders and Preferred DNS servers, which are your ISP's DNS servers. This way you effectively shield your network and enable the use of private IP addresses. The DNS server information is given to the clients via DHCP. When a client requests an external web address, the request first goes to the SBS DNS server. If the request can not be resolved, it gets forwarded to the preferred DNS server at your ISP, which will either resolve the query or forward it on to the next DNS server up the line.

By default, DNS is an Active-Directory Integrated-Zone and there should be no additional configurations required unless you decide to, say, host your own Internet-accessible DNS server, which is not recommended. To Access the DNS management console and view settings, on the run command type **dnsmgmt. msc** or go to **Administrative** Tools, DNS.

Domain Name Server (DNS)

DNS provides clients with name resolution services for the local network, so you must use the IP address of the internal NIC of the SBS server.

DNS Domain Name

DNS Domain Name provides client computers with the fully qualified domain name (FQDN). Therefore, you must enter the full DNS name of your local network like DomainName.local, if you used the default DNS for the internal domain. (More on DNS in Chapter 10, *Installing and Configuring Windows Server 2003.*)

Windows Internet Naming Service (WINS)

WINS provides local network name resolution for computers running NT 4.0 and Windows 98 and earlier. Specify the IP address of the SBS server in the WINS server option of the DHCP server/router device. WINS is enabled by default on the SBS server and would normally not require any additional configuration beyond the default SBS configuration. WINS is covered in depth in Chapter 10, *Installing and Configuring Windows Server 2003.*

Manage Networks Using Simple Network Management Protocol

Use of the Simple Network Management Protocol (SNMP) goes way back. This is an industry standard for talking to and managing devices on a network and includes devices beyond the server machine such as switches, routers, firewalls, and the like. SNMP management software is used to monitor any device configured with SNMP agent software. The SNMP agent, which is an optional component of Windows Server 2003, interacts with third-party SNMP software to enable the flow of network status information between monitored devices and applications and the management systems that monitor them. SNMP traps are the "messages" sent that communicate performance information.

To be brutally honest—SNMP is beyond the scope of a "day in the life of an SBSer," and as such, doesn't demand much of your attention in preparing for the 70-282 exam (or deserve much space on the limited pages we have in this book). SNMP environments typically have hundreds or thousands of nodes that would be difficult or costly to monitor.

> IMPORTANT: To learn more about SNMP in your free time, visit Microsoft TechNet at www.microsoft.com/technet and search on the keyword "SNMP" and you'll have over 500 hits returned. The following title is very detailed and highly recommended: How SNMP Works—Networking Services: Windows Server 2003 (Windows Server 2003 Technical Reference). You can also subscribe to the monthly Microsoft TechNet Disc library. TechNet is a great 70-282 exam preparation resource!

Okay, let us also give a tip of the hat to the instant gratification crowd. Whereas this book has a laser focus on the Small Business Specialist Partner community and the 70-282 exam in particular (as it should), here is an instant treat for you! If you want to see how the SNMP area applies, in the REAL WORLD, to the small and medium business space, visit these two SMB and SBS friendly ISVs and read about their management services and monitoring products:

- Level Platforms: www.levelplatforms.com
- HyBlue: www.hyblue.com

It is here you can observe real world SNMP applications in the SMB and SBS areas. Be sure to revisit the SNMP topic again in Chapter 9 of this book.

Configure Messaging and Collaboration

There is an old saying in the SBS community: You already know more about Exchange Server 2003 than you think you do. How can this be? Exchange Server 2003 is essentially installed and configured for you when you deploy SBS 2003. Its configuration level out of the box will likely meet 90 percent of your needs with the product. End of story.

The remaining 10 percent of Exchange Server 2003 that you "don't know" out-of-the-box is something you likely don't really need to know for the 70-282 exam. There are parts of Exchange that really don't relate to the SBS space, such as site connectors to link multiple Exchange locations together.

Experience counts for something in the worlds of SMB and SBS (thank goodness) and this really manifests itself in Exchange Server 2003. More than other SBS components, there is nothing like Exchange Server 2003 experience to prepare you for the 70-282 exam.

> IMPORTANT: Be discerning in the amount of information you are prepared to digest in preparation for the 70-282 exam. Sure, you could do a deep dive into the Exchange Server 2003 internals for the sake of satisfying your own interests. However, that would be INEF-FICIENT from a 70-282 exam preparation time management point of view. Rather, using your very best judgment, ask critically, "Do I really need to know that?" We like data dumps as much as anybody, but find a balance that prevents brain freeze due to overload.

One bona fide Exchange Server 2003 tip that you might not know and need to know relates to the number of Exchange servers and stores allowed on an SBS network. Briefly:

- Multiple Exchange server machines are allowed on an SBS 2003 network, assuming you purchased the extra Exchange product licenses.

- Only one store is allowed on the Exchange version (standard edition) contained in SBS 2003. With the Exchange enterprise edition, multiple Exchange stores are allowed.

Outlook Web Access

Outlook Web Access (OWA) is one of the coolest features that just work straight out of the box in SBS 2003. In case you've been living in a cave along the Tex\Mex border and don't know about OWA, it's a rich web page that allows you to check your Exchange-based mailbox. It's popular with everyone on Planet Earth who uses SBS 2003. There is no server-side configuration required except:

- Using the user templates to assign a mailbox in the Add User Wizard. This will assign appropriate permissions to user accounts for OWA access.

- Running the CEICW and selecting **Outlook Web Access** under **Allow access to only the following Web site services from the Internet** on the **Web Services Configuration** page.

There is no configuration required on the remote client site (e.g., hotel business center). It is recommended that you use at least Internet Explorer (IE) 5.01 or later. Macintosh and UNIX operating systems and browsers are supported by OWA. For UNIX users, OWA is the primary solution for e-mail, calendar, and collaboration.

OWA comes in two versions:

Outlook Web Access Basic

Hey, if you are used to the old version of Outlook, it's okay to use basic OWA, especially if you have a slow Internet connection. Basic OWA was designed to work in browsers that support HTML 3.2 and the European Computer Manufacturers Association (ECMA) script standards. It provides a subset of the features available in Outlook Web Access Premium that allow you to read and send messages as well as access some parts of your calendar and your contacts. If you are accessing OWA using Windows 98 or NT, Outlook 2003 will not install and you will have no choice but to use the basic version of OWA.

Outlook Web Access Premium

OWA premium has an enhanced user interface and several new features, including the new enhanced features for Exchange 2003. This includes a server-side spellchecker, Quick Flags, and Personal Tasks, allowing attachments to be opened from the reading pane, auto signatures, public folders displaying in their own window, two-line view, meeting requests that can be forwarded, access to GAL property sheets within an e-mail message, and numerous more improvements.

However, some of the features will not work unless you are using IE 6.0. If you log on to OWA through RWW, you automatically get the premium version of OWA. Or, if you have forms-based authentication enabled in your browser when you access OWA directly over the Internet, you will be given the choice of using either the premium or basic version, where premium is selected by default.

Configure Outlook Web Access

OWA is easily configured by running the CEICW (Connect E-mail and Internet Connection Wizard) and checking the Outlook Web Access checkbox on the Web Services Configuration screen. SBS will automatically make the web services available to host the OWA site and users with access permissions will be able to access OWA over the Internet.

> IMPORTANT: In the SBS 2003 time frame, OWA now operates under HTTPS over Port 443 to create a more secure session. Contrast this with prior SBS releases when OWA could run over Port 80 (HTTP) with less security.

Configure Windows SharePoint Services

Windows SharePoint Services (WSS) is the intranet (intraweb) of the company and is automatically installed during the SBS installation. The WSS site is a collaborative platform that allows businesses to organize and manage information in a browser-based and office-integrated environment.

Understanding WSS

Central to understanding WSS are the following high-level concepts:

- WSS replaces the COMPANY share. Older versions of SBS had a network shared folder called COMPANY (the path was <drive letter>:\Company Share Folders). Now, in the SBS 2003 time frame, you are directed to place your bona fide company-related documents and data in the WSS repository. The WSS repository is a SQL Server-type database file and isn't part of the NTFS storage system (NTFS can be thought of as the "yellow folders" you are familiar with from MyDocuments or Windows Explorer).

- WSS has alerts and NTFS does not. You will want to configure the alerting capabilities in WSS, to advise you when documents have been checked out, help desk tickets entered, etc.

- Full Search. SBS 2003 Standard Edition uses the Windows MSDE engine to manage WSS. SBS 2003 Premium Edition uses the MSDE engine from SQL Server 2000 to manage WSS and has superior search capabilities.

- More than a document management system. In the real world, it's easy to view WSS as only a document management system (and a darn good one for free out-of-the-box in SBS 2003). However, that is not the only way MICROSOFT VIEWS IT (remember the 70-282 exam is based on Microsoft viewpoints). In fact, you won't even see the words "document management" on Microsoft's SharePoint page at www.microsoft.com/sharepoint. Here is the current WSS description from Microsoft's site:

  Windows SharePoint Services is a collection of services for Microsoft Windows Server™ 2003 that you can use to create team-oriented Web sites to share information and foster collaboration with other users on documents. You can also use Windows SharePoint Services as a development platform for creating collaboration and information-sharing applications.

Different strokes for different folks. There are numerous ways to access WSS that are fair game on the 70-282 exam:

- CompanyWeb. This is the default home page in Internet Explorer for a client computer connected to an SBS 2003 network. See Figure 7.9.

- My Network Places. WSS folders can be published as network places.

- File, Open. Office 2003 applications can directly open and close documents in WSS.

- Shared Attachments. A new form of e-mail attachment interacts directly with WSS. Very cool!

Configuring WSS

There are several customizations you can perform after installation to make the intranet more useful for your clients and/or organization. WSS is comprised of different web parts that can be modified, moved or removed, and added.

Notes:

You can configure WSS by using **Tasks** located in the **Server Management** console under the **Internal Web Site** link where you can manage:

- Importing files—Using the Import Files Wizard, files, and subfolders can be moved into the SharePoint site from shared folders.

- Add link—Allows you to add an internal or external link to the company's intraweb site.

- Change name—You can change the name of the intranet displayed on the intranet site.

- Change homepage layout—Lets you modify the layout of the site.

- Manage access—Here you can specify roles for users to manage user access.

- Manage your company's internal website—Where you can manage intranet site settings.

- Central administration—Used to configure server, virtual server, security, and component settings for SharePoint services.

You may also configure WSS in other ways from the CompanyWeb page. For example, you can create sub-webs from CompanyWeb. Sub-webs are like mini-web pages created to collaborate on a specific project.

> IMPORTANT: WSS has very generous permissions. A user added to the SBS 2003 network is given the second-highest level of permissions in WSS: Web Designer. This allows users to create sub-webs by default and enter Help Desk tickets. Contrast that with the restrictive default NTFS shared network folder permission setting for a user on the SBS 2003 network: read-only (actually read, execute, and list—but effectively read-only).

The above comparison of WSS and network share permissions is presented to touch on two points in the 70-282 exam. WSS is considered cool by Microsoft and will certainly be on the exam. And I've offered you a security example. Microsoft takes security very seriously.

So the WSS section ends with a couple of homework assignments. First, use WSS as experience and you will find no better teacher for this section of the

70-282 exam. Keep in mind the exam still covers WSS version 2.0, unlike the 70-631 exam which covers WSS version 3.0! Visit www.sharepointknowledge.com and look for postings on the SBS newsgroups (detailed in Appendix A) from SBS-MVP Chad Gross.

Configure Real-Time Communications

Small businesses expect to have real-time communication capabilities just as seen in the enterprise. With SBS, you can offer mobile solutions that allow for increased productivity, collaboration, and communication. These solutions are enabled through core services of Windows Server 2003 and taken advantage of by SBS in different forms.

> IMPORTANT: Beware of semantics and "plays on words," as we say in the Western world. Microsoft removed the built-in Instant Messaging (IM) communications from Exchange Server 2003 in the SBS 2003 time frame. (IM was available via Exchange 2000 Server in the SBS 2000 time frame.) Microsoft replaced the IM functionality for SBS 2000 owners who purchased its Software Assurance prior to October 1, 2003, by giving these select owners a free copy of its Live Communications Server (http://office.microsoft.com/en-us/communicationsserver/default.aspx). Here is my concern. It would be easy from the above section headline (taken from the 70-282 exam objectives) to infer that Microsoft might test you on this very limited offer to restore IM functionality via the Live Communications Server product. And it's even easier to assume that all this somehow relates to configuring real-time communications in the context of the 70-282 exam. Such is not the case. You are not tested on IM functionality and Live Communications Server on SBS 2003. Whew!

Recommend and Implement an E-mail Solution

E-mail access can be configured in many different flavors in SBS. If you installed Exchange, you have a robust e-mail solution that can be extended beyond receiving messages at the desktop. The default approach is to have SMTP-based e-mail, which is discussed above and in other book sections. But, even if your client or organization still uses POP3 as its primary e-mail retrieval method, which many small businesses prefer, you will be able to take advantage of all the features that Exchange has to offer.

Configure the POP3 Connector

SBS can automatically download messages from POP3 e-mail boxes and deliver them to the proper Exchange mailbox with the Microsoft Connector for POP3 mailboxes. The POP3 connector is disabled by default and the Microsoft Connector for POP3 mailboxes service does not start until you add the first POP3 mailbox through either the CEICW or the POP3 Connector Manager in the Server Management/Advanced Management node. You can add, remove, and edit POP3 e-mail boxes in the POP3 Connector Manager and set delivery schedules.

 The Exchange server supports one single global POP3 mailbox that allows all e-mail sent to your domain to be delivered to a single mailbox managed by your ISP. You do not need to assign individual POP3 e-mail boxes to individual user accounts.

When you add POP3 mailboxes to the POP3 connector, you tell the e-mail server to retrieve from a POP3 domain (e.g., Pop3.atsomedomain.com) and add the POP3 username and password to be able to access the e-mail at the ISP. You then fill in the Mailbox information for Exchange choosing **User Mailbox** as the type and then selecting the user account that should be receiving the e-mail. You continue adding individual POP3 mailboxes in the POP3 Connector this way until you have entered every user account that should receive messages. When the POP3 Connector retrieves e-mail from the ISP's POP3 mailbox, it will automatically distribute e-mails to the appropriate Exchange mailboxes.

IMPORTANT: The POP3 Connector cannot deliver e-mails to a Public Folder in Exchange even though a Public Folder has an SMTP e-mail address. Why, you ask? Because a Public Folder is not a real Active Directory object and is merely a mailbox. It's these little tricky tidbits (and thinking about tricky tidbits) that will help get you over the passing bar on the 70-282 exam.

Migrating Mailboxes from POP3 to Exchange

If you have been using the POP3 Connector, mailboxes don't really get migrated from POP3 to Exchange. You already have an Exchange e-mail box and you are really just changing the e-mail retrieval method to an e-mail delivery method. This can be done by:

1. Configure the **CEICW**.

2. Select **Enable Internet e-mail**, then the e-mail delivery option.

3. Uncheck the **Use the Microsoft Connector for POP3 Mailboxes** checkbox.

To use Exchange server only, you need a static IP address and must set up an mx record at your ISP or Name Service Provider, pointing to your static IP address.

Outlook Web Access

As discussed earlier, OWA allows remote access to Exchange Server 2003. But here is another take on OWA. Besides having an improved User Interface (UI), OWA has undergone several improvements in functionality and security. Some security enhancements include:

- S/MIME support (Internet Explorer 6 and Microsoft Windows 2000 or later is required).

- Spam beacon-blocking to help protect your e-mail address privacy from spammers.

- A hidden destination site to help protect your privacy when viewing a URL from a message in Outlook Web Access.

- Attachment blocking so you can selectively disable attachments being viewed from outside the firewall. You can also prevent sensitive documents from being downloaded outside your network.

- A session inactivity timeout using forms-based authentication that enables support for a timed log off after a period of inactivity; Outlook Web Access enables you to log off securely even if the browser is left open with a current session to the server.

Performance improvements include the choice between basic and premium versions of Outlook and a choice between the basic client version from the forms-based authentication logon page when you use Netscape and IE5.01 and earlier. Other substantial performance improvements have been made for dial-up, low-bandwidth wireless networks, and when using SSL after enabling GZip compression.

Cell Phones and Mobile Devices

Cell phones and connected mobile devices are starting to make the inroad to small business and have support through Outlook Mobile Access (OMA) for use of PDAs, Pocket PCs, or SmartPhones. SBS offers an easy way to add these devices to your network, by use of the *Assign Applications Wizard* (shown in Figure 7-9) which sports a special area for *Mobile Client and Offline Use* configuration. By selecting the *Install Active Sync 3.8* check box, you are now enabling mobile devices such as SmartPhones and Pocket PC Phone editions to synchronize with client machines and the SBS server. Once you connect your Pocket PC to a client computer, a wizard will pop-up and walk you through the synchronization settings. And remember, you already configured a self-signed certificate in the CEICW, which will now be automatically downloaded and installed on the mobile device. All settings in the Exchange server have been preconfigured for mobility, and voila – you just added the device in less than five minutes to your SBS network.

Figure 7-9

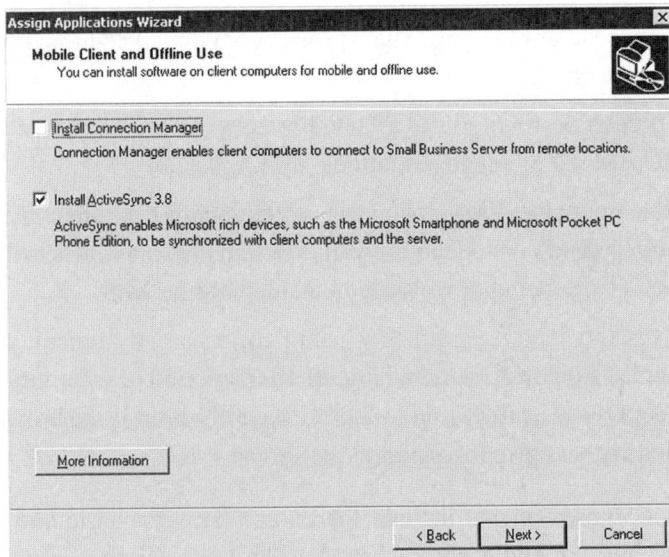

OMA

Exchange 2003 supports Wireless Application Protocol (WAP) 2.*x* and XHTML browser-based devices, and has support for full HTML browsers as well as i-Mode devices such as mobile phones and personal digital assistants (PDAs). Mobile phone browsers in Japan can now access servers running Exchange Server by using compressed HTML (CHTML) on i-Mode devices. OMA is configured through the CEICW. Please take a closer look at Figure 7-9.

Active Sync

Exchange Active Sync allows Pocket PCs, Pocket PC Phone Editions, and Windows Mobile-Based SmartPhones to stay in direct contact with the Exchange 2003 server. This means you have the capability to:

- Synchronize your e-mail messages, calendar, and contact list.
- Receive SMS messages from the Exchange Server.

Select your synchronization method from on-demand or scheduled synch. Coupled with OMA you can also get your tasks list and GAL.

> IMPORTANT: As mentioned in this book a couple of times, mobility is HOT in the SBS 2003 time frame and you will most certainly be held accountable for it on the 70-282 exam. The free Chapter 8 from *Windows Small Business Server 2003 Best Practices* explores OMA and the Small IT Solution for Mobility (a cool solutions accelerator) at https://partner.microsoft.com/global/products solutions/smbsolutions/ really explores the topics in great detail!

Outlook 2003

Outlook 2003 client is included with SBS, and there is no reason why your clients or organizations shouldn't be using it. All I have to say is, "Hey, its free!" Besides being free, Outlook 2003 also provides an integrated solution for managing and organizing e-mail messages, schedules, tasks, notes, contacts, and other information. Often end-users find Outlook so feature-rich they are scared of it and ask to keep Outlook Express. Of course, as a sensible consultant, I don't allow that on any network.

There are so many benefits to using Outlook 2003, I don't know where to start. Always focusing on the client side, I first point out that you can:

- Manage all e-mail in one place.
- Easily organize the Inbox.
- Access calendar, tasks, and contacts quickly in one location.

Outlook also integrates with SharePoint Services and has the junk folder and search folder options. One really cool item is being able to restore deleted items directly from the Outlook client. By going to **Tools/Recover Deleted Items**, users can bring back deleted items from as far back as you set the deleted item retention in the Configure Backup Wizard.

> IMPORTANT: The best way to answer any Outlook 2003 question on the 70-282 exam is to simply use Outlook 2003 in your day-to-day life. Seriously—it's not necessary to read a big, thick book on Outlook 2003 for the 70-282 exam. Simply use it, try new things, and poke around. You'll do fine on the exam section.

IMAP4

Exchange 2003 supports IMAP4 (Internet Message Access Protocol Version 4) allowing clients to access messages in public and private folders on the server. Users with IMAP4 clients are able to retrieve their e-mail without downloading the entire mailbox to their computer. With IMAP, a client can retrieve specific messages or portions of a message like an attachment.

IMAP does not send mail—that is handled by SMTP. The difference between IMAP and POP3 is that IMAP allows you to access and manage e-mail on the server, where POP3 is a retrieval method that downloads e-mail to an Inbox.

Implement a Website Hosting Configuration

First of all, I want to let you know that hosting a website on your SBS server will put you at greater risk to be attacked by hackers, script kiddies, and other malicious thingamajiggies floating around on the Internet. You have just placed your server out there and said, "Come hit me!" The only way I would personally host a website off my SBS domain using a second server hosting the site and using ISA server to take the brunt of the attacks. Hosting will require having your server patched and locked down at all the times. I'd rather pay someone else who does website hosting for a living to have all the headaches. So the moral of the story is: Do not host a public site on your SBS machine!

So why would this topic be on the 70-282 exam if knowledgeable SBSers are opposed to hosting a public website (even Microsoft itself discourages hosting public websites on an SBS 2003 server)? Because some line-of-business applications require a public-facing website on an SBS server using Port 80. Small businesses, advised of the problems of hosting a website on the SBS server (security risks and performance concerns), may elect to host a public-facing website to support their beloved line-of-business applications.

Granting Non-Admin Access Permissions

You decide to go ahead and create a new website in IIS and set it to allow Anonymous Access. Anonymous Access is enabled by default when you create a new website in IIS. To observe or change the settings in IIS:

1. Go to the **Server Management** console and expand **Advanced Management.**

2. Expand **Internet Information Services,** expand **ServerName,** and then expand the **Web Sites** node.

3. Right-click on the **SiteName,** then click on **Properties**.

4. Click on the **Directory Security** tab, then on **Edit. Y**ou should see that **Anonymous Access** is enabled by default.

You can use the **Authenticated access** section in the dialog box to choose another method for client authentication and uncheck the **Enable anonymous access** box.

> IMPORTANT: You can fine-tune Anonymous Access permissions by configuring the NTFS permissions of the folder that holds the website files.

1. In **Windows Explorer**, go to the folder and select **Properties**, then the **Security** tab.

2. Click the **Advanced** tab and the select the **IUSR_USER** and click on **Effective Permissions**.

Configure Firewall Settings to Publish the Website

To open up the SBS firewall to host the website, you must run the CEICW again and choose to **Enable Firewall** on the firewall page. Then on the Web Services Configuration page, select **Business Web site (wwwroot)**. You can select this individually or choose the radio button to **Allow access to the entire Web site from the Internet**. If you do so, when you click **Next**, you will be warned that you are exposing the entire website and allowing users to gain access to all the website directories on the server's default website via the Internet. Not a smart thing to do!

Configure the File Transfer Protocol

There once was the client who tried to send 10 MB-size e-mail attachments to her clients and complained that the e-mail never made it. After receiving a lengthy explanation as to why she shouldn't send such a big file attachment, the user retaliated a week later by trying to send out an e-mail to three recipients with an 18 MB-size attachment, inadvertently crashing the Exchange server. Clearly a better approach would be to use the File Transfer Protocol (FTP).

Installing the FTP Service

The FTP service is not installed by default and it is not managed out of the Server Management console, but directly from the IIS console. To install the FTP service, you must first:

1. Go to the **Control Panel** and click on **Add or Remove Programs**.

2. Click on **Add/Remove Windows Components** in the left pane and select the **Application Server**.

3. Click on **Details** and select the **Internet Information Services**.

4. Click on **Details** and select the **File Transfer Protocol (FTP) Service** checkbox.

5. Click **OK** twice and then click **Finish** (you may get prompted for the SBS installation CD, so have it ready).

6. IIS then installs the default FTP site to C:\Inetpub\FTProot.

IMPORTANT: Once FTP is installed, you must rerun the CEICW to allow access for external users and open the firewall. If you have a separate hardware firewall, be sure to open Port 21. If you have a UPnP hardware firewall, SBS will configure the port for you.

Configure FTP Permissions

Once you have installed the FTP site, you may want to add a welcome or exit message for the external users or some different directory security settings. This must be configured from the IIS management console.

1. In the **Server Management** console, expand **Advanced Management,** expand the **Internet Information Services**, expand your **ServerName,** then **expand** the **FTP Sites** container.

2. Right-click the **FTP Sites** container, then click on **Properties**.

3. Click the **Security Accounts** tab and select the **Allow only anonymous connections** checkbox. This prevents users with valid accounts from sending their credentials in clear text and thereby increases security.

4. Click on the **Messages** tab to enter a Welcome or Exit message.

5. Click on the **Home Directory** tab to choose the FTP files folder location.

6. Click on the **Directory Security** tab and select either **grant** or **deny** for specific IP addresses. This is useful if you want to enable only certain users and know their IP addresses.

IMPORTANT: If the FTP site will not be used for a long time, it is a good practice to stop the FTP site by right-clicking the site in IIS and choosing **Stop.** Start it up again when it is needed.

Configure Disk Quotas

Beware that SBS enables disk quotas on the volume or partition where the Users shared folder is located by default. Disk quotas are not enabled on other volumes or partitions unless you turn them on. Quotas can be assigned only to volumes that have a drive letter. Quotas can be set for individual users or groups or enabled for all users.

By default, quotas are set to 1 GB and send a warning message to the users at 900 MB. When quotas are enabled, you can set or modify different options from:

- Deny disk space to users exceeding quota limit.

- Limit disk space to ... (you can specify the limit).

- Set warning level to ... (where you can specify the warning level).

- Log event when a user exceeds his quota limit.

- Log event when a user exceeds his warning level.

Disk quotas do not apply to administrators, unless you explicitly set them so.

> IMPORTANT: Avoid setting individual quotas. It is better to manage quotas for all users unless you absolutely have to single out an individual.

If you have special quota settings, like the boss gets more room than others or certain groups get a different amount of disk space, and you find yourself having to implement or move them to a different volume, you have the ability to import and export quotas.

You can also create quota reports on the fly by simply dragging them from the quota entries window into an Excel spreadsheet.

Create and Configure Public Folders

Public Folders is a feature of Microsoft Exchange Server that provides an effective way to collect, organize, and share information with others. Typically, public folders are used by project teams or user groups to share information on a common area of interest. Public Folders appears in the Outlook Folder List, can be managed from Outlook, and can contain messages, appointments, contacts, tasks, journal entries, notes, forms, files, and postings. You can also add a shortcut to any public folder to the Favorites folder under Public Folders.

Creating a Public Folder

You can create a public folder by creating a distribution group with the Add Distribution Group Wizard and choose to send all e-mail messages to the public folder. If you select the **Create a public folder to archive all e-mail messages sent to this group**, a public folder with the DistributionGroupName Archive will be added as a member to the group.

If you check the box **Enable this Group to receive e-mail message from users outside of your network**, the distribution group will be able to communicate with users outside the network. If the group is to be used internally only, clear this checkbox.

You can also manually create a public folder:

1. Go into the **Server Management Console**. Expand the **Advanced Management** node, click on the **Exchange** node, and expand **Folder**, then **Public Folders.**

2. **Right-click Public Folders** and select **New, Public Folder.** Type a name into the **Name** box.

3. Click **Apply** and **OK.**

Configuring Public Folders

Now that you have created the new public folder, you would want to configure permissions on who can create and read items in the public folder. To specify different access permissions:

1. **Right-click** on the folder and select **Properties**.

2. Click the **Permissions** tab and you will be able to configure **Client Permissions**.

Practice Questions

Question #1:

Which statement best describes the purpose of Domain Local Groups?
(Choose the best answer.)

a. Domain local groups are used to group users within a single domain. Only users from the parent domain can be included in a domain local group.

b. Domain local groups are used to assign permissions throughout an entire forest. The primary function of domain local groups is to facilitate the use of transitive trusts to form the secure communications within domain-forest relationships.

c. Domain local groups are used to assign permissions to resources within the local domain. Universal groups, global groups, or user accounts from any domain can be placed into a domain local group.

d. Domain local groups provide the backward capability needed to facilitate upgrades from SBS 2000 and earlier versions. Local group functionality has since been replaced with the introduction of universal groups.

Question #2:

Acme Marketing recently moved their corporate HQ to a new location on the opposite side of town. Their new broadband connection is with the same ISP but now requires authentication directly at the server and not the modem. What has to be done to successfully get them working in the new environment? Their server is a 2.4 GHz P4, with 2 GB RAM, 36 GB RAID 1 OS Volume, 60 GB RAID 5 data volume, and dual 10/100/1000 NICs?. (Choose the best answer.)

a. Run CEICW and in the Firewall section choose "**Authenticate with ISP (WAN).**" Answer the questions, ensuring that the proper NIC is selected for the external connection.

b. Run CEICW and in the Network section choose "**Broadband connection requiring a username and password (PPOE).**" Answer the questions with the information provided by the ISP, ensuring the proper NIC is selected for the external connection.

c. Create a user using the details provided by the ISP. Set the user login type to "Automatic," and assign it to the local resource NIC 1 (External). Modify the DNS server properties to not attempt name resolution until after successful authentication (DNS_ON_AUTH=TRUE).

d. Reinstall SBS 2003 and choose the correct broadband connection type.

Question #3:

The specifications you are handed for the new SBS 2003 Premium edition installation are as follows:

- Internal name resolution is to occur transparent to the external network.

- Local PC's are not to have references to external name servers, but Internet name resolution should operate transparently.

- IP Addresses for local pc's are to be assigned automatically and include transparent updating of name server records.

Which of the following would meet these requirements? (Choose the best answer)

a. Disable DNS on the local SBS server, point to the ISP's DNS at the SBS server, create an internal alias referencing the external DNS server and push to local PC's with DHCP.

b. Provide proper information during the installation wizard to enable DNS and DHCP on the Server. After installation has completed, go to **All Programs** >**Administrative Tools** >double click the DNS icon, Right click on the server icon and choose "properties". Select the "Forwarders" tab. Enter the IP addresses of the ISP's primary and secondary DNS servers in the domain forwarders IP address list.

c. This operation cannot be completed on SBS 2003. It requires an upgrade to Windows Server 2003 Standard Edition.

d. Go to **All Programs** >**Administrative Tools** >double click the DHCP icon, Highlight and authorize the server node and then expand it. Right click on "Server Options", choose "Configure Options", enable option

134 "External Client Name Resolution Forwarded (transparent)", and option 128 "Local Client Lookup (local)."

Question #4:

You want to provide Internet name resolution, management, Internet mail, automatic addressing, and plug and play functionality. Which of the following are accurate acronyms for the technologies required? (In the proper order.)

a. ARP, SNMP, UPS, SMTP, UDP

b. DNS,SMTP,SNMP,DHCP, UPnP

c. LAPD, UPMC, DNS, RDP, POP3

d. DNS, SNMP, SMTP, DHCP, UPnP

Question #5:

You would like to provide terminal services for some of the users in an SBS 2003 environment. What has to be done to enable this functionality?

a. Install SBS 2003 Premium Edition, enable **Terminal Services Applictions Sharing Mode** in the To Do list.

b. Install SBS 2003, enable **Terminal Services Applictions Sharing Mode** in the To Do list. Apply the **Power** User template to all users requiring access.

c. Terminal services are only available in **Remote Administration mode** on SBS 2003. In order to provide Terminal Services in Application Sharing mode, a separate server must be installed.

d. Install SBS 2003 with the **/app_mode** switch which unfortunately removes much of the functionality of the product.

Question #6:

Which of the following options are available when implementing Disk Quotas (Choose all that apply)

a. Limit the total disk space which can be consumed by a user on a volume.

b. Limit the total disk space that can be consumed by a user on all volumes.

c. Send the user a warning that they are approaching their maximum allocated value.

d. Limit total space that can be consumed within selected folders by a user.

e. Deny disk space to users who have exceeded the quota limit.

Question #7:

SBS 2003 comes with Microsoft Exchange preconfigured to operate in the small business environment. Which of the following statements are true about Exchange and SBS? (Choose all that apply.)

a. The implementation of additional message stores within an SBS environment requires an upgrade to another version of Exchange.

b. SBS 2003 comes with "Exchange Lite," which is not fully functional.

c. Outlook Web Access is by far the most popular e-mail software, principally because of the high purchase price for the full Outlook 2003 client.

d. Multiple licensed Exchange servers are supported on an SBS network.

Question #8:

Which of the following are true statements concerning the POP3 connector implementation in SBS 2003? (Choose all that apply.)

a. The POP3 connector can connect to multiple POP3 servers to retrieve e-mail messages for multiple users but must save them in a single global POP3 mailbox.

b. The POP3 connector can be configured to deliver e-mail to multiple SMTP recipients, including Public Folders, as long as its e-mail address has been properly defined.

c. The POP3 connector can connect to multiple POP3 servers to retrieve e-mail messages for multiple users. The e-mail can then be saved in a single global POP3 mailbox, or distributed to the appropriate users' Exchange mailboxes.

    d. The POP3 connector is disabled by default but the service will automatically start once the first POP3 user is added.

Answers:

Question #1: Answer: c

1A: Incorrect! Domain local groups are not used to group users, but rather to provide a convenient mechanism to assign permissions to resources within a single domain.

1B: Incorrect! Never pass up an opportunity to use "transitive trusts" in a sentence. There's certain poetry in the phrase – or is it just me? Domain local groups have nothing to do with trusts, only permissions within the local domain.

1C: Correct! The idea being that resources are local to the machine and the starting point collection of objects within a forest is of course a domain. Domain local groups can contain users, other local groups (from the same domain), global groups, or universal groups. Remember AGDLP - Accounts into Global into Domain Local and then grant Permissions. Or All-Guys-Definitely-Love-Pizza! OK, maybe the food thing just works for me.

1D: Incorrect! Domain local groups are used to assign permissions to resources within the domain. Earlier versions of NT and Windows also had the concept of local groups (though not necessarily *Domain* local groups) that backwards compatibility is certainly an added benefit.

Question #2: Answer: b

a. Incorrect! Though CEICW is the correct tool, *Firewall* is the wrong section.

b. Correct! Did I mention that CEICW is your friend? Never underestimate its usefulness. Changes like this one which may seem complicated are usually resolved by simply rerunning CEICW and providing the new information – in this case the network section. I'm not sure what all has to happen under the hood to convert from direct connect to PPOE, but I am reasonably sure there is a

long list of "gotchas" if attemped manually. Thank you SBS wizard Wizards! (Hmmm, wuz that redundant?)

c. Incorrect! Nothing near as complicated as this - just run CEICW and choose PPOE!

d. Incorrect! With a hearty and soul-felt *Thank You!* Just visit our friend CEICW and choose PPOE. Then have a nice day!

Question #3: Answer: b

a. Incorrect! The SBS 2003 server can handle local resolution and forward lookups to external DNS servers as required.

b. Correct! DHCP will provide the clients with their IP addresses and will point them to the SBS server for DNS. The SBS server will provide DNS resolution for all of the local nodes because it is authoritive for the domain. Any resolution requests received for non local nodes will be sent to the defined "forwarders" for resolution. The SBS DNS server will cache the results to minimize internet traffic for subsequent lookups.

c. Incorrect! SBS 2003 IS Windows Server 2003 Standard Edition at the core.

d. Incorrect!. There are no DNS forwarding server options under DHCP.

Question #4: Answer: d

a. Incorrect!

b. Incorrect. Many people confuse SNMP and SMTP

c. Incorrect!

d. Correct! Domain Name Services, Simple Network Management Protocol, Simple Mail Transport Protocol, Dynamic Host Control Protocol, Universal Plug and Play.

Question #5: Answer: c

a. Incorrect! Unlike previous versions of SBS, terminal services cannot be run in application mode on SBS 2003 – period. If Application Sharing mode is required, a separate Terminal Server server must be installed. The SBS 2003 server can be configured act as the license server, however.

b. Incorrect! Doesn't matter what template is applied. The users Application Mode terminal services cannot be enabled on an SBS 2003 server.

c. Correct! SBS 2003 only support Terminal Services in remote administration mode. The SBS 2003 server can be configured to act as the license server for another server running Terminal Services in application sharing mode.

d. Incorrect! Application Mode terminal services cannot be enabled or installed on an SBS 2003 server.

Question 6: Answer: a,c,e

a. Correct! Disk Quotas are implemented at the volume level for each user.

b. Incorrect! Disk Quotas are implemented at the volume level for each user. You cannot control disk quotas across multiple volumes.

c. Correct! Users can be sent a warning message when a preset amount of disk space has been consumed.

d. Incorrect! Disk quotas can only be implemented on a volume, not at the folder level.

e. Correct! When a user has consumed the assigned amount of disk space on a volume they are prevented from using more by the disk quota process. This is obviously the basic reason for implementing disk quotas to begin with - to make sure users don't consume all of the disk space on a volume.

Question #7: Answers: a,d

a. Correct! Microsoft Exchange (Standard Edition) which supports only a single message store, is implemented on the SBS 2003 server. Microsoft Exchange (Enterprise) would have to be installed to support multiple message stores.

b. Incorrect! The fully functional version of Microsoft Exchange (Standard Edition) is implemented on SBS 2003. In fact the only thing removed is the complex installation procedures!

c. Incorrect! The Outlook 2003 client is provided free and its use is included in the client license purchased with the SBS 2003 server.

d. Correct! Multiple licensed Exchange servers can be present on an SBS network.

Question 8: Answers: c,d

a. Incorrect! Delivering messages to a single global mailbox is an option but it is not required.

b. Incorrect! The POP3 connector cannot be configured to deliver to a public folder.

c. Correct! This makes the POP3 connector very powerful, allowing for the immediate integration of the current mail environment into Exchange. It also makes the process of migrating from a POP3 environment a much less stressful task. With a greater likelihood of success.

d. Correct! The first user can be added either by CEICW or via the POP3 Connector Manager.

Summary

That was one monster-length chapter and represents the deepest dive into the SBS product stack that this book will take. No SBS technology was left untouched, if you think about it. We started with domain groups and moved on to SBS networking technologies. In this look at SBS networking, we took a look at the "SBS way," including walking through much of the To Do List and a few special wizards. The networking section ended with a look at specific networking components like DHCP and DNS. Terminals Services was followed by a tip of the hat to SNMP. Then an important area of discussion was presented: messaging and collaboration. The chapter concluded with discussion of web hosting, FTP, and resource sharing. It was a grand chapter, but don't ever lose sight of the fact that all this information was presented in the context of successfully passing the 70-282 exam. That's why we're here. Onward to Chapter 8.

CHAPTER 8
Supporting and Maintaining Windows Small Business Server 2003

Managing Windows Small Business Server 2003

Well, is it really about just managing the SBS server, or is it about managing the desktops? Should we manage users? Server management essentially is not only about the server, but also about the entire network and its user culture. Therefore, server management requires a holistic view that includes client computers, network connections, and users.

The SBS management console reveals the most excellent management tools; but let's not forget that we are sitting on top of a Windows Server 2003. In order to get the whole pie, not just a piece, it is imperative that you brush up on your Group Policy Object (GPO) knowledge. To achieve a well-balanced network environment, happy users, desktop security, and a healthy server, you need to employ all the tools you can get.

Using the Server Management Console

The Server Management console is the portal from which all SBS management-related tasks are performed. The Server Management console first appears automatically after the initial install of SBS opening the To Do List; it will always open up by default when you log on as the administrator as well. If it does not launch for you automatically, go to Start, and on top of the Start bar, click on Server Management. In one view, you are presented with the Server Management Home Page and its individual nodes, the Standard Management node and Advanced Management node, and shortcut icons to manage the most common management tasks for administrators.

Standard Management Options

The Standard Management node includes most actions that are **task-based,** and unless you require special configurations, you will be able to perform most tasks here. The Standard Management node has a plethora of tasks that will surprise you. So, before you go about managing and using the native Windows Server 2003 tools, make sure to check for hidden jewels in the Server Management console. Need strong Texas talk to get the point? Always use the Server Management console! The Standard Management node is broken down into several taskpads. Since there are so many options, you will find combined taskpad functions and tasks in Table 8.1 for a quick overview.

> IMPORTANT: It's reasonable to assume the 70-282 test will high-light the Server Management console. Spend 30 minutes working through Table 8.1 by actually clicking through the server management console.

Notes:

Table 8-1

The Standard Management Taskpads, Tasks, Tools, and Links.

Standard Management		
Taskpad	**Tasks**	**Tools & Links**
To Do List	• Network Tasks - View Security Best Practices - Connect to the Internet - Configure Remote Access - Activate your Server - Add client Licenses • Management Tasks - Add a Printer - Add Users and Computers - Configure Fax - Configure Monitoring - Configure Backup	All items listed here are tasks, which means that a wizard will be opened up to assist you in completing the task. The To Do List contains the first tasks you should complete, preferably in the order listed. If you did an upgrade vs. a clean install, tasks will display different options. After an upgrade you will also have a change users permissions task.
Information Center	• Downloads and Updates • Documentation • Community Web site • Technical Support	The Information Center contains quick links to facilitate administration.

Notes:

Standard Management		
Taskpad	**Tasks**	**Tools & Links**
Internal Web Site	• Import Files 　- Performs file import from anywhere into the Share-Point file library. This is very useful when you want to copy entire folders of shared drive locations into SharePoint. • Add Link 　- Creates a New Item Link in SharePoint	Here you will also find tools that allow you to configure or have access to: • Change Name • Change Homepage Layout • Configure Alerts • Manage Access • Manage Your Company's Internal Web Site • Central Administration
Fax (local)	• Configure Fax Services 　- This wizard helps you configure SBS to send, route, and receive faxes and to fax routing groups (into ... Outlook 2003 e-mail in boxes), a SharePoint fax folder, or a shared folder	Here you will also find tools to: • Manage Fax Jobs • Manage Cover Pages and links to: • Configure Phone and Modem Options • Manage Printers
Monitoring and Reporting	• Set Up Monitoring Reports and Alerts 　- This wizard assists in setting up scheduled server reports, configures alert notifications that will be sent to you by e-mail, and enables application logging	In this category you will also find tools to: • View Services • View Event Logs • Open Task Manager • Change Server Status • Report Settings • Change Alert Notifications • A link to: View Usage Report

Standard Management		
Taskpad	**Tasks**	**Tools & Links**

Internet and E-mail	• Add Licenses
	
	  - With this wizard you can add client access licenses to the server. You should already have the license codes on hand and will be able to activate client access licenses over the Internet.
		There are several additional tools found here to manage the Internet and E-mail. With these tools you can:
		
		• Synchronize E-mail
		• Change Server IP Address
		• Change Broadband Connection Password
		• Change Dial-up Connection Password
		• Change E-mail Password
		• Configure Network Connections
		• Configure Phone and Modem Options
		  ...and links to:
		• Manage POP3 E-mail
		• Manage Distribution Groups

Shares (local)	• Add a Shared Folder
	
	  - The Share a Folder Wizard shares a folder on the Server computer and sets the appropriate client access permissions on the folder.
		Tools include:
		
		• Configure MyDocuments Redirection
		  ...and links to:
		• View Connected Users
		• View Open Files

Standard Management		
Taskpad	**Tasks**	**Tools & Links**
Backup	• Configure Backup - This wizard assists in configuring backup to tape or a hard disk (or other location), allows you to specify excluded folders, defines a backup schedule, selects a user to manage backup media, and sets deleted item retention and the space allocated for VSS snapshots.	Here you will also find tools to: • Configure MyDocuments Redirection ...and the link to open up Help files to: • Learn How to Restore the Server • Restore Individual Files • Restore SharePoint Files
Printers	• Add a Printer - This wizard assists in installing a printer and making printer connections. If you are using a USB, IEEE 1394, or infrared printer, you will not need to use this wizard. Attach and turn on the printer and Windows will install it.	There is a link provided to: • Manage Fax Printers
Distribution Groups	• Add a Distribution Group - This wizard assists in adding a distribution group and defines the group membership.	There are links to: • Manage POP3 E-mail, and • Manage Security Groups

Standard Management		
Taskpad	**Tasks**	**Tools & Links**
Security Groups	• Add a Security Group - This wizard assists in adding a security group and defines the group membership.	There is a link to: • Manage Distribution Groups

User Templates	• Add a Template
	
	  - Launches the Add Template Wizard discussed in detail in Chapter 6 under **Small Business Server User Templates.**
	
	• Import Templates
	
	  - This wizard imports templates.
	
	• Export Templates
	
	  - This wizard exports templates.
		There is a link to:
		
		• Manage Users

Even though the Server Management console is represented in a combined view here, there is no substitute for actually going to, clicking around, and looking at all the tools and tasks named above.

You may have noticed some tool and link repetition in different nodes. At times we need to engage several different tools, and the links make it easier to follow the logical order. In the next release of SBS, it would be nice to see one wizard where you can just add tools and tasks as needed without having to leave the wizard.

Tools differentiate from **tasks** in that they open directly into a utility window so you don't have to rerun an entire wizard. An example of this is the Change Server IP Address under the Internet and E-mail node. This will save you time from going through the entire Configure E-mail and Internet Connection Wizard (CEICW) again.

IMPORTANT: You should use tools whenever you can. A good example is the Change Server IP address tool. Run this instead of manually changing the IP on the Server Local Area Connections Properties page, because it will reconfigure all network services for the SBS server to work with the new IP address, instead of just changing the NIC properties.

Each node also lists a **More Information** link that will open the SBS online Help on the specific subject. Don't ignore the online Help; there are some real nuggets of wisdom at your fingertips and this should be your first avenue for finding valuable information for all things SBS before you spend hours scavenging the Internet.

Another way to complete some tasks is by clicking on the node. An example of this is the **Client Computers** and then clicking the **Action** command in the tool bar. Point is, the Server Management Console is very feature-rich. Even though it appears simple at first sight, it is surprisingly well-thought-through and capable of managing most common tasks very efficiently.

Advanced Management Options

Now that we've covered Standard Management options and discussed that these are task-based, let's look at the Advanced Management options, which are tool-based. The Advanced Management node gives fast access to management tools listed here in order:

- Active Directory Users and Computers
- Group Policy Management
- Computer Management (local)
- Exchange System Manager
- POP3 Connector Manager
- Terminal Services Configuration
- Internet Information Services
- Migrate Server Settings

Interestingly enough, when you click on some nodes, the right pane will display shortcut options, like in Standard Management, as well as the full native option, so take your pick. At times you just want to dive down and check a specific setting, especially Exchange and IIS settings, and this lets you drill down without having to leave the Server Management Console. The Advanced Management tools give you the same shortcut options as the task-based tools, except they are organized by application.

One thing to point out though, is the **Migrate Server Settings**, which not only has the Import and Export Templates option for SharePoint, but also has additional configuration options like:

- Import Health Monitor Configuration – This is helpful if you have several SBS server installations and you want to standardize Health Monitor across all your client locations. You would first configure settings as desired on one SBS server, then export the settings to a file, to import them at another SBS server as needed.

- Export Health Monitor Configuration – After you create the perfect configuration, use this wizard to export configured settings to a floppy disk or USB key for later import at another server.

- Migrate E-mail and Internet Connection Settings – Provides steps on how to modify config.vbs, which is the script that runs the EICW. It is located in the Program Files\Microsoft Windows Small Business Server\Networking\ICW folder. This is useful if you want to migrate Internet connection settings to another computer running SBS.

Whew, lots of options here. It will take a while for you to get used to using the Server Management Console and not reaching for native tools, but once you get the hang of it, you'll never go back. After you've set up your server, there should be little need for special configurations outside the Server Management Console. You'll even become accustomed to using the Group Policy Management node out of the Advanced Management node—hey, it takes seven clicks to open it the native way: Start, Administrative tools, Active Directory Users and Computers, right-click the domain, Properties, Group Policy tab, and click on Open. Forget that—I get a cramp in my finger just thinking about it.

Using the Group Policy Management Console

Windows Server 2003 includes the new Group Policy Management Console (GPMC) from where you can manage all Group Policy tasks. If you have not acquainted yourself with this yet, it is high time. Even though the GPMC is meant to manage a collection of GPOs and multiple domains and forests, it is also useful to manage our lonely SBS domain. To manage the content of a single GPO, you still use the Group Policy Object Editor, formerly known as GPedit.

With the GPMC you can:

- Drag-and-drop (cool)
- Backup
- Restore
- Import
- Copy
- Run GPO reports

The GPMC runs only on a Windows 2003 Server operating system and can also be installed on a Windows XP SP1 machine.

Applying and Configuring Group Policy By the Group Policy Management Console

Before we even go there, I would like you to be keenly aware of where your SBS organizational unit (OU) is actually located. Figure 8-1 shows the MyBusiness OU being used for all things SBS in the left pane. A word to the wise: Do not move users or groups outside this OU. You can create users in the regular user container in AD then move them into the MyBusiness OU, but never, ever move them out. Better yet, just get into the habit of creating user accounts using the SBS templates. Okay, off the soap box and on with life…

Notes:

Figure 8-1
MyBusiness OU.

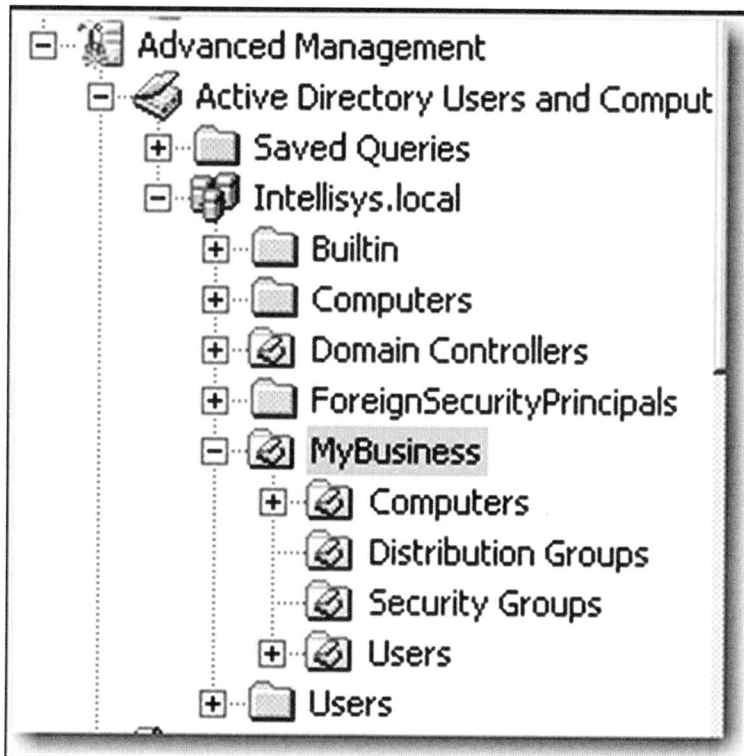

GPO settings can only be applied if the GPO is linked to a site, domain, or OU. In Figure 8-2 you can see the GPMC tree view with GPO links being displayed as child nodes under the domain. For instance, you can see a SUS policy under the GPOs, but the SUS GPO does not show up in the left pane under the domain node. SUS in this case is linked to the MyBusiness OU as shown in Figure 8-2.

Notes:

Figure 8-2
Linking in the GPMC.

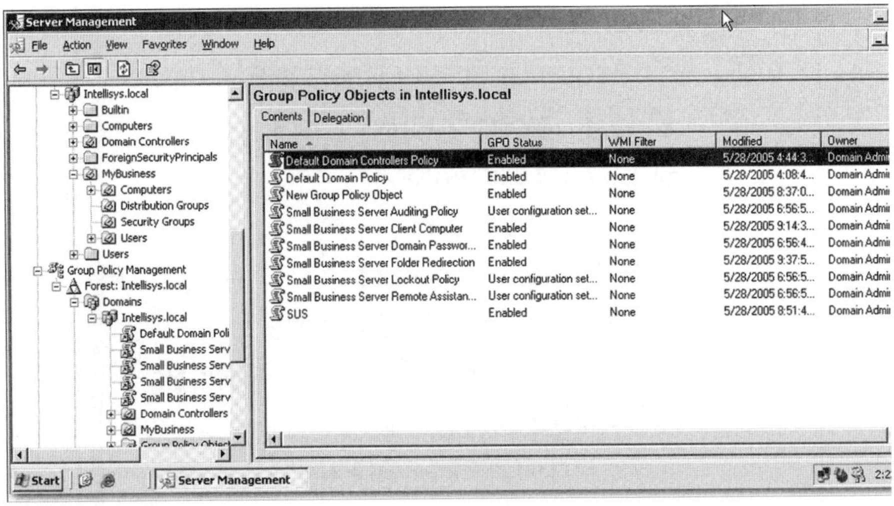

So, for you to apply a GPO, it must first be created and then **linked** to the site, domain, or OU. This can be easily achieved in one step by right-clicking **the object** of your desire (site, domain, or OU) and then choosing **Create and Link GPO here.** This is analogous to clicking **New** in the old Group Policy before GPMC.

Okay, the cool part is the drag and drop functionality. You can grab any GPO from the **Group Policy Objects** node and just drag it over to the site, domain, or OU.

Editing Group Policies

Initially, when a new GPO is created, it has no settings defined. You can edit a Group Policy Object by right-clicking the **GPO** in the GPMC and selecting **Edit.** This opens the **Group Policy Object Editor** displaying the Computer Configuration and User Configuration. At this point you just have to path your way to the object where you want to edit the setting and choose either:

- Not Configured

- Enabled

- Disabled

Not Configured means exactly that, and when GPOs are processed, the settings will not conflict with any other setting. The Enabled setting allows the GPO setting to be processed, whereas a Disabled setting will not process the GPO. It is recommended that you switch all unused objects to Disabled instead of leaving them on Not Configured to speed up processing.

Not that you will be using this in an SBS environment (but you never know) and just in case you encounter this in the exam, let's touch on inheritance for a moment.

GPO Inheritance

When studying for the MCSE, you had to repeat the mantra of site, domain, and OU (SDOU) in just that order—which is the way group policy is applied. First, the local computer policy is applied during logon. Then the computer checks for site policies, then domain, and then OU. The last policy applied (OU) in this case would overwrite previous applied policies. Then came Block and Overwrite into the equation, which was not a hard concept to grasp, but could be tricky, to say the least. Especially if you were working in an enterprise environment where multiple GPOs would be applied across sites and domains and issues arose and you had to start sifting through the policy quagmire.

The default inheritance behavior is altered by several Group Policy options:

- **Link Order** – The GPO with the #1 under the **Link Order** has the highest precedence, then #2, and so on.

- **Block Inheritance** – Allows an OU to block inheritance from a parent container. This will prevent domain GPOs from being applied to an OU, for instance, unless the domain GPO was set to **Enforced.**

- **Enforced** – Previously known as "Overwrite," this will enforce the GPO on an OU or domain, regardless whether the domain or OU is set on **Block Inheritance**.

- **Link Enabled** – Since GPOs must be linked to a site, domain, or OU for settings to be applied, you could also choose to uncheck the **Link Enabled** setting when right-clicking on a **GPO**. This will exclude the GPO from being processed.

Configuring Folder Redirection

In Small Business Server you can redirect the MyDocuments folder of all clients (Windows XP and Windows 2000) to a single shared folder on the server or a network share with the **Client Document Redirection** tool. It is recommended that you choose the **Redirect all MyDocuments folders to the default shared folder for users on the Small Business Server** for numerous reasons, including:

- Folders are automatically included in the SBS Backup
- Deleted files can easily be recovered through Volume Shadow Service
- If users log onto another machine on the network, their documents will always be available.

When you redirect the MyDocuments folder, it will still appear as a local folder on the user's desktop, but the target path will point to the **Users Shared Folders** folder on the SBS server.

> IMPORTANT: Folder redirection is cool and you should anticipate 70-282 exam questions in this area.

Disk quotas are enabled by default on the same volume where the **Users Shared Folders** folder resides and default settings are both:

- Quota limit: 1 GB
- Warning level at: 900 MB

Essentially, the MyDocuments redirect tool configures the **Small Business Server Folder Redirection** GPO, linking it as a node in the domain container and pointing the root path to *SBSServerName*\\Users.

To manually create this policy setting, you would have to go to the Advanced Management tasks and create and link a GPO in the GPMC to the domain or OU container. You would then drill down under the **Users Configuration** to the **Windows Settings** and expand **Folder Redirection,** right-click on **MyDocuments**, click the **Properties** tab, and in the **Target** tab manually enter your preferred settings.

Resultant Set of Policies (RSoP)

Resultant Set of Policies (RSoP) is an addition to Group Policy that simplifies GPO troubleshooting. RSoP consists of two modes:

- Planning Mode
- Logging Mode

The **Planning** mode simulates the effect of policy settings that would be applied to computers and users and the **Logging** mode reports on existing policy settings for computers and users currently logged on. RSoP helps determine a set of applied policies and in which order they are applied (precedence). It details settings including:

- Administrative Templates
- Folder Redirection
- Internet Explorer Maintenance
- Security Settings
- Scripts
- Group Policy Software Installation

You can run the wizard by right-clicking the **Group Policy Results** folder in **Group Policy Management**. (See Figure 8.2). RSoP needs a Windows Server 2003 or Windows XP machine to run. It cannot retrieve Windows 2000 Group Policy data, but this can be simulated with Group Policy Modeling.

Manage and Troubleshoot Small Business Client Computers

SBS has come a long way since its first inception way back when. I remember looking at the SBS 4.x console and observing the meager choice of management tools and deciding to skip the entire console altogether and just going about my business with the NT 4.0 native tools—essentially breaking the SBS console and disliking it even more, then insisting that it did not function. I call that MCSE job security!

Today, when you open the Server Management Console, the Home Page displays several "most common" tasks icons in the right pane, and in the left pane you have all the taskpads at your fingertips. From the manage **Client Computers** taskpad you can create computer accounts to assign applications, view event logs, and perform other advanced tasks. You can also find help for troubleshooting the most common Windows Small Business Server 2003 issues. The SBS server tools no longer break if you use native tools, but at this point the question is: Why bother? You can perform just about any client management task right from here.

Adding and Removing Clients

If you remember the dark days of the magic disk, fear no longer, because here comes http://SBSServerName/connectcomputer—and it works! This is about the easiest way to join clients to a domain if you are coming from a peer-to-peer network. If your client is coming from another SBS domain or domain in general, well, we'll cover that one in a minute. First of all, the question arises: What client operating systems are supported on the SBS network? Well, since we are dealing with Active Directory, the easiest client operating systems to join to the network are:

*   Windows XP Professional
*   Windows 2000 Professional clients

We can do so by running http://*SBSServerName*/connectcomputer in the browser UI of the client to be joined. And even though they are not really supported by Active Directory, you can also join the following:

*   Windows 98
*   Windows Me
*   Windows NT 4.0 SP6a / IE4.0
*   Mac OS X clients

IMPORTANT: On the 70-282 exam, assume it is nearly always correct to try and upgrade legacy clients to Windows XP Professional if the budget allows.

Now, do we recommend this? Well, NO...but if you *have* to go this route you can. Just be prepared to perform several manual steps along the way. So, let's get started and look at the easy way first.

> IMPORTANT: The 70-282 exam tends to emphasize the easy way, which is the Microsoft way of thinking.

Small Business Server Network Configuration Wizard

Once again, you can type http://SBSServerName/connectcomputer into the client workstation Internet Explorer browser address bar to initiate the Small Business Server Network Configuration Wizard. This is the simplest way to establish a network connection and join a Windows XP Professional or Windows 2000 Professional workstation to the domain after you created a computer account with the Set Up Computer Wizard. This wizard will join a workgroup client to the SBS domain. During the process of joining the client, the wizard will:

- Make the workgroup computer a member of the SBS domain.

- Migrate existing local user account profiles.

- Install operating system service packs (optional):

    - Shadow Copy client.

    - Internet Explorer 6.

- Install the Outlook 2003 client (optional) and configure Outlook Profile settings.

- Install the Shared Fax client and configure fax settings (optional).

- Install printer drivers (optional).

- Install printers (if published in Active Directory).

- Install additionally assigned software (optional).

- Configure Remote Desktop Assistance and enable Remote Desktop.

- Add the selected user account (for the specific computer) to the local administrator's group.

- Set the Internet Explorer Home Page to http://companyweb (pointing to the internal SharePoint site).

The "Other" Clients

When joining Windows 98, Me, or NT 4.0 SP6a / IE4.0 clients, you do not have to create the computer account with the Set Up Computer Wizard. You will have to manually join the client to the domain since the http://*SBSServerName*/connectcomputer method would not work here. Also, you will have to manually install the client applications located at the *SBSServerName*\clientapps folder. This folder includes:

- Shadow Copy client located in *SBSServerName*\clientapps\Shadow-Copy (only works with Win98 SE and Me).

- Shared Fax client located in *SBSServerName*\clientapps\faxclient.

- Outlook 2003 (will not install on Win98 or NT 4.0).

- SBScert.

- Connection Manager.

- Internet Explorer 6 client located in *SBSServerName*\clientapps\ie6.

- If running ISA, the firewall client located in *SBSServerName*\mspclnt.

Client files will have to be manually installed and configured; shared printers need to be added as well.

Windows 98 and Windows Me require the Active Directory client extensions. You will find the files on any Windows Server 2000 CD in the \Clients\Win9x folder.

NT 4.0 SP6a requires the files for NT 4.0 on the SBS Disc #3 in the \SBSSUPPORT\ADCLIENT folder. The Active Directory client provides:

- Support for Dfs (Distributed files system).

- NTLM ver.2 (stronger authentication).

IMPORTANT: Remember that data stored on WIN98 is available to anyone that has physical access to the WIN98 machine. If security is an issue, it is better to upgrade to Windows 2000 Professional or Windows XP Professional and use NTFS permissions and EFS for file encryption.

The client extensions also DO NOT support certain Active Directory features. For instance, there is no support for:

- Kerberos, which requires kernel-level extensions for security and is only available in Windows XP and Windows 2000 clients.

- Group policies, which cannot be created or deployed to computer objects with client extensions.

- Windows NT 4.0 clients will need to use the NT administrative templates (.adm files) and the NT system policy editor (poledit.exe).

- Windows 98 clients need to be manually managed with system policy editor.

- IPsec and L2TP. This requires an upgraded network stack which is available in Windows 2000 and later. Client extension can not provide this functionality. However, there is a separate Microsoft client for IPsec and L2TP connectivity for legacy clients.

A Special Word About Macs

Be aware that when you connect Mac OS X clients, they do not get along with the .local DNS extension that SBS uses by default for the internal domain name. Windows systems use SMB (Server Message Blocks) as the default file sharing protocol and Macs have an issue with that unless you are running Mac OS 10.4 or OS 10.3 with special configurations for Active Directory Access and disabled SMB encryption. Another way around this is to either choose a different DNS name extension, like .prv or .office, or not to join the Mac to the Windows domain at all. Mac clients will still be able to access shares and happily participate on the network, unless you are running ISA. And this is where the discussion ends today.

Migrating Profiles

Yes, migrating profiles still is a lively topic at many SBS meetings, and even though Microsoft recommends using the Files and Settings Transfer Wizard included in XP, it will not preserve all user settings of the domain account nor will it pick up certain files you would think should be included, like the .pst file. You have to be sure and specifically tell the Files and Settings Transfer

Wizard which file extensions to transfer. For more information about the Files and Settings Transfer Wizard, go to: http://www.microsoft.com/technet/prodtechnol/winxppro/deploy/mgrtfset.mspx.

One workaround, when moving from an old to a new domain, is to create a separate local user account with administrative rights on the computer and then copy the domain profile of the old user account into a specific folder using the **Control Panel\System Tools\Advanced\Settings and Copy to Profile** option. You then go to the **Local Users and Groups Console**, right-click the newly created user account, click the **Profile** tab, and type the path to the folder holding the copied **Profile** into the **Profile Path** box. You then switch the computer from being a domain member to a workgroup computer and join it to the SBS domain using the newly created user account.

Removing Clients

Removing clients from the network is rather simple. Go into the **Standard Management Console** to the **Client Computers** container, right-click the computer object you want to delete, and select **Delete**. This will remove the computer account from the Active Directory domain. Don't forget to disjoin the client from the domain and revert it back into a workgroup.

Assigning Applications to Clients

Assigning applications is one of the easiest tasks in SBS. If you don't want to dabble with GPO application deployment, you can just use the Assign Application Wizard and be done with it. Of course, experienced admins can still use GPOs; just make sure to stick with one way or another to standardize the deployment procedure and not have a hodge-podge of methods.

SBS uses the SBS_LOGIN_SCRIPT.BAT logon script that is automatically assigned to all domain user accounts. When a user logs on, the script launches Setup.exe in the *SBSServerName*\Clients\Setup folder. Setup.exe parses the Apps.dat file in the *SBSServerName*\Clients\Response\ *ClientComputerName* folder that contains the information of each setup program for an assigned application.

Assign Application Wizard

Once you've launched the Assign Application Wizard from the link located in the Client Computers container, you will be presented with default available programs:

- Client Operating System Service Packs
- Internet Explorer 6
- Microsoft Office Outlook 2003
- Shared Fax Client

These are all located in the \Clientapps folder. If checked, these applications will automatically be installed when a user logs on to the client computer. You can also add your own additional applications here by choosing the **Edit Applications** button, which will launch the Set Up Client Applications Wizard. It makes sense to place your application into its own shared folder in the \ClientApps folder to keep all applications together.

Administrative Install

If you are deploying Microsoft Office, make sure to do an administrative install by using **setup.exe /a** to extract the .cab files into a shared folder before you launch the Set Up Client Computer Wizard. On a side note, if you use the administrative install, make sure to always patch the clients from the same location using the full Office patches which are entire file replacements, and disallow clients to patch through Windows Update, which are only binary patches. If you mix and match these patch files, you will get funky Microsoft Office behavior. Also, do not remove the original install files from the shared location or you will lose the resiliency of the self-repair function since clients have the source install path hard-coded in their registry and will check this location to repair damaged files.

Additional Applications assigned in the Assign Application Wizard will appear as a desktop shortcut icon on the user's computer next time she logs on. The user will then have to initialize the install by clicking on the icon (it will have a UNC path to the executable). The disadvantage here is that you cannot control if and when a user installs the application or decides to simply delete the desktop icon.

On the same screen, the **Advanced** button allows you to configure Internet Explorer Settings, Outlook 2003 profile settings, Desktop Settings, Fax printer and Fax settings as well as Fax configuration information, and Remote Desktop.

There are also two checkboxes (as shown in Figure 8-3), if you mark:

- **During client setup, allow the selected applications to be modified** allows a user who is installing applications to change the default application installation location or to deselect applications.

- **After client setup is finished, log off the client computer** will log off the client workstation after the installation and prevent other users accessing the computer.

Figure 8-3
Assigning Applications with the Assign Applications Wizard.

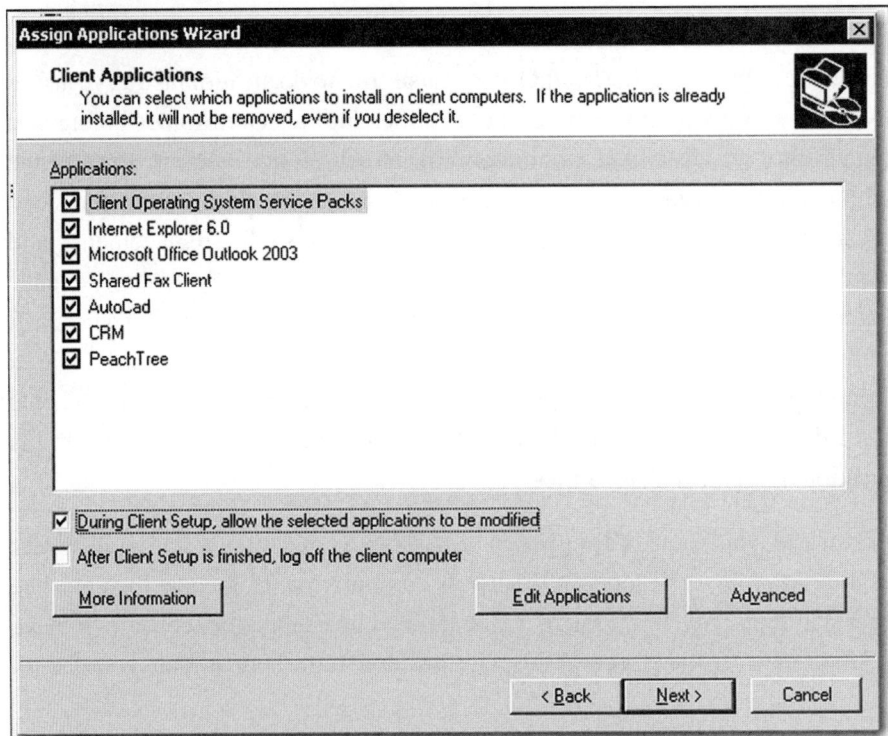

Managing Assigned Applications

A quick and easy way to view and modify assigned applications is by using **View Computer Settings**. You have just got to love this! Go to the **Client Computers** container and click on the

View Computer Settings link. You will get a display with all client computers and can expand each node to access the **Assigned Applications, Client Setup Settings,** and **Client Setup Configuration Options** (as shown in Figure 8-4). You can expand each of those nodes and then just right-click on a setting or option displayed and change it.

Figure 8-4

Viewing and modifying assigned applications in the Server Management Console.

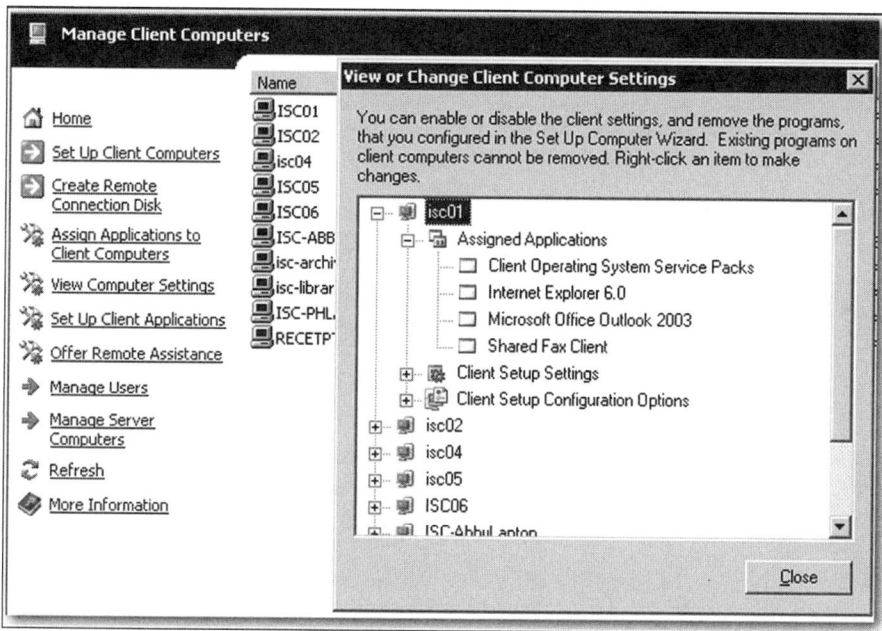

IMPORTANT: Chapter 10 *Installing and Configuring Windows Server 2003* covers Managing User Environments with GPOs, which is an alternative way on the SBS server to manage assigned applications.

Setting Up a Client Computer

Setting up the client computer account in SBS is done through the Server Management Console with the Set Up Computer Wizard. Launch the wizard from the **Standard Management Console**, click **Client Computers,** and click the **Set Up Client Computers** link. The wizard will launch and first ask you to specify the name for the client computer account. In the

- **Client Computer Names** screen, you can add multiple computer accounts at once. This is called the **bulk-add tool**. Adding computer names here will create a machine accounts in Active Directory. The next screen is the

- **Client Applications** screen as discussed in the section above, where you add or edit client applications. Following is the

- **Mobile Client and Offline Use** screen, where you can select to

- **Install Connection Manager** to create the download Connection Manager in Remote Web Workplace for easy client VPN configuration. More on this topic in the following section.

- **Install Active Sync 3.7,** which will push down the Active Sync application to the client computer during the network join process. This will allow devices such as SmartPhones and PocketPCs to synchronize with the client computer and SBS. Matter of fact, if you have a PocketPC with the 2003 OS version, when setting it in the cradle to sync the first time, set it to sync with the Exchange server and it will be automatically configured for wireless access. If you are using GPRS or Wi-fi, you will be able to sync your e-mail, contacts, and schedule from wireless from there on.

IMPORTANT: As of this writing, the 70-282 exam assumes the use of Active Sync 3.7 (even though SBS SP1 upgrades this component to version 3.8). Visit www.smbnation.com and click on the 70-282 Upgrade link to get the latest exam news!

At this point you are done setting up the client computer and are prompted to go to the client machine and type http://*SBSServerName*/connectcomputer into the browser to launch the Network Configuration Wizard.

Now that you have typed http://*SBSServerName*/connectcomputer into the browser on the client computer, the process of adding the client computer physically to the domain will be initiated. You will be presented with the

- **Network Configuration screen**, which will ask you to **Connect to the Network Now** and then give you a Security Warning dialog box if you want to install the SBS Network Configuration Wizard. The first page that appears will be the

- **Assign users to this computer and migrate their profile** page, where you have the choice of adding **local user accounts** to the **Users assigned to this computer** box. You can assign more than one user to the computer. On this same page you choose to **preserve existing settings** by selecting the assigned user and pairing them with **current user settings.** This is how the local profile gets migrated into the domain profile. The next page will be the

- **Computer Name** screen where you select the computer account name for the client machine. If the machine currently has a different computer name, it will be renamed.

You then complete the Network Configuration Wizard by clicking **Finish** and the client machine will reboot and go through an automatic logon using the **sbs_netsetup** profile, joining the client to the domain, and boot again.

At this point you can log on with the application install, Outlook 2003 will be installed and automatically configured, so when the user clicks designated user account for this client machine, thereby logging on, you will be prompted to install the assigned application packages or to postpone installation until later. While on the Outlook icon, he will be presented with a fully configured e-mail client.

Setting Up Server Computers

Yikes! Turns out there is a lot to these wizards. Learning to trust and use them to your advantage will make your life so much easier. Recently, I developed a training course for an enterprise-level class using Windows Server 2003 Enterprise, and it made me realize how much I have become accustomed to the SBS way of doing things. Even though there is the Add Server Roles Wizard in the "other" Windows server versions, it doesn't come anywhere near the ease of setup and management that you have with SBS.

A word about joining additional servers to the SBS domain. I can't tell you how many times I was told that after joining a server to the domain, people experienced somewhat funky server behavior ranging from permission problems to plain odd intermittent connectivity issues. Every time, when I asked how the second server had been joined to the domain, it turned out that the Set up Server Wizard had not been used. No comment.

Setting up a server to be joined to the domain is very similar to joining a client and will be covered in Chapter 9, *Expanding the Windows Small Business Server 2003 Network*.

Configuring Remote Client Computers

SBS is all about mobility and remote connectivity. Setting up a remote client and configuring a VPN connection or Remote Web Workplace access is easy. Note: Do not try to join remote clients to the domain via VPN. Having to push the applications out over the VPN link would be excruciating to say the least. It is better to join a client to the domain in the office, and then ship the client workstation to its final destination. If security is a concern, joining a client to the domain will support not using an L2TP VPN, since we then have computer authentication. On the other hand, if security is not a concern, there is no reason why a remote client needs to join the domain.

Regardless, whether joined to the domain or not, if you want to set up VPN connectivity, you can achieve this in two ways:

• Create a **Remote Connection Disc.**

- Use the **Connection Manager** download link in Remote Web Workplace.

To create the Remote Connection disk, click on the Create Remote Connection Disk link in the Client Computers container. It will prompt you for a floppy at the finish to load the setup.exe file on it. You could transfer this file to other media, like a thumb drive, burn it to a CD, or plain e-mail it (it has a very small footprint). The setup.exe file will have to be executed on the target machine and will create an icon on the desktop that will just require the username and password to log on to the server remotely.

The **Download Connection Manager** link appears in **Remote Web Workplace** by selecting the **Install Connection Manager** checkbox on the **Mobile Client and Offline Use** screen in the **Assign Applications Wizard.** Well, they had to stick this somewhere and this seemed like the most logical place.

Now, none of this will allow remote access or configure remote access settings, unless you run the Remote Connection Wizard, which is located on the **To Do List**, Step #3 in the Network Tasks, right below the Configure E-mail and Internet Connection Wizard.

> ATTENTION: Just a note on the side - to gain full functionality without having to do any client-side configuration, you must use the fully qualified domain name (FQDN) with this wizard. If you use an IP address, you will have to manually configure the VPN client. Just a minor glitch where the developer of the wizard stated, "DUH...I never thought about that..."

As you can see, even though the Server Management Console is laid out very logically, you should have some hands-on time to become familiar with the whereabouts of individual wizards and how they play together.

Configure Offline Mail Synchronization

With the Outlook 2003 client came a new feature called **Cached Exchange Mode** that is very useful for mobile users. The cached mode creates a full copy of all the current items in the user's mailbox. It also creates an offline copy of the address book. This process is called **synchronization.** Items synchronized are:

- Utility folders.
- Calendar.
- Contacts.
- Drafts.
- Inbox.
- All other folders (defined by the user).
- Sent Items.
- Deleted Items.
- Public Folder Favorites (added by user).

The Outlook client is set to use Cached Exchange Mode by default. You can manually turn Cached Exchange Mode on or off by:

1. Go into **Control Panel**, **Mail**, and click on your current **Profile Properties**.

2. Click on **E-mail accounts** and **view or change existing e-mail account**.

3. Select the **Microsoft Exchange Server** account and click **Change**.

4. On the **Exchange Server Settings** screen, under the Exchange server entry, there will be the checkbox **Use Cached Exchange Mode**.

5. Once you have verified that Cached Exchange Mode is set, you can go to **File** and deselect **Work Offline.**

The first time the inbox will is synchronized, it will appear empty until the calendar, contacts, and draft folders are synchronized. Once synchronized, you can take the computer offline and all mailbox contents will still be fully accessible. When the client connects back to the network and detects the Exchange server, it will detect the difference between the mailbox and the local cached mailbox and start synchronizing the changes.

Usually, Outlook 2003 configures the optimum synchronization setting based on the connection speed. You can configure them manually as shown in Figure 8-5 and select from the following:

- Download Full Items
- Download Headers and then Full Items
- Download Headers
- On Slow Connections, Download Only Headers

Your choice will depend on whether you have a fast connection or are on a dial-up connection. Slow connections are considered 128 kilobits or slower.

Figure 8-5

Exchange Download Options in Outlook 2003.

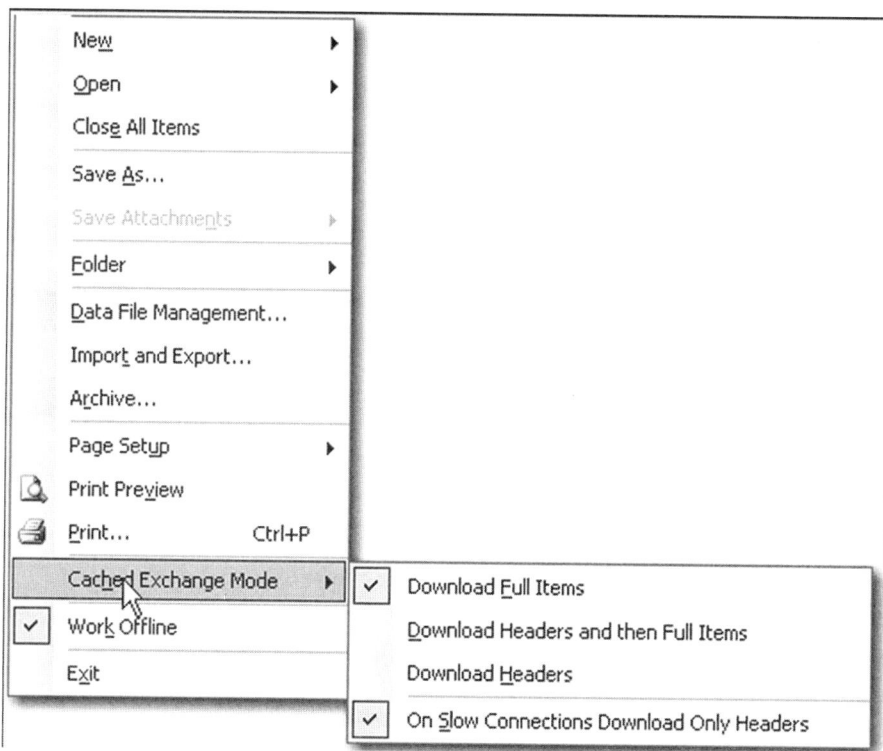

When you have a fast online connection, the e-mail headers are retrieved, followed by the full contents of the message, and the OAB (online address book) is updated every 24 hours.

When you have a slow online connection, only the e-mail headers are retrieved and you will have to click **Download the rest of this message now** to download the full message from the server. The OAB is not updated.

The cached file (outlook.ost) is located at C:\Documents and Settings \ Administrator\Local Settings\Application Data\Microsoft\Outlook.

> IMPORTANT: It is still a best practice to back up your e-mail inbox to .pst occasionally. In case all hell breaks loose and you find yourself having to recover e-mail from the client side, recovering them from the .ost file can be cumbersome. There is no import/export option for the .ost files as there is for the .pst file and you will find yourself looking at expensive third-party tools.

Configure SUS Using Group Policy

The automatic Software Update Service (SUS) is a free tool for deploying patches to client workstations. You can download SUS from the Microsoft Web site and install and configure it to either of the following:

1. **Host the SUS updates locally**, where the client computers get all updates installed from the local computer. This will require only a single download to patch all clients, but be sure to have at least 6 GB of space on the server. The first time you download SUS, it will take a considerable amount of time.

2. **Keep the updates on a Microsoft Windows Update Server** to which you will direct the clients. This will have each individual client connect and download, taking up considerable bandwidth, but will not take up any considerable amount of space on the server.

Updates should be checked and approved at least once a month, if not weekly. The easiest way to deploy SUS to the clients on the network is by creating a new Group Policy Object. To configure the GPO settings,

1. Go into the **Adavanced Management Console** and expand **Group Policy Management** down to the **MyBusiness** container.

2. Right-click the **MyBusiness** container and click on **Create and Link a GPO Here**.

3. Give the **New GPO** a descriptive name, like SUS, and click **OK**.

4. Expand the **MyBusiness** container and **right-click** on the **SUS policy object** and click **Edit**.

5. Go to **Computer Configuration, Administrative Templates, Windows Components** and click on **Windows Update** to expand the settings.

6. Click on **Configure Automatic Updates,** then click **Enable**.

In the **Configure Automatic Updates Properties,** you can now select to either:

- **Notify for download and notify for install** – This will create a local notification message to prompt the download and installation.

- **Auto download and notify for install** - This will automatically download updates and prompt for the install.

- **Auto download and schedule the install** - This will automatically download and install the new updates.

You can also choose the **scheduled install day** as well as the **scheduled install time**. If you want the clients to get updated from the local SUS server:

1. Click on **Next** and choose **Enabled** in the **Specify intranet Microsoft update service location Properties** box.

2. Type the address of the SUS server, **http://*SBSServerName***, in both boxes and click **OK**.

Important: Yes, we are aware that Small Business Server 2003 R2 is out – but the fact remains that the current 70-282 exam is based on the original version of Small Business Server 2003. Visit www. smbnation.com and click on the 70-282 Update link to get the latest status on the 70-282 exam, if anything changes we will be sure to let you know!

Resolve Client Computer Connectivity Issues

It never fails, regardless of how much you plan a new install, there will always be the oddball machine that has to act differently than any other machine on the network, and despite having the same hardware, etc., displays its own individual behavior by refusing to play nice. Or you will have an installation that has been running smoothly for the longest time and for no apparent reason (i.e., nothing obvious you can immediately pinpoint) the network connectivity has become flawed. Mostly these will be isolated incidents pertaining to individual computers, but at times it will bedevil several machines simultaneously, leaving you stumped and clueless as to where to start tracing the issue.

SBS comes with some troubleshooting information included in the **Small Business Server Help and Information** file, and at http://www.microsoft.com/ sbs there is a **Support** link that will lead you to several support choices including a **Troubleshooting** link that refers to the top troubleshooting issues for SBS 2003. If none of these resolve your current issue, you need to reach for the network troubleshooting utilities.

Network Troubleshooting Utilities

There are several utilities available that help diagnose and resolve networking problems. Besides checking the above-mentioned troubleshooting help files, there is also TechNet (http://www.microsoft.com/technet) and, of course, the built-in troubleshooting tools in Windows Server 2003. You can start troubleshooting by using:

- Event Viewer
- Network Diagnostics
- Command Line tools

The **Event Viewer** records events in the Application, Security, and System logs. The SBS server will also have Directory Service, DNS Server, and File Replication Service logs. By first checking the event viewer, you can find out about possible hardware, software, or system problems that could be the cause of your network connectivity issue. Usually, the Event Viewer will provide a

Source and an **Event ID**, which you can then use to investigate the issue on TechNet or Google. (Yes, Google is an excellent search tool for Microsoft Event IDs). More on the Event Viewer later in this chapter.

The **Network Diagnostics** tool, which is located in the **Help and Support Center**, performs a series of tests to help isolate causes of network-related issues. It will check the system for network connectivity and whether network related programs and services are running on the computer. To access Network Diagnostics:

1. Click on **Start,** then click on **Help and Support.**

2. Click on **Tools** and in the left pane expand the **Help and Support Center tools.**

3. Click on **Network Diagnostics** in the left pane, then click on **Scan your system** in the right pane. You can click on **Set scanning options** to see the several choices for which Network Diagnostics will gather information.

There are too many command line tools to cover them all, but you can see the entire list in the Help and Support Center Tools by clicking on Tools by Category and then selecting Network Services Management Tools. There are some all-time favorites to help you troubleshoot network connectivity on you network, like:

•   Arp – Arp a displays the Address Resolution Protocol (ARP) cache for stored IP addresses and their resolved MAC address.

•   Ipconfig – Ipconfig /all displays the full TCP/IP configuration for all adapters, including subnet, gateway, and IP address.

•   Nbtstat – Nbtstat displays the NetBIOS name resolution statistics. This requires your Windows XP machine or Windows 2003 server to be configured with WINS. Eventually, WINS should go away.

•   Pathping – Pathping *IPaddress* will provide information on network latency and network loss between intermediate hops between the source and a destination. It will help you determine the degree of packet loss at any given router or link.

Of course, there are also Ping, netstat, netdiag, NSLookup, and Network Monitor as well as additional tools that can be installed from the SBS Disc #1 Support Tools folder or from the Windows Resource Kit. Either way, make sure to be familiar with individual troubleshooting tools including their command line switches. Please visit the list in the Help and Support Center for descriptions on command line tool switches.

IMPORTANT: More troubleshooting and utilities discussion later in this chapter and Chapter 10.

Back Up and Restore Windows Small Business Server 2003.

Recently, I went on a 25-city Hands-On-Lab training tour that included a Disaster Recovery Session for SBS. Microsoft had wanted a bare-metal restore lab. If you have done a bare-metal restore before, you know that according to Microsoft SBS white paper ideology, you first reinstall the operating system from Disc #1 of the SBS disc set, then after the reboot of the GUI portion install, and before going into the Small Business Server 2003 Installation Wizard, you connect your backup media device, load the drivers, and then do a full restore to the server. That of course goes with the assumption that the data on the backup media was placed there by running the Configure Backup Wizard. Now, the Configure Backup Wizard is a cool wizard to have when you don't know anything about backing up data, but as it turns out, most IT professionals choose a third-party backup solution, which was confirmed every time I posed this question.

So, why is there so much discontent? The reasoning echoed is that the Configure Backup Wizard really uses the NTbackup utility in Windows Server 2003 (configured by the Small Business Backup.bks script located in %systemdrive%\ program files\Microsoft Windows Small Business Server\Backup folder), which has had a bad rap in the past. Fickleness and oddities about NTbackup utility behavior have made this utility a great discussion topic, as well as creating many frustrated system admins.

Volume Shadow Copy technology (covered in a bit), which is new to Windows Server 2003 and being embraced by many consultants, plays a big part in the SBS data availability and recovery model.

Creating a Backup Job Using the Backup Configuration Wizard

The Backup Configuration Wizard is located under the **Backup** link in the Standard Management Console. The wizard not only allows you to make a full system backup, it also lets you set the **Deleted Item Retention** for Exchange e-mails and the size of the Volume Shadow Copy snapshot. Having all tools in one wizard follows the "keep it simple" SBS methodology and kudos to the person who thought this up. It's like having the "one-stop-backup-shop." Of course, as several Hot-Lab attendees have pointed out, there is always room for improvement, but remember that the wizards and entire SBS methodology was designed for nontechnical people. Good thing Microsoft didn't succeed all the way, or we would be looking for work.

Backup Configuration Wizard

Once you launch the wizard, the first screen will ask in what location to place the backup data. Two choices are offered:

- Back up to a tape drive [recommended].
- Back up to a local hard disk or network share.

By default, the backup wizard will back up ALL data on the server (except for default excluded files) including the System State comprised of:

- Boot files, including the system files.
- Files protected by the Windows File Protection (WFP).
- Registry.
- Performance counter configuration information.
- Component Services class registration database.

Also backed up are all other data folders, as well as the Exchange database, SharePoint database, and SQL databases, including open files with the help of the Volume Shadow Copy Service (explained more in a bit).

Exclude Folders

You can then manually select to exclude certain folders from the backup. This option is useful when you, say, have a 60 GB hard disk and only a 20 GB tape drive; you would want to exclude all the junk data (disposable data that would not have a financial or operational impact on the business if it wasn't restored immediately after a disaster) and select to leave only the pertinent high-value (mission-critical, immediate financial, or operational impact) data folders included in the backup.

Define Backup Schedule

By default, the Define Backup Schedule page starts the backups at 11 p.m. and has Monday – Friday selected. Here you can change the schedule and select a different time of day. You can only create one backup job with the Backup Configuration Wizard. If you would want to set up a nightly differential backup and a Friday full backup, you will still have to use NTbackup to define a more sophisticated backup job.

Tape Changer

You have the ability to select the tape changer—no, that is not your tape backup device. In this case it will be the person designated as the official "Tape Changer," who will be in charge of manually changing the tapes in the server. Setting this option will send a reminder e-mail to the person at a designated time; you can also set it to send a monthly tape drive cleaning reminder.

IMPORTANT: It strikes both authors that this type of oddity is the type of thing that could appear on the 70-282 exam.

Storage Allocation for Deleted Files and E-mail

Here you can set the option to **Retain copies of permanently deleted e-mail messages**, which will allow you to bring back deleted e-mails, even if they were deleted with the Shift+Ctrl keys. By default, this is set to 30 days and you can bump it up to any number of days you would like. Just keep in mind that even though the deleted item does not count against your 16 GB mailbox store limit, this will take up space in the Recovery store, so you don't want to overdo it. Keep it at about 120 to 160 days. By configuring this setting in the

Backup Configuration Wizard, you don't have to go into the Exchange System Manager. Deleted e-mails can then be retrieved from the Outlook client under **Tools** by clicking on **Recovery Deleted Items.**

The **Enable periodic snapshots of users' shared folders** option will let you configure the amount of space you can allocate for the Shadow Volume Copy snapshot. When you redirect the user's MyDocuments folder (covered earlier in the Standard Management section), this will be the amount allocated to store the snapshot. More on VSS later in this chapter.

Excluded Files

Now, when we say "backs up ALL files," that is, of course, with the exclusion of "default-excluded files," like temporary files, such as:

- Pagefile.sys
- Hiberfil.sys
- Win386.swp
- 386spart.par
- Backup.log
- Restore.log.

If you are backing up from a network share on a remote computer, backup skips these files if they are in use at the time of the backup.

Volume Shadow Service (During Backup)

Volume Shadow Service (VSS) requires NTFS as the file system. VSS is a copy technology that provides an instant copy of the original volume. When the backup is initiated, a shadow copy of the volume is made even though the original volume continues to change as the process continues. The shadow copy of the volume will remain constant. Users can continue to access files while you are running the backup job. Once the data is backed up to media, the shadow copy will be deleted.

You can summarize VSS advantages to include benefits such as:

- Computers can be backed up while applications and services are running.

- Files will not be skipped during the backup process.

- Files that are open at the time of the shadow copy appear closed on the shadow copy volume.

- There is no need to shut down applications or services to ensure a successful volume backup.

IMPORTANT: **Caveat Emptor!** The NTFS volume stores the difference between the original volume and the shadow copy volume in a record, and the data on the shadow copy volume exists only while the shadow copy is being taken. There has to be sufficient disk space available for the volume shadow copy, or the service will shut down and Backup will skip the open files.

If you purchase a third-party backup solution, make sure to verify that it can register with writer interfaces and make use of the Volume Shadow Copy technology.

Volume Shadow Service (Periodic Snapshots)

Volume Shadow Copies are enabled by default in SBS. You can check the settings by going to **C:**, clicking on the local disk properties, then clicking the **Shadow Copies** tab. Its purpose is to keep previous versions of users' files and is therefore called "Previous Versions." Accessing previous versions can be useful when users need to:

- **Recover accidentally deleted files.**

- **Recover from accidentally overwritten files.**

- **Compare different file versions.**

Previous Client Version

Snapshots are taken at 7 a.m. and 12 noon, Monday through Friday, and can be manually modified to fit a different schedule. Shadow Copies will keep up to 64 versions before overwriting the last one.

The snapshot is being taken on the volume that occupies the **Users Shared Folders** by default. When you have **Client Document Redirection** enabled, documents that are placed into the MyDocuments folder on a user's computer are automatically placed in the Users Shared Folders where Volume Shadow Copies Service will take the snapshot. If a user accidentally deletes a file, he can right-click on his **MyDocuments** folder where he has the **Previous Versions** tab and be able to recover the previous version of the document from that point in time when the last snapshot was taken.

Backup Location and Media Considerations

Historically, the preferred backup location has been a tape drive, as the tape can then be moved off-site after the backup is completed. With disaster recovery becoming a more prominent item due to HIPAA compliance and other legislative requirements, terrorist acts, hurricanes, and the likes, technology is switching to support, not only recovery - business continuity despite a catastrophe. There are more solutions available and affordable now with dropping hardware prices and technology improvements, allowing more small businesses to afford RAID arrays, NAS storage, and other previously too-high-priced-to-afford solutions. Small businesses back up to removable hard drives, DVDs, network shares, even over the web, and in general have become more sophisticated about disaster recovery and prevention.

A balance must be struck between the price of the recovery solution and the availability and cost of the backup media. There is no point in having an inexpensive solution if it will take you days to recover and get back to the point of being operable. In the meantime, the business may have lost a million dollar contract or been unable to deliver on a deadline. Then again, there is no point in spending dollars on having the latest high-tech recovery solution only to use it to back up not just mission-critical data, but also junk data that has no business on the server or should have been removed eons ago.

Unfortunately, there is no one-size-fits-all formula, and considerations of media and backup location will have to be carefully weighed against the impact of financial and operational loss that will be caused due to irrecoverable data.

Restoring From a Backup Job

So, the unexpected happened and you had corrupted or damaged data to the point where you have to recover the entire server. One business where I was performing a backup job got hit with the "I love you" virus just as I was running the backup. After containing the outbreak, we started to restore from the backup tape and guess what? It all started over again! Well, lucky enough, we were on a regular rotation schedule and ended up only losing one day's worth of work, but the impact could have been much worse.

In a rosy-rose world (the Microsoft exam view), you are on a regular tape backup schedule, there are no tapes that fail, and, of course, you are able to recover to the same hardware as before. So now you are ready to use the backup utility and have a backup on a tape, hard drive, or network share.

You can launch the NTbackup utility by typing **ntbackup** in the **Run** command. You want to select the **Advanced Mode** and click on the **Restore and Manage Media** tab.

Select the media you will be restoring from and decide whether to restore to one of the following:

- **Original location** – if you had to replace a failed drive for instance.
- **Alternate location** – especially if you are not sure of the data integrity and only have to restore a few files, you should not restore into the original location.

If the restore turns out to be bad, and you restored the entire tape into the original location, you just shot your last chance of possibly doing a last resort data recovery of the hard drive.

Before you initiate the actual restore, click on **Advanced** and make sure that you have:

- **Restore security,**
- **Restore junction points, restore file, and folder data under junction point to the original location,**
- **Preserve existing volume mount points** checked.

Click **OK** and wait and see! The restore will finish and display a message that the restore is completed. Click **OK** again. You may want to also check the Report to ensure the successful restore.

Another method for restoring individual files would be using the **Previous Versions Client** to restore individual files. Some installations will have an entire hard drive dedicated to take a snapshot of an entire volume. You can enable the snapshot by modifying the settings in the Local Disk Properties on the **Shadow Copies** tab. First disable the current snapshot, then click on **Settings.** You can use the dropdown in the **Storage area** to select the drive you dedicated for the volume snapshot and set the **Maximum size** to **No limit.** Then click on **Schedule** and set your preferences.

Monitor and Troubleshoot Windows Small Business Server 2003

SBS 2003 comes with the Monitoring Configuration Wizard from which you can set up alert notifications and enable application logging. The Monitor Configuration Wizard will configure settings in **Health Monitor** which for some reason is no longer part of the Server Management Console. To access Health Monitor, click on **Start, Administrative Tools,** then **Health Monitor.** You will have to first run the Monitoring Configuration Wizard before the Alerts show up in Health Monitor. Another great monitoring tool is the **Performance Monitor**, which will require manual configuration.

Configuring Monitoring and Alerts

You set up Monitoring by way of running the Monitoring Configuration Wizard which will create server performance and usage reports that can either be e-mailed or viewed from Server Management or on the intranet. In the Server Management Console,

1. Click on **Monitoring and Reporting** to launch the wizard.

2. On the **Configuration Mode** screen, select **Modify existing settings** and click **Next**.

3. On the **Reporting Options** screen, under **Performance Report,** select **Receive a daily performance report in e-mail**, and under the **Usage Report**, check **View the usage report in Server Management** and **Receive a usage report in e-mail every other week.**

4. Enter an **E-mail address** on the **E-mail Options** screen.

5. Specify who you want to have access to the usage report by adding respective user names.

6. On the **Alerts** screen, select **Send me notification of performance alerts by e-mail** and enter your e-mail address. Now the Monitor Configuration Wizard will configure the:

- Data Store
- Data Collection
- Alert Threshold
- Configure Reports

Performance data is collected hourly, so it will take a bit before you can view your first report. By selecting to receive the report by e-mail on a daily basis, you configured the Server to send you a report every morning at 6 a.m., which is a default setting that can be changed to a different time. I do prefer the 6 a.m. schedule because this way I know first thing in the morning that the server is up and running. If there are critical events or alerts, it is still early enough for me to look over the issue and remote manage the server and not have to interrupt my clients in the middle of the day in case the server requires a reboot.

Performance, Usage, and Server Status Reports

What can I say, they are cool! In SBS 2000 we had the xml reporting tool, which provided great information but was a bit cumbersome to use because you had to save the files and, and, and—there were just too many steps involved. Being able to receive the reports now in e-mail in html format has made life as an administrator so much easier. The performance report contains detailed information about the overall health of the server. The daily server performance report includes:

- **Server Specifications** – displays information on the OS, Processor, Speed, and the amount of RAM.

- **Performance Summary** – displays Memory in use, free disk space, disk busy time, CPU use, and the rate of change/growth over the last month.

- **Top 5 Processes by Memory Usage** – displays the process using up the most memory.

- **Top 5 Processes by CPU Usage** – displays the processes using up the most CPU cycles

- **Backup** – displays whether the Backup completed successfully or with errors.

- **Auto-started Services Not Running** – displays services that are set to auto start and should be running, but are not.

- **Critical Alerts.**

- **Critical Errors in the Event Logs.**

You can also attach event viewer log files and the backup log status to be sent with the daily performance or the usage report. To attach the files, you have to go into the **Change Server Status Report Settings** tool and select from:

- **Application Event Log**

- **IIS Log**

- **SBS Backup Logs**

- **Security Event Log**

- **System Event Log**

In a daily performance report, as shown in Figure 8-6, you first get a summary view, which, if there are any problems, lets you drill down to **Details** and provide an Event Viewer view of the log file, including Event ID and Source.

Notes:

Figure 8-6
Daily Performance Report Summary View.

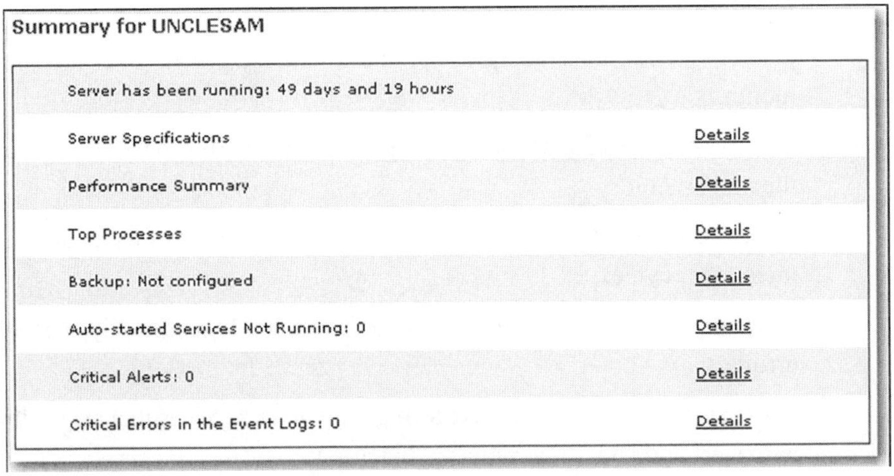

```
Summary for UNCLESAM

    Server has been running: 49 days and 19 hours

    Server Specifications                              Details

    Performance Summary                                Details

    Top Processes                                      Details

    Backup: Not configured                             Details

    Auto-started Services Not Running: 0               Details

    Critical Alerts: 0                                 Details

    Critical Errors in the Event Logs: 0              Details
```

Usage Reports are a great tool for business owners to get a quick glimpse of what is going on. If you have an owner who wants to know everything from web usage to applications used, I suggest you install ISA Server which is an excellent reporting tool.

> IMPORTANT: Remember that reporting and configuring are not the same actions.

The Usage report is composed of:

- **Web Activity by Computer** – displaying the total active and average active hours per day.

- **Web Traffic by Hour** – displays the total connection and average connections per day.

- **E-mail Sent** – displays the amount of internal and external e-mail sent, including the size in MB.

- **E-mail Received** – displays the amount of internal and external e-mail received, including the size in MB.

- **Mailbox size** – displays the mailbox starting size and ending size for the last two weeks and the rate of change in %.

- **Outlook Web Access Activity by User** – displays who accessed OWA, how many visits, and the average visits per day.

- **Outlook Web Access Usage by Hour** – displays the hours of the day and total and average visits during these hours.

- **Remote Connection Activity by User** – displays the user name and total VPN connections and the average time and average connections per day.

- **Remote Connection Activity by Hour** – displays the hours and average connections per day during these hours.

- **Fax Sent** – displays faxes sent to destination, total faxes, average amount of pages, the average transmission time, and average number of faxes per day.

- **Faxes Received** - displays faxes received from, total faxes, average amount of pages, the average transmission time, and the average number of faxes per day.

- **Faxes sent by User** – displays faxes sent by user to, total faxes, average amount of pages, the average transmission time, and the average number of faxes per day.

- **Fax Traffic by Hour** – displays fax traffic by the hour of the day, total faxes, and average number of faxes per day.

It is good business to e-mail forward the usage reports to the business owners, as well as the performance reports on a regular basis. This way your client sees that you are truly monitoring her network, as well as helping her keep tabs on employees. We recently had a case where a user started working from remote. When the first usage report came in, we discovered the user had connected only once in two weeks for less than 30 minutes! Needless to say, the employer that had been paying a full-time salary was able to take corrective action based on the report. Certainly this would have been discovered eventually, but why not find out sooner and have it documented?

In Figure 8-7 is a detail cut-out on E-mail Received, which tells us right away who is giving out their business e-mail address to Internet sites they should stay OFF! (And this is after the spam filter…)

Figure 8-7
E-mail received cutout from a Usage Summary Report over a two-week period of time.

E-mail Received						
User Name	Internal E-mail	Size (MB)	External E-mail	Size (MB)	Total E-mail Received	Size (MB)
James Taylor	0	0.0	690	3.6	690	3.6
Diane Welford	2	0.1	153	4.0	155	4.0
Debbie Dye	3	0.1	52	0.4	55	0.5
Tim Heffernan	2	0.1	48	1.1	50	1.2
Laura Peery	4	0.0	16	0.0	20	0.1
Administrator	2	0.1	1	0.0	3	0.2
Liz Dye	2	0.1	1	0.0	3	0.1
Lynda Pritchard	2	0.0	1	0.0	3	0.0
Andrea Wilson	0	0.0	1	0.0	1	0.0
Jennifer Walter	1	0.0	0	0.0	1	0.0
Company Total	18	0.6	963	9.1	981	9.7

Changing Alert Notifications

You can configure a change alert notification by going to the **Health Monitor** snap-in and right-clicking the **Actions** node, then clicking on **New.** You will be able to configure an Action as a response to an Alert. You can configure the following Actions:

- **Command Line** – executes a file that can be run from the command line.

- **E-Mail** – Sends SMTP e-mail to a specified recipient.

- **Text Log** – Writes text that you specify to a specified test-based log file.

- **Windows Event** – Generates a event that will be written to the application log in the Event Viewer.

- **Script** – Runs a WSH (Windows Scripting Host) that you specify.

An alert is generated when a defined threshold is crossed, and the action is a response to the alert.

Small Business Server Troubleshooter Utilities

SBS comes with a variety of built-in troubleshooter utilities. These utilities will help you diagnose and solve technical issues. The troubleshooters are interactive and will require you to answer a series of questions about the problems you have encountered. Each troubleshooter utility addresses a different problem, based on the answers you provide. Troubleshooters are listed in table 8-2.

Table 8-2
Small Business Server Troubleshooter Utilities.

Troubleshooter	Identifies and resolves problems related to:
System Setup	Installing and setting up Windows.
Startup/Shutdown	Starting up and shutting down your computer.
Display	Video cards and video adapters, including your computer screen, outdated or incompatible video drivers, and incorrect settings for your video hardware.
Home Networking	Setup, Internet connections, sharing files and printers.
Hardware	Disk drives (including CD-ROM and DVD drives), game controllers, input devices (such as keyboards, mice, cameras, scanners, and infrared devices), network adapters, USB devices,modems, and sound cards. Also see the more specific hardware device troubleshooters below.
Multimedia and Games	Games and other multimedia programs, DirectXdrivers, USB devices, digital video discs (DVDs), sound, joysticks, and related issues.
Digital Video Discs (DVDs)	DVD drives and decoders.
Input Devices	Keyboards, mouse and trackball devices, cameras, scanners, and infrared devices.

Troubleshooter	Identifies and resolves problems related to:
Drives and Network Adapters	Hard discs, floppy discs, CD-ROM and DVD drives, network cards, tape drives, backup programs.
USB	USB connectors and peripherals.
Sound	Sound and sound cards.
Modem	Modem connections, setup, configuration, and detection.
Internet and Connection Sharing	Connecting and logging on to your Internet service provider (ISP).
Internet Explorer	Browsing the web, downloading files, saving your favorites, using IE toolbars, or printing web pages.
Outlook Express	Outlook Express and Windows Messenger Service.
File and Print Sharing	Sharing files and printers between computers, connecting to other computers in a network, installing network adapters, logging on.
Printing	Printer installation and connection, printer drivers, print quality, printer speed, and fonts.

Troubleshoot Outlook Web Access

Remember the problem where your client accessed Outlook Web Access (OWA) one day, simply checked some e-mails, and then the next day she couldn't get into the site? You hadn't installed new service packs or applications on the server and the log files all came up clean, but OWA just decided on its own to not work that day. There are so many factors that come into play when troubleshooting OWA, from possible issues with Exchange and IIS to web browser settings and authentication methods used.

Outlook Web Access Basic/Premium

When accessing OWA, you may receive one of the following error messages:

- HTTP 401.1 – Unauthorized: Logon Failed
- Access is Denied
- Page Cannot Be Displayed

Or you can log on successfully but will be prompted to enter your credentials again. If you fail to type your user name in the **domain/username** format, you get be faced with one of the following:

- Logon failed or cancelled message.
- After you provided the correct credentials, the OWA page doesn't load.
- You can log on with Netscape, but not use any other browsers.

Most of these issues occur if users have not been granted the correct permissions or use an incorrect authentication method. Also, a combination of IIS 6.0 on a Windows Server 2003 with Exchange Server 2003 requires entering the **domain\username**. (This has been fixed with KB831464.)

By default, Integrated Authentication is enabled in Exchange Server 2000 SP3 and later on the Outlook Web Access folder. You should try using basic authentication when:

- Integrated Windows Authentication between the client browser and the web server isn't functioning and a proxy server exists between the client browser and the web server.
- Integrated Windows Authentication fails because there is a time difference between the client and the server.
- Web Proxy clients using SecureNAT in ISA Server experience issues trying to authenticate to OWA.

There are workarounds to these issues. You could also try to:

- Remove Integrated Windows Authentication from the OWA site.

- Add the FQDN, the IP address of the Outlook Web Access server, or both to the Do not use proxy server for addresses beginning with list in the advanced proxy settings of the LAN settings in the Internet Explorer options.

- Install the ISA firewall client and add the FQDN of the OWA site to the local domain table in ISA Server.

Okay, the point is — use TechNet. There are several KB articles on troubleshooting OWA access and when I went to the Knowledge Base and entered, "Outlook web access," it came back with 100 KBs! There is something for everyone.

OWA Client-Side Troubleshooting Remedies

If you are experiencing trouble accessing OWA, try these steps on the client first before changing any settings on the server side.

- Clear the browser cache and history. Also check http://windowsupdate.microsoft.com for critical updates for the operating system and browser.

- Delete temporary Internet files and cookies.

- Reset all Internet Explorer settings to default.

- Ensure you are using IE5.01 or later to use the premium version of OWA. (Some features will work only with IE6.0.)

- Set the browser to use SSL.

- Accept and install the site certificate.

- Set the browser to accept cookies.

- If OWA loads but the right pane is stuck on "loading," make sure to add the site to your trusted sites.

- If you use Windows 98 or 98SE and you are using IE6.0 and the right pane remains empty, you may need to install the Java plug-in for IE.

Notes:

Troubleshoot Company Network Connections to an Internet Service Provider (ISP)

Once in a while you will have issues with Internet connectivity, and your ISP will tell you it's your server, at which point you have to pull out the tools to show them otherwise. We have already discussed some troubleshooting tools useful for LAN issues, and some of those tools work for Internet connectivity as well.

- GetMac – GetMac.exe is a quick way to get your MAC address.

- IPConfig – IPConfig displays the current configuration of your IP stack.

- Network Connectivity Tester – Netdiag.exe gathers static network information and tests the network driver, protocol driver, send/receive capability, and well-known target vulnerabilities.

- Nslookup – Nslookup.exe performs DNS queries and examines content of zone files on local and remote servers.

- Trace Route – Tracert.exe traces the connection pathways between the source and destination including the amount of hops and the time.

- Network Monitor – Netcap.exe monitors network traffic and captures information to a log file.

- Netsh – Netsh.exe is a command line scripting utility that displays and lets you modify network configuration.

There are several command line switches with these tools. We recommend you check them out individually by going to http://www.microsoft.com and typing each command into the Microsoft Search. Also, see the section, "Troubleshooting Utilities" in Chapter 10.

> IMPORTANT: Given that a common call to SBS consultants from customers is, "I can't connect to the Internet," don't you think it's likely there would be this type of question on the 70-282 exam?

Event Viewer

When it comes to troubleshooting, the Event Viewer should always be the first tool checked for logged error messages. It will give you clues to help discover problem areas with the server as well as the applications running on it. The Event Viewer allows you to view, clear, save, filter, and find Events.

Events are broken down into Event Types as shown in table 8-3. Each event is a particular type, and there are five types of events that are reported. Event logs include the date, time, source, category, and Event ID.

Table 8-3
Event Types

Event Type	Description
Information	This indicates a significant, successful operation—for example, an event indicating that a service has started.
Warning	Warning events indicate problems that are not immediately significant, but could cause problems in the future. Resource consumption is a good example of a warning event.
Error	Error events indicate significant problems the user should know about. Error events usually indicate a loss of functionality or data.
Failure Audit	Failure audit events are security events that occur when an audited access attempt fails. A failed attempt to open a file (due to lack of permissions) is an example of a failure audit event.
Success Audit	Success audit events are security events that occur when an audited access attempt succeeds.

Now, you open the Event Viewer and are inundated with a gazillion log entries. Don't cry; simply specify a filter that limits the type of information that you want Event Viewer to display. To filter events:

1. Click **Start**, **Programs**, **Administrative Tools**, and then **Event Viewer.**

2. In the console tree, right-click the appropriate log file, and then click **Properties**.

3. Click the **Filter** tab.

4. Type the appropriate information that you would like to filter and click **OK**.

You can filter for an event based on the five event types or by source, user, computer, or date of the event. This really helps when sorting through large log files. Now that events are filtered by your particular criteria, you may want to find an event based on a user name or computer within the filter, a category, or a source. To use the Find function:

1. Click **Start**, **Programs**, **Administrative Tools**, and then **Event Viewer**.

2. In the console tree, right-click the appropriate log file.

3. On the **View** menu, click **Find**.

4. Type the appropriate information you would like to find in the dialog box, and then click **Find Next.**

Make the Event Viewer your friend and combine it with other troubleshooting tools and the TechNet Knowledge Base, and you will rarely have to call Product Support Services.

IMPORTANT: By the way, an old trick Microsoft Certified Partners have used to obtain an MCSE is to "burn" or use one of their five free Product Support Service incidents to get the smarties at Microsoft to walk the caller through a tough exam area. That is, burn a support incident as a study tool. In your case, you might have to find a partner with support incidents left to burn. Try a local user group meeting to meet such a person.

Practice Questions

Question #1:

In SBS 2003 what is the purpose of the "Tape Changer"? (Choose the best answer.)

a. It is the library attachment that automatically changes the tape in the tape drive when full.

b. The person who changes the tape in the tape drive.

c. Software utility designed to reformat disk-based .bkf files to raw tape format for off-site storage.

d. The person who is designated to receive an e-mail message reminding them to change the tape in the tape drive.

Question #2:

You have configured your customer's SBS server's backup jobs but there appears to be a problem. Examination of the backup logs reveals several errors related to files being in use and the backup jobs never complete cleanly. Which of the following would you investigate as a possible cause of this issue? (Choose the best answer.)

a. The backup process is running under the wrong user context and does not have the privileges required to lock files for non-exclusive use.

b. The VSS service is stopping because of inadequate disk space. As a result open files cannot be backed up.

c. The directories dedicated for backup share processing have not been globally shared.

d. Client Document Redirection is not enabled on the affected volumes.

Question #3:

Which of the following are included in the SBS 2003 Performance Report? (Choose all that apply.)

a. Mailbox Size.

b. Top 5 processes by memory.

c. Critical Alerts.

d. Fax traffic by hour.

e. Backup.

Question #4:

Which of the following are included in the SBS 2003 Usage Report? (Choose all that apply.)

a. Mailbox Size.

b. Top five processes by memory.

c. Critical Alerts.

d. Fax traffic by hour.

e. Remote Connection Activity by User.

Question #5:

Your customer's sales force travels a great deal and it is important that they have the ability to keep the e-mail on their laptops as up-to-date as possible whether their current internet connection is extremely fast or not. It is also important for them to read and work on their e-mail while they are not connected at all, with assurance that once they are connected any e-mail they have modified or created is sent and new e-mail is received. Which of the below technology will meet these requirements? (Choose the best answer.)

a. Remote Web Workplace (RWW).

b. Cached Exchange Mode.

c. Remote Desktop Protocol (RDP).

d. Exchange Web Access.

e. Connection Manager.

Question #6:

You installed SBS 2003 with 25 CALs and 25 workstations for your customer a year ago. He now wants to purchase the additional licenses and workstations necessary to add five additional local users and computers to the SBS network. Which of the following are some of the utilities you will need to access in order to properly complete the tasks necessary to add the users and computers? (Choose all that apply.)

a.   Client Computer menu item.

b.   Connection Manager.

c.   Active Directory Users and Computers.

d.   Server Management Console.

e.   Users menu item.

Question #7:

You've created the users and computer accounts and want to complete the installation of the five additional workstations. Which of the following is the browser command required to finish the installation of the workstations? (Choose the correct answer.)

a.   http://www.microsoft.com/SBS/WindowsClient.aspx

b.   http://SBSServerName/connectcomputer /WS:_new

c.   http://SBSServerName/Net_Add -WS1,WS2,WS3.WS4,WS5

d.   http://SBSServerName/connectcomputer

Question #8:

Which of the following may be an issue for MAC clients in an SBS 2003 domain? (Choose the best answer.)

a.   domain.prv

b.   domain.local

c.   domain.mac

d.   domain.office

Question #9:

Your SBS 2003 customer wants a Group Policy defined that will force user applications to be installed automatically when they logon. How is this accomplished? (Choose the correct answer.)

a.   Use the Group Policy Management Console to create and link a GPO to the MyBusiness container to publish the desired application.

b.   Use the Group Policy Management Console to create and link a GPO to the Computers container to publish the desired application.

c. Use the Group Policy Management Console to create and link a GPO to the MyBusiness container to assign the desired application.

d. Use the Group Policy Management Console to create and link a GPO to the Computers container to assign the desired application.

Question #10:

Your customer is complaining that his SBS 2003 backup never completes before the tape in the tape drive is full. What can you do to try and alleviate the problem? (Choose the correct answer.)

a. Relocate the user directories to another SBS volume.

b. Insure all users are logged off before the backup utility is invoked.

c. Open the Server Management Console and run the Backup wizard. Use it to exclude directories and subdirectories from each of the volumes.

d. Upgrade the capacity of the tape in the tape drive.

Question #11:

What utility is invoked to determine which GPOs are being applied to an object within active directory? (Choose the correct answer.)

a. Group Policy Management Console.

b. GPMC.

c. RSoP.

d. Precedence Tool.

Question #12:

Which of the following can be successfully joined to an SBS 2003 domain using the http://SBSServerName/connectcomputer browser command. (Choose all that apply.)

a. Windows ME

b. Windows 95

c. MAC OS X

d. NT 4.0 SP4a

e. Linux

Question #13:

Your customer wants to retain deleted Exchange e-mail for up to 6 months. Where is this configured. (Choose the correct answer.)

a. Backup link in the System Management Console.

b. Exchange Administrator, SMTP, deleted items retention tab.

c. In Outlook 2003 mailbox properties.

d. Using the ExMerge /retention command.

Question #14:

Your customer is concerned about down time. He would like his system and backup configured in such a way as to minimize data loss, while at the same time provide a means to restore operation as quickly as possible should a disaster occur. Which would be the proper choice for this customer? (Choose all that apply.)

a. RAID 1 (mirrored) disks, with full backups to tape.

b. RAID 1 (mirrored) disks, with full backups to disk.

c. RAID 1 (mirrored) disks, with full backups to rotated external disk drives.

d. RAID 0 disk, with incremental backup to tape.

Answers

Question #1: Answer: d

a. Incorrect. Though it seems this is the obvious hardware answer, it is not the correct one.

b Incorrect! Though nearly correct. Read all of the presented answers before deciding which one is correct.

c. Incorrect! There is no such utility.

d. Correct! It is the person designated to receive the e-mail reminding them to mount a fresh tape. It can also be configured to notify when the tape drive requires cleaning.

Question #2: Answer: b

a. Incorrect! The backup process runs under a special service account named (of all things) "backup user," but even so that would not be the problem. "Locking" files for "non-exclusive use" seems somewhat contradictory, doesn't it?

b. Correct! The Volume Shadow Service (VSS) will take a "snapshot" or instant copy of the data to be backed up. If there is not enough disk space available for the temporary file containing the shadow copy file, the VSS service will stop and open files will not be backed up.

c. Incorrect! Backup does not require special directories to be created and "global sharing" is not a valid option anywhere.

d. Incorrect! Would not affect backup at all.

Question #3: Answer: b, c

a. Incorrect! Mailbox size is not a performance or health indicator.

b. Correct! A listing of which five processes use the most memory would be a performance or health indicator.

c. Correct! Critical alerts would be a health indicator.

d. Incorrect! The amount of fax traffic per hour is not a performance or heath indicator.

e. Correct! The status of the server backup would be considered a health indicator.

Question #4: Answer: a, d ,e

a. Correct! Mailbox size would be an indicator of disk space usage.

b. Incorrect! Top five processes by memory is a dynamic indicator and does not affect permanent resource usage.

c. Incorrect! Critical alerts would be a health indicator.

d. Correct! The amount of fax traffic per hour does reflect the amount of time the resource is in use.

e. Correct! Remote Connection Activity by User does reflect the amount of time the resource is in use.

Question #5: Answer: b

a. Incorrect! RWW will allow you to connect remotely but does not provide any services when you cannot connect.

b. Correct! Cached Exchange Mode does not only what is asked from an e-mail perspective, but also provides similar functionality for the Calendar, Contacts, and defined Public and other folders as well.

c. Incorrect! RDP will allow you to connect to a remote system, but provides no functionality if you cannot get a connection.

d. Incorrect! Exchange Web Access is a window into the folders on the Exchange server and does not update folders on the user's laptop. It also does not provide any functionality without connectivity.

e. Incorrect! Connection Manager will download the components and configure the laptop for a VPN connection. Although it will provide the protocols necessary to connect securely to the Exchange server, it has no other involvement in the e-mail process. It provides no functionality without connectivity.

Question #6: Answer: a, d, e

a. Correct! The Client Computer menu item will add the new computers to the network and assign applications to them.

b. Incorrect! The Connection Manager is used to configure a VPN connection for remote users and does not apply here.

c. Incorrect! Definitely No! Resist all temptation to use this tool even if you have been using it for years in a Windows Server 2xWhateverxx environment (especially on the exam). Instead, rely on the task items within the Server Management Console to do the right thing – and they will!

d. Correct! This is your gateway to all things correct and properly configured in an SBS environment. Use it and you will be rewarded, Grasshopper. (Whoops, showing my age (again)).

e. Correct! The Users menu item will create the users and put them in the proper OU with all the correct privileges for you – ain't life grand?

Question #7: Answer: d

a. Incorrect! Not a valid link.

b. Incorrect! Not a valid switch.

c. Incorrect! Not a valid command.

d. Correct! This will initiate the Small Business Server Network Configuration Wizard to properly join the workstation to the domain, install assigned software, add users to the local administrators group, install published printers, and additional required tasks.

Question #8: Answer: b

a. Incorrect! This domain name should not be an issue.

b. Correct! Macs do not get along with the .local DNS name extension. It is recommended a different one is chosen or do not join the Mac to the domain.

c. Incorrect! This domain name should not be an issue.

d. Incorrect! This domain name should not be an issue.

Question #9: Answer: c

a. Incorrect! A published application is available to be installed but is not installed until it is required.

b. Incorrect! SBS client computers are not located in the Computers container.

c. Correct! An assigned application is automatically installed when the user logs in. The MyBusiness container is correct.

d. Incorrect! SBS client computers are not located in the Computers container.

Question #10: Answer: c

> a. Incorrect! The SBS 2003 backup job will backup all of the data on all of the volumes by default, including Exchange. Moving data from one volume to another does not change the total amount of data being backed up, only its location.
>
> b. Incorrect! Logging users off will have no impact on this issue.
>
> **c. Correct! Exclude directories and subdirectories on all volumes until the amount backed up does not exceed the capacity of the tape drive.**
>
> d. Incorrect! If only it were so easy.

Question #11: Answer: c

> a. Incorrect! The Group Policy Management Console will allow you to define. Set, and apply Group Policy, but does not allow you to directly see the result of the GPOs applied.
>
> b. Incorrect! GPMC is Group Policy Management Console.
>
> **c. Correct! Resultant Set of Policies (RSoP) allows you to see how existing GPOs are applied and their effect (logging mode). RSoP can also simulate the effect of GPOs on an object for planning and troubleshooting purposes.**
>
> d. Incorrect! No such utility.

Question #12: Answer: a, c

> **a. Correct! But just because you can doesn't mean you should!**
>
> b. Incorrect! Not supported.
>
> **c. Correct! Some manual setup may be required.**
>
> d. Incorrect! Must be SP6a with IE4.0.
>
> e. Incorrect! Not supported.

Question #13: Answer: a

> **a. Correct! The backup utility wizard allows you to set the deleted message retention time.**
>
> b. Incorrect! Invalid administrative function.

c. Incorrect! This setting would be global and not apply to a single user.

d. Incorrect! Invalid ExMerge function.

Question #14: Answer: c

a. Incorrect! Though this will back up the data, it does not allow for a speedy rebuilding of the system. Tape drives are very slow for backup or recovery as compared to backing up to a disk drive.

b. Incorrect! But better. Backing up to disk allows for much faster recovery should an issue occur, but because only a single external disk is attached there is no offsite storage of data.

c. Correct! Backing up to disk allows for much quicker backup and recovery and because the external drives are rotated one can be taken offsite for safekeeping. The RAID 1 array further minimizes the chances for data loss to begin with.

d. Incorrect! Not a good answer at all. RAID 0 provides no data protection.

Summary

This chapter represents a deep dive into SBS administration and support functions supporting the core Windows Server 2003 operating system in a small business environment. Special attention was paid to the configuration and deployment of Group Policy Objects. This is an area of much improvement in the Windows Server 2003 time frame and you should expect this to appear on the certification examination. Traditional functions such data protections, monitoring and basic troubleshooting were covered. The emphasis was clearly on SBS 2003 and how it interacts with the underlying Windows Server 2003 operating system.

CHAPTER 9
Expanding the Windows Small Business Server 2003 Network

Technology in the small business arena would be an oxymoron for many readers of this book if they were to step back in time about 30 years. Only the most successful small businesses, such as well-heeled law firms, had "technology" that included an expensive photocopier and a new thing called a "fax" machine. The good old IBM Selectric typewriter was the order of the day. A few years later, the local area network (LAN) concept was developed that allowed small offices to share an expensive printer and other resources. It worked well, it was simple, and sharing was the reason for being.

Fast forward to the Twenty-first Century. Small businesses are truly starting to embrace technology and trust their entire operations to IT infrastructure. That alone is a huge step for some SMBs. For many of these business people, one server is enough for their immediate needs. However, as those businesses start to grow and business owners learn to take advantage of the IT infrastructure, these SMBs find the need for more flexible solutions and increased storage space. E-mail storage, proprietary line-of-business applications requiring their own server, regulatory compliance, and the 24/7 mindset of service and data availability is changing the landscape. Hardware costs have decreased dramatically, making additional server purchases a viable SMB consideration.

SMBs are learning to operate with enterprise-level technology and have an elevated expectation set that they can do "more with less." And SBS delivers. SBS 2003 now has the ability to add additional domain controllers (DC) to the SBS 2003 network. Being untied from the single-server model, SBS has become a more robust computing environment, an option for some branch office solutions, and an easy way to expand and grow your business.

Adding and Managing Member Servers in a Windows Small Business Server 2003 Domain

Member servers are historically used as file servers storing data or applications to be shared by users. Member servers, being part of a domain, are not domain controllers and do not handle any sort of logon functions. In their purest form, they are plain dedicated to managing file, printing, or application services.

Time to think outside the server box! The above paragraph gives the "corporate speak" viewpoint of the generic role of a member server in a Microsoft networked environment. But, there really is more you can do with a member server. A member server makes an excellent platform to run Terminal Services in Application Sharing Mode and support important line-of-business applications. So, kinda like the "Zen of golf," where you are advised to meditate and "be the ball," please do the following: Drop down into the yoga "downward facing dog" pose. Take a few deep breaths via your nose. Be the member server! Get excited about the possibilities of introducing a member server into your SBS network!

So, time to run for a moment before we walk. After joining a member server to the domain, you have the ability to promote the server to a domain controller and participate in Active Directory replication, make it a global catalog server, and enjoy all the rights bestowed upon a DC in a Microsoft Windows Server 2003 networked environment. However, any additional server (as either a member server or a domain controller) you join to an SBS 2003 network will necessarily assume a subservient role to the SBS 2003 server machine. That is because the SBS 2003 server machine must be the ROOT OF THE ACTIVE DIRECTORY FOREST (yes—I'm shouting for emphasis). This was discussed in passing in Chapters 4 and 5 of this book.

IMPORTANT: Take the adding a member server discussion in this section very seriously. Microsoft and the SBS-MVPs do. In these paragraphs you'll see a simple procedure for adding a server to an SBS 2003 domain. At first blush, the keystrokes are simple. But, did you know that adding an additional server to an SBS 2003-based network is one of the top product-support issues?

Verify the Hardware Requirements

Before you dive in and add the additional server to the network, you want to verify that it is capable of handling its destined role, be it a file and print server, terminal server or a server to run a specific line-of-business application. For starters, you cannot join a server that is running the Microsoft Windows NT® Server 4.0 operating system to a Windows SBS domain because Windows NT® Server 4.0 does not support the Active Directory directory service. Instead, you must either migrate the server to the Windows 2000 Server operating system or back up your application data and restore it on a new installation of Windows Server 2003. Once you have decided on the operating system to use you should first:

- **Run the preinstallation hardware and software compatibility check.**

- Run the operating system disc from the command line using **x:\i386\ winnt32\checkupgradeonly**. This will not begin the upgrade or installation process.

- **Check the Windows Server Catalog** – located at http://www. microsoft.com/windows/catalog/server. If your hardware is not listed in the Server Catalog, contact the hardware manufacturer to find out whether there is a Windows Server 2003 compliant driver available.

- **Check drivers and BIOS** – upgrade to the latest BIOS and check that you have the latest device drivers for your hardware. You can check this at http://v4.winodwsupdate.microsoft.com/en by clicking on **Scan for Updates,** then **Driver Updates**. If you cannot find a driver here, check with the device manufacturer directly.

- **Check all 16-bit or older hardware devices** – inventory your current hardware and check whether devices use Plug and Play.

Adding a Server to the Windows SBS Domain

Joining a member server can be done through the Set up Server Computers Wizard in the Server Management Console as shown in Figure 9-1. The two basic steps are (1) the wizard will ask for the server name and (2) either a static IP or a dynamic IP will be assigned. To set up the server:

1. Open the Server Management console. To do so, click **Start**, and then click **Server Management.**

2. In the console tree, click **Server Computers,** when the **Set Up Server Wizard** begins, click **Next.**

3. Type the server name in the **Server Name** text box. The server name must follow standard naming conventions: no more than 15 alphanumeric characters and no spaces or other reserved characters. Click **Next.**

4. In the **IP Address Configuration** dialog box, select the method that the new server uses to obtain IP addresses. If you select **Use the following Static IP address**, make sure your address is excluded from the DHCP scope that is used on your network. Click **Next.**

5. Review the **Completing the Set Up Server Wizard** page. It contains a summary of the configuration of your new server.

6. Click **Finish** and a dialog box will advise you to go to the server to be joined and run http://sbsservername/connectcomputer in the browser to be joined to the domain.

Figure 9-1
Adding a member server with the Set Up Server Computers Wizard.

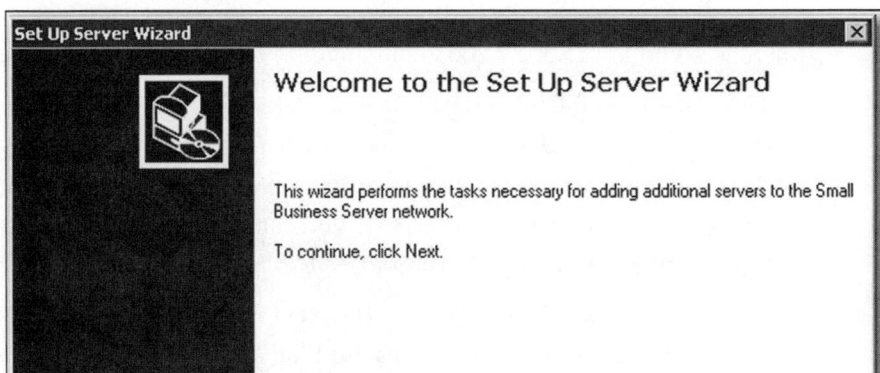

This is the appropriate way to create a machine account in the SBS domain and it sets up the member server with the correct trust relationship. You want it to play nice with the SBS domain controller. Now you are ready for the next step, which is configuring your member server. (Installing and Configuring Windows Server 2003 is covered in detail in Chapter 10.)

Configure the Additional Server

The configuration steps on the additional server will depend on whether this is a newly installed Windows Server 2003 or an already existing Windows Server 2003. We will walk through the steps of an existing Windows Server 2003 below. New installation and configuration steps for Windows Server 2003 are covered in Chapter 10. Once you have walked through a new installation, retrace the steps below if needed to configure the additional server to join the SBS domain.

1. Log on with administrator rights and click **Start, Control Panel.**

2. Click on **Licensing;** make sure Windows Server is selected in the product drop-down list. Click Per Device or Per User, and then click OK. This mode is used whether your Windows SBS CALs are per device or per user. The number of licenses must equal the total number of Windows SBS CALs on the server that is running Windows SBS.

3. Click **System**, click the **Computer Name** tab, and then click **Change**. Type the new name of the server in **Computer name**. You must use the same name that you added to **Manage Server Computers** in Windows SBS.

4. If the server was a member of another domain, you have to remove it from the domain and join a workgroup, in the **Member of** section, click **Workgroup**. Type a new workgroup name (such as WORKGROUP), and then click **OK.**

5. **To change the network settings, click Network Connections, right-click the name of your connection (usually Local Area Connection), and then click Properties. Click Internet Protocol (TCP/IP), making sure the checkbox is selected, and then click Properties. If you want** the server to use DHCP, click **Obtain an IP address automatically**.

If instead you want the server to use a static IP address, click **Use the following IP address.**

Run the Connect Computer Wizard

Now that the additional server is a member of a workgroup and has the proper IP address configured it is ready to join the SBS domain.

1. Open **Internet Explorer,** click **Tools**, click **Internet Options.**

2. Click the **Security** tab, click **Trusted Sites,** click **Sites**, and then in **Add this Web site to the zone**, type **http://***SBSServerName*, where *SBSServerName* is the name of your server that is running Windows SBS. Click **Add.**

3. Make sure that the **Require Server Verification (https:) for all sites in this zone** check box is clear, and then click **Close.**

4. In the Internet Explorer address bar type: **http://***SBSServerName***/ConnectComputer**, where *SBSServerName* is the name of the server that is running Windows SBS. Hit **Enter.**

5. Click **Connect to the network now.**

And that is it! When the configuration finishes, the additional server will be a member of the SBS domain. All the steps you would usually take to manually join a server to a Windows domain have been scripted and placed into the Connect Computer Wizard. This may be a painful step for technicians who like to do things the native way, but remember, if not done properly (the SBS way) you may find yourself calling Product Support Services. So for real life and exam purposes, just stick with the SBS way!

Synchronizing the New Server's Time Clock

With the SBS being the root of the domain, SBS is also the authoritative time server of the domain. The newly added server will look to the SBS server for time synchronizations. Windows servers use the Windows Time Service (WTS), and WTS uses the Network Time Service (NTS) connecting across the Internet to other synchronized time servers at time.microsoft.com. It is important to have the time clocks of the servers synchronized to ensure consistency and in order for Active Directory replication to function if you decide to upgrade the member server to a domain controller. WTS will set the internal clock accurately within a tenth of a second to the SBS server. First configure SBS to synchronize with the Internet time clock. On the SBS server:

1. Click **Start, Run** and type **gpedit.msc** and click **OK.**

2. In the tree pane, click **Computer Configuration, Administrative Templates, System,** and then **Windows Time Service.**

3. In the details pane, double-click **Global Configuration Settings.** Click **Enabled,** and then click **OK.**

4. In the details pane, double-click **Time Providers,** double-click **Enable Windows NTP Client,** click **Enabled,** and then click **OK.**

5. In the details pane, double-click **Time Providers and** double-click **Configure Windows NTP Client,** and then click **Enabled.**

6. In the **NtpServer** text box, type the IP address or fully-qualified domain name of the Internet time provider you want to use. You must append **,0x1** without any spaces to the end of the time provider, otherwise the time service fails (see figure 9-2).

7. Ensure the **Type** drop-down list is set to **NT5DS, click OK.**

8. Double-click **Enable Windows NTP Server,** click **Enabled,** and then click **OK.** Close **Group Policy Object Editor.**

9. Next step is to restart the Windows Time Service. Click **Start,** click **Run,** type **services.msc,** and then click **OK.**

10. In the details pane, click **Windows Time.** In the toolbar, click the **Restart Service** button.

11. Double-click **Windows Time.** Verify that the startup type is set to **Automatic.** Click **OK.**

Now you have configured the external time source for the SBS server, and configured the SBS server as the authoritative time source on the network.

Notes:

Figure 9-2
NtpServer configuration

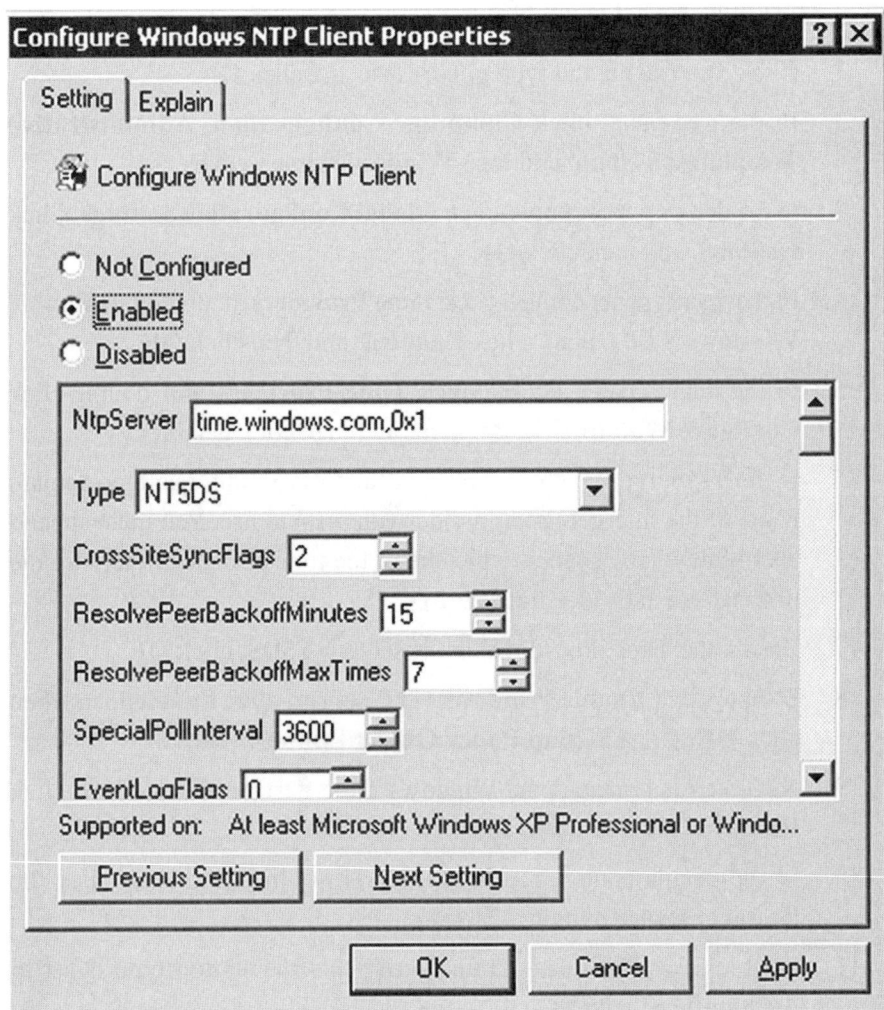

Editing the Logon Script

This is the final step which needs to be performed on the SBS server. In order for the time to be synchronized with SBS on the additional server (as well as all clients on the network) you need to edit the logon script.

1. Open **Windows Explorer** on the SBS server.

2. Browse to %*SystemRoot*%\SYSVOL\sysvol\%*DomainName*%\scripts, where %*SystemRoot*% is your installation directory for Windows SBS and %*DomainName*% is the NetBIOS domain name for your Windows SBS network.

3. Right-click **SBS_LOGIN_SCRIPT.bat**, and then click **Edit.**

4. At the end of the file, type net time *SBSServerName* /set /y, where *SBSServerName* is the NetBIOS name of your server that is running Windows SBS. Be sure to include the spaces where the example indicates.

5. Save the changes to the batch file.

Next time you log on to the additional server, the logon script will run and synchronize time with the SBS server.

Server Roles

At this point you would go about configuring the server roles on the additional server to act as either a domain controller, a terminal server, or an application server. There are no specific roles for database servers or line-of-business servers.

Once you have brought your member server online, the Manage Your Server Wizard will appear and ask you to configure a server role. You could choose to add a server role as a:

- File server
- Print server
- Application server (IIS, ASP.NET)
- Mail server (POP3, SMTP)
- Terminal server
- Remote Access / VPN server
- Domain Controller (Active Directory)
- DNS server
- DHCP server
- Streaming media server
- WINS server

Not all roles would fit the SBS bill, and most realistic choices will be the File, Print, Application, Mail and Terminal Server. If you select the Mail server option and plan on using Exchange, you must have a separate license for the Exchange server as well as the Terminal server, which will require separate licenses away from your SBS CALs. (Please see Chapter 10 for more information on server roles.)

Promoting Additional Windows 2003 Servers to Domain Controller Status

Now that you have joined an additional server to the domain, you can opt to bring it up to DC status. An interesting historic data point and not part of the 70-282 exam is that the dearly departed and discontinued BackOffice 2000 product had a "branch office setup wizard" that did exactly what we are describing herein.

When promoting a Windows Server 2003 member server to a DC, use the Manage Your Server Wizard and choose to add the Domain Controller role which will launch the Active Directory Installation Wizard. The steps are outlined in Chapter 10. (No, we are not trying to take short-cuts but want to conserve trees! You will find that Chapter 9 and 10 go hand in hand and we didn't want to duplicate information unnecessarily). The key is to know when to use SBS and when to use native Windows Server 2003 functions. Upgrading a member server to a DC is clearly a Windows Server 2003 function, despite it having joined an SBS network!

Adding a Domain Controller to a Remote Office

You may have clients who are expanding their businesses over multiple sites and require multiple servers. There are some considerations for SBS which would be centrally located and managed and have additional domain controllers at remote offices.

There are several reasons to locate an additional domain controller at a remote office, including reasons to reduce authentication time and providing security services. There are some items that should be taken into consideration before deploying a multiple-site operation:

- There will be a greater need for high-speed dedicated network connections. It is possible to handle remote office connectivity across a DSL or cable modem where you can route authentication, file sharing, e-mail, and application traffic to the main office. Performance will depend on the number of users and what type of traffic is involved.

- Backing up data locally is a must. If remote offices maintain servers and data, you must plan for a backup and restore method. Volume Shadow Copy Services and Folder redirection are doable over a WAN connection, except that the performance is likely not acceptable. Therefore, you are better off creating a local backup system for remote data.

Essentially, the steps to adding a domain controller to a remote office are:

1. Build the server at the main office site.

2. Join it to the SBS domain.

3. Configure the domain controller server role.

4. Synchronize Active Directory.

5. Move files and folders.

6. Load the applications.

7. Ship it to the remote office.

Contrary to popular belief, you may upgrade more than one additional server to domain controller status. You can add servers as you have licenses. Each additional Windows Server, regardless of whether member server or domain controller will require one client access license to access the SBS server, besides its own Windows server license. All clients on the SBS domain will be able to access the additional servers using their existing SBS client access licenses, meaning you DO NOT have to purchase additional client access licenses in order to access the additional servers on the SBS domain.

Notes:

Migrate from Windows Small Business Server 2003 to Windows Server 2003

So, your client with thirty users decides to partner with another company. Or the company is going to outgrow the 75 CAL limitation by the end of the year. Doesn't matter what the reason is, if there is a need to move into a full-blown "back office" solution using full server products, Microsoft has an elegant migration path called the "Transition Pack." The Transition Pack is a Disc you can purchase (SKU available at http://www.mircosoft.com/sbs; click on **How to Buy and Select the License** link) that includes a wizard for transitioning out of the SBS limitations and into a fully functioning Windows Server 2003 solution. There are really two transition packs: standard and premium.

Transition Pack

With the Transition Pack, you can remove all the limitations that have been placed upon SBS 2003. If you encounter a question on the transition pack during the exam, remember the restrictions placed on SBS such as:

- **75-user or device license restriction** (limiting users and workstations that can access a component or server program to a total of 75).

- **Trust-relationship restriction** (you are not permitted to create explicit trusts with NT-based or Active Directory directory service domains).

- **Creating child domains.**

- **Joining other domains.**

- **Moving FSMO roles** - SBS must hold all FMSO roles (see Chapter 10 on FSMO roles).

- **Moving Exchange Server 2003** to another server (all components must be installed on SBS).

- **Moving SQL Server 2000** to another server (all components must be installed on SBS).

- **Moving ISA Server 2000** to another server (all components must be installed on SBS).

- Using Terminal Services.

- **2-CPU restriction** (SBS only supports up to two physical CPUs and up to four virtual CPUs with hyperthreading).

The advantage of using the transition pack (standard and premium editions) is that it REMOVES ALL SBS LIMITATIONS and you will not have to reinstall your network or make any changes, and you get to keep the:

- Shared Fax Service,

- Remote Web Workplace and

- all the SBS wizards to boot!

Standard Transition Pack

The Standard Transition Pack applies to SBS Standard Edition, and comes with:

- One license for Windows Server 2003 Standard

- One license for Exchange Server 2003, Standard Edition

- Five Client Access Licenses

Note that Exchange Server and five CALs were part of the original SBS Standard purchase. The Transition pack removes limitations, but does not strip licenses!

Premium Transition Pack

The Premium Transition Pack applies to SBS Premium Edition, and comes with:

- One license for Windows Server 2003 Standard

- One license for Exchange Server 2003, Standard Edition

- One license for ISA Server 2000, Standard Edition with Service Pack 1

- One license for SQL Server 2000, Standard Edition with Service Pack 3a

- Five Client Access Licenses

IMPORTANT: The 70-282 exam is based on technology that was introduced to the market in late 2003. The exam is not continually updated when a new Service Pack or component update is introduced to market. This can be confusing to the test taker, especially in our case where the technology is four years old and the market has long moved on to newer components (i.e. ISA 2004, SBSR2, etc.).

Don't get too focused on the "bits" surrounding the Transition Pack SKU. The Transition Pack is also a financial concept! The Transition Pack is sold at a price point that has three financial implications:

- Going Up to Market. The Transition Pack effectively charges the customer the full cost of the Microsoft technologies being implemented. Basically, if you are going to go up to the full server SKUs, shouldn't you pay the cost of doing so? Read the next point for an exception.

- Rebates Are Us. The Transition Pack is priced to effectively credit you for the original cost of the SBS 2003 product. That's a nice touch and akin to getting trade-in value on your used car when you purchase a new car.

- Rollback. The CAL count is rolled back to five CALs and you must then "re-purchase" sufficient full server SKU CALs to become legal and compliant with Microsoft's licensing scheme. For example, an SBS 2003 site with 65 CALs that implemented the Transition Pack would rollback to five CALs and need to purchase 60 new full-server SKU CALs. Consulting Best Practices

Enough ducking and dodging. Table 9-1 shows the different Transition Pack SKUs, including the CALs.

Notes:

Table 9-1
Transition Pack information with prices in USD:

Transition Pack Standard Edition	$1,769 T72-00346
Transition Pack Premium Edition	$3,522 T75-00039
5-Pack Transition CALs	$194 Device: T74-01130 User: T74-01131
20-Pack Transition CALs	$776 Device: T74-01132 User: T74-01133

Expect to see at least one question on the 70-282 exam regarding the Transition Pack, because Microsoft thinks it's cool AND Microsoft is adamant about communicating that you're not "locked" into SBS as your firms grows! There is indeed an elegant migration path with the Transition Pack.

Create an Application Migration Strategy

There once was a client who had about twenty different applications on the server and insisted he used them all. My job was to move five of those critical applications to a new member server. In this case, I first inventoried the existing applications and categorized them by their relative business value and dependencies. I then called the manufacturer to find out if there were any updates available or special considerations when moving the applications and data to a new location. (Hey, beats reading documents for three nights in a row). I estimated the amount of time it would take to do the migration, then doubled that amount. Such is real life. When it comes to taking the exam, we may as well skip all third-party talk and focus on migration of Microsoft applications, and look at the way Microsoft recommends it being done. We call it the "Microsoft Way," because (you guessed correctly) that is the only "right" way when you answer exam questions.

Application Compatibility Toolkit

Talking about third-party, most applications are written to support the Windows operating system. One way to make sure they will work with Windows Server 2003 and not just with Windows 2000 or NT 4.0, is to use a really cool new tool—the **Application Compatibility Toolkit** - which is used by Microsoft developers themselves to test application compatibility. Test-driving an application with the analyzer in the toolkit will tip you off immediately if there are going to be issues. The tool kit has been a real time-saver in the past. You can download the tool kit at http://technet.microsoft.com/en-us/windowsvista/aa905066.aspx.

Migration Considerations

The term "migration" is often used to describe the process of migrating mailboxes from one Exchange-based computer to another Exchange-based computer by using the Exchange Server Migration Wizard or its command-line equivalent. The migration process is actually a copy process where the source mailbox object is not deleted or changed in any way by the migration process.

Microsoft recommends that you migrate in phases. This means that there will be a period of co-existence when part of the company uses the old mail system (source), which could be Lotus cc:Mail, Novell, GroupWise or Microsoft Mail, Exchange Server 5.5 or Exchange Server 2000, and another part of the company uses Exchange (target). Exchange includes several mail gateways, also called connectors, that allow mail systems to co-exist with Exchange. The connectors also support directory synchronization. This means that Exchange users are represented in the address book of your other mail system, and users of the other mail system have objects that represent them in the Exchange address book (Active Directory). The Migration Wizard permits you to view the Active Directory objects that are going to be converted before you start the process. It also permits you to change the pairing of migrated users to Active Directory objects.

Microsoft provides three tools to facilitate migration to and from Exchange Server version 5.5 and Microsoft Exchange 2000 Server:

- The Move Server Wizard
- Exmerge
- Exchange Migration Wizard

Move Server Wizard

The Move Server Wizard is a tool used to reconfigure a single server so you can move the server between sites and organizations, basically allowing the existing server to belong to a new Exchange Server site or organization. You would use the Mover Server Wizard to:

- Work with Exchange Server 5.5.
- Move large numbers of mailboxes between sites or organizations.
- Merge large sites or organizations.

Exmerge

Exmerge is a tool that was created by Product Support Services (PSS) to make extracting and importing bulk mailboxes easier. Exmerge has many uses besides moving between organizations. The Exmerge tool is included on the Exchange 2000 CD. It is a tool used for bulk export and import using personal folders (.pst) files. This tool can be used in many different situations. Exmerge does not preserve access control to mailboxes, public folders or reply-to capabilities. You would use Exmerge to:

- Work with Exchange Server 5.5.
- Work with Exchange 2000.
- Move multiple mailboxes but not the entire server (it does not migrate mailbox directories).
- Move mailboxes to new hardware (a mailbox and user account must exist on the target system prior to the import).
- Recover mailboxes.

Exchange Migration Wizard

The Exchange Migration Wizard provides a simple process for exporting and importing mailboxes from Exchange Server 5.5 to Exchange Server 2000 or migrating from Exchange Server 5.5 to a different Exchange 2000 organization. Even thought the Exchange Migration Wizard moves mailbox-based contacts, it does not migrate or move Active Directory-based custom recipients or distribution lists. And like Exmerge, it does not preserve access control or public folders. You would use the Exchange Migration Wizard to:

- Work with Exchange Server 5.5.

- Migrate an Exchange Server 5.5 system to a new and separate Exchange 2000 system without upgrading the Exchange Server 5.5.

- Preserve mailbox directory information during migration.

- Move to new hardware when moving between organizations.

- Move to Exchange Server 2000.

The Exchange Server Migration Wizard is designed to migrate mailboxes between separate domains. The exception to this is the option to migrate mailboxes to personal storage (.pst) files instead of to an Exchange-based computer. However, it is more common to use the Microsoft Exchange Mailbox Merge program (Exmerge.exe) for this purpose. The option to migrate from cc: Mail, MSMail, Novell GroupWise, Lotus Notes and other programs has always been present in the Exchange 2000 Migration Wizard. The option to migrate mailboxes from Exchange Server 5.5 to Exchange 2000 Server came available with the Exchange Server 2000 Service Pack 1 (SP1) and migrating mailboxes from Exchange 2000 Server to Exchange 2000 Server came available with Exchange 2000 Server Service Pack 2 (SP2).

Working with the Exchange Migration Wizard

In order to work with the Exchange Migration Wizard you have to first establish a trust relationship between the source and target domains. The original source user domain account is used by the migration process to connect to the newly created Exchange Server 2000 or Exchange Server 2003 mailbox. During this process, the migration wizard will create disabled user accounts on the target server which are associated with the source user accounts that connect to the mailbox. The disabled user accounts on the target server should be left as they are, and should not be enabled.

Migration from Exchange Server 5.5

When running the Exchange Server Migration Wizard, on the "Account Migration" page, select the Exchange Server 5.5 mailboxes that you want to import. If the mailboxes do not yet exist in Active Directory on the target domain, the Migration Wizard will create new Active Directory users. If an Exchange 5.5 mailbox already exists in Active Directory, the Migration Wizard matches the Exchange 5.5 mailbox with the contact and then converts the contact to an Active Directory user. After the Migration Wizard created the new users, it will migrate the mailbox data to the Exchange mailbox stores. There are several migration strategies available based on the needs of the organization.

Example: You could set up an Active Directory Connector (ADC) prior to the migration, updating Active Directory and maintaining a co-existence between the Exchange Server 5.5 or Exchange 2000 organization with the Exchange Server 2003 organization. This is the best strategy if users need to have access during the migration process. Another option would be using the Active Directory Migration Tool (ADMT, covered in Chapter 5) if you have a large organization where you don't want to manually grant permissions after the migration. The ADMT will retain any permissions that were assigned to user accounts prior to the migration.

Migration from Exchange Server 2000

If you are migrating from an Exchange Server 2000 organization to another Exchange Server 2000 or Exchange Server 2003 organization, you can use the Exchange Migration Wizard (Exchange Server 2000 SP2 version) with the ADMT. The Migration Wizard is not a full-featured user account migration tool (hence the disabled user accounts in the target domain). If you want to turn on these accounts you should use the ADMT to migrate the user accounts with their security identifiers (SIDs). The use of ADMT with the Migration Wizard has been tested and is a supported and recommended procedure for migrating user accounts with their corresponding mailboxes.

There are two recommended ways you can employ the ADMT together with the Migration Wizard to import user accounts and their corresponding mailboxes:

- First use the ADMT to migrate user accounts and their SID, creating user accounts in Active Directory which are turned on, then use the Migration Wizard to import the mailbox information.

- First use the Migration Wizard to import mailbox information, creating user accounts in Active Directory that are turned off, and then use the ADMT to import the user accounts into Active Directory. Here you would need to use the Active Directory Cleanup utility (ADClean) to remove duplicate account information. (Discussing ADClean is beyond the scope of this book. Please refer tohttp://www.microsoft.com/reskit).

Terminal Services

Windows Server 2003 contains a Terminal Server component that delivers Windows desktop and Windows-based applications from a centralized server to virtually any client computer. Terminal Services (TS) transmits the user interface of the program to the client computer, which then sends keyboard and mouse clicks back to the TS.

In SBS, Terminal Services is available only in Remote Desktop for administration (a.k.a. Terminal Services in Remote Administration Mode) and enabled by default for access by two administrators for server administration purposes only. (This is not application-sharing mode.)

Any member of the Administrators group with access to the Terminal Service's administrative utilities can remotely manage all aspects of the SBS server. However, a user created with the Power User Template may log on remotely via Terminal Services to the SBS 2003 server machine (say from a remote location like a hotel room) and perform administration tasks ONLY from the locked down Server Management console. This "power user" cannot access other parts of the server machine interface and is not allowed to log on locally to the server machine (at the server machine console back at work).

But, what if you would like to save some money and enable Terminal Services to host user desktops? First know that you **cannot** convert Terminal Services to Application Sharing Mode on the SBS 2003 server machine. Okay, once more with feeling: **It cannot be done**. So, don't be duped into believing it can be, by a tricky question on the 70-282 exam. If you want a Terminal Services Applications Sharing Mode scenario, you'd want to perform such feats on an additional server machine, either a domain controller (not recommended) or a member server (recommended) approach.

The official Microsoft statement of why you cannot run Terminal Service on SBS is as follows: *Terminal Services is optimized for the desktop experience, it does not coexist well with the rest of the applications and services that Windows Small Business Server includes. Terminal Services and Windows Small Business Server contend for the same resources and can conflict with one another, degrading the performance of both. Also, Windows Server 2003 and Windows Small Business Server 2003 are more secure by default than previous versions, making coexistence with the domain-controller capacity of Small Business Server unfeasible.*

Understanding Terminal Services

With Terminal Services you can run any installed program on the server. Because it is optimized to run Windows-based applications, you can deliver the Windows desktop itself to just about any computing device, even those that cannot run Windows. Clients connect to Terminal Services using RDC (Remote Desktop Connection), which is built into Windows XP and Windows Server 2003. Clients who do not have RDC installed can download the RDC client at http:// www.microsoft.com/windowsxp/downloads/tools/rdclientdl.mspx. The client can be run on:

- Windows 9x,
- Windows Me,
- Windows NT 3.51,
- NT 4.0,
- Windows 2000,

- Mac OS-X, and
- Windows CE-based handhelds.

RDC can also be run on 16-bit-based computers running Windows for Workgroups with MS TCP/IP-32. RDC uses RDP (Remote Desktop Protocol) to connect to the server and has support for:

- 24-bit color
- Audio redirection
- Smart card redirection
- COM port redirection
- Local network printer redirection
- File system redirection
- Disk drive redirection
- 128-bit encryption

The client and server communicate via RDP 5.2 with high encryption (128-bit RC4) protocol. RDP is designed to support many different types of network topologies, like ISDN, POTS, IPX, NetBIOS, TCP/IP, and other LAN protocols. The current version of RDP will run only over TCP/IP and use port 3389 by default. RDP provides 64,000 separate channels for data transmission, but is used only on a single channel for keyboard, mouse, and presentation data.

Configure Terminal Services

Since the SBS server cannot be the host you will have to add an additional Windows Server 2003 server to the SBS network and configure it with the Terminal Server role. For security reasons (you have multiple users with access to all directories unless you lock down the machine), you would want the TS server to only be a member server and not a domain controller to host Terminal Services in Application Sharing Mode. To configure Terminal Services on a **Windows 2003 Server** (not the SBS server), you would:

1. Go to the **Manage Your Server** page and click **Add or remove a role**.

2. Select **Terminal Server,** click **Next**, and click **Next** on the **Summary of Selection** screen. Click **OK**.

IMPORTANT: In order to administer the additional server, you must log on using a domain administrator account that was created with the **Add User Wizard**. A domain administrator account that was created using any other method does not work for administering an additional computer on a Windows Small Business Server network. (Please refer to Chapter 6 for creating user accounts.)

Now that the terminal server role has been configured you want to make sure the client can communicate with the terminal server. The following operating systems will already have the Remote Desktop Connection tool installed by default:

- Windows Server 2003
- Windows XP
- Windows CE (most versions)

There may be some situations where you will have to reinstall or newly install the **terminal services client;** in this case:

1. From the client computer, click **Start**, click **Run**, and then type\\Server-Name\clientapps (where *ServerName* is the SBS server).

2. Click **tsclient**.

3. Double-click the Win32 folder, and then double-click **Setup.exe**.

4. Follow the instructions and click **Finish.**

Configure and Activate Terminal Services Licensing

Terminal Server will run an evaluation period of 120 days from the date of the first client logon. After 120 days it will no longer allow client connection unless it locates a Terminal Server license server issuing client licenses. Each client computer that connects to the terminal server requires a terminal server client access license. To configure Terminal Server licensing:

1. Click **Start**, click **Control Panel**, and then click **Add or Remove Programs**.

2. Click **Add/Remove Windows Components**.

3. In the **Components** dialog box, click **Terminal Server Licensing**, and then click **Next**.

4. On the **Terminal Server Licensing Setup** page, click **Next** to accept the default on that page.

5. Provide the file system location where the license server database should be installed on the Terminal Server license server, click **Next**, and then click **Finish**. The default location for the license server database is *systemroot***System32\LServer**.

To configure activation:

1. Click **Start**, click **Control Panel**, click **Administrative Tools**, and then click **Terminal Server Licensing**.

2. In the console tree, right-click the Terminal Server license server you want to activate, and then click **Activate Server** to start the Terminal Server License Server Activation Wizard.

3. In **Activation method**, select **Automatic connection** (recommended), and then click **Next**. Follow the instructions in the wizard.

IMPORTANT: By default, Terminal Server licensing is set to **Per Device** mode. To change to **Per User** mode, click **Start**, click **Control Panel**, and then click **Administrative Tools**, and then click **Terminal Services Configuration**. In the console tree, click **Server Settings**. In the details pane, double-click **Licensing**. In the **Licensing Mode** dialog box, click **Per User** from the drop-down list box, and then click **OK**.

Folder Redirection

By default, users' My Documents folders are saved with the user profiles on the terminal server. Unless you want to configure an additional backup method for users' data stored on the Terminal Services server, it is recommended that you redirect users' My Documents folders to the server running Windows Small Business Server 2003 and apply volume quotas to the folders. (Please see Chapter 8 for SBS Backup.)

Installing Client Applications

The best practice is to install the client applications from the ClientApps install folder located on the Small Business Server. Terminal Server is able to run Windows-based applications as well as third-party applications (check with manufacturer for compatibility). For the purposes of the exam we will focus on installing Outlook 2003 and the Fax service. To install Outlook 2003:

1. On the Windows Server 2003, log on using the domain administrator account.

2. Click **Start**, click **Run**, and then type *ServerName* (name of the SBS server).

3. Double-click **ClientApps**, and then double-click **Outlook2003**.

4. Double-click **Setup.exe**, and then follow the Setup instructions.

5. To close Outlook Setup after installation, click **Next**, and then click **Finish**.

To configure Fax Services the Small Business Server must be configured as a fax server (see Chapter 7 for fax service). To configure Fax Services for Terminal Server users, you need to configure the terminal server and each client computer that will use the service. To configure the terminal server, on the terminal server:

1. Click **Start**, click **Control Panel**, and then click **Add or Remove Programs**.

2. Click **Add/Remove Windows Components**.

3. Select the **Fax Services** check box, and then click **Next**.

4. Click **Do not share this printer**, and then click **Next**, click **Finish.**

To configure client computer for the Fax Service, open the remote desktop connection to the terminal server:

1. From each client computer, click **Start**, click **Programs**, click **Accessories**, click **Communications**, click **Remote Desktop Connection**, and then log on to the terminal server using the Remote Desktop Connection.

2. Click **Start**, click **Printers and Faxes**, and then double-click **Add a printer**. The Add Printer wizard starts.

3. Click **Next**.

4. Click **A network printer, or a printer attached to another computer**, and then click **Next**.

5. Click **Find a printer in the directory**, and then click **Next** .

6. In the **Find Printers** dialog box, click **Find Now**.

7. In the search results list, a printer named **Fax** should appear. Select the printer named **Fax**, and then click **OK.**

Changing the Session Encryption Level

By default, all Terminal Services sessions connect using high encryption, which provides bi-directional security using a 128-bit cipher. However, some older versions of the Terminal Services client do not support this high level of encryption. Clients that do not support this level of encryption will not be able to connect. Therefore, the encryption level can be set to "client compatible" to provide the highest encryption level supported by the client. Both levels use the standard RSA RC4 encryption.

Changing the encryption level is performed within the Terminal Services Configuration utility, located under Advanced Management, Terminal Services Configuration. Right-click the Connections folder and click on Properties. The General tab will show the Encryption dialog box where you can select:

- Low
- Client Compatible
- High
- FIPS compliant

Remote Desktop User Group

Instead of adding users to a list in the Terminal Services Connection Configuration (TSCC) program, you can simply make them members of the **Remote Desktop Users** (RDU) group. For example, the administrator can add the "Everyone" group to the RDU group to allow everyone to access the terminal server.

Maximum Connections

You may want to set the amount of maximum connections; if so, best practice dictates using Group Policy. Go to **Group Policy Management** and in the appropriate container:

1. Click on **Computer Configuration** and expand **Administrative Templates.**

2. Expand **Windows Components**, expand **Terminal Services,** and double-click the **Limit number of connections** setting. Click **Enabled** and enter the number of maximum connections allowed.

We recommend that you use Group Policy for Terminal Services Configuration in general. For more information on this topic, go to http://www.microsoft.com and do a search on "Terminal Server Best Practices." (The URL is too long to list here.)

Terminal Services Manager Utility

The Terminal Services Manager can be used to monitor sessions, users, and processes and to manage the Terminal Server. The utility can be accessed under **Advanced Management**, **Terminal Services Configuration**, and by clicking on **Terminal Services Manager** in the right pane or typing **tsadmin.exe** on the Run command line. By clicking on **Actions** in the Terminal Services Manager toolbar, you can:

- **Connect** – connects a user to another session. This will disconnect the current session but not delete it. You can use this to switch between sessions.

- **Disconnect** – disconnects as user from a session. The session remains attached and currently running applications continue to run. The user will be reconnected to the session when logging back on, even when connecting from a different computer.

- **Log off users** – logs off users without warning and can result in data loss for that session. All processes will be ended and the session is deleted from the server.

- **Reset** – deletes a session instantly, without warning the user, and can result in loss of data at that session. Use this if a session has stopped responding.

- **Remote Control** – allows monitoring a user's session and will interact if needed.

- **Status** – enables the administrator to monitor session-related counters, such as incoming and outgoing bytes.

- **Send Message** – allows the administrator to send a message to a session and to remotely control sessions.

- **End Processes** – allows the administrator to end a process running in a user's session.

Wow, that was quite a bit. Go take five, grab a cup of java and come back here to load up on more exam information when you are ready.

DNS (Domain Name System)

Understanding of DNS names, zones, name server roles and replication is absolutely a must in order to configure and maintain a properly functioning intranet and connect to the Internet. In this chapter we will cover basic terms and techniques you will have to master for the 70-282 exam. Let's get started!

When you type a URL into the address bar of Internet Explorer, you type an easily remembered web address like www.smbnation.com, which is considered a friendly name and is easy for human beings to understand, but not for computers. To be understood by a computer it must first be resolved to an Internet Protocol (IP) address using DNS. To facilitate resolving names to IP addresses, DNS servers manage the logical namespace in a hierarchical order throughout the Internet. There are three components of DNS:

- **The domain namespace and resource records:** DNS defines a specification for a structured namespace that looks like an inverted tree and resource records, which are used to configure the DNS database server, and contain resources by their name and IP address.

- **Name servers:** Name servers store resource records and information about the tree structure and resolve client queries.

- **Resolvers:** Resolvers are programs that run on DNS clients and DNS servers and query name servers for information.

IMPORTANT: DNS traffic uses the UDP port 53 and TCP port 53.

DNS Names, Domains, and Subdomains

A fully qualified domain name (FQDN) uniquely identifies a host within the DNS hierarchy and contains both the host name and domain name. The FQDN is broken down into the following levels, separated by a period:

- The **top-level** domain identifies the type of organization, such as a government organization (gov) or a commercial organization (com).

- The **second-level** domain indicates a specific domain within that top-level namespace.

- The **third-level** indicates a specific host within that domain.

For example, in support.smbnation.com, **.com** is the top-level domain, **smbnation** is the second-level domain, and **support** is the name of the host computer.

The very top hierarchy in the DNS namespace on the Internet is called a **Root domain.** (This would not be included in the FQDN) The root domain uses a null label, which is written as a single period (.). In the United States, the Internet Assigned Names Authority (IANA) manages several Root domain name servers. The Root domain stands above all top-level domains, which are assigned by the organization type or country. Some common top-level domains are:

- .com – Commercial organizations in the United States.
- .edu – Educationial organizations in the United States.
- .gov – United States governmental organizations.
- .mil – United States military organizations.
- .net – Networking organizations.
- .org – Non-commercial organizations.
- .uk – United Kingdom, where "uk" is the code for the country.

DNS Zones

A zone is a database record that defines a contiguous portion of a domain in the DNS namespace and is stored on one or multiple DNS servers. The zone file contains information that defines mappings between domain names and IP addresses and can also contain reverse mappings that can resolve IP addresses into domain names. Windows Server 2003 provides an option for four different zone types:

- **Primary zone:** The primary zone maintains the master writable copy of the zone in a text file.

- **Secondary zone:** The secondary zone stores a copy of an existing zone in a read-only text file. A primary zone must already exist before a secondary zone can be created.

- **Active Directory–integrated zone:** The Active Directory–integrated zone stores zone information within Active Directory. This allows for additional features, such as secure dynamic updates and replication.

- **Stub zone:** The stub zone maintains only a list of authoritative name servers required to identify the authoritative DNS servers for that zone. The purpose of a stub zone is to ensure that DNS servers hosting a parent zone are aware of authoritative DNS servers for its child zones. This zone is new in Windows Server 2003.

Zone Transfers

Zones are replicated through zone transfer. A primary DNS server or master name server transfers its zone files to a secondary DNS server. Zone transfers occur for all zones for which a DNS server is a secondary name server. From startup and on an ongoing basis the secondary DNS server ensures that the most current information about the zone is reflected in the local zone file. The two types of zone transfers are full and incremental.

- **AXFR:** Asynchronous full zone transfer.

- **IXFR:** Incremental zone transfer.

Full Zone Transfer (AXFR)

A full zone transfer is the transfer of an entire zone file regardless of how much (if anything) has changed in the file since the last transfer. The full zone transfer goes through the following process:

1. The secondary server waits until the next refresh time (as specified in the SOA resource record) and then **queries** the master server for the **SOA resource record** for the zone.

2. The master server **responds** with the **SOA resource record**.

3. The secondary server checks the Serial Number field of the returned SOA resource record. If the serial number is higher than the serial number of the locally stored zone file, changes have been made to the zone file on the master server and a zone transfer is needed. The serial number in the SOA resource record is updated every time a resource record is changed on the master name server.

4. The secondary server sends an **AXFR** request (a request for a full zone transfer) to the master server.

5. Then the secondary server initiates a TCP connection with the master server and **requests all** the **records** currently in the **zone database**. The Serial Number field in the SOA record of the local zone file will then match the Serial Number field in the SOA record of the master server after the zone transfer had been completed.

If there is no response to an SOA query received by the secondary server, it will retry SOA queries using a retry time interval specified in the local zone SOA resource record. The secondary server continues to retry until a specified expiration time specified in the SOA resource record in the local zone file is reached. Once the expiration time is exceeded, the zone file is closed by the seondary server which will stop answering subsequent queries. The secondary server will continue to attempt a zone transfer, and when the zone transfer succeeds, the local zone file will be opened and used for subsequent queries.

Incremental Zone Transfer (IXFR)

Performing full zone transfers can consume a large portion of processing resources and network bandwidth. How much depends on the size of the records and frequency of transfer. In this case you can perform an incremental zone transfer which will only transfer the resource records that have been added, deleted or modified.

To perform an incremental zone transfer, the secondary server performs the same query for the SOA record and comparison of the Serial Number field. If there is a change, the secondary server sends an **IXFR request** (a request for an incremental zone transfer) to the master server. The records that have changed will be sent by the master server, and the secondary server builds a new zone file. The new zone file will be built combined from the records in the incremental zone transfer and the records that have not changed.

Resource Records

For small networks, DNS name resolution is simpler and more efficient by having the DNS client query a DNS server that is maintained by an ISP. SBS does a great job of this, so you never have to know about resource records, because SBS has been scripted to manage the internal DNS server for you. Once you enter the pertinent ISP DNS information into the CEICW, your job is done.

But this will not suffice for the 70-282 exam. So let's dig a bit deeper and see what else is going on. After a zone is created, resource records must be added. The following table lists the most commonly used resource record types.

Table 9-2
Common DNS Zone Types

Zone	Description
SOA	Identifies the start of a zone of authority. Every zone contains an SOA resource record at the beginning of the zone file, which stores information about the zone, configures replication behavior, and sets the default TTL for names in the zone.
A	Maps an FQDN to an IPv4 address.
AAAA	Maps an FQDN to an IPv6 address.

Zone	Description
NS	Indicates the servers that are authoritative for a zone. NS records indicate primary and secondary servers for the zone specified in the SOA resource record, and they indicate the servers for any delegated zones. Every zone must contain at least one NS record at the zone root.
PTR	Maps an IP address to an FQDN for reverse lookups.
CNAME	Specifies an alias (synonymous name).
MX	Specifies a mail exchange server for a DNS domain name. A mail exchange server is a host that receives mail for the DNS domain name.
SRV	Specifies the IP addresses of servers for a specific service, protocol, and DNS domain.
WINS	Indicates the IPv4 address of a WINS server for WINS forward lookup. The DNS Server service in Windows Server 2003 can use a WINS server for looking up the host portion of a DNS name.
WINS-R	Indicates the use of WINS reverse lookup, in which a DNS server uses a NetBIOS Adapter Status message to find the host portion of the DNS name given its IPv4 address.
ATMA	Maps DNS domain names to asynchronous transfer mode (ATM) addresses.

Most resource records are represented as a single line of text in text-based DNS database files. This is an example of what the resource record would look like:

Example: Server1.sales.smbnation.com   3600   A   IN   65.43.17.2

The record starts with record owner's information (**server1.sales.smbnation.com**), followed by the TTL (Total time to live) of **3600** seconds (that is one hour), type **A** (address record), class **IN** (Internet) and the RDATA (resource data, 65.43.17.2).

DNS Server Service Configuration

The DNS Server service can be configured by right-clicking the DNS server within the management console and selecting the **Properties** option (or go to Run and type dnsmgmt.msc). We encourage you to click around the DNS management console to make yourself familiar with it. The following properties can be configured (see Figure 9-3 below):

- **Interfaces:** Specify individual IPv4 addresses (interfaces) to listen for and receive incoming DNS traffic.

- **Forwarders:** Specify a list of IP addresses to forward DNS queries that cannot be resolved.

- **Advanced:** Determine the data format for name checking, determine the location from which zone data is loaded, and enable automatic scavenging of stale records.

- **Root Hints**: Configure the set of root DNS server for iterative queries.

- **Debug Logging:** Record and use the packets that are sent and received for troubleshooting. Debug is disabled by default.

- **Event Logging:** Log errors, warnings and all events to be displayed in the Event Viewer. Logging is enabled by default for all events.

- **Monitoring:** Test and verify configuration by manually sending queries against the DNS server. Select iterative and recursive queries to run at a specified interval.

- **Security:** Specify access control list (ACL) users and groups for DNS server administration.

Notes:

Figure 9-3
Configurable DNS Server Properties, Root Hints tab open

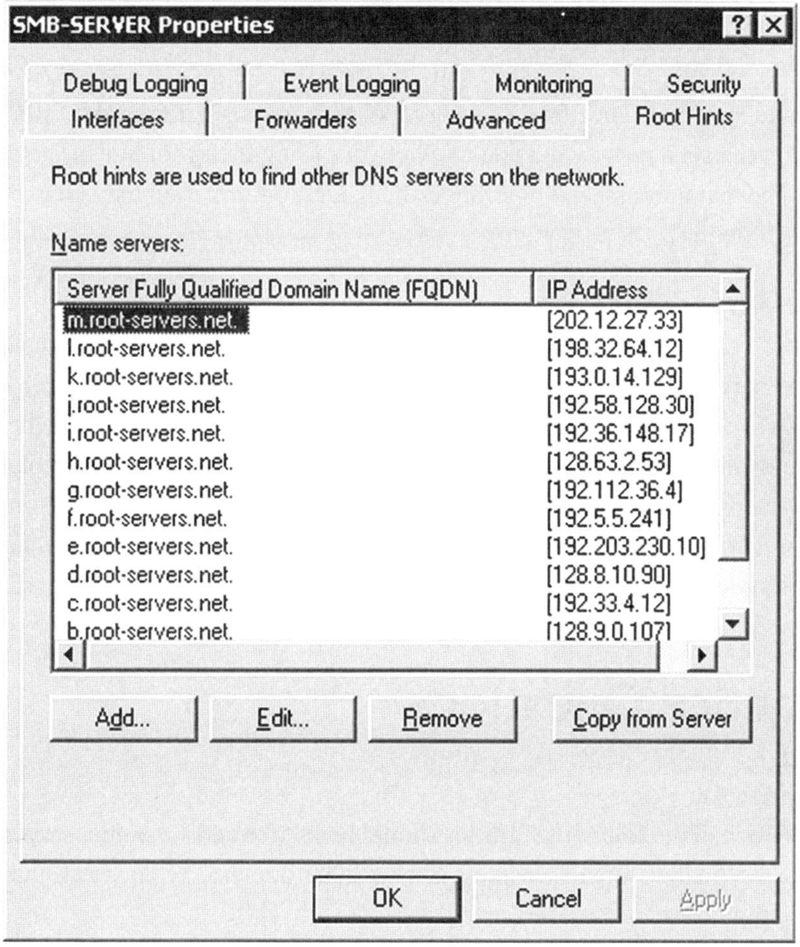

DNS Forwarders

Often a DNS server must communicate outside of its local network. If the DNS server cannot resolve a query locally, it forwards the request to another DNS server. A forwarder is an entry pointing to other DNS servers. A DNS server that has forwarding configured will behave differently (and faster) than one that does not have a forwarder configured. The forwarder should always be configured for the following reasons:

- It will attempt to resolve a query using the primary and secondary DNS server which is designated as the forwarder.

- It will forward the query DNS server designated as the forwarder if the query cannot be resolved locally.

Without having a specific DNS server designated as a forwarder, all DNS servers can send queries outside of a network using their root hints. The result could be that internal, and possibly critical, DNS information may be exposed on the Internet.

The Root Hints File

To resolve domain names on the Internet, a default file provided with the DNS Server service in Windows Server 2003 (root hints file) contains the records for the root servers of the Internet. The root hints file, also known as the cache file, contains the names and addresses of root name servers. For installations not connected to the Internet, the file should be replaced to contain the name servers authoritative for the root of the private network. This file is named Cache.dns and is stored in the systemroot/System32/Dns folder.

Practice Questions

Question #1:

Which of the following utilities should be used to add a member server to a Windows Small Business Server 2003 domain? (Choose all that apply.)

a. Add a computer wizard.

b. Connect Computer wizard.

c. Setup Server Wizard.

d. Server Management Console.

Question #2:

Your customer recently added a second location that is connected to the main office via a VPN implemented over the respective offices DSL connections. Users in the remote office have been complaining

about slow or unresponsive logins. How would you resolve this issue?
(Choose the best answer.)

a.   Implement simple passwords to reduce the latency caused by complex
     security processing over the VPN.

b.   Disable domain processing on PC's in the remote office.

c.   Install a domain controller in the remote office.

d.   Suggest that the customer stagger the start times of the users in the
     remote office to reduce login traffic.

Question #3:

Which of the following of the following statements are true about the
Exmerge utility? (Choose all that apply.)

a.   Exmerge will move Exchange 2000 or Exchange 5.5 servers to
     Exchange 2003.

b.   Exmerge will move Exchange 2000 or Exchange 5.5 mailboxes to
     Exchange 2003.

c.   Though Exmerge will move mailboxes, it cannot recover them.

d.   Exmerge will preserve contacts.

Question #4:

Your SBS 2003 customer would like to provide terminal services access
for some of his users. What is the best way to implement terminal
services in this environment? (Choose the best answer.)

a.   If the server was upgraded from SBS 2000 you could use the terminal
     server software installed on it.

b.   Install a new member server with terminal server installed on it.

c.   Configure the SBS 2003 server to run in terminal server supplication
     mode.

d.   Terminal services is NOT supported in an SBS2003 environment.

Question #5:

You installed a new member server in an SBS 2003 environment to
run terminal services. The customer has two offices in the same public

facility connected by a dedicated link with a firewall router in between. After the implementation you have found that the local users can run terminal services without issue, but none of the users in the remote office can, including a terminal server user that recently relocated to the remote office. Which of the following could potentially be the cause of the problem? (Choose all that apply).

a. Port 443 not open on the firewall.

b. Port 3389 not open on the firewall.

c. Affected users are not members of the Remote Desktop Users group.

d. Incorrect gateway or static route definition on the terminal server.

e. The terminal server is not configured for application mode.

Question #6:

You installed a new member server in an SBS 2003 environment to run terminal services. The customer has two offices in the same public facility connected by a dedicated link with a firewall router in between. After the implementation you have found that the local users can run terminal services without issue, but only some of the users in the remote office can. Which of the following could potentially be the cause of the problem? (Choose all that apply.)

a. Port 443 not open on the firewall.

b. Port 3389 not open on the firewall.

c. Affected users are not members of the Remote Desktop Users group.

d. Incorrect gateway or static route definition on the terminal server.

e. The terminal server is not configured for application mode.

Question #7:

Which of the following statements is an accurate description of the DNS INXFR zone transfer process? (Choose the best answer.)

a. The primary server's SOA record is read by the secondary server and compared to its own. If the Serial Number values do not match, an IXFR notification is sent and the entire database is pulled down by the secondary.

b. The primary server's SOA record is read by the secondary server and compared to its own. If the Serial Number values do not match, an IXFR notification is sent by the primary, instructing the secondary to push the entire database back.

c. The primary server's SOA record is read by the secondary server and compared to its own. If the Serial Number values do not match, an IXFR notification is sent and the primary will send database changes to the secondary to rebuild its database.

d. None of the above.

Question #8:

Your customer's SBS 2003 server is set up as a DNS forwarder. Which of the following accurately describes the DNS name resolution process? (Choose the best answer.)

a. The workstation will send a DNS request to the SBS 2003 server. If the SBS 2003 server is the authoritative DNS server for the domain holding the node it will resolve the node name and answer the query with the proper TCP/IP address. If the SBS 2003 server is not authoritative it will first check the contents of the cache and if possible will answer the query from the cache. If the node is not in the cache, the DNS query is forwarded to the defined external DNS servers. The query response will then be returned to the SBS 2003 server which will then be used to respond to the original query. The SBS 2003 server will also update its cache with the response.

b. The workstation will send a DNS request to the SBS 2003 server. The SBS 2003 server will forward the query to the defined external DNS servers. If the external DNS servers cannot resolve the query, a NORESP is sent back to the SBS 2003 server which will then check its local table and will respond with the proper IP if the node is listed. If the external DNS servers can resolve the query, the response is sent directly back to the originating workstation.

c. The workstation will send a DNS request to the SBS 2003 server. If the SBS 2003 server is the authoritative DNS server for the domain holding the node it will resolve the node name and answer the query with the proper TCP/IP address. If the SBS 2003 server is not authoritative, it will first check the contents of the cache and, if possible, will answer the query from the cache. If the node is not in the cache, the DNS query is forwarded to the defined external DNS servers. The query response will then be sent directly back to the originating workstation.

d. The workstation will send a DNS request to the SBS 2003 server. If the SBS 2003 server is the authoritative DNS server for the domain holding the node it will resolve the node name and answer the query with the proper TCP/IP address. If the SBS 2003 server is not authoritative it will generate an IXFR zone transfer with the authoritative DNS server of the affected zone. The SBS 2003 server will then configure itself as a stub zone server for the authoritative zone to ensure that future resolution requests are processed in a more efficient manner.

Question #9:

What is the purpose of DNS PTR record? (Choose the correct answer.)

a. The DNS PTR record provides a pointer to the primary DNS server for a DNS zone.

b. The DNS PTR record is used to match non-standard Microsoft SRV records to standard DNS "A" and "AAAA" records. This ensures that down-level DNS servers properly resolve records outside of the primary zone.

c. The DNS PTR record provides the ability to look up the FQDN of a node by IP address.

d. The DNS PTR is used in conjunction with the A record to form the individual components that make up an ATMA entry.

Question #10:

Which of the following valid ways to invoke the DNS management interface? (Choose the correct answer.)

a. Double click the DNS icon under Administrative tools.

b. Type dnsmgmt.msc at the Run prompt.

c. Right click the DNS server within the management console and select properties.

d. All the above.

Question #11:

Which of the following should be changed to resolve issues with RDP clients running older versions of terminal services client? (Choose the correct answer.)

a. Change Terminal Server Global Parameters to use only 48 bit bi-directional security.

b. Modify the session manager to use any security option other that RSA RC4 encryption.

c. Modify the tsconfig.inf file and remove the REMARK statement from the **Client Compatible** line at the end of the file.

d. Change the encryption level within the Terminal Services Configuration utility to "**Client Compatible.**"

Question #12:

Which of the below will **not** be included in the Standard Transition Pack. (Choose all that apply.)

a. One license for Exchange Server 2003, Standard Edition.

b. One license for SQL Server 2000, Standard Edition with Service Pack 3a.

c. One license for Windows Server 2003 Standard.

d. One license for ISA Server 2000, Standard Edition with Service Pack 1.

e. Five Client Access Licenses.

Question #13:

What utility can be used to verify migrated applications will work properly with Windows Server 2003? (Choose the correct answer.)

a. Application Compatibility Toolkit.

b. WinApp.exe /compat.

c. Setup.exe /CheckUpgrade.

d. Transition Pack Premium (Upgrade Edition).

Question #14:

Which of the following would not be allowed on an SBS 2003 server. (Choose all that apply.)

a. 4 Processors.

b. Terminal Services Administration Mode.

c. Terminal Services Application Mode.

d. 65 Users.

e. Creating a child domain.

Answers

Question #1: Answer: b, c, d

a. Incorrect. Not appropriate for a server, only a desktop system.

b. Correct! All of the steps necessary have been scripted to properly add the new system to the SBS 2003 domain.

c. Correct! This will define the server within AD so it is added to the correct location when joined to the domain.

d. Correct! The Server Management Console is where the Setup Server Wizard lives. So we start here.

Question #2: Answer: c

a. Incorrect! Complex passwords do not slow down the authentication process, unless of course you are some nasty evildoer who happens to be trying to break into a system. Rather, consider the fact that the domain controller, which one must talk to in order to authenticate, is only available across the relatively slow DSL link. Hmmmmm…

b. Incorrect! There is no such thing as turning off domain processing. But let's just say that not participating in domain security (by using a workgroup instead) is not a good idea and removes all of the added value gained from the SBS 2003 environment.

c. Correct! Placing a domain controller in the remote office will allow user authentication occur local to the users and not over the much slower DSL VPN link.

d. Incorrect! But sounds logical, doesn't it? We know no one picked this answer! (We hope.)

Question #3: Answer: b

a.Incorrect! Exmerge only works with individual mailboxes not the entire server.

b. Correct! Exmerge will move mailboxes via .PST files. It does not, however, preserve permissions and will not migrate mailbox directories.

c. Incorrect! Exmerge can be used to recover mailboxes.

d. Incorrect! Exmerge only works on mailboxes.

Question #4: Answer: b

a. Incorrect! The SBS 2003 server cannot host terminal services in application mode.

b. Correct! The only way you can have terminal services running in application mode in an SBS 2003 environment is to host it on a separate server.

c. Incorrect! The SBS 2003 server cannot be configured to host terminal services in application mode.

d. Incorrect! As long as a separate server is the applications terminal services host it's not a problem.

Question #5: Answer: b, d

a. Incorrect! Port 443 is the SSL port and is not used for terminal services connectivity.

b. Correct! Port 3389 is used by clients to communicate with the terminal services serve. If port 3389 is blocked by the firewall the clients would not be able to connect. There are of course other reasons why connections may fail, but the key information here is that NONE of the remote clients could connect, while local users did not have an issue. This would lead us to look at the firewall because only remote users pass through it.

c. Incorrect! Though this is always a possible cause, in this case it is most likely not the main issue. Remember none of the remote users can connect. This includes the relocated terminal server user who it is implied could connect while in the local office. Most likely the cause is related to an improper firewall port configuration.

d. Correct! The fact that a firewall router is involved means that the local and remote offices are on different TCP/IP subnets. A route or routes needs to be defined so computers on each subnet can communicate with one another. Most often this happens automatically but is often missed in manual configurations.

e. Incorrect! Since the users in the local office are operating normally this means that terminal services are working properly.

Question #6: Answer: c

a. Incorrect! Port 443 is the SSL port and is not used for terminal services connectivity.

b. Incorrect! The fact that some of the remote users are working properly means that that port 3389 is open properly in the firewall.

c. Correct! This is the most likely cause. Chances are that the users from the remote office who were recently configured for terminal services access were not added to the Remote Desktop User group.

d. Incorrect! Since other remote users are working fine, the network configuration must be OK.

e. Incorrect! Since some of the users, local and remote, are operating properly, then the terminal server host must be configured properly.

Question #7: Answer: c

a. Incorrect! Only the updates are sent not the entire database.

b. Incorrect! The IXFR is sent by the secondary. The primary will send only the updates to the secondary which will then rebuild its database.

c. Correct! If the secondary's Serial Number does not match the primary, an IXFR will be sent to the primary. The primary will then send the changes to the secondary, which uses them to rebuild its database.

d. Incorrect! C is the correct answer

Question #8: Answer: a

a. Correct! If not the authoritative name server for the domain of the queried node, the SBS 2003 server will forward the request to its defined external DNS servers. The response is then used to answer the original query from the workstation.

b. Incorrect! The SBS 2003 will always check its database first and there is no such thing as a NORESP.

c. Incorrect! The query response goes back to the SBS 2003 server, which will then respond to the workstation.

d. Incorrect! Zone transfers are between DNS servers and are not initiated by DNS name queries. If the SBS 2003 server had to reconfigure itself as a stub zone for all domains for which it was not authoritative it wouldn't have time for anything else.

Question #9: Answer: c

a. Incorrect! A PTR record is a pointer but not to the primary DNS server.

b. Incorrect! The PTR record has nothing to do with SRV records.

c. Correct! Allows the resolution of a TCP/IP address to a node name.

d. Incorrect!

Question #10: Answer: d

d. Correct! Each of the methods listed (a,b,c) will invoke the DNS management interface.

Question #11: Answer: d

a. Incorrect!

b. Incorrect!

c. Incorrect! There is no tsconfig.inf file.

d. Correct! Change the encryption level by opening the Server Management Console, click on Advanced Management, Terminal Services Configuration. Click on the Connections folder to open it up, right click on the RDP-TCP connector and click on Properties. Choose Client Compatible as the encryption method.

Question #12: Answer: b, d

a. Incorrect! Exchange Server 2003, Standard Edition is part of SBS 2003 Standard so a license will be included.

b. Correct! SQL Server 2000, Standard Edition is an SBS 2003 Premium Edition component and is not included in the Standard Edition Transition Pack.

c. Incorrect! Exchange Server 2003, Standard Edition is part of SBS 2003 Standard so a license will be included.

d. Correct! ISA Server 2000, Standard Edition is an SBS 2003 Premium Edition component and is not included in the Standard Edition Transition Pack.

e. Incorrect! Five client access packs are included with both the Standard and Premium versions of the Transition Pack.

Question #13: Answer: a

a. Correct! The Application Compatibility Toolkit is a toolkit used by Microsoft developers themselves to test application compatibility.

b. Incorrect! WinApp.exe is not a valid application.

c. Incorrect! Setup.exe does not have a /CheckUpgrade switch.

d. Incorrect! Transaction Pack Premium (Upgrade Edition) is not a valid application.

Question #14: Answer: a, c, e

a. Correct! SBS 2003 is limited to two physical and four logical processors.

b. Incorrect! SBS 2003 does support terminal services in administration mode.

c. **Correct! Application mode terminal services is not allowed on SBS 2003.**

d. Incorrect! SBS 2003 will support up to 75 users.

e. **Correct! SBS 2003 cannot become a member of another domain or create child domains.**

Summary

Subliminally, this chapter is here to avoid having you develop a narrow-minded viewpoint of the 70-282 exam wherein you want to stay inside your SBS world. Hopefully, this chapter expanded your mind by getting you to think about expanding an SBS 2003 network. It's not sacrilegious to go beyond the SBS 2003 server box and there are appropriate times and places to do so.

You learned about adding a member server to an SBS 2003 network. Then you were taught how to promote the member server to a DC and what the ramifications would be. You delved into the nuts and bolts of migration strategies and execution, and added a little bit of Terminal Services, DNS and WINS, so now you have a better picture of what technologies are essential when expanding a network. And, as always, the materials presented in this chapter focus on the 70-282 certification exam!

CHAPTER 10
Installing and Configuring Windows Server 2003

Here comes the part where we have to remind you that the 70-282 exam is a Microsoft exam oriented toward a particular segment - small and medium businesses. The 70-282 exam is unique with its segment approach and isn't focused solely on a specific product. Rather, the 70-282 exam is focused on both SBS and the underlying Windows Server 2003 network operating system. Therefore, as odd as it seems, readers lucky enough to have Microsoft Certified System Engineer (MCSE) knowledge under their belts will find such knowledge helps them greatly!

Windows Server 2003

For the purpose of the 70-282 exam, you should have a general understanding of the differences between each server edition and know when one should be recommended over the other.

Standard Edition

The Windows Server 2003, Standard Edition includes:

- Maximum 4 GB RAM and minimum 128 MB RAM.
- Four-way symmetric multiprocessing (SMP).
- Designed for small organizations, workgroups and branch offices.
- File and printer sharing, the Active Directory directory services centralized management, web services and secure Internet connectivity.

Enterprise Edition

The Windows Server 2003, Enterprise Edition includes:

- Maximum 32 GB RAM for the 32-bit version (x86-based).
- Maximum 64 GB RAM for the 64-bit version (Itanium-based).
- Minimum 128 MB RAM for both, the 32-bit and 64-bit versions.
- Supports up to eight processors (for both the 32-bit and 64-bit version).
- Designed for medium- to large-sized organizations.
- Has all features of the Standard Edition.
- Supports clustering – not available in Standard Edition.

Datacenter Edition

The Windows Server 2003, Datacenter Edition includes:

- Maximum 1 TB RAM, minimum 512 MB RAM.
- Supports up to 64 processors (64-bit version) and 32 processors (32-bit version).
- Designed for large enterprise organizations.
- Must be purchased through an OEM.
- Supports clustering.

Web Edition

The Windows Server 2003, Web Edition includes:

- Maximum 2 GB RAM, minimum 128 MB RAM.
- Designed for small organizations needing to build and host web applications and services.
- Incorporates ASP and .NET framework functionality targeted towards developers and ISPs.

IMPORTANT: The 70-282 isn't just about SBS! The 70-282 exam will be very Windows Server 2003-centric, interwoven with SBS questions. Be sure to have your Windows core knowledge polished very well.

Installing Windows Server 2003

Insert Disc 1 and go! Hee, hee, I am just being silly, but that is how I feel about server installs. There was a time when I was installing several servers a week, and I can still remember dreaming about the text mode setup at night and having visions of BSODs (blue screens of death). The installation for NT required hitting the F8 key several times before you got to the end of the EULA. Nightmares!

Much time has passed since I encountered a BSOD during an install, and the SBS install is no different. Obviously with SBS running on top of Windows Server 2003, Disc 1 of the SBS Disc Set contains all the Windows Server 2003 installation files, located in the \i386 directory. Okay, enough talk. Let's move on.

Windows Server 2003 Standard Edition System Requirements

The Windows Server 2003 system requirements are shown in Table 10-1. Please don't laugh—just remember the minimum recommendations for the exam, so we made sure we got it straight from the horse's mouth.

IMPORTANT: The exam is looking for the Microsoft's version of the truth. Not what you think should be minimum requirements. Microsoft is testing you if you know their minimum recommendations. Treat Microsoft communications, such as presented here, as gospel!

Notes:

Table 10-1
Windows Server 2003 Standard Edition minimum system requirements

Component	Requirement
Computer and processor	PC with a 133-MHz processor required; 550-MHz or faster processor recommended. (Windows Server 2003 Standard Edition supports up to four processors on one server).
Memory	128 MB of RAM required; 256 MB or more recommended; 4 GB maximum.
Hard disk	1.25 to 2 GB of available hard-disk space.
Drive	CD-ROM or DVD-ROM drive.
Display	VGA or hardware that supports console redirection required. Super VGA supporting 800 x 600 or higher-resolution monitor recommended.

IMPORTANT: Do not install Windows Server 2003 on a compressed hard disk unless it was compressed with the NTFS file system. Drive Space or Double Space volumes should be uncompressed before running the Windows Setup.

Preparing for the Installation

Regardless of whether you have a brand new system or are recycling another system, before performing the installation you should prepare and verify several tasks to ensure a smooth install.

- Verify the hardware is listed in the Windows Server Catalog.

- Verify that components meet the minimum system requirements.

- Disable any disk mirroring during the setup process.

- Disconnect uninterruptable power supplies (UPS) or other serial connections (they could interfere detecting devices during the setup.

- Have the driver for SCSI, RAID, or Fibre Channel hard disks available.

- Ensure the BIOS is set to boot of CD-ROM or PXE-based network boot.

IMPORTANT: When you install Windows Server 2003 Standard Edition, any previous operating system must be completely removed from the partition. However, dual boot is still supported with Windows Server 2003.

Performing the Installation

The most common methods of installing Windows are for mass installations. These require automating the setup and deployment process using different methods like:

- Sysprep.

- Remote Installation Services (RIS).

- Answer files.

For the purpose of this exam we cover a manual server installation to show the basic installation process. There are several setup phases

- **Preinstallation** (optional phase if setup is run from Windows PE or a MS-DOS-based boot disk and copies the necessary files to boot the server into the text-mode Setup).

- **Text-mode Setup**

    - Examines the hard disk.

    - Determines what hardware is installed.

    - Performs limited plug and play detection.

    - Creates registry and files systems.

    - Partitions and formats the disks.

    - Checks for minimum system requirements.

    - Checks for adequate disk space.

    - Copies minimal installation files for the GUI-mode setup.

If you have SCSI, RAID, or Fibre Channel hard disks, you must engage the F6 key at the beginning of the text-mode setup, so you can provide the driver files.

- **GUI-mode Setup**

  - Detect and install devices found on the computer.

  - Configure each device, install and configure network components.

  - Copy installation files that were not copied during the text-mode setup.

  - Write the setup log files to the installation directory.

During GUI mode, the Windows Server 2003 Setup Wizard will complete the installation by requiring the following steps:

- Select regional and language settings.

- Provide name and organization.

- Ask for the 25-character product key.

- Choose a licensing mode.

- Ask for a computer name.

- Configure system date and time.

- Configure network components.

- And ask to join either a workgroup or domain. Often you first deploy Windows Server 2003 in workgroup mode and then make a decision about creating a domain (using the Configure Your Server Wizard discussed next which effectively runs the dcpromo command). However, in some cases you might have the Windows Server 2003 machine join an existing domain during the setup phase. You will need to make the proper choice depending on your situation.

The **First Boot will** complete the setup process and Windows will be ready for further configuration.

IMPORTANT: Even though you are not required to know exactly how other deployment processes work, i.e. Sysprep, RIS, it is a good idea to be familiar with the terminology and concept of these Microsoft methods. We focus on covering knowledge necessary for the 70-282 exam and encourage you to visit www.microsoft.com\reskit if you require further study.

Setup Command-Line Parameters

You can run the install from a network location from a computer that contains the Windows Server 2003 source files by running **x:\386\winnt.exe** (x is any drive letter), or by booting directly from the CD-ROM. The setup process for a single server can be streamlined by using command-line parameters. To use a parameter, use the command prompt window and type x:\winnt32.exe[parameter] (x is any drive letter). Table 10-2 contains common parameters:

Table 10-2
Command-Line Parameters

Parameter	Function
/checkupgradeonly	Runs a compatibility test to check for problems that may interfere with upgrading the operating system.
/cmdcons	Enables the Recovery Mode Console at boot time to repair failed installations.
/copydir:[folder name]	This parameter can be used several times. It names additional folders that setup can use to copy additional drivers or other files if needed.
/s:[sourcepath]	Specifies a Windows setup files location in case the default setup file location fails to search for needed files.
/syspart:[drive letter]	
/unattend	Upgrades the previous Windows version in unattended mode.

Troubleshooting Setup Issues

There are numerous erroneous and weird things that could happen to you during setup. If you stick with the guidelines and are not experimenting, then you should have smooth sailing. Table 10-3 contains a list of common and easily identifiable setup issues and the solutions to them.

Table 10-3
Common setup issues and their solutions

Problem	Solution
Media errors	Use a different CD. (Get a burned copy from your buddy.) (Just kidding! Call Microsoft.)
Non-supported CD-ROM drive	Replace the CD-ROM drive OR use a different install method, like across the network.
Insufficient hard disk space	Create a larger partition using the setup program.
Unable to contact the Domain Controller	Check the NIC first, as well as all physical connections. Check that the server running the DNS server service is online. Verify that the domain name is correct. If this is a reinstall using the same computer name, delete and re-create the computer account on the server.
Failure of Windows Server 2003 family to install or start	Check that the operating system detects all hardware and that such is listed in the Windows Server Catalog.
Bad device driver	A bad device driver can manifest itself in numerous ways including causing a failed setup. Ugly!

There could also be issues where setup just freezes in the middle of the installation or another type of failure occurs. There is a complete list of troubleshooting tips in the Microsoft online Knowledge Base at http://support. microsoft.com/winsrv2003.

Configuring Windows Server 2003

After a successful install of the operating system, there will be important configuration steps to perform. The server needs to be set up for its intended role on the network which can be done by either using the Manage Your Server window or the Configure Your Server Wizard. The Configure Your Server Wizard will appear by default the first time you log on to the server with administrative rights.

Configure Your Server Wizard

When setting up the first server in a domain, it will first check for other servers on the network. When it can't find other servers, the Configure Your Server Wizard will offer a Configuration Options page offering a choice of using the First Server option or choosing the server roles individually. By using the First Server option, the Configure your Server Wizard will walk you through the configuration process of setting up Active Directory, DNS, and DHCP.

A list of server roles the wizard can install and configure is in Table 10-4.

Table 10-4

Windows Server 2003 Standard Edition components and server roles

Component or server role	This wizard:
Administration across the network	Turns on Remote Desktop for Administration so this server can be administered from another computer.
A Dynamic Host Configuration Protocol (DHCP) server	Installs DHCP and starts the New Scope Wizard.
A DNS server	Installs DNS and starts the Configure DNS Wizard.
A domain controller (Microsoft Active Directory Service)	Starts the Active Directory Installation Wizard and effectively runs the dcpromo command.
File server	Limits the amount of hard disk space allocated, toggles indexing on or off, and installs a utility to manage folders.
The Post Office Protocol 3 (POP3) Service	Installs the POP3 Service.
Print server	Starts the Add Printer Wizard and the Add Printer Driver Wizard that installs printers and printer drivers on this server.

Component or server role	This wizard:
A server running Session Initiation Protocol (SIP)	Installs SIP on this server. SIP enables communication sessions like instant messaging, data collaboration, and file transfer.
Remote access server	Starts the Routing and Remote Access Setup Wizard.
A server running Microsoft Windows SharePoint Services 2.0	Installs Windows SharePoint Services and turns on the indexing service.
Streaming media server	Installs WMS (Windows Media Services).WMS delivers real-time multimedia content or prepares and streams stored content.

Configure File and Print Servers

File and print services are the heart of a business, regardless of its size. Windows Server 2003 has several wizards of its own, and the most prominent one is the Manage Your Server Wizard from which you can assign server roles and configure server settings. Quite honestly, I recommend installing Windows Server 2003 in either virtual PC or on an old machine floating around in your garage (as long as it meets minimum requirements) and getting some hands-on with the product so you don't walk into the exam totally cold. It helps the confidence level to have seen and touched it. You can acquire a copy of Windows Server 2003 Standard by downloading a trial version or purchasing the Action Pack from the Microsoft Partner site.

Configuring a File Server

In the following, we walk you through the steps of setting up a shared folder, turning on the indexing service, and setting permissions on the shared folder.

1. Click **Start** and then click **Manage Your Server**.

2. On the **Manage Your Server** page, click **Add or remove a role**.

3. On the **Preliminary Steps** page, review the preliminary steps and then click **Next**.

4. On the **Configuration Options** page, click **Custom configuration** and then click **Next**.

5. On the **Server Role** page, click **File server** and then click **Next**.

6. On the **File Server Disk Quotas** page, click **Next**.

7. On the **File Server Indexing Service** page, select **Yes, turn the Indexing Service on,** and then click **Next**.

8. On the **Summary of Selections** page, review the options you have selected, and then click **Next**.

9. On the **Welcome to the Share a Folder Wizard** page, click **Next**.

10. In the **Folder path** field, type **c:\shared\projects** and then click **Next**.

11. Click **Yes** to create the c:\shared\projects path.

12. On the **Name, Description, and Settings** page, in the **Share name** box, verify that **Projects** is displayed, and then click **Next**.

13. On the **Permissions page**, click **Administrators have full access; other users have read and write access**, and then click **Finish**.

14. On the **Sharing was Successful** page, review the options you selected and then click **Close**.

15. On the **This Server Is Now a File Server** page, click **Finish**.

That was pretty simple and we managed to configure basic settings in one swoop task. You probably noticed that we turned on the **Indexing Service**, which is a service that can scan files on servers and workstations and then build content and property indexes.

Indexing Service

The Indexing Service will allow you to search thousands of files in the index in different formats and languages by using key words, phrases, or properties. You can start a search by either clicking **Start** and then **Search** or through a **Web browser**.

After the Indexing Service has been configured, its operations run automatically, including index creation, updating, and crash recovery. The Indexing Service requires little maintenance and is designed to run continuously. Indexing Service properties can be configured through the MMC snap-in. It can be configured to use minimal resources for indexing, or configured to be a dedicated index server using all available resources.

To perform a search for a document that contains "OWA" in close proximity to "SBS," you would type **OWA NEAR SBS AND @filename=*.doc** in the Indexing Service query window.

To configure the Indexing Service:

1. Click **Start**, point to **Administrative Tools**, and then click **Computer Management**.

2. In the console tree, expand **Services and Applications** and then click **Indexing Service.**

3. On the **Action** menu, click **Properties**.

4. In the **Indexing Service Properties** dialog box, click the **Generation** tab and select the options you want:

    - **Index files with unknown extensions**. This option indexes documents with unknown extensions (those for which you do not have filters installed). Indexing Service extracts whatever content and properties it can from the documents.

    - **Generate abstracts**. This option produces abstracts of documents to present in the list of results. In the **Maximum size** box, type or select the maximum number of characters for the abstracts.

5. Click the **Tracking** tab, select the **Add Network Share Alias Automatically** checkbox if you want Indexing Service to use the share name of any shared directory as the alias for that directory, and then click **OK**.

6. On the **Action** menu, click **Stop** and then click **Start** for these changes to take effect.

IMPORTANT: To be honest, the Indexing Service typically has a supporting actor role in a small or medium-sized network. You don't really "use" the Indexing Service directly. However, the Indexing Service has a huge background role. It supports the searching capabilities of native operating system tools. But in my humble opinion, the real benefit of the Indexing Service is the supporting actor role for line-of-business applications. For example, when you install Microsoft CRM 1.2, a line-of-business application used for customer relationship management, the Indexing Services is required to be installed and properly configured. That is a key dependency you should understand.

Configuring a Print Server

A print server is a server that routes print requests and job status information on the network. This does not need to be a dedicated computer and servers usually share the printer server function with other duties. First you would physically attach a printer to the network using the Add Printer Wizard in the Printers and Faxes system folder. Needless to say you must be an Administrator on the print server. The Add Printer wizard guides you through the steps of adding a printer for a print device that is shared on the network or directly connected to the print server. Once you add a printer to the network and share it, you will be prompted for:

- The printer port on the server to which the print device is attached.
- The printer driver for the local print device.
- The printer name.
- The share name that allows users to connect to the printer.

After adding the printer to the network, you must run the Manage Your Server Wizard and choose first to **Add or remove a role** and then **Print Server** role. The wizard will then guide you through the rest of the installation configuring the particular settings the printer requires.

IMPORTANT: We can't emphasize enough the importance of exact terminology and we're starting to run out of chapters in this book to make that point! Read the following carefully, because some exam questions will invoke terminology trickery. A "print server" is a server that routes print requests and job status information on a network. A "printer" is the print device that performs the printing. A "logical printer" is the software interface on the print server.

Connecting to Printers on the Network

Once the network printer has been created, users can connect to it and use it like a local printer. To manually connect the printer:

1. Access the **Printer and Faxes** folder.

2. Double-click **Add Printer** to start the Printer Wizard.

3. Click select a **Network Printer** and click Next.

4. In the **Specify a Printer** dialogue box choose from one of the available options:

    a. **Find a Printer in the Directory.** (Select this option if you want search the Active Directory service for a printer.)

    b. **Type the Printer Name or click Next to Browse for a Printer.** (Select this option if you want to browse the network for shared printers.)

    c. **Connect to A Printer on the Internet or On Your Intranet.** (Select this option if you want to enter the URL for an Internet printer.)

5. Once the selection is made, click OK.

Configure Internet Printing

With Internet printing, you can print or manage documents from a web browser. You can also manage any shared printer on the print server from a browser. If you are using a computer that is running Microsoft Internet Explorer 4.01 or later, you can print to a printer over an intranet or the Internet by typing the address of the print server in the **Address** box. For example, type http://*printservername*/ printers/ (*printservername* is the name of you print server).

Internet printing is turned on automatically on a Windows Server 2003-based computer when you install Microsoft Internet Information Services (IIS) and then turn on Internet Printing through the IIS Security Lockdown Wizard. Printing is implemented by way of the Internet Print Protocol (IPP), which is encapsulated in the Hypertext Transfer Protocol (HTTP).

Connecting a Printer by Using a Web Browser

You can connect to a Web browser by typing http://*printservername*/printers/ (*printservername* is the name of you print server). Once connected, the print server downloads the appropriate printer driver to your computer. When you click **Connect** on the printer's web page a .cab file containing the appropriate printer driver files is generated and downloaded by the server. After the installation is complete, the printer's icon is added to the Printers folder on your computer. You can use, monitor, and administer the printer as if it were attached to your computer.

Internet Printing Security

The authentication method for Internet printing can be configured through IIS on the print server. The following authentication methods are available:

- Enable anonymous access.
- Integrated Windows authentication.
- Digest authentication for Windows domain servers.
- Basic authentication.
- Microsoft .NET Passport authentication.

Setting Group Policy for Printers

It is easy to manage printer policies using Group Policy.

1. Start Group Policy according to the object you want to set the printer policy to.

2. Select the properties page of the object to manage and select the Group Policy node.

3. If you want the policy to apply to users, expand the **User Configuration** node.

4. Expand **Administrative Templates** and then expand **Control Panel.**

5. Double-click **Printers** to open a listing of policies.

6. Select the printer policy, double-click and on the **Policy** tab, enable or disable the policy.

Active Directory Overview

If you have worked with SBS up to this point or with single Windows Server 2003 installations but not in multi-server environments, please do a bit of reading up on Active Directory (AD) at http://www.mircosoft.com/reskit for a deeper dive. We will give you a quick down and dirty overview in the following pages, but take this to heart: SBS is built on Windows Server 2003 using AD, and despite the management of AD through SBS wizards, reality is that you need to know AD, its tools and utilities, its functions and how to access and manage AD. Ergo: **Do not skip this part!**

Active Directory is a structured data store providing information about objects on the network in a logical, hierarchical organization of directory information. Active Directory objects are shared resources such as servers, volumes, printers, network users, computer accounts, and other distributed resources. Distributed environments require a central repository of information and integrated services that provide the means to manage the objects (network users, services, devices, and additional information).

Active Directory provides:

- A central location for network administration and delegation of administrative authority.

- Information security and single sign-on for user access to network resources.

- Scalability. (Active Directory includes one or more domains, each with one or more domain controllers, enabling you to scale the directory to meet any network requirements).

- Flexible and global searching. (Users and administrators can use desktop tools to search Active Directory).

- Storage for application data.

- Systematic synchronization of directory updates. (Updates are distributed throughout the network through secure and cost-efficient replication between domain controllers – see Replication, below).

- Remote administration.

- Integration of object names with DNS.

- Lightweight Directory Access Protocol (LDAP) support. (Active Directory supports LDAPv3 and LDAPv2).

Replication

Large sites with multiple domain controllers replicate updates on Active Directory objects between them to keep a replica of the directory partitions synchronized. Domain controllers in the same domain are commonly placed in separate sites. Replication must occur within sites and between sites to keep the domain data consistent.

Knowledge Consistency Checker

The Knowledge Consistency Checker (KCC) is a distributed application that runs on every domain controller and is responsible for creating the connections between domain controllers. The domain controllers form the replication topology collectively. The KCC uses Active Directory data and determines how connections are created from the source domain controller to the destination domain controller.

File Replication Service

The File Replication Service (FRS) is a multimaster replication service that is used to replicate files and folders in the system volume (SYSVOL) shared folder on domain controllers and in Distributed File System (DFS) shared folders. FRS uses the replication topology that is generated by the KCC to replicate the SYSVOL files to all domain controllers in the domain. It works by detecting changes to files and folders and then replicating the updated files and folders to other replica members, which are connected in a replication topology.

Data Store

The data store (referred to as the directory) is located in the Ntds.dit file on the domain controller. The data store is separated into:

- **Private data**: Stored securely and not replicated.

- **Public data**: Stored in a shared system volume and replicated to other domain controllers.

The public data store replicates the following data with other domain controllers:

- **Domain data**: Contains information on objects in the domain such as user and computer account attributes, e-mail contacts, and published resources.

- **Configuration data**: Contains a list of all domains, trees and forests, and the locations of domain controllers and global catalogs.

- **Schema data**: Contains the definitions for all objects in the directory. Schema data is made up of object classes and attributes. Every new object created in the directory is validated against the schema object definitions.

- **Application data**: Can be replicated to a specific domain controller or a set of domain controllers anywhere in the forest and is not part of the directory data store by default.

To keep directory data on all domain controllers consistent and up-to-date, Active Directory replicates directory changes on a regular basis. Following are the two types of methods of replication:

- Intra-site replication: Replication within a website using remote procedure call (RPC).

- Inter-site replication: Replication to domain controllers in different sites using RPC over TCP/IP or SMTP.

Global Catalog

A global catalog (GC) is a domain controller that stores a full copy of all of its host domain objects and a partial copy of objects of all other domains in the forest. The global catalog enables users to perform searches for directory information throughout all domains in the entire forest. By default, the first domain controller in a domain is a global catalog server. When adding additional domain controllers, you will have to manually enable the global catalog. Perform the following steps to enable or disable the global catalog:

1. Open **Active Directory Sites and Services**/Sites/Your_Name DC site/Servers/Your_Server_Name.

2. Right-click **NTDS Settings** and click **Properties.**

3. Select or clear the **Global Catalog** check box to enable or disable the global catalog.

The Global Catalog performs the following roles:

- **Finds objects**. The GC enables searching the directory for information throughout all domains in a forest. If you search for a person or printer from the Start Menu and choose the Entire Directory option, the query is routed to port 3268 and sent to a global catalog for resolution.

- **Supplies user principal name (UPN) authentication**. The GC resolves the UPN if the authenticating domain controller does not have the knowledge of an account.

- **Supplies universal group membership information in a multiple domain environment**. Universal group membership is stored in the global catalog compared to global group membership which is stored in each domain. (More on group memberships later in this chapter.)

IMPORTANT: If there is only one domain in a forest, obtaining universal group memberships for users is not necessary when logging on. Active Directory detects that there are no other domains in the forest and will prevent a query to the global catalog for this information.

Active Directory Functional Levels

Introduced in Windows Server 2003 Active Directory services, functional levels enable advanced Active Directory features on the domain controller. There are different functional levels for domains and forests so Active Directory capabilities can be maximized within each domain or forest.

Functional levels protect against incompatibility. Before raising a functional level, Active Directory verifies that all domain controllers are running the correct version of the operating system. After raising the functional level, Active Directory no longer allows the introduction of a domain controller that is running an incompatible version of Windows Server.

Forest and domain functional levels are restrictive for domain controllers only. Clients can interact with Active Directory regardless of the domain or forest functional level that is in effect. In a domain that has a functional level of Windows Server 2003, domain controllers can still authenticate computers that are running earlier versions of Windows.

> IMPORTANT: Raising domain and forest functional levels is required to enable certain new features as domain controllers are upgraded from Windows NT 4.0 and Windows 2000 to Windows Server 2003. Even for a new installation of Windows Server 2003 Active Directory (as opposed to an upgrade), an administrator must raise functional levels to obtain the full capabilities of Windows Server 2003 Active Directory.

Domain Functional Level

This level is an extension of the mixed and native domain modes that were available in Microsoft Windows 2000 Server operating system. Domain functional levels affect the domain only. There are four domain functional levels:

- Windows 2000 mixed (default functional level)*.
- Windows 2000 native.
- Windows Server 2003 Interim.
- Windows Server 2003.

Some of the features enabled in the domain functional level, for instance, allow drag and drop functionality by dragging objects from container to container, more efficient search capabilities, saving search parameters for reuse in AD and universal group membership caching and many other advanced functions.

Forest Functional Level

This is a new level in Windows Server 2003. It enables Active Directory features across all domains in the forest. There are three forest functional levels:

- Windows 2000 Server (default functional level)*.
- Windows Server 2003 Interim.
- Windows Server 2003.

Advanced features enabled at the forest functional level include all default Active Directory features and features such as enabling group nesting, Security Identifier (SID) history, enabling universal group membership for both, distribution and security groups and using netdom.exe, a management tool to prepare for a domain controller rename.

* New Windows Server 2003 Active Directory deployments where the domain controller is the root domain, the forest functional level of the newly created forest is Windows 2000 and the domain functional level is Windows 2000 mixed domain mode.

> IMPORTANT: After the domain functional level has been raised, it cannot be reversed. After this, domain controllers that are not supported at that level cannot be introduced.

Promoting to a Domain Controller

A server can be promoted to a domain controller by installing Active Directory. Once promoted, the server will contain a writable copy of the AD database, participate in AD replication and be able to control access to network resources. You install Active Directory through the **Manage Your Server** page and choosing the domain controller role, which will then launch the Active Directory Installation Wizard. You have to be a member of the **Domain Admins** group, be a member of the **Enterprise Admins** group or have been **delegated the appropriate authority** to perform this procedure. The Active Directory Installation Wizard will ask you if you want to create a:

- Domain in a New Forest.
- Domain Tree in an Existing Forest.
- Child Domain in an Existing Domain Tree.

The wizard will continue and ask for:

- NetBIOS domain name.
- Active Directory Database and log file location.
- Shared System Volume (SYSVOL) folder location.
- Whether to install and configure DNS.
- Permissions for user and group objects to be compatible with previous Windows versions.
- Directory Services Restore Mode Administrator Password.

After all the above information is provided, the Active Directory Installation Wizard installs Active Directory and promotes the server to a domain controller. The following consoles will be added to the Administrative Tools menu:

- Active Directory Domains and Trusts.
- Active Directory Sites and Services.
- Active Directory Users and Computers.

You must restart the Windows Server 2003 after the Active Directory Installation Wizard finishes, where the server will then be converted to a domain controller and the consoles will be added.

Install Active Directory Steps

To install Active Directory from the command-line type:

Dcpromo

To install Active Directory from the Administrative Tools:

1. Click **Configure Your Server Wizard**.

2. Select **Domain Controller** (Active Directory) to configure your domain controller.

3. After the Configure Your Server Wizard finishes, the Active Directory Installation Wizard begins.

To install Active Directory on a Windows Server 2003-based member server from media:

1. Go to the **Run** dialog box.

2. Type **dcpromo /adv**.

3. Click **OK.**

4. The wizard then prompts you for the installation source.

Demoting a Domain Controller

Demoting a DC comes just as easily as promoting a DC.

1. Launch **dcpromo** (preferably from the Run command but you can use the wizard as well).

2. In the **Active Directory Installation Wizard** click Next.

3. On the **Remove Active Directory** page click Next and follow the wizard to finish.

Before you start the domain controller demotion you want to verify that this DC is not the only **global catalog** and that it doesn't hold an **operations master** role.

• If this domain controller currently holds one or more operations master roles, transfer the operations master roles to another domain controller before demoting it.

• If this domain controller is a global catalog, ensure that another global catalog is available to users before demoting it.

• If this domain controller is the last domain controller in the domain, demoting this domain controller will remove this domain from the forest.

- If this domain controller holds the last replica of one or more application directory partitions, you must first remove the last application directory partition replicas from this domain controller before you can demote it.

Operations Master Roles

The multimaster replication of Active Directory between all DCs makes the DCs practically peers. There are some changes that would not be practical to replicate and therefore the requests for those changes are handled by one domain controller only, the one which holds the role of **operations master.**

There are at least five operations master roles that are assigned to one or more domain controllers. Forest-wide operations master roles must appear only once in every forest. Domain-wide operations master roles must appear once in every domain in the forest.

The operations master roles are also called **flexible single master operations (FSMO)** roles.

Forest-wide Operations Master Roles

Each forest must contain the following roles:

- **Schema master.** The schema master domain controller controls all updates and modifications to the schema.
- **Domain naming master**. The domain controller holding the domain naming master role controls the addition or removal of domains in the forest.

There can only be one Schema master and one Domain naming master in the entire forest.

Domain-wide Operations Master Roles

Every domain in the forest must contain the following roles and each role can only be represented once in each domain.

- **RID master.** The RID master allocates sequences of relative IDs (RIDs) to each of the various domain controllers in its domain. Whenever a domain controller creates a user, group, or computer object, it assigns the object a unique security ID (SID). The SID consists of a domain SID, which is the same for all SIDs created in the domain, and a RID, which is unique for each SID created in the domain.

- **PDC emulator master.** If the domain contains computers operating without Windows 2000 or Windows XP Professional client software or if it contains Windows NT backup domain controllers (BDCs), the PDC emulator master acts as a Windows NT primary domain controller. It processes password changes from clients and replicates updates to the BDCs. The PDC emulator master is also responsible for synchronizing the time on all domain controllers throughout the domain. The PDC emulator role supports two authentication protocols:

  - Kerberos V5

  - NTLM

- **Infrastructure master.** The infrastructure master is responsible for updating references from objects in its domain to objects in other domains. The infrastructure master compares its data with that of a global catalog. Global catalogs receive regular updates for objects in all domains through replication, so the global catalog data will always be up to date.

IMPORTANT: Unless there is only one domain controller in the domain, the infrastructure master role should not be assigned to the domain controller that is hosting the global catalog. If the infrastructure master and global catalog are on the same domain controller, the infrastructure master will not function. The infrastructure master will never find data that is out-of-date, so it will never replicate any changes to the other domain controllers in the domain.

NTDSUTIL

The NTDS utility is a command-line tool that provides management facilities for Active Directory and can be used to move or seize FSMO roles. At times there is a need to move or seize a FSMO role, for instance, when the domain controller is failing.

To move a role using the command line (here we use the RID master):

1. Open the command prompt, type **ntdsutil.**

2. At the ntdsutil command prompt, type **roles.**

3. At the FSMO maintenance command prompt, type **connection.**

4. At the server connections prompt, type **connect to server***Domain Controller*.

5. At the server connections command prompt, type **quit.**

6. At the FSMO maintenance command prompt, type **transfer RID master.**

Other parameters could be used for **moving** master roles under Step 6, for instance, transfer domain naming master|transfer infrastructure master|transfer PDC|transfer schema master.

Other parameters could be used for **seizing** master roles under Step 6, for instance, seize domain naming master|seize infrastructure master|seize PDC|seize RID master|seize schema master.

You have to be a member of the Domain Admins group, a member of the Enterprise Admins group or have been delegated the appropriate authority to transfer FSMO roles. To Transfer the schema master role you must be a member of the Schema Admins group.

Ntdsutil.exe is also used for Active Directory maintenance, including performing metadata cleanup, authoritative restores, configuring LDAP policies, setting the DSRM (Directory Services Restore Mode) password and other tasks.

Configure Networking, Hardware

After Windows Server 2003 Setup completes, you have to configure your server's network settings to get the system to basic working order. That includes verifying that Setup completed properly, adding devices and configuring the server's network settings, and setting the server up for one of the roles covered previously in this chapter.

Check for Setup Issues

It is recommended that you check for Windows Setup issues or device problems after the Windows installation is complete. Here are some areas to check:

Setup Error log. Open Explorer and go to C:\Windows\setuperr.log. If the file does not exist or is empty you had a clean install.

Log Files. Click Start, go to Administrative Tools, Click Computer Management, select Event Viewer and then click System. Review the Application, Directory Service and other logs.

Devices. Click Start, go to Administrative Tools, Click Computer Management, select Device Manager and check for missing or problem devices.

Disk Management. Go to the **Run** command box, type **diskmgmt. msc**. The Disk Management console will open. Check that all hard disks and partitions are there.

Enable Remote Administration

Remote Desktop is not enabled by default and should be the first thing you enable, unless you like to spend much time in the server closet. Remote desktop will allow you to manage the server from your desktop as if you were sitting in front of the server.

> IMPORTANT: Make sure to only administer the server from a secure workstation and not a public terminal to mitigate the risk of compromise. It is preferred that you not use e-mail or browse the web from the machine where your are administering the server from.

To enable Remote Desktop:

1. Click Start, select the **Control Panel** and go to the **System Properties.**

2. Click the **Remote Tab** and select **Enable Remote Desktop on this computer.**

3. Members of the Administrators Group are given permission by default to remotely connect to Remote Desktop after it has been enabled.

4. Select any additional Users that need remote access to the server.

5. If Windows Firewall is enabled you must select the Remote Desktop exception in the Windows Firewall (Start > Control Panel > Windows Firewall > Exception) and select the Remote Desktop checkbox. Remote Desktop uses port 3389.

Configure Devices

Windows Server 2003 will detect and configure devices automatically unless it cannot find drivers or there is a resource conflict. You want to reconnect the UPS and add any plug and play (PnP) devices you had disconnected before the installation.

Device Console Utility

Devices can be managed from the command line or with Device Manager. To administer a device from the command line, use **Devcon.exe**, a Windows Management Instrumentation Command-line (WMIC) found under the support tools on the product CD.

This command-line tool brings many of the functions of Device Manager to the command window. Devcon enables, disables, installs, configures, and removes devices on the local computer and displays detailed information about devices on local and remote computers.

Device Manager

You can also use the graphical user interface for Device Manager by going to:

1. **Start, Programs, Administrative Tools** and clicking on **Computer Management.**

2. Expand the **System Tools** node and click on **Device Manager.**

or by going to:

1. **Start,** click on **Run** to open the dialog box.

2. Type **devmgmt.msc.**

Device Manager is a central repository for device information Windows has detected on your system. Nonfunctioning devices will be displayed with an exclamation point indicating a problem with the device or a red "x" over the device icon, indicating a disabled device.

By clicking on the device properties you can now administer the device and have the choice of:

-   Scanning for Hardware changes.

-   Update the device driver.

-   Uninstall the device.

-   Disable/Enable the device.

Configure Networking

The following section will give you step-by-step network configurations. For a deep dive on the following topics (despite us trying to cover these here in Chapter 9 and Chapter 10), TCP/IP, DHCP, WINS and DNS are far to extensive to elaborate in this book and many great entire books have been written on these topics. But you can get the whole enchilada for free at http://www.microsoft.com/reskit.

No, the team is not trying to cop out and head to the pub early. This is our way of subliminally suggesting that Windows networking is a core part of any network administrator's knowledge. We actually have grown quite fond of the Windows Server Resource kit and have found it an excellent study guide in the past, especially if we needed concepts explained or needed knowledge beyond the usual expectations. Moving on.

The Windows Server 2003 should have already been properly configured during the setup but you need to know how to add or change settings for the core network components. Components could be clients, services and protocols. You can access these through the **Network Connections** folder.

1. Click Start, then **Control Panel** and right-click the **Local Area Connection.**

2. Choose **Properties.**

The **Local Area Connection Properties** dialog box will open where you can view and change the servers networking components.

Configure TCP/IP for Dynamic Addressing

By default, computers running Windows Server 2003 operating systems attempt to obtain the TCP/IP configuration from a DHCP server on the network. You would only perform the following steps if a static TCP/IP configuration had been used previously.

1. Open **Network Connections.**

2. On the **General Tab** or **Networking Tab** click **Internet Protocol (TCP/IP)** and click **Properties.**

3. Click **Obtain an IP address automatically**, click OK.

To perform this procedure, you must be a member of the Administrators group or the Network Configuration Operators group on the local computer. (See Chapter 6 for more information.)

Configure TCP/IP for Static Addressing

Usually you would not configure a static IP address for a device on the network. Managing TCP/IP addressing through DHCP is the easiest and most reliable way to distribute IP addresses. In order to manually configure the TCP/IP address

1. Open **Network Connections.**

2. On the **General Tab** or **Networking tab** click **Internet Protocol (TCP/IP)** and click **Properties.**

3. Click **Use the following IP address** and do one of the following:

a. For a local area connection in **IP address, Subnet mask,** and **Default gateway** type the IP address, subnet mask and default gateway address.

b. For all other connections in **IP address**, type the IP address.

4. Click **Use the following DNS server addresses.**

5. Type in **Preferred DNS server** and **Alternate DNS server**, the primary and secondary DNS server addresses.

To perform this procedure, you must be a member of the Administrators group or the Network Configuration Operators group on the local computer. (See Chapter 6 for more information.)

Configure TCP/IP for Automatic Addressing

Automatic Private IP Addressing (APIPA) is a TCP/IP feature in Windows XP and Windows Server 2003 that automatically configures a unique IP address from the range 169.254.0.1 through 169.254.255.254 with a subnet mask of 255.255.0.0. By default, the TCP/IP protocol is configured for automatic addressing in computers running Windows XP and Windows Server 2003 operating systems. If a DCHP server is not available, the APIPA alternate configuration setting is selected automatically. The APIPA range of IP addresses is reserved by the Internet Assigned Numbers Authority (IANA) for use on a single subnet. IP addresses within this range are not used on the Internet.

To configure APIPA follow the same steps as outlined above under *Configure TCP/IP for dynamic addressing*, because APIPA will automatically assigned if a DHCP server is not detected.

DHCP

Windows Server 2003 Dynamic Host Configuration Protocol (DHCP) reduces the complexity and administrative overhead involved in managing network-client IP addressing and configuration. DHCP enables you to assign IP addresses to network clients automatically and dynamically, as needed, and to automate, centralize, and simplify IP address and option configuration and distribution across your network. This protects against common configuration errors that occur when values are entered manually at each computer and helps to prevent address conflicts.

Some commonly used DHCP configuration options are:

- Subnet mask.
- Default gateway.
- Domain suffix.
- DNS server addresses.
- WINS server addresses.
- Scope options.
- Class options.
- Reservation options.

There are over 70 available options that you can assign using a Windows Server 2003 DHCP server, but DHCP client computers running Windows Server 2003 and Windows XP only request these options listed in the following table:

Table 10-5
Common DHCP Options

Option	Description
001 Subnet Mask	Specifies the subnet mask associated with the leased IPv4 address. The subnet mask is configured with a scope and does not need to be separately configured as an option.
003 Router	Specifies the IPv4 address of the default gateway of the host.
006 DNS Servers	Specifies the IPv4 addresses of DNS servers.
015 DNS Domain Name	Specifies the connection-specific DNS domain suffix to be used by the DHCP client.

Option	Description
031 Perform Router Discovery	Specifies whether the DHCP client uses Internet Control Message Protocol (ICMP) router discovery as a host, as specified in RFC 1256.
033 Static Route	Specifies a set of IPv4 network destinations and their corresponding router IPv4 addresses that DHCP clients add to their IPv4 routing tables.
043 Vendor-specific Information	Specifies that vendor-specific options are requested.
044 WINS/NBNS Servers	Specifies the IPv4 addresses of WINS servers.
046 WINS/NBT Node Type	Specifies the type of network basic input/output system (NetBIOS) over TCP/IP name resolution to be used by the client.
047 NetBIOS Scope ID	Specifies the NetBIOS scope ID. NetBIOS over TCP/IP (NetBT) hosts will communicate only with other NetBT hosts that are using the same scope ID.
249 Classless Static Routes	Specifies a set of classless routes that are added to the IPv4 routing table of the DHCP client.

DHCP traffic uses the following ports:

- **UDP port 67:** DHCP clients listen on this port.
- **UDP port 68:** DHCP servers listen on this port.

IMPORTANT: The DHCP Server service is installed on Small Business Server 2003 by default. Other editions of Windows Server 2003 require you to install the DHCP Server service through the **Add or Remove Program** applet under **Add/Remove Windows**

Components. Under **Components**, click **Networking Services**, **Details** and in the **Subcomponents of Networking Service**, select **Dynamic Host Configuration Protocol**. After the DHCP Server service is installed, the DHCP server should be **authorized** and a **scope activated** before it is able to assign addresses to clients.

DHCP Relay Agent

A relay agent is a small program that relays DHCP/BOOTP messages between clients and servers on different subnets and should comply with RFC 1542. The DHCP Relay Agent is a routing protocol component included in the Routing and Remote Access service in Windows Server 2003.

Perform the following steps to install the DHCP Relay Agent:

1. Open Routing and Remote Access/server name/IP Routing.

2. Right-click **General** and select **New Routing Protocol**.

3. In the **Select Routing Protocol** section, select **DHCP Relay Agent**.

IMPORTANT: You cannot use the DHCP Relay Agent component on a computer running the DHCP service, the network address translation (NAT) routing protocol component with automatic addressing enabled, or Internet Connection Sharing (ICS).

DHCP Scope Configuration

A DHCP scope is an administrative grouping of IP addresses for computers on a subnet. Each subnet can have only a single DHCP scope with a continuous range of IP addresses. The scope defines the parameters used by clients on that subnet. The scope includes:

- IP address range (included or excluded addresses for DHCP lease offering).

- Subnet mask.

- Scope name.

- Lease duration values.

- DHCP scope options, such as DNS server, WINS server, and so on.

- Reservations (optional) to ensure a DHCP client retains the same IP address.

- Exclusion ranges: Exclusion ranges are set for IP addresses within the scope that should not be offered for DHCP lease assignment. Excluded IP addresses can be active on the network, but need to be manually configured on the host.

After a scope has been configured, it must be activated to start serving clients. Perform the following steps to activate the DHCP scope:

1. Open **Administrative Tools** and click **DHCP.**
2. Select **DHCP server/scope.**
3. Right-click **Activate** from the drop-down.

DHCP Scope Types

Following are the types of DHCP scopes:

- **Scope:** Distributes IP addresses to computers on the network.

- **Superscope:** Allows multiple logical IPv4 subnets on the same physical subnet grouped under a single name.

- **Multicast Scope:** Distributes a group of IP multicast network addresses to computers on the network.

Backing Up the DCHP Database

The default DHCP database backup path is systemroot\System32\Dhcp\Backup. There are three backup methods supported by the DHCP Server service:

- Synchronous backups that occur automatically. The default backup interval is 60 minutes. These are performed while the DHCP Server service is running.

- Asynchronous (manual) backups are performed by using the **Backup** command on the DHCP console. These can be performed while the DHCP Server service is running.

- Backups using Windows Backup (ntbackup.exe) or non-Microsoft backup software.

When a synchronous or asynchronous backup occurs, the entire DHCP database is saved, including the following:

- All scopes, including superscopes and multicast scopes.

- Reservations.

- Leases.

- All options, including server options, scope options, reservation options, and class options.

- All registry keys and other configuration settings (for example, audit trail settings and folder location settings) set in DHCP server properties. These settings are stored in the following registry subkey: HKEY_LOCAL_MACHINE\SYSTEM\CurrentControlSet\Services\ DHCPServer\Parameters.

Restoring the DHCP Database

You can restore the DHCP database from a backup copy of the database file, Dhcp.mdb, located at systemroot\System32\Dhcp\Backup. The **Restore** command is located on the **Action** menu in the DHCP console. When you restore the DHCP database from a backup copy of Dhcp.mdb the following information is restored:

- All scopes, including superscopes and multicast scopes.

- Reservations.

- Leases.

- All options, including server options, scope options, reservation options, and class options.

- All registry keys and other configuration settings (for example, audit trail settings and folder location settings) set in DHCP server properties.

IMPORTANT: The DNS dynamic update credentials (user name, domain, and password) that the DHCP server uses when registering

DHCP client computers in DNS are not backed up with any backup method; therefore, they are not restored during the restore procedure. After restoring your DHCP database, you must configure credentials for your server.

WINS

Contrary to popular belief, WINS is still alive and well. You may just encounter it during the exam so we will not deprive you of yet another Microsoft core networking component that used to be an integral part of a Microsoft Network until Active Directory showed up. So again we'll keep it short and sweet and you will find further reading at http:\\www.microsoft.com\reskit.

The Windows Internet Naming Service (WINS) is a NetBIOS name resolution service that allows client computers to register their NetBIOS names and IP addresses (name-to-IP address mapping) in a distributed database. WINS is the Microsoft implementation of NBNS (refer to NetBIOS). NetBIOS names of network resources can then be queried and resolved back to the respective IPv4 addresses. WINS supports dynamic registering of NetBIOS computer names using the DHCP services to provide ease of configuration and administration of a Windows-based TCP/IP network. WINS is used in a routed environment. Most routers are not configured to forward broadcasts among subnet masks and the WINS server resolves this problem by automatically updating the WINS database.

WINS Benefits

Following are the benefits of WINS:

- Pre-Windows Server 2003 clients can locate domain controllers not on their local subnet.

- Centralized management of NetBIOS name-to-IP address mapping.

- Eliminates the need for LMHOSTS files (static mapping).

- Dynamic, distributed database for registering, and resolving NetBIOS names.

- Reduces broadcast traffic.

IMPORTANT: WINS is installed by default on Windows Small Business Server 2003 but not on any other Microsoft Windows Server 2003 Standard Edition. For Windows Server 2003 Editions, you need to add WINS as a service through the **Add or Remove Programs** applet.

WINS Database Replication

For a host computer that registered its NetBIOS name with WINS server01 to communicate with a host computer that registered with WINS server02, both WINS server01 and WINS server02 are required to first replicate their databases to each other. The replication will allow the WINS server01 to resolve the NetBIOS names that were registered with the WINS server02 and vice versa.

WINS servers can be configured like the following partners:

- Push partner: Notifies other WINS servers when changes are made to WINS server database.

- Pull partner: Requests database changes from other WINS servers.

- Both Push and Pull: It performs the actions of both the push partner and the pull partner.

WINS Rule of Thumb

A good rule of thumb to follow for WINS is as follows:

- If WINS servers are connected by slow links, configure a pull partner so that replication can be scheduled.

- If WINS servers are connected by fast links, configure a push partner so that replication can occur when changes are made to the database.

IMPORTANT: WINS servers replicate only new entries in the WINS databases. Servers do not replicate the entire WINS databases each time replication occurs.

Backing up the WINS Database

The WINS management console allows you to configure periodic backups of the WINS server database. Perform the following steps to configure periodic backups for the WINS server database:

1. In the WINS Server Properties window, you can specify a backup location. The server will create a wins_bak\new folder in the specified location and backup the local database at a regular interval of every three hours.

2. On the Properties tab, select the Back Up database during server shutdown check box. Alternatively, right-click WINS server and click Back Up database from the drop-down for an immediate backup.

Restoring the WINS Database

The WINS service must be stopped before restoring the database.

Perform the following steps to restore the WINS database:

1. Right-click WINS server and select Restore Database.

2. Specify the location where the backup folder is located. The database backups can also be restored to a new computer.

Integrating WINS with DHCP

When you configure a network to use both DHCP and WINS, set the DHCP lease period to be equal to or greater than the WINS renewal period. This prevents a situation in which the WINS server fails to notice that a DHCP client computer has released a DHCP-assigned IP address. Specifically, the client computer cannot send a WINS renewal request because it did not renew the IP address.

Secure Windows Server 2003

First install Windows Server 2003 SP1—wait, that's not included in the exam as of this writing. We must focus on the pre-SP1 era and consider how to secure communications between the server and clients going out to the Internet as well as those coming in from public unsecured networks. There are numerous ways to secure and lock down the server, but let's not get away from Microsoftology and look at natively included options in Windows Server 2003.

Configure and Secure Internet Access

NAT (Network Address Translation) configured through RRAS (Routing and Remote Access Service) translates private, internal IP addresses to external public IPs. This protects the private network from unauthorized access by hiding the private IP from the public networks (as explained previously in Chapter 6). To implement NAT in RRAS, you can use the Manage Your Server Wizard and follow these steps:

1. Click **Start,** then click on **Manage Your Server.**

2. On the **Manage Your Serv**er page, click **Add or remove a role.**

3. On the **Preliminary Steps** page, click **Next**.

4. On the **Server Role** page, click **Remote access/VPN server**, and then click **Next**.

5. On the **Summary of Selections** page, review the selected options, and then click **Next**.

6. On the **Welcome to the Routing and Remote Access Server Setup Wizard** page, click **Next**.

7. On the **Configuration** page, click **Network address translation (NAT)** and click **Next**.

8. On the **NAT Internet Connection** page, select the interface to connect to the Internet.

9. Clear the **Enable security on the selected interface by setting up Basic** Firewall checkbox and then click **Next**.

10. On the **Name and Address Translation Services** page, click **Enable basic name and address services,** and then click **Next.**

11. On the summary information page click **Finish.**

This is too easy, the enterprise people are supposed to use command lines and scripts and stuff like that. Who allowed them to have wizards?

Configure a VPN Connection

RRAS not only manages NAT, but also provides VPN services. RRAS encrypts the data as it is sent over an unsecured network, encapsulating the data with a header that provides routing information, and acts like a point-to-point link on a private network. Even if data is intercepted, it cannot be read without the encryption key. This is also called a VPN tunnel.

There are two tunneling protocols:

- PPTP – uses user-level PPP (Point-to-Point Protocol) authentication methods and MPPE (Microsoft Point-to-Point encryption).

- L2TP/IPSec – (Layer 2 Tunneling Protocol with Internet Protocol Security) uses user-level PPP authentication methods over an IPSec encrypted connection. IPSec requires either Kerberos, Certificates, or Shared Secret Keys for authentication.

- Used for secure communications between a remote client and a corporate network across the Internet.

- Used for secure communications between branch offices.

For L2TP, both the client and server must support L2TP and IPSec. Client support for L2TP is built into the Windows XP remote access client, and VPN server support for L2TP is built into the Windows Server 2003 family. The L2TP server support is automatically installed when you install RRAS. Based on your choices during the RRAS Setup Wizard, L2TP can be configured for as few as five or as many as 128 L2TP ports.

By using a L2TP enabled VPN with IPSec for authentication, data transfer is as secure as a LAN in a corporate network. Before you can configure a VPN server role, you must:

- Identify the network interface connecting to the Internet and the remote interface connecting to your network.

- Decide whether to assign IP addresses to clients through the VPN server or the DHCP server on the network.

- Decide whether you want the VPN server or RADIUS to authenticate connection requests from VPN clients.

Before being able to configure VPN, you must add the Remote access/VPN server role. You must be a member of the administrator's group on the local computer. If you are not a domain admin, you can have the domain admin add the server computer account to the RAS and IAS security server grouping Active Directory. This action can also be performed on the command line by typing **netsh ras add registeredserver smbnation server1.** This would register the server1 in the smbnation domain.

You can check whether the RAS is already registered in AD by typing **netsh ras show registeredserver smbnation server1.**

To configure RAS for the VPN connection, you would open the **Manage Your Server** console and **Add or remove a role** and choose **Remote access/VPN server.** On the **VPN Connection** page, you select the NIC that will receive the connections from the VPN clients. On the **IP Address Assignment** page, you choose to either have the server generate the IP addresses by leaving the default selection on **Automatically** or select **From a specified range of addresses** option. You then choose to use RAS to authenticate connection requests locally by using Windows authentication, and then complete the wizard.

> IMPORTANT: Ensure that you configure enough ports to support all simultaneous connections. PPTP and L2TP ports are configured through the RAS console by expanding the **Ports** node and clicking **Properties**, highlighting the port to configure, and clicking **Configure.**

> IMPORTANT: It is easy to overthink and debate in your head and trot down the wrong test-taking path. Here is what I mean in the context of the above discussion. Many real-world SMB consultants are revisiting the assumption that all mobility must include a VPN connection. There are alternatives, such as tunneling in an ISA Server.

> However, for the 70-282 exam, keep it simple and keep it straight! Microsoft, as you would infer from the section above, is thrilled by

advances in its VPN-related capabilities. Please be sure to share the same excitement level when you take the 70-282 exam.

Manage Windows Server 2003

First off, perform the following simple task so you have an overall view of managing a Windows Server 2003 machine. In the Administrative Tools program group, open each item and poke around. Don't commit changes, but understand that a simple look-and-see exercise (also known by certification instructors as "daze and amaze") is an effective learning approach. It's uncanny that on an exam, such as 70-282, you'll say to yourself "I've seen that before!" You are able to utter such remarks and answer the test question correctly because you used playtime (that's the poking around part) as learning time. So go play and explore the items in the Administrative Tools group and come back here in one hour. Bye! Okay—welcome back from your playtime recess hour! Let's do a deep dive into the world of group policy objects. From the Manage Your Server page to the new Group Policy Management Console (GPMC) and built-in remote administration, many improvements have been made in managing the Microsoft Server world. Managing a server is becoming easier, more mundane tasks are optimized through the use of wizards, and hey, we are getting a lot fewer blue screens and headaches. I know there are some of you out there who like to do things the old way, but the nature of IT is that it is constantly changing. I used to laugh at people when the mouse first came out, thinking they were lazy because with a mouse you didn't have to remember keyboard commands. Well, was I ever wrong! I finally accepted mouse-use and managed to move on with my life. So let this be a lesson, and embrace all the new wizards and anything that will save you time, like using the GPMC. I know—it's hard to relearn something in a different way, but truth be told, the time you spend learning a new tool vs. the time you would spend sticking with the old way will pay off a hundredfold.

Managing User Environments with GPOs

If you are looking for a way to bullet-proof and lock down the environment, Group Policy is the dot on the "i" in controlling the user environment. The Group Policy feature provides powerful capabilities for automatically managing and configuring servers and workstations in distributed Windows environments. With Group Policy you can distribute software, control IE (Internet Explorer) configuration, redirect folders, and much more.

You can apply Group Policy to users and computers to:

- **Manage users and computers** – You can ensure that users get the same desktop every time they log on, even from different computers. Local folders can be redirected to a central location, where they can be backed up as well as made available to the user regardless of which computer the user uses to log on. Group Policy includes administrative templates that allow you to manage

    o Shared Folders,

    o Control Panel access,

    o Start Menu and

    o Taskbar settings, and other computer settings.

- **Deploy software** – You can ensure all users have the software available they require for their job function, even when a user logs on from a different machine. You can also ensure that computers in a specific department have specific software available, regardless of who logs on. You can also deploy hot fixes and service packs with Group Policy.

- **Enforce security settings** – Security settings for local and domain policies can be centrally applied through Group Policy to protect the user environment. You can use it to set:

    o The minimum number of characters in a password,

    o Audit policy,

    o User rights assignment (like load and unload device drivers), and

    o Security options (e.g., not displaying the last logged-on username).

- **Ensure consistent desktop settings** – With logon scripts you can ensure users get a specific environment, like always having the same mapped drives and printers available, regardless of which computer they use to log on. The logon script will run every time a user logs on to the network.

By default, Group Policy settings are **not configured** and you should decide whether to **enable** or **disable** a Group policy setting. The easiest way to configure security policy is by creating an mmc (Microsoft Management Console) and adding the Security Configuration and Analysis Snap-in and the Security Templates Snap-in.

Then you can run an analysis against your current policy settings and apply a template that is configured with the minimum security configuration settings.

GPO Assigned vs. Published

If you use a GPO to deploy software packages, you can force an application installation based on a user configuration policy or computer configuration policy. The installation can be forced in the

- **computer configuration**, by choosing the **assign** option for an application,whereas under the
- **user configuration container**, you have to option to either **publish** or **assign** the application

When **assigning** an application, it will be **automatically installed** the next time the user or computer logs on. When an application is **published**, the icon will be **made available** in the Add/Remove Control Panel and under the Programs Menu, but the application will not be installed until it is actually required. The install can be triggered by either clicking the application install option in the **Add/Remove Programs**, or by a user clicking on a file extension that calls for the program, i.e., clicking on a file with the .xls extension that will then trigger the install of Excel.

When using GPO to push out patches and updates, you know have the ability to remove the application if no longer needed by removing the GPO.

IMPORTANT: Chapter 6 *Supporting and Maintaining Small Business Server 2003* covers Using the Group Policy Management Console and Applying and Configuring Group Policy

User Profiles

Here we would like to add a quick word on user profiles. User Profiles control startup features for the user's session, the desktop settings, programs that are available and drive mappings. Every user has a user profile stored in the Windows environment, regardless of whether the profile is:

- Local
- Roaming
- Mandatory

Local Profiles are kept in c:\Documents and Settings\UserName.UserDomain\ *Ntuser.dat* This profile will only be available if the user logs on to the local workstation where this profile is kept. If the user logs on to the network from another machine, the profile settings (from the regularly used workstation) will not be available to the user, and the (other) workstation will create its own user profile for this user.

Roaming Profiles are stored in a shared directory on the Windows Server 2003. You can access a user's profile properties through Active Directory Users and Computers, selecting the **user account**, clicking on **Properties** and choosing the user's **Profile Tab**. Here you can type a path to the shared folder that contains the user's profile. For example: \\servername\SharedUserProfiles\SusanDoe. The profile is then stored in the **Ntuser.dat** file in the shared folder. During network logon, the Ntuser.dat file will be copied over to the workstation supplying all user profile features so the user will have his desktop icons, programs, shortcuts and certificates available consistently, regardless of the workstation being used. Now there will be a copy of Ntuser.dat on the workstation and server, and when the user logs off, any changes to the profile will be updated, both locally and on the server.

Mandatory Profiles are profiles that are controlled by the administrator. The profile is kept on the server in a **Ntuser.man** file. The purpose of the Ntuser. man profile is to ensure a consistent local environment for all users. When a user logs on to a workstation the same desktop icons, programs and shortcuts are available all the time, for everyone. If a user makes changes to the environment during a session, changes are not saved once the user logs off. This way a user cannot change the network environment permanently.

Software Restriction Policies

Software Restriction Policies are not to be taken lightly, they can adversely affect end users if not tested and implemented properly. Software restriction policies are downloaded with other Group Policy objects when Windows starts up or a user logs on. Software restriction policies are also checked every time a new program launches.

- **Unrestricted** – Enabling systems to run specific applications that would usually be disallowed for low security user accounts.

- **Disallowed** - Locking down systems to prevent users from running specific applications by blocking the application.

Software restriction policies use the following rules which control whether programs are allowed or disallowed, and are applied in the following order:

- **Hash rules**. Software is identified by unique file characteristics and translated into an algorithmic hash. Even if a program is renamed or moved, the unique hash will identify the program.

- **Certificate rules**. Software is identified by its digital signature.

- **Path rules**. Software is identified by file path or registry location.

- **Internet Zone rules**. Windows Installer packages (.msi) are identified by Internet Explorer zone, i.e. Trusted Sites, Intranet, so packages can be downloaded and installed.

- **Default rule**. Set to **Unrestricted** by default and applies to all software. Can be changed to Disallow, blocking unidentified software.

To create a software restriction policy follow these steps:

1. Create and open a new GPO.

2. Select **User Configuration** or **Computer Configuration** in the console tree.

3. Click on the **Windows Settings**, click on **Security Settings.**

4. Right-click on **Software Restriction Policies** and select **New Software Restriction Policies.**

5. Select the **Security Levels** container, right-click a security level and click **Set as Default** from the shortcut menu.

6. Click the **Additional Rules** container to create a rule to identify the software and select one of the following options:

    a. **New Certificate Rule**

    b. **New Hash Rule**

    c. **New Internet Zone Rule**

    d. **New Path Rule**

7. Double-click the **Enforcement** item in the Software Restriction Policies container to specify how policies are enforced.

8. Double-click the **Designated File Types** item to control which file types should be included in the software restriction policies.

9. Double-click the **Trusted Publishers** item to control who can determine if certificates are trusted when opening digitally signed programs or Active X Controls.

IMPORTANT: If you set the default security rule to disallow, be sure to create path rules that allow all locations from which Windows runs login scripts. If you change or delete the path rules it could prevent users from logging on or block the execution of Windows programs.

Delegating Administration

Delegating administration of various tasks that could be performed by nontechnical personnel or staff helps distribute the administrative workload. You could delegate less technical and more frequently-used tasks to the office manager at a business. This way you can keep the support costs down and help the office to function more autonomously. You would not make the office manager a member of the Administrators group to perform this task, but set appropriate permissions. In this case you would want to make the office manager a member of the Account Managers Operators group, which is an already built-in group in Active Directory.

You can delegate administrative control by using the Delegation of Control Wizard to specify users or groups within any OU within the domain tree. Active Directory defines specific permissions and user rights to help assign the most appropriate administrative scope for a particular person. This can be assigned at the domain level, a single OU within the domain, all OUs in the domain, or on an object within an OU.

With the Delegation of Control Wizard you can allow a user to:

- Create, delete, and manage user accounts.
- Reset user passwords and force password change at the next logon.
- Read all user information.
- Create, delete, and manage groups.
- Modify the membership of a group.
- Modify Group Policy Links.
- Generate RSoP (Planning and Logging).
- Create, delete, and manage inetOrgPerson accounts. Active Directory provides support for the inetOrgPerson object class and its associated attributes.
- Reset inetOrgPerson passwords.
- Read all inetOrgPerson information.

IMPORTANT: Several third-party Lightweight Directory Access Protocol (LDAP) and X.500 directory services use the InetOrgPerson object class which is used to represent people within an organization. Support for InetOrgPerson makes migrations from other LDAP directories to Active Directory more efficient.

1. Go to **Active Directory Users and Computers**.
2. **Expand** the domain node.
3. In the console tree, right-click the container or OU where you want the user or group to have control. Click **Delegate Control**.
4. On the **Welcome to the Delegation of Control Wizard** page, click **Next**.

5. On the **Users or Groups** page, click **Add**.

6. In the **Select Users, Computers, or Groups** dialog box, in the **Enter the object names to select** box, type the users or groups to whom you want to delegate authority and then click **OK**.

7. On the **Users or Groups** page, click **Next**.

8. On the **Tasks to Delegate** page, in the **Delegate the following common tasks** box, select the tasks to delegate and then click **Next.**

9. On the **Completing the Delegation of Control Wizard** page, click **Finish**.

IMPORTANT: The Delegation of Control Wizard changes permissions on specified objects according to the users, group objects, and tasks that were indicated. To undo changes, the object must be modified manually. Therefore you should use groups instead of individual users, because you can just remove users from the group and not the object.

Also, from a 70-282 testing perspective, understand that Microsoft is keenly interested in administration delegation in the small and medium networking space. It views such efficiency gains as the only way to truly grow the SMB space worldwide. Remember — for today — think like MICROSOFT!

Protecting Against Data Loss

This section presents discussion on protecting against data loss.

Shadow Copies

One of the cool features in Windows Server 2003 is Shadow Copies. Shadow Copies allow users to restore their own files and not have to bother you and wait for them to be retrieved from a tape backup. Shadow Copies come in handy for:

- Recovery of accidentally deleted or overwritten files.

- Version-checking a document.

Shadow Copy will take a snapshot of the file at specifically set intervals. You must first enable Shadow Copies on the server and on the client. You must copy the Shadow Copy client file **twcli32.msi**, from the **%systemroot\system32\cleints\twclient\x86** folder to the client workstation.

To enable Shadow Copies on the server:

1. Go to **My Computer**, right-click, then click on **Manage.**
2. In the console tree, right-click the **Shared Folders** and point to **All Tasks**.
3. Click on **Configure Shadow Copies** and click **Enable.**

Once installed and enabled, this will create a **Previous Version** tab in the network share properties.

> IMPORTANT: To use Shadow Copies in Windows 2000 you must have Service Pack 3 or later installed.

Previous Versions Tab

Many end users are not aware of the **Previous Versions** tab located in the **Properties** of the **My Documents** shortcut. The Previous Versions tab enables users to restore files on their own, without the assistance of an administrator.

Folder Redirection

There are four folders that are part of the user profile that can be redirected:

- My Documents
- Application Data
- Desktop
- Start Menu

By redirecting them to a centrally-stored location on the network, you can ensure the folders are available regardless of the client computer the users logs on to. Since the files are stored centrally, there will be no storage space used on the client machines and confidential data will not remain on the client computer. In case a workstation is lost and the operating system on the client needs to be reinstalled, the user's files are protected and will not be lost.

These are the choices when redirecting folders:

- **Redirect folder to the following location:** All users' folders will be redirected to a common area and will be accessible by other users (not private). When redirecting, choose **Basic,** and in the **Target Folder location** field to **Redirect folder to the following location.**

- **Create a folder for each user under the root path:** All users' folders will be redirected to a private area, accessible only by the individual employee. When redirecting, choose **Basic,** and in the **Target Folder location** to **Create a folder for each user under the root path.**

- **Advanced — specify locations for various user groups:** Where you can redirect folders to different locations based on the user's security group membership.

IMPORTANT: When using Folder redirection to create the folders, permissions will be assigned automatically and there is no need for manual NTFS configuration. If you create the folders manually, make sure to set the appropriate NTFS permissions.

Also note that folder redirection is often mentioned as a cool GPO in public-facing Microsoft presentations. Hint-hint!

Backup Utility

With the built-in Backup Utility (NTbackup), you can back up the entire system or choose to back up specific files and folders or system state data and schedule backup jobs. Backup uses the Volume Shadow Copy service, which is enabled by default. This allows you to back up open files and they will not be skipped.

With the backup utility, you can back up to a selection of storage media and devices, including CD-ROM, removable disks, network drives, tape drives, and logical drives.

Backup allows for five different types of backups, as shown in Table 10-6.

Table 10-6

Backup types available in the Backup Utility

Type	Description	Archive Attribute cleared?
Normal or Full	Backs up all selected files regardless of archive attribute setting.	Yes
Copy	Identical to Normal other than it does not change the archive attribute.	No
Differential	Creates backup copies of files that have changed since the last Normal or Full backup.	No
Incremental	Creates backup copies of the files that have changed since the last Normal or Incremental backup.	Yes
Daily	Backs up files based on the file modification date and ignores the current state of the archive attribute.	No

So what does the archive attribute setting really dictate? If you did a Normal backup on each Friday, the archive bit gets reset. Then on Monday through Thursday you could create a Differential backup that does not reset the archive bit. That means on Monday you back up all changed files since Friday. On Tuesday you back up all changed files since Friday, since the Monday Differential did not reset the archive bit. So goes Wednesday and Thursday. In this case if you were to have a server crash on Wednesday, you would perform the restore using the Friday Normal backup tape and the Tuesday Differential tape, since the Tuesday backup contains all files changed since last Friday.

New scenario. You perform a Friday Normal backup, but make Incremental backups every night of the week. The Incremental backup resets the archive bit, which means after the Monday backup, the Tuesday backup only backs up files that have changed from Monday to Tuesday. The Tuesday Incremental backup resets the archive bit again and on Wednesday, the Incremental backup only backs up changed files since Tuesday. When you suffer a server crash on Wednesday, to restore you will need the Friday Normal backup and the Monday AND Tuesday Incremental backup tapes! So all this has its pros and cons. Whereas the Differential backup will take longer to back up by Thursday, it will also restore more quickly compared to an Incremental backup, since it only requires two tapes (Friday's Normal tape and the Differential tape of last backup).

The Incremental backups will be faster, but the restore will take longer because we now need the Friday Normal tape and every Incremental tape up to the last backup tape.

There are numerous backup strategies and methods which are beyond the scope of this book and I recommend further reading on the Microsoft website on the backup utility to fully understand all of its functions and capabilities.

> IMPORTANT: This is a classic certification testing area. Tradition-ally, Microsoft has held you responsible for a rich understanding of backup approaches. Let's just say you needed to know the "finer points" to become an MCSE!

> Here is the conceptual challenge you will face on the 70-282 exam. It is easy to think real world and say, "Oh…I always do Full backups each day." Perhaps such is the case and it makes sense because it's easy and you've got plenty of room to store backup data at the SMB level. However—the real world and 70-282 exam reality are often NOT the same. So even if you couldn't care less about Differential or Incremental backup methods, PLEASE care about these approaches for the 70-282 exam!

Automated System Recovery

The Automated System Recovery Wizard is included in the backup utility in Windows 2000, Windows Server 2003, and Windows XP. It is an automated recovery that requires the use of the original system CD and an ASR disc. The ASR is not a Full backup and should only be used in conjunction with another Full backup.

When you create an ASR backup, it will back up:

- The system state data.
- Windows file-protected files.
- System services and minimal system files.

The ASR does not back up data files. ASR works best with NTFS and it does not support FAT partitions larger than 2.1 GB and does not support 64 KB clusters. When you create an ASR backup, it will prompt you to insert a floppy on which the backup will create two files:

- Asr.sif
- Asrpnp.sif

These files will contain all the disk signatures along with volume and partition information. Do not confuse the ASR floppy with the ERD floppy under NT. The ASR floppy contains enough information to restore partitions and volumes to the proper configurations, remembers the location of the last backup, and automatically connects to the last backup location pulling the backup data, all without requiring any user interaction.

To perform an ASR restore, you insert the Windows Server 2003 Disc and hit the F2 key when prompted. The system restore will be automated from that point on, and when it finishes the restore, you have a fully bootable system.

Beware: Since the ASR does not back up data files, use it only in conjunction with your regular backups.

RAID

Whoa, another topic entire books have been written about! Implementing RAID (redundant array of independent disks) allows increasing data integrity and availability by creating redundant copies of the data. RAID can also improve disk performance depending on how it is implemented. Mind you that you are taking a Microsoft exam, so I doubt that you will find a question concerning hardware RAID there. The reason you want to make yourself familiar with Windows Server 2003 RAID, is not a question of whether hardware RAID is superior to Windows software RAID. Fact is that it is available in Windows Server 2003 and you are expected to know about it. 'Nuff said.

Windows Server 2003 offers support for three different RAID levels:

RAID 0 – **Disk striping** which offers NO redundancy but performance gains. Data is broken into blocks (stripes) and written sequentially to all drives in the striped set. RAID 0 requires a minimum of two disks.

RAID 1 - **Disk mirroring** which offers redundancy. Requires two volumes on two drives that are identically configured. Data is written to both drives simultaneously and if one drive fails, the other drive contains an identical copy of the data.

RAID 5 – **Disk striping with parity** uses three or more volumes on three separate disks, creating a striped set with parity error checking. In case one of the disks fails, the other two disks will be able to generate the missing data of the third disk by combining the blocks of data with the parity record. If two disks fail simultaneously, well that's when you bring Plan B into play.

Creating a RAID 1set

To create a RAID 1 volume you must be a member of the Backup Operators group, Administrators group or have been delegated proper rights on the local computer.

1. Click **Start, Control Panel** and double-click **Administrative Tools.**

2. Click **Computer Management (Local),** click **Storage**.

3. Click **Disk Management** and right-click the unallocated space on one of the dynamic disks where you want to create the RAID 5 volume.

4. Click **New Volume**, the New Volume Wizard will open, click **Next** and **Mirrored** and continue to follow the instructions on the screen.

In the event of disk failure, disk operations continue on the remaining disk. You may have to break the mirrored set. The data on the breaking mirror will not be deleted.

1. Click **Start, Control Panel** and double-click **Administrative Tools.**

2. Click **Computer Management (Local)**, click **Storage.**

3. Click **Disk Management** and right-click the one of the volume copies in the mirror.

4. Click **Break Mirrored Volume.**

Windows Server 2003 will break the mirror and you will have two independent volumes. To replace a mirror in the mirrored volume, you must have a dynamic disk with unallocated space that is as large as the healthy disk. If you are replacing one of the disks in a mirrored system volume it is better to use an identical disk to the one you are replacing. Otherwise, startup problems might occur.

Repairing and Resynchronizing a Mirrored Set

Sometimes data on a mirrored set gets out of sync, for instance if you have one disk offline due to failure or maintenance. In order to repair and resynchronize the mirrored set you would take the next steps after having broken the mirror:

1. Both drives of the mirrored set should be online. The status should read **Failed Redundancy** and corrective actions are based on the failed volume's status

2. If the status is **Missing** or **Offline**, right-click the failed volume and click **Reactivate Disk**. The status should show **Regenerating** and then switch to **Healthy** once done.

3. If the status shows Online with **Errors**, right-click the failed volume and select **Reactivate Disk.** The status should show **Regenerating** and then switch to **Healthy** once done.

4. If a volume shows **Unreadable**, select the volume and select **Rescan.**

5. If none of these actions bring the disk back to **Healthy**, and you have to physically replace the disk, right-click the failed disk and select **Remove Mirror.**

6. After replacing the failed disk, right-click on the volume to be re-mirrored and click **Add Mirror.**

RAID 1 Basics:

- .• You can create mirrored volumes only on computers running Windows 2000 Server, Windows 2000 Advanced Server, Windows 2000 Datacenter Server, or Windows Server 2003 operating systems

- You need two dynamic disks to create a mirrored volume.

- You can mirror an existing simple volume.

- Mirrored volumes cannot be extended.

- Both copies (mirror) of the mirrored volume share the same drive letter.

Creating a RAID 5 Set

To create a RAID 5 volume you must be a member of the Backup Operators group, Administrators group or have been delegated proper rights on the local computer.

1. Click **Start, Control Panel** and double-click **Administrative Tools.**

2. Click **Computer Management (Local)**, click **Storage.**

3. Click **Disk Management** and right-click the unallocated space on one of the dynamic disks where you want to create the RAID 5 volume.

4. Click **New Volume**, the New Volume Wizard will open, click **Next** and **RAID-5** and continue to follow the instructions on the screen.

To repair a RAID 5 volume:

1. Click **Start, Control Panel** and double-click **Administrative Tools.**

2. Click **Computer Management (Local)**, click **Storage.**

3. Click **Disk Management.**

4. Right-click the Missing or Offline disk and click **Reactivate Disk.**

RAID 5 Basics:

- You can create RAID 5 volumes only on computers running Windows 2000 Server, Windows 2000 Advanced Server, Windows 2000 Datacenter Server, or Windows Server 2003 operating systems.

- You need at least **three** (but **no more than 32**) dynamic disks to create a RAID 5 volume.

- RAID 5 volumes provide fault tolerance at a cost of only one additional disk for the volume. For example, if you use three 10 GB disks to create a RAID 5 volume, the volume will have a 20 GB capacity. The remaining 10 GB is used for parity.

- RAID 5 volumes cannot be extended or mirrored.

- Operating system files and boot files cannot reside on a RAID 5 set.

Monitoring Server Performance

It makes sense to monitor system performance on the server routinely. Best practice would have you create a baseline established over several months, giving you the ability to compare your performance data when you have to diagnose a problem. This can reveal issues, such as high demand on a specific resource, that end up creating a bottleneck. This can affect the entire system, so it is a good idea to baseline your four subsystems:

- Memory
- Processor
- Disk
- Network

Reasons for bottlenecks are:

- Insufficient subsystems, like not having adequate memory.

- Uneven distribution of workload, e.g., using old parts in a new server.

- Failing subsystem—before a motherboard or hard drive fail, you will experience odd occurrences.

- A runaway program or process, interfering with other application performance.

There are built-in tools in Windows Server 2003 that can collect and view real-time system data in the System Monitor. The Performance Logs and Alerts allows you to configure logs, record performance data, and create system alerts.

System Monitor obtains information on how the system and applications are functioning, helping prevent bottlenecks by keeping an eye on resource usage. The collected data can be displayed in a text file or bar graph, which can be viewed in a browser, saved as an HTML file, or printed.

The Performance Logs and Alerts console contains the following utilities:

- **Counter Logs** – Based on performance objects and counters, these logs record data sampled from hardware resources and system services. You have the ability to set the interval time for sampling data from several seconds to minutes or hours.

- **Trace Logs** – These measure performance statistics such as disk and file input/output, page faults, and thread activity.

- **Alerts** – These logs are useful to monitor specific counters you actively monitor and will send you notification when a specific threshold value has been reached or exceeded. Alerts can be set to send a network message, run a program, or start a log file.

Please be sure to take a quick look at additional monitoring tools like Task Manager (right-click the **Start** bar to access) and Disk Defragmenter (select from the **System Tools** program group under the **Accessories** program group). A quick peek-and-poke session is all you need.

IMPORTANT: You will like this tip! Instead of referring you to another information source for more studying, I can now say that the above discussion on performance monitoring is SUFFICIENT for your 70-282 exam preparation purposes! While I think the entire monitoring area is really cool and a service revenue opportunity for SMB consultants, the fact of the matter is that Microsoft historically does not test extensively on this topic. Personally, I think it's a bummer, but it's to your benefit for managing your study time to pass the 70-282 exam. In the old days, there was an MCSE exam that had a major testing objective focused on performance monitoring. When I took the test, there was only ONE question on Performance Monitor. What a letdown!!!

Microsoft Operations Manager

MOM (Microsoft Operations Manager) can centrally monitor user actions, application software, and desktop computers and servers for several thousand computers. There are several features included in MOM that allow you to manage servers and applications:

- **Alerts** – MOM rules can be configured to create specific alerts with associated severity levels. Alerts can be set to trigger e-mail messages, SNMP traps, pages, and scripts to notify other management systems. Alert history and associated events can be traced and looked up in the Microsoft Knowledge Base.

- **Rules** – Administrator-created rules allow MOM to react in a predetermined event pattern, triggering administrative alerts or specific actions. With MOM rules, events can be linked to the Knowledge Base articles providing probable-cause guidance and links to additional information.

- **Distributed Event Management** – MOM uses a repository for all system and application events stemming from the Windows-based systems within a network. Events can be consolidated and specific information on a detailed event stream can be viewed in a single desktop console view.

- **Performance Monitoring** – MOM can be configured to monitor key performance thresholds. New rules can be added and existing rules can be customized to allow system and application performance to be monitored. Reports can be used for baseline reporting and capacity planning.

- **Web Reporting** – MOM can be configured to generate HTML snapshots of all generated reports. HTML reports can be exported and hosted on a web server for browser viewing.

- **Graphical Reporting Tool** – In addition to the web console, preconfigured performance data reports and charts can be viewed at a glance by administrators in the MOM MMC.

- **Management Packs** – There are preconfigured MOM-rule sets and Knowledge Base articles for specific applications and services. MOM

Management packs are available for Active Directory, IIS, and ISA Server 2004.

Troubleshoot Windows Server 2003.

Well, we all wouldn't have a job if this stuff would just work. So yes, once in a great while, we experience a minor glitch, weird symptoms, servers with attitude, and just plain misconfigured servers like a recent server I ran into. A client called me in to oversee continuing e-mail issues. They were using the POP3 e-mail retrieval method for external e-mail and also had separate internal e-mail set up—get this—by first using separate POP3 accounts at the ISP. The business was running a Windows 2000 server and—hold on to your hats—it was not being used as a domain controller. To further explain the situation, all network users had local user accounts set up on the server (since it's not running AD you can do that), and they connected using mapped drives and using ICW to get Internet access. They were using NTFS permissions, and every time someone changed their password on their respective workstation, they could no longer connect to the server. Yes, the previous consultant (always the bad guy) had also enabled Group Policies, and I found some server-side scripts, and to make a long story short, I sold them on Small Business Server 2003, which will be installed in the very near future.

But back to troubleshooting a system. If it's your creation, you usually have some clue what the issue is; if it is an adopted system, like the one I mentioned above, you cannot rule out anything. Windows Server 2003 comes with a whole barrage of troubleshooting utilities included, as well as downloadable tools from the resource kit and free third-party tools.

Troubleshooting Utilities

All right, so where do we start? There are oodles of troubleshooting tools and utilities available for Windows Server 2003 appearing in all sorts of flavors. You just have to know where to find them. We can separate Windows Server 2003 troubleshooting tools into:

- **Operating system tools** – These are installed as part of the default Setup program. You can view a list of them by going into the Help and Support Center for Windows Server 2003 and clicking on **Tools** and then on the **Command-line reference A-Z** or **Windows interface administrative tool reference A-Z**.

- **Help and Support Center Tools** – These are user-friendly trouble-shooting tools built into Help and Support Center and are designed for interactively troubleshooting problems with a remote user.

- **Support Tools** – These optional tools are not installed by Setup, but you can find them on the Windows Server 2003 Disc under **\Support\Tools\ Suptools.msi**. Double-click the **.msi file** and follow the instructions to install them. This will add a Windows Support Tools folder shortcut to the Start menu.

- **Downloadable Debugging Tools** – Debugging tools are available at http://www.microsoft.com/windows/reskits/webresources. If you need to diagnose a Stop error, such as Stop 0x0000000A, IRQL_NOT_ LESS_OR_EQUAL error, you can use a kernel debugger to determine the issue.

- **Windows Resource Kit Tools** – These tools are part of the Windows Server 2003 deployment kit and must be downloaded and installed separately. You can download these tools from http://www.microsoft. com/ windows/reskits.

For more information on all Windows Server 2003 troubleshooting tools, I highly recommend that you do a search and download **SPTCC_TOL.doc** on the Microsoft website. It covers many tools included with the family operating system that are distributed separately and are useful for troubleshooting hardware and software problems in Windows Server 2003.

The main troubleshooting tools you will be working with mostly of the time are:

- **Event Viewers** – which maintains the Application, Security, System, Directory Services, DNS Server, and File Replication Service log. Here you can usually get the event error code which can then be researched on the Internet (use Google—it's faster then the Microsoft site) for KB Articles.

- **GPResult** – which is a command-line tool that can be used to view Group Policy settings on a local computer if you need to troubleshoot issues with missing or wrongly applied GPO.

- **Performance Logs and Alerts** – discussed earlier in this chapter.

- **Program Compatibility Wizard** – a cool built-in tool that allows you to set compatibility modes if you need to run a legacy application that doesn't play quite nice in XP, for instance.

- **Runas** – Okay, so this isn't a troubleshooting tool, but it allows you to run programs using different user credentials and comes in handy when you are troubleshooting issues on client workstations, especially if they are experiencing quirky behavior when connecting to applications and folders on the server. This helps diagnose a permission issue on the fly.

- **Task Manager** – immediate information on processes, applications, and CPU statistics as well as memory utilization and process performance. Helps you weed out unwanted processes by being able to right-click them and kill the process.

- **DcDiag** – a domain controller diagnostic tool—the coolest and will run 27 tests (AD, DNS, NIC, etc.) against a DC and is the first tool you should run if you suspect issues on the domain controller.

- **DNSLint** – use this if you suspect DNS issues in the domain; it will return any issues related to incorrect or missing DNS records in the domain.

- **DS-tools** – Dsquery, DSget, DSadd, DSmod, DSmove, and DSrm, obviously Active Directory tools with different functions. I suggest you take time and play with all of them to get acquainted.

- **ADLB** – Active Directory Load Balancing tool, new in the Windows Server 2003 resource tool kit, a cool enterprise tool which handles connection objects between sites, allowing staggering replication intervals between connection objects owned by a bridgehead server.

As you can see, there are many troubleshooting tools available. I didn't even touch the tip of the iceberg here. Key is, you need to know most of these, not only for the exam, but for real-life support of your networks.

Practice Questions

Question #1:

The RFP (Request for proposal) you are working on for a new customer includes the following requirements:

- Dual processor server.

- 4 GB RAM.

- File and printer sharing.

- Active Directory Support.

- HW RAID.

- Two node cluster.

Which version of Windows Server 2003 would you recommend for this customer? (Choose the best answer.)

a.   Windows Server 2003 Web Edition.

b.   Windows Server 2003 Datacenter Edition.

c.   Windows Server 2003 Enterprise Edition.

d.   Windows Server 2003 Standard Edition.

Question #2:

Which of the following occur during the, "Text Mode" phase of Setup? (Choose the best answer.)

a.   Choose a licensing mode.

b.   Detect Plug and Play devices.

c.   Partition and format the system disk.

d.   Configure system date and time.

Question #3:

Which of the following commands will check for problems that may occur during an upgrade to Windows Server 2003 (Enterprise Edition)? (Choose the best answer.)

a.   x:\i386\setup.exe /UpgradeChk /log=VerifyConfig.log

b.   x:\i386\winnt32.exe /checkupgradeonly

c.   x:\i386\winnt.exe /checkupgradeonly

d.   x:\i386\setup32.exe /UpgradeChk /log=VerifyConfig.log

Question #4:

Which of the following are components you may expect to find as part of the "Configure Your Server Wizard"? (Choose all that apply.)

a.   Domain Controller.

b.   VB.Net Application Server.

c.   Streaming media server.

d.   Remote access server.

e.   RADIUS Server.

Question #5:

Which of the following are Forest Functional Levels? (Choose all that apply.)

a.   Windows Server 2003 Interim.

b.   Windows Server 2003.

c.   Windows Server2000 mixed.

d.   Windows 2000 Native.

e.   Windows 2000.

Question #6:

Which of the following are Domain Functional Levels? (Choose all that apply.)

a.   Windows Server 2003 Interim.

b.   Windows Server 2003.

    c.   Windows Server 2000 mixed.

    d.   Windows 2000 Native.

    e.   Windows 2000.

Question #7:

Which of the following statements about the Global Catalog or Global Catalog Servers are true? (Choose all that apply.)

    a.   Domain controllers are by default Global Catalog Servers.

    b.   The first domain controller in a domain is automatically a Global Catalog Server.

    c.   The Global Catalog Server search mechanism uses port 3107 for queries.

    d.   The Global Catalog Server enables users to perform searches for directory information throughout all domains in the entire forest.

Question #8:

Which of the following are accurate statements about Active Directory? (Choose all that apply.)

    a.   Active Directory allows domain lookups of private information such as is required by Sarbanes-Oxley.

    b.   Synchronization is achieved using time-stamped configuration and registry files that are passed from server to server by Domain controllers which happen to be GCs.

    c.   Active Directory provides a central location for network administration and delegation of administrative authority.

    d.   Active Directory's scalability will meet the requirements of nearly any network.

    e.   LDAPv3 and LDAPv2 are fully supported.

Question #9:

What is the purpose of the Ntds.dit file? (Choose the correct answer.)

    a.   Ntds.dit provides the backup data for Exchange Server.

b. Ntds.dit is the Active Directory data store, in other words the Active Directory database file. It contains domain data, schema data, application data, and configuration data.

c. Ntds.dit is the file used to schedule the replication activites defined within the Knowledge Consistency Checker (KCC). The KCC recreates the Ntds.dit after each successful replication cycle.

d. Ntds.dit is the NT distributed services data information table. It holds all pointers required to provide distributed file service (DFS) functionality within a domain.

Question #10:

Which of the following are forest-wide operations master roles? (Choose the correct answer)

a. Domain Naming Master.

b. RID Master.

c. Infrastructure Master.

d. PDC Emulator Master.

e. Schema Master.

Question #11:

Which of the following are domain-wide operations master roles? (Choose the correct answer.)

a. Domain Naming Master.

b. RID Master.

c. Infrastructure Master.

d. PDC Emulator Master.

e. Schema Master.

Question #12:

The Windows Server 2003 system you are responsible for is scheduled for a full backup every Friday, incrementals each weekday at 11:00 p.m. and a differential on the 15th of the month. The data drive crashes on Tuesday the 17th at 11:00 a.m.. Which backup sets should be restored to restore the data in the fewest number of steps? (Choose the correct answer.)

a. Saturdays full, Sundays differential.

b. Saturdays full, Sundays differential, Monday and Tuesdays incremental.

c. Sundays differential.

d. Saturdays full, Sundays differential, Mondays incremental.

Question #13:

Bill restored his system using the Automated System Recovery (ASR) disk he created, and finds that all his data files that were stored on another volume (D:\) are missing, and only the operating system files on C:\ were restored. What is the issue? (Choose the correct answer.)

a. The ASR backup can only backup the system state and system services.

b. Bill did not configure the ASR properly and let it run using only the default settings.

c. The ASR backs up to a floppy only and the backup should have been created on CD or other removable media with greater capacity.

d. The ASR disk is a recovery utility, it does not backup files.

Answers

Question #1: Answer: c

a. Incorrect! Windows Server 2003 Web Edition is only for hosting web applications and services.

b. Incorrect! Though Windows Server 2003 Datacenter Edition will meet and exceed all of the listed requirements the customer would have to get it directly from the OEM. Datacenter Edition is tested and certified on specific HW. This allows the OEM and Microsoft to provide the highest level of support and stability to mission critical systems.

c. Correct! Enterprise supports clustering (as does Datacenter Edition) which is one of the customer's requirements. A cluster is multiple nodes that utilize shared storage technology to provide "failover" to a standby node should the designated active node become unavailable. Clustered systems allow for a much higher level of availability than non-clustered systems.

d. Incorrect! Windows Server 2003 Standard Edition does not support the clustering requirement.

Question #2: Answer: b, c

a. Incorrect! Licensing mode selection occurs during the GIU phase.

b. Correct! Detecting Plug and Play devices is essential for even the installation process itself. How else would the system know the hardware configuration so it can load and install the proper drivers?

c. Correct! The system disk is where all files and folders go, as well as where the operating system is built, so it must be created and formatted very early in the Text mode phase.

d. Incorrect! The system time and date are set in the GUI phase of setup.

Question #3: Answer: c

a. Incorrect! This can be a tricky one since setup.exe is most often the program used for installations. In this case x:\i386\winnt.exe is the program used.

b. Incorrect! winnt32.exe does not exist. winnt.exe is the utility name.

c. Correct! x:\i386\winnt.exe /checkupgradeonly will look for issues or known driver incompatibilities that may cause an upgrade to fail.

d. Incorrect! setup32.exe does not exist.

Question #4: Answer: a
a. Correct!

b. Incorrect.

c. **Correct!**

d. **Correct!**

e. Incorrect.

Question #5: Answer: a, b, e

a. **Correct! Windows Server 2003 Interim mode was created to support environments that are upgrading from Windows NT 4.0. The first Windows NT 4 domain controller that is upgraded to Windows Server 2003 (the PDC of course) auto-magically has the forest functional level set to Windows 2003 Interim mode. Like the Windows 2000 forest functional level it has none of the improved forest functionality of Windows Server 2003 with the exception of improved Global catalog replication if both servers involved are Windows Server 2003.**

b. **Correct! The Windows Server 2003 forest functional level brings all of the new features to the party such as cross-forest trust relationships, the ability to rename domains and/or domain controllers, application directory partitions, and universal group membership caching. There is a catch though. All domain controllers must be Windows Server 2003 machines or you cannot raise the forest level to Windows Server 2003.**

c. Incorrect! Mixed mode is not a valid forest functional level.

d. Incorrect! Windows 2000 Native is not a valid forest functional level.

e. **Correct! This is the default level for upgraded domain controllers, with the exception of upgraded NT 4 domain controllers – they are set to Windows Server 2003 Interim mode. Windows 2000 is also the default mode for newly installed domain controllers.**

Question #6: Answer: a, b, c, d

a. **Correct! Windows Server 2003 Interim mode was created to support environments that are upgrading from Windows NT 4.0. In fact, the only domain controllers that are allowed in a Windows**

Server 2003 Interim domain are NT 4 and Windows Server 2003 – not Windows Server 2000.

b. Correct! But all domain controllers must be running Windows Server 2003 before you can get there. The Windows Server 2003 Domain functional level brings all of the new features to the party such as the ability to rename domains and/or domain controllers, application directory partitions, and universal group membership caching.

c. Correct! This is the default level for the first domain controller running Windows Server 2003 in a new domain. This functional level allows for other domain controller types such as Windows 2000 and Windows NT 4.0. Mixed mode was how Windows Server 2000 integrated with Windows NT 4.0 domain controllers. Windows Server 2003 uses mixed mode in much the same way.

d. Correct! Windows 2000 Native allows windows Server 2003 to join and participate in a Windows 2000 Native domain. Like the Windows 2000 implementation NT 4.0 controllers are not supported in a native mode domain. This is the highest domain functional level allowed in a mixed Windows 2000 and Windows Server 2003 environment.

e. Incorrect! Windows 2000 is a forest functional level; Windows 2000 Native is the domain counterpart.

Question #7: Answer: b, d

a. Incorrect! Only the first domain controller in a domain is by default a GC. Any other domain controllers must have GC functionality manually enabled.

b. Correct! Each domain must have at least 1 GC, though it may not be queried in a single domain environment. The installation process will automatically make the first domain controller within the domain the GC to fulfill this requirement.

c. Incorrect! Port 3268 is used for queries.

d. Correct! This lookup functionality is one of the main examples of Active Directories powerful feature set.

Question #8: Answer: c, d, e

a. Incorrect! AD allows storage for application data, serves as the central repository for information security, provides the mechanism to manage objects within the environment, and provides authentication and single sign-on services for the environment.

b. Incorrect! AD synchronization is achieved through the process of replication which ensures that identical copies or replicas of the AD directory partitions are present on each domain controller. Only domain controllers hold replicated directory data, not standard member servers.

c. Correct! This particular statement is usually the "elevator pitch" describing AD, but is only a small part of the functionality of Active Directory.

d. Correct! Because AD is basically a security database it is extremely expandable and extensible. AD can start with a single domain and its associated objects. Additional domains can easily be added within the forest and AD will determine and enforce the object relationships.

e. Correct! Lightweight Directory Access Protocol (LDAP) is based on the X.500 standard and is the defined industry protocol that describes how directory information is stored and accessed.

Question #9: Answer: b

a. Incorrect! Ntds.dit is the AD data store file.

b. Correct! Ntds.dit is the AD database itself!

c. Incorrect! Sounds good – but I made it up.

d. Incorrect! Sounds even better, but I made it up too.

Question #10: Answer: a, d

a. Correct! Domain Naming Master is forest-wide role.

b. Incorrect!

c. Incorrect!

d. Correct! Schema Master is a forest-wide role

Question 11: Answer: b, c

a. Incorrect!

b. Correct!

c. Correct!

d. Incorrect!

Question #12: Answer: d

a. Incorrect! Misses files created Monday.

b. Incorrect! Tuesday's incremental hasn't yet occurred.

c. Incorrect! Misses files created on Monday.

d. Correct!

Question #13: Answer: b

a. Incorrect! A default ASR backup is set to backup the system state and services of the operating system components. You can configure the ASR manually to do a full backup of the entire system, all data on all volumes.

b. Correct! Bill did not configure the ASR to do a full backup, and by default it will only backup the system state and services of the operating system components.

c. Incorrect! The floppy disk is not used to backup data but contains the Asr.sif and Asrpnp.sif files which contain drivers for the NIC card or USB drive (if needed) and points to the location where the backup data file is stored.

d. Incorrect! ASR is a backup utility and can be found in the NTbackup utility.

Summary

IMPORTANT: Before we leave the chapters in the 70-282 exam preparation section of this book, let's talk about performance anxiety (also known as test-taking tension). And we'll talk about it in the context of the last section on troubleshooting.

First, feeling anxious is normal, natural, and a good thing. It means you care, and it's your body's natural reaction to stress. So celebrate anxiety! You might be concerned about successfully completing the troubleshooting sections of the 70-282 exam because you are not an SBS or SMB technology guru and have limited experience. It's a completely understandable concern.

But, I've got a little secret for you. Just as you might be fretting over the troubleshooting problems on a certification exam, I can attest that the test writers STRUGGLED to write decent troubleshooting questions! It's true for many reasons. Test writers often sit around and ponder such conundrums as "How can we test troubleshooting? Troubleshooting is something you just do on a case-by-case basis." And troubleshooting lends itself to third-party interactions, like antivirus vendors, backup vendors, hardware vendors, and line-of-application vendors. Microsoft Legal will never ever allow third-party vendors to be mentioned in its exams, so think about the functional constraints that the poor test writers had to live under. If misery loves company, you and the test writers are soul mates!

So what can you expect in troubleshooting testing scenarios? Historically, such exam questions have been generic, high-level, and aimed at testing your conceptual thinking rather than measuring your super-deep technical knowledge. Microsoft's 70-282 exam has a strong business component and this would be the place to test your analytical reasoning capabilities. So in addition to just picking the correct answer on a troubleshooting question, think about the troubleshooting steps you are undertaking and whether the flow is logical.

Examination.

In this chapter, you were brought into the world of Windows Server 2003 stand alone edition and how it is positioned in the small- and medium-sized business segment.

To be honest, this chapter, reflecting the 70-282 examination guidelines, is a soup-to-nuts all-inclusive view of the underlying network operation system. You were schooled on installation, deployment, configuration and administration topics. The chapter ended by presenting troubleshooting topics.

A few final notes that may be helpful.

1. Both authors, upon reflection, recall more questions specific to Windows Server 2003 than might have been anticipated. Take this topic seriously.

2. Read the examination questions carefully. It is easy to overlook whether the question related to Windows Server 2003 or SBS 2003. Such an oversight cold be costly and cause you to answer the question incorrectly.

3. Go and schedule the 70-282 examination right now before you forget, then return and start reading the final few chapters!

Section III ❧ Exam 70-631

Chapter 11
Configuring for and Deploying Windows SharePoint Services

Chapter 12
Crash Course: Administering Windows SharePoint Services

Chapter 13
Managing Windows SharePoint Services Security

CHAPTER 11
Configuring for and Deploying Windows SharePoint Services

Welcome to the first of three chapters designed to help you cram for the 70-631 exam. In this chapter, we'll look at some of the objectives surrounding configuring the network environment for Windows SharePoint Services 3.0, creating secure installations, and deploying in server farms and in extranet scenarios. We'll close the chapter with a quick look at installing WSS, both in a standalone installation and to upgrade an existing installation of Windows SharePoint Services 2.0.

I've noted SBS-specific information where possible; though the exam itself is not geared to SBS (it's merely an option to get a specialist designation).

Let's get started!

Network Infrastructure

Being a Web-based application, Windows SharePoint Services requires some attention in regard to your network. In this section, we'll cover topics specific to deploying and integrating WSS 3.0 within your network structure, including name resolution, balancing loads using Windows Server 2003's Network Load Balancing feature, establishing WSS's presence in perimeter network scenarios, and publishing WSS 3.0 if you have ISA Server 2004 deployed.

Names Resolution

Resolving canonical names to IP addresses, as you probably know, is handled by the Domain Name Service, or DNS. Windows Server 2003, which is required to run Windows SharePoint Services 3.0 (WSS), contains a DNS system that is straightforward to configure. It works perfectly if your SharePoint site is designated for exclusive use by internal clients. However, if your WSS site is destined to be available to users both inside your network and external to your organization, there are some DNS and name resolution issues to contend with:

- How will external clients resolve the name of your SharePoint site, particularly if you would like to use host headers to distinguish the WSS site from the name of your SBS server?

- How will your internal clients access the SharePoint site—using the fully-qualified domain name of the site, which would by default be routed to the external network interface card—or will they simply use an internal reference?

The Split-DNS Architecture

For WSS sites that are supposed to function correctly to both internal and external users, a split-DNS architecture is recommended. The split-DNS architecture scenario consists of a set of internal nameservers that are used within the corporate computing environment in daily operations. There are also one or more nameservers facing externally to the Internet, which outsiders use to connect to your corporation's electronic services, but they are separated from the internal nameservers for security. Outsiders who query for information from your external nameservers won't be able to obtain information on your internal network structure and composition because the external nameserver is completely separate from the internal nameservers that hold this data. The external nameservers hold records only for externally-facing servers and not for your entire internal domain. This technique is called the split-DNS architecture because DNS information is split between the inside and the outside of an organization.

NOTE: By default, Small Business Server 2003 is set up with the split-DNS architecture, wherein local clients use the businessname. local zone for references and external users access the network via the publicly accessible name, businessname.com (or other top level domain).

There are two points to note about using the split-DNS architecture for name resolution:

- The external set of nameservers is not authoritative for the internal, Active Directory-based DNS structure. They are authoritative only for external, Internet-based requests.

- If your ISP has been providing hosting for your nameservers, there's no reason it can't continue doing so. In fact, this is simpler to administer than hosting both sets of nameservers on your own premises.

How would you go about setting up this architecture in a from-scratch environment? Here's a general guide to doing so:

1. Create two sets of servers—one for in front of the firewall, and one for behind it. Install the DNS service on both. Or, if you will have an ISP host your externally accessible DNS records, only create one server for your internal DNS services.

2. Make every nameserver point to itself for its own DNS information; you do this within the network card properties where you indicate the IP address. There's no need to configure a secondary nameserver for each of these.

3. Copy any external records your internal users might need to the internal zone. This includes web, mail, and FTP servers. Remember, if you don't do this, your users won't be able to resolve the names of anything outside the firewall.

4. Configure external forwarders—these are the machines to which your internal nameservers will forward requests so that your internal users can resolve Internet names.

5. Slave the internal set of nameservers to these external forwarders you created in the previous step. This shields them from the Internet's blinding eye.

6. Configure all machines on the internal network to use only the internal nameservers. This allows them to register with Active Directory if appropriate and to find internal resources, which they couldn't find if directed to the external nameservers outside the firewall.

Network Load Balancing

Network load-balancing (NLB) clusters allow for the high availability of services that rely on the TCP/IP protocol. You can have up to 32 machines running any edition of Windows Server 2003 and Windows 2000 Server participating in an NLB cluster. NLB is a very inexpensive way to achieve TCP/IP high availability for servers that run web services or other intranet or Internet applications. In effect, NLB acts as a balancer, distributing the load equally among multiple machines running their own independent, isolated copies of IIS. NLB only protects against failure, in that if a copy of IIS on a machine fails, the load will be redistributed among the other servers in the NLB cluster. Dynamic web pages that maintain sessions don't receive much benefit from this type of clustering because members of the cluster are running independent, unconnected versions of IIS and therefore cannot continue sessions created on other machines. However, much web content is static, and some implementations of dynamic web sites do not use sessions. Thus, chances are that NLB can improve the reliability of a site in production.

NOTE: Other services that can take advantage of NLB are IP-based applications such as FTP and VPN.

Before we dig deeper in our coverage of NLB, let's discuss a few terms that you will see. Some of the most common NLB technical terms follow.

• **NLB driver**: This driver resides on memory on all members of a cluster and is instrumental in choosing which cluster mode will accept and process the packet. Coupled with port rules and client affinity (all defined on the following pages), the driver decides whether to send the packet

up the TCP/IP stack to the application on the current machine, or to pass
on the packet because another server in the cluster will handle it.

- **Unicast mode**: In unicast mode, NLB hosts send packets to a single
  recipient.

- **Multicast mode**: In multicast mode, NLB hosts send packets to multiple
  recipients at the same time.

- **Port rules**: Port rules define the applications on which NLB will "work
  its magic," so to speak. Certain applications listen for packets sent to
  them on specific port numbers—for example, web servers usually listen
  for packets addressed to TCP port 80. You use port rules to instruct NLB
  to answer requests and load-balance them.

- **Affinity**: Affinity is a setting which controls whether traffic that origi-
  nated from a certain cluster member should be returned to that particular
  cluster node. Effectively, this controls which cluster nodes will accept
  what types of traffic.

Creating an NLB Cluster

To create a new NLB cluster, use the Network Load Balancing Manager and
follow the instructions shown next.

1. From the Administrative Tools folder, open the Network Load Balancing Manager. The main screen is shown in Figure 11-1.

Figure 11-1
Network Load Balancing Manager

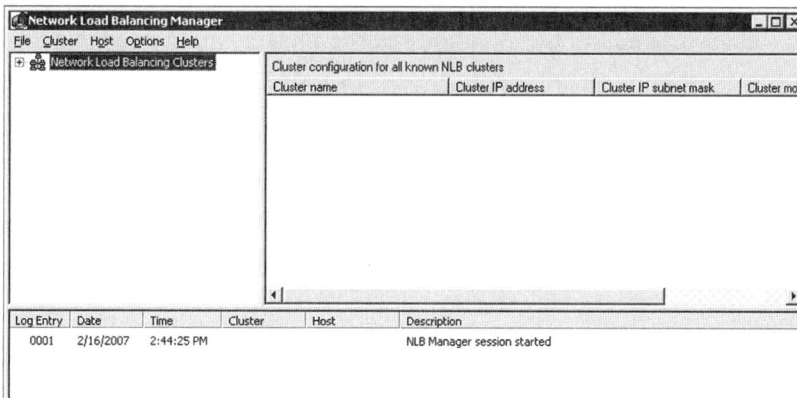

2. From the Cluster menu, select New.

3. The Cluster Parameters screen appears, as shown in Figure 11-2. Here, you specify the name of the cluster and the IP address information by which other computers will address the cluster. Enter the IP address, subnet mask, and full Internet name (i.e., the canonical DNS name). Also choose unicast or multicast mode, as discussed in the previous section. Click Next to continue.

Figure 11-2
Cluster Parameters screen

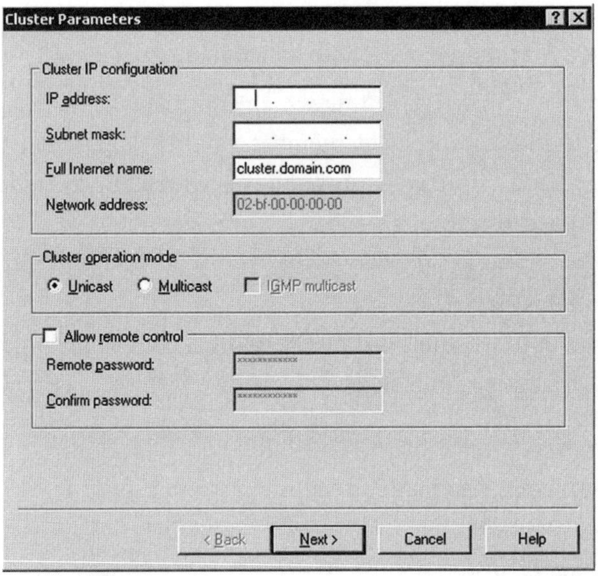

4. The Cluster IP Addresses screen appears, as shown in Figure 11-3. Here, enter any additional IP addresses the cluster might need. You might want this for specific applications; it's not required for a standard setup. Click Next when you've finished, or if there are no other IP addresses by which this cluster will be known.

Notes:

Figure 11-3

Cluster IP Addresses screen

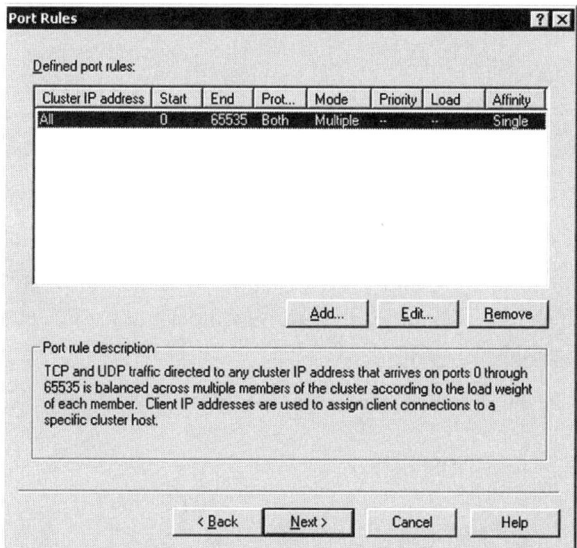

5. The Port Rules screen appears, as shown in Figure 11-4. Enter and configure any port rules you'd like, as discussed in the previous section, and then click Next when you're done.

Figure 11-4

Port Rules screen

6. The Connect screen appears, as shown in Figure 11-5. Here, enter the IP address or DNS name of the host which will be added to the cluster first. Then click Connect. The list in the white box at the bottom of the screen will be populated with the network interfaces available for creating a cluster. Click the public interface, and click Next.

Figure 11-5
Connect screen

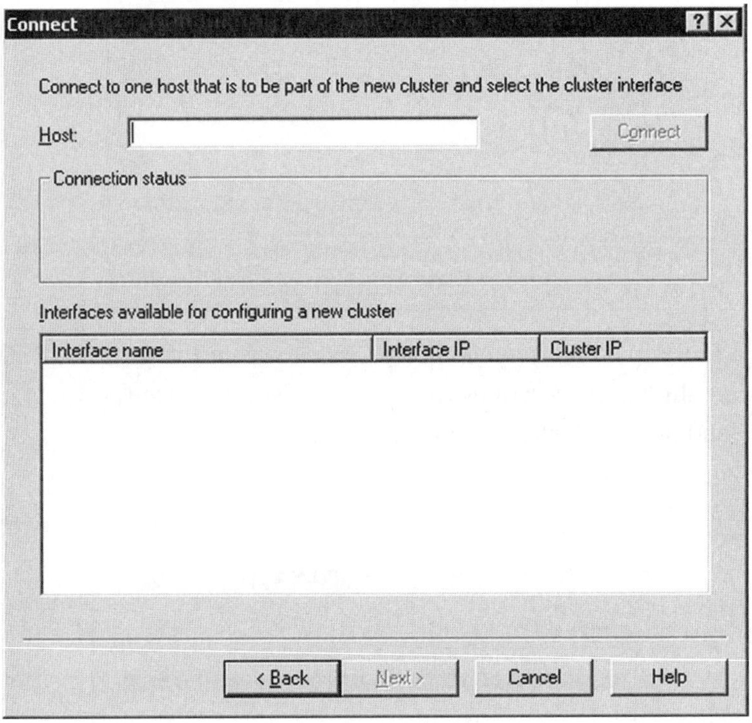

7. The Host Parameters screen appears, as seen in Figure 11-6. On this screen, enter the priority for the host of the cluster, the dedicated IP that you'll use to connect to this specific member node, and the initial state of this host when you first boot up Windows Server 2003. Click Finish to complete the process.

Notes:

Figure 11-6

Host Parameters screen

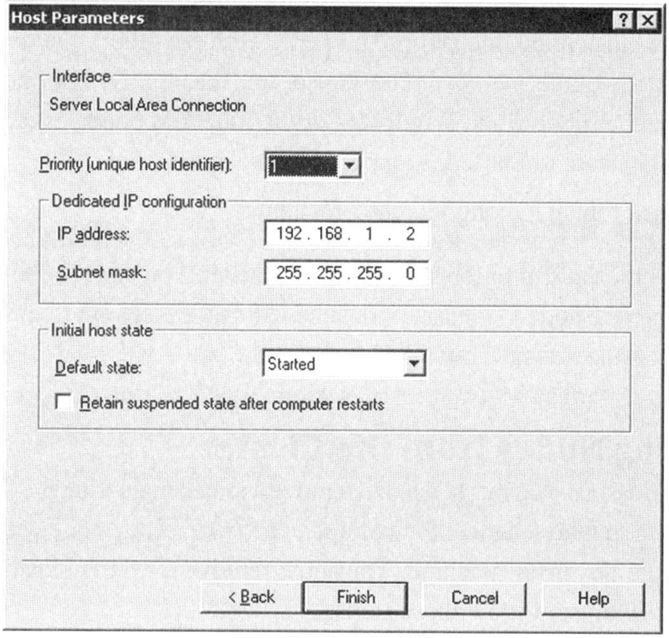

The NLB cluster is created, and the first node is configured and added to the cluster.

Adding Other Nodes to the Cluster

Chances are good that you want to add another machine to the cluster to take advantage of load balancing. To add a new node to an existing cluster, use the following procedure:

1. From the Administrative Tools menu, open the Network Load Balancing Manager console.

2. In the left pane, right-click the cluster to which you'd like to add a node, and then select Add Host to Cluster from the pop-up context menu.

3. The Connect screen appears. Type in the DNS name, or the IP address, of the host to join to the cluster. Click the Connect button to populate the list of network interfaces on that host, and then select the card that will host public traffic and click Next.

4. The Host Parameters screen appears. Enter the appropriate priority of the host (a setting which allows you to specify which machine should get the largest number of requests—useful if you have two machines in a cluster and one is more powerful than the other), the dedicated IP address of this member of the cluster, and the initial state of the potential member node when Windows Server 2003 first boots. You can set the initial state to Started, Stopped, or Suspended.

5. Click Finish to complete the procedure.

The node is then added to the selected NLB cluster. You can tell the process is finished when the node's status, as indicated within the Network Load Balancing Manager console, says, "Converged."

Removing Nodes from the Cluster

For various reasons, you might need to remove a joined node from the cluster—to perform system maintenance, for example, or to replace the node with a newer, fresher, more powerful machine. You must remove an NLB cluster member gracefully. To do so, follow these steps:

1. From the Administrative Tools menu, open the Network Load Balancing Manager console.

2. Right-click Network Load Balancing Clusters in the left pane, and from the pop-up context menu, select Connect to Existing.

3. Enter the host to connect to, and then click Connect. Then, at the bottom of the Connect screen, select the cluster on the host, and click Next.

4. Finally, back in the console, right-click the node you want to remove in the left pane, and select Delete Host from the pop-up context menu.

This removes the node.

If you are only upgrading a node of the cluster and don't want to permanently remove a node from a cluster, you can use a couple of techniques to gradually reduce traffic to the host and then make it available for upgrading. The first is to perform a drainstop on the cluster host to be upgraded. Drainstopping prevents new clients from accessing the cluster while allowing existing clients to continue until they have completed their current operations. After all current clients have finished their operations, cluster operations on that node cease.

To perform a drainstop, follow these steps:

1. Open a command-line window.
2. From the command-line, type wlbs drainstop <IP Address>:<hostID>, replacing the variable with the cluster IP address and the HostID with the unique number set in the Host Parameters tab in NLB properties.

For example, if my cluster was located at 192.168.1.20 and I wanted to upgrade node 2, I would enter the following command:

```
Wlbs drainstop 192.168.1.20:2
```

In addition, configure the Default state of the initial host state to Stopped, as you learned in the previous section. This way, that particular node cannot rejoin the cluster during the upgrade process. Then you can verify your upgrade was completed smoothly before the cluster is rejoined and clients begin accessing it.

Considerations for WSS and Your Perimeter Network

The perimeter network is the network that is closest to a router over which you exercise no control. Essentially, it's the last step before parts unknown, meaning that such a network forms the perimeter of your area of control, your zone of security and authority. It's also the first network that inbound traffic originating from the Internet encounters when destined for your network. In short, the perimeter network separates a trusted network from an untrusted network. Sometimes this network is physical, as with a de-militarized zone, or DMZ, but many times this "perimeter" network is virtualized and the term refers only to the logical boundaries of packets and not to the placement of machines themselves.

Typically, when SharePoint is used to form an extranet, a machine or a group of machines is placed in some form on the perimeter network. Here are a couple of examples of how WSS can be deployed in a perimeter network situation.

A Single-Screened Subnet

In the single-screened subnet scenario, the perimeter network is bounded by one firewall, with three interfaces—one to the Internet, one to the internal network, the final one to the perimeter network. WSS is deployed on one or a number of machines on the perimeter network. This scenario is shown in Figure 11-7.

Figure 11-7
Single-Screened subnet scenario

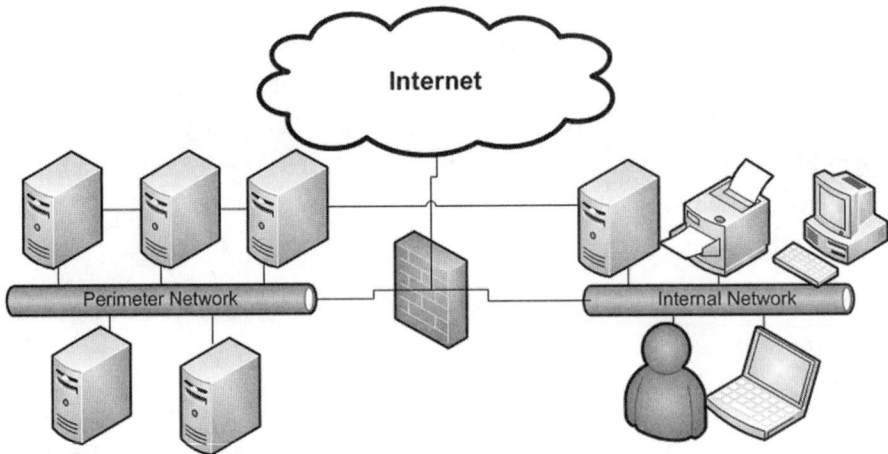

A Dual-Screened Subnet

In the dual-screened subnet scenario, the perimeter network, where WSS is deployed, is sandwiched between two firewall devices. The internal network is doubly protected against threats from the Internet, and another layer of security is added for packets traveling in the perimeter network, further protecting internal assets. This is more secure than the single-screen subnet scenario. This scenario is shown in Figure 11-8.

Figure 11-8
Dual-Screened subnet scenario

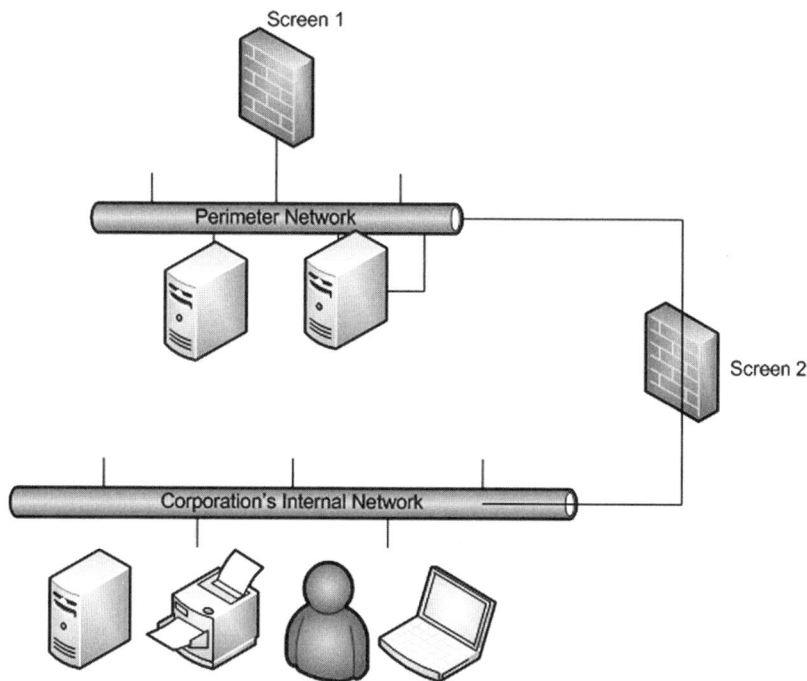

Publishing WSS with ISA Server 2004

Publishing Windows SharePoint Services with ISA Server 2004 involves creating a Web listener, creating a web publishing rule, and then configuring the HTTP filter. All of these pieces work together to make WSS securely accessible through ISA Server 2004.

To create a web listener:

1. In the ISA Server Management console, click Firewall Policy.

2. From the toolbox, click Network Objects, and then select New and Web Listener.

3. The New Web Listener Definition Wizard opens. Give the listener a name and click Next.

4. On the IP Addresses screen, as shown in Figure 11-9, select the network on which to listen for requests—most likely this will be External, to represent all connections on the "other" side of the firewall. Click Next.

Figure 11-9
Select the network on which to listen for requests on the IP Addresses screen

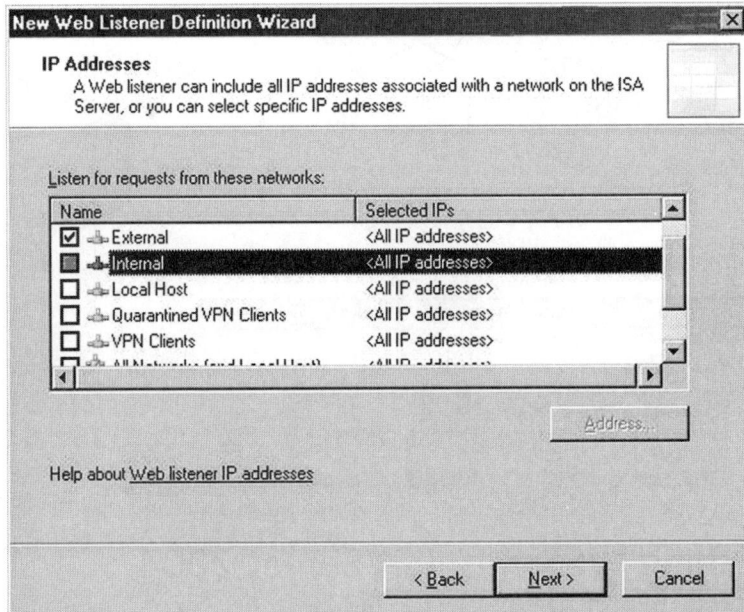

5. On the Port Specification page, select Enable HTTP and then enter port 80. Click Next.

6. Click Finish.

7. Click Apply in the console to apply the changes and activate the new filter.

To create a web publishing rule:

1. Within the ISA Server Management Console, right-click on Firewall Policy, and choose Web Server Publishing Rule from the New sub-menu.

2. The New Web Publishing Rule Wizard appears. Give the rule a friendly name and click Next.

3. Select the Allow action and click Next.

4. On the Define Website to Publish page, enter the name of the machine running WSS version 3.0. Check the "Forward the original host header instead of the actual one (specified above)" box, and then enter the path to the site in the Path box. The URL will be combined for your review in the grayed-out Site box. Click Next once everything is correct.

5. On the Select Web Listener page, as shown in Figure 11-10, choose the listener you created in the above procedure from the drop-down list box. Click Next.

Figure 11-10
Choose the listener on the Select Web Listener page.

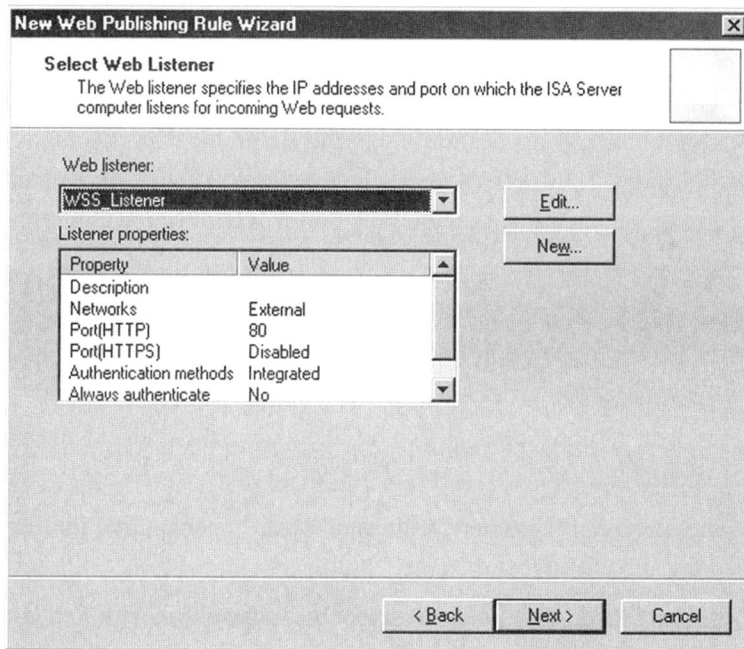

6. Click Next and then Finish to close out the wizard.

7. Click Apply back in the ISA Server Management console to activate the rule.

To configure the HTTP security filter setting:

1. Find the new web publishing rule you just created in the previous procedure.

2. Right-click the rule and select Configure HTTP.

3. The property screen will appear. On the General tab, uncheck "Verify normalization" and if you will be using an international language, like German, with special characters, uncheck "Block high bit characters," as well.

4. Click OK.

Enabling Secure Sockets Layer (SSL) Across Both Connections

If security on both ends of the connection—both from the client to the ISA Server and from the ISA Server to whatever machine WSS 3.0 is running on internally for you—is important to you, then you can enable secure Web publishing with host-header forwarding. By doing so, the SSL connections are bridged, so while it appears seamlessly to the client, his data is actually going across two separate, but vetted, secure connections. This involves creating a secure web listener, creating a secure Web publishing rule, and configuring the HTTP security filter.

To create a secure web listener:

1. In the ISA Server Management console, click Firewall Policy.

2. From the toolbox, click Network Objects, and then select New and Web Listener.

3. The New Web Listener Definition Wizard opens. Give the listener a name and click Next.

4. On the IP Addresses screen, select the network on which to listen for requests—most likely this will be External, to represent all connections on the "other" side of the firewall. Click Next.

5. On the Port Specification page, as shown in Figure 11-11, uncheck "Enable HTTP" and check "Enable SSL" and then enter port 443. Click Next.

Figure 11-11
Port Specification page

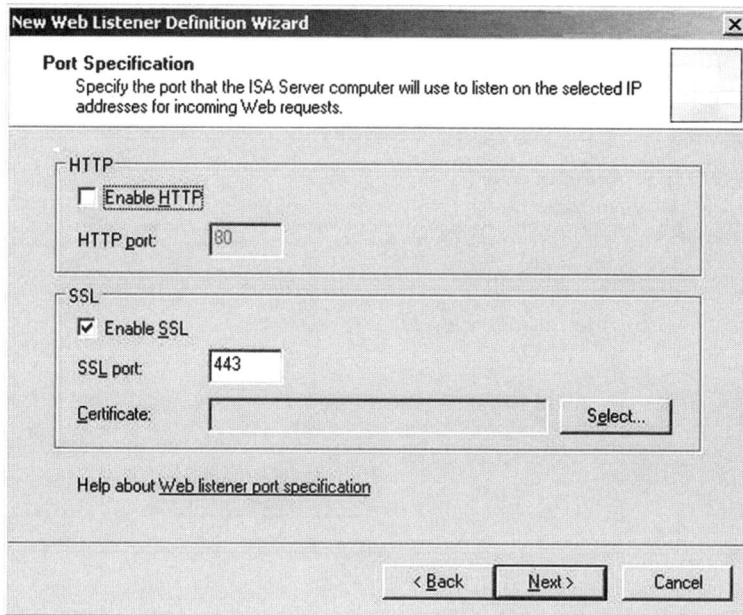

6. Select the proper secure certificate. This is one you either self-signed or purchased from a third-party secure SSL certificate vendor. Click OK.

7. Click Next and click Finish.

8. Click Apply in the console to apply the changes and activate the new filter.

To create a secure web publishing rule:

1. Within the ISA Server Management Console, right-click on Firewall Policy, and choose Secure Web Server Publishing Rule from the New sub-menu.

2. The New SSL Web Publishing Rule Wizard appears. Give the rule a friendly name and click Next.

3. The Publishing Mode page appears; select SSL bridging and click Next.

4. Select the Allow action and click Next. The Bridging Mode screen appears, as shown in Figure 11-12. Choose "Secure connection to clients and Web server," and click Next.

Figure 11-12
Bridging Mode screen

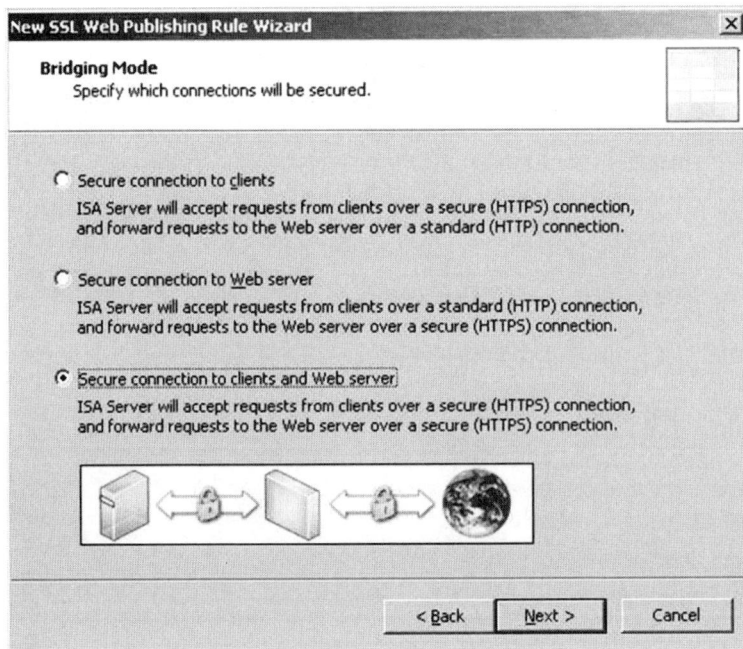

5. On the Define Website to Publish page, enter the name of the machine running WSS version 3.0. Check the "Forward the original host header instead of the actual one (specified above)" box, and then enter the path to the site in the Path box. The URL will be combined for your review in the grayed-out Site box. Click Next once everything is correct.

6. The Public Name Details page appears. Choose to accept requests for any domain name, and click Next.

7. On the Select Web Listener page, choose the listener you created in the above procedure from the drop-down list box. Click Next.

8. On the User Sets page, you can specify any predefined user set from which to accept connection requests. Add users as necessary, or choose All Users, and click Next.

9. Click Finish to close out the wizard.

10. Click Apply back in the ISA Server Management console to activate the rule.

To configure the HTTP security filter setting:

1. Find the new secure web publishing rule you just created in the previous procedure.

2. Right-click the rule and select Configure HTTP.

3. The property screen will appear. On the General tab, uncheck "Verify normalization," and if you will be using an international language, like German, with special characters, uncheck "Block high bit characters," as well.

4. Click OK.

Server Roles and Topology

Windows SharePoint Services 3.0 is designed to scale from one machine to many machines. To handle large loads, you can deploy Windows SharePoint Services in a server farm environment. Don't let the term "farm" fool you—a farm can be two servers or two hundred. In a server farm for SharePoint, there is at least one machine running SQL Server 2005 or SQL Server 2000 running Service Pack 3a or later.

There is also at least one machine, if not more than one, running Windows Server 2003 and Internet Information Services. These function as front-end servers, and you can choose to deploy just a Web front-end server during the installation of Windows SharePoint Servers. This role allows the machine to serve Web content, while handing off the database duties to the database server in the farm. For sites that require high-availability, network load balancing is generally used in a WSS server farm where more than one WSS machine is installed in the Web server role.

You can have a dedicated set of machines that run the search service and have all WSS sites linked to specific search servers. Search in WSS is similar to the full version found in SharePoint Server. However, it only indexes SharePoint content. You can't configure it to index external databases, file shares and other content sources. In addition, it only returns results from a single site collection. It is not able to aggregate results from various site collections.

Installation

Actually deploying Windows SharePoint Services version 3.0 is, of course, where you get hands-on with the process. If you're deploying WSS standalone, and not upgrading, then the procedure is a piece of cake—just get a couple of fundamental pieces of software and then run the installation process, and a few minutes later, you have a live SharePoint site. If you are upgrading an existing machine running WSS 2.0 to version 3, then the process is a little more involved. In this section, I'll talk about both deployment methods, some "gotchas," and how to actually proceed through the deployment.

Raw Installation

Installing WSS 3.0 is a very simple process. There are a couple of prerequisites, however:

- You must be running Windows Server 2003 and have Internet Information Services installed.

- You must install the .NET Framework 3.0, as this includes Windows Workflow Foundation (WF), which is a vital component of WSS.

Before starting the installation process, decide on the version of SQL Server to be used as the content repository. WSS can be installed on either of the following:

- Microsoft SQL Desktop Edition (MSDE). A lightweight version of SQL Server with a limited store size and no user interface. Suitable for small departments and team collaboration sites.

- Microsoft SQL Standard/Enterprise editions. The full-blown version of SQL which provides for better storage capacity and can be installed on a separate box for performance and scalability. More often used by enterprise deployments and active sites with large amounts of content and high traffic.

To install WSS version 3, and if needed, the components mentioned above, follow these steps.

1. Install and configure IIS. If you are running SBS 2003, this has already been done for you. For a standard Windows Server 2003 machine, use the Configure Your Server wizard and add the Application Server role (which includes IIS and ASP.NET support).

2. Install Microsoft's .NET Framework version 3.0. You can get the appropriate package from the Microsoft Download Center—you need the Microsoft .NET Framework 3.0 Redistributable Package. Be sure to get the right version, either x86 or x64, depending on the processor architecture necessary.

3. Enable ASP.NET 2.0, if it's not already enabled. Use IIS Manager, and in the Web Services Extensions folder under the IIS server name, right-click ASP.NET v2.0.50727 and click Allow.

4. Download the WSS version 3 distribution package.

5. Run the installation and accept the Microsoft Software License Terms.

6. Click **Continue**. The next screen presents you with two installation options:

    a. **Basic.** Uses default answers to all questions the installation program asks. Along with WSS, you get MSDE. This is the fastest way to get WSS installed.

    b. **Advanced.** Gives you the option of either installing WSS as a web-front end server or as a stand-alone. Choosing the **Web-Front End** option will install only the components which are required by WSS. It is the only option that allows you to configure WSS to run on Standard and Enterprise editions of SQL Server, which is usually installed on a separate box. The **stand-alone** option will install and run on MSDE.

To take a look at the installation options available, choose **Advanced** and select the **Stand-alone** option. This will install all the components required for SharePoint to work, including MSDE as shown in Figure 11-13.

Notes:

Figure 11-13
Select the type of installation

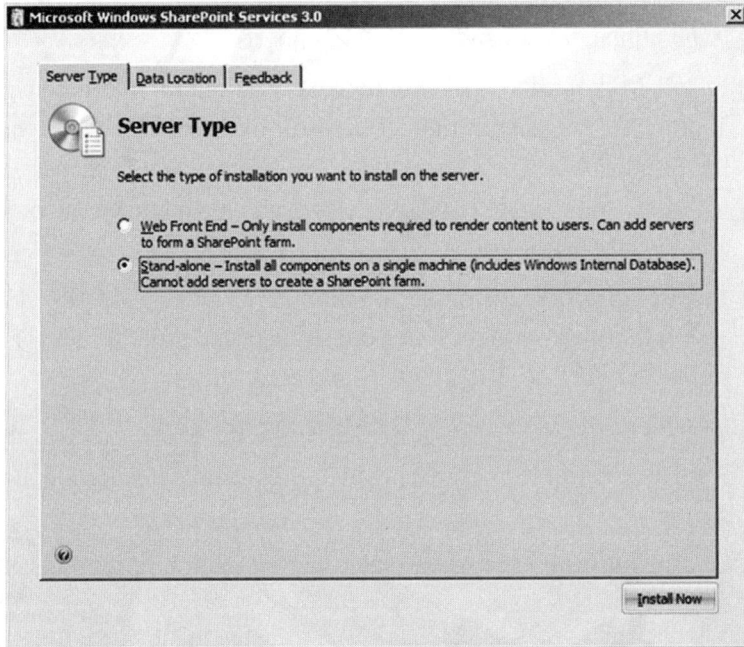

Click on the **Data Location** tab to select the path used to store search index files. In WSS, the search index is stored on the local hard drive. The rule of thumb is to select a location that is approximately half the size of the content to be stored in SharePoint. Choose to accept the default location as shown in Figure 11-14.

Notes:

Figure 11-14
Default data location

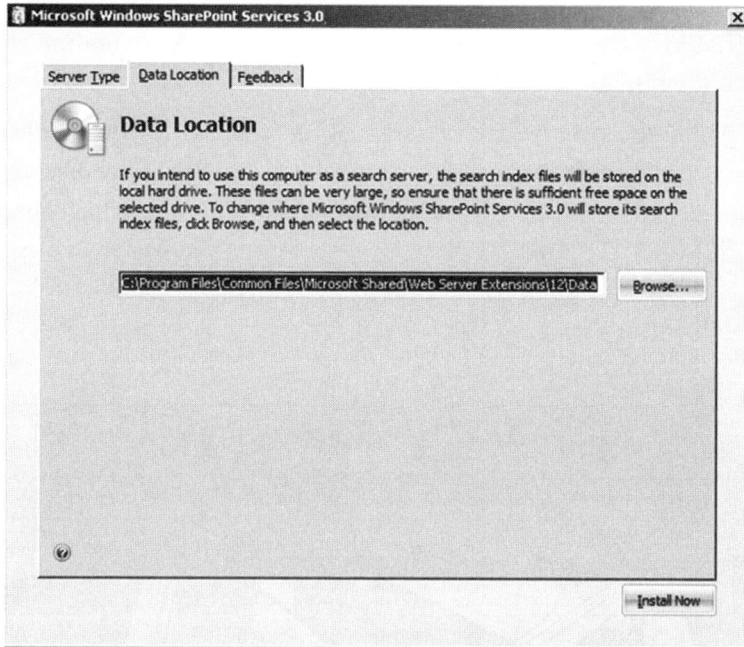

Click on the **Feedback** tab and choose whether you would like to participate in Microsoft's Customer Experience program. If you decide to do so, content such as error logs would be sent to Microsoft anonymously.

7. Finally, click on the **Install Now** to start the installation process. When the installation process is finished, you will be presented with the option to run the "SharePoint Products and Technologies Configuration Wizard." Ensure that the option is checked and click **Close**.

   If, for some reason, you closed the dialog without running the wizard, you can always get back to it by selecting **Start | All Programs | Administrative Tools | SharePoint Products and Technologies Configuration Wizard** from the Start menu.

8. On the splash screen of the SharePoint Products and Technologies Configuration Wizard, click **Next**. Click **Yes** to allow the wizard to stop the Internet Information Services, SharePoint Administration Service and the SharePoint Timer Service if required.

9. The wizard will start the configuration process which will take about 10-15 minutes, depending on the server's configuration. While its running, sit back and relax – you won't be asked for additional input until the configuration is complete. When the configuration is done, click **Finish**.

At this point, you may be asked to reboot, in which case you should do so before proceeding any further with configuration. After the restart, you can access the default WSS site by navigating to http://localhost, which appears in Figure 11-15.

Figure 11-15
Going to http://localhost will bring up the default SharePoint site

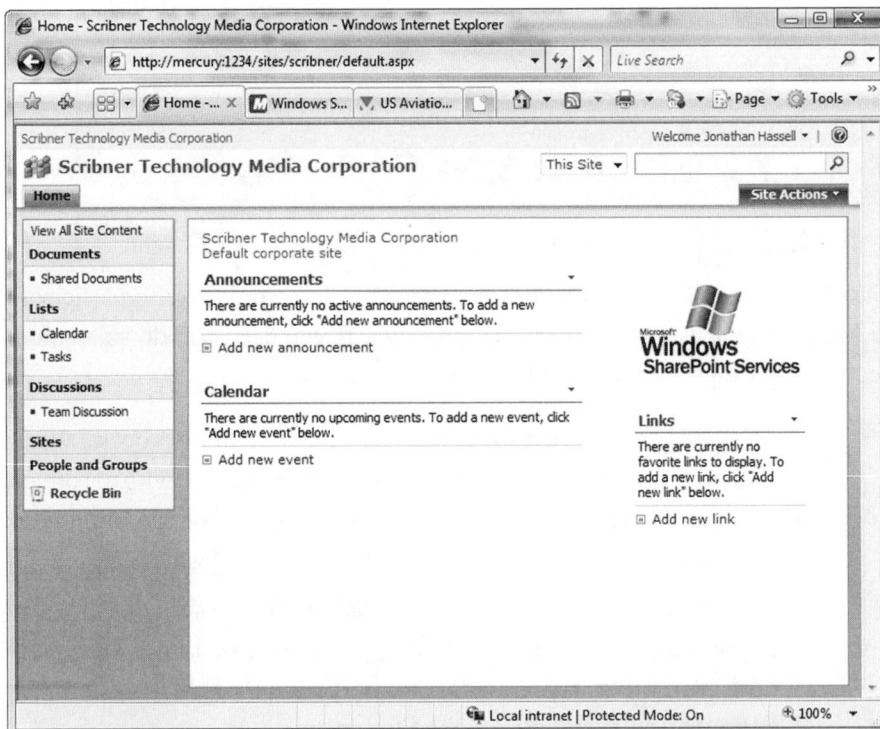

Upgrading from Previous Versions of WSS

Upgrading from Windows SharePoint Services 2.0 to version 3.0 is a more involved procedure than simply installing it new. You can choose to perform an in-place upgrade or a gradual upgrade. With an in-place upgrade, all SharePoint sites on a given server are immediately and entirely upgraded. A gradual upgrade involves optional final update steps to web part and site customizations and is best suited to larger deployments of WSS, mainly because it allows the administrator to decide for himself or herself exactly how many site collections to upgrade at one time. You can host non-upgraded sites on the same server as upgraded sites, so the gradual upgrade does not mandate having multiple machines for sites in different stages of being upgraded.

How does the actual upgrade take place? Upgrading WSS involves several steps, almost all of them at the server level.

1. The WSS 3 installer upgrades the existing underlying SharePoint installation to the latest version.

2. It then upgrades the database used by WSS to the latest WSS version 3 schema.

3. It then reconfigures user rights, site groups, and cross-site groups to new user permissions, permission levels, and SharePoint groups in version 3.

4. In the case of a gradual upgrade, the installer may upgrade the Web Part customizations or it may not.

5. In the case of a gradual upgrade, the installer may or may not upgrade the site customizations done by SharePoint Designer, for instance.

While the technology upgrades are generally performed under the supervision of a system administrator, there are some implications for WSS site owners and designers when their sites are part of an upgrade from version 2 to version 3.

•   Site owners and designers should notify administrators if any customizations are present on their sites, and if so, whether those customizations were made with an approved tool like SharePoint Designer.

•   Site owners should note the theme associated with each of their sites. Since themes differ between the versions of SharePoint, site designers should create a custom theme if they want the same design elements to be present after the upgrade has been completed.

- Once the administrator notifies site owners and designers that the upgrade from WSS version 2 to WSS version 3 is complete, site owners should verify that everything works on their sites.

To actually perform the upgrade from WSS 2.0 to WSS 3.0, follow these steps:

1. Install Microsoft's .NET Framework version 3.0. You can get the appropriate package from the Microsoft Download Center—you need the Microsoft .NET Framework 3.0 Redistributable Package. Be sure to get the right version – either x86 or x64, depending on the processor architecture necessary.

2. Download the WSS version 3 distribution package.

3. Run the installation and choose the in-place or gradual upgrade option. Note that if you are installing WSS 3.0 on an SBS server, you cannot perform an upgrade. You must install WSS 3.0 alongside WSS 2.0 or you will break the integration between the SBS management tools and wizards and SharePoint.

Uninstalling Windows SharePoint Services

To uninstall WSS, simply select Add or Remove Programs from the Control Panel. Click Microsoft Windows SharePoint Service 3.0 and click **Remove**. After WSS is uninstalled, you will be required to reboot the server.

Practice Questions

Question #1:

You are a consultant asked to deploy Windows SharePoint Services securely for use by both internal employees and a set of business partners. In this extranet, the customer has asked for his internal assets to be fully protected from misuse by both the external partners and anonymous connections from the Internet. He has hardware available to support this deployment scenario, and security is of the utmost importance. Of the following, which is the best logical network layout to achieve this goal?

a.   Host the WSS site internally and establish accounts with dial-in or VPN permissions for the customer's business partner.

b.   Use two firewalls or ISA Server machines and deploy WSS 3.0 in the perimeter network. Establish the firewalls on both sides of the perimeter network.

c.   Configure the firewall to allow any type of access on port 80 for traffic destined for the IP address of the computer running Windows SharePoint Services.

d.   Use a tri-homed firewall and connect the perimeter network to this firewall; deploy WSS in the perimeter network.

Question #2:

You are a consultant asked to deploy Windows SharePoint Services securely for use by internal employees *only*. The customer has asked for employees to be able to access intranet content from home. Security is of the utmost importance. Of the following, which is the best logical network layout to achieve this goal?

a.   Host the WSS site internally and establish accounts with dial-in or VPN permissions for the customer's employees.

b.   Use two firewalls or ISA Server machines and deploy WSS 3.0 in the perimeter network. Establish the firewalls on both sides of the perimeter network.

c.   Configure the firewall to allow any type of access on port 80 for traffic destined for the IP address of the computer running Windows SharePoint Services.

d.   Use a tri-homed firewall and connect the perimeter network to this firewall; deploy WSS in the perimeter network.

Question #3:

You are a consultant asked to deploy Windows SharePoint Services securely for use by both internal employees and a set of business partners. In this extranet, the customer has asked for all requests to and responses from the server to be encrypted. He has hardware available to support this deployment scenario, and security is of the utmost importance. Of the following, which is the best logical network layout to achieve this goal?

a. Install ISA Server 2004 and configure it to listen for requests on the external network.

b. Install ISA Server 2004 and configure it to listen for requests on the internet network.

c. Configure the ISA server to listen to port 443 on the internal network.

d. Configure the ISA server to listen to port 443 on the external network.

Question #4:

You have just deployed a Windows SharePoint Services 3.0 server farm. At first everything seems to be working fine. However, as customers begin accessing the sites hosted on that farm, they find that while they can make use of document libraries and other features, they are unable to find specific information via the search facility on each WSS site. What is the most likely cause of this problem at this point?

a. You need to reboot the server after configuring the Indexing Service.

b. The Indexing Service has not been scheduled to run.

c. You did not initially configure the Windows SharePoint Services Search feature on every search server in the server farm.

d. The indexing service is not running in full-text mode.

Question #5:

Your customer is running Windows Small Business Server 2003, Premium Edition and has requested to use Windows SharePoint Services 3.0 instead of WSS 2.0, which is bundled with the product. You agree to assist the customer in this deployment. What steps will be necessary? (More than one answer may be correct.)

a. Back up the SBS server.

b. Install Microsoft .NET Framework 2.0.

c. Install Microsoft .NET Framework 3.0.

d. Download the WSS 3.0 distribution package.

e. Perform a standalone installation.

f. Perform an in-place upgrade.

g. Perform a gradual upgrade.

h. Deploy WSS on a different server.

Question #6:

Your customer is running Windows Server 2003, and has requested to use Windows SharePoint Services 3.0 instead of WSS 2.0. The site has been customized extensively. You agree to assist the customer in this deployment. What steps will be necessary? (More than one answer may be correct.)

a. Back up the database server.

b. Install Microsoft .NET Framework 2.0.

c. Install Microsoft .NET Framework 3.0.

d. Download the WSS 3.0 distribution package.

e. Perform a standalone installation.

f. Perform an in-place upgrade.

g. Perform a gradual upgrade.

Question #7:

You have a Windows SharePoint Services 2.0 site that has been customized with a theme that is not present in Windows SharePoint Services version 3.0. You intend to upgrade to version 3, but want to maintain the theme. What is the most straightforward course of action?

a. Create a custom theme with the desired settings, back it up, and then deploy the existing theme after the upgrade is complete.

   b.   Use Microsoft FrontPage to save a copy of the site and reupload it after the upgrade is complete.

   c.   You cannot maintain the theme across versions.

Question #8:

A customer has requested you to upgrade a small collection of department websites built on WSS 2.0 to Windows SharePoint Services 3.0. The website is used by a group of 100 employees on an occasional basis. You have analyzed the site and found that the site has *not* been customized extensively. Which approach would be most ideal to upgrade the site?

   a.   Perform an in-place upgrade. Perform a one-time upgrade of the content and configuration information on the server.

   b.   Perform a gradual upgrade. Install WSS 3.0 side-by-side on the same server. Migrate existing codes and functions to the new platform. Upgrade site collections one-by-one to minimize site downtime.

   c.   Install WSS 3.0 on a separate server. Migrate existing codes and functions to the new platform. Manually migrate content to the new WSS 3.0 sites.

Question #9:

A customer has engaged you to install and deploy Windows SharePoint Services 3.0. He has requested that the site be available 99.9% of the time. The customer has the necessary hardware resources to implement such a site. Which network configuration would be the most suitable?

   a.   Install WSS 3.0 on a stand-alone machine. Use MSDE as the back-end content repository.

   b.   Install WSS 3.0 on a single web-front end server. User SQL Server Enterprise as the back-end content repository.

   c.   Install two WSS 3.0 web-front end servers on separate machines. Use a network load balancer to distribute traffic between the two servers. Connect the WSS 3.0 servers to a back-end SQL Server cluster.

   d.   Install two WSS 3.0 stand-alone servers on separate machines. Use a network load balancer to distribute traffic between the two servers.

Question #10:

You have a customer who wishes to deploy Windows SharePoint Services 3.0. The customer, a corporation, has 200 employees and expects heavy use of the SharePoint sites, as they are intended to function as an intranet. Of the following choices, what is the most appropriate topology scenario for deploying WSS according to this customer's objectives?

a. One standalone machine with WSS installed.

b. One Web front-end server and one database server running SQL Server 2005.

c. Two or more Web front-end servers and one database server running Access.

d. Two or more Web front-end servers and two database servers running MSDE.

e. Two or more Web front-end servers and one database server running SQL Server 2005.

Answers

Question #1: Answer: b

This scenario, the dual-screened subnet scenario, offers the most security because the internal network is protected in two places from outside customers and connections. The internal employees can still access the perimeter network, while the extranet partner remains unable (by default) to access the local, internal network.

Question #2: Answer a

Unlike the previous scenario, the site will only be accessed by employees on the intranet. The most secure configuration for employees to access content from home will be through a virtual private network.

Question #3: Answer: a,d

For two-way encryption, the ISA Server must be configured to listen for all requests on the external network and only allow connections that go through SSL on port 443.

Question #4: Answer: c

Search is a server role available in WSS 3.0. You can have dedicated search servers to index SharePoint content. However, you must ensure that the Windows SharePoint Services Search Service is running on all Search servers.

Question #5: Answer: a,c,d,e

WSS requires the 3.0 version of the .NET Framework, and any sort of upgrade procedure is completely unsupported on SBS machines and may break integration features.

Question #6: Answer: a,c,d,e,g

Gradual upgrades are recommended to sites that have been customized extensively.

Question #7: Answer: a

Site owners and designers can apply custom themes across versions.

Question #8: Answer: a

In-place upgrades are best suited for small sites that have not been customized extensively.

Question #9: Answer: c

For high-availability scenarios, always plan for redundancy. The web-front end servers can act in active-active cluster with the help of network load balancers. The back-end should be a clustered SQL server in active-passive mode. Should any of the servers fail, there is at least one other server that can take over its functions immediately.

Question #10: Answer: e

Since the customer expects heavy use of the sites, two or morefront-end servers seems appropriate given the user count. The database should run either SQL Server 2000 SP3a+ or SQL Server 2005 and must be on a separate machine than the WSS installations themselves because if one of the nodes hosts the database and goes down you don't have an effective front end load balanced cluster. The DB is always not on the front end machines so it must be on a separate machine than the WSS installations.

Summary

In this chapter, we:

- Looked at name resolution issues, including the split DNS architecture.

- Discussed how to configure network load balancing.

- Explored perimeter network deployments for WSS 3.0.

- Published WSS securely using two methods with ISA Server 2004.

- Covered server farm topologies and the Web front-end server role.

- Installed WSS 3.0 in standalone mode.

- Discussed considerations and the process for upgrading from WSS 2.0 to WSS 3.0.

CHAPTER 12
Crash Course: Administering Windows SharePoint Services

Welcome to the second of three chapters designed to help you cram for the 70-631 exam. In this chapter, we'll look at administering Windows SharePoint Services version 3 once you have deployed it, including managing from the site level, from the server level, and from the farm level. We'll look at managing via the graphical user interface and from the command line, and talk about disaster preparedness and recovery (an essential part of system administration).

Then, we'll move on to customizing SharePoint sites, including the concepts of master pages and page layouts, and then spend some time with SharePoint Designer, the new application specifically geared toward users who want to directly edit their SharePoint sites and the contents therein.

We'll wrap up the chapter with some information on monitoring, both via the facilities offered by Windows SharePoint Services and also generically via Windows Server 2003.

Without further ado, let's begin!

Administration

Windows SharePoint Services is a complex beast, and of course there are settings and knobs to twirl everywhere. In this section, we'll talk about the various interfaces to site, server, and farm administration, and also discuss administering backup and restore services within SharePoint.

Before we do so, let's take a brief look at the various levels in which you can configure SharePoint. At the very top level, we have the server farm. A farm can host several web applications. Within a web application, you can store multiple site collections which in turn contain sites. At the bottom of the hierarchy are the pages and lists stored within individual sites as shown in Figure 12-1.

Figure 12-1
Pages and lists hierarchy stored within an individual site

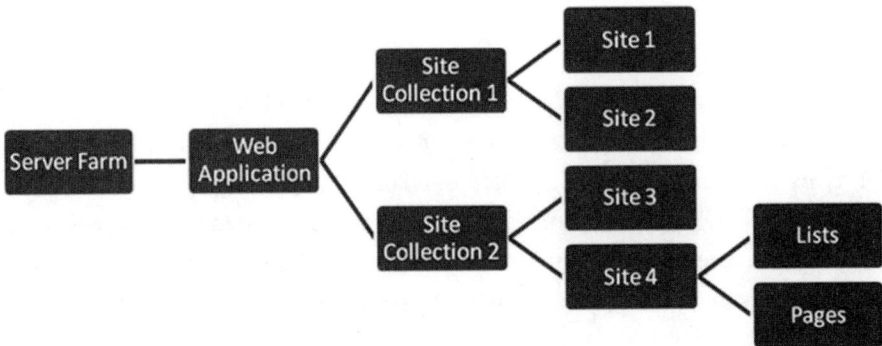

SharePoint provides the flexibility of configuring settings at every level. Let's start by looking at the configuration settings at the site level.

Site Settings

Each individual site within Windows SharePoint Services has its own group of site-specific settings, including users and permissions, look and feel, galleries of Web parts and layouts, site administration features, and site collection administration links. You can access the Site Settings screen for any site by clicking Site Settings from the drop-down Site Actions menu in the right corner of any page with default layout. The Site Settings screen is shown in Figure 12-2

Notes:

Figure 12-2

Site Settings screen

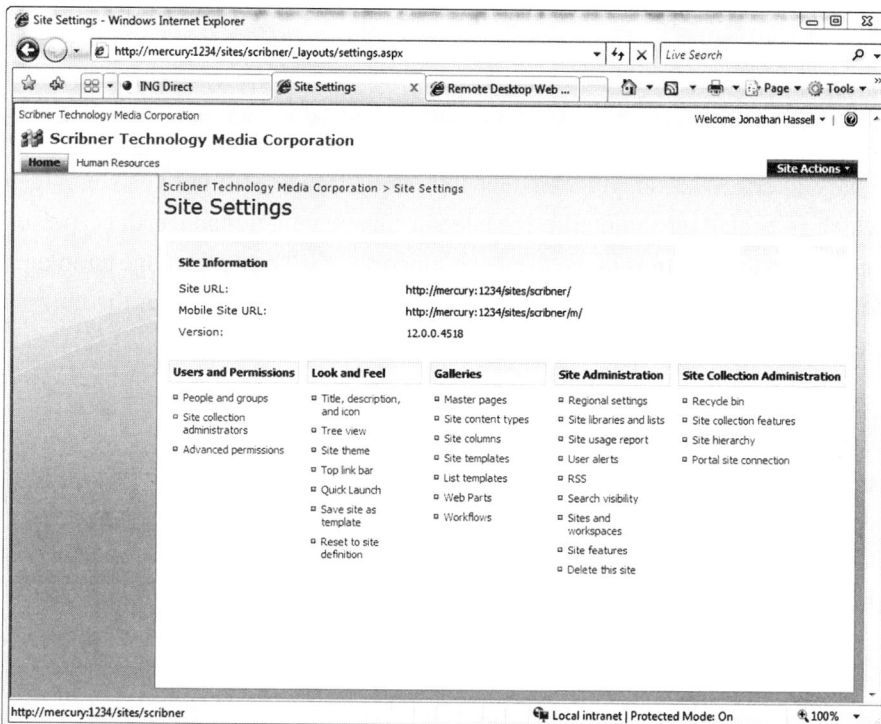

Users and Permissions

In the Users and Permissions section, you can configure user rights for the site. The first site in the collection will contain the "Site collection administrators" option which allows you to specify and manage the list of administrators for all sites within the collection. By default, a sub-site will automatically inherit the permissions of its parent site, but you can override the settings to give each site its own unique set of permissions. Managing users and permissions is a hotspot in the exam and we will have a more in-depth discussion about this in the next chapter.

Look and Feel

In the Look and Feel section of the Site Settings screen, you can configure the site's title and description, configure the associated logo and logo description, enable the quick launch and tree view portions of the main site layout, configure the theme of the site (for example, Belltown, Breeze, Lacquer, or Verdant), add links to the Top Link bar at the top of any given page, save the current site as a site template, and reset the site to its original definition.

Galleries

In the Galleries section, you can do a number of things: configure master pages (which is explained in detail a bit later in this chapter), manage the types of content and the columns in the database supported by the site, manage templates for lists created in the site, store and retrieve Web parts for use in the current site, and define workflows and their statuses in the site.

Site Administration

In the Site Administration section, you can define regional or geography-dependent settings, define the number and names of site libraries and lists, view the site usage report if one is set up (see later in this chapter for more on usage analysis processing), look at alerts users have defined, configure really simple syndication (RSS) feeds for the current site, view sites and workspaces that have been configured underneath the current site, define features available for the site, or delete the current site.

Site Collection Administration

In the Site Collection Administration section, administrators can configure the site collection's Recycle Bin, define features of the site collection (like a three-state workflow), view and manage individual sites in the site collection's hierarchy, and connect the site collection to a portal site.

WSS Central Administration

SharePoint 3.0 Central Administration is the go-to spot for configuring any option or functionality that relates to the overall WSS installation or deployment. It is NOT a place to configure site- or workspace-specific features; rather, the administrator can use SharePoint 3.0 Central Administration to configure the server farm, web application and site collection settings. The Central

Administration page is broadly divided into two sub-areas: **Operations** and **Application Management**.

The Operations section gives you the option to configure topology, running services of a deployment, the overall security configuration of an installation (including the presence of rights management software), logging and reporting, farm features, access mappings, backup and restore, and database configuration settings.

The Application Management section has options for configuring settings for applications and components that reside on the server; or the server farm as the deployment case may be. For example, you can create or extend web applications, manage site collections, specify the authentication mode, and configure external service connections.

Figure 12-3 shows the Operations tab of the Central Administration site, and Figure 12-4 shows the Application Management tab of the site. As part of the preparation for the exams, it is probably a good idea to click through each link within the Central Administration to find out what each option does. Also, read the documentation available onhttp://technet2.microsoft.com/windowsserver/ wss/en/library/6181fe5b-90ca-40cf-aade-abd59cf3c9071033.mspx?mfr=true for how-tos and step-by-step walkthrough of each configuration option.

Notes:

Figure 12-3
Operations tab of the Central Administration site

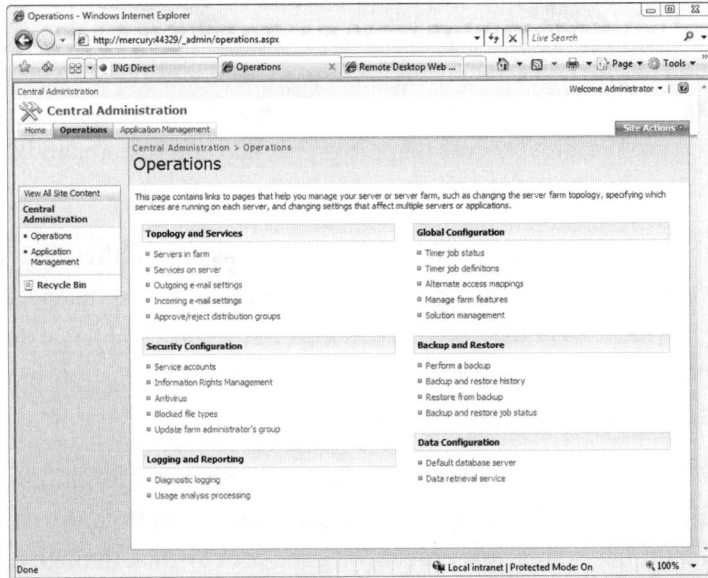

Figure 12-4
Application Management tab of the site

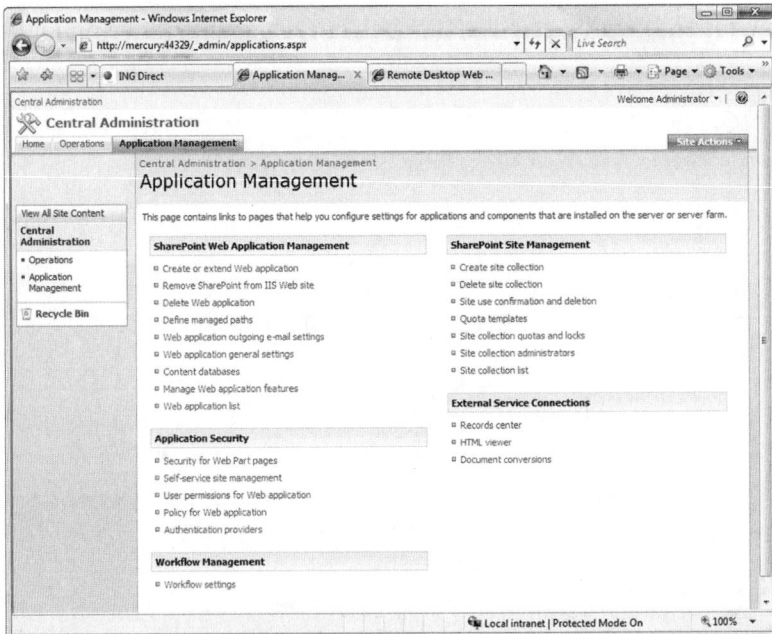

Some definitions of commonly referred to features and terminologies are included here, as well as directions for accessing them within the Central Administration site:

- **Web application**: This is the most commonly-used administrative option within Central Administration. When creating a new SharePoint Web application, a database is created and an authentication method is defined to allow certain users access to certain parts of the new application. A Web application involves a new or existing IIS website and a new or existing database from SQL Server 2005 or MSDE, and both are extended (read: customized) to work specifically with Windows SharePoint Services 3.0.

- **Content database:** This is the database, that contains the data for any given site. You can configure, add, and delete content databases using the Manage Content Databases link on the Application Management tab of Central Administration.

- **Workflow**: A SharePoint-based workflow is a set of rules, based on business processes, that help users route objects to and from different areas and users on the SharePoint site. On the Workflow Settings link on the Application Management tab of Central Administration, you can select an application and then choose whether or not to allow users to define their own workflows on a site. You can also configure how users external to a SharePoint site can get notifications if they have activities pending their attention based on a configured workflow.

- **Timer job:** The Windows SharePoint Services timer job is like a print spooler, in that it handles the scheduling and execution of regular maintenance and administration tasks. If you take a look at the Timer Job Status link on the Operations tab of Central Administration, you can see the dozen or so tasks that the Timer service takes care of, including changing out log files (no, not like dirty diapers!), running disk quota checking and sending out quota warnings, cleaning up workflow remnants, and refreshing the search functionality of WSS.

- **Site collection:** A site collection is a complete intranet, extranet, or Internet implementation of Windows SharePoint Services—it generally contains one or more sites, within a distinct, separate part of a site collection that you generally mentally associate the term "SharePoint site" with.

- **Quota templates:** Quota templates define storage limits for sites. You can apply a quota template to a site by clicking Site Collection Quotas and Locks on the Operations tab of Central Administration. Select a site collection to which to apply the quota template, and then choose the template to apply.

Looking at the Farm

On the first page of the SharePoint 3.0 Central Administration site, you can view a list of administrator tasks that Microsoft has pre-defined to appear after a SharePoint deployment. You can also look at the current farm and its topology, including all of the servers in a given farm and a specific list of services running on those servers. See Figure 12-5 for an example.

Figure 12-5
Farm topology

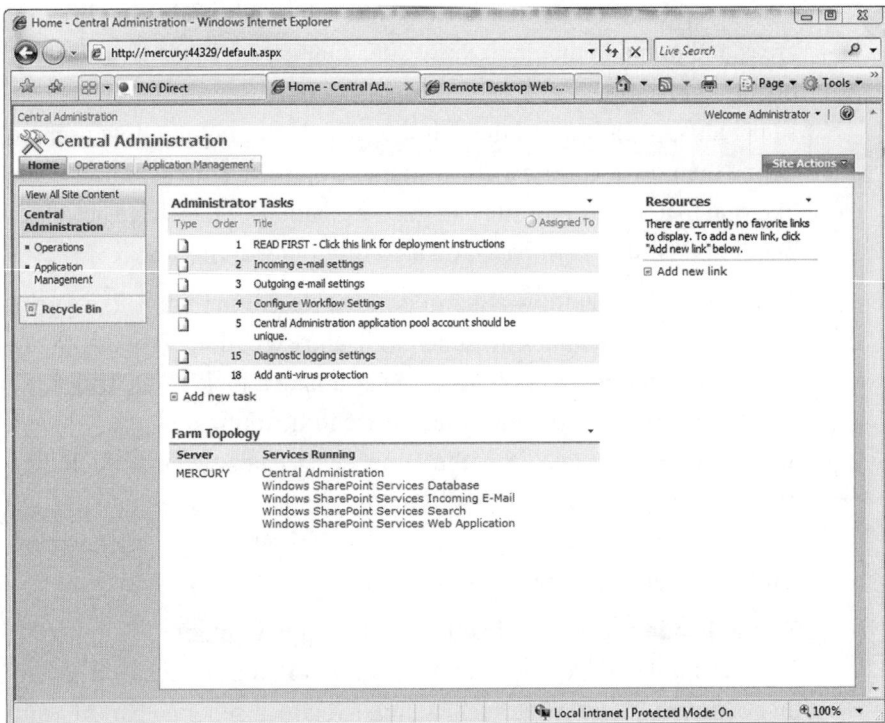

STSADM

STSADM is the command-line counterpart to the SharePoint 3.0 Central Administration site. It offers access to almost all of the interfaces, configuration options, functions, and features of WSS 3.0 from a command line. This is most useful in creating scripts, as command-line utilities are far better suited to being called in common batch scripting languages than are visual dialog- or web page-based configuration screens. You can find the STSADMIN utilities in the `C:\Program Files\Common Files\Microsoft Shared\web server extensions\12\bin` directory.

You can get an idea of what STSADM can do by executing STSADM –help, which will list all functions supported by the program. To drill down into the specific syntax for any particular feature, use STSADM –help featurename to get more details. Here are the functions supported by STSADM. You can also find extensive documentation on the STSADM utility online http://technet2. microsoft.com/windowsserver/wss/en/library/a8ae94e2-0866-4790-a8f4-4a75de6e885b1033.mspx

- Operations:
  - activatefeature
  - addalternatedomain
  - addcontentdb
  - addpath
  - addpermissionpolicy
  - addsolution
  - addtemplate
  - adduser
  - addwppack
  - addzoneurl
  - authentication
  - backup
  - backuphistory
  - binddrservice
  - blockedfilelist
  - canceldeployment
  - changepermission-policy
  - copyappbincontent
  - createadminvs
  - creategroup
  - createsite
  - createsiteinnewdb
  - createweb
  - databaserepair
  - deactivatefeature
  - deleteadminvs
  - deletealternatedo-main
  - deleteconfigdb
  - deletecontentdb
  - deletegroup
  - deletepath

- deletepermission-
  policy
- deletesite
- deletesolution
- deletetemplate
- deleteuser
- deleteweb
- deletewppack
- deletezoneurl
- deploysolution
- deploywppack
- disablessc
- displaysolution
- email
- enablessc
- enumalternatedo-
  mains
- enumcontentdbs
- enumdeployments
- enumgroups
- enumroles
- enumservices
- enumsites
- enumsolutions
- enumsubwebs
- enumtemplates
- enumusers
- enumwppacks
- enumzoneurls
- execadmsvcjobs
- export
- extendvs
- extendvsinwebfarm
- forcedeletelist
- getadminport

- getproperty
- getsitelock
- geturlzone
- import
- installfeature
- listlogginglevels
- localupgradestatus
- managepermission-
  policylevel
- migrateuser
- provisionservice
- refreshdms
- refreshsitedms
- registerwsswriter
- removedrservice
- removesolutionde-
  ploymentlock
- renameserver
- renameweb
- restore
- retractsolution
- retractwppack
- scanforfeatures
- setadminport
- setapppassword
- setconfigdb
- setlogginglevel
- setproperty
- setsitelock
- setworkflowconfig
- siteowner
- spsearch
- spsearchdiacritic-
  sensitive
- syncsolution

- unextendvs
- uninstallfeature
- unregisterwsswriter
- updateaccountpass-
  word
- updatealerttem-
  plates

- updatefarmcreden-
  tials
- upgrade
- upgradesolution
- upgradetargetwebap-
  plication
- userrole

Disaster Preparation and Recovery

A big part of Microsoft's certification emphasis lately is on disaster preparation and recovery—what can an administrator or consultant do to help a business prepare for a disaster? And in the unfortunate event that a disaster does indeed happen, what can that person do to restore normal operations in as rapid a manner as possible? It's a tall order, of course, but SharePoint provides a backup and restore facility that helps ensure against server failure and data loss. Let's take a look at how to use it.

Backing Up

Backup is, of course, of critical importance for any installation of Windows SharePoint Services. You generally perform backups of WSS installations, and recoveries of those backups, manually from within the Central Administration interface. You'll find the needed functionality and switches on the Operations tab, shown in Figure 12-3 above.

Backups consist of saved information in a series of files that are written to a target folder. Generally, this is a network location, and you must ensure you have the correct permissions for SharePoint to write to that folder. You will need to grant the following accounts Modify, Read and Execute, List Folder Contents, Read and Write permissions:

- The SQL Server or MSDE account running SharePoint.

- Your personal account, under which you will manually start backup jobs.

- The server from which Central Administration is accessed.

- The accounts running both the Shared Services and Central Administration application pools.

To perform a backup:

1. Open the SharePoint 3.0 Central Administration tool.

2. From the Operations tab, under the Backup and Restore section, click Perform a backup.

3. Select the farm item to back everything up, or an individual portion of the farm to get only a subsection of the WSS installation.

4. Click Continue to Backup Options.

5. The Start Backup page appears. Enter the location of the target folder, where you will store your backups, and then click OK.

Backups are typically scheduled via the Windows SharePoint Services Timer service, so in much the same way as a print spooler works, you might not notice your backup job starting immediately after you click the OK button to fire it off.

You can also perform a backup using the STSADM utility. This is particularly useful for scheduling backups on a regular basis. You can write a *.bat file containing the backup command and use windows scheduler to run it. The command to use is:

Stsadm –o backup –url <url> -filename <filename>

Alternatively, you could backup the entire WSS site using the following command:

Ststadm –o backup –directory <UNC path to backup folder> -backupmethod <full | differential>

Restoring a Backup

After you have successfully completed a backup operation, restoring that backup is a very simple procedure.

1. Open the SharePoint 3.0 Central Administration tool.

2. From the Operations tab, under the Backup and Restore section, click Restore from backup.

3. Choose the backup package to restore, and the portion of the farm to restore.

4. Click OK to start the restoration procedure.

NOTE: Lots of experienced SharePoint administrators use the backup and restore functionality to move development environments, where they've been testing new setups, workflows, and other features, to production environments once everything is set in stone and fully tested.

You could also use the STSADM utility to perform the restoration of a specific site:

Stsadm –o restore –url –filename

Or to perform a full restore of all sites:

Stsadm –o restore –directory <UNC path to backup folder> -restoremethod <overwrite | new>

Customization

Everyone wants to make a site their own, and SharePoint sites are no exception. In fact, a business can gain significant productivity and efficiency improvements merely from customizing a SharePoint deployment to better fit its needs, from a simple branding change to adding workflows and specific page layouts more suited for the company's internal processes. In this section, I'll discuss the basics of SharePoint customization, including master pages and page layouts, and briefly introduce SharePoint Designer as an option for graphically designing your sites.

Notes:

Master Pages and Page Layouts

Master pages provide consistent navigation and a single page layout structure across a site, independent of the content that is actually displayed on that page. The page layout provides the content that a user sees on a page. Tough distinction? Maybe. Let's take a closer look.

Master pages are often referred to as the trim, or the chrome, of a site. New sites automatically come with a default master page, called default.master, and it is responsible for the structure and overall "feel" of a good number of site pages. However, there is another master page, known as the application master page, which is used across site collections and affects all of those site collections equally. You can edit each of these master pages and change the chrome of various parts of the site. The crux of the matter, though, is this - since there are two master pages in use, if you don't edit the application master, you won't always have a consistent look and feel, whereas if you actually do indeed edit the application master, you may introduce another set of inconsistencies since changes apply across sites.

Is that all? You might ask. To be perfectly true and technically correct, it's not. Indeed there are several other master pages that SharePoint uses in various capacities, including some for administration pages, or some for particular templates, and so on. You can check out all of the master pages SharePoint uses by navigating to `C:\Program files\Common Files\Microsoft shared\web server extensions\12\template\layouts`.

There is a suggested workaround for avoiding the layout inconsistency problem. Create a new LAYOUTS directory for each web application. Create a new directory under `C:\Program files\Common Files\Microsoft shared\web server extensions\12\template`, and then within the IIS Manager console, change the Local Path for the virtual layouts directory to the directory you just created. Copy the necessary pages into the new layouts folder, and then you will have separate application master pages just for that specific web application and the site collections contained thereon.

> NOTE: Do NOT use SharePoint Designer (the application) to edit any file in the LAYOUTS directory; otherwise, you will corrupt the file.

You can create new page layouts, which really define the structure for the actual data that will appear on the SharePoint page. Creating page layouts involves defining site columns, defining a content type, editing the page layout specifically, and then publishing the page layout. The site columns are essentially types of data stored in a column—for example, single line of text, currency, date/time, or HTML. The various types of site columns are below:

- Single line of text.
- Multiple lines of text.
- Choice.
- Number.
- Currency.
- Date/time.
- Lookup.
- Boolean.
- People.
- URL.
- Calculated.
- HTML.
- Image.
- Hyperlink.
- Summary.
- Business data.
- Audience.

Site columns are used by content types, which are then used to create new page layouts. Once the new layout is created, you must check in the page layout, publish it, and then approve it; then it will be available for use by site owners.

Content types have a different practical role to play when assigned to lists. They determine the list of choices that appear when you click on the "New" button. If you have a list that supports two content-types, e.g. Document and

Picture, users will find two different options when they click "New" as shown in Figure 12-6.

Figure 12-6
Selecting different content types

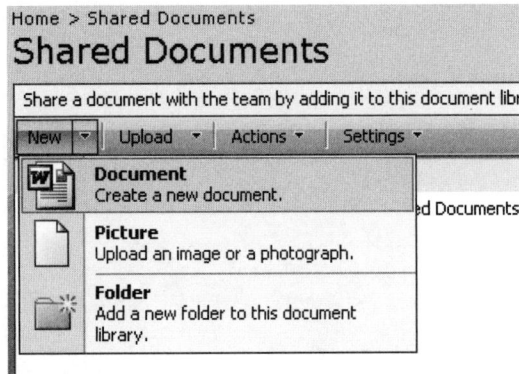

For a practical hands-on guide to creating content types and columns and assigning them to a list, refer to: http://office.microsoft.com/en-us/sharepointserver/HA101734541033.aspx.

SharePoint Designer

SharePoint Designer is a Microsoft product that replaces the old Microsoft FrontPage web design application. It's part of Microsoft Office and is not freely available, so you'll need a license to use it, but as of this writing, there is a free trial available for download from Microsoft at http://www.microsoft.com/downloads/details.aspx?FamilyId=BAA3AD86-BFC1-4BD4-9812-D9E710D44F42&displaylang=en.

SharePoint Designer is destined to become the editor of choice for customizing team sites running on SharePoint. You can see the many options and features of this editor simply by looking at the default screen, shown in Figure 12-7

Notes:

Figure 12-7

SharePoint Designer destined to become the editor of choice for customizing team sites

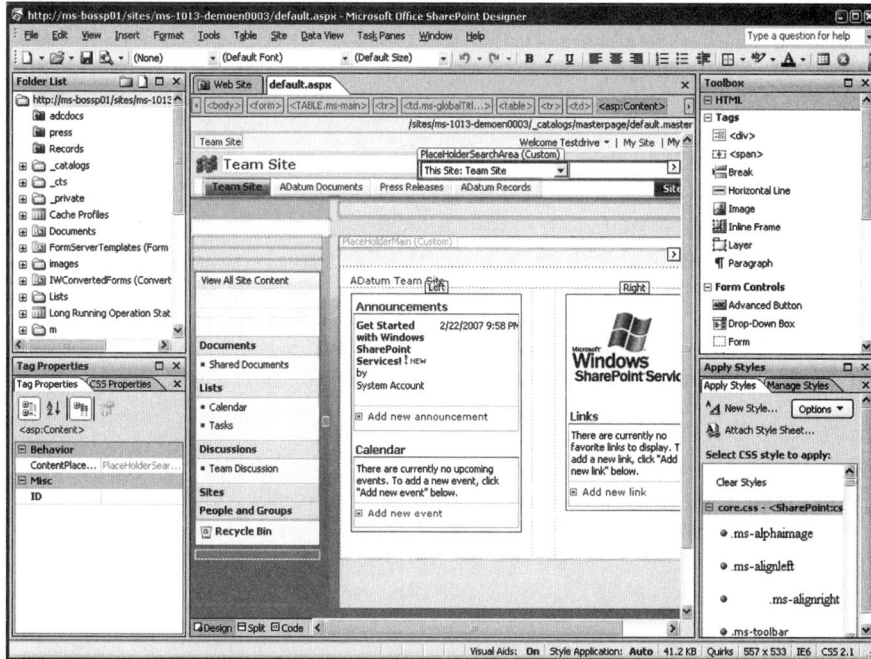

You open SharePoint sites for customization and editing by choosing the Open Site option from the File menu. SharePoint Designer will fetch the site from the server and open its various elements within the editing environment. The folder list view will display all sites, libraries, and lists defined within the site. Any of these elements can be opened from within the program.

In addition, you can add custom web part zones to the page layout from SharePoint Designer. Simply place your mouse cursor on the area you would like to insert the zone and select **Insert | SharePoint Controls | Web Part Zone** from the menu. Note that by design, you can only add web part zones to page layouts and not to master pages.

Authoring Pages

One of Windows SharePoint Service's biggest selling points is the ease in which end-users with varying levels of technical know-how can quickly build web sites. You don't have to know sophisticated HTML and script programming to publish content. All you need are basic word processing skills and you are well on your way to being a web publisher.

For example, to edit a page, simply click **Site Actions** followed by **Edit Page**. The page automatically transforms itself to display editable areas. For example, if template designers have included web part zones as part of the page layout design, you can click on the **Add a Web Part** button to include your own set of web parts.

Note that while being able to customize a page is a great feature to have, adding faulty web parts may cause pages to display incorrectly. To fix the problem, either ensure that all custom web parts are built to handle unexpected exceptions; or go to the web part maintenance page (simply append the querystring, contents=1, to the page's URL e.g. http://mywss/default.aspx?contents=1) to delete the faulty web part from the page. Figure 12-8 below shows how the default page looks like in edit mode.

Figure 12-8
Default page in edit mode.

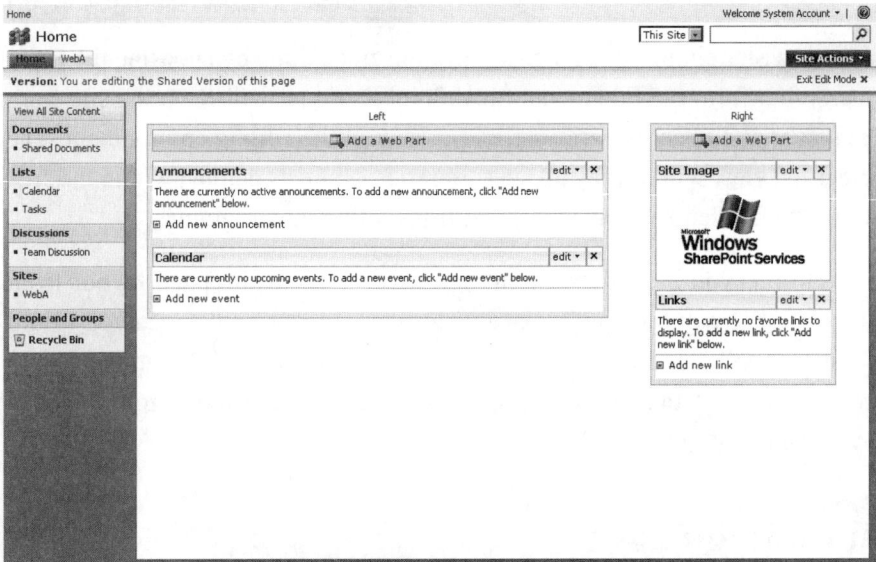

Probably one of the most useful features available to authors is the recycle bin. When a document, list item or page is deleted, it is automatically sent to the user's personal recycle bin. There, they can retrieve documents that have been accidentally deleted without having to bother an administrator. To access the recycle bin, simply click the "Recycle Bin" link on the left menu bar.

What happens if the user unwittingly deletes an important document, promptly empties her recycle bin and suddenly realizes that her much-needed sales report has been trashed? Not to worry, all items that have been deleted from the user's recycle bin are sent to the site collection's recycle bin. There, site collection administrators can recover "lost" files.

Recycle bins automatically purge files that are older than 30 days. However, if you would like to change this limit, you can do so from the **SharePoint Central Administration | Application Management | Web application and general settings** link.

Workflows

You could use workflows to manage the lifecycle of a document, list item or page. Out-of-the box, Windows SharePoint Services ships with a three-state workflow process. Essentially, the workflow monitors the progress of a list item and creates tasks and email notifications based on its status. Take for example the case of a bug database. The three-state workflow could be configured to perform the following:

- When the issue is "new," create a task for the developer and send him an email notification to inform him that there's a new task pending.

- When the issue is "resolved," create a task for the end-user who raised the bug report. An email notification would also be sent to the user to let her know that the bug has been fixed. Perhaps the user will need to re-test the fix.

- When the issue is "closed," the workflow process completes.

If you need to perform more complex tasks with workflows, you could use SharePoint Designer to quickly create custom workflows. And for really complex workflows with tricky business rules, you can use Visual Studio to build custom workflows using Windows Workflow Foundations.

Features

Features are SharePoint's answer to deploying customized modules across WSS sites. For example, you could have created a custom list for containing all progress reports for the Finance department. Before long, you will find that the Technology Department is requesting for the same list type. You could choose to re-build the list definition from scratch. However, Windows SharePoint Services 3.0 now provides a more efficient way to manage customized modules – you could package them as Features.

Take a look at some of the out-of-the box features provided by SharePoint. Choose **Site Actions | Site Settings | Site Features** (located in the Site Administration section). The following screen shot shows the Team Collaboration Lists feature. You could click on the **Deactivate** button to remove the option to support such lists on the site as shown in Figure 12-9.

Figure 12-9
Activate or Deactivate capabilities for standard lists.

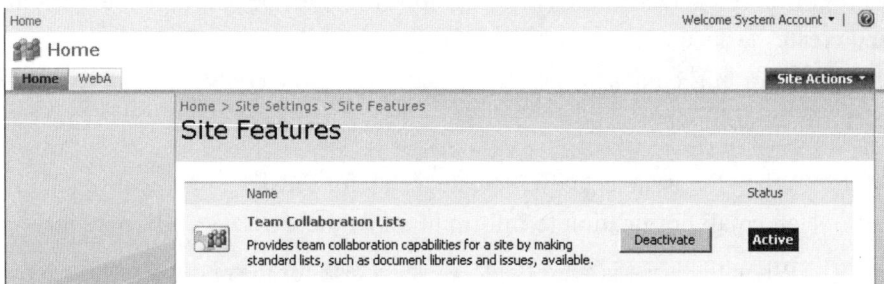

Creating a feature involves building a set of XML files to be added to the `C:\ Program files\Common Files\Microsoft shared\web server extensions\12\template\features` folder. You probably won't be tested on the building of feature files in this exam. However, do watch out for questions that ask about the installation of features. Features first have to be installed on a server using the STSADM utility:

> Stsadm –o installfeature – filename -name

After a feature has been installed you can use the Site Features web page to activate it for a particular site. Or, you could run the following command using the STSADM utility:

> Stsadm –o activatefeature –filename –name –url

Note that if you are planning to uninstall a feature, you will have to deactivate it first.

Solutions

When deploying customized modules, more often than not, it will involve the process of migrating custom features, site definitions, templates, web parts and assemblies. In Windows SharePoint Services 3.0, you can package these files as solutions. A solution file is essentially a compressed cabinet file that has a *.wsp extension.

Using solution files to deploy custom code has several advantages over a manual approach. Solution files can be upgraded so modified code can easily replace existing code-bits. In addition, you can retract a solution anytime. If you accidentally deployed a faulty version of a module, you can recall it without affecting the availability of the WSS site.

Solution files are usually created as part of the development process. As a WSS administrator, you will probably be expected to install them. To install a solution, you will have to run the following command from the STADM utility:

> Stsadm –o addsolution -filename

Monitoring

Part of being a good system administrator is knowing what your systems are up to—the processes running on them, how they're performing, if any errors are cropping up in day to day operations. In this section, we'll take a look at two of the facilities that SharePoint offers for monitoring itself, and then briefly discuss two features of Windows Server 2003 that can be used to look for systemwide errors, not just WSS problems, and also the overall performance and health of the server machine itself.

Logging and Reporting

SharePoint generally logs errors, information events, and warnings to the Application, System, and Security event logs. This allows the administrator to view what's happening in SharePoint installations across the network in a place he is used to looking for that sort of information. As a bonus, it also gets collected in any event forwarding or collection processes that administrator has configured. But SharePoint can also write information to a separate, distinct logging system that is new to WSS 3.0—this is called the Unified Logging Services, or ULS.

The ULS is a collection of text-based files stored by default in `C:\Program Files\Common Files\Microsoft Shared\web server extensions\12\LOGS`. All of the files that make up the ULS contain a .LOG extension. You can configure how, when, and to what degree events are written to the ULS through a module in the SharePoint 3.0 Central Administration site. From within Central Administration, navigate to the Operations tab, and have a look at the Diagnostic Logging link in the Logging and Reporting section. A portion of that page, scrolled to the meaty stuff, is shown in Figure 12-10.

Notes:

Figure 12-10

Diagnostic Logging link in the Logging and Reporting section

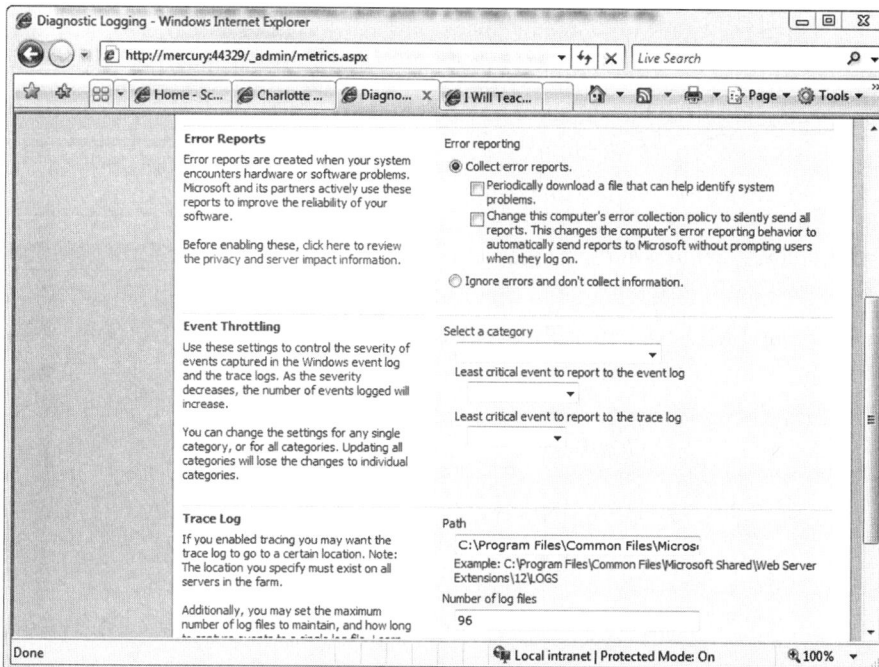

The Diagnostic Logging page contains options for participating in Microsoft's Customer Experience Improvement Program. It also has an Error reports section where you can choose to download a file periodically to help identify solutions to hardware and software problems when they occur. You could also silently send error reports to Microsoft. Note that while these are useful features, they do not actually write any events to the ULS.

The last two sections on the Diagnostic Logging page—the Event Throttling and Trace Log sections—are the heart of this section.

In the Event Logging section, you can control what kinds of errors are captured in the Windows Event log and ULS. As the screen says, if you configure a low severity level, you will receive a lot of events in the logs, whereas kicking the severity threshold up a couple of notches (you can choose from None, Error, Warning, Audit Failure, Audit Success, and Information) results in fewer events being recorded. You can also configure the minimum threshold for logging events to the trace log (you can choose from None, Unexpected, Monitorable, High, Medium and Verbose).

In the Trace Log section, you can specify the path to the ULS logs, how many log files to keep on hand, and the number of minutes SharePoint will write to any specific log file. For instance, if you choose to keep 96 log files, and each log file is written to for 30 minutes, you will have ULS log information for any 2,880 minute period, which translates to 48 hours, or two days.

Unfortunately, Microsoft didn't see fit to include a viewer for the information and events contained in the ULS log files, but on the other, slightly more fortunate hand, the text files are generally pretty easy to parse with just your eyes. You could, however, download free text editors that display the tab-separated lines in an easy-to-read format. Here's a sample:

```
Timestamp                    Process              TID
     Area                          Category
     EventID      Level      Message      Correlation

02/20/2007 15:53:19.95      OWSTIMER.EXE (0x0BAC)     0x1174
     Windows SharePoint Services      General
     0           Medium           Entering MRU trim routine.

02/20/2007 15:53:19.95      OWSTIMER.EXE (0x0BAC)     0x1174
     Windows SharePoint Services      General
     0      Medium           Initial table size: 0 in 0 entries

02/20/2007 15:53:19.95      OWSTIMER.EXE (0x0BAC)     0x1174
Windows SharePoint Services      General
     0      Medium           Final table size: 0 in 0 entries

02/20/2007 15:53:19.95      OWSTIMER.EXE (0x0BAC)     0x1174
     Windows SharePoint Services      General
     0      Medium           Exiting MRU trim routine.

02/20/2007 15:55:18.30      w3wp.exe (0x1C60)          0x1ACC
     Windows SharePoint Services      General
     0      Medium           Entering MRU trim routine.

02/20/2007 15:55:18.30      w3wp.exe (0x1C60)          0x1ACC
     Windows SharePoint Services      General
     0      Medium           Initial table size: 20004691 in 132 entries
```

Portal Usage Reporting

Portal Usage Reporting is a service that allows you to track how many people use any given SharePoint farm, what they are doing with the site, and so on. It's a great way to keep tabs on the traffic the WSS site is receiving, what the most popular pages are, and so on. You can configure portal usage reporting through SharePoint 3.0 Central Administration; on the Operations tab, under the Logging and Reporting section, click Usage Analysis Processing. The resulting page is shown in Figure 12-11.

Figure 12-11
Usage Analysis Processing

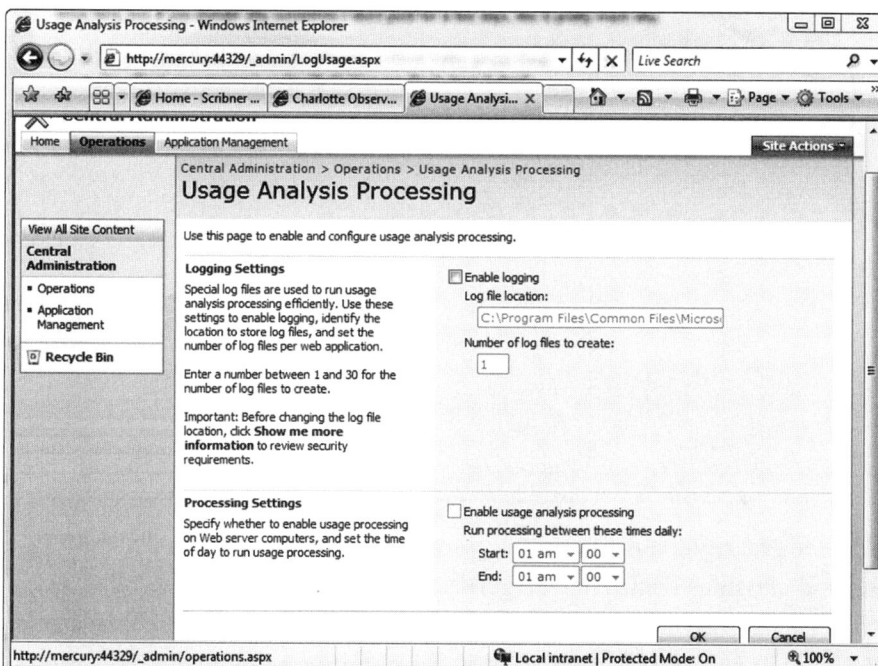

To set up usage analysis processing, click the two checkboxes, "Enable logging," and "Enable usage analysis processing," and configure the times at which the analysis will run.

Windows Server 2003 Event Viewer

The Event Viewer allows you to look at events in three event logs by default. Other applications can add their own logs into the Event Viewer console. Figure X.13 shows a typical Event Viewer console, with the three default logs as shown in Figure 12-12.

Figure 12-12
Event Viewer

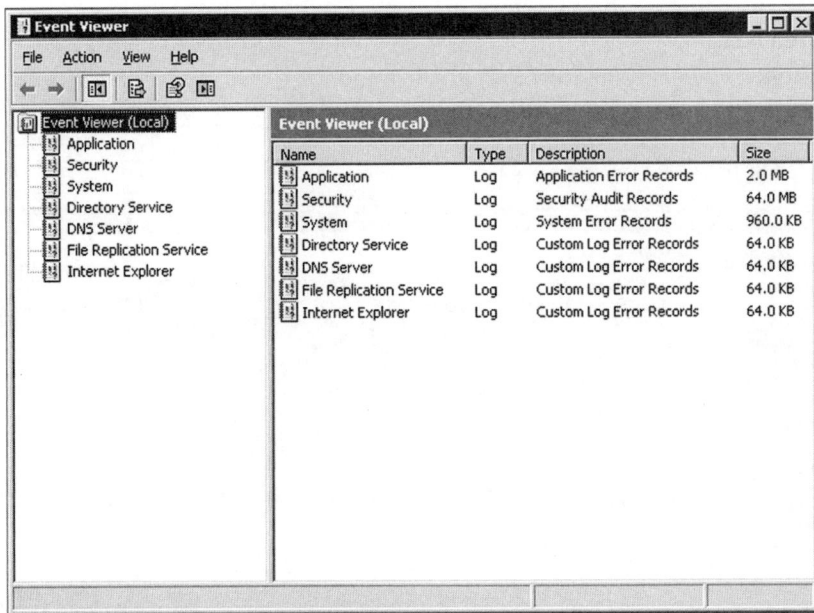

First, the security log displays successes and failures with regard to privilege use, and classifies them into categories such as object access, account logon, policy change, privilege use, directory service access, and account management. The remaining event logs have three different classes of entries: errors, informational events, and warnings. The application log consists of information reported from programs running on the system. The system log consists of events and exceptions thrown by Windows itself. All users can see the system and application logs, but only members of the Administrators group can see the security log.

To clear all events from your Event Viewer console, choose Clear All Events from the Action menu.

Performance Monitor

You can monitor your server over a period of time in relation to discreet activities it carries out during operation—like how often the various SharePoint services are spiking your CPU, for example, although there are numerous other measurements you might make. You use the Performance Monitor to grab this data.

To start the Performance Monitor, do the following:

1. Click on the Start menu then select Administrative Tools.

2. Select Performance.

Processes on a Windows Server 2003 can be analyzed over time using objects known as counters. The System Monitor displays the output of these counters in a chart, a sample of which is shown in Figure 12.13.

Figure 12:13
  Performance Monitor

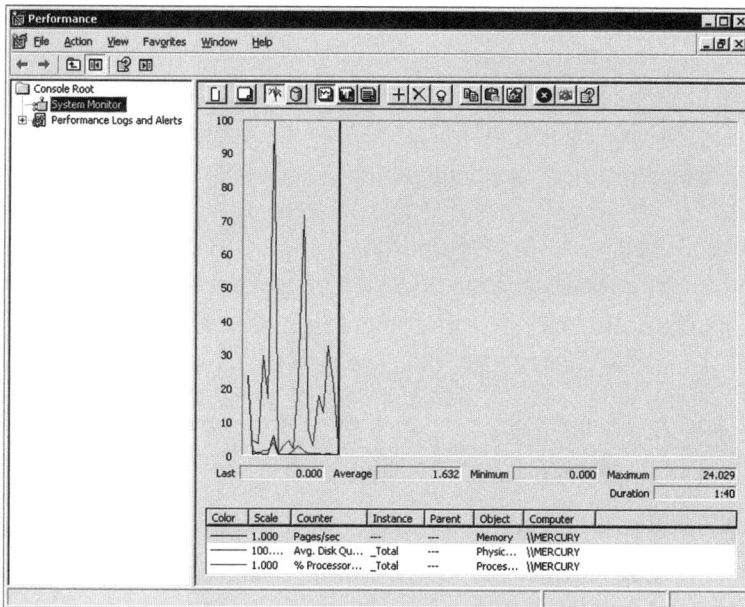

The counters currently selected are displayed underneath the graph. You can monitor the criteria for each counter in this table, as well as use it as a key to decipher which color on the graph represents which counter.

If you want to add a new counter to the set you are monitoring, do the following:

1. Right click anywhere on the System Monitor screen then select Add Counters.

2. If you are selecting counters from your server, select the radio button beside Use local computer counters.

3. The Performance Object is the category of information you wish to monitor, with objects such as Processor, Memory and Network available for selection. When you select a new object, the list of available counters for that object is displayed below. You can then scroll through the list of counters and use the Add button to add each new counter to the graph. Click Explain to find out more details about each counter.

Alerting

Alerts are great as they constantly monitor certain counters for peaks and troughs, and alert you when that counter's value reflects a threshold you've set. It's a nice way to be alerted to potential performance problems on your machine before they become critical. Alerts are sent to the Application event log on the server on which the alerts are configured.

To configure alerts, do the following:

1. Under Performance Logs and Alerts, highlight Alerts. Then in the right hand details pane, right click and select New Alert Settings.

2. Give the alert a meaningful name, then click OK.

3. Add the counters you wish to alert on, for example Processor time.

4. Add a limit, for example 50 percent.

5. Click the Action tab.

6. Click Log an entry in the Application Event Log. If you want to, you can also send the alert to a specified email address.

7. When you're finished, click OK.

Monitoring a Server Farm

When monitoring multiple servers in a farm, consider using Microsoft Operations Manager 2005 or System Center Operations Manager 2007. Microsoft has shipped a management pack for WSS 3.0 that, amongst other things, monitors events placed in the application event log. From a single interface, you can collect information about all servers in a web farm and get recommendations about how to fix problems when they occur. You can download the WSS 3.0 management pack from Microsoft's download center: http://www.microsoft.com/downloads/details.aspx?FamilyId=DB1CADF7-1A12-40F5-8EB5-820C343E48CA&displaylang=en.

Practice Questions

Question #1:

> You have deployed a WSS site for a customer. The customer has complained that the site is not sending out email alerts to users who have subscribed to changes in list content. You suspect that the background timer job has failed to run. What should you do to log the error?
>
> a. On the Diagnostic Logging page, configure the Error Reports feature to periodically download files. Check the downloaded file for possible solution.
>
> b. On the Diagnostic Logging page, sign up for Microsoft's Customer Experience Program.
>
> c. On the Diagnostic Logging page, configure Event-throttling to log "Timer job" errors with a minimum level of "Error" and view the ULS for the error details.
>
> d. On the Diagnostic Logging page, configure Event-throttling to log "Workflow infrastructure" errors with a minimum level of "Error" and view the ULS for the error details.

Question #2:

You have deployed 3 WSS servers to a farm. The customer has requested for the administrator to be notified automatically should any of the servers lose connectivity with the backend database server. Which solution would you propose?

a. Install Microsoft Operations Manager 2005 and use the Windows SharePoint Services 3.0 Management Pack to monitor the event logs of all servers. Configure MOM to send alerts should there be any connectivity issues to the database.

b. Use WMI to write a windows service application to monitor the event logs of all servers. Automatically send an e-mail to the administrator should the logs detect any database connectivity issues.

c. Create a performance counter on the database server. When the counter detects zero connections to the database, send an alert to the administrator.

d. From one of the WSS servers, create a shared folder to map to the ULS directory of the other servers. Write a windows service application to monitor all activity in recorded in the logs. Automatically send an e-mail to the administrator should the logs detect any database connectivity issues.

Question #3:

A customer has requested for a new "Press Release" section to be created within an existing WSS site. Each press release page will consist of a headline, a story (in full HTML) and a ratings web part for users to rate the quality of the article. The ratings web part has been programmed to store the results in a separate database table. How would you create the "Press Release" section? (choose 2 options)

a. Create a custom content type for "Press Releases". The custom content type will have columns for the headline and story.

b. Create a custom content type for "Press Releases". The custom content type will have columns for the headline, story and ratings web part.

c. Create a page based on the existing "Blank Web Part Page" page layout.

    d. Use SharePoint Designer to create a custom master page. Add a custom web part zone for the ratings web part.

    e. Use SharePoint Designer to create a custom page layout. Add a custom web part zone for the ratings web part.

    f. Use SharePoint Designer to customize the "Blank Web Part Page" page layout. Add a custom web part zone for the ratings web part.

Question #4:

A developer has created a custom web part and made it available online for everyone to use. A user has complained that the page crashes each time the web part is added to a page. What should the developer do to ensure that the web part does not cause pages to crash?

    a. Restart the World Wide Web Services for the latest version of the web part code to be deployed.

    b. Add try-catch statements to the web part code. When an error occurs, display a friendly error message on the web part.

    c. Deploy the web part to the global assembly cache. This will ensure that all users are using the same version of the web part.

    d. Use SharePoint Designer to add the web part. Do not allow users to add it to the page themselves.

Question #5:

You are a consultant developing a WSS site for a client. The development work in on the verge of completion and you would like to move the content from the development server to the production servers. As development work has not been finalized, the client has requested for both the development and production to be synchronized at 12 midnight everyday for one week. What should you do?

    a. Manually copy content from the development server over to the production server on midnight every week for one week.

    b. From SharePoint Central Administration, trigger a backup operation on the development server every midnight. Similarly, use SharePoint

Central Administration to trigger a restore operation on the production server after the backup on the development completes.

c. Write a batch job to call the stsadm –o backuprestore procedure on the development server. Use windows scheduler to perform the backup at midnight.

d. Write a batch job to call the stsadm –o backup procedure on the development server. Use windows scheduler to perform the backup at midnight. Write another batch job to call the stsadm –o restore procedure on the production server to recover content.

Question #6:

You received a frantic call from the sales manager that one of his employees has accidentally deleted an important file from the WSS document library. He has tried recovering it from his recycle bin but it appears that he has recently just emptied it. What should you do?

a. Go to the site collection recycle bin and recover the deleted file.

b. Restore a previously backed up version of the site on a separate server and retrieve the file from there.

c. Go to the recycle bin on the user's windows desktop and recover the deleted file.

d. Go to the version history of the document library and retrieve the file from previously saved versions of the document.

Question #7:

A developer has created a solution package that deploys a feature that activates the use of a custom master page file. How would you deploy it?

a. Use the STSADM utility to run the installfeature command.

b. Use the STSADM utility to run the addsolution command.

c. Use SharePoint Central administration to add the solution to the web application.

d. Use SharePoint Central administration to add the feature to the web application.

Question #8:

A developer has created a custom feature that adds a new list type. How should you deploy it? (Choose 2 options)

a. Use the STSADM utility to run the installfeature command.

b. Use the STSADM utility to run the uploadfeature command.

c. Use the STSADM utility to run the activatefeature command for sites that require it.

d. Use the STSADM utility to run the deployfeature command.

Question #9:

A customer has requested that a specific content database, DatabaseA, will host the content of only one site collection. All other site collections should be created in DatabaseB. What should you do? (Choose 2 options)

a. Use SharePoint Central Administration to take DatabaseB offline.

b. Use SharePoint Central Administration to make DatabaseB the default database.

c. Use SharePoint Central Administration to make DatabaseA the default database.

d. Use SharePoint Central Administration to take DatabaseA offline.

Question #10:

You have created a list to track project issues. When new issues are raised, you would like to create tasks and send email notifications to the appropriate person. Similarly, when an issue has been closed the person who raised the issue should review the changes. What is the easiest way to accomplish this?

a. Use SharePoint Designer to create a custom workflow.

b. Activate the three-state workflow feature for the issue list. Configure the workflow to start whenever a new item is created.

c. Use Visual Studio to create a custom workflow based on Windows Workflow Foundation.

d. Write an event handler to capture the status of the list item and create tasks and email notifications whenever the status of the object changes.

Answer Key

Question #1: Answer: c

Use event throttling to configure the minimum threshold level to log events for specific SharePoint services. In this case, we are looking for errors with the timer job. Answer A is incorrect because the files downloaded by the Error Reports feature refer to answers sent out by Microsoft to known problems. The Customer Experience Program in Answer B sends information about your server anonymously to Microsoft and does not help determine why the timer job did not run. Answer D is incorrect because we are looking at errors related to alerts and not workflow.

Question #2: Answer: a

Microsoft Operations Manager 2005 was built to monitor the health of multiple servers in a farm. The WSS MOM pack contains tools that specifically monitor events for Windows SharePoint Services, including checking for connectivity issues with back-end databases. Answers B and D are not the best solutions as they requires a significant amount of coding to work. Answer C is incorrect because zero connections to the database may not necessarily mean that the server is offline. It could just mean that there is no one accessing the server or running any jobs on it.

Question #3: Answer: a, e

SharePoint Designer is the primary tool for customizing page layouts. In this case, we don't need to create a master page as we are interested in configuring the page content, not the overall look and feel of the site, therefore answer D is incorrect In addition, we should not customize the existing page layouts unless we are absolutely sure that no other pages will be affected unfavorably by the change, hence answers C and F are incorrect Answer B is not the best solution because the ratings web part stores information in a separate SQL table, therefore the page does not need to have a custom column to store ratings information.

Question #4: Answer: b

Developers should always handle unexpected errors that may occur within a custom web part. While restarting the WWW service and deploying to the global assembly cache are useful for deployment custom web parts, they do not help in the troubleshooting process, hence Answers A and C are incorrect. Answer D is not the solution either as the problem is with the way errors are handled within the web part. Even if administrators were to add the web part to the page, it will still cause unexpected errors.

Question #5: Answer: d

The easiest way to accomplish this is to use the STSADM tool to write batch jobs that can be called from Windows Scheduler. Note that you have to call backup and restore as two separate operations. The backup/restore options from the SharePoint Central Administration does not provide an immediate way to schedule backup/restore operations on a periodic basis hence Answer B is incorrect. Answer A is not the best solution as it requires someone to be physically present at midnight to perform the migration. Answer C is incorrect as there is no such thing as a 2-in-1 backuprestore command.

Question #6: Answer: a

You should use the site collection recycle bin to recover items that have been purged from the end-user's recycle bin. Answer B is used only when absolutely necessary (e.g. when the site collection recycle bin has also been emptied). Answer C is incorrect as documents are not sent to the recycle bin on the user's desktop. Answer D does not work because version histories are no longer available when the document has been deleted.

Question #7: Answer: b

Only the STSADM utility provides the command for adding solutions. From SharePoint Central administration, we can delete solutions but not add new ones hence Answers C and D are not correct. Answer A is incorrect because the developer has packaged the feature as part of a solution file (*.wsp). The solution has to be added to SharePoint first before the installfeature command is called.

Question #8: Answer: a, c

You need to run the installfeature and activatefeature commands of the STSADM utility to deploy a feature. Answers B and D are incorrect because those commands do not exist.

Question #9: Answer: b, d

To prevent new sites from being created in DatabaseA, use SharePoint Central Administration to take it offline. To ensure that all new sites are created in DatabaseB, make it the default database. Answers A and C are incorrect because we want all other site collections to be created on Database B.

Question #10: Answer: b

Use the three-state workflow to monitor the status of items and send email notifications. Answers A, C and D are workable solutions but are not the best given the scenario as they require significantly more work.

Summary

In this chapter, we:

- Covered administration managing from the site level, from the server level, and from the farm level.
- Discussed Site Settings
- Learned about SharePoint 3.0 Central Administration
- Introduced the command-line utility STSADM
- Discussed backup and recovery of SharePoint farms
- Covered customizing SharePoint sites,
- Developed an understanding of master pages and page layouts
- Introduced SharePoint Designer
- Discussed logging and reporting via SharePoint

- Discussed the Windows Server 2003 Event Viewer

- Learned how to configure the Performance Monitor and derive monitoring information from there

CHAPTER 13
Managing Windows SharePoint Services Security

Welcome to the final chapter in our "exam cram" for the Windows SharePoint Services, the Configuring Exam! In the past two chapters we've talked about deployment considerations, planning for a server farm, installing and upgrading WSS, setting it up, user roles and site settings, general administration, customization, and monitoring. In this chapter, we'll touch on some aspects of Windows SharePoint Services security, including configuring authentication methods, code security, and user permissions. We'll finally wrap up with a bit about integrating information rights management software with WSS.

You're close to the finish line – let's go ahead and get this wrapped up! Dive in.

Authentication

Configuring authentication for the Windows SharePoint Services installation is actually pretty simple when you're doing so as part of the initial installation procedure. The wizard interface that you run just after setup helps you get all of the details in order, including your database server and authentication provider.

But first, before we get started, a little background. SharePoint 3.0 generally uses what is termed as Microsoft Windows Integrated Authentication to authorize and verify users and their credentials. This is great because in an Active Directory environment or a secure workgroup environment, users sign on to a system once and their credentials—since they are "integrated" into their session—work in every application that supports Windows-integrated authentication. Within Windows integrated authentication, there are actually two protocols that provide the standard challenge/response authentication that makes up a secure session:

- **NTLM**: According to Microsoft, NTLM refers to "a secure protocol that is based on encrypting user names and passwords before sending the user names and passwords over the network. NTLM authentication is required in networks where the server receives requests from clients that do not support Kerberos authentication." In other words, if you don't have Kerberos authentication support (more on that in the next bullet), you are required to use NTLM.

- **Kerberos**: The Kerberos protocol is based on ticketing, like going to a theater. A user presents his username and password to the authentication server—in this case, a machine like a domain controller that might be running Active Directory, for example. Assuming all is well with the credentials the user gives, the authentication server gives that user a ticket. The ticket can be used on the network, over and over again, to gain access to other, protected parts of the network. Kerberos requires that both the client and the server have a trusted connection to the domain Key Distribution Center (KDC). Those clients and servers must also be compatible with Active Directory.

There are also a couple of other supported methods of authentication which aren't necessarily as common as NTLM or Kerberos authentication, but yet are still important:

- **ASP.NET Forms-based authentication**. This is the ticket to using a SQL database of usernames and passwords, or authenticating against an LDAP-compatible directory (but not Active Directory—for that you would use NTLM or Kerberos). Typically used to authenticate users not within your Active Directory domain - for example, customers and partners.

- **Web Single-Sign-On (SSO) authentication**. This allows authentication into SharePoint against Active Directory Federation Services—allowing cross-security boundary authentication and trust—or other federated identity management solutions.

Implementing Forms Authentication

Let's take a closer look at implementing forms authentication for a site. When users log in to a site that implements forms authentication, instead of being prompted with a windows login dialog, they will be presented with a login web form as shown below in Figure 13-1. The form, login.aspx, is located in the C:\Program Files\Common Files\Microsoft Shared\web server extensions\12\ TEMPLATE\LAYOUTS directory.

Figure 13-1
Web login form

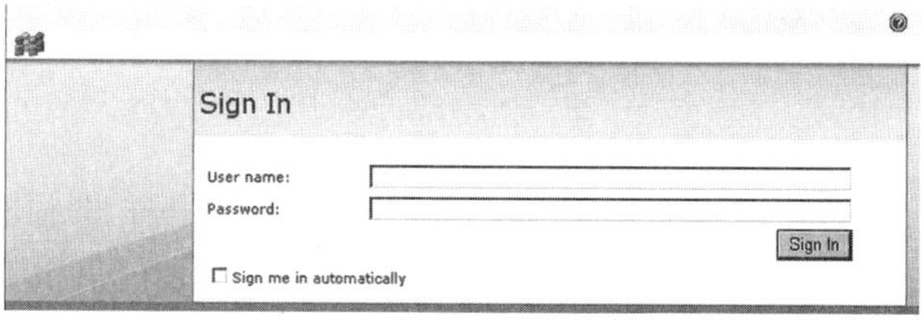

To illustrate how forms authentication is configured, we will attempt to authenticate against a list of user accounts stored in an SQL database table.

1. First, we will install the application services database for SQL Server. To do so, run the following command from the command prompt. You may have to change to the c:\Windows\Microsoft.NET\Framework\ v2.0.50727 folder for the command to be recognized:

```
aspnet_regsql.exe -E -A all -S [Enter name of
database server]
```

2. Next, we will add the first user by running the following script using Microsoft SQL Management Studio against the **aspnetdb** database. For details on what each parameter in the script does, take a look at this article: http://msdn2.microsoft.com/en-us/library/aa478949.aspx.

```
declare @now datetime

set @now= GETDATE()

exec aspnet_Membership_CreateUser 'appName',
'user1', 'password', '', 'user1@somewhere.com',
'', '', 1, @now, @now, 0, 0, null
```

The script adds an account with the id, user1.

3. Now that the database has been created and the first user added, we need to configure WSS to recognize the existence of the database. To do so, we will open the web.config file located in the c:\inetpub\wwwroot\wss\virtualdirectories\(sitename)(portnumber) folder and add the following connection string just before the </configuration> tag:

```
<connectionStrings>

<add name="SqlProviderConnection" connectionStr
    ing="server=[Enter name of database server];
    database=aspnetdb; user=[Enter database access
    account]; password=[Enter database access
    account password]" />

</connectionStrings>
```

4. For the site to recognize the SQL database table as a user account store, we need to register it as a membership provider. We will do that by entering the following membership settings between the first set of <system.web> tags, just below the </authorization> tag:

```
<membership defaultProvider="AspNetSqlMembership
    Provider">

<providers>

<remove name="AspNetSqlMembershipProvider" />

<add name="AspNetSqlMembershipProvider"

type="System.Web.Security.SqlMembershipProvider,

System.Web, Version=2.0.3600.0, Culture=neutral,

PublicKeyToken=b03f5f7f11d50a3a"

description="Stores and retrieves membership data
    from the Microsoft SQL Server database"

connectionStringName="SqlProviderConnection"

passwordAttemptWindow="10"

enablePasswordRetrieval="false"

enablePasswordReset="true"

requiresQuestionAndAnswer="true"
```

```
applicationName="appName"
requiresUniqueEmail="false"
passwordFormat="Hashed" />
</providers>
</membership>
```

5. Repeat steps (3) and (4) for the web.config of the SharePoint Central Administration site. Don't worry, it won't turn on forms authentication for the administration site. Rather, this step is crucial for the administration site to recognize user accounts stored in the database.

6. We are almost done. We will now configure the WSS site to use forms authentication. From SharePoint Central Administration, click **Application Management**.

7. In the Application Security section, click **Authentication providers**. Select the application for which you would like to configure and click on the zone you would like to configure forms authentication for.

8. In the Authentication type field, select **Forms**.(See Figure 13-2). In the Membership provider name section, enter the name of the membership provider, which in this case is **AspNetSqlMembershipProvider**.

Notes:

Figure 13-2
Forms Authentication

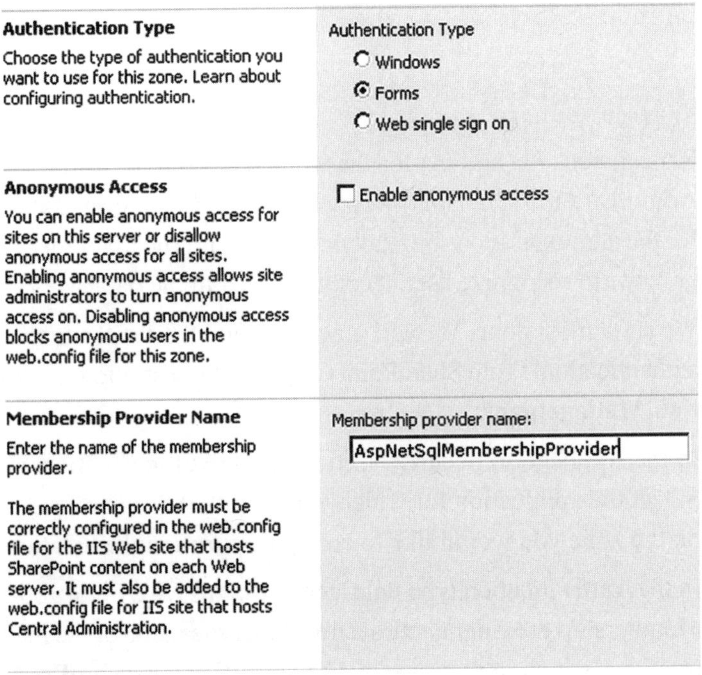

Authentication Type	Authentication Type
Choose the type of authentication you want to use for this zone. Learn about configuring authentication.	○ Windows ● Forms ○ Web single sign on
Anonymous Access	☐ Enable anonymous access
You can enable anonymous access for sites on this server or disallow anonymous access for all sites. Enabling anonymous access allows site administrators to turn anonymous access on. Disabling anonymous access blocks anonymous users in the web.config file for this zone.	
Membership Provider Name	Membership provider name:
Enter the name of the membership provider. The membership provider must be correctly configured in the web.config file for the IIS Web site that hosts SharePoint content on each Web server. It must also be added to the web.config file for IIS site that hosts Central Administration.	AspNetSqlMembershipProvider

9. When done, click **Save**.

As a final step, add user1 (or whatever the first account created earlier was) as the site collection administrator. You can then use that account to add other users to the site.

The next time you attempt to access any page on the site, you will be prompted to login using the credential of an account stored in the SQL database table.

Configuring Anonymous Access

When authentication is applied on a site, users will be prompted to login using their credentials whenever they request for a page. In some cases, like those of Internet-based dot-com sites, requesting users to enter a user name and password is as good as waving a "Do not enter" banner across the site.

Typically, for such sites, you would like to enable anonymous users to view site content.

To do so:

1. When configuring the authentication provider for the site, simply check the Enable Anonymous Access option.

2. In addition, navigate to the site you would like to turn on anonymous access for and select Site Actions | Site Settings.

3. Click Site Permissions from the quick launch menu on the left.

4. In the Site Permissions page select Settings | Anonymous access. Here, you are given the following options:

    a. Entire website. Select this option to give anonymous users read access to all lists, views, folders and pages on the site.

    b. Lists and libraries. Choose this option to give only lists and library access to anonymous users.

    c. Nothing. Select this option to deny anonymous users access to all areas of the site.

When done, click **OK** to save the settings.

Now when users make a request for pages on a site, they will not be prompted for a user name and password. For authors and administrators who need to access protected areas and functions, they will have to click on the "Sign In" link at the top of the page to enter their credentials.

Extending a Website across Zones

Today's Windows SharePoint Services sites are accessed by users across multiple locations. For example, a WSS site hosted on the intranet could be shared with partners accessing the site from the extranet.

More often than not, the authentication mechanism for employees on the intranet will be different from those of, say, partners accessing the site from the extranet or internet. Most organizations will prefer for employees to use their windows credentials to access the intranet site. However, partners will most likely use alternative authentication mechanisms, such as forms authentication, to access the site.

To facilitate this, WSS provides the ability to extend an existing web application across up to five different zones, namely:

- Default
- Intranet
- Internet
- Custom
- Extranet

To have a better understanding of how extending a site works, let's roll up our sleeves and extend the default WSS site that was created during the installation process:

1. From the SharePoint Central Administration page, click **Application Management**.

2. In the SharePoint Web Application Management section, click **Create or extend Web application** (the first link on the page).

3. Choose to **Extend an existing Web application**. Here, you can configure a separate IIS application to host the same web application on a different zone. Figure; 13-3 below shows the section where you specify the zone in which the site will be located.

Figure 13-3
ExtendSiteZones

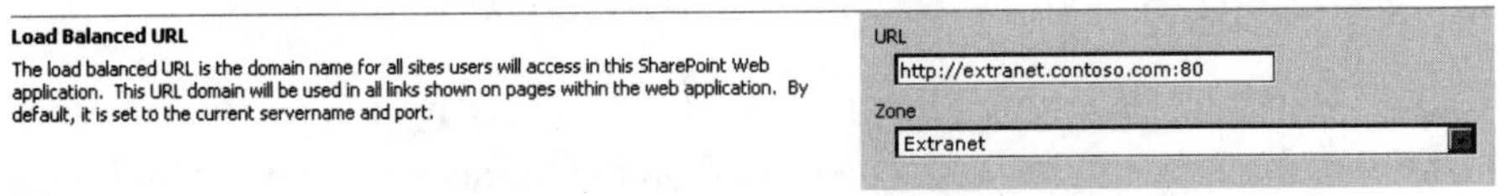

4. Click **OK** to save the settings.

Once the site has been extended, you can specify different authentication mechanisms for each zone. For example, if you wish to specify forms authentication for the extranet site:

1. From the SharePoint Central Administration page, click **Application Management**.

2. In the Application Security section, click **Authentication Providers**.

3. You will see a list of authentication providers for each zone your site has been extended to. In our case, we have two zones - the default and the extranet zones as shown in Figure 13-4.

Figure 13-4
AuthenticationProvidersZones

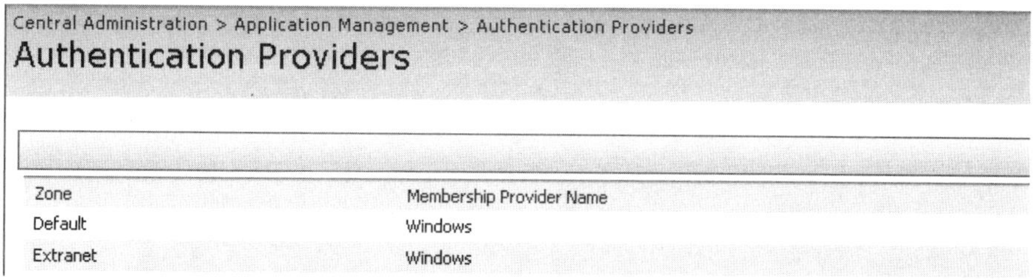

Central Administration > Application Management > Authentication Providers
Authentication Providers

Zone	Membership Provider Name
Default	Windows
Extranet	Windows

4. Click **Extranet** to change the authentication provider for the zone. You can choose between the following authentication types:

    a. Windows

    b. Forms

    c. Web single sign on.

5. Click **Save** to complete the configuration.

Alternate Access Mappings

Earlier, we discussed how the same site can be accessed across multiple zones. Sometimes, you may also be required to give different URLs for each website. For example, employees may access the intranet using intranet. contoso.com while partners will access the same site on the extranet using extranet.contoso.com.

To facilitate the use of multiple URLs, Windows SharePoint Services provides an option to configure alternate access mappings. Say, for example, the extranet site we created earlier has the URL http://www.contoso.com:14379 . To configure it to be accessed via the URL http://extranet.contoso.com:

1. From the SharePoint Central Administration page, click **Operations**.

2. In the Global Configuration section, click **Alternate access mappings**. Figure 13-5 shows a list of all websites on the server and their extended zones.

Figure 13-5
AlternateAccessMappings

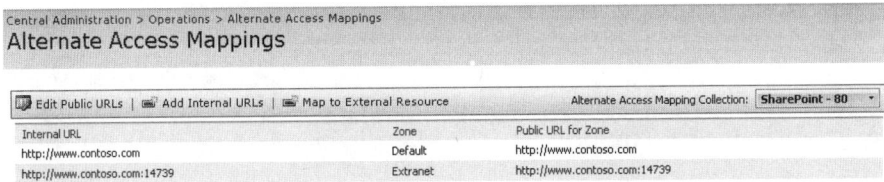

Central Administration > Operations > Alternate Access Mappings
Alternate Access Mappings

Internal URL	Zone	Public URL for Zone
http://www.contoso.com	Default	http://www.contoso.com
http://www.contoso.com:14739	Extranet	http://www.contoso.com:14739

Edit Public URLs | Add Internal URLs | Map to External Resource　　Alternate Access Mapping Collection: SharePoint - 80

3. To change the public URL of a site, click **Edit Public URLs**. In the Extranet field, enter http://extranet.contoso.com. Click **Save**. See Figure 13-6.

Figure 13-6
EditPublicZonesURL

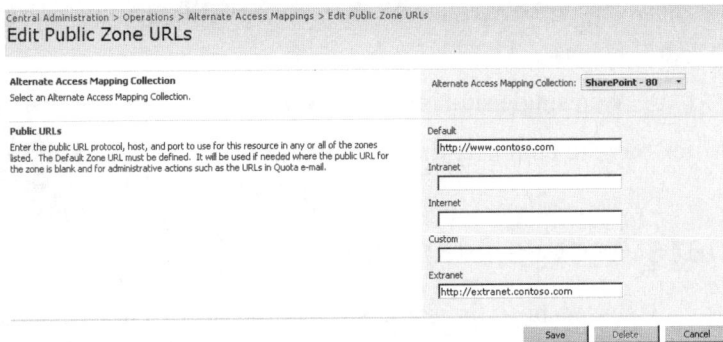

Central Administration > Operations > Alternate Access Mappings > Edit Public Zone URLs
Edit Public Zone URLs

Alternate Access Mapping Collection
Select an Alternate Access Mapping Collection.

Alternate Access Mapping Collection: SharePoint - 80

Public URLs
Enter the public URL protocol, host, and port to use for this resource in any or all of the zones listed. The Default Zone URL must be defined. It will be used if needed where the public URL for the zone is blank and for administrative actions such as the URLs in Quota e-mail.

Default
http://www.contoso.com
Intranet

Internet

Custom

Extranet
http://extranet.contoso.com

Save　Delete　Cancel

Now, when you access the site using http://extranet.contoso.com, SharePoint will automatically respond with the extranet site.

The alternate access mappings feature can also be used to map a single external URL to multiple internal URLs which is useful in the following scenarios:

- When you have published a site using a reverse proxy server. Users request for the site using, for example, http://www.contoso.com. However, the reverse proxy modifies the request and forwards it to another address, or to another port number (e.g.http://intranet.contoso.com:888). In this case, you can add the internal address to the alternate access mapping collection by clicking the **Add Internal URLs** button.

- When you publish a site that is load balanced across multiple servers, some load balancing solutions may modify the URL of the site. For example, if a user requests for the site, http://www.contoso.com, the load balancer forwards the request to one of the internal servers. During the process, the URL could be translated to that of the internal servers. You can add the internal addresses to the alternate access mapping collection so that users will continue to see only the original URL.

Using SSL with Web Applications

SSL, or Secure Sockets Layer, is the accepted standard for secure communications across the web and under other circumstances, too. SSL is a reasonably secure way to encrypt data coming to and from a website, and you can configure WSS to use SSL. More specifically, you are configuring the virtual web server on which Windows SharePoint Services is running to use SSL in its communications with clients.

You can use Internet Information Services Manager to configure SSL. Note that if you want to use SSL for the virtual server used by SharePoint Central Administration, you must also use the setadminport command-line operation to enable SSL in Windows SharePoint Services.

To use SSL on any given WSS installation:

1. Open IIS Manager.
2. Expand the tree in the left until you get to websites.
3. Right-click the virtual server you want to change, and then click Properties.
4. On the Directory Security tab click Edit in the Secure Communications section.
5. Check the Require secure channel (SSL) box, and then click OK. Figure 13-7 shows this screen.

6. Click OK again to close the Properties dialog box.

Figure 13-7
Companyweb Properties Secure Communications tab

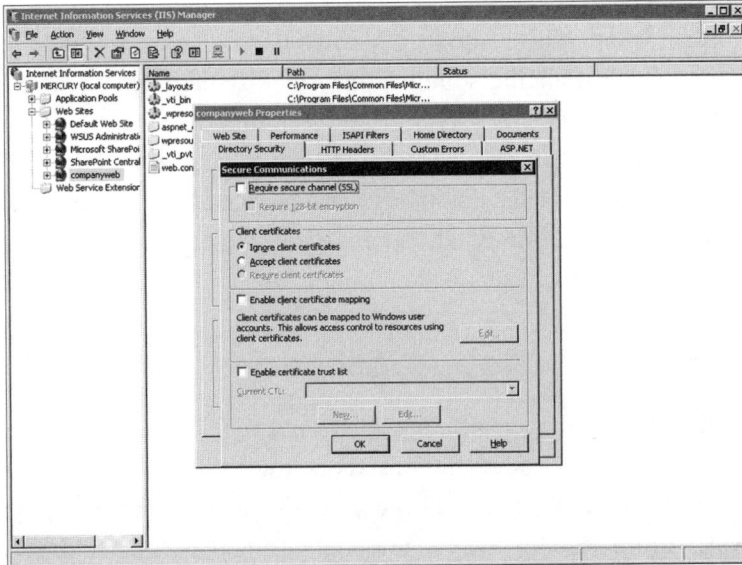

If you want to use SSL on the Central Administration pages, you need to use the command line. First off, if you have a server farm, use the STSADM utility to set the port used for remote administration of your Windows SharePoint Services installation. Issue the following command on the machine running WSS:

```
stsadm.exe -o -setadminport -p 443
```

You don't need to perform that step if you only have a single server running WSS. Finally, use STSADMIN to instruct WSS to communicate via SSL. Type the following at a command line on the machine running WSS (or, in the case of a server farm, each machine in the server farm):

```
stsadm.exe -o -setadminport -ssl
```

Once SSL has been enforced, all requests to the site will require the HTTPS protocol. If you attempt to access the site using the regular HTTP protocol, the request will fail.

Configuring NTLM and/or Kerberos Authentication

Setting up the authentication method for WSS is actually a pretty simple process. You do it all through SharePoint 3.0 Central Administration:

1. Open SharePoint 3.0 Central Administration.

2. Open the Application Management tab.

3. Click the Authentication Providers link.

4. Click the Edit Authentication link. You'll see the screen depicted in Figure 13-8.

5. Under Authentication type, choose Windows to enable the option to choose either NTLM or Kerberos authentication.

6. Under the IIS Authentication section, choose either Negotiate (Kerberos) or NTLM, see Figure 13-8.

Figure 13-8

Selecting the Authentication type

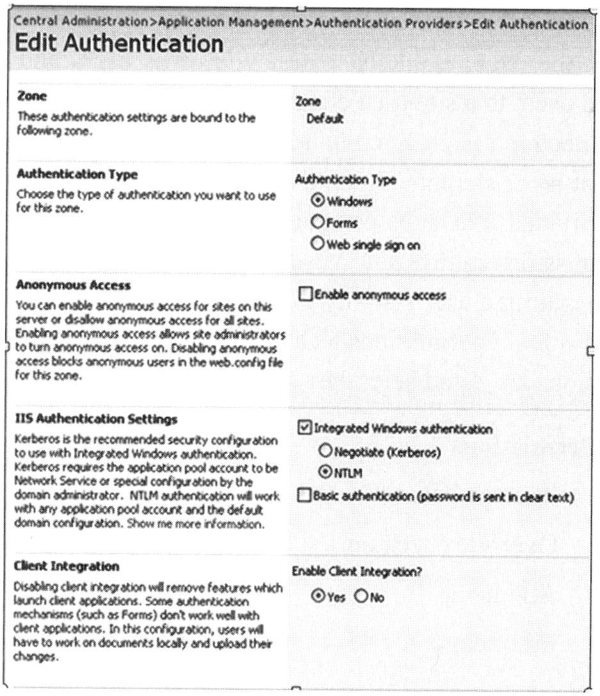

If you choose Kerberos authentication, there are some additional steps you need to take:

- Configure the web application to use the Kerberos authentication mechanism. You do this from within IIS Manager.

- Specify a Service Principal Name (SPN) for the user account on the domain that is used within the application pool's identity. You can manage this from with IIS Manager as well.

- Finally, you then need to register the Service Principal Name for the domain user just mentioned within Active Directory so it's accessible.

Permissions and Access Policies

In this section, we'll talk about the inevitable – keeping honest people honest, and dishonest people from screwing things up for you - by setting up permissions and code security access policies.

Roles and Site Permissions

A big hotspot the exam is likely to test you on is users and permissions. When you add users to a site (just click New and Add User under People and Groups), you need to assign a certain set or group of permissions to that user to control what he or she may do on the site. There are actually 33 granular permissions, divided into three categories, that SharePoint lets you assign a user. *List* permissions control how a user can create and manage lists on a site; *site* permissions limit a user's ability to modify content and the look and feel of a site; and *personal* permissions let a user control his personal content. All of the permissions are listed here; they are fairly self-explanatory:

- **List Permissions**
  - Manage lists
  - Override check out
  - Add items
  - Edit items

- Delete items
- View items
- Approve items
- Open items
- View versions
- Delete versions
- Create alerts
- View application pages

- **Site Permissions**
  - Manage permissions
  - View usage data
  - Create subsites
  - Manage website
  - Add and customize pages
  - Apply themes and borders
  - Apply style sheets
  - Create groups
  - Browse directories
  - Use self-service site creation
  - View pages
  - Enumerate permissions
  - Browse user information
  - Manage alerts
  - Use remote interfaces
  - Use client integration features
  - Open
  - Edit personal user information

- **Personal Permissions**
  - o　Manage personal views
  - o　Add/remove private web parts
  - o　Update personal web parts

It is important to understand that when you add a user to a site, you're by default adding that user to one or more SharePoint groups. That SharePoint group contains rights from the associated permission levels you've configured. For instance, by default, you have a site group called "<site name> Members," which has Contribute permissions for that site. There are also two other groups by default, called "<site name> Owners," and "<site name> Visitors," which have full control and read permissions respectively. There are also other default groups that don't show up:

- Approvers
- Designers
- Hierarchy managers
- Quick Deploy Users
- Restricted Readers

If you're familiar with assigning permissions to users and groups within Windows Server 2003 itself, you'll understand the framework and scenario around users, SharePoint groups, and permission levels.

A special feature of SharePoint groups is their ability to allow users to request to join or leave a group by sending an e-mail to a specified address. Administrators can monitor the requests in the mailbox and grant permissions to the requestor accordingly. You can even allow the group to auto-accept requests as shown in Figure 13-9.

Notes:

Figure 13-9

RequestGroupMembership

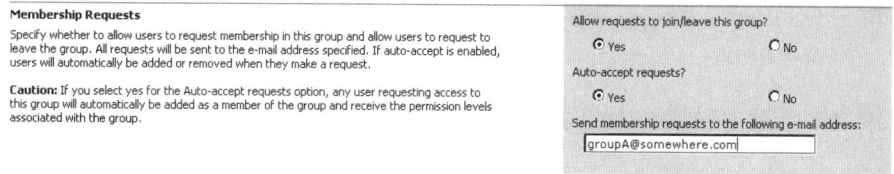

Code Access Security & Access Policies

Since Windows SharePoint Services is primarily an ASP.NET application, it follows the same security procedures and regulations as any web-based .NET application. This means it is by default most likely restricted from accessing certain resources on the network, especially ones that might be useful to include in web parts and other dynamic elements supported by Windows SharePoint Services. This type of security—restricting code from accessing potentially sensitive information across an enterprise—is known as code access security.

Code access security for any given IIS server is dictated by a set of configuration files that are packed with thousands of settings; of course, in this discussion, we're concerned with but one of those groups of settings. One of these configuration files dictates the code access security level for an entire server—this file is located at C:\windows\Microsoft.NET\Framework\v2.0.50727\CONFIG, and the name is web.config. Open it up and take a look. Scroll down to the section labeled <securityPolicy>. In this section, you can see five levels of security, known as levels of trust, defined:

- Full
- High
- Medium
- Low
- Minimal

Notes:

Figure 13-10 shows you a sample:

Figure 13-10
Code Access Security levels for the entire server located in the web. config file

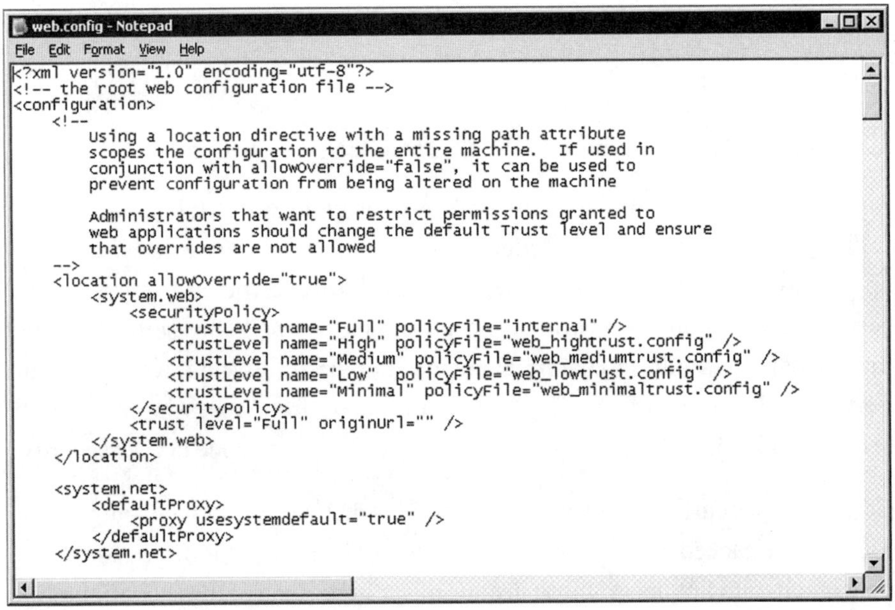

```
web.config - Notepad
File  Edit  Format  View  Help
<?xml version="1.0" encoding="utf-8"?>
<!-- the root web configuration file -->
<configuration>
    <!--
        Using a location directive with a missing path attribute
        scopes the configuration to the entire machine.  If used in
        conjunction with allowOverride="false", it can be used to
        prevent configuration from being altered on the machine

        Administrators that want to restrict permissions granted to
        web applications should change the default Trust level and ensure
        that overrides are not allowed
    -->
    <location allowOverride="true">
        <system.web>
            <securityPolicy>
                <trustLevel name="Full"    policyFile="internal" />
                <trustLevel name="High"    policyFile="web_hightrust.config" />
                <trustLevel name="Medium"  policyFile="web_mediumtrust.config" />
                <trustLevel name="Low"     policyFile="web_lowtrust.config" />
                <trustLevel name="Minimal" policyFile="web_minimaltrust.config" />
            </securityPolicy>
            <trust level="Full" originUrl="" />
        </system.web>
    </location>

    <system.net>
        <defaultProxy>
            <proxy usesystemdefault="true" />
        </defaultProxy>
    </system.net>
```

You can see that, within that master web.config file, each of those levels has defined for it a separate individual trust level file. For example, the "high" level of trust refers to web_hightrust.config, and so on. If you take a look at each of those files, you get a better idea of exactly what permissions and access is entrusted to code running at any given trust level.

Apart from that web.config file, there are individual web.config files that correspond to individual ASP.NET applications; these web.config files are found in `c:\inetpub\wwwroot\wss\VirtualDirectories\{your web application}`. Just as the previous master web.config file had a section called <securityPolicy>, these individual web.config files have <securityPolicy> sections as well, and if you take a look at the web.config file associated with the SharePoint ASP.NET application, you'll find that here you get an extra two levels of trust defined:

- `WSS_Medium`

- `WSS_Minimal`

Check it out in Figure 13-11

Figure 13-11
Two additional trust levels defined in web.config

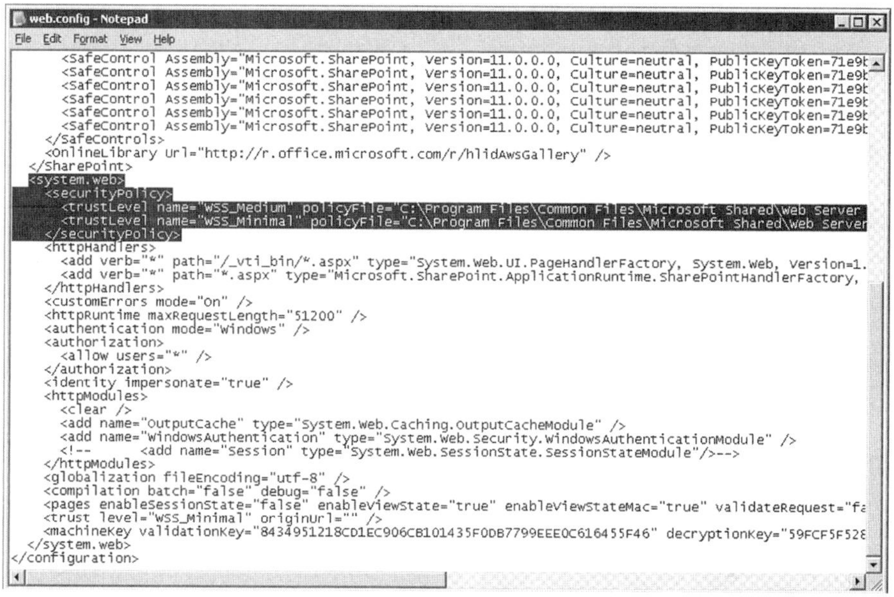

For a variety of technical reasons that are beyond the scope of this discussion (and the exam topic itself), you'll find that web parts within SharePoint, when configured with one of the previous two trust levels, are severely limited in what they are able to do. In a good number of circumstances, you will want to raise the trust level under which specific web parts run in order to allow them access to juicy enterprise resources like databases and other collections of data.

You have three options.

1. Raise the trust level for all Windows SharePoint Services sites by modifying the web.config file in `c:\inetpub\wwwroot\wss\VirtualDirectories\{your web application}`. Just define the level directly in the text file, like this:
   `<trust level="WSS_Medium" originUrl=""/>`

2. You can deploy all of your web parts into the Global Assembly Cache, or GAC. Code running in the global assembly cache automatically runs at the Full trust level. The downside is that if you have a special or sensitive web part, it becomes available to all sites on the WSS machine when you deploy it in the GAC. You add a web part to the GAC by simply using the following command at the command line:
   `gacutil -i [name of web part assembly.dll]`

3. If the previous two options don't appeal to you, then you could create your own policy file. This is the most granular way to achieve the effect that you want, but at the same time it's quite a bit of work to build and test. This is the recommended best practice. If this option appeals to you, I recommend the following website for more information on building a custom policy: http://dikov.blogspot.com/2006/12/configuring-code-access-security-in.html

Information Rights Management

In this section, we'll take a look at rights management software—what it is, what it is supposed to do, and the particulars of how to integrate its features and capabilities into Windows SharePoint Services.

What is IRM?

Information Rights Management, or IRM, is the concept that above the layers of technical permissions that are implemented in software—meaning user A and group B having read and write access to resource C while being denied delete privileges to printer D—there should be another level of rights to control what people actually do with the information they have access to. Think of all of the personal and corporate details that are leaked to press, other media, and even competitors. These types of leaks are achieved not because server permissions are set incorrectly; after all, it's part of this person's job description to manage, edit, and have general access to sensitive information. Rather, it's because there were little or no controls on what that individual could do in terms of transmitting and recording that information outside of its native format.

Microsoft defines information rights management, in the context of Office 2003, as follows:

Information Rights Management (IRM) technology in Microsoft® Office 2003 helps to give organizations and information workers greater control of their sensitive information. IRM is a persistent file-level technology from Microsoft that allows the user to specify permission for who can access and use documents or e-mail messages, and it helps to prevent sensitive information from being printed, forwarded, or copied by unauthorized individuals. Once permission for a document or message has been restricted with this technology, the usage restrictions travel with the document or e-mail message as part of the contents of the file.

Integrating IRM with Windows SharePoint Services

Windows Rights Management Services is the preferred rights management software for integrating with Windows SharePoint Services. As they're both Microsoft products, both of the products benefit from some rather tight integration services and a relatively simple configuration process. And while Windows Rights Management Services, or WRMS, doesn't require SharePoint by any means—it can be used just to protect Office documents themselves—it ties in with SharePoint nicely.

There are a few administrative items to get out of the way before implementing WRMS tying into WSS. For one, you need the actual server bits of WRMS to install on your machine, and you also should download the WRMS client software, which must be deployed to all client machines before you can implement rights management enterprise-wide—whether WRMS is protecting just Office documents, SharePoint, or both. The SharePoint server itself also needs the WRMS **client** bits installed so it can be used to configure document libraries and the associated protections.

Once you have all of the requisite software downloaded, you need to do some preparatory work on the machine that will host the WRMS server software. The software prerequisites:

- Application server role installed (meaning IIS with ASP.NET is installed and enabled).

- The .NET Framework 1.1 must be installed.

- Microsoft Message Queuing software must also be installed (this can be installed through the Add/Remove Programs☐ Windows Components tool, and the software is on the Windows Server 2003 distribution CD or DVD).

After the prerequisite software is installed, it's time to configure IIS:

1. Open IIS Manager.

2. Expand the tree on the left until you can see Web Service Extensions.

3. Make sure you can see ASP.NET v1.1.4322 in the list at the right. (If you can't, click the Add link and browse to the aspnet_isapi.dll file for the 1.1.4322 version of the .NET Framework.)

Then, install the RMS server software. Once the installation is complete, you need to do a bit more configuring:

1. Open Windows RMS Administration from the Start menu.

2. Click the Provision RMS on this Web Site link.

3. Select Remote Database.

4. Provision a service account for the RMS Service to use while operating.

5. Enter a password, and then a strong password for the RMS Private Key and a contact name.

6. Clear or check the proxy box if the current machine uses or doesn't use a proxy server (make the appropriate selection for your environment), and then finally click Submit.

7. Wait for the provisioning process to finish.

After the website has been provisioned, go back into Windows RMS Administration, and then click the Administer RMS on this Web Site link. Click the RMS Service Connection Point link, and then press the Register URL button and browse to C:\Inetpub\wwwroot\WRM_wmcs\Certification\ServerCertification.asmx. Right-click on that file, choose Properties, click the Security tab, and click the Add button. Type in Authenticated Users, click Check Names to get that security group in the permissions box, and then click OK until you get out of all of the property pages.

Now that the server itself has been properly provisioned and configured, you need to set up Windows Rights Management Service for use with SharePoint. You can set this up through Central Administration, but remember that before you can set up RMS with WSS, you absolutely must install the client piece of WRMS on the SharePoint server or servers in question.

Once the client software is installed, use the following instructions to finalize the configuration:

1. Open SharePoint 3.0 Central Administration.
2. Click the Operations tab.
3. Click the Information Rights Management link in the Security Configuration section.
4. Click the Use the Default RMS Server Specified in Active Directory option.
5. Then, to enable WRMS on the document libraries themselves, go to any WSS site and click the Document Center tab.
6. Click the Documents library.
7. Select Document Library Settings from the Settings menu, and go to the Customize page.
8. Click the Information Rights Management link.
9. Check the box called Restrict Permission to Documents in This Library on Download.
10. Give the policy a name – for example, "Restricted"—and then enter an appropriate description, like "Secured documents." Then click OK.

Notes:

Practice Questions

Question #1:

You have deployed a Windows SharePoint Services 3.0 site at the address http://www.mywsssite.com. However, the marketing department has decided that the address be changed to http://www.mysuperwsssite.com. You have already built the site based on the original address. What should you do?

a. Extend the site, http://www.mywsssite.com, to a different zone. Configure the new zone to use the address http://www.mysuperwsssite.com.

b. Use Internet Information Services to create a dummy website with the address http://www.mysuperwsssite.com. Write a script within the web application to redirect all requests to http://www.mywsssite.com.

c. Use the alternate access mapping option to set the external address for http://www.mywsssite.com to http://www.mysuperwsssite.com.

d. Use the alternate access mapping option to set the internal address for http://www.mywsssite.com to http://www.mysuperwsssite.com.

Question #2:

A customer has requested that documents stored on the Windows SharePoint Services 3.0 document library be protected. Only authors and editors will have access to edit documents. Everyone else will only be able to read them. How should SharePoint be configured?

a. Install Windows Rights Management on the WSS server. Create two Windows groups: One for authoring/editing and another for reading. Configure WRM to allow only users in the author/editing group to edit documents.

b. Create two windows groups: One for authoring/editing and another for reading. Use Windows Explorer to give the relevant "Read" and "Write" permissions for the groups on the document library.

c. Create two SharePoint groups. Give one group "Design" rights and assign authors/editors as users of the group. Give the other group "Read" access and assign everyone else to the group. Assign both groups to the document library.

d. Create two SharePoint groups. Give one group "Contributor" rights and assign authors/editors as users of the group. Give the other group "Read" access and assign everyone else to the group. Assign both groups to the document library.

Question #3:

A customer has requested for documents stored on the Windows SharePoint Services 3.0 document library to be protected. Only authors and editors will have access to print documents. Everyone else will only be able to read them. How should SharePoint be configured? (Choose three options.)

a. Install Windows Rights Management Client on a central rights management server.

b. Install Windows Rights Management Client on the WSS server.

c. Use the Information Rights Management option in the document library to allow users to print documents.

d. Install Windows Rights Management Server on a central rights management server.

e. Install Windows Rights Management Server on the WSS server.

Question #4:

You are deploying a Windows SharePoint Services 3.0 site that will be accessed by users from both the intranet and the extranet. You have been requested to authenticate users accessing the site from the extranet against an existing SQL table that contains a list of valid user accounts and credentials. What are the steps required to achieve this? (Choose three options.)

a. Modify the web.config file of the SharePoint Central Administration site.

b. From the SharePoint Central Administration page, configure the site to use forms authentication.

c. Modify the web.config file of the site you are configuring forms authentication for.

d. Modify the machine.config file of the server.

e. Create a form for users to enter their user names and passwords. Write a script to connect to the existing SQL database table to validate the user's credentials.

f. Write an HTTP module to intercept all requests to the site and check to see if the user has been authenticated before. If the user has not been authenticated, redirect the user to the login form.

g. From Internet Information server, change the directory security to Digest.

h. Enable anonymous access for the site you are configuring forms authentication for.

Question #5:

You are implementing forms authentication for a Windows SharePoint Services 3.0 site. When users log onto the site, they complain that regardless of the account credentials entered, they can't get past the login page. What is the most likely cause?

a. You did not specify the correct settings in the web.config file of the site for which you are configuring forms authentication.

b. You did not give the correct permissions on the application folder located in the wwwroot\inetpub\.

c. The Active Directory service for the domain is offline.

d. You did not specify the correct security type in Internet Information Services for the web application.

Question #6:

You are implementing an Internet site for a company using Windows SharePoint Services 3.0. The site should allow all visitors to view content without having to enter a username and password. What should you do?

a. Implement web single-sign on for the site.

b.   Implement Windows authentication for the site. Provide instructions on the page for users to configure their browsers to "automatically sign on with their current user name and passwords."

c.   Configure the site to allow anonymous users.

d.   Give the account "NT Authority\Authenticated Users" read access to the site.

Question #7:

You have deployed a web part created for use throughout the SharePoint Portal Server sites. A colleague reports that when their Windows Sharepoint Services 3.0 page loads the web part, they get System. Security exceptions. What should you do to fix these errors? (Choose two options.)

a.   Send the web part back to the developer. Ask the developer to catch unhandled errors in a try-catch block.

b.   Add the web part assembly to the "bin" directory of the web application.

c.   Add the web part to the <safecontrols> list in the site's web.config file.

d.   Configure the website to run using the WSS_Minimal trust level.

e.   Configure the website to run using the WSS_Medium trust level.

f.   Create a web part file (*.dwp) and import it to an existing page using the Import Web Part option.

Question #8:

You have deployed a web part created by your colleague. However, when the Windows SharePoint Services 3.0 page loads the web part, you get System.Security exceptions. What should you do to fix these errors? (Choose two options.)

a.   Send the web part back to the developer. Ask the developer to catch unhandled errors in a try-catch block.

b.   Add the web part assembly to the global assembly cache (GAC).

   c.   Add the web part to the <safecontrols> list in the site's web.config file.

   d.   Configure the website to run using the WSS_Minimal trust level.

   e.   Configure the website to run using the WSS_Medium trust level.

   f.   Create a web part file (*.dwp) and import it to an existing page using the Import Web Part option.

Question #9:

You have deployed Windows SharePoint Services 3.0 on a load-balanced cluster. A user has provided feedback that the URLs returned by the search service are not consistent. Sometimes the results contain the URLs of one server in the cluster and at other times, the URLs of the other servers in the cluster. What can you do to ensure that the URLs returned by the search service are consistent?

   a.   Host the search service on a separate WSS server. Configure all web-front-end servers to use the search on the WSS server.

   b.   Host the search service on each WSS server. Configure the web-front-end servers to use the search service locally.

   c.   Write a script on the search page to programmatically alter the URLs of the result set.

   d.   Use alternate access mappings to map the addresses of all servers in the load-balance cluster as internal addresses to the external URL.

Question #10:

You have developed an RSS Feed Reader web part that allows users to subscribe to a personalized list of RSS feeds. You deploy the web part to a Windows SharePoint Services 3.0 server that is hosted behind a proxy server that requires authentication for all requests to the Internet. You notice that the custom RSS Feed Reader web part that you have built always fails with the error "Access denied" by the proxy server. Which of the following is the best solution?

   a.   Raise the trust level of the site hosting the web part to "Full."

   b.   Install the web part's assembly in the global assembly cache.

 c. Configure the web browser to "automatically logon with current user name and password."

 d. Implement Kerberos authentication for the site.

Answers

Question #1: Answer: c

You should use the alternate access mapping feature to map a site's address to an alternative external address. Answer A is incorrect because while we could extend the site to a different zone and configure the new zone to use the alternate address, it is not the best solution in this scenario. Answer B is not efficient as the redirects will generate unnecessary loads on the web server. We are attempting to map an internal address to an external address, hence answer D is incorrect.

Question #2: Answer: d

Use WSS to configure who has read/write access to libraries and lists. We should use SharePoint to manage SharePoint permissions and groups, hence Answers A and B are incorrect. Answer C suggests the use of the "Designer" role which manages users who can also create page layouts and master pages – more than what the scenario is asking for.

Question #3: Answer: b, c, d

Use Windows Rights management server to manage rights for printing and uploading documents. Answer A is incorrect because we need the WRM client to be installed on the WSS server, not the WRM server. And answer E is incorrect because the WRM server should preferably be installed on a separate central server.

Question #4: Answer: a, b, c

To implement forms authentication, you will have to modify the web. config files of both the target site as well as the SharePoint Central Administration. In addition, on the Application Management page, you will have to specify the name of the membership provider of the target site. Answer D is incorrect as we do not need to modify the machine.

config file on the server. We could use SharePoint's out-of-the box login form, therefore we do not need to create a custom form as suggested in Answer E. Answer F is wrong as it incurs additional overheads and is not the right way to implement authentication. Answer G works only if you are using Windows authentication which is not the correct answer in this scenario. There is no need to turn on anonymous access unless the site specifically requires it, hence answer H is not correct

Question #5: Answer: a

The most likely cause of failure to authenticate against a SQL store if user accounts are typos or errors in the membership provider settings in the site's web.config file. If the permissions on the application folder have not been applied correctly, users will receive a windows login prompt instead, hence Answer B is not correct. In this scenario, we are using forms authentication, therefore Answer C is irrelevant. Answer D is wrong because the security type is specified in SharePoint's Central Administration and in the application's web.config file.

Question #6: Answer: c

To allow all users access to a site without having to enter credentials, give anonymous users read-access to the site. Answers A, B and D are not the best solutions as they still require users to have valid credentials before viewing content.

Question #7: Answer: b, c, e

For most custom web parts to run without security issues you will have to raise the trust level to at least WSS_Medium. In addition, you will have to register the assembly in the web.config's safe control list. Answer A will not work as the error is caused by SharePoint's code security feature. Even if the developer traps the error, the web part will still not work correctly. By default, SharePoint runs in with the trust configuration set to WSS_Minimal which is insufficient for web parts with assemblies stored in the "bin" directory, hence Answer D is incorrect. Answer F will only load the web part on a page, it will not solve the security exception error.

Question #8: Answer: b, c

When a web part assembly is added to the GAC, it is automatically executed in full trust mode. However, you will still have to register the assembly in the web.config's safe control list. . Answer A will not work as the error is caused by SharePoint's code security feature. Even if the developer traps the error, the web part will still not work correctly. With the assembly in the GAC, setting the trust level to either WSS_Minimal or WSS_Medium makes no difference as they have been configured to execute libraries in the GAC in full-trust mode. Therefore Answers D and E are incorrect. Answer F will only load the web part on a page, it will not solve the security exception error.

Question #9: Answer: d

You can also use alternate access mappings to map a single external address to multiple internal addresses in a load-balancer scenario. Answer A is incorrect as the URLs will still be inconsistent, depending on which front-end server the search service crawls. If Anwer B is deployed, users will still experience inconsistent URLs when they get redirected from one WFE to another by the load balancer. Answer C is not the best solution as it is expensive to implement and maintain.

Question #10: Answers: d

The ticket issued by Kerberos can be used to authenticate the user against the proxy server. Answers A and B are incorrect because the error is not caused by code access security. Answer C will not work because the RSS Feed reader requires two hops – the first from the user's browser to the WSS server. And a second from the WSS server to the proxy server. Configuring the browser to "automatically logon with the current user name and password" will handle only the first hop.

Notes:

Summary

In this chapter, we:

- Discussed authentication in general.

- Looked at how to configure NTLM and Kerberos authentication.

- Discussed setting up sites for SSL access.

- Covered how to set up the SharePoint 3.0 Central Administration site for SSL.

- Went over the various permissions available to SharePoint users.

- Discussed code access security and how it affects web parts.

- Looked at three methods of securely deploying web parts that have actual functionality instead of being neutered by security restrictions.

- Discussed information rights management.

- Learned how to integrate Windows Rights Management Services within SharePoint.

Section IV ❧ Additional Exams and Assessments

Chapter 14
Exam 74-134
Preinstalling Microsoft Products Using the OEM Preinstallation Kit

Chapter 15
Small Business Sales and Marketing Skills Assessment

CHAPTER 14
Exam 74-134—Preinstalling Microsoft Products Using the OEM Preinstallation Kit

The Small Business Specialist program has a certification examination requirement, and you can choose which examination to take. As of this writing, there are two certification exams you can select one from: (1) the 70-282 exam covered extensively in this book (Chapter 3-10) or the 74-134 exam covered in this chapter. This chapter will serve as a "primer" for the 74-134 exam and point you to additional resources to properly prepare you.

> IMPORTANT: Look for updates to this book to reflect inclusion of additional certification exams that will satisfy the testing requirements of the Small Business Specialist Community. Microsoft has signaled that it intends to add qualifying certification exams to the mix over time. By registering your book, you'll be notified of this additional content.

It seemed in the early 2000 time frame that you couldn't attend a Microsoft workshop without having a PowerPoint slide deck presenting the Original Equipment Manufacturer (OEM) Preinstallation Kit, affectionately called the OPK. The OPK exists for a variety of Microsoft products spanning the underlying operating systems, etc. This set of tools helps the OEM partner or system builder automate the installation of Windows Server 2003, Windows XP, Windows Small Business Server 2003 and other support products, saving valuable time and increasing revenue opportunities.

So what gives? Why the interest in the OPK? Microsoft is learning that the low-hanging fruit of the SMB segment has been harvested and eaten. That is, the low-hanging law firms and doctors offices are now successfully using SBS 2003 and other SMB product stack solutions. So Microsoft has turned its focus toward the system builder community, ever loyal, as fertile hunting grounds. The system builder community, a very loyal and enthusiastic group, benefits from using the OEM Preinstallation Kit tools, and passing the 74-134 exam can validate such expertise.

Steps to Passing the 74-134 Exam

This section outlines suggested steps for passing the 74-134 exam. Understand that you'll have to commit the necessary hours of preparation to successful pass the 74-134 exam. The good news is people are doing exactly that, each and every day!

Purchase Microsoft Action Pack

If you haven't already done so, as explained in Chapter 2 of this book, go purchase Microsoft Action Pack at www.microsoft.com/partner. Offered for the first year price of $299 USD, this is a library of Microsoft front office and back office software and partner guides. More importantly for system builders and relating to the 74-134 exam, Action Pack is one place to easily acquire the OPK for numerous Microsoft products.

Review the Exam Objectives

Believe it or not, as of this writing, the public-facing Microsoft web page for the 74-134 exam is actually a hidden link when you visit Microsoft Learning (www.microsoft.com/learning). So you will need to very carefully type in the following URL in your web browser: http://www.microsoft.com/learning/exams/74-134.asp and your page should look like Figure 14-1.

Figure 14-1

The comprehensive Preparation Guide for Exam 74-134

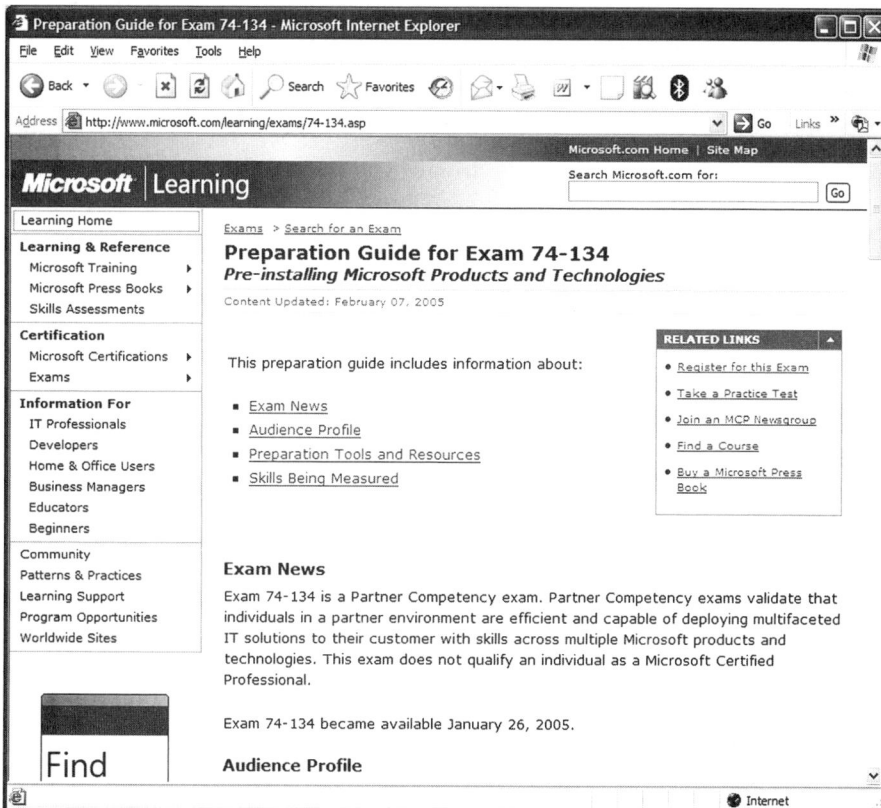

IMPORTANT: Passing the 74-134 exam does not qualify you to hold the Microsoft Certified Professional title. Passing the 70-282 exam DOES qualify you to hold the Microsoft Certified Professional title. For that reason, if you have the choice in your professional field, the authors prefer that you complete the 70-282 examination to meet the one certification test requirement to join the Small Business Partner Community.

When you review the 74-134 examination site, pay careful attention to the **Skills Being Measured** section. This is an excellent matrix that relates the exam objectives to preparatory learning resources. In effect, Microsoft tells you what's on the exam and then tells you were to go find target information to prepare for specific exam objectives. This is a very nice touch and much richer than on the 70-282 examination site (http://www.microsoft.com/learning/exams/70-282. asp) where you're told that every 70-282 exam objective is covered by the three-day Microsoft Official Curriculum course 2395a (true but an expensive course to attend).

> IMPORTANT: Complete the following step now. Print this web page and use it as your roadmap to prepare for and complete the 74-134 examination. Place the print out in a notebook or folder labeled 74-134. You'll add more resources to this shortly.

Visit the Microsoft OEM Site

Consider the following URL to be your portal for tapping into both 74-134 exam and system builder resources: http://www.microsoft.com/oem/default.mspx. Your first step here is to register by clicking the Register Now button. Much of the excellent information on this site is controlled and requires registration to access. Go ahead and do that now. I found the registration process took less than ten minutes.

Once you've registered and performed a site logon, your screen should look similar to Figure 14-2.

Notes:

Figure 14-2

Welcome to the system builder site. Take 30 minutes to explore the sub-sites linked from the left side to rapidly immerse yourself in the system builder community.

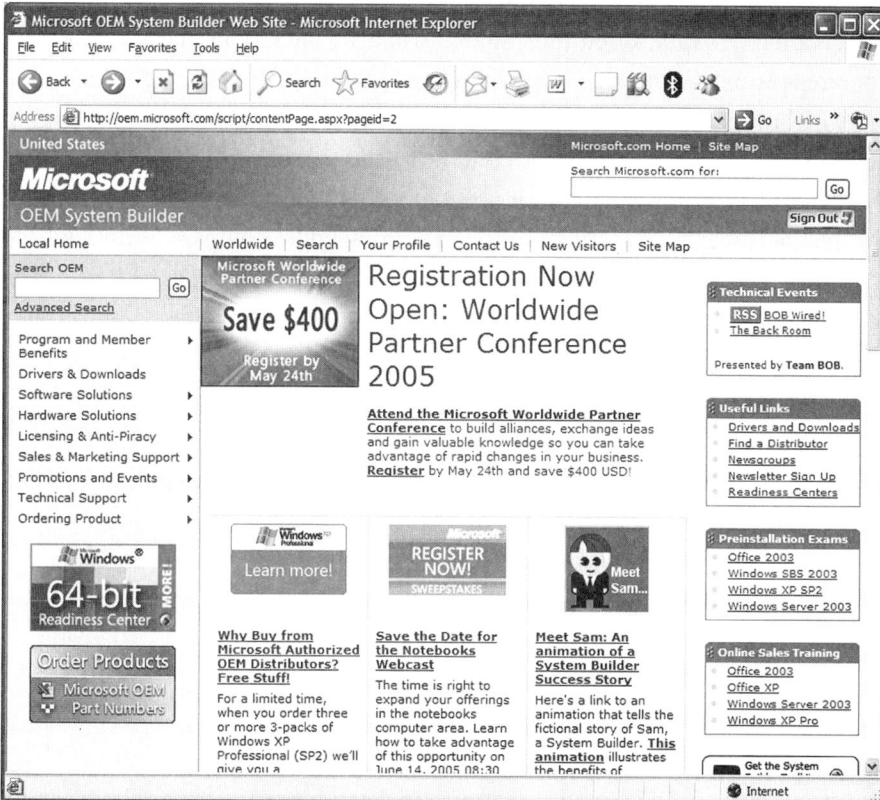

Get To Know BOB!

As you explore the Microsoft OEM and system builder site, you'll bump into the BOB team. BOB, which stands for US System Builder Technology Team, is really a group of Texans in Building 121 at the Microsoft Redmond campus. Not only are they as friendly as the day is long in Alaska in mid-June, but their hearts are truly as large as Texas. I found Steve and the other partners to be some of the most exciting Microsoft blue badges I'd met in a long while (harkening back to the early days of the SBS 4.x development team). What's important about that sage observation is team attitude speaks volumes about partner momentum. When you've got a jacked-up team behind a partner program, as is the case with system builders, it's a good trend line and suggests you should jump on board!

Be the Webcast Warrior

Educational delivery, often the subject of long-winded speeches at academic conferences and the like, is ever evolving and changing. With the higher adoption rates of broadband technology, Microsoft (like many technology vendors) is cost-effectively delivering cool content to the masses using Webcasts. The system builder program and your ability to effectively and efficiently prepare for the 74-134 exam benefit from this emerging education paradigm! And did I mention that the vast majority, if not all, of these Webcasts are FREE! (See – we just paid for the price of this book.)

> IMPORTANT: A few years ago, after gaining much weight writing books and serving a portfolio of real-world customers as an ardent SMB consultant, I hired a personal trainer to right my life and return me to good health. Steve Rhoades, this athletic angel in disguise, provided some invaluable advice on day one: sign up for as many classes at my athletic club as I could.
>
> In the same vein, I offer a similar suggestion to you. Sign up for as many system builder Webcasts as you can muster and tolerate! Not only are these Webcasts immediately applicable to your cause of passing the 74-134 exam, but you might just meet a famous author or two along the way (Hint: see Figure 11-3). The System Builder Events page, found at http://oem.microsoft.com/script/contentPage. aspx? pageid=4078 is where you join the Webcast fun.

N otes:

Figure 11-3

Look closely. Co-author Harry Brelsford presented that June 22, 2005 Webcast while traveling in Dublin with his SMB Nation Summit workshop tour. Co-author Beatrice Mulzer presented the June 29th Webcast on ISA 2004 (she wrote the ISA 2004 chapter in the Advanced Windows Small Business Server 2003 Best Practices book).

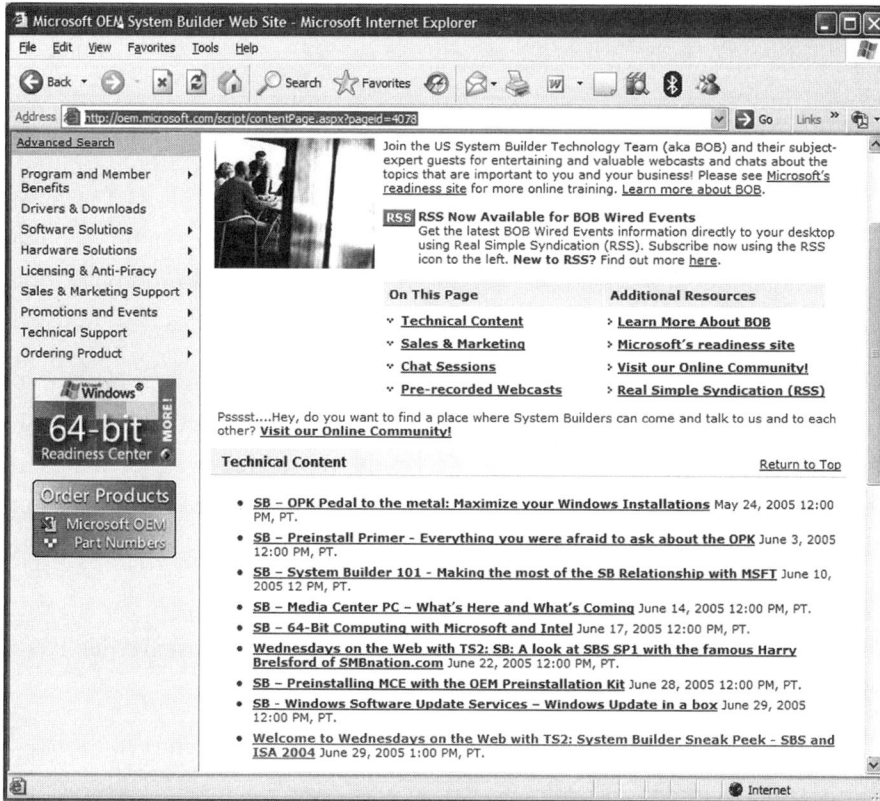

IMPORTANT: Use the system builder Webcasts wisely to prepare you for the 74-134 exam. First attend at least a handful of applicable Webcasts related to the OPK and other 74-134 exam topics. While attending, take a critical step: ASK LIVE QUESTIONS. What better way to prepare for the 74-134 exam than to have your exam-related questions answered by the Microsoft experts!

Second, view past Webcasts. Figure 11-3 displays a link for "Pre-recorded Webcasts." This is especially applicable for newcomers who missed the live delivery of important content and international readers who don't live on Pacific Standard Time (PST), which is GMT -8. Microsoft, located in PST in the Pacific Northwest, tends to have a timing bias towards West Coast USA working hours. That translates into missing a wee bit of pub time in Dublin, Ireland when you are giving a high noon Webcast on Redmond time! I speak from experience.

Complete Applicable Coursework

There are more learning resources online at Microsoft for the 74-134 exam than you can shake a stick at. If you plan to follow our advice in this section, you should budget for approximately 20-hours of study time to complete these learning opportunities.

First, let's do it by the book and observe how the applicable courses map to the 74-134 exam. To accomplish that, go to your Preparation Guide for Exam 74-134 printout and carefully review the Skills Being Measured section. Here you'll see how the XP and Server course, SBS course, OPK Documentation (discussed in the next section of this chapter) and the Windows XP Sp2 Webcast align with specific 74-134 exam objectives.

Second, peruse the following three courses listed under Course for this Exam on your Preparation Guide for Exam 74-134 printout:

- Preinstallation of Windows XP and Windows Server 2003 (http://oem. microsoft.com/downloads/ABCs_OPK/ABCs_updated/ABC'sOPK/ Bin/default.hta). See Figure 14-4.

- Using the OEM Preinstallation Kit to Preinstall Windows Small Business Server 2003 (http://members.microsoft.com/partner/profile/learningcenter.aspx?courseid=442). See Figure 14-5.

- Windows XP SP2 Recorded Webcast (http://oem.microsoft.com/script/ ContentPage.aspx?pageid=551604)

Figure 14-4

The Windows XP and Windows Server 2003 preinstallation learning opportunity.

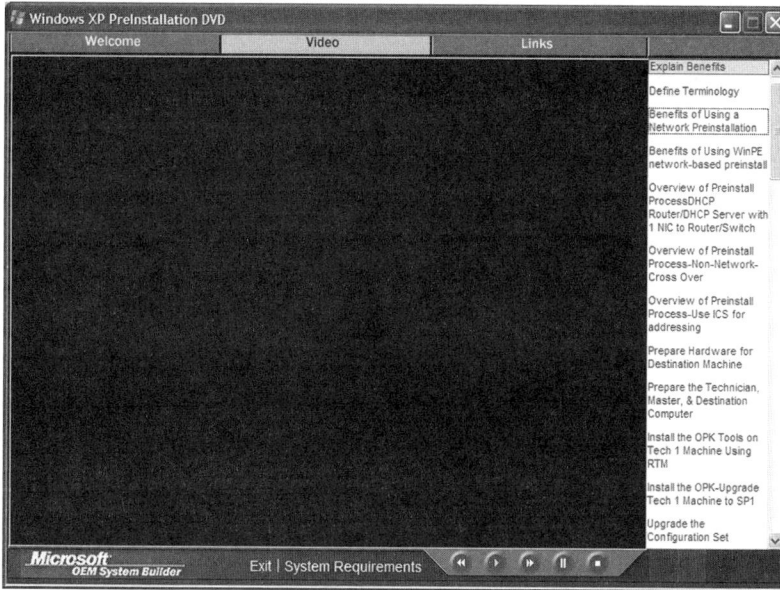

Figure 14-5

The SBS 2003 preinstallation learning opportunity.

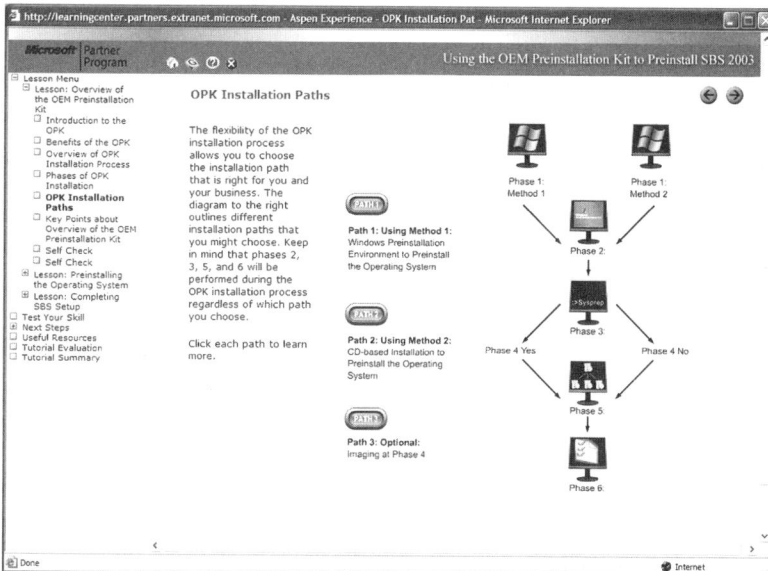

Third, complete the following learning opportunities that weren't explicitly listed in the Preparation Guide for Exam 74-134.

- Under Training and Readiness on the main Microsoft OEM System Builder site, there is a link to the Windows XP SP2 Readiness Center (http://oem.microsoft.com/script/contentpage .aspx?pageid=551796). Visit that page and peruse the Essential Information: Preinstall Windows XP SP2 PowerPoint slide deck (which has its own URL of http://oem. microsoft.com/static/Worldwide/file/OEM_ Preinstallation_ Win_XP_ SP2.ppt).

- After performing a registered member logon at www.microsoft.com/ oem, visit this URL: http://oem.microsoft.com/script/content page. aspx?PageID=552172, which is the System Builder Training and Readiness Center. Select the Online Training link (http://oem.microsoft .com/script/contentpage.aspx?pageid=500972) and complete the following learning opportunities, as shown in Figure 14-6.

  - Windows XP

  - Windows Small Business Server 2003

  - Windows Server 2003

Figure 14-6
A gold mine of online learning opportunities.

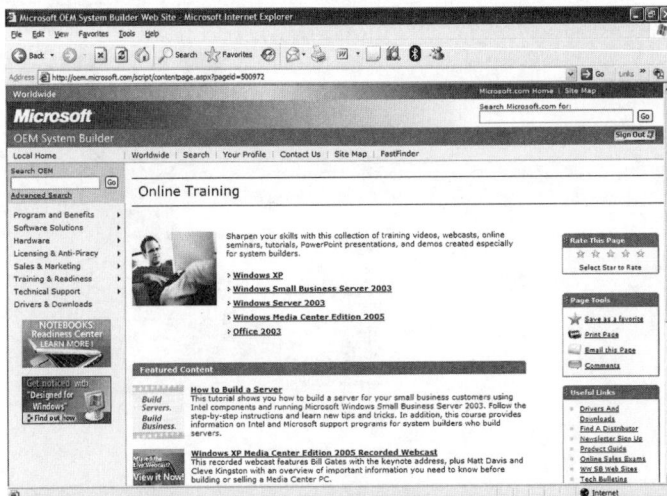

IMPORTANT: You do not need to complete the Windows Media Center or Office 2003-related online learning course to prepare for the 74-134 exam, but you can certainly return at a future date and do so (after you pass the 74-134 exam!).

- Complete the product-specific training courses by selecting the product of your choice on the left drop menu at Software Solutions Overview page (http://oem.microsoft.com/script/contentpage.aspx ?PageID=4022). For example, drilling down into the Servers link, Windows Small Business Server, will result in the page displayed in Figure 14-7 (found at http://oem.microsoft.com/script/contentPage. aspx ?pageid=554992).

Figure 14-7

Note the SBS-related training and hands-on lab. Complete this for SBS 2003. Complete at least the How to Install Microsoft Small Business Server 2003 course.

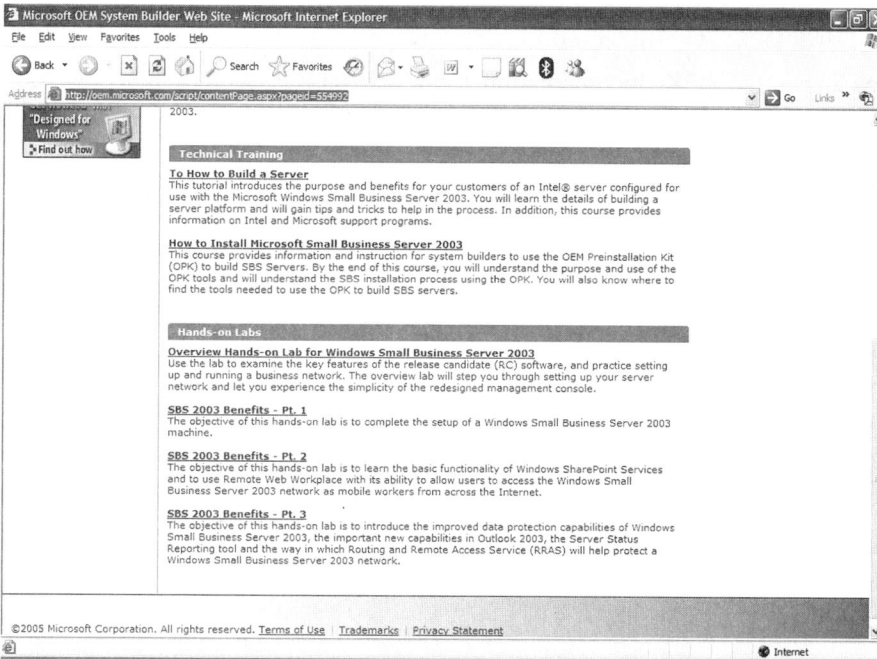

- Also complete the learning opportunities for Windows Server 2003 and Windows XP accessed at the above-mentioned site (http://oem.

microsoft.com/script/contentpage.aspx?PageID=4022). Ignore the coursework for Windows 2000 products.

IMPORTANT: Here's an insider tip directly from one of the internal Small Business Specialist Community team members at Microsoft. Search on the term "OPK" at the OEM System Builder Training and Readiness site at http://oem.microsoft.com/script/contentpage.aspx ?PageID=552172. This will return numerous new and updated curriculums that have emerged since this book was published. It's your way to stay current!

Well, were we right or what? That above "game plan" should have taken approximately 20 hours to complete. Trust us, though. It was time well spent!

Read OPK documentation

The cliché of a droning college professor admonishing his weary students to "...read the book" truly applies to the 74-134 exam. In this case, the required reading is the OPK documentation for Windows XP, Windows Server 2003 and Windows Small Business Server 2003, as per your Preparation Guide for Exam 74-134 printout.

There are two ways to review the all-important OPK documentation. First, you can simply access the OPK Discs contained in Action Pack and open the applicable documentation. Second, you can click over to the following links for the following readings:

- Windows XP (http://oem.microsoft.com/script/contentpage.aspx ?pageid=512504)
- Small Business Server 2003 (http://oem.microsoft.com/script/content-page.aspx?pageid=550830)
- Office 2003 (http://oem.microsoft.com/script/contentpage.aspx ?pageid=550618)

IMPORTANT: Even though the 74-134 exam doesn't explicitly hold you responsible for Office 2003 matters, the above link is recommended because there is enough OPK "table talk" that you can benefit from a casual reading of that document. Note that I didn't instruct you to take the Office 2003 OEM, System Builder or OPK online courses because the time consumption outweighed the value received vis-à-vis that 74-134 exam. In an inconsistent way, I believe I'm being consistent here!

Complete Online Assessments

Ah, now for the fun part. You've meticulously followed our suggested steps and arrived at the payoff point: you get to take some sample exams.

Click over to http://oem.microsoft.com/script/contentpage.aspx?PageID =552866 (Figure 14-8) and complete the following assessments:

- Microsoft Office 2003 Preinstallation Exam (12-questions, worth a try but don't dwell on this)

- Windows Small Business Server 2003 Preinstallation Exam (12 questions, very important)

- Windows XP Service Pack 2 (SP2) Preinstallation Exam (25 questions, very important)

- Windows Server 2003 Preinstallation Exam (25 questions, very important)

IMPORTANT: Use leverage to your advantage. Earn your Microsoft Preinstallation Specialist designation too! That's right! With a few extra steps, a tad more moxie and a little bit more gumption, you can complete the online assessments and hold this title in addition to your soon-to-be-awarded Small Business Specialist Community title!

Notes:

Figure 14-8

Details of the Microsoft Presinstallation Specialist program and your access portal to the online assessment exams. These will assist you immensely in preparing for the 74-134 exam.

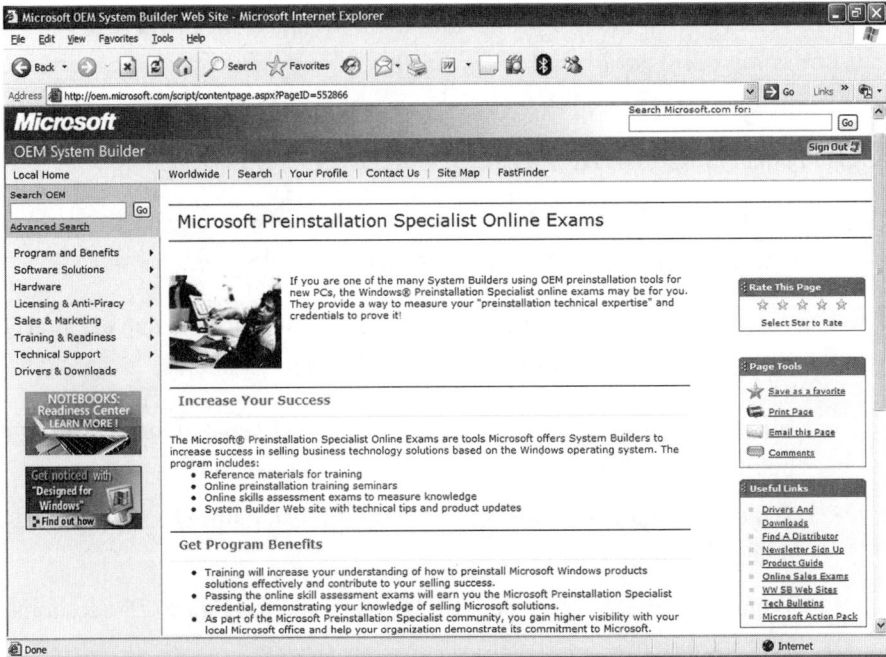

Finally, visit the generic Microsoft Skills Assessments site for other interesting and applicable tests: http://www.microsoft.com/learning/assessment/default.asp.

> IMPORTANT: You will notice this chapter does not contain sample questions. Please register your book with the registration form at the back of the book and we'll be delighted to provide you with some online sample 74-134 test questions on our site!

Schedule and Take Test

Time to make it happen. Register for the test. Visit the Microsoft Learning exam registration page at http://www.microsoft.com/learning/mcpexams/register/default.asp and pick from either PearsonVue or Prometric.

IMPORTANT: Schedule the exam a couple weeks out if you feel you need sufficient preparation time. The important point is to schedule the exam and put yourself under a wee bit of pressure to perform! Deadlines do wonders for writers and test-takers. Trust us!

74-134 Certification Secrets

Shhh! Don't tell anyone, but here are a few secrets to increase your odds of success on the 74-134 exam. I gained these insights from behind closed doors in Redmond, water cooler talk and whispers in the hallways. These secrets are presented here for your benefit!

- **Tools.** The 74-134 exam is very tools centric. There is little emphasis on strategy and design (which play significant roles on the 70-282 exam). Truly your best bet is to learn and use the tools. Have an appreciation for why the tools were created but don't dwell on this aspect. Rather, remain tactile (touch) rather than tactical (strategy) for the 74-134 exam.

- **Interface.** Your short-term memory will likely be tested on the 74-134 exam because a premium is placed on graphical user interface (GUI) recall. Hopefully you're fortunate to have something of a photographic memory and you can "burn" the screen images into your cerebellum. Such image recall will be immensely useful in passing the 74-134 exam.

- **Can Do. Will Do. Done!** Active learning rules! Equal with the 70-282 exam, you need to use the OPK. Want some free advice? Create a Microsoft Virtual PC environment (http://www.microsoft.com/windows/virtualpc/default.mspx) and just DO IT. Use the OPKs to install the various operation systems. Use the Action Pack OPK bits to achieve this. You read it here first!

- **Intent.** When in doubt, you can always revisit what the intent of something was to seek clarification. To assist you in using the intent framework in the 74-134 realm, remember that Microsoft wants you to "preinstall" correctly to avoid a "reinstall!"

- **Scorecard.** As long-time college instructors and trainers (both authors bring this background to the table), it was a true pleasure to bump into the OEM system builder scorecard generated when you complete the assessment path to earn the Preinstallation Specialist designation. This is shown in Figure 14-9 and provides that critical dimension necessary to any successful transfer of knowledge and assessment: FEEDBACK!

Figure 14-9
Scorecard...use it! Very cool!

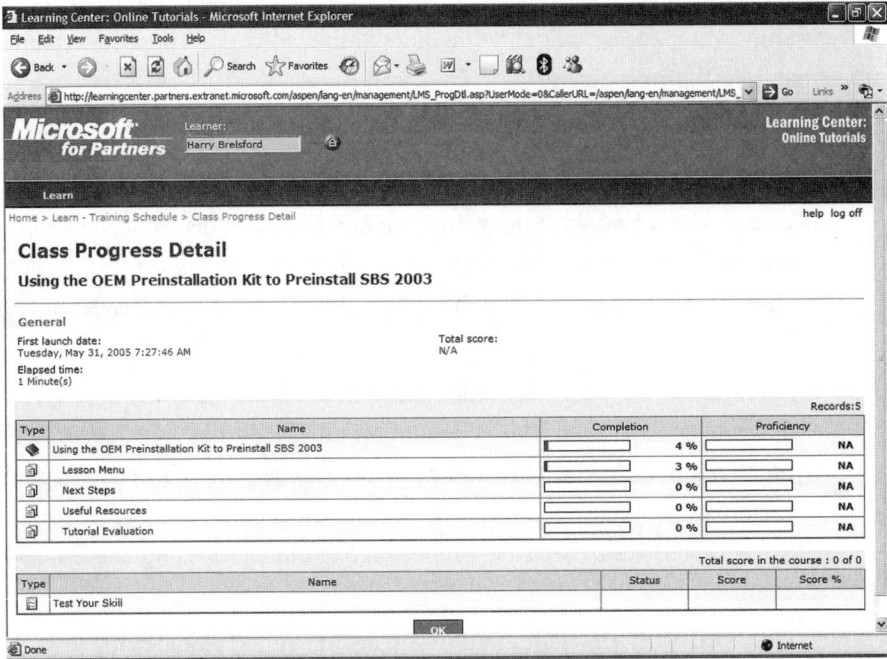

- **Read** *Reseller Advocate Magazine* **(RAM).** Co-author Beatrice Mulzer writes a monthly column for a leading USA system builder magazine and she and other writers share applicable community insights at www. reselleradvocate.com. Bookmark it!

- **Appendix A.** By all means, help yourself to the resources listed in Appendix A of this book to pass both the 74-134 exam and become a Small Business Specialist Community member!

Summary

Alternatives are a good thing, and it's a good thing Microsoft placed the 74-134 exam in the mix as a certification alternative for the Small Business Specialist Community program! We applaud that. This chapter provided you a detailed strategic plan to go forth with God Speed and slay (we mean pass) the 74-134 exam.

You were introduced to the OPK concept and the system builder community. Then we asked you to purchase Microsoft Action Pack. We directed you to the 74-134 exam preparation guidelines that we highly recommend you print out and use as a roadmap. Then it was time to go off and read, study and learn from a library of rich OPK resources. An assessment process followed, and then a gentle nudge to go schedule and actually take the 74-134 exam. At the end of the chapter, a few extra secrets were provided to get you over the top of the pass bar!

CHAPTER 15
Small Business Sales and Marketing Skills Assessment

This guest chapter was written by Arlin Sorensen, founder and CEO of Heartland Technology Solutions, Harlan, Iowa.

Many people want to take cheap shots at Microsoft about its small business strategy. There are many differing opinions on what that strategy should look like (and we can argue that point until we are all blue in the face and never come to an agreement), but the good news is that Microsoft has put a stake in the ground and created something specific and completely focused on this segment of the market through the creation of the Small Business Specialist Community (SBSC). With all its warts and issues, it is still a great step toward helping identify Partners who are truly engaged with small businesses. It creates a way for that group of very specialized folks to differentiate themselves in the marketplace.

This chapter is devoted to helping you pass the required sales and marketing assessment so you can become SBSC certified and have a designation to use in your marketing and customer-facing materials. Having been a Partner in this space for over 20 years, and being somewhat vocal in requesting a way to create a "brand" for our company in this customer segment, I am pleased with the steps that have been taken. Sure, there are many things that can yet happen to make it more valuable, but we have to start somewhere and Microsoft has done exactly that. So I encourage you to study and pass this first step in joining the SBSC. Although that alone doesn't do anything for your company (you have to actively use it in marketing and customer touch), Microsoft has done their part. The rest will be up to you!

First, a little history on myself and my company. I am privileged to serve as the CEO/president of Heartland Technology Solutions, with global headquarters in Harlan, Iowa. Now my bet is that you have never heard of Harlan, maybe not even Iowa. Harlan is a small town of 5,000 Danish- and German-heritage residents in the southwest quarter of Iowa. We are an hour west of Omaha and an hour and a half east of Des Moines. Who cares? Well that fact gives you hope.

Today HTS has over 75 full-time staff serving customers from eight offices in five Midwestern states. We are Microsoft Gold certified and have five competencies as well as the SBSC designation. But the rest of the story is that our headquarters is in the middle of an Iowa cornfield. There are no customers for miles. You see, when I started my business as a hobby in 1985 I had no idea what would develop. So after five additions to the office with over 12,000 square feet attached to the south side of the farm house I grew up in as a kid, we now manage our regional solution integration business from the "technofarm," as I like to call it. We have merged with or acquired five other companies over the last five years and grown from that one-man shop which my wife and I ran for five years, to what we have today. With offices in Harlan and Ames (Iowa), Joplin (Missouri), Wichita, Newton and Hutchinson (Kansas), Muskogee (Oklahoma) and Omaha (Nebraska), I am never at a loss for things to do. The moral of the story is that I don't want to hear about anyone struggling to find success in the small business space. Our company is living, breathing proof that there is opportunity everywhere if you truly serve customers. The phrase "if you build it they will come" is never truer than in the case of HTS. Iowa truly has been a "Field of Dreams" for me, and that has become a reality as we continue to serve SMB customers all over the Heartland.

Why Are We Here?

Passing the Small Business Sales and Marketing Skills Assessment is a required component for gaining acceptance in the Small Business Specialist Community. The skills covered in this chapter are more important than the SBSC Assessment, but that is our first and primary goal for now – to pass the exam.

What is the bottom line on the examination and assessment? You must successfully complete (pass) one certification examination. As of this writing, you can select from three Microsoft Certified Professional (MCP) certification exams: 70-282, 71-630 and 74-134. Any one of these three exams, in combination with the successful passing of the online Small Business Sales and Marketing Skills Assessment and a valid subscription to Microsoft Action Pack (MAPS), will fulfill the requirements for SBSC.

In explaining the Small Business Specialist program to me, Microsoft was insistent that the Small Business Sales and Marketing Skills Assessment not be called a test or examination. It is an online assessment that you can attempt multiple times until you achieve a passing score. The goal of this chapter is to give you the background necessary so you can do it on the first attempt!

Another goal of this chapter is to provide you some foundational information you can use to become a sales and marketing guru, or at least competent to get things moving in your business. **Nothing happens in business until the sale is made.** You can be the best technical genius in the world, but if you never sell anything, all that talent is for naught. And before sales typically are made, a consistent marketing approach needs to be in place. Not to say that you can't have some success with selling without structured marketing, but if you intend to grow and sustain your business over time, you will need to have a marketing plan and consistent execution to continue to move to new heights.

The Life We Lead

If you are like the majority of small business technology consultants, then you wear many different hats. As a small business yourself, you must perform many tasks including sales and marketing (finding the customers), management (managing the business and customer relationship), finance and accounting (billing and collecting from the customer), service delivery (actually performing the technical work for the customer), and a variety of other chores like cleaning the office and mowing the grass! But in the end, one thing is clear - business is all about the customer. It is not about you or me, but them. Without the customer we all are looking for a new job. Customer service that exceeds their expectations is a key to leading a successful business. There are many other people trying to do what you do in the market you serve. You need to differentiate yourself by how you do what you do – which is the essence of customer service.

Hunter or Farmer

In this area of sales and marketing, we typically see people in one of two roles. A hunter is one who is out continually looking for opportunities that can become customer engagements. This role is driven by the thrill of discovery and making the sale. They are "cold call" focused and are uninhibited in their ability to go speak to new people and businesses about how they can help take the pain out of the customer's situation. Once they have created the initial relationship, they are on to the next opportunity. They often do not do well in building deep relationships that take significant time. They want action and they want it now.

The farmer role is one that is suited to taking an established relationship with a customer and turning it into an ongoing source of revenue. Farmers love to build deep relationships and see their role as being one of "customer satisfaction" rather than initiation. They "farm" the customer year after year, bringing new ideas and opportunities to the table and making sure that the service and support being provided is meeting all the customer's expectations. This person likes "warm calls" and very seldom is excited about the idea of having to work with people they don't know.

It is rare indeed that any one person can fulfill these two roles. In many companies these are split between outside sales people who hunt and customer support people who take the handoff once the initial project is in place. The reality is that for many of us in the small business space, we don't have the luxury of having those roles split, so we are tasked with handling both sides of the fence ourselves. That creates some interesting internal conflict as we need to be looking for new customers while not ignoring our current customer base all at the same time. The work never ends……

Beside those two basic sales roles, you also serve as the marketing director. Too often in the small business space, marketing is ignored as it just never makes it high enough on the priority list to get any attention at all. That creates some major issues when you decide you are ready to scale your company and need to grow. Without a consistent marketing strategy and plan, it is very difficult to keep a flow of potential prospects in the pipeline so a hunter can bring them on board. Don't ignore marketing. It is one area you can effectively outsource and leverage the skills of an outside organization.

Where You Fit In

The important thing to identify at this point is where your skills lie in running your business. Time for some real truth telling and honesty here, it is not a crime to be inadequate in some aspects of running your business. In fact, if you are not, then you are a special breed indeed. Most people leading small businesses are not good at all the tasks that are required for success. The important thing is to recognize your weaknesses and then surround yourself with people who have strengths in those areas, either as employees or as outsourced services. Failing to do that will cause your business to grow much more slowly than it needs to. I have had to do that on numerous fronts as HTS has grown. The bigger we get, the less I know and the more I need to hire essential skills. Those people are available out there. You may not find them quickly, but they can be found.

Execution is often the key problem for most of us as small business owners. It isn't usually that we don't know what to do – the issue is getting it done. We react to the immediate rather than the important I see that disease in many small businesses I consult with and mentor. In order to truly grow and be successful, you have to get away from the day-to-day rat race and spend time working "on" your business, not just "in" it. That is one of the most difficult transitions that most small business owners have to make, but it is critical if you want to succeed.

Enough Already – Let's Get on With It

So it is time to learn the elements of sales and marketing that are essential to your business and to equip you to pass the assessment test for the SBSC program. As we begin to discuss the area of sales and marketing, remember that nothing happens until the sale is made. There are many other aspects of business management that are important, but closing business through the sales process is critical. Microsoft offers many aids in this area of sales training which are listed below. Take time to study some of these key trainings as they will expand your view of the sales process and help you become more proficient in the marketplace. Visit the Microsoft Partner site and look at the *Small Business Market and Sell Series* (you must have Registered Member status) located at (https://partner.microsoft.com/US/program/40015881), where Microsoft offers several free training opportunities.

In Microsoft speak, the sales process is broken down into different stages from start to finish. These describe the process from the time an initial contact is made with a prospect until an actual order is placed for a product or service. The terminology is important to learn as it is how all Microsoft employees view the sales process and how they discuss things like pipeline and opportunities in regard to your business.

These terms may not come up during the SBSC Assessment, but as you become engaged with the Microsoft field team, you will hear them over and over. It is important to speak the Microsoft language so that you can work effectively with field resources. Taking the time to learn the system will show your interest in working with them and that you are worth investing in.

So What Do I Need to Know to Pass

The Small Business Sales and Marketing Assessment focuses on many commonsense realities of serving the SMB space. Don't overanalyze the questions. Many of the responses will be things you have dealt with before if you have been working in this market for any length of time. Most of you have seen major changes over the past few years as the Internet has become prevalent in business. Companies want their employees to be able to work anywhere, at any time. They want access to information on the go using mobile devices. The trend is for more and more people to work in teams and the increased demand for customer service comes from all directions. People just expect more and technology has become a key to achieving more. As an SMB consultant, your role is to help customers identify how technology can help them stay focused and do more with less. You are expected to enable teamwork both in the office and across the wire. You are expected to give them customer relationship management (CRM) systems that will allow them to provide enhanced customer service and support capabilities.

The world has changed significantly. Microsoft calls this change the "**One World of Business.**" People do their work from all over the place – home office, library, Starbucks, even driving down the road with the new cellular data cards. It is no longer work as usual from a stationary location. People work in teams that are not in the same building or even on the same continent. Groups are created that put the right talent and resources together and technology is the glue that makes that happen. Businesses face competition from all over the world, not just the shop down the street. The Internet has leveled the playing field between companies and the virtual store is now bringing competitors right to the desktop of your customers. Creating a call center, once an extremely expensive proposition, can be done very inexpensively and can be done anywhere in the world using readily available labor markets. Traditional barriers to doing business across the country or around the world are surely reduced if not gone. Overnight shipping is dependable, communication readily accessible and technology allows people to work seamlessly from different places in different cultures with different languages. We truly have become "One World of Business."

Microsoft offers an online tutorial, *Selling Microsoft Solutions to Small Businesses* which is an integral study tool for the Small Business Sales and Marketing Assessment. You can find the tutorial at Microsoft Partner University at http://www.msreadiness.com or through a link on the 'Small Business Specialist Exams and Training' page on the Microsoft Partner site.

The New Wave

All these changes have caused a need for an entire new wave of products from Microsoft. Windows Vista, the new desktop operating system, Microsoft Office 2007, Exchange Server 2007, and the Unified Communication and Collaboration tools like Live Communication Server respond to these new demands. There are dozens of other products that have been, or will soon be, released. These products simplify how people work, make them more productive, protect and manage the huge amounts of content that businesses have, and make all this manageable. Of course security and cost reductions are expected as part of this new wave. These products also make it easier to find information and use it to lead businesses to success. A pretty tall order for the new wave of products Microsoft is bringing to market.

Microsoft Solutions

Vista is certainly one of the biggest products in the next wave. It comes in numerous versions designed to meet every need a customer could have. It is designed for small companies as well as the largest enterprise and brings some key functionality that is an improvement from previous Microsoft operating systems. The Instant Search feature allows people to find things much more quickly. Improved mobility and networking make it easier than ever to be connected. There are dozens of other enhancements, but the bottom line is that Vista is designed to help people focus on the work at hand and get things done more quickly and effectively.

The Microsoft 2007 Office System is now a series of products and servers that significantly beef up the tools that information workers need to get their jobs done. There are many flavors of the Microsoft Office 2007 desktop suite designed for every business configuration, from individuals to small business to enterprise. People should upgrade not because the previous version, Microsoft Office 2003, is no longer supported or not a solid performer. People should upgrade because of the enhancements that have been added to the new product line. There are dozens of new capabilities targeting the individual user all the way to those needing group productivity. New features, like the ribbon toolbar and true "see it before you change it" graphics, make the interface superior to previous versions. With InfoPath and SharePoint, true workflow is now available and simple to implement. And putting the entire suite into use gives you a fantastic toolbox to handle the sales and marketing needs of any business. It streamlines tasks from creation of marketing materials to sales graphs and reports. The product speaks for itself if you give it a test drive.

Exchange Server 2007 is much more than a new version of an email server. It now includes the foundational pieces for Unified Communication and Collaboration (UCC). What is that you may wonder? UCC is a set of tools that allow you to use Exchange as your one source for all communication needs – email, calendaring, contact management, voice and voice mail, conferencing, live meeting and other ways to connect. It has tight integration for communication features that previously were somewhat disconnected. That makes it a simpler solution to deploy and maintain, and with its competitive pricing, it is sure to be a very solid performer for businesses in the years ahead. Finally, one source for every communication need. Add into the mix the enhanced security of spam and phishing protection and you have a real value for your customers.

The Mindset

These new technologies are all as strong as standalone products, but they truly are "**Better Together**." Surprisingly, or probably not so, Microsoft has created a campaign called just that. It isn't a product but rather a mindset. The focus of the program is to cross sell the entire technology platform when you are building a customer solution. When these solutions are implemented in conjunction with each other, customers are able to experience all the new functionality and feature sets to the fullest. You don't necessarily get the complete experience if you don't install Office 2007 with Vista, for example. The Better Together campaign includes Vista, Office and Exchange. Any of these is a great product on its own, but together they really shine. Sell the stack!

One key new area is the advent of the productivity group known as the "Information Worker" today. This is a Microsoft term that describes employees who use technology to manage information day to day. Typically heavy users of the Microsoft Office product suite, these people are tasked with the manipulation and management of information to make decisions and provide data that drive business.

The People in Our Space

Another set of people you serve in the SMB space are the decision makers. While some small businesses have one person filling multiple roles, in many there are different people who make decisions. The Business Decision Maker (BDM) is typically the owner or someone else with a focus on how a decision will impact the business itself. These individuals are often focused on the return on investment (ROI) and are not usually all that excited by the "wow" factor, but are excited by the profit factor. Another common decision maker is the Technical Decision Maker (TDM) who looks at how the technology works and what it does, with less interest in the profit impact. These two individuals need to be sold to very differently, so it is important to know your audience and how to approach them. Using a ROI approach on a TDM will not generate great results while trying to "wow" a BDM will almost always backfire. Know who you are speaking to and tailor the discussion appropriately.

To be successful in the real world of selling technology, work closely with the Microsoft field resources in your area. There are dozens of people placed strategically in cities all across the world who help drive the Microsoft message and sales process. Their titles include a number of acronyms which you should understand so you can be effective in working with them. Here are some common employee groups that will be of most value to you.

> **Partner Account Manager (PAM)** –works with Microsoft Partners in building their business in a specific geography. Typically they work with a set of Gold and Certified Partners who are assigned to them.
>
> **Partner Community Manager (PCM)** – has region-wide responsibility for the broad Partner channel. This role is the communication point for all things Microsoft that matter to Partners.
>
> **Telephone Partner Account Manager (TPAM)** – another version of the PAM but the engagement happens via phone, which enables this group to touch many more Partners than a traditional PAM would.
>
> **Technical Specialist (TS)** – is responsible for a certain area of technology, such as those for Information Workers, and works with Partner organizations to build their expertise in these technologies.

There are dozens of other field resources available but these are the most prevalent for SBSC companies. The important thing to remember is that there are thousands of Partners in your space who are vying for attention from the field staff. You need to be proactive and work diligently to meet your field resources and let them know about your company and the market you are focusing on. They can be very beneficial in helping with marketing, programs, event resources and many other things. They are the face of Microsoft to you, so I encourage you to make the necessary effort to get involved with them as soon as possible. They have a huge task and you are not their entire focus, so respect their time and manage your expectations appropriately. These people work with all good Microsoft Partners within the guidelines they are given. Sometimes Partners who have not built a relationship with a local field resource think their resource person appears to be helping a competitor. But Microsoft resources are not in the business of trying to push certain people out of the market. Sometimes a competitor gets more attention because the competitor has taken the initiative to build a relationship, participate in the programs and execute successfully over time. The Microsoft field resource is not your enemy, if you fulfill your part of the relationship by reaching out.

The Role of Services

While selling the Microsoft product line can be a great business in and of itself, the real opportunity for most of us involves the addition of services to the sale. The obvious ones involve implementation, installation and ongoing support services. Today the buzz is to create managed services, which means a flat fee support program where you agree to provide the needed support for an environment for a set cost each month. This can be a somewhat frightening service offering until you have some experience. Many Partners I talk with struggle to get it off the ground. But once in place, it can be a hugely profitable service model.

Other services can include assessments to analyze the customer's requirements, or a business process evaluation to make sure the solution you propose will actually meet the needs of the customer. One large area of opportunity involves making the Microsoft product stack work with other products, either line-of-business applications that run on the Microsoft platform or actually building systems that pull or push information to completely different technologies. Your sales process should include a variety of services as you build your consulting practice. You may not be able to offer all possible services yourself, but you should partner with another company(ies) to offer the full plate of services your customer base may need.

Partner Tools You Can Use

Microsoft has really stepped up to help us work more effectively with SMB prospects and customers. They have recently revised the Business and Technology Assessment Toolkit (https://partner.microsoft.com/assesssmbneeds) which is designed to help Partners communicate with their prospects and customers and identify the pain that a small business is experiencing so that technologies can be identified to help remove the pain. The tool is simply a series of questions that probe for opportunity for a consultant to help this business move forward. It covers the key Microsoft products discussed earlier and is now customizable so you can build your own assessments or use one of the predefined templates. The foundation of the tool is to "peel the onion," and become a trusted advisor for the business you are working with. These results often follow:

a) You create a foundation for lifelong relationships.

b) You better understand the short- and long-term business goals.

c) You build win-win relationships where both you and the prospect/customer win.

d) You gain insights into their processes and procedures so you truly understand their business.

The toolkit is a service, not a product. Sell it as such. One creative way to do it is to sell an assessment for a price, then rebate back that amount if they take your recommendations and use your company to provide the products you have recommended.

Note: The toolkit is covered in Chapter 3, *Analyzing the Existing Environment*

Real World

The toolkit requires InfoPath 2007 to load, and it installs on your notebook or desktop PC. It has a self-updating feature which allows it to get new updates via the Internet. It includes a number of templates which cover different size customers as well as different technology areas. The resulting documentation can be the creation of an executive summary, a three year IT plan, proposals, and many other deliverables. Samples for these documents are located on the web at the Toolkit Readiness Center (https://partner.microsoft.com/US/40029617). What you can provide depends on the expectations you set up front. The key is to take the information you gather, create a report and allow the customer to prioritize what matters most to his business. From there you can create a plan and solution that meets his goals and needs.

Partners often make the mistake of not clearly setting the expectations for the customer about the assessment process. First, it takes time to do the interview and to develop the deliverables. It will take at least an hour or two for the simplest assessment, and I have experienced many that were 20 hours or so from start to finish, including the interview, gathering information, preparing the summary, review and prioritization, creating a plan, building a solution proposal and then getting a decision.

When you throw in a technical assessment, the time required is expanded even more. Obviously something of that magnitude is worth a significant service engagement – we have charged up to $5,000 for something that size. I would never give away that type of assessment because it has significant value to the customer whether they chose to use your recommendation or not. Sometimes Partners believe they have to give things away to get in front of prospects and customers. If they will not pay for an assessment, they will likely dispute every bill you ever send them and are not a good candidate to become a lifelong customer. We walk away from those engagements. Not every prospect can become a good customer and the goal should be to surround your business with good customers.

So what happens at a first meeting? It is those initial impressions that often set the tone for the way things go from that point forward. Prepare well. Study the prospect/customer's website. You should know as much about them as possible before walking in the door. Review the assessment questions thoroughly before the meeting. It is best to do some practice runs, either on your own company or with a very close customer, to get some experience in using the tool. The conversation needs to flow seamlessly and that only happens if you are comfortable with how the tool works and with the questions being used.

Make sure proper time has been set aside. Don't rush things. You will know when you have exceeded their interest. Adapt things on the fly. If you hit an area they have no interest in or cannot answer, move on. This is not a test but a conversation. Don't get caught up in the questions. Not every one has to be answered. Have a pad of paper with you to jot down questions you may come up with on as you go.

Now with the new customization ability, you can add those to your assessment tool so those questions can be used again in the future. Make sure you have explained the process. This is not magic; it is hard work and will only result in good things if the answers are thorough and complete. Don't sugar coat the experience; completely prepare yourself and the people you will engage. You are not selling anything but yourself in this assessment process. If it is done right, you will have gained the trust of this company. You will have a customer for life.

Licensing

During the assessment process, licensing almost always comes up. You need to understand the licensing programs that Microsoft offers. They are not difficult but do require some study. There are really only a few ways to purchase Microsoft products for small businesses:

> **OEM** – preinstalled on equipment purchased from hardware vendors like HP or Dell.
>
> **Volume Licensing** – paper only – there are several licensing programs that fit the SMB space including Open Business and Open Value License products. There are minimum purchases to get started in these programs.
>
> **FPP** – full package products in retail boxes.

Most customers do not attempt violate licensing rules. They often have no idea what they own or what the requirements are. One surefire way to become a trusted advisor is to understand this area well. In many cases, we find some pirated software in customer environments. Part of the assessment process should involve gathering information on the licensing they legally own and comparing it with what is installed. The discussion should be about having "Genuine Software," or legally licensed software for all the installations at a customer site. There are some strong penalties for companies that don't heed that requirement.

More information can be found at http://www.microsoft.com/piracy/default. mspx

http://download.microsoft.com/download/3/6/3/363e4976-3abd-4eab-b2e2-a643342bc869/Yankee_Group_Piracy_Research_Whitepaper.pdf

You are not there to be the licensing police, but to educate the customer and identify gaps in their licensing situation. Keep the discussion positive and focus on the value of the products, messaging around the "New World of Business," staying competitive with the competition and the "Better Together" value. There are so many reasons to purchase the correct licensing that beating them with the fear stick shouldn't be necessary. And with some of the creative payment options in the Open Value program, payments can be spread across three years to make it affordable, too. Be sure to stay current with the Microsoft promotion site which has a list of the current promotions. You can find it at: https://www.microsoftincentives.com.

Another common area of licensing concern involves the ability to downgrade or upgrade to past or current versions. There are a lot of rules about this area, and I direct you to the End User Licensing Agreement (EULA) for details. You can normally (not always) downgrade to a previous version of the software you own. When you upgrade, unless you own Software Assurance (SA) which gives you upgrade rights, you normally have to purchase something, either an upgrade SKU or the new version of the product. Customers don't get free upgrades unless they have paid for them in some form, typically through the SA program.

One key thing to remember about Microsoft licensing – typically they don't give any licenses away for free. They often have discounted programs or bundles, but free doesn't typically fit their style when it comes to licensing. They do add much value to their products with free tools, programs, marketing and on and on, but they protect their software investment and sell their licenses!

On another note, free software, like Linux, isn't really free. The cost to support "free" products normally is more than the cost of buying a comparable Microsoft product. Don't fall for the "free" card. As my parents taught me, "If it seems too good to be true, it is," definitely applies to this area.

Prices that are way below market often indicate pirated or copied software and free stuff usually is far from free over time. There is a reason that so many emails fly with pricing that is way below the market. They are non-legitimate and are selling licensing that is not legal. Don't fall prey to that scheme.

SWOT Analysis Exercise

In the MBA world, there is an exercise called SWOT. This stands for Strengths, Weaknesses, Opportunities and Threats. It's a valuable assessment exercise and I present it here as a tool to prepare you for the Small Business Sales and Marketing Skills Assessment that you'll take at the end of the chapter. Strengths and weakness are internal matters ("my strength is…"); opportunities and threats are external ("our competitor's new service is a threat to our livelihood). Take some time now and complete this table by applying this SWOT analysis to you individually and your small business technology consulting practice. This is one of the most valuable parts of the Microsoft Business and Technology Assessment Toolkit.

Table 15-1
Small Business Specialist SWOT Analysis

Strengths	Weaknesses	Opportunities	Threats
Example: Creative problem solver	Example: Weak at C# programming	Example: Merge with John's Computer Repair Shop	Example: Linux consultants calling on my SBS customers

IMPORTANT: With the above exercise, I hope to move you into the assessment mind-set. I also hope the information you provided above will be useful as you begin building your practice. There is nothing like self-inspection to really get started building your company.

Off To School

Thoughtful study, not haste, will prove to be your ally as you prepare for the Small Business Sales and Marketing Skills Assessment. This section provides advice on properly preparing yourself.

Online Study Resources

The good news is that no trip to the book store to purchase over-priced texts is necessary. Microsoft has leveled the playing field between worldwide "haves" and "have-nots" by posting many excellent study resources for immediate dissemination via no-cost downloads. One or two education resources are fee-based but the majority are at no cost. That means FREE! The one fee-based course I would recommend is the Microsoft Solution Selling Course that was referred to earlier in this chapter. It is only $60 and that gives you access for 12 months. You can access all the online training resources from the training and events page on the partner.microsoft.com home page:

http://www.msreadiness.com/

https://training.partner.microsoft.com/plc/trainingprefs.aspx

https://partner.microsoft.com/US/trainingevents/webcasts

You Are Ready!

Your dedication to the study of small business technology consulting is admirable. It's now time to complete the Small Business Sales and Marketing Skills Assessment. First, trot over to Small Business Specialist Community website and select the assessment. A back door direct link is:

https://training.partner.microsoft.com/plc/register.aspx?publisher=3&coursei
d=542

https://partner.microsoft.com/US/program/smallbusinessspecialist/sbsbenefits

The assessment is open book, but if you have read the material in this chapter
you are ready to proceed. Microsoft wants you to be successful. You may take
the assessment multiple times if for some reason you are not successful. So
don't worry, take a run at it and rely on what you have read. You are ready
to succeed!

Starting the exam

After completing authentication as a registered Partner at the Microsoft Partner
site, proceed to the Small Business Sales and Marketing Skills Assessment page
as illustrated.

Notes:

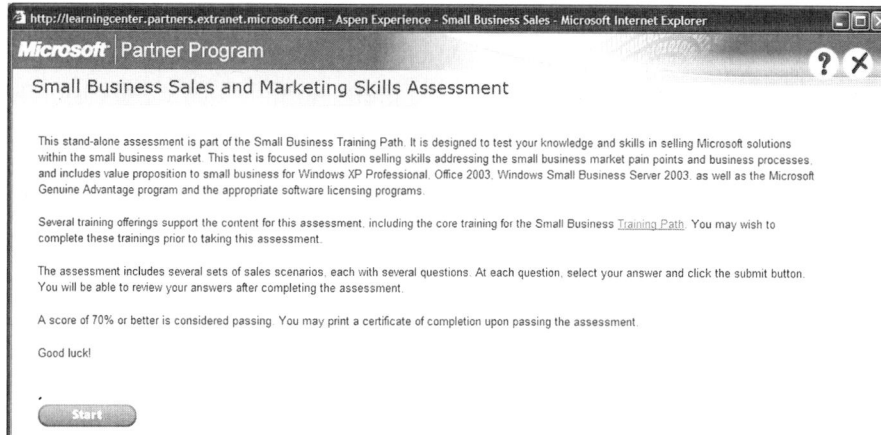

Once you get to this site, you have the option to begin the sign-up process to become a Small Business Specialist. The three steps for membership are clearly defined here in a Ready – Set – Go display. Being **ready** means you have become a part of the Microsoft Partner Program (MSPP) by signing up to be at least a Registered Member. Of course Certified or Gold Members can also apply to become SBSC authorized. As a Registered Member you also need to subscribe to the Microsoft Action Pack, which provides licensing to Microsoft products to be used to run your business. The quantity of licenses varies based on your membership level, but suffice it to say it is a great value

Set refers to taking the next step in the process, which is to get trained and then take the Small Business Marketing and Sales Assessment. That needs to be followed by having one certified MCP who has passed one of the three tests that qualify for the SBSC designation (70-282, 74-134, or 70-631).

Notes:

Go is all that remains, which is to sign up to be an SBSC member. This is a simple web application that provides Microsoft with the information it needs to put you into the SBSC. The process is pretty straightforward and simple to follow.

The exam questions are based on real-world scenarios. When I took it, four scenarios were profiled and five questions were asked about each scenario (for a total of 20 questions). What I really liked about the scenarios was that I only had to read the descriptive paragraph once before proceeding to answer five follow-on questions. I was able to positively leverage my time.

With Microsoft's permission, I'm allowed to show you one assessment question so you can appreciate the look and feel of the online assessment environment. A bona fide assessment question before your very eyes!

> **Question**: Stan was surprised to receive a call from one of his small business clients, with whom he had been working for a while, complaining about the level of pricing. "I am getting offers over the Internet of the same software for much cheaper," the client had said. Which of the following arguments did Stan use to convince the client?

Notes:

a) Beware of such Internet deals, they are very common spam, but unfortunately they are illegitimate.

b) What kind of support do they offer their clients? What happens if something goes wrong? I am here for you. Will they be?

c) Be careful that you are getting the version your small business needs. Microsoft list prices are listed on their web site as well as their promotions. Anything else should be scrutinized.

d) All the above.

e) If you save more than US$50 per license, I'd buy it from that source with my eyes closed. The Internet is always cheaper.

Answer: d

It is important for Stan to help his client delve a little deeper into the offer and whether or not it is legitimate. In most cases, ridiculously priced offers on Microsoft licenses are scams. A perceived saving even of US$10 might end up costing a lot more in case of fraud or bad support.

Completion

I have been part of the SBSC community since the program was originally announced. In fact, I was the first in the state of Iowa. The program has grown and developed significantly since the early days, and Microsoft continues to add more value. Now you have achieved the Sales and Marketing part of the process. Pass that MCP exam, sign up and you will be part of the family of SBSC'ers from all over the world.

Notes:

Next Steps

So now you have passed the Small Business Sales and Marketing Skills Assessment and are well on your way to your SBSC membership. But this is just the beginning of the value of sales and marketing to your company. The keys are to put into practice a disciplined approach to marketing your business, use the Microsoft Business and Technology Assessment Toolkit and then initiate the sales process so you can create and manage a consistent pipeline of opportunities for your future. Achieving this designation as an SBSC is an important step, but remember, nothing happens until the sale is closed. So get out there and put your hard-earned learning to work immediately. You will refine the process over time, but it is best to jump in and "just do it," as one famous marketing company has shown.

Notes:

Summary

Here I have covered the mandatory Small Business Sales and Marketing Skills Assessment portion of the Small Business Specialist Community program. I hope I was able to deliver more value to you than simply passing the Small Business Sales and Marketing Skills Assessment.

You've reached the end of this chapter on the Small Business Specialist Community. But you've only begun your career as an SBSC member. This step is a crucial part of your future in the technology industry. It is the foundation from which you can grow a thriving business, serving a very special group of individuals who run SMBs. We serve a different group of customers than our enterprise-focused brethren, but our service can be equally or even more rewarding than what they do with the "big boys." We can get to know our customers intimately and truly impact their bottom line by the way we meet their technology needs. Time to go get it done!

Appendices

Appendix A
SBS 2003 Resources

Appendix B
More SNMP Stuff

Appendix C
Third Party 70-282 Viewpoint: Andy Goodman,
David Anderson, Greg's Stuff

Appendix D
More Questions and Answers

Appendix A
Small Business Specialist Resources

This appendix lists resources that will be useful in your quest to become a Small Business Specialist and better utilize SBS 2003. Many of these resources have previously been listed in the book, but many new resources are added here as well. Bottom line: Use these resources plus the search engines of your choice (ahem – Guess which one) and visit our site www.smbnation.com often.

Small Business Specialist Community Sites

- **All You Really Need To Get Going:** Visit www.smbizspecialist.com and become SBSC!

- **Overview:** https://partner.microsoft.com/global/smallbizspe coverview

- **Benefits and requirements:** https://partner.microsoft.com/global/ smallbizspecbenefits

- **Training and exams:** https://partner.microsoft.com/global/ smallbiztraining

- **Readiness site:** https://partner.microsoft.com/global/smallbizreadiness

Certification Sites

- Microsoft Learning: http://www.microsoft.com/learning

- *Certification Magazine*: http://www.certmag.com

- *MCP Magazine*: www.mcpmag.com

- Transcender certification testing software. http://www.transcender.com/

- MeasureUp software: http://www.measureup.com.

- Self-test certification testing software: http://www.selftestsoftware.com/

SBS-MVP Sites and Blogs

Meet the SBS-MVPs and click over to their blogs: http://www.microsoft.com/windowsserver2003/sbs/community/default.mspx. One site in particular that I want to highlight that leads to many other sites is that of Susan Bradley: http://msmvps.com/blogs/bradley/default.aspx.

Microsoft Windows SBS Sites

- www.microsoft.com/windowsserver2003/sbs/default.mspx

- www.microsoft.com/sbserver

- www.microsoft.com/sbs

- Microsoft Learning SBS course: Designing, Deploying, and Managing a Network Solution for the Small- and Medium-Sized Business (three-day SBS course): www.microsoft.com/traincert/syllabi2395afinal.asp

- Exam 70-282: Designing, Deploying, and Managing a Network Solution for the Small- and Medium-Sized Business: www.microsoft.com/learning/exams/70-282.asp.

Microsoft Partners-Related Sites

- Microsoft Partner's SBS site: www.microsoft.com/partners/sbs

- Main Microsoft Partner site: www.microsoft.com/partner

- Microsoft SBS Partner Locator Tool: sbslocator.cohesioninc.com/ apartnerlocator.asp

- Microsoft Certified Partner Resource Directory (how to find a Certified Partner): directory.microsoft.com/resourcedirectory/ solutions.aspx

- Action Pack: members.microsoft.com/partner/salesmarketing/ partner-market/actionpack/default.aspx

Additional Microsoft or Microsoft-Related Sites

- Microsoft TS2 Events: www.msts2.com

- Microsoft Connections: http://www.microsoft.com/connections

- Eric Ligman's Microsoft Small Business Channel Community site: www.mssmallbiz.com/default.aspx

- Microsoft TechNet: www.microsoft.com/technet

- Microsoft Office templates: officeupdate.microsoft.com/ templategallery/

- Great Plains: www.microsoft.com/greatplains

- Microsoft Visio: www.microsoft.com/visio

- Asentus: www.asentus.net

- Hands On Lab: www.handsonlab.com

- Granite Pillar: microsoft.granitepillar.com/partners/

- Entirenet: www.entirenet.net/registration

- Directions on Microsoft: www.directionsonmicrosoft.com

- Microsoft Solution Selling: www.solutionselling.com/mspartners/ fusion.html

- Dr. Thomas Shinder's ISA Server Web site: www.isaserver.org

- Bill English's SharePoint Web site: www.sharepointknowledge.com

Third-Party SBS-Related Sites

- Susan Bradley's Small Biz Server Links: http://www.sbslinks.com/ (and try www.sbslinks.com/really.htm for a really good time)
- Andy Goodman's site: www.sbs-rocks.com
- Wayne Small's SBS Web site: www.sbsfaq.com
- Another SBS FAQ site: http://www.smallbizserver.net/

Newslists, User Groups, Trade Associations, Organizations

- SBS—Microsoft Small Business Server Support: http:// groups.yahoo. com/group/sbs2k/
- Small BizIT "Small Business IT Consultants" newslist at Yahoo: groups. yahoo.com/groups/smallbizIT

Seminars, Workshops, Conferences

- SMB Nation: www.smbnation.com
- Microsoft TS2 events: www.msts2.com
- Microsoft Connections: http://www.microsoft.com/connections
- Microsoft Momentum Conference: http://www.microsoft.com/partner/ events/wwpartnerconference/
- ITEC: www.goitec.com
- Guerrilla marketing and sales seminars: www.guerrillabusiness.com
- Who Moved My Cheese seminars: www.whomovedmycheese.com
- Myers-Briggs Type Indicator: www.apcentral.org
- Millionaire Mind / T. Harv Eker: www.peakpotentials.com
- TechMentor: www.techmentorevents.com

Business Resources

- US Small Business Administration: www.sba.gov

- Palo Alto Software for business planning: www.paloaltosoftware.com

- PlanWare: www.planware.org

- Presentations: www.presentations.com

- CardScan: www.cardscan.com

- Plaxo: www.plaxo.com

Media

- SMB Advisory newsletter: http://www.smbnation.com
- CRN: www.crn.com
- SBS Maven Andy Goodman posts SBS-related articles at http://www.12c4pc.com.
- Small Business Computing: www.smallbusinesscomputing.com
- PC Magazine Small Business Super Site (www.pcmag.com/category2/0,4148,13806,00.asp)
- Mary Jo Foley's Microsoft-Watch: www.microsoftwatch.com
- NetworkWorldFusion SMB portal: www.nwfusion.com/net.worker/index.html
- Microsoft Certified Professional Magazine: www.mcpmag.com
- Certified Magazine: www.certmag.com
- Windows and .NET Magazine: www.winnetmag.com
- CRMDaily: www.crmdaily.com
- TechRepublic: www.techrepublic.com
- VAR Business: www.varbusiness.com
- Small Business Technology Report: www.smallbiztechnology.com

- Win2K News: www.w2knews.com
- SmallBizTechTalk: www.smallbiztechtalk.com
- Eweek: www.eweek.com
- ComputerWorld: www.computerworld.com
- Kim Komando Show: www.komando.com
- WinInformit: http://www.wininformant.com/
- Entrepreneur Magazine: www.entrepreneur.com
- INC Magazine: www.inc.com
- Fortune: www.fortune.com
- Bizjournals: www.bizjournals.com
- CNN: www.cnn.com
- Business Week: www.businessweek.com
- CBS MarketWatch: www.marketwatch.com
- USA Today: www.usatoday.com
- Money Magazine: www.money.cnn.com
- NPower, not-for-profit technology agency: www.npower.org
- eBay: www.ebay.com
- GeekSquad: www.geeksquad.com
- Geeks On Call: www.geeksoncall.com
- Soft-Temps: www.soft-temps.com
- Insurance for technology professionals: www.techinsurance.com
- Robert Half International salary survey: www.rhii.com
- AOL for Small Business: aolsvc.aol.com/small_biz
- eProject: www.eproject.com

Appendix B
More SNMP Stuff

Manage Networks by Using Simple Network Management Protocol (SNMP)

SNMP is a widely used network management standard on TCP/IP and IPX networks. SNMP can manage nodes (servers, workstations, routers, bridges, and hubs) from a centrally located host. You can use SNMP to configure remote devices, monitor their network performance, detect faults or inappropriate access, and audit network usage. The centrally located host is referred to as an SNMP manager and the network nodes are called SNMP agents.

SNMP Services

Both agents and management systems (SNMP manager) use SNMP messages to inspect and communicate host information. SNMP messages are sent using UDP and IP is used to route messages between the two. The information will be contained in a management information database (MIB). Information like hard disk space is requested using messages. Message requests are sent as **Get, Set, GetNext, Getbulk** requests by the manager and agents will respond with the information. **Notify** would be the only agent-originated message if traps have been set.

The SNMP Service will first have to be installed through the **Add/Remove Windows Components** in **Control Panel** by an administrator. Once installed, the service will automatically start and can be configured for the management of computers on your system. Under the **Agent** tab in the SNMP **Service Properties**, you can select:

- **Physical** – The computer manages physical devices, such as a hard disk partition

- **Management of logical devices** – The computer uses applications that send data using the TCP/IP protocol suite. This service should always be enabled.

- **Datalink and subnetwork** – The computer manages a bridge.

- **Internet** – The computer functions as an IP gateway (router).

- **End-to-end** – The computer functions as an IP host. This service should always be enabled.

Configure Agent Properties

The SNMP agent responds to management system requests for information. Any computer running SNMP agent software is an SNMP agent. The agent responds to information requests from the management system. To configure agents:

1. Go to **Start, Administrative Tools**.
2. In the dropdown, click **Services**.
3. In the details pane, click **SNMP Service**.
4. On the **Action** menu, click **Properties**.
5. On the **Agent** tab, in **Contact**, type the name of the user or administrator for this computer.
6. In **Location**, type the physical location of the computer or the contact.
7. Under **Service**, select the appropriate checkboxes for this computer, and then click **OK**.

Management hosts and agents belong to an SNMP community. The community is a collection of hosts that is grouped together for administrative purposes. Defining communities provides security by allowing only management systems and agents within the same community to communicate. You can configure agents, traps, and security from the SNMP **Properties** tab as shown in Figure B-1.

Figure B-1

SNMP property configurations.

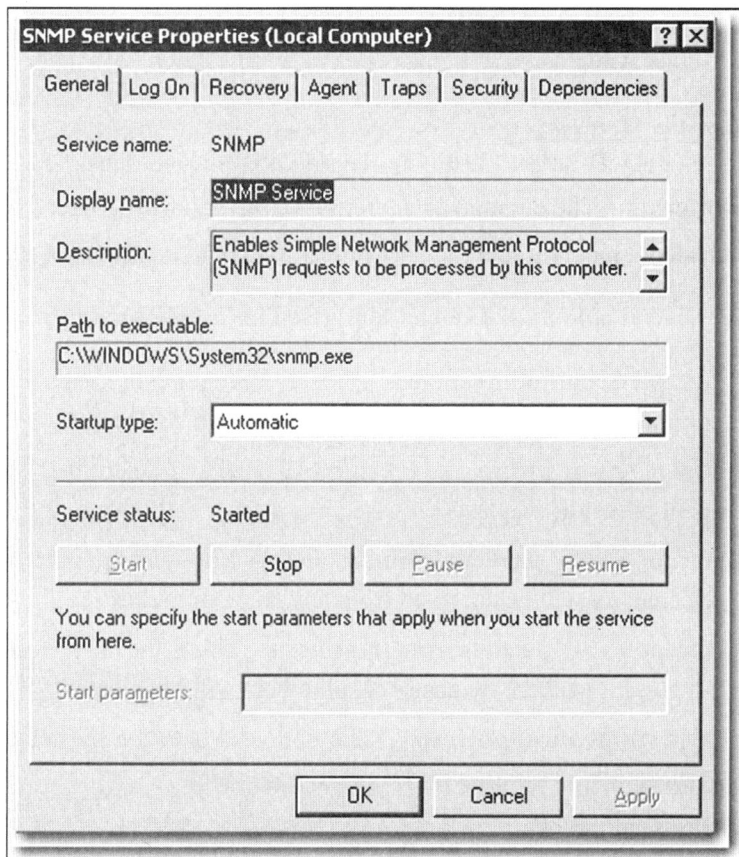

Configure Traps

A trap message is the only agent-initiated SNMP communication. A trap is an alarm-triggering event on an agent, such as a system reboot or illegal access, which provides enhanced security. To configure traps:

1. Go to **Start, Administrative tools**.
2. In the dropdown, click **Services**.
3. In the details pane, click **SNMP Service**.
4. On the **Action** menu, click **Properties**.
5. On the **Traps** tab, under **Community name**, type the case-sensitive community name to which this computer will send trap messages,

and then click **Add to list**.

6. In **Trap destinations**, click **Add**.

7. In **Host name, IP or IPX address**, type information for the host, and click **Add**.

Configure Security

SNMP provides security through the use of community names and authentication traps. SNMP communications can be restricted for the agent, allowing it to communicate with only a specific list of other SNMP management systems.

There are several options that can be configured for SNMP security.

- **Accepted community names** – The service requires at least one default community name; the default of **Public** should be changed.

- **Rights** – A permission level can be selected and determines how the agent processes requests.

- **Accept SNMP packets from any host** – No SNMP packets will be rejected; all will be accepted from any name or address.

- **Accept SNMP packets from these hosts** – This is the list of hosts from which sent packets are accepted; all others will be rejected.

- **Send authentication trap** – This option is checked by default and verifies that host names and addresses are valid.

To configure security:

1. Click **Start, Administrative tools**.

2. In the dropdown, **click** on **Services**.

3. In the details pane, click **SNMP Service**.

4. On the **Action** menu, click **Properties**.

5. On the **Security** tab, select **Send authentication trap** if you want a trap message sent whenever authentication fails.

6. Under **Accepted community names**, click **Add**.

7. Under **Community Rights**, select a permission level for this host to process SNMP requests from the selected community.

8. In **Community Name**, type a case-sensitive community name, and then click **Add**.

9. In **SNMP Service Properties**, specify whether or not to accept SNMP

packets from a host:

- To accept SNMP requests from any host on the network, regard less of identity, click **Accept SNMP packets from any host**.

- To limit acceptance of SNMP packets, click **Accept SNMP pack ets from these hosts**, click **Add**, type the appropriate host name, IP or IPX address, and then click **Add** again.

Important: If you remove all the community names, including the default name **Public**, SNMP does not respond to any community names presented.

Appendix C
Third-Party 70-282 Viewpoints

Near the end of writing the book, two strong SMB consultants who focus on Windows Small Business Server 2003 stepped forward to provide some excellent content and outside context on the 70-282 exam.

Andy Goodman, SBS-MVP

It is with great pleasure that we have been granted permission by *MCP Magazine* (www.mcpmag.com) to reprint Andy Goodman's 70-282 exam review. But first things first: we revised the MCP Magazine article slightly to fit a book format. Now meet Andy in Figure C-1.

Figure C-1
Andy Goodman is a long-time SBSer!

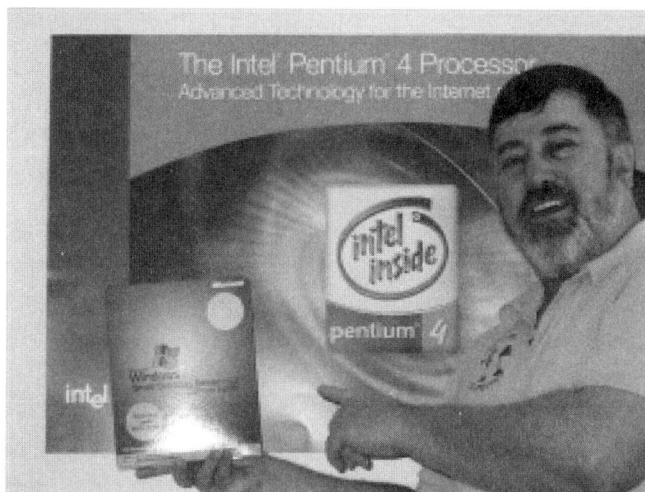

Visit www.microsoft.com/technet for the latest updates for any Microsoft product.

Exam Review

70-282: Planning, Deploying, and Managing a Network Solution for the Small- and Medium-Sized Business

This exam covers Windows 2003 Server and Small Business Server 2003, including Network Planning, Security, Backup, SUS, and Maintenance Group Policies.

by Andy Goodman

February 2004 — So you've heard the rumors that there is money to be made in the SMB Space. And you're wondering how to show your knowledge fits the market. Well, Microsoft has just released a new exam to do just that.

In this review, I try to give you an idea of what to expect. Of course, I can't give you the actual questions or the answers. But I can give you an idea of what is involved.

The Main Areas Tested Break Down as Follows

Analyzing the Existing Environment

Make sure you know how to "walk the job," looking for what

70-282: Planning, Deploying, and Managing a Network Solution for the Small- and Medium-Sized Business

Reviewer's Rating
This exam is hard, especially if you have not used the product in real life. If you've just been reading about, do yourself a favor and get the trial and use it.

Status
Available as of December 16, 2003.

Exam Title
Planning, Deploying, and Managing a Network Solution for the Small and Medium-Sized Business (70-282)

Who Should Take It
People with real world experience, wanting to prove it, this exam is also an elective for 2003 Server MCSE

Preparation Guide
http://www.microsoft.com/learning/exams/70-282.asp

---

existing equipment and software can be used or will need to be replaced. What licenses does the customer already have? Should you offer a software audit? Keep in mind the HCL is your friend. Where is the data stored now and what is it going to take to gather it together? Where are the bottlenecks? What is the customer's "Business Need" ?

Designing a Business Technology Solution for a Small- or Medium-sized Business

This is where you will put the information gathered previously into use. Keep in mind this exam is mostly about SBS, so you should know what tools it offers and especially what tools are new to the 2003 version. What business goals does the new technology infrastructure solve? Which version is right for which customer? There is now a whole family ofWindows Servers; make sure you know the differences between them and when to use which one. You should know which products fill which customer's needs.

Installing and Configuring Windows Small Business Server 2003

Although you won't find a lot of licensing stuff, there is some. Make sure you understand the different types of licenses new to SBS. Prior versions did not have this confusion. Remember, in SBS we use the console whenever possible. There are improved tools for adding users and computers, and you should know how to use them. Make sure you know the installation limitations—what can go where. Make sure you know how to set up a user's access to the new Remote Web Workplace. Become familiar with the To Do List and the CEICW—what it does and why you need to use it. Remember, they took away some things that used to be included in SBS. You should know what's not there anymore. Know how to configure a DHCP scope, and how DNS works.

Supporting and Maintaining Windows Small Business Server 2003

The improved backup that comes with SBS is actually a functional tool now. Make sure you know how to schedule backups and do restores. Install and configure SUS on your test machine; get to know how to manage it with Group Policies.

Under the hood of SBS is Active Directory and Group Policy Objects. You should understand how they work and why they might not. Study up on delegating administrative tasks and configuring a console for these limited administrators. Also, you want to clearly understand remote administration of the server.

Expanding the Windows Small Business Server 2003 Network

When the customer outgrows SBS, you need to know how to move them to the full-blown products. What are the upgrade options to get them there? Can it be done little by little or must it be all or nothing? This section seemed to be pretty light if my memory is correct.

Installing and Configuring Windows Server 2003

Whether you are dealing with an additional domain controller, a stand-alone server, or the new Web server edition, make sure you know the basics of setting up and configuring a Windows Server.

10 Things To Practice

1. Install, configure, and get to know SBS 2003!
2. Learn how to get around in the Administrator Console.
3. Learn how to set up Users and Computers correctly and how to restrict their permissions
4. Learn to create and use Group Policies to save trips to the desktops.
5. Discover the Built-in Backup Utility.
6. Learn to administer SharePoint. This is one of the two biggest things MS marketing will be pushing, so it is only reasonable they will be testing you on it.
7. Set up and use Remote Web Workplace. See Number 6.
8. Set up SUS and learn how to manage it—more trips to the desktop saved.
9. Learn how to use MBSA to scan your server and your entire network

10. Learn the Windows Server Family Product Line. It's not just one product

Okay, here's my take...

When I took the test, it was still in beta. I did it as a favor to one of the authors of the test—kind of a test of the test. I finished it in about half the allowed time and didn't find it too difficult. So, I was surprised when I talked to some of the other test takers afterwards. Many folks whom I highly respect as being SBS experts confessed they had a hard time with it; some even ran out of time before they could finish.

My theory is this: While these people have been working toward becoming SBS experts, and most are MCSEs or better, their knowledge has come from studying and taking tests. My knowledge comes from actually being in the field and tracking down reference books whenever I had to research a problem. I'm not here to say one way to learn is better than another, but I do know that on-the-job training, getting down and dirty with the product, is a great way to really learn your stuff. So, if you want to pass this test—and not just pass but *know* the material—get the demo and install it a few times. Then break it and try to fix it. Don't just do it once, but a few times. And read the marketing literature. This test is not just testing you on the technology, but whether you can sell the right product to the customer, based on that customer's needs. If you don't know the marketing hype, you won't know what to recommend when or for whom.

Final Report

This exam is tough! If you've just started to work with SBS, and especially Windows Small Business Server 2003, make sure you get some hands-on experience before trying to take this exam. Plan on going to a TS2 event (www. msts2.com), if one happening is near you. Listen to the pitch; you will find it very helpful. Good luck!

Andy Goodman, MCP, SBS-MVP, has more than 25 years of experience in computer-related fields. He's the owner of DownHome Computers, a small computer shop in Kernersville, NC, specializing in Microsoft Small Business Server. He has been involved with SBS since its initial release. He's also the online

SBS Forum Moderator for MCPMag.com's "SBS Forum." He hosts a monthly technical chat on MCPmag.com about SBS with Harry Brelsford. His work can be found scattered about the Web on sites such as ServerWatch.com, SWYNK. com, and Admin911.com as well as on his own site www.SBS-Rocks.com. You can contact Andy about "70-282: Planning, Deploying, and Managing a Network Solution for the Small- and Medium-Sized Business at andy@SBS-Rocks.com *or meet him face to face at a SMB Nation Event, www.smbnation.com.*

David Anderson, SBSer (Mercer Island, Washington)

David shared this letter of hope which speaks towards all aspects of becoming a Small Business Specialist and passing the 70-282 exam.

July 15, 2007

Dear (original recipient's name & address have been removed for privacy:),

I am happy to provide assistance with your current project. It is a very worthwhile endeavor which will significantly help people interested in Microsoft's SBS program. This document is in follow-up to your telephone call last Tuesday (7/10/2007). Some of this information summarizes what we have previously discussed. Other topics are further amplified with specific references cited. In addition, a considerable amount of new information is provided. I should be clear that my goal in writing this document is to record in one place a summary of the wealth of information that I have been able to discover to date as it applies to your project's topics. Special emphasis has been directed towards the resources available to prepare for Microsoft's 70-282 exam. It is left to you to distill some of this large body of information into a useful format for your presentations. I have the easy part of this project.

As I understand your project's goal, you wish to create two presentations for Microsoft. One has to do with how a person would go about starting a new SBS-oriented consulting business. The other has to do with how a person would learn the technical aspects of SBS specifically as they apply to passing the required Microsoft 70-282 exam.

Having acquired an extensive teaching background as well having worked as a technical consultant and manager in small and large organizations for many years, it occurs to me that you are facing a Herculean task. In such a short period of presentation time, it seems the best outcome you can expect is to inspire people with some basic information and then provide them with excellent reference sources for additional information and training. Hopefully this document will be of assistance in that regard.

Starting an SBS Business

One might surmise that I should know quite a bit about starting a new SBS business. After all, back in the mid-eighties as a Dean's List student at the University of Southern California's Graduate School of Business which I attended on a computer fellowship, I was the computer consultant for USC's famous Entrepreneur Program. So you might think that with an MBA from USC along with a computer fellowship that required providing various services to all the people associated with the Entrepreneur Department, I should know something about starting an entrepreneurial business. However, it's actually the practical experience, not all the formal education, which has proven to be the most memorable and beneficial. There's no substitute for years of conducting business in the real world. Before recently moving to the Seattle area, my computer consulting business did quite well in the Cleveland region. It was fortunate to win numerous awards year after year as the best of its kind in Cleveland and northeast Ohio. But I digress.

You stated that one of your presentations will be focused on how to start a new SBS consulting business. During our telephone conversation I mentioned that Harry Brelsford's books offer a practical foundation for this topic. I recommend his *SMB Consulting Best Practices* published in 2003 and his *MCSE Consulting Bible* published in 2001. Since you are already familiar with them, I won't elaborate. Another useful book is *From Serf to Surfer - Becoming a Network Consultant* (2000). It's irreverent and somewhat dated, but it contains useful information on your topic. Another interesting book is *Start Your Own Computer Business – the Unembellished Guide* (2002). You can gage people's opinions about all these books by looking at the reviews written by readers at Amazon. com. I frequently use Amazon to evaluate the usefulness of such books.

The SMB Nation website also has several additional books that might be helpful and/or inspirational to new SBS consultants. For example *Making It Big In Small Business* (2005) tells the stories of fifteen MVP SBS people. Lest you think that I am some sort of Brelsford/Mulzer groupie, I assure you that I am offering my best objective opinions. While it is true that Beatrice still owes me the beer that I won from her in June (her e-mail two weeks ago suggested that we settle up at the forthcoming SMB Nation Conference), it appears to me that the SMB Nation website remains among the very best sources of useful information for the SBS world.

The SMB Nation site also includes access to some additional books on the hot topic of managed services. This may be of interest to your audience. For the past three years managed services has been a major subject of conversation in the SBS world. You may want to provide new people with some basic information about this subject. There's a plethora of managed services books, websites, and "managed services gurus" available for reference. However, since presenting a comprehensive discussion about managed services is well beyond the scope of your project, I'll refrain from elaborating further.

Learning SBS for a Professional Career

Simply studying for the 70-282 exam is clearly a different project than learning SBS for the long-term as a professional computer consultant who specializes in SBS. If someone really wants to learn SBS, they could carefully read the *Microsoft Windows Small Business Server 2003 R2 Administrator's Companion* (2006). And really comprehend all of it. That is what some of my most knowledgeable colleagues have done. Yes, that's a difficult and time-consuming task, but it is a worthwhile endeavor in my opinion. In addition to gaining fundamental knowledge through focused SBS studying, I think real-world practical experience is clearly the best teacher. However, as a supplement to this real-world experience, Microsoft's Hands-On-Labs-Online (HOLO) for SBS 2003 and Windows Sever 2003 can provide additional preparation. These HOLOs are discussed later in this document.

As much as I respect the *Administrator's Companion* book, it may be expecting too much for some new SBS people to read and comprehend the complete book before taking the 70-282 exam. Absorbing those 700 pages of technical information takes much time and effort. Plus they may have such little practical experience that they won't be able to relate to some of the more technical sections. Many people will never get around to taking the exam if they first attempt to absorb everything in the *Administrator's Companion*. And that book only covers SBS 2003, not Windows Server 2003. One suggestion is to at least read the book's basic chapters as well as the glossary so as to become familiar with the fundamental information, terms, and acronyms.

So in addition to studying the *Administrator's Companion* book and gaining practical experience with HOLOs and real-world projects, what else is advisable for a new SBS person to learn in order to become a professional SBS consultant? I recommend that they set up a functional SBS lab in their office. Trial versions of SBS are available from Microsoft for just a $12 shipping charge. SBS is also included as part of the Action Pack. Although purchasing an HP or Dell server for the office is advisable, one can actually set up SBS on almost any extra PC that's available since SBS hardware requirements are quite moderate. And SBS can also be set up in a virtual environment as well.

There are some other books I would recommend for people who really want to learn SBS on a professional basis (not just preparing for the 70-282 exam). Begin with Brelsford's *Windows Small Business Server 2003 Best Practices* (2003). New SBS people need a good place to start. Later move on to his subsequent book *Advanced Windows Small Business Server 2003 Best Practices* (2005). This was written by a group of knowledgeable SBS experts and has won critical acclaim from many SBS professionals. In addition to the two editions of the *Administrator's Companion* books (2004 and 2006) discussed elsewhere, one final book I would strongly recommend is *Microsoft Small Business Server 2003 Unleashed* (2006) which even includes informative sections on using Macintosh clients in an SBS network.

Yes, it's hard work to fully digest all this technical material. But it all seems relatively easy compared to the vast amounts of detailed information that I was required to quickly assimilate in business school and medical school. In my opinion it's all just part of the process of acquiring the fundamental knowledge needed to be truly worthy of the title of Microsoft Small Business Specialist. If a person wants to be recognized as a professional SBS consultant, they should do the required preparation. It's that simple.

Learning SBS for the 70-282 Exam

It needs to be recognized that fully comprehending all these SBS technical books provides such a formidable barrier that few people will ever complete such an arduous task before they finally take the 70-282 exam. And remember that the exam covers Windows Server 2003 in addition to SBS 2003. Therefore, the remainder of this document will be devoted to my recommendations and experiences regarding learning about SBS and preparing for the 70-282 exam as opposed to the far more comprehensive project of learning SBS as a professional Microsoft Small Business Specialist. Although these two projects are closely related, they actually involve achieving different goals and so they require different approaches. I have spent considerable time and effort researching what is available with regard to learning resources for the 70-282 exam. It turns out that I have a quite a bit to say about this subject. Hopefully you will find some pieces of information you can use in your presentations.

While there is a wealth of good material about SBS and the 70-282 exam available (actually an overwhelming amount), the resources tend to be scattered and sometimes difficult to find. From the perspective of a new person starting an SBS business and learning about the technical aspects of SBS, the most important accomplishment you could achieve in your project is to create a manageable roadmap for these people to follow. In addition to Microsoft's SBS team, great credit is deserved by both the SMB Nation people and Microsoft's BOB team because they have each done such a good job of creating and organizing relevant information for new SBS people.

So where should a new SBS person start? Probably the first step should be to visit Microsoft's website and read about the Small Business Specialist Program. They need to become familiar with the many benefits of joining the program so that the various kinds of costs associated with joining it will equate to a good investment from their perspective. New people may feel intimidated by this undertaking so presenting them with a clear roadmap to success is important. These people need to become familiar with the details of the SBS program, the various requirements to join, the Action Pack subscription, and how to become a Registered Microsoft Partner. They also need to print out the document entitled "Preparation Guide for the 70-282 Exam" which includes a list of the exam topics. I won't elaborate on this subject further since you are obviously familiar with all these fundamental materials.

Using the "Red Book"

Here is a fact your audience may find interesting. The SMB Nation book entitled *Microsoft Small Business Specialist Primer & 70-282 Exam Preparation Guide!* (2005) actually goes through Microsoft's test topics section by section in chapters three through ten. The strength of this correlation is not entirely obvious until you compare the test topics stated in Microsoft's "Preparation Guide for Exam 70-282" directly to the topic and subtopic headings in the table of contents of the "red book". And then it becomes clear and makes perfect sense. Harry and Beatrice apparently used this Microsoft test guide as their writing outline for the "red book".

The "red book" is the most important test preparation resource for the 70-282 exam. However, this book has some vocal critics so you may want to be aware of what they have to say. Some people complain that the book doesn't cover enough material and is too basic. Others say it refers to Harry's other books too often rather than teach the desired material. Some people dislike its "folksy" style which is so different from standard technical books. And other people don't care for the end-of-chapter questions because sometimes the question's answer is not specifically covered in the chapter. And still others wish there was much more information on Windows Server 2003 (vs. SBS 2003). These are all fair criticisms to some extent.

So why am I such a major advocate of the "red book"? I'll discuss that answer in the following paragraphs. The essential fact, however, is that the "red book" is still the only book on the market that specifically addresses how to prepare for the 70-282 exam. It surprises me that neither Microsoft Press nor any of the various test-prep companies have yet to publish a competitor book. Sometimes in life you need to go with what is, not what should be. And therefore the "red book" is my primary recommended resource to prepare for the 70-282 exam.

It might interest you to know that Beatrice told me just two weeks ago that she is currently involved with preparing a new edition of this book.

What do I like about the "red book", and why do I disagree with its critics? The topic by topic layout provides an excellent format for learning the test material because it directly corresponds to Microsoft's stated test topics. There's plenty of information to learn, and the depth is satisfactory although not sufficient by itself to pass the exam. To cover everything about SBS 2003 and Windows Server 2003 in eight chapters of one *Primer* book is simply expecting too much. The authors' frequent references to other more in-depth information sources are an appropriate way to handle this matter in my opinion. However, it is obvious that there is a market for a more comprehensive 70-282 exam-prep book.

The end-of-chapter questions are very helpful because they are representative of Microsoft exam questions whose unique scenario-style may be new to many readers. It doesn't concern me that the correct answers to these questions are not always directly covered in the chapter text. The explanations of why answers choices are right or wrong are very instructive. However, I recently spoke with Beatrice about this particular criticism and recommended it be plainly stated that these Q&A were simply intended as examples of Microsoft-style scenario test questions and that not all answer choices would be covered in the chapter text. The Q&A could even be put in a separate section of the book instead of at the end of each chapter. This approach might alleviate some unnecessary criticism in the upcoming edition.

Did you know that there are valuable free supplements to the "red book" that are available for download from the SMB Nation website? One supplement includes twenty-five more 70-282 sample questions with explanations of answers. These Q&A provide valuable practice with dealing with this scenario style of question. Another exceptionally valuable supplement is entitled "70-282 Exam Update Guide". It covers numerous topics and contains an extensive section on technical subjects primarily related to Windows Sever 2003. Although this section is written as an overview, it contains significant detail. This supplement also includes another thirty test questions divided by topic. I would strongly recommend downloading and reading this "update guide" because of the wealth of valuable information it includes on a variety of important subjects. The supplement's section that lists available SBS resources is particularly helpful as is Appendix A of the "red book" entitled "SBS 2003 Resources".

In my opinion the "red book" might be even more valuable if it clearly emphasized the usefulness of additional learning resources such as Microsoft's Hands-On-Labs-Online (HOLO), Microsoft's 70-282 study groups and boot camps, the BOB team's SBS resources, the MOC 2395A course, and the e-learning Collection 5974. Each of these resources is discussed later in this document.

The "red book" along with its supplements could be described as several books in one. The first two chapters (Section 1) are an introduction to the book and the world of becoming an SBS consultant. It contains the type of information a potential SBS person would want to know about. Chapters three through eight (Section 2) are devoted to the SBS 2003 technical material covered on the exam. Chapters nine and ten deal with Windows Server 2003 material. The remaining chapters (Section 3) and the appendices cover diverse topics including reference material sources plus how to prepare for and then take the 70-282 exam. There's even a chapter on the infamous online test that is entitled "Small Business Sales and Marketing Skills Assessment". Each technical chapter includes ten end-of-chapter questions which are valuable because they teach new test-takers about dealing with Microsoft-style scenario questions. In addition to the sections containing recommendations about preparing for and taking the 70-282 exam, many other valuable hints about taking this test are offered throughout the book.

The previously mentioned "70-282 Exam Update Guide" contains Windows Server 2003 summary information and provides a technical overview of some very important exam topics. The creation of this guide may have been influenced by last year's 70-282 exam "update" by Microsoft test designers. Although Microsoft's current exam guide is exactly the same as the old guide and the list of test topics is identical, Microsoft "updated" the test in early 2006. It is not clear to me exactly what the practical ramifications are of this "update". I hear that there may now be more in-depth emphasis on Windows Server 2003 and related technical topics.

Since I mentioned the online marketing exam requirement, I have a hint for your audience. If someone doesn't pass the online marketing exam the first time, they should carefully review all the questions and answers of their failed exam to learn what was marked right and wrong. The "correct" answers are not always obvious so write them down. Chances are very strong that they will see some of those very same questions again on their marketing exam re-take.

Using the Administrator's Companion book(s)

The second major book I recommend for preparing for the 70-282 exam is the *Windows Small Business Server 2003 R2 Administrator's Companion*. This is generally considered the most comprehensive and well-written of all the SBS books currently available.

It should be noted that there are now two *Administrator's Companion* books (published in 2004 and 2006). The new book from 2006 with "R2" added to its title contains several important changes. It's almost 100 pages longer (701 versus 620) with new chapters and appendices. The new R2 features and changes are covered in detail. There's been some reorganization of the material. A fair amount of text has been revised and added. And the name of one of the three original authors has been omitted. Unfortunately the new book is less visually appealing because the text font is now smaller and the attractive blue topic headings have been changed to plain black. However, the newer R2 edition is obviously the better investment of the two books because the R2 version of SBS is what most of us will be installing for the foreseeable future. The only significant topic missing from the new R2 edition of the book is an appendix covering the installation of ISA Server 2000 and SQL Server 2000.

Saving Money

Here are some suggestions on ways new people can save some money while pursuing their new SBS careers. Most people already know that all these reference books can be bought at discount on Amazon.com from non-Amazon sellers. Significant savings can be achieved. Also, people might want to save money on their exam fee by obtaining an exam voucher which generally can save about 30% depending on the particular offer they discover. Probably the easiest way to get an exam voucher is to simply call the SBS people at Microsoft and ask if they have one available. They can often just e-mail a voucher code to you. The live online 70-282 exam preparation seminars by the BOB team and TS2 team sometimes offer discounts for attendees. Microsoft's live events presenters often know of available discount programs as well (particularly the TS2 people). SMB Nation's website and their 70-282 exam study blog is another great source for information on discounts. Even conducting searches at Amazon and Google will often uncover some deals.

Discounts are frequently available for both Microsoft exams and commercial Q&A vendor products. Currently I have a free Microsoft exam voucher and a five free Q&A vouchers to Self-Test Software. But these particular deals I discovered are much better than the usual discounts you can find which are generally in the 30% off range. One important caution with all these discount opportunities is to be very aware of their expiration dates.

And speaking of saving money, prospective SBS consultants will want to know that the Microsoft Action Pack Subscription (MAPS) costs only $299 per year. It is an invaluable asset. As we discussed during our telephone call, a person must become a partner to purchase it. Recently I learned that in November 2007 new requirements for MAPS will go into effect which will include passing one of the e-learning courses. MAPS is a great deal and readily available to various computer-related entities who agree to abide by its reasonable restrictions. Details and requirements are available at various places on Microsoft's website. A currently active Action Pack subscription is a requirement to obtain the Small Business Specialist certification.

Being currently registered as a Microsoft partner is another requirement for the SBS program. People will be interested to know how simple it is to become a Registered Microsoft Partner. And it's free. They don't even have to pass a Microsoft certification exam (why not?). As with the Action Pack subscription, you must renew this partnership each year to maintain an active partner status with Microsoft. But renewal is easy and without cost. It simply involves updating your partner profile and accepting Microsoft's terms of partnership.

This kind of information about topics like becoming a Registered Microsoft Partner, obtaining an Action Pack subscription, and finding test-related discounts are the types of information new people might want to know about in your presentations. Please don't assume "everybody already knows this". Many do not. Speaking from personal experience, I had been an active computer consultant for many years before becoming aware of the great benefits of teaming up with Microsoft as a partner. It should be noted that the "red book" and the SMB Nation website discuss these topics. One final point that deserves emphasis is that obtaining active Microsoft Partner status is required to access some of the best technical reference materials, test preparation materials, and marketing/sales materials. For example, I believe that access to the valuable Hands-On-Labs-Online requires partner status.

Using HOLOs

One of the most valuable test-preparation resources that hardly anyone ever mentions is Microsoft's Hands-On-Labs-Online (HOLO). This is true of even the most knowledgeable sources of information like SMB Nation and the BOB team. HOLOs are very valuable learning tools! For example, an SBS 2003 HOLO lets you work with a simulated SBS 2003 server and a Windows XP client for about eighty minutes by connecting to a special Microsoft website from your personal computer. There are numerous guided exercises available that teach you step-by-step how to accomplish important tasks in the server environment. Some of these free exercises are the same ones that are used in the high-priced courses. The instructions for the exercises can either be followed on the screen in a narrow column beside the server window, or they can be printed out to serve as a review of the procedures. These interactive HOLOs provide a far better learning experience than just looking over menu items on an SBS box or trying to remember procedure steps from a book.

It is very important to know that in addition to following the guided exercises, you can also work ("play") with the virtual SBS server and try out different menu choices and then observe the outcomes. You can look through all the buried menu options and read the help screens for more information. When you reach the end of the eighty minutes time period, you can just sign on again. It should be emphasized that following the structured exercises is optional. Working and experimenting with this simulated client/server environment takes the fear out of ruining your own office's SBS setup if you make a mistake. The HOLOs are a great learning tool that are seldom mentioned.

There are many different kinds of HOLOs. Do a search to find them. In addition to SBS 2003 HOLOs, you can also work with the Windows Server 2003 HOLOs as well. This is important because the 70-282 exam covers both SBS 2003 and Windows Server 2003. Some people seem to be under the mistaken impression that it's just an SBS exam, and they underestimate how much Windows Server 2003 knowledge is required. Those are the same people who will need the "free re-take" offers and the "exam insurance" deals.

Using MOC 2395A and E-Learning Collection 5974

In addition to the HOLOs, another important study resource that is hardly ever mentioned is Microsoft's MOC 2395A classroom course entitled "Designing, Deploying, and Managing a Network Solution for the Small and Medium-Sized Business". Sound familiar? This course has exactly the same name as the 70-282 exam. The best part of this course is its well-written textbook which is quite comprehensive and contains many practical exercises. I'm not sure if someone would be able to obtain this excellent course book without actually enrolling in the course.

This MOC 2395A course covers both SBS 2003 and Windows Server 2003 in nine modules over three days. There are numerous lessons, guided exercises, and interactive multimedia presentations in each module. The first of the nine modules covers designing a business network solution. The next four modules cover SBS 2003, and the last four modules cover Windows Server 2003 topics. A great deal of material is covered in the course book. Some of the instructive exercises are similar to the ones available in HOLOs.

The MOC 2395A course is somewhat expensive as is common in the training industry. The one company I checked currently has it listed at $2,695 per student. Better deals must be available. After earning my MBA from USC, I was eventually promoted to the general manager position of one of the country's major computer training companies located in Los Angeles. Therefore I know from experience that steep discounts and negotiated prices can generally be obtained for courses at these training centers.

Two years ago I helped negotiate a deal for this MOC 2395A course for the members of my Cleveland SBS group. We got the price reduced by about fifty percent to around $700 per student, and some of my colleagues sent their employees to take the course. Although this MOC 2395A course may be listed as available by various teaching centers, apparently it is often cancelled due to a lack of sign-ups. One person flew a thousand miles from Texas to take the Cleveland course, and he said it was the only MOC 2395A course he could find anywhere in the country that was actually being conducted. I have heard similar stories from other people as well.

Apparently several years ago this MOC 2395A course was originally intended to be offered as an online course as well as being taught in a classroom setting. According to certain Internet sources, its online course title was supposed to be exactly the same name as the classroom course title. It's not clear whatever happened to that original plan.

So if you can't find or afford the MOC 2395A course, what can you do? You can enroll in Microsoft's little-known online e-learning course entitled "Collection 5974". I've been told that this is a relatively new offering by Microsoft. Its official course collection title is "Designing, Deploying, and Managing a Network Solution for a Small and Medium-Sized Business". And of course that is exactly the same name as the 70-282 exam's title as well as the MOC 2395A course title. The price is $224 and consists of a combination of seven individual $40 courses whose titles correspond to the various topics being tested in the 70-282 exam. Although this "collection" of individual courses isn't called MOC 2395A and the titles of the seven individual courses don't exactly match the titles of the nine modules in MOC 2395A, it appears to be about the same course. This Collection 5974 seems like a good deal if you like online e-learning courses. However, a person might wear out their printer trying to re-create a textbook from it. I tried out a sample demo of an e-learning course a few weeks ago and it looked good.

Teaming Up with the BOB Team, SMB Nation, and Microsoft's SBS Program

So moving on to other places to find training, I believe you are already familiar with the large number of Microsoft resources available from the Small Business Specialist Program. It is also my understanding that you are knowledgeable about the many resources available at SMB Nation. Therefore, I won't elaborate on the abundant amount of information available from these two places.

Here is one of my favorite Microsoft groups. The BOB team (Builder of Boxes) has created many valuable training resources. If you watch one of their recent 70-282 Study Group presentations (May 2007 was the latest one), at the end of their slide deck you'll see a long list of links to their training and reference resources. By going to http://oem.microsoft.com, you enter a portal with access to many valuable links including their instructional "BOBcasts" on many technical topics, the "BOBwired" webcasts and chats, the "BackRoom" page resources, and a discussion forum in their "Community" page. There are slide deck presentations, blogs, plus Q&A with partners. The list of links is extensive.

The BOB team is an example of a Microsoft group that is really doing a great job. The resources available from the BOB team for the SBS people are commendable. Moreover, this group's helpful spirit truly distinguishes it within the huge Microsoft bureaucracy. These BOB team people radiate such a helpful attitude that it transforms the gigantic Microsoft Corporation down to a small group of knowledgeable people dedicated to do all they can to assist SBS people in addition to supporting their core OEM constituency. They are a major credit to Microsoft.

As a computer consultant who primarily works with small organizations, the great resources available within Microsoft often seem scattered and hard to find. This situation must be particularly challenging for a new SBS person. It's not a lack of information that is the issue. In fact I feel overwhelmed by all the information sent to me and available on the vast Microsoft website. What is needed by a new SBS person is to have all this great information be more organized, focused, and simplified. Yes, simplified. Too much information can be as bad as too little information. Scattered information is as bad as missing information. What would be helpful is a clear and relatively simple path to follow for new and aspiring Microsoft Small Business Specialists. Pull things together and connect the dots. I suspect that is part of what you are hoping to accomplish with your important project.

During our telephone discussion I mentioned that the SMB Nation website has a link to their 70-282 exam study group. It's regularly monitored and commented on by Harry and Beatrice. It has become quite extensive and informative. People ask a variety of questions and others offer useful information. In a similar manner, the BOB team's blogs and their Q&A related to the 70-282 exam study group are also quite helpful. Recently a particularly insightful and instructive posting regarding 70-282 exam preparation was featured on the BOB team's 70-282 section. And on the SMB Nation's 70-282 study group site, a person just posted a document with links to all the online Microsoft 70-282 study group presentations as well as another six pages of critical "need to know" information for the exam. Your audience may want to hear that these helpful study groups are freely available to anyone and how they can find them.

Learning with Q&A

Another test-preparation topic is the Q&A practice material available from various places on Microsoft's website as well as from the many commercial Q&A companies. It seems to me that using Q&A as a learning tool should only be utilized after a person has thoroughly studied the material elsewhere. Q&A should not be the primary source of learning new material. If someone decides to purchase a Q&A product, I would recommend only dealing with the major companies like Self-Test, Transcender, and MeasureUp. Stay away from all the others to avoid problems with this notorious business segment. Each of the major Q&A companies offers about ten free Q&A for the 70-282 exam so their sites might be worth a visit.

One hint related to Q&A is to carefully study why the "wrong answers" are wrong. I actually printed out Transcender's entire database of 70-282 exam Q&A to study it section by section like it was a book. Knowing why an answer is wrong can be as instructive as knowing why an answer is right. Another hint regarding Q&A is to take the practice exams in a timed mode to gage how fast you have to work in order to stay on schedule with these unique scenario-based questions with all their excess text and superfluous information.

I recommend extensive use of Q&A as a tool in test preparation. However, there are so many good 70-282 Q&A freely available now that a person may not need to purchase a Q&A package from one of the commercial vendors. Many Q&A are available in the "red book" because at the end of each of the eight technical chapters, there are ten test questions with explanations of answers. In addition, one "red book" supplement contains twenty-five more questions, and then the "70-282 Exam Update Guide" supplement contains another thirty questions. Also, as mentioned earlier, each of the major commercial Q&A vendors offer about ten free Q&A for the 70-282 exam. In addition, Microsoft's website also offers about thirty Q&A as a pretest assessment. And finally, a large number of Q&A from Self-Test Software are available from Microsoft's 70-282 boot camps and study groups. If you know where to look, there are many free 70-282 Q&A available.

Learning with Online Presentations

You are probably quite familiar with the numerous multi-session 70-282 exam preparation seminars conducted by the BOB team and the TS2 team. They're available online and can be found with a search for 70-282 web seminars. They range from two session "boot camps", to five session Q&A presentations, to twelve and eighteen session "study groups" which combine lecture presentations with Q&A sessions. The most recent one was presented by the BOB team in May 2007. Their website has all the slide decks as well as the answers to questions from the audience. Let me know if you want individual evaluations of these various groups of presentations because they are each a little different.

It would be a serious mistake to assume that merely listening to a group of these online presentations would adequately prepare a person for passing the exam. These online sessions are helpful and easy to listen to. But the recommended books have far more depth, and they seem like a more appropriate test preparation resource for a professional computer consultant. These online presentations tend to focus on the bare essentials of what you might get asked on the exam. While the instructors have done a good job in presenting these sessions, they are "easy listening" for students. They should not be considered a substitute for serious book-oriented studying which is time-consuming and hard work.

These online presentations are helpful but surprisingly time-consuming. Here are some tips for your audience on additional ways to utilize these presentations. Print out the slide decks and use them like a supplementary "Cliff Notes" for exam preparation. Each slide deck contains excellent summary information on the topics presented. Another suggestion is to practice Q&A skills by using the numerous Microsoft Q&A 70-282 prep sessions presented by the BOB team and the TS2 team. As mentioned earlier, their test questions come from Self Test Software's question database and seem representative of Microsoft-style scenario questions.

Organizing the 70-282 Exam Project and Employing Learning Strategies

It may be quite a while between the time a person first starts preparing for the 70-282 exam and when they actually get around to taking the test. Busy people often get diverted from this difficult and time-consuming project. So here are a few suggestions which have proven useful to me in business school, medical school, and preparing for the 70-282 exam.

First, stay organized. Keep related materials in labeled manila folders. Keep all the folders together in a multi-pocket organizer. Keep relevant books together as well. To remember what has been read and studied, I use a yellow highlighter for important material, a green highlighter for extra important material, and a red pen to underline important terms like technical vocabulary and acronyms. This technique becomes easy with practice. After the initial reading, I go back and re-read the highlighted material and then write out a summary of each section on notepad paper. This technique is time-consuming but very effective. Memorization is enhanced. When it eventually comes time to take the test several months later, the final preparation process is both fast and thorough. Simply review the highlighted text and study the written summary notes. It would also be advisable to review the HOLOs and go through all the menu choices again in both SBS 2003 and Windows Server 2003.

It is also important to design an effective study program which identifies and lists the necessary individual tasks to be completed during this project. The number of tasks for this project will be extensive. This list of tasks needs to be accompanied by a schedule of completion dates for the individual tasks. As with any management project, it is important to include a timeframe for individual task completion in order to keep the project on schedule. Creating an Excel spreadsheet is one way to organize such a project. Ideally a person could set aside a month or more to focus on this project and be totally devoted to completing it.

Another hint for new SBS people has to do with managing the innumerable Internet resource links and keep them easily accessible. As one works with SBS, the number and variety of websites you bookmark can soon become overwhelming. Right from the start, it is advisable to create Favorites folders and subfolders by topic and/or information source. Otherwise, the reference sites become scattered and lost in the vast crowd of other favorites. For example, I keep links to official Microsoft web pages grouped together and always make sure that an official favorite's name starts with the word "Microsoft" to differentiate it from other non-Microsoft related favorites. Then I group the Microsoft sites into subcategories. In addition, I often change the name of a favorite so that the new name becomes more meaningfully and descriptive in the context of my professional work. And one last obvious suggestion is to actively bookmark the good sites as soon as they are discovered. It's so easy to forget to create a favorite, and then it's so frustrating when you can't find them again.

And Finally a Few Last Suggestions

Since students tend to remember less than 50% of what is actually said in a presentation, it would be advisable to have your slide decks available for a PDF printout. Based on my experience with these presentations, printing a slide deck during the live online presentations can be quite distracting (especially when the PDF slide deck isn't available until midway into the presentation). Maybe the PDF deck could be made available for printing a few minutes before the presentation starts. Moreover, you might be interested to know that some people have had significant difficulty at times printing PDFs from the previously recorded Microsoft presentations. That may become a problem with presentations like yours which will probably be recommending numerous websites and references so a printout will be very important.

One thing you might want to cover in your presentations is where and how to find training on Microsoft's vast website. It's an important skill that new people need to learn. A summary of the different kinds of training that are available would be useful. Effective search techniques could also be included in the discussion, or an actual demonstration could be performed. Suggested search terms might include SBS, Small Business Server, HOLO, and 70-282.

At our recent PSSBS user group meeting in May at Microsoft's headquarters in Redmond, a DVD partially entitled "March 2007 - Partner Group Community Resource DVD" was made available to everyone at the table. I suspect you have a copy so I won't elaborate on all the contents. However, one of the DVD's topic titles was "Small Business Training Path". It covers the relevant core training resources available from Microsoft in both the sales and technical areas. There are even links to some SBS HOLOs. It provides excellent information so I thought it might be useful to call your attention to this valuable DVD. Some of those recommended resources are mentioned in this document, but many others are not.

I hope some of this information proves helpful in completing your project. There is actually far more I could add, but this summary should suffice for now. You might be surprised at how many additional paragraphs I've actually written but later decided to delete in order to decrease this document's length. It's fair to say that this summary includes the major resources that come to mind at this point in time. If I recall something else important, I'll contact you. Please let me know if I can be of further assistance. Best of luck with your project!

David Anderson
DavidAnderson5@gmail.com

Appendix D
Practice Questions

Question #1

As the IT admin at your company, you must select a new server from the following choices. Considering resources, what is the best option?

A. A server with one Pentium III 500 MHz processor, 256 MB RAM, a 4 GB hard drive and two NICs

B. A server with three Pentium III 300 processors, 1 GB RAM, two 20 GB hard drives, one NIC

C. A server with two Pentium III 500 MHz processors, 512 MB RAM, two 8 GB hard drives, one NIC

D. A server with two Pentium III 300 processors, 512 MB RAM, two 8 GB hard drives, two NICs

Question #2

You are the IT admin at a small interior design firm. There are six Windows 98 computers and four Windows 95 computers on a peer-to-peer network. Data files are spread out over the individual computers. There is a shared broadband connection. Users have POP3 e-mail accounts to retrieve their e-mail. Your employer wants you to implement centralized storage for the data files. He also wants to start using the company's domain name, Spacedesign.com, for e-mail, and give users the ability to send and receive faxes from their desktop. You are to implement the most effective and least costly solution. Which steps should you take? Choose all correct answers.

A. Install a modem on each client computer.

B. Upgrade client computers to Windows XP Home Edition.

C. Purchase a low-cost fax application and install on each client station.

D. Install a modem on the Small Business Server.

E. Install Small Business Server 2003, Standard Edition.

F. Upgrade client computers to Windows XP Professional Edition.

G. Install Small Business Server 2003 and Exchange 2003.

H. Purchase a low-cost fax application and install on the Small Business Server.

Question #3

Springers Ltd. currently has three Windows 2000 computers and three Windows XP Professional machines. The company uses a peer-to-peer network. Because they have recently hired additional staff, the owner has ordered four more Windows XP Professional computers. Springers Ltd. will also be purchasing a proprietary application that requires its own server. As the admin, you suggest implementing an SBS 2003 server and purchasing a second Windows Server 2003 to host the proprietary application. You are thinking about going with the device licensing model. How many client access licenses must Springers Ltd. purchase on top of the five licenses that come with SBS 2003?

A. 0

B. 5

C. 10

D. 15

Question #4

You are the administrator for Springers Ltd. and manage a Small Business Server 2000 domain with 15 Windows XP clients and eight Windows 98 clients. Your boss finally coughed up the bucks to purchase an SBS 2003 upgrade. The SBS 2000 server machine has two 36 GB hard drives with two FAT32 partitions each. You plan to do the upgrade over the weekend and want to perform for the upgrade with minimal effort. Prior to installing SBS 2003 on the current domain controller, you should:

A. Move all data onto one drive and create a mirror for redundancy.

B. Convert the system partition to NT file system (NTFS).

C. Run chkdsk on drive 0.

D. Format the system partition with NTFS.

E. Convert both drives to NTFS.

Question #5

Heartland Tractor Supply has called you to provide an assessment of their needs for a new platform to operate their business upon. Their parent company has told them that NT 4 will no longer be supported, and they must move to a new operating system. Before they invest any money, they want to be sure that whatever they chose will meet their needs. They currently have three locations with 45 employees. You discover during the interview process that they spend a significant amount of time each month trying to keep the line of business parts application updated. Each location currently has a NT 4.0 server that is used to run this LOB app. They receive a DVD set each month which must be loaded onto each location's server. This can take four to eight hours per machine, as their existing servers are old and slow. They also struggle to maintain the remote machines and their part-time IT manager spends hours driving back and forth to the remote locations to fix minor issues. They mentioned a desire to bring their e-mail in house, as their ISP has not been reliable in providing mail services. They have decent connectivity via a VPN between locations, but don't really use it for more than connection to the LOB app. Based on these facts, what do you do?

A. Recommend they continue to use NT 4.0, as it has worked for them for years and provides a source of regular support revenue for you

B. Recommend a Windows 2003 server replace of each of the NT 4.0 servers to bring them up to a current platform

C. Recommend replacing the individual NT 4.0 servers with three SBS 2003 servers

D. Recommend a single SBS 2003 server with a second Windows 2003 server running terminal services at the head office location

E. Recommend a single Windows Server 2003 server with a second server running terminal services at the head office location

Question #6

You receive a call from an accounting firm regarding some network issues. You determine they need to upgrade their NT 4.0 operating system to be able to operate the new tax software they purchased. Upon review of their situation, you discover there are five people in their main office, four people in a remote office, and two part-time users who operate from their homes. The tax software vendor has recommended SBS 2003 Premium edition, which you agree is the best solution. During most of the year, only eight people need access to the network. Only during tax season do all 11 need network access. You will configure the network with a VPN connection between the two offices and VPN access from the two part-time work-at-home users. How would you quote the licensing for SBS 2003 to this accountant?

A. Purchase SBS Premium 2003 with 5 CALs, and 4 additional CALs to cover the full-time workers

B. Purchase SBS Premium 2003 with 5 CALs, and 6 additional CALs to cover all the staff

C. Purchase SBS Premium 2003 with 5 CALs, and 1 additional 5 pack of CALs to cover the full-time workers

D. Purchase SBS Premium 2003 with 5 CALs, and 2 additional 5 packs of CALs to cover all the staff

E. Purchase SBS Premium 2003 with 5 CALs and ignore the remote workers

Question #7

You are called to provide advice to a prospective customer about what solution he should install in his business. Since you are a long way from this prospect, you ask him to send you an e-mail with some basic information you can use to put together an interview to define the solution. Which of the following pieces of information gives you enough information to begin formulating a recommendation?

A. One dedicated fax line that is not currently in use

B. An Internet connection

C. Three computer workstations

D. Pentium 4 – 2.4GHz server with 40 GB hard drive

E. 70 employees

Question #8

Your local chamber of commerce wants to be able to generate marketing information and communicate better with its members. Tim, the chamber director, comes to you for help in making this happen. They have a small office of six people, some of whom work from home part-time. From the following possible scenarios around SBS, which would give the best functionality for the feature it describes:

A. Purchase a color inkjet to connect to each workstation.

B. Install a 56K internal fax modem in the server

C. Talk to the ISP to set up e-mail accounts

D. Configure a remote Web workplace for outside access

E. Use file shares on local hard drives to allow others in the office to get to files

Question #9

One of your existing customers is running a single Linux server using Samba to provide file sharing for the 12 Windows XP Pro SP2 workstations they have. They also use the same server to host a simple web server with four static pages. They would like to have a shared calendar solution as well as publish the web site. They have also expressed some interest in working from home. They currently have a 512K up/down DSL connection to the Internet with static IP address. They back up the Linux server to one of the XP workstations using the built in Windows XP backup. The Linux server is a P4 2 GHz machine with 1GB RAM. What solution best fits their needs? Budget is a major concern for this project.

A. Replace the existing server with a new Small Business Server 2003 Premium Edition.

B. Back up the Linux server. Run the Small Business Server Wizard to upgrade the Linux server to Small Business Server 2003.

C. Back up the Linux server. Load Small Business Server Premium on the existing server, then create the users and file shares and restore the data from the backup.

D. Have them use the existing Linux server and install Exchange Server 2003 on it.

Question #10

A new startup company, The Recycle IT Co., receives various pieces of electronic equipment from people who do not want them anymore and do not want to just throw the equipment in the Dumpster. They do a good job of stripping equipment and recycling the parts. Recently a large firm upgraded an entire department and sent Recycle IT several servers. They would like to start keeping track of the equipment they receive; they also want to be able to receive and send faxes from their desktops. They currently have three Windows XP workstations with Office 2003 Standard on each and a dedicated fax machine. They do not have any type of network currently, so any documents they create they save to a USB memory stick then run it to the other computers. They were also recently at a training center and received a free five-user version of Small Business Server 2003 Standard. The following is a list of four servers they received that might be used. Which machine will be able to run SBS 2003 Standard without upgrading? Select all that apply.

A. Compaq Proliant 1000: Pentium 90MHz, 128MB, RAID 5, four 2GB drives

B. Dell 4400: PIII 500 MHz, 512MB, 4GB drive (400MB used for diagnostic partition)

C. Whitebox: PII 300 MHz, 384MB, two 10GB drives

D. Dell 4400: PIII 500 MHz, 2GB, no hard drive

Question #11

Springers Ltd. has three traveling sales managers that use Windows 98 on their laptop computers. The sales managers each also have a desktop computer at work with Windows 2000 Professional installed on them. Springers is on an SBS 2003 network and as the administrator you are asked to implement a low-cost remote access solution. What are the least costly remote access implementations? (Choose two.)

A. Add a member server to the network.

B. Install terminal services on the SBS 2003 server.

C. Enable remote desktop administration.

D. Configure Remote Web Workplace.

E. Install terminal services on the member server.

F. Upgrade the Windows 2000 Professional machines to XP Pro.

G. Configure SharePoint services.

H. Upgrade the Windows 98 machines to XP Pro.

Question #12

SpaceDesign, Inc., will be implementing an SBS 2003 network that consists of 40 Windows 2000 Professional computers and a domain controller with four SATA hard drives. The DC will be used as the file server and needs to be continuously available. How should you configure the hard drives? (Choose two.)

A. Create a system partition on one disk.

B. Create a RAID 1 volume and use one disk for shadow copy.

C. Create a spanned disk set with three disks.

D. Mirror the system partition and create a two-disk RAID 5 volume.

E. Create a RAID 5 volume with three disks.

Question #13

Schnitzelbank, Inc., is a prestigious law firm located in Paris, Texas, that plans on opening an additional office in Chicago, Illinois. Both offices will have a high-speed Internet connection and will be equipped with an SBS 2003 network. The paralegals at each location must be able to securely retrieve confidential client information at the other office. As the consultant, you are asked to implement an inexpensive, efficient, secure, and reliable solution with low administrative overhead. You propose to:

A. Install member servers with Terminal Services at each office.

B. Configure clients at each office with the "Connection Manager."

C. Install PC Anywhere.

D. Configure a router-to-router VPN.

E. Enable Remote Desktop.

Question #14

A bank officer at a small regional bank calls and asks for an assessment of their upgrade options. They are currently running on a competitive platform and want to consider options for migrating to a Microsoft Windows solution. They are concerned about security and how they can comply with the Gramm Leach Bliley Act (GLBA) regulations in the banking industry. (The GLBA is a comprehensive law requiring financial institutions to protect the security, integrity, and confidentiality of consumer information.) They connect to a larger bank system to have their data processed. Because this connection is currently across a dedicated T1, which is cost-prohibitive to continue, they want to evaluate options for making a secure connection to their processing service center via the Internet while still remaining compliant and secure. There are 30 employees in their bank, all of whom use an office suite and some bank-specific applications. They access the processing service center for account information and balances across their connection. Based on discussions with the vendors, you determine that all their applications will run on the Windows platform. As their partner and consultant, you have been asked to lay out a plan that will meet these requirements and concerns. Which of the following actions do you take? (Select all that are appropriate.)

A. Recommend that they install SBS Premium immediately and run ISA for security.

B. Sit down with the IT manager and management team to lay out a long-term plan for the bank.

C. Recommend that they upgrade their current competitive platform to keep it simple.

D. Schedule a meeting or conference call with their host bank to determine what connectivity options are available.

E. Research local ISP providers and the prices and plans offered.

Question #15

A small business owner who works out of his home calls after attending a Microsoft event that featured SBS. He describes his situation as a two-person company, just he and his wife, selling pet health care products. They have been doing this successfully, using a printed catalog and receiving most of their orders via the fax in their home. He wants to upgrade to a web-based business to expand his ability to take orders and make it easier for his customers to do business with them. He also wants to secure a domain name so they can have e-mail. He currently has one computer on which he runs a simple personal accounting system. He and his wife fight over who can get to the computer to do their part of the accounting entry. He is convinced he wants to set up an SBS-based network so he and his wife can become web-enabled. They have access only to a dependable low-speed connection. Based on this information, you recommend that they:

A. Install SBS and set up a web site to be hosted on it along with e-mail and network faxing.

B. Sell them a second PC and create a peer-to-peer network.

C. Install SBS and set up e-mail and network faxing, but recommend they host their web site at an offsite hosting service.

D. Tell them to continue to do business the same way, since they have been getting along just fine.

E. Sell them a laptop and wireless access point so they can work in different rooms.

Question #16

Al, a local contractor, has just experienced a server failure and lost data due to poor backups and data management. He calls you to help configure a new server to meet his needs with a special emphasis on data security. He never wants to experience this loss again. You have determined that SBS is the appropriate operating system for his business and now need to recommend some ways to safeguard his data. He wants optimum data security. Cost is a secondary concern. You recommend these as good solutions:

A. Manually copy all the data from his server to a CD each evening.

B. Create a backup rotation using a tape drive with daily, weekly, and monthly tape rotations and store the tapes offsite each day.

C. Configure his server using RAID 0.

D. Subscribe him to an offsite backup service over the Internet.

E. Configure his server using RAID 5.

F. Purchase SBS-specific backup software.

Question #17

Sally Smith calls you from her clothing store and wants your help in putting in a server to manage her company. She has attended one of your SBS seminars and believes that is the correct product based on the features she has seen through the demonstrations and talking with one of your sales people. You drop by the store to evaluate the equipment she has accumulated to see what might integrate with the new SBS server she is purchasing. During a discussion with her, you learn the following: 1) it will be running a LOB clothing application requiring SQL; 2) she is very interested in knowing what her employees are doing on the Internet during work hours; 3) she wants to use the fax services in SBS; and 4) simplicity of install and ease of management are important. Based on this information, which of the following items could be implemented or utilized with the SBS Premium server?

A. Hardware-based firewall, which you will configure to sit behind ISA, and split to a separate server.

B. Old fax/scan/print device with no drivers past Windows 98.

C. New laser printer with drivers for XP.

D. Hardware-based firewall, which you will configure to sit ahead of ISA on the SBS server.

E. Macintosh notebook running OS 10.

F. Linux machine running spam filter software.

Question #18

The ABC Records Company warehouses paper records for several local firms in the area. Each customer has a separate space; the location of each file box is marked with the date of arrival. Currently they have high-speed Internet access in the office and use an Excel spreadsheet to keep track of the location of each file box. They have five Windows 2000 desktop machines and a single NT 4.0 server that is used for file and print services. The owner would like to have secure remote access from home to the server. The four office workers currently open and close the Excel spreadsheet and save it. The office workers would like to be able to share the information and be able to look back at the changes made to the spreadsheet and know who made them. They recently have had to restore the Excel spreadsheet from tape backup and had to key back in the entire day of recent arrivals. The owner wants to implement the most cost-effective solution. What would solve both issues?

A. Replace the NT 4.0 Server with Server 2003 Standard Edition.

B. Replace the NT 4.0 Sever with SBS 2003 Standard and configure SharePoint.

C. Replace the NT 4.0 Server with SBS 2003 Premium and configure SharePoint.

D. Setup SharePoint and Routing and Remote Access Service (RRAS) on the NT 4.0 Server.

Question #19

The local police station has a small network comprised of two Windows 2000 Pro workstations, three XP Pro workstations, and one XP home laptop workstation the chief uses. They have a 1.5MB Internet connection and a DSL modem shared by one of the XP workstations.

They have been asked by the state to secure the network and been advised that the current method is not acceptable. They need to have a true firewall. They must also be able to log all the login activity to the network. The chief mentions it would be nice if they could have their own e-mail there. He says he has changed Internet providers three times in the last year and each time has to set up new e-mail accounts. He also tells you that he only has 30 days to comply with the rules or his office will be fined $1000/day. What solution makes the most sense?

A. Put in a new SBS 2003 Standard Server. Upgrade his XP home laptop to XP Pro. Join all the machines to the new domain. Set up SharePoint.

B. Put in a new SBS 2003 Premium Server. Upgrade his XP home laptop to XP Pro. Join all the machines to the new domain.

C. Set up Server 2003 with ISA 2004. Upgrade the XP home laptop to XP Pro. Join all the machines to the new domain.

D. Set up SBS 2003 Premium Server. Join the machines with Pro to the new domain and tell the chief he needs to buy a new laptop.

Question #20

You are the consultant for Chelsea, Inc., a Title company. Chelsea, Inc. requests a proposal for implementing a client server network; specifically, they need to implement fault-tolerant document sharing. Users need to access shares from any location within the network without having to remember drive letters or share locations. Chelsea, Inc. uses a third-party application that only works with UNC path names. You propose Small Business Server 2003 and a second Windows Server 2003 file server. For the requested shared solution, what do you propose? (Select the best choice.)

A. Configuring Windows SharePoint Service

B. Configuring a stand-alone distributed file system (DFS) root

C. Configuring a domain-based DFS root

D. Configuring RAID 1

E. Configuring RAID 5

Question #21

You are both a CPA (accountant) and in-house IT resource at the regional accounting firm. You are a proud member of the Microsoft Professional Accounting Network (MPAN) program which is how you heard about the Small Business Specialist Community. You have five Windows Server 2003 servers that support over 125 users using laptops and desktops running Windows XP Pro SP2. Two of the aforementioned servers act as DNS servers and provide DNS database redundancy and performance enhancements. One such server is configured as the primary DNS server; the other server is the secondary DNS server machine (both of these servers act as Domain Controllers). Your specific need is to perform zone updates from either DNS server. You will complete this task with which of the following approaches?

1. In the Properties dialog box for the Zone, select the General tab and click the Change button beside the Zone Type. Select the Option to store the Zone in Active Directory.

2. In the Properties dialog box for the Zone, select the Zone Type and click the Change button. Select the Active Directory-Integrated option.

3. In the Properties dialog box for the DNS server, select the Zone Type tab and click the Change button. Select the Active Directory-Integration option.

4. In the Properties dialog box for the DNS server, select the Zone Type tab and click the Change button. Select the option to store the zone in Active Directory.

Question #22

You are the founder, owner and network administrator for your own privately-held company. The server machines have been upgraded to Microsoft Windows Server 2003 and the client computers are running Microsoft Windows XP Professional. The DNS service has been installed on a member server within the company domain. You want to provide fault tolerance for your zone so that name resolution can still continue if the DNS server goes offline. To accomplish this goal, you wisely plan to add another DNS server to the domain. However, you realize that you need to configure the new DNS server role in the appropriate role. How will you accomplish this?

1. Configure the new server as a Master name server.

2. Configure the new server as a secondary DNS server.

3. Configure the new server as a caching-only server.

4. Configure the new server as a DNS forwarder.

Question #23

You are the network administrator for the Total Supply Company (with over 300 employees). All of the legacy Windows NT and Windows 2000 Server servers have been upgraded to Microsoft Windows Server 2003. You have delegated the marketing.totalsupply.net zone to another DNS server on the network. You want to ensure that the name server for totalsupply.net is notified anytime a new authoritative name server is added to the marketing.totalsupply.net zone. What will you do at this point?

1. Configure all zones to store information within Active Directory.

2. Configure a DNS server within the bayside.net zone to be a secondary server to the sales.bayside.net zone.

3. Configure a stub zone on the DNS server within the parent domain.

4. Using the Name Servers tab from the sales.bayside.net zone, configure the DNS server to notify the DNS server in the parent domain of any changes.

Question #24

You are the network administrator for your professional services company. All of the servers run Windows Server 2003 and the client computers run Windows XP Professional. You have installed the DNS service on SMB-DNS1. You want to configure this DNS server to forward queries that it cannot resolve to another DNS server on the network. You log on to SMB-DNS1 using a user account that belongs to the DNS Admins group. When you display the Forwarders tab in the properties of SMB-SRV1 (the root of the AD forest DC) in the DNS console, the option to enable forwarders is unavailable. What should you do?

1. Configure SMB-DNS1 as a secondary DNS server.

2. Enable Round Robin on SMB-DNS1.

3. Add your user account to the Enterprise Admins group.

4. Delete the root DNS zone on SMB-DNS1.

Question #25

You are the network administrator for the Klondike Creek Inc. All servers are running Microsoft Windows Server 2003. Klondike has five offices located in different parts of the United States, typically in mountain regions (including Alaska). The central office in Seattle hosts the primary DNS server. All remote office locations have their own DNS servers configured as secondary servers. The offices are currently connected by slow WAN links, with no plans to upgrade them. The annual IT capital budget allows for a second DNS server at each of the locations. However, you do not want any more traffic generated from zone transfers on the WAN or the local networks. What should you do?

1. Configure the new server machines as Standard secondary DNS servers.

2. Configure the new server machines as Standard primary DNS servers.

3. Configure the new server machines as Caching-only servers.

4. Configure the new server machines as Master name servers.

Question #26

CoolBeans, Inc. is expanding their office space from 6 Windows XP Pro SP2 desktops and adding 8 new hires and Windows XP Pro SP2 workstations. The network has a single SBS 2003 server and a hardware firewall. The office is set up in an old building where you have to traverse several corners and hallways to get to the individual offices. In the past, the administrator didn't mind manually updating the workstations, but realizes that this is becoming too much work and wants to automate the Windows Update process. Client workstations need to receive their updates in a timely manner and should not receive patches that are not necessary. CoolBeans, Inc. is on a metered Internet connection and wants to use the least amount of bandwidth. How should the administrator implement this?

A. Set all client workstations to automatically download all new patches in the Security Center every night at 3 a.m. and select "download updates for me, but let me chose to install them" and then remote to the system once a week and approve the downloads.

B. Configure Automatic Updates on the SBS 2003 Server and select "notify me but don't automatically download or install them," and approve the updates once a week.

C. Install SUS on the SBS 2003 Server, set it to download the updates locally and edit the GPO for the client computers to download updates from the SBS Server.

D. Install MBSA (Microsoft Security Baseline Analyzer) and configure it to run the Security scan once a day and to automatically download required updates. Edit the GPO for the client computer to download updates from the SBS server.

Question #27

You are the administrator for a national defense contracting firm. The firm uses Windows SBS 2003 Premium. There are 15 Windows XP Professional computers in the office and 43 Windows XP Professional laptops. Your firm got a new contract and the server now contains highly sensitive data and all communications should be secured when needed. How should you configure the server? (select all that apply)

A. Assign the Server IPSec (Request Security) policy to the server

B. Assign the Secure Server IPSec (Require Security) policy to the server

C. Assign the Server IPSec (Request Security) policy to the client computers

D. Assign the Client IPSec (Respond only) policy to the client computers

E. Assign the Client IPSec (Respond only) policy to the server

Question #28

You administer an SBS server for a small travel agency in town. There are 60 Windows XP Professional computers, 3 Windows 2000 Professional machines, a color laser printer and 12 black and white laser printers. The travel agency is run by the owner, who employs several travel agents, three professional ad writers, and two marketing people. The owner doesn't want the travel agents using the color laser printer, but uses it for herself, the ad writers and marketing people. How will you configure printer permissions on the color printer?

A. Create a color printer security group. Add the owner, ad writers group and marketing group to the color printer security group. Grant the Allow Print Permissions to the color printer group and select Deny for the Everyone group.

B. Create a color printer distribution group. Add the owner, ad writers group and marketing group to the color printer distribution group. Grant the Allow Print Permissions to the color printer group and remove the Everyone group.

C. Create a color printer security group. Add the owner, ad writers group and marketing group to the color printer security group. Grant the Allow Print Permissions to the color printer group and remove the Everyone group

D. Create a color printer security group. Add the owner, ad writers group and travel agents group to the color printer security group. Grant the Allow Print Permissions to the color printer group and remove the Everyone group

Question #29

The Sinclair Group uses SBS 2003 Standard edition, and the office manager is in charge of managing the server. There are 23 Windows XP Professional computers on the network and employees are split up into different security groups. There are some folders that the office manager wants to be accessible by everyone, but only he should be able to add, remove or edit files in those folders. The office manager creates the "Company" share and wants to assign only the least required permissions. The office manager user account is in the office manager group. Which share permissions should be assigned?

A. Assign the Allow – Full Control permission to the Office Manager group for the Company share. Assign the Allow – Read permission to the Everyone group for the Company share.

B. Assign the Allow – Change permission to the Office Manager group for the Company share. Assign Allow – Read permission to the Everyone group for the Company share.

C. Assign the Allow – Full Control permission to the Office Manager group for the Company share. Assign the Allow Read & Execute permission for the Company share.

D. Assign the Allow – Change permission to the Office Manager group for the Company share. Assign the Allow – Read & Execute permission to the Everyone group for the Company share.

Question #30

You manage an SBS 2003 server for a small medical office. Due to government regulations that need to be complied with, you are now asked to install ISA Server 2000. The medical office is running a custom application that allows access to a special medical database over the Internet. This custom application uses port 4008 (TCP) to communicate. You install ISA Server 2000 and lose the ability to communicate with the remote database server. What should you do? (select all that apply)

A. Create a port proxy rule for access though port 4008

B. Create a protocol rule for access through port 4008

C. Create a port protocol definition

D. Create a port proxy forwarding definition

E. Create an IPSec policy for the custom application

Question #31

You manage a network consisting of a SBS 2003 server and 43 Windows XP Professional client computers. You check the security log in the event viewer and see several endless denied log on requests on a valid user account. This appears to be the work of a malicious intruder, attempting to gain access to the network. The user account "lsmith" belongs to Linda who should never be prevented from logging on to the network, even after you implement new security measures. You want to accomplish this with the least amount of administrative effort on your part. What should you do?

A. Set the Account Lockout Policy to 5 failed logons

B. Delete Linda's user account and create a new user account for her

C. Rename Linda's user account to "l_sm1tH"

D. Disable Linda's user account and have her use your account until the failed attempts stop.

Question #32

You are the administrator of a small law firm. The firm has an SBS 2003 Server and 12 Windows XP Professional laptops. There are 15 Windows XP workstations used by paralegal staff. Several attorneys travel nationwide for high-profile cases and are out of the office for weeks at a time. The owner of the firm does not allow the use of Remote Web Workplace. Attorneys need to have secure access to data on the server. You ran the Remote Access Configuration wizard, but attorneys with their hectic schedule don't want to be bothered with client VPN installation instructions. You have enabled Outlook Web Access and RPC over HTTP. The attorneys need to have access ASAP. What will be the easiest way with the least amount of effort for the users to install the VPN connection?

A. Run the Assign Applications wizard and assign the VPN client to the laptops. Next time when users are in the office, the client will automatically be pushed out.

B. Run the Create Remote Connection Disk in Server Management. Copy the file to a zip file and e-mail it to the attorneys

C. Run the Create Remote Connection Disk and overnight the floppy to the attorneys

D. Create a GPO that will assign the VPN client automatically next time an attorney connects their laptop in the office.

Question #33

You are the consultant at a non-profit research group. The non-profit has nine Windows XP Professional computers in a peer-to-peer configuration and will be adding four additional computers. Staff usually spends numerous hours on the Internet conducting research. They have a dial-up connection. Security is not a concern as much as being able to retrieve Internet research pages as fast as possible. Their budget was not approved for a faster Internet connection, but was approved for SBS 2003 Premium Edition and several hours of your consulting service. What would benefit the non-profit most?

A. Join the computer to the domain, install ISA 2000 in firewall mode on the SBS 2003 Premium Server, and install the firewall client on the server and the client workstations.

B. Join the client computers to the domain and install ISA 2000 in caching mode and increase the HTTP caching TTL on the SBS Premium Server.

C. Join the client computers to the domain and install ISA 2000 in caching mode on the SBS 2003 Premium Server and install the caching client on all client computers.

D. Join the clients to the domain, copy the ISA 2000 CD into a shared folder in clientapps\ and run the Assign Applications wizard.

Question #34

Your company has one SBS 2003 server, 17 Windows XP Pro SP2 client workstations, and 11 laptops with Windows XP Pro SP2. The laptop users bring their laptops to office meetings at least twice a month. You have configured SUS for Windows Updates and want to ensure that users do not download updates themselves; you especially want to prevent the laptop users from downloading and installing security updates that are not tested and approved. You decide to use Group Policy to ensure this policy. Where do you configure these settings?

A. Open the User configuration\Administrative Templates\Windows Components\Windows Update and enter the URL of the SUS server under **Specify intranet Microsoft update service location**

B. Open the Computer Configuration\Administrative Templates\Win-dows Components\Windows Update and enter the URL of the SUS server under **Specify intranet Microsoft update service location**

C. Open the User configuration\Administrative Templates\Windows Com-ponents\Windows Update and select and enable **Configure Automatic Updates** with automatic updating set to 5.

D. Open the Computer Configuration\Administrative Templates\Win-dows Components\Windows Update and select and enable **Configure Automatic Updates** with automatic updating set to 5.

Question #35

Realty Inc. has SBS 2003 that is being used for faxing, e-mail, printing, file server and has the real estate LOB application installed on it. There are 40 agents in the office who use Outlook 2003 and 30 agents who remote in with their laptops. Most of those agents use Outlook Express for e-mail, but some use Outlook Mobile Access on their SmartPhones. Users have also been told that they can access Outlook Web Access by typing http://www.realtyinc.com/exchange in any browser. You just purchased a new hardware firewall and must ensure security but more importantly, that e-mail workflow will not be interrupted. What ports should be opened on the firewall? (select all that apply)

A. 80

B. 25

C. 110

D. 443

E. 4125

Question #36

You are a network administrator for your Springer Spaniels Limited. The network consists of server computers running Microsoft Windows Server 2003 and client computers running Microsoft Windows XP Professional. The DNS service is installed on SPRINGER1. It hosts a zone file called contoso.com. SPRINGER2 is configured as an FTP server to accommodate customer's large file requests. The following resource records exist in the zone file for SPRINGER2.

- Host (A)

- Alias (CNAME)

- Service Location (SRV)

- Well Known Service (WKS)

You decide to change SPRINGER2 to use Transmission Control Protocol (TCP) port 1022 as the control port for FTP. You need to ensure that the port is defined correctly in DNS. Which resource record should you update?

1. Host (A)

2. Alias (CNAME)

3. Service Locator (SRV)

4. Well Known Service (WKS)

Question #37

You are the network administrator for Springer Spaniels Limited. You have installed the DNS service on all the Windows Server 2003 domain controllers in the SPRINGERS domain. Zone information is stored within Active Directory. You want to verify that zone data is being updated between DNS servers. Which tool can you use to verify this?

1. DNS management console

2. DNS Debug logging

3. Replication Monitor

4. System Monitor

Question #38

All servers at Springer Spaniels Unlimited are running Microsoft Windows Server 2003. Client computers are running Windows XP Professional. You are the network administrator at this fine company. You have just finished installing the DNS service on a Windows Server 2003 member server in the springers.net domain. You need to add a record into the zone file to identify the mail server in the domain. What should you do?

1. Create an MX record on the DNS server.
2. Create a PTR record on the DNS server.
3. Create a CNAME record on the DNS server.
4. Create an A record on the DNS server.

Question #39

You are the network administrator for an insurance company, Snapper Inc. Client computers are running Microsoft Windows XP Professional SP2. You have upgraded all servers to Microsoft Windows Server 2003. You are trying to determine the hostname associated with the IP address of 192.168.0.33 using the NSLookup command from SnapW2, but you are unsuccessful. You know the IP address is assigned with SnapW1 and you can successfully resolve other hostnames on the network using this command. What is most likely the cause of the problem?

1. There is no A record for SnapW2.
2. There is no PTR record for SnapW1.
3. There is no PTR record for SnapW2.
4. There is no A record for SnapW1.

Question #40

You are the network administrator for the Springer Spaniels Limited with the domain controllers running Microsoft Windows Server 2003 and the client computers running Microsoft Windows XP Professional. A user reports that she is having problems resolving certain hostnames to IP addresses at her laptop. You recently made changes to some resource records in the zone file. Because you are an experienced SMB technical professional, you draw on your experience. You suspect there are outdated entries in the client resolver cache. Note that no other users are reporting this problem. What should you do?

1. Use the ipconfig /flushdns command on the client computer.
2. Uninstall the DNS server service.

3. Delete the cache.dns file.

4. Use the Clear Cache option from the Action menu within the DHCP console.

Question #41

You are the administrator for a glass manufacturing company. You performed an upgrade from Windows NT 4.0 to SBS 2003 and added a second Windows Server 2003 server. The client computers were also upgraded from Windows 98 to Windows XP Professional. The application that runs the glass cutting equipment, which was previously installed on all the Win98 computers, has been removed and is now installed on the Windows Server 2003 computer. The client computers now use Terminal Services to access the application on the server. When clients connect to the application and try to use full-screen mode, it only opens in a small window on their monitor. You test the terminal services connection and find out that this only happens with this application, not with any others. In order for employees to effectively use the application, it must show in full screen mode. What can be done to fix this?

A. Configure the application to run in NT 4.0 compatibility mode on the Windows Server 2003 computer

B. Configure the application to run in 640 x 480 screen resolution

C. Run Terminal Services in Windows 98 compatibility mode when connecting to the application

D. Configure the application to run in 256 colors

Question #42

You are the administrator of Widgets, Inc. The network consists of one SBS 2003 Standard Edition server, a Windows 2003 server and sixty Windows XP Professional client computers. The Windows 2003 server is configured as a file server. The file server has five hard disks, Disk 0, Disk 1 through Disk 4, and runs a RAID 5 array on Disk 2, Disk 3 and Disk 4. The system partition is located on Disk 1 and mirrored to Disk 0. Each hard disk has 300 GB of space. There are sixty users on the network and you need to implement disk quotas so everyone gets the same amount of storage space on the volume. What steps should you take? (select all that apply)

A. Format the volume with NTFS

B. Enable FRS

C. Configure disk quotas to be 10 GB per user

D. Configure disk quotas to be 15 GB per user

Question #43

You are the consultant to a call center in town. The network is set up with one SBS 2003 Standard Edition server and four Windows 2003 member servers, all located in separate branch offices and connected with a 128Kbps WAN link to the main office where the SBS domain controller is located. Users come in at the same time in the mornings and complain about the time it takes to log on to the domain. How can you fix this in the most cost-effective way?

A. Create a connection bridge between the servers

B. Create a sub-site and site link for each connection

C. Add the Domain controller role to each Windows Server 2003

D. Install compression technology

Question #44

You administer a Windows SBS 2003 network for a regional sales office of herbal products. The server is configured with two NIC's and a hardware firewall. There are 34 agents out in the field with Windows XP Professional SP1 computers and 22 with Windows 2000 Professional SP2 computers. Sales agents need to securely connect to the network for about 10 minutes a day to transfer data. Agents are calling to say that they are unable to connect via VPN to the server. There is no way of telling at what time agents will connect and you want to change current practices. How can you remedy this situation?

A. Assign Group Policy to the sales agents and specify a VPN logon time

B. Add additional VPN ports in RAS

C. Configure the hardware firewall for multiplexing

D. Upgrade the amount of bandwidth available from your ISP

Question #45

You administer a network consisting of an SBS 2003 Server Premium and four Windows Servers 2003. The SBS server is located at the main office site in Denver, CO and the member servers are located in branch offices in Orlando, Dallas, and San Jose. Users from all branch offices regularly connect to the main office Windows 2003 member server named HQ, which is configured as a terminal server to run an application. The client computers deployed all have Windows XP Professional with the latest service packs and patches installed. One new user in the Dallas office is unable to print reports from the application on HQ to his local printer. Other users do not have this problem and can print from HQ to their respective client computers. How can this be fixed?

A. Add the user to the Remote Desktop Users group on HQ

B. Configure automatic printer redirection

C. Configure manual printer redirection

D. Configure bi-directional printing

Question #46

You administer a network consisting of an SBS 2003 Server Premium and four Windows Servers 2003. The SBS server is located at the main office site in Denver together with three Windows 2003 member servers. All Windows member servers have terminal services enabled and are frequently used by remote employees. What is the most convenient way to connect to terminal services on member servers?

A. Type *mstsc* into the command line and then enter the IP address of the server in the Remote Desktop Connection box

B. Use Remote Web Workplace and then select to "connect to my computer at work" and then select the member server you want to connect to

C. Open a remote Desktop Connection

D. Use the Terminal Services client

Question #47

You are the administrator of a small software development company. Currently there are eight Windows XP Professional computers in a peer-to-peer configuration. You decide that you will benefit greatly from a client/server environment that facilitates collaboration, e-mail and faxing. Your company develops software that needs a dedicated SQL server. How can you implement this in the most cost-effective way?

A. Install SBS 2003 Premium, Windows Server 2003 Standard and SQL 2000

B. Install SBS 2003 Premium

C. Install SBS 2003 Standard, Windows Server 2003 Standard and SQL 2000

D. Install Windows Server 2003 Standard and SQL 2000

Question #48

You are the administrator for a company with a SBS 2003 domain. The domain also has four additional domain controllers, two Windows 2003 Domain controllers and two Windows 2000 domain controllers, and 60 Windows XP Professional computers spread over four branch locations, all connected with high-speed broadband. You would like to securely manage all the domain controllers remotely from your office in one desktop monitor without having to log in and out of the remote domain controllers. Which tool will let you manage the domain controllers cost effectively and with the least administrative effort?

A. Remote Desktop

B. Remote Assistance

C. SMS (System Management Server)

D. Telnet

Question #49

You manage a SBS 2003 network with two additional Windows Server 2003 domain controllers. They are called SBS1, Server2 and Server3. Fifty-five clients use applications on all three domain controllers. You make a full backup of each domain controller every Friday and run differential backups Monday through Thursday. On Wednesday, the hard drive on Server 2 seizes. You have a spare on hand and install the new disk immediately. What will you have to do to get the server back into the most recent operable state?

A. Start Server2 in Directory Services Restore mode

B. Start Server2 in safe mode

C. Recreate all volumes as they were on the previous disk

D. Hit the F2 key in the text mode installation

E. Authoritatively restore the system state data from the full backup

F. Non-authoritatively restore the system state data from the full backup

G. Do a full restore from Friday

H. Restore the Tuesday differential backup

Question #50

You are the administrator at Paletti Bicycles, Inc. and you just added an additional Windows Server 2003 named TS1 to the network using the add Server Computer wizard to your SBS 2003 network. You install the Terminal Server role on the server and load the multi-session application. You send an e-mail to the RemoteSales group outlining the steps of connecting to the terminal server via Remote Web Workplace. Twenty minutes later, users are calling you, stating that they get this message: "The local policy of this system does not permit you to logon interactively" and are unable to logon. What should you do to enable the RemoteSales group to log on with the least amount of permissions?

A. Add all users to the Power Users group in the Domain

B. Add all users to the Domain Admins group in the Domain

C. Add the RemoteSales group to the Power Users group in the Domain

D. Grant the RemoteSales group "Log on locally" rights on TS1 using a GPO

    E. Add the RemoteSales group to the Remote Desktop Users group on TS1

    F. Add the Mobile User group to the Remote Operators group

Question #51

You are the network administrator for Springer Spaniels Limited and of course all servers are running Windows Server 2003. The network has both WINS and non-WINS clients. Four of the six subnets contain WINS servers. Several users report that they are unable to browse hosts on other subnets. At first blush, it appears the malady only impacts non-WINS clients. What should you do?

1. Configure a DHCP relay agent on each subnet.

2. Configure static mappings for the non-WINS clients.

3. Install a WINS proxy on each subnet that does not have a local WINS server.

4. Configure replication between the three WINS servers.

Question #52

You are the network administrator for Springer Spaniels Limited. Unless otherwise instructed, the networks are running Windows server 2003. The network consists of several subnets. All clients are WINS-enabled and capable of updating their records dynamically. Each of the subnets has its own WINS server. One of the subnets contains a UNIX server. Hosts on this local subnet can communicate with the UNIX server; however, hosts on other subnets are unsuccessful. Clients can resolve NetBIOS names for hosts on other subnets. It is you job to make sure that clients on all subnets be able to resolve the NetBIOS names of the UNIX server. What are you planning to do?

1. Configure static mappings for the UNIX server.

2. Configure the WINS servers to back up their local databases.

3. On each of the subnets, configure a secondary WINS server on each subnet.

4. Configure the WINS servers as replication partners.

Question #53

You create a small business network, using Windows Server 2003 and Windows XP Pro in a virtual environment using Microsoft Virtual PC. This is for research, design and testing purposes before deploying the solution in the "real world" at a customer site. The server machine acts as the domain controller running Active Directory and has the DHCP service. You're very pleased with the outcomes from your testing and you want to recreate the exact DHCP server configuration in a production environment as fast as possible. Select the best answers.

1. Backup the current DHCP database (virtual environment) and then restore it to the DHCP server in the production environment.

2. Replicate the current DHCP database from the virtual environment to the production environment using the reconcile command.

3. Replicate the current DHCP database and then copy-and-paste the log file to the production server running DHCP.

4. Backup the current DHCP log file and copy it from the virtual environment to the production environment.

Question #54

Springer Spaniels Limited has a network running Windows Small Business Server 2003 R2 as its network infrastructure. Many of the dog trainers (20) work remotely and to best utilize the Microsoft CRM 3.0 SBE application, they established a VPN connection via RRAS PPTP. You limit the DHCP scope on the server to 25 IP addresses due to the address limit on the network firewall. You add ten new clients to the SBS network. The dog trainers report that their laptops can only connect to the SBS 2003 network intermittently from the Internet. The users also report that they can only connect to the Internet intermittingly and your research so this is never more than 15 computers at a time. You have reason to believe the no more than 10 have every connected remotely at the same time. You need to ensure that all computers can always connect to the Internet with restricting access to the RAS client computers. What should you do?

1. Shorten the DHCP lease time to 60-minutes

2.   Change DHCP in RAS to static scope

3.   Set up new client computers with reserved addresses

4.   Change the DNS server entry on new computers.

Question #55

Springer Spaniels Unlimited is running Windows Server 2003 with Active Directory. The server is configured with a static IP address, subnet mask and default gateway. The DHCP service is installed from the Manage Your Server MMC. Checking the Services MMC, you see that the DHCP service is will start automatically. Finally, you create a DHCP scope with a range of static IP addresses excluded (including the server IP address).   Your users have a mixture of Windows XP Pro and Windows 2000 Professional client computers. These client computes are configured to receive their addresses dynamically. After starting one of the client computers, you notice that it isn't receiving a dynamically assigned IP address from the server machine. What should you do?

1.   Fix the incorrect IP address in the client computer reservation in the DHCP MMC.

2.   Configure the scope in the DHCP MMC with the proper IP address.

3.   Run arp –a from the command prompt at the server.

4.   Authorize the DHCP server in Active Directory.

Question #56

As the administrator of AdvantaCorp., you manage a SBS 2003 server and 35 client workstations with XP Professional. Every year, AdvantaCorp hires 5 college students to help over the summer and also hires students throughout the year. Students usually stay on for specific assingments only. Since the students are temporary, you want to secure and only allow the minimum access to folders that is required, as well as enforce disk quota limits. What would be the most efficient way to do this?

A.   Create a user account using the Add User wizard. Create a security group called "SummerHelp" and enter quoata limits. Set this user account up as a template.

B. Create a user template and create a security group called "Summer-Help." Add quota restrictions. Use the Add User wizard to create the new accounts.

C. Create a security group called "SummerHelp" and add a quota. Use the Add User wizard and assign the new user to the security group.

D. Create a user template and create a distribution group called "SummerHelp." Add quota restrictions. Use the Add User wizard to create the new accounts.

Question #57

You are the new administrator at AdvantaCorp. The company has a SBS 2003 server and two member servers and 35 client workstations running XP Pro. The company uses shared folders and mapped drives. Users connect to a member server to which you just installed Terminal Services. About four months later users can no longer gain access to the terminal server. What should you do?

A. Deploy Terminal Server licensing server on the member server in per user mode.

B. Push out terminal server user licenses with a GPO

C. Add terminal server user licenses on the SBS server with the Add license wizard

D. Deploy an activated terminal server domain license server on the SBS server

Question #58

Springers Ltd. consists of an SBS server, a Windows 2000 member server, 5 NT 4.0 workstations, 4 Windows 2000 Professional and 7 Windows XP Pro clients. Springers uses software that requires clients to communicate using NetBIOS names. You also need to be able to use FQDNs. You want to make sure you have fault tolerance for the FQDN and NetBIOS name resolution. How can you implement this? (multiple choice)

A. Configure each client as a proxy client

B. Configure the member server as a proxy client

C. Configure the member server as a DNS server

D. Configure the member server as a WINS server

E. Configure SBS 2003 as a proxy client

F. Configure SBS 2003 as a DNS server

G. Configure SBS 2003 as a WINS server

H. Configure the DHCP scope on the member server

I. Configure the DHCP scope on SBS 2003

Question #59

DentalTech.Inc is hiring you to perform an upgrade of their current SBS 2000 server to SBS 2003 Standard Edition. The company is using Exchange to host their e-mail and ISA 2000 as a firewall. In preparation for the upgrade you should: (multiple choice)

A. Scan the M:/ drive

B. Install ISA Service Pack 1

C. Remove discontinued Exchange Server components

D. Uninstall ISA

E. Disable the external NIC

F. Reformat the system drive

Question #60

You are the administrator of Kabrifam, Inc and just installed a new SBS 2003 server. There are 20 users on the network using XP Pro machines. In the past, users have inadvertently overwritten or deleted documents which were stored in the My Documents folder. You want to implement a fault tolerance solution and an easy retrieval method for files and folders stored in the My Documents folder by users. What should you do?

A. Enable shadow copies

B. Run the "Configure My Documents Redirection" wizard on the clients

C. Use a GPO to redirect the folders to the user shares on the SBS server

D. Run the "Configure My Documents Redirection" wizard on the server

E. On the client machines, go to the My Documents folder properties and change the target folder.

Question #61

Kabrifam, Inc just completed an upgrade from SBS 4.5 to SBS 2003. There are 12 XP Pro clients, 4 NT 4.0 workstations and 4 Windows 98 clients. After the upgrade users on the NT workstations and Windows 98 machines complain that they cannot logon to the network. You should:

A. Make the SBS 2003 server a WINS server

B. Release and renew the IP address on the NT 4.0 and Windows 98 clients

C. Type *flush dns* on the command prompt on the NT 4.0 and Windows 98 clients

D. Install Dsclient.exe on the NT 4.0 and Windows 98 clients

E. Configure DNS recursion

Question #62

Kabrifam, Inc. has a SBS 2003 server called Kabri1. The company has been expanding and decides to add another server to the network. Kabrifam purchases a Windows 2003 server license and has the local computer store build a white box server. After installing the server operating system and naming the server Kabri2 you want to join the new member server to the domain. What steps do you have to perform? (multiple choice)

A. Run the client computer wizard and add the server to the domain

B. Run the server computer wizard and add the server to the domain

C. Run http://kabri2/connectcomputer on Kabri1

D. Run http://kabri1/connectcomputer on Kabri2

E. Run dcpromo on Kabri2 and opt to become a child domain

F. Run dcpromo on Kabri1 and join Kabri2 to the SBS domain

Question #63

The Legal Aid non-profit group currently runs on a SBS 2000 server and seven Windows 98 client computers. Even though funding is short, due to compliance regulations they are forced to upgrade the server software to a new operating system. Currently the server has 256mb RAM and a Pentium 450 mhz processor and a 4 GB hard drive. There is no funding for new hardware in sight and the non-profit has to choose the best option, but does not want to lose the e-mail and fax capabilities. What should you upgrade to?

A. Upgrade the server to Windows XP Professional

B. Upgrade the server to Windows SBS 2003 Standard Edition

C. Upgrade the server to Windows SBS 2003 Premium Edition

D. Upgrade the server to Windows Server 2003

Question #64

You are the administrator of SMB Nation and have just purchased the upgrade CD from Windows SBS 2000 to SBS 2003 Standard Edition. Currently you are running Exchange Server 2000, IIS, ISA Server 2000, Terminal Server in Application Sharing mode DHCP and DNS. You plan to perform an in-place upgrade. What must you do to ensure a successful upgrade? (select all that apply)

A. Exmerge all mailboxes from Exchange and export all mailbox rules

B. Uninstall ISA Server 2000

C. Uninstall IIS

D. Disbable DNS and DHCP

E. Uninstall Terminal Server

F. Uninstall Exchange Server components that are incompatible with SBS 2003

G. Install Windows SBS 2000 SP1

Question #65

Trial Attorneys, Inc. just purchased a new server and would like SBS 2003 Standard Edition installed. The server contains four disks and you have to think of the best fault tolerance option for the attorneys. When attorneys prepare for trial, there cannot be any interruption or slow down on the system. After formatting all four drives with NTFS, you decide to use disk 0 as the system partition and use the remaining three disks for fault tolerance. What should you do? (select all that apply)

A. Configure two disks to a RAID 0 volume

B. Configure two disks as a RAID 1 volume

C. Configure three disks as a RAID 1 volume

D. Configure two disks as a RAID 5 volume

E. Configure three disks as a RAID 5 volume

F. Convert all disks to dynamic disks

G. Configure one disk as an extended partition

H. Configure one disk for Volume Shadow Copy repository only

Question #66

In the spirit of customer service, you've added a WifFi HotSpot router over the weekend to your espresso café lobby. This is connected to the same subnet as the Windows Small Business Server 2003 network you run for internal business operations purposes. This Monday afternoon you went to a local big box retailer and purchased a new laptop computer for a assistant book keeper. You attempt to connect the computer to the SBS 2003 network, over the wired LAN, via the Connect Computer Web-based approach but the Web page returns a 404 error (which means can't be found). None one else is experiencing computer usage problems. What do you believe has happened?

1. The WifFi router is running a DHCP service on the same subnet as the SBS 2003 server machine.

2. The SBS 2003 server machine has shut down its DNS server service.

3. The SBS 2003 server machine has shut down its DHCP service.

4. The new laptop can easily use Wifi network instead of the SBS 2003 network.

Question #67

You are an aspiring Small Business Specialist and you are soliciting business from a new account. This customer site runs SCO UNIX and plans to slowly transition to SBS 2003 (perhaps waiting for the next release known by the code name Longhorn). You want to better understand how the Windows-based workstations acquire IP addresses. At the Unix command line, what type of service will you view?

1. DHCP

2. BOOTP

3. DNS

4. KILL

Question #68

Arizona Housing Corporation (AHC) has grown rapidly and it is investing in newly created opportunities in India. AHC has opened offices in Delhi, Mumbai and Bangalore. Essentially the firm connects these multiple offices via an over-the-Internet PPTP-based VPN. All servers are Windows Server 2003 standard edition and all users run Windows XP Pro. Back at the home office in Phoenix, you recently terminated your relationship with the local Telco for both voice and Internet connectivity. Instead, you accept the competitive offer from a cable company and you installed the cable modem following the basic configuration sheet. Late that night, you are awakened by a call from Mumbai where one of the users reports that she cannot logon to the HQ server in Phoenix. What do you suspect?

1. The cable company might be blocking port 1720 and other ports related to VPN and PPTP-based communications.

2. The cable modem was configured with port forwarding for the applicable ports

3. The users should upgrade to Windows Vista Business in order to make a VPN-based connection over cable infrastructure.

4. Introducing a cable modem on a network requires you to reconfigure your firewall.

Question #69

You have a Windows Server 2003 server machine with the following static IP address assigned to the internal network adapter card: 131.107.0.2. The Default Gateway is 131.107.0.1. What is the default Subnet Mask for this scenario?

1. 255.255.255.248

2. 255.255.0.0

3. 255.0.0.0

4. 255.255.255.0

Question #70

You are the network administrator at Springer Spaniels Limited and it has a single Active Directory domain (springers.local). The company has its headquarters in Seattle, Washington with offices in London, Tokyo, Lima, Mexico City and New York. You want to apply Group Policy to each of these locations and to the departments that employees belong to (Marketing, Accounting and Finance, Management, Dog Trainers). Select a efficient strategy to accomplish this (select all that apply).

1. Reconfigure the network to have multiple domains (a domain for each location) and use trust relationships to establish company-wide communications.

2. Apply GPOs at each local office using a decentralized management paradigm.

3. Create sites in Active Directory via the Active Directory Sites and Services MMC.

4. Create organizational units (OUs) for each functional department,

5. Apply GPOs to both sites and OUs to achieve the most efficient and effective form of configurations.

Question #71

Race Brook Publishing has 29 Windows XP Pro SP1 client computers, 10 Windows Professional SP3 computers, an SBS 2003 server and 2 Windows 2000 servers on the network. Your boss has asked you to implement standard policy across the network. There is one accounting application that should only be accessed by certain users and others need to have access to different proprietary applications and their respective files. Where can you install the GPMC (Group Policy Management Console) to manage users? (check all that apply)

A. Install the GPMC on the Windows 2000 servers

B. Install the GPMC on a Window 2000 Professional Computer

C. Install the GPMC on the SBS 2003 Server

D. Install the GPMC on a Windows XP Pro client

Question #72

As a promotional gig you give away a 20 hours of free consulting to a non-profit group in town. As you survey their network, you discover that they have ten Windows 95 computers and seven Windows XP Pro Machines. They purchased SBS 2003 Standard and expect you to help them install the server and enable the clients to communicate with the SBS domain. Currently the non-profit uses the sneaker network and wants to implement SBS as their file server and Internet connection with the least amount of your time used. What could you do? (select two)

A. Set up a separate DHCP scope for the Windows 95 clients. Install the Active Directory client extensions on Windows 95 computers and assign static addresses.

B. Set up a separate DHCP scope for the Windows 95 clients. Install the Active Directory server extensions on the Mac clients.

C. Install Active Directory client extensions on the Windows 95 machines.

D. Disable SMB signing on the SBS server.

Question #73

ABC Insurance has one SBS server located in the Headquarters office. They have four additional Windows Server 2003 servers in four branch office locations, connected with a T1. There are 15 client Windows XP Pro client workstations at each location and a backup is performed every night at the Headquarters office. You have been noticing errors in the DNS event log and want to check the SBS 2003 server errors. Which tool should you use?

A. DNS console

B. NSLookup.exe

C. Dcdiag.exe

D. Health Monitor

Question #74

You are the consultant for Travel, Inc., a small travel agency. You just installed SBS 2003 and connected 23 Windows XP Professional workstations and 12 Windows 2000 Professional computers to the network. Employees use e-mail to communicate with clients and the Internet for research. The owner wonders if there is a way to monitor e-mail and web usage inexpensively. He also asks you to check the event logs on a daily basis. How can you configure this with the least amount of administrative effort?

A. Run system monitor and create a base line. Create alert thresholds and set the action to send e-mail when the threshold is exceeded. Write a script to send Exchange and Internet information from the collected logs to the owner.

B. Run the Monitoring Configuration wizard and create custom alert thresholds, and set the actions to send e-mail when a threshold is exceeded. Write a script to send you the daily system event log.

C. Run the Monitoring Configuration wizard and add the owner's user account to the report recipients. Run the Change Alert Notification wizard and attach the system event log files to your e-mail notification.

D. Run the Usage Report wizard and add the owner's user account to the report recipients. Run the Monitoring Configuration Wizard and attach the system event log files to your e-mail notification.

Question #75

You administer a network for a restaurant chain. The main office runs an SBS 2003 server, a Windows Server 2003 and six Windows XP Professional computers. The chain has several branch locations that feed their transactions via Terminal Services into the Windows Server 2003. The server has the restaurant point of sale system installed, and uses a SQL database. The server is configured with three disks. The system sits on disk 0, the SQL database is located on disk 1 and the transaction log is located on disk 2. You run a full backup every two hours. The last full database backup finished at 9 p.m. Transactions are continuing in this sequence:

9:05 p.m. – Transaction 313 starts

9:07 p.m. – Transaction 314 starts

9:08 p.m. – Transaction 315 starts

9:15 p.m. – A differential backup begins

9:17 p.m. – Transaction 316 starts

9.17 p.m. – Transaction 315 commits

9:21 p.m. – Transaction 317 starts

9:22 p.m. – The differential backup ends

9:23 p.m. – Transaction 313 commits

9:25 p.m. – The transaction log backup starts

9:29 p.m. – The transaction log backup ends.

Disk 1 fails at 9:24 p.m. You replace disk 1 and restore the database and transaction log. To what state can you recover the database?

A. To the state at 9 p.m. of the last full database backup

B. To the state at 9 p.m. and all transactions up until 9:24 p.m.

C. To the state where transaction 315 is committed

D. To a state where transactions 313 and 315 are committed

Question # 76

Spanferkel, Inc. is running one SBS 2003 and two Windows Server 2003 Standard Edition Servers and 35 client computers with Windows XP Pro SP2. The Internet connection is a broadband connection, there is a hardware firewall and the SBS server has two NICs installed. Due to construction in the inner city, the consultant has been having a hard time responding in a timely manner to client support requests. The consultant suggests using remote support in SBS 2003 first, before having to come on-site in person. The very next day, the consultant gets a support request call from an employee who is having trouble with his e-mail. You want to start the troubleshooting process remotely. How can remote support be initiated?

A. Ask the employee to send a Remote Assistance invitation via e-mail to your e-mail address.

B. Remote into the SBS Server and offer Remote Assistance to the employee from the Server Management console.

C. From Remote Web Workplace, use the "Download Connection Manager" to connect to the employee's computer.

D. Use PC Anywhere to connect to the employee's computer.

Question #77

Your company has a SBS 2003 server, 15 Windows XP Pro SP1 computers and 9 Windows 98 computers. There is a backup tape drive connected to the server. The Backup is set to run Monday through Thursday as a differential backup at 11 p.m. On Friday, there is a full backup at 11 p.m. On Wednesday the server gets hit with a worm at 4 p.m. Even though quickly contained, it destroys the data to a point where a recovery is the best option. What information will be lost?

A. Monday and Tuesday information will be lost.

B. Monday, Tuesday and Wednesday information will be lost.

C. Only Wednesday information will be lost.

D. Tuesday and Wednesday information will be lost.

Question #78

You are the office manager at Fishhooks, Inc. in Florida. Your company receives the latest fishing reports from all major fishing locations on a daily basis via fax. The company uses SBS 2003 primarily as a file and print server. The SBS server has a dial-up modem and two NICs installed. In the past you printed out a report for every employee and put it on their desk. At times, users would misplace their report so they had to make additional copies, which interrupted the workflow. You want to stop using all this paper and find a better solution so employees will not lose their copy of the fishing report and have it at their fingertips at any time. What would be the easiest way to accomplish this?

A. Configure the SBS fax service to route the fax to a shared folder on the network

B. Configure the SBS fax service to print the report at each user's local printer

C. Configure the SBS fax service to route the fax to the SharePoint fax folder

D. Configure the SBS fax service to route the fax to each user's My Document folder.

Question #79

You are the administrator of Stockbridge Construction Co. There are 20 Windows XP Pro clients on the network and one SBS 2003 server that is used as a file server and application server. The server has three volumes: Volume 1 holds all the by-default installed SBS shares, Volume 2 holds the applications and Volume 3 holds the Data share. In the past, users have been storing their documents in the My Documents folder on the desktop despite having been told to store documents on a network share called Data on the server. This has resulted in lost and overwritten documents that have not been backed up. You are thinking about redirecting the users' My Documents folders to a share on the server to be on the safe side. How can you accomplish this? (select all that apply)

A. Set the Group Policy in User Configuration\Administration \Redirect-Documents to point to the Data Share

B. Set the Group Policy in User Configuration\Administrative Temp-lates\ Desktop\Prohibit user from changing My Documents path to enabled and configure it to point to the Data share.

C. Run the My Document Redirect wizard in the Server Management console and select the Data share.

D. Enable Shadow Copies on the Volume where the Data share resides.

Question #80

You are the administrator of a regional start-up cosmetics sales office. The office runs on SBS 2003 server and most company staff is working outside sales and on the road most of the time. Sales agents want to be able to access their e-mail, shared folders and personal data on the server. Sales Agents want to know what the most efficient way will be to access Remote Web Workplace using a 56k dial-up modem. You recommend that:

A. Users type http://www.mycosmeticscompany.com/remote

B. Users select: Modem (56Kbps) in the Connection Speed drop down on the Remote Web Workplace logon screen.

C. Uses connect to Remote Web Workplace and select: Download Connection Manager.

D. Users de-select the "I'm using a public or shared computer" on the logon screen.

Question #81

Which are the following reasons to use Active Directory-integrated zones? (Choose all that apply).

1. Active Director-integrated zones are more secure and should be sued in the screened subnet.

2. Active Directory-integrated zones provide improved fault tolerance for zone transfers because all servers are primary and can perform zone replication.

3. Active Directory-integrated zones are compatible with standard secondary zones on Windows NT 4.0 or BIND 4.9.7

4. Active Directory-integrated zones provide faster and more efficient replication than Windows NT 4.0.

Question #82

You work for a bottled juice manufacturer in India that has a mainframe in a single location (HQ). Every plant connects to this central location through its 56 Kbps leased lines. All IT management is in the central location, along with all resources. The users run Windows XP Pro and the on-site servers are running Windows Server 2003 standard edition with the SNA protocol. What is your IT structure from a business requirements perspective? (Choose all that apply)

1. Centralized IT but resource management is decentralized.

2. Centralized IT and resource management is centralized.

3. User management is centralized and resource management is decentralized.

4. User management is centralized and resource management is centralized.

5. All users are centrally located.

6. All users are not centrally located.

Question #83

You have been hired by a mid-sized company to improve IT security. The company is very concerned about securing its network. It's also concerned about preventing unauthorized access to its network. Which of the following features in Windows Server 2003 can enable the company to authorize and authenticate its users? (Choose one answer)

1. ACLs, Kerberos, PKI, NTLM, RADIUS

2. RADIUS, LM, PKI, NTLM, L2Tp, NTLM v2

3. Kerberos, NTLM, RADIUS

4. Kerberos, NTLM, PKI

Question #84

Karla is the domain administrator at Company One and will planning the Active Directory for the company's Windows Server 2003 network, she decides on implementing the Group Policy structure. What are the possible reasons for doing so?

1. Automate software integration

2. Manage security settings

3. Redirect folders to the server

4. Implement scripts

Question #85

Springer Spaniels Limited has one domain that spans a multisite WAN. The WAN is comprised of one site in Germany and one in New York, each with a domain controller. Directory information must be widely distributed, but this must be balanced with the need to optimize network performance. If the directory updates are constantly distributed to all other domain controllers in the domain, they will consume the company's network resources. How does Windows Server 2003 use sites and replication change control to optimize replication? (Choose all that apply)

1. Occasionally re-evaluating which connections are used.

2. Using multiple routes to replicate changes.

3. Replicating all the information on each DC.

Question #86

You have a client that has Windows 2003 domain controller, 7 Windows XP Professional clients, 15 Windows 2000 Professional and 9 Windows 98 clients. The business uses a third-party application that uses a small but essential database. The domain controller has one volume which is C:\ and holds all files. You set up a backup schedule with an ASR backup using the ASR backup wizard once every Saturday backing up to an external tape drive. On Tuesday your domain controller experiences a fatal crash. You perform the ASR restore and even though your domain controller boots fully restored and functional, the third-party database is missing on the restored domain controller. All the user accounts are in Active Directory and the domain controller appears to have had a successful restore. Why did the application database not restore?

A. The ASR floppy disk was corrupt

B. The ASR backup does not work properly with external tape drives

C. The ASR backup only backs up minimal Windows system files and system state

D. You forgot to hit the F2 key during the restore operation

Question #87

You are the admin for TeleNut, Inc., which has three Windows Domain controller 2003 servers named SERV1, SERV2 and SERV3. All client computers run Windows XP Professional. TeleNut, Inc., is a single domain implementation. You set up SERV3 as the SUS server since this is the only server connected to the Internet. SERV2 is also a SUS server and gets the updates from SERV3. All clients are configured to receive automatic updates from SERV2. You download the latest Windows updates to SERV3 and notice that the clients are not receiving any updates. You check all connectivity and find everything in working order. What must you do to ensure that clients receive the updates?

A. Configure clients to receive updates from SERV3

B. Set a GPO to push the updates out to SERV2

C. Install the SUS connector on the clients

D. Approve the updates on SERV3

E. Approve the updates on SERV2

Question #88

You are the outside consultant for a huge company. You help manage the Active Directory domain for the huge company. The Active Directory domain consists of four Windows 2003 domain controllers and two Windows 2000 domain controllers, and Windows XP Professional and Windows 2000 computers. You have been asked to implement a GPO for several OUs in the Active Directory structure. Before you deploy the GPO, you would like to know how it will affect the OUs. How can you anticipate this with the least amount of administrative effort?

A. Use the gpresult.exe command line utility

B. Use the RSoP MMC snap-in

C. Use the repadmin/ showreps command

D. Use the replmon.exe command line utility

Question #89

You are the administrator for Gadgets, Inc. Gadgets, Inc. consists of one Active Directory domain. The domain consists of 6 Windows 2003 domain controllers and 300 Windows XP Professional computers. Two Windows 2003 servers, DNS1 and DNS2, are the DNS servers for the domain. DNS1 hosts the standard primary DNS zone and DNS2 hosts the standard secondary zone. Both DNS domain controllers are configured with forwarders to external ISP DNS domain controllers. There have been too many requests for the DNS servers lately and requests have been forwarded to the external ISP DNS servers. You want to delegate some of the workload to another server in the domain. You create a new zone and install a new server, DNS3. How can you implement delegation with the least amount of administrative effort?

A. Set the forwarders on DNS1 and DNS2 to point to DNS3

B. Create an A record for DNS3

C. Create an NS record for DNS3

D. Run the New Delegation Wizard on DNS3

Question #90

Your company uses a SBS 2003 Standard Edition server and two Windows Server 2003 member servers to store data files. The owner of the business requests that you create a folder named Mangement and a folder named Confidential, which both should be secured and only accessible by the Managers Group and no other employees should be granted access. What technology can you use to ensure the appropriate level of security?

A. Share permissions

B. NTFS permissions

C. EFS

D. IPSec

Question #91

You administer an SBS 2003 server and two Windows Server 2003 member servers. Users report that access to one member server is very slow and you want to investigate the cause of this. You employ Network Monitor to analyze packets going back and forth from the member server and notice that there is a lot of DNS related traffic. What would be the next step to find the cause of the DNS related traffic?

A. System Monitor

B. Task Manager

C. Event Viewer

D. Netdiag.exe

Question #92

You are the IT admin at Response, Inc. You manage a network with four Windows 2003 domain controllers and two Windows 2000 domain controllers, and 350 Windows XP Professional client computers. The company has a high turnover rate and you are adding and removing user accounts on a weekly basis. Usually you do full backup on all servers on Friday nights and differentials on Saturday through Thursday. Wednesday you are adding five user accounts. The next day you realize that you accidentally deleted an entire OU with all user accounts in it. This has already replicated across the entire Active Directory domain. You want to be able to restore the OU without losing the newly created user accounts in Active Directory. What should you do?

A. Quit

B. Perform an authoritative restore of the OU only from the last full backup

C. Perform a non-authoritative restore of the last full backup

D. Perform a non-authoritative restore of the last full backup and perform an authoritative restore of the OU from the last full backup

E. Perform an authoritative restore of the last full backup

Question #93

You are the consultant for a medium-sized business that has 1 Windows Server 2003 domain controller and 70 Windows XP Professional client computers. All applications are loaded on this one server under C:\apps. The server has a single hard disk configured as drive C:\. You notice that the C:\ drive is going to run out of space before long. As a temporary fix until a new additional server arrives, you install a new drive as drive formatted with NTFS as D:\ and decide to mount a new disk to C:\apps but are unsuccessful. What can you do to remedy this?

A. Use Diskpart to move data from drive C:\ to drive D:\

B. Convert drive D:\ to a basic volume

C. Convert drive C:\ to NTFS

D. Convert drive D:\ a dynamic volume

Question #94

Your Domain Controller, which is also your GC (global catalog) server fails. What group or user can still log on to the network?

A. Power Users

B. Domain Administrators

C. Enterprise Administrators

D. Network Configuration Operators

Question #95

Your company has been experiencing unprecedented growth. The company business is of a sensitive nature and has employees world-wide that need to connect to the Windows Server 2003 and upload their findings. The owner is concerned about corporate espionage when employees connect to the network, so a new company policy has been put in place. The VPN has to be at the highest level of authentication and encryption possible without spending any additional money. What can you implement? (select all that apply)

A. PPTP

B. L2TP

C. IPSec

D. PEAP

Question #96

As the domain administrator, you are aware of the limitation of Group Policy Objects (GPOs). Which of the following statements are true?

1. Multiple sites and OUs may use a single GPO.

2. GPOs are inherited across domains.

3. Multiple GPOs may be associated with a single OU.

4. GPOs are not inherited.

Question #97

Bob is designing the Active Directory for his company. He is not sure about name restrictions. He is especially concerned about the use of characters that are allowed when naming the domain. What characters are not allowed as part of the domain name?

1. Backslash

2. A-Z, a-z

3. Period

4. 0-9

5. Hyphen

6. Underscore

Question #98

The events company you serve as a Small Business Specialist wants to elevate its customer list management beyond Business Contact Manager (BCM). Making the situation more complicated, the firm recently opened an office in Mumbai, India to focus on the growing APAC market. The company currently has three servers, all running

Windows Server 2003. You recommended a migration from BCM to CRM 3.0 SBE. What database issues will it encounter?

1. None. The Jet database is common between CRM 3.0 SBE

2. The firm must purchase and implement SQL Server 2005.

3. None. The firm can simply use Microsoft Access found in several of its Office Professional installations (on workstations running Windows XP Professional)

4. It cannot be done. CRM 3.0 SBE is designed for small businesses and cannot run on Windows Server 2003.

Question #99

You are the administrator at Springers, Ltd. in London. The Windows Server 2003 server that you manage is part of an Active Directory domain that has trust relationships with other domains. The Windows server also has SQL 2005 and ISA Server 2004 installed. You are concerned about users accessing resources on you Windows Server 2003 server. When should you consider performing a backup of ISA Server 2004?

1. When a new trust relationship is established

2. When new users are added to the domain

3. When the firewall policy is changed

4. When there is a change to the SQL database

Question #100

Which client supports user-level authentication in ISA Server 2004?

1. Secure NAT client

2. Web Proxy client

3. VPN client

4. Firewall client

Question #101

You administer an SBS 2003 network for a call center that sells logo wear and other printable marketing items. There are 21 Windows XP Pro computers and 10 Windows 2000 Professional computers. Besides phone calls, the call center receives several hundred fax orders a day. Too many times the fax machine has run out of paper or orders were neglected because there was no one there to manage the fax. The company hires two new staff people just for the purpose of handling the fax orders. Faxes should be received and processed on the desktop, but only by the two new hires. You create the new user accounts with the Add User wizard. What else should you do?

A. Create a security group called "FaxPersonnel" and add the user accounts of the new hires to the new security group

B. Create a distribution group called "FaxPersonnel" and add the user accounts of the new hires to the new distribution group

C. Run the Configure Fax Service and select the "Use the Route through e-mail routing method"

D. Run the Configure Fax Service and select the "Use the Route through distribution group method"

Question #102

You administer an SBS 2003 network for a small doctor's office in town. The server is configured with two NICs and there are seven Windows 2000 Professional and four Windows 98 computers on the network. Due to regulatory compliance regulations, you decide to add a UPnP hardware firewall to the SBS installation. After you add the UPnP hardware firewall device, users are no longer able to log on to Remote Web Workplace and internal users can't update their medical application which uses port 4008. To fix this with the least amount of administrative effort, what should you do? (select all that apply)

A. Access the firewall interface and open port 4125, 1723 and 4008

B. Run the CEICW and when prompted that there is a UPnP firewall device detected, let the CEICW configure it

C. Access the firewall interface and set port forwarding for port 80 to port 4125

D. Run the CEICW and in the Web Server Certificate screen, add a certificate

E. Add port 4008 in the Services Configuration screen in the CEICW

F. Access the firewall interface and set port forwarding for port 4008 to the SBS server

Question #103

You installed an SBS 2003 network at a paper recycling plant. There are 15 Windows XP Professional computers and the server has a proprietary recycling software solution installed. You, the office manager and the owner have the ability to administer the server from remote locations. You get a call from the plant and remote into the server, to find after logging on that you get a blue desktop background but no icons or start bar and are unable to manage the server. You drive over to the plant and find two disconnected sessions from the office manager and owner. What can you do to ensure this won't happen again?

A. Install Terminal Services on the SBS 2003 Server

B. Add additional user accounts to the Remote Desktop Administration on the SBS 2003 Server

C. Configure the server to "set a time limit for disconnected sessions" to 5 minutes

D. Configure the server to allow "automatic reconnection"

Question #104

You are the consultant for XYZ Title Company. XYZ runs an SBS 2003 server, one Windows 2003 Server and 14 Windows XP Professional computers. XYZ has grown its client base and its folder structure on the server to a point where collaboration and a document repository needs to be implemented. You suggest SharePoint as a solution. XYZ tested SharePoint with several individual client files before deciding to go ahead and move all the documents in existing shares from the two servers. What will take the least administrative effort to upload the documents into SharePoint?

A. Instruct users to create their own sites and upload all the files they are responsible for using the Upload Document button

B. Migrate the files with the SharePoint migration tool

C. Use the Import File Wizard

D. Move the files using the stsmigrate.exe command line tool

Question #105

You are the consultant for ASAP, an auto supply and parts distribution center. ASAP has an SBS 2003 server and six client computers. The SBS server has two NICs, one fax modem and an external backup tape drive. Currently ASAP is getting inundated with fax orders and customers are complaining about having to do numerous re-dials before the fax goes through. Users send and receive faxes from their desktops acknowledging orders and faxing shipping information. ASAP purchased a competitor and expects to receive double the amount of orders than it is currently receiving within the next couple of months. How can you set up ASAP to be able to manage the increasing fax demand with the lowest expenditure and fewest changes to their business processes so users do not need to be retrained?

A. Purchase two new standalone Fax machines that are capable of high-volume faxing

B. Set up an Internet Fax service to manage the fax volume and forward the faxes by e-mail to your business

C. Add three additional fax modems to the SBS machine

D. Add one additional fax modem the SBS machine

Question #106

You administer a SharePoint site for New Construction, Inc. on a SBS 2003 Server with ISA installed. The company has ten Windows XP Professional computers in the office and has numerous contractors on job sites that are required to have Windows XP Professional SP2 computers with Microsoft Office 2003 loaded on them. The construction company wants contractors to be able to access the SharePoint site for specific projects and be able to discuss, add, edit and delete items on the lists. They should not be able to create their own lists or modify existing lists. You already have a user account template setup for contractors. What group should also be assigned to the contractor's template and how should you change permissions on existing contractor accounts? (select all that apply)

A. Distribution

B. Reader

C. Contributor

D. Power User

E. Run the Change Permission wizard

F. Add the appropriate Group through the users account properties tab in Active Directory

G. Create a Group Policy that assigns the appropriate access to the Contractors Security Group

Question #107

Callaway Antiques is a new client of yours that already has SBS 2003 server installed. There are two existing Windows 2000 Professional computers and the owner purchased two new Windows XP Pro computers he would like to add to the network. He also wants Office 2003 Professional installed on the new computers and would like to be able to backup MyDocuments data for all users in a central location. He wants you to spend the least amount of time and effort implementing a solution. What should you do?

A. Configure a GPO under Computer Configuration\Software Settings and add a software installation package for the Office 2003 installation. Configure the MyDocument redirect GPO and configure NTbackup to run a nightly backup of the Users Shared folder.

B. Insert the Office 2003 CD into the Server CD tray and share the CD. Run the Configure My Documents redirection wizard and run the Configure Backup Wizard.

C. Copy the Office 2003 CD into a folder in the clientapps folder and share it. Configure the Assign Application wizard and run the Configure My Documents redirection wizard. Configure the Configure Backup Wizard.

D. Copy the Office 2003 CD into a folder in the clientapps folder and share it. Run the Configure My Documents redirection wizard and run the Assign Application wizard and add the Office 2003 files. Configure the NT backup wizard to include the system state.

Question #108

You are the IT manager for a local delivery company Express, Inc. Express Inc. just purchased SBS 2003, 13 Windows XP Professional computers and 10 PocketPCs with Windows Mobile for PocketPC2003 installed. Express Inc. has a registered domain name. The delivery staff is constantly on the run and you would like to implement the PocketPCs to synchronize e-mails and schedules without having the delivery staff constantly calling the office. You run the CEICW and enable OMA and a self-signed Web Server certificate. You run the Assign Application wizard and add Active Sync 3.7 to the assigned applications and then join the new client computers using the Network Connection wizard. What are the next steps you should take to configure the PocketPCs?

A. Set the PocketPC into its cradle and let it sync with the Windows XP computer; when prompted to sync with the local computer or Exchange, select Exchange.

B. Set the PocketPC into its cradle and let it sync with the Windows XP computer; when prompted to sync with the local machine or Exchange, select the local computer.

C. Set the PocketPC into its cradle and let it sync. Copy the SBS Web Server certificate onto the PocketPC and then go to Settings\Con-nections and add the URL for the SBS server.

D. Set the PocketPC into its cradle and let it sync. Go to Settings\ Connections and add the URL of the SBS server. Install the SBS Web Server certificate over the wireless connection when prompted.

Question #109

Your company is moving from a peer-to-peer network to SBS 2003. Currently the e-mail accounts are held at the ISP and downloaded with POP3 clients. There are 23 Windows XP Pro computers on the network. The owner wants to be able to use calendar sharing features in Exchange, as well as OWA, but does not want to change the POP3 accounts at the ISP. How can the administrator implement that?

A. Install the POP3 connector from SBS Disc #4 to the server and set the client machines to pull their POP3 e-mail from the server. Have the ISP push out the POP3 e-mail to the SBS server.

B. Run the CEICW and select the "POP3 connector" box in the e-mail configuration screen. Add a POP3 connector for each individual user and point it to the appropriate Exchange mail account.

C. Run the CEICW and select the "POP3 connector" box in the e-mail configuration screen. Add the mailbox retrieval information for each individual POP3 account and point it to the appropriate Exchange mail account.

D. Run the CEICW and select the "POP3 connector" box and de-select the Exchange Server box in the e-mail configuration screen. Configure clients to retrieve their e-mail from the SBS POP3 connector.

Question #110

Magic Inc. uses an SBS 2003 server as their e-mail and file server. Magic has 30 actors working for them who are constantly on the road. The actors expressed that they would like to receive their e-mail on their SmartPhones and PocketPCs. The actors would also like to have a central scheduling method and secure access to the main office. As the consultant you want to guarantee secure access using certificate services in the most cost-effective manner with the least amount of administrative effort. What should you configure? (select all that apply)

A. Purchase a commercial certificate and install it through the CEICW

B. Select the Outlook Mobile Access checkbox in the Web Services Configuration screen in the CEICW

C. Set up an Enterprise Certificate Authority (CA) on the SBS server

D. Install the Enterprise CA on the client computer

E. Add the commercial certificate in the Web Services Configuration screen in the CEICW

F. Configure the CEICW to use a self-signed certificate

G. Select the enable Outlook Mobile Access check box in the Mobile Services Properties in Exchange

Answer Key

Question #1: Answer: C

The minimum system requirements to install Small Business Server 2003 are a 300 MHz CPU speed, 256 MB of RAM, and a 4GB hard disk. Answer C is correct because it offers the most resources: two CPUs and 512 MB of RAM. Answer A would work, but is incorrect because this solution does not have the most available resources. Answer B is incorrect because Small Business Server 2003 can only accept a maximum of two CPUs. Answer D would work, but has fewer resources than Answer C.

Question #2: Answer: D, E, F

The correct steps would be to install Small Business Server 2003 Standard Edition, which already includes the full version of Exchange 2003 Standard and Microsoft Shared Fax Services. You would not have to purchase a separate copy of Exchange Server, nor a third-party fax application. You would have to install a fax modem on the server to receive the faxes, but would not have to install modems on the client machines, as SBS will allow you to send and receive faxes in your Outlook client on each individual workstation routed through the SBS server. You would want to upgrade client machines to Windows XP Professional, since the Home version does not support being joined to the domain.

Question #3: Answer: C

The correct answer is ten. Ten more CALs need to be purchased on top of the five CALs that come with SBS. There are a total of ten client machines and one member server, which brings the device number on the SBS network to 11. Since licenses come in packs of five, you would have to purchase two five-packs, bringing you up to a total of 15 CALs.

Question #4: Answer: B

Windows Small Business Server 2003 requires NTFS for Active Directory and Exchange 2003 and, therefore, you must convert the system partition to NTFS. Moving all data to one drive and creating a mirror for redundancy or running chkdsk will not convert the FAT32 partitions, so you could not do the upgrade. Formatting the system partition with NTFS would erase all data. (Hey, nothing like starting out with a clean system!) Converting both drives (even that would be the better choice) would not meet your objective of "minimal effort."

Question #5: Answer: D

The need for e-mail in a company with 45 employees makes SBS a logical choice. Coupled with the fact that they want to reduce maintenance of their LOB app and remote desktops, a terminal server running as a member server provides them a very manageable platform that achieves the customer needs. Answer A is incorrect because NT 4.0 is no longer a supported application and should be replaced to provide a stable platform to build their business upon. Answer B is incorrect because simply replacing the current servers with updated ones does not address their need for mail or management of the remote sites. Answer C is incorrect because you cannot have three SBS servers on a single domain. Answer E is incorrect because it does not address the mail issue. SBS is the most cost-effective way to provide mail to this client, as well as providing a number of other valuable features they will enjoy.

Question #6: Answer: D

SBS 2003 Premium comes with five CALs, and additional user CALs are sold only in five-packs. Each person who will authenticate to the SBS server must have a CAL. All other answers are incorrect because they either do not cover all the users or are not legitimate ways to purchase CALs.

Question #7: Answer: A

This is the only piece of information complete enough to provide guidance. Answer B is incorrect as you do not know whether the connection is dial-up, DSL, cable modem, or a dedicated line of some sort. It also may be part of some frame network from another source. Answer C is incorrect as you do not know the operating system of the machines or their specifications. Answer D is incorrect because of a lack of specifications. RAM would be the first area to probe. Answer E is incorrect because you are unsure how many of these employees are actual users of the network. It is possible that the actual network users may only be a fraction of the entire employee count.

Question #8: Answer: B, D

The fax modem will allow for group faxing and an easy way to route incoming faxes. Option D allows users to work effectively from home. Answer A is incorrect. Inkjet printers are costly to use, and on a network, a better use of funds would be to purchase a color laser printer for output. Answer C is incorrect. SBS comes with Exchange for e-mail. While an ISP could do this for the Chamber, it would not provide the best functionality for their work. Answer E is incorrect. All data files should be maintained on the server to make sure they are backed up and protected. At a minimum, shared folders should be created on the server. The best solution would be to use SharePoint for this, as it is designed as a perfect collaboration tool for this type of situation.

Question #9: Answer: C

Answer A is not a good solution because of the budget constraints. Answer B is not correct because there is no direct upgrade migration. Answer D is not correct because Exchange 2003 cannot be run on Linux.

Question #10: Answer: C

Answer C meets all the minimum requirements. Answer A does not meet the RAM or processor requirements. Answer B does not have enough free space on the hard disk. Answer D has no hard drive, so cannot be installed.

Question #11: Answer: D, F

The least costly implementation would be to upgrade the Windows 2000 Professional desktops in the office to XP Pro and run the CEICW to configure Remote Web Workplace. Adding a member server to the network and installing terminal services would be much more expensive. You cannot install terminal services on the SBS domain controller. Upgrading the Win98 laptops to XP Pro does not help the solution. You can access Remote Web Workplace from most Internet browsers regardless of the operation system. Configuring SharePoint will not allow remote access.

Question #12: Answer: A, E

You should create a system partition on one disk and create a RAID 5 volume using the other three disks. In a RAID 5 array, you can continue working without interruption when one disk fails. Creating a RAID 1 volume and using shadow copy on another disk will still cause interruptions in the workflow by taking time out to break the mirror or having to restore from shadow copy. A spanned disk set offers no redundancy. It takes at least three disks to create a RAID 5 array.

Question #13: Answer: D

Installing a router-to-router VPN allows secure communications where authorized routers have to identify themselves when initiating the connection. Installing member servers and terminal services would be a more expensive solution. Using the Connection Manager icon on each client workstation creates more administrative overhead than using one router-to-router VPN and is not as efficient. Enabling Remote Desktop would not be as efficient or secure as the router-to-router VPN. PC Anywhere? Remember this is a Microsoft exam. And in the real exam this would never even be given as an option.

Question #14: Answer: B, D, E

These three are needed to provide solid direction to the bank. Answer A is incorrect since you do not have enough information to make that recommendation. It may well become the solution, but before you can make a recommendation you need to get the facts. Answer C is incorrect for the same reason.

Question #15: Answer: C

Without a dependable high speed Internet connection, web hosting would be a mistake. It is not a best practice to host a web site on a single SBS server even with a high-speed connection. Network faxing would be beneficial to handle the continuing orders that come by fax, and e-mail can be effective even across low bandwidth connections. The other answers do not achieve the goals expressed by the customer. The key to successful assessment is listening to the customer and meeting or exceeding his expectations.

Question #16: Answer: B, D, E

Answer B is correct in that some sort of removable backup solution is critical to protect loss of data. Tape- or disk-to-disk solutions are effective. Answer D is a good solution for those customers who are paranoid about data protection and want another level of offsite backup protection. This requires an Internet connection with adequate speed to transfer the data. Answer E is the best configuration to provide the highest level of data security in his SBS server. Answer A is too labor-intensive and not practical, although it would work. Answer C is a legitimate solution, but not as effective as RAID 5. Answer F is not necessary unless his environment contains multiple servers that need to be backed up to his SBS server.

Question #17: Answer: C, D, E

The laser printer will work fine. A hardware firewall can effectively be used in front of an ISA server to provide depth of defense for security. A Mac with a current operating system will attach to an SBS server. Answer A is incorrect. You cannot split ISA from the SBS server. Answer B is incorrect. You would not be able to support this fax as a solution in your SBS environment. Driver issues will prevent it. Answer F is incorrect. With the new filtering available in Outlook and Exchange, it is unlikely you need the Linux solution. It would add much complexity to the environment and would not significantly reduce spam.

Question #18: Answer: B

This will allow secure remote access via VPN from the owner's home to the server and SharePoint will fulfill the team collaboration needs of the office workers. Answer A is incorrect because it does not address all issues. Answer C would not be the most cost-effective solution. Answer D is incorrect because SharePoint is not supported on NT 4.0

Question #19: Answer: B

Answer A is not correct because it does not resolve the main problem of firewall. Answer C is not correct because it does not cover the e-mail issue. Answer D is not correct because there is no need to buy a new laptop.

Question #20: Answer: C

Configuring a domain-based DFS root will allow for fault tolerance and does not require users to know where the actual share is located. The domain-based DFS root stores information in Active Directory, which will automatically be replicated. In Answer A, SharePoint Service would almost work, except shares were requested and the third-party application is dependant on a UNC path name which would not work with WSS. In Answer B, a stand-alone DFS root keeps information stored in the registry and would therefore not be fault tolerant. Answers D and E make for fault tolerance but do nothing for sharing data.

Question #21: Answer: 1

To change the zone type, right-click the zone within the DNS management console and click Properties. In the Properties dialog box, make sure the General tab is selected and click the Change button beside the zone type. Select the option to store the zone within Active Directory.

Question #22:   Answer: 2

The new server should be configured as a secondary server. It will then maintain a copy of the DNS zone file. If the original DNS server goes offline, name resolution can still occur.

Question #23: Answer: 3

By configuring an authoritative DNS server within totalsupply.net to host a stub zone for the marketing.totalsupply.net zone, any updates made to the authoritative name server resource records will be updated within the parent zone as well. The other options do not satisfy the scenario.

Question #24: Answer: 4

Because a root DNS zone exists on the DNS server, you will not be able to configure a DNS forwarder. You must delete this file before you can proceed.

Question #25: Answer: 3

By having and configuring caching-only servers within each location, you can decrease the name resolution response time for users. Since caching-only servers do not maintain any zone information, no traffic is generated from zone transfers.

Question #26: Answer: C

Installing and configuring SUS to download locally will require only one download to service all client computers. You can edit a GPO to force the clients to update from the local source instead of the Windows update site. That would be the most efficient solution. Answer A. would have client workstations do individual downloads taking up more bandwidth, and remoting into the client would create more work for the administrator. Answer B. would only download updates to the server and not the clients. Answer D. The MBSA can be used in conjunction with SUS, but cannot be set to download updates automatically on a schedule.

Question #27: Answer: B, D

The Secure Server IPSec (Require Security) policy ensures that communication with the server is protected. The client IPSec (Respond only) policy is a good choice for computers that do not need secure communications the entire time. With this policy applied, the client will only use secure communications if another computer requests it. Answer A. This would allow unsecured communication if the client computer does not have IPSec enabled. Answer C. Assigning this policy to the clients would make the client request secure communications and not the server. Answer E. This is only for computers to respond to requests for secure communications. We want to ensure that the server only uses secure communication, and this answer would not achieve the objective.

Question #28: Answer: C

You should create a color printer group and add all groups that should have print permissions for the color printer. You must assign print permissions to the color printer group and remove the Everyone group, which has printer permissions by default. This way the rest of the travel agency employees will not be able to print to this printer. Answer A. would not work because when you set Deny permissions for the Everyone group, that will deny everyone from printing to this printer, including the color printer security group since a deny will overwrite everything else. Answer B. Distribution groups cannot be assigned permissions, they are merely for e-mail purpose. Answer D. This solution will also allow the travel agents to print to the printer and would not meet the objective.

Question #29: Answer: B

There are two types of permissions: share and NTFS permissions. The share permissions are Read, Change and Full Control. Since we only want to use the principle of least permissions, the office manager should have change permissions and not full control permissions. The Read permission allows limited access, to view files and folders in the share, but will not allow adding, deleting or modifying folders. Answer A. This gives Full Control to the office manager and would not follow the principle of least amount of permissions. Answer C and D. Read & Execute is a NTFS permission and not available under the share options.

Question #30: Answer: B, C

In ISA Server 2000 you should first create a protocol definition for the protocol and then create the protocol rule that will allow the custom protocol port to be used. Answer A and D. There is no such thing as a port proxy rule or definition in ISA. Answer E. Creating an IPSec policy will not open ports.

Question #31: Answer: C

You should rename her user account to make it harder on the person attempting to access her account. Answer A. If you set the account to lock out, this will lock out Linda as well. Answer B. Creating a new user account will require migrating her profile settings and creating additional administrative effort and she would not keep the exact settings that she has now. Answer D. Disabling the account will not allow Linda to have access to the network.

Question #32: Answer: C

Running the Create Remote Connection Disk wizard will create a floppy disk that will just have to be inserted and the executable sbspackage.exe launched. This will be the easiest way for attorneys to set up the VPN client. Answer A. You cannot only assign applications with the Assign Applications wizard; it will not configure the VPN client. Answer B. This would require the user to unzip the file and save it to a folder in the laptop. Way too many steps! Answer D. You would have to create a script and place it in the GPO, which is too much administrative effort on your part, plus, the client needs access ASAP.

Question #33: Answer: B

Install ISA 2000 Server in Cache mode to facilitate accelerated Internet browsing. This way, the server will cache recently accessed Internet sites and if several users request the same site or page, will be served up from cache instead of having to request the data across the Internet. Increasing the HTTP TTL (total time to live) will allow you to keep cached information longer in Cache. Answer A. Do not install the firewall client on the ISA 2000 Server. Ever. Answer C. There is no such thing as a caching client. Answer D. This is a server product designed to be installed on a server operating system and not to be pushed out to clients.

Question #34: Answer: B

To set the client computer, you must go to Computer Configuration/ Administrative Templates/Windows Components/Windows Update/ Specify intranet Microsoft update server. There you specify an intranet server to host updates from the Microsoft Update web sites. You can then use this update service to automatically update computers on your network. This will allow you to test updates first and then approve them on the SUS server. Laptop users will only be able to get updates when they are connected to the SUS server. Answer A and C. There is no setting for SUS under User configuration. Answer D. This selection would allow the local admin to choose the configuration modes and would not achieve the objective.

Question #35: Answer: B, C, D

Port 25 is SMTP and needed to send e-mail. Port 110 POP3 is needed for the Outlook Express clients to download their e-mail. Port 443 HTTPS is needed for Outlook Web Access and Outlook Mobile Access. Answer A. Port 80 is not called for in this scenario, which would be for browsing the internet. Answer E. Port 4125 is for Remote Web Workplace, which is also not called for.

Question #36: Answer: 3

Update the SRV record. The SRV record identifies services that are running on a host, the port used by the service, and the protocol.

Question #37: Answer: 3

If the support tools have been installed, you can use Replication Monitor to ensure that replication between DNS servers is occurring on a regular basis.

Question #38: Answer: 1

Mail servers are identified within a zone file using Mail Exchanger (MX) records.

Question #39: Answer: 2

If the hostname cannot be resolved using the NSLookup command, adding a PTR to the zone file will allow you to resolve the IP address to a hostname.

Question #40: Answer: 1

The /flushdns command line extension will clear and refresh the client resolver cache. Note that this command is commonly needed when using virtual environments in order to get the name caching properly aligned.

Question #41: Answer: B

You should configure the Terminal Services to run the application in a lower resolution. On the client computer, right-click the Remote Desktop icon and click Properties and then the Compatibility tab, select Run in 640 x 480 screen resolution. When the screen displays small and centered on the monitor, it is an indication that the screen resolution is set to high to run the program in full-screen mode. Answer A. Running the application in compatibility mode is not necessary because it is functioning on the Windows Server 2003 computer. Answer C. The Remote Desktop Client comes built into XP Pro and does not need to be run in compatibility mode. Answer D. You would use the 256 color option only if the application displays the wrong color.

Question #42: Answer: A, C

The volume needs to be formatted with NTFS in order to use Disk Quotas. Disk Quotas are not available on a FAT volume. Since we are running a RAID 5 array with three disks totaling 900 GB, one third is being used for striping so we really only have 600 GB total space available. With 60 users, this makes for 10 GB per user. Answer B. FRS is used for replicating data. Answer D. If you configure 15 GB of storage per user, the volume will physically run out of space before anyone will reach their limit.

Question #43: Answer: C

Adding the domain controller role to the member servers allows for logons to be authenticated locally and do not need to cross the WAN-link. This will increase logon speed. Answer A. A connection bridge allows you to bridge two subnets and would not increase logon speed. Answer B. Site links are used to control Active Directory replication between domain controllers in each site. This would not speed up logons. Member servers do not use replication. Answer D. This would require a third-party application and, thus, be an expenditure.

Question #44: Answer: B

You would add additional VPN ports in the RAS console by expanding the Ports node and then click Properties, highlight the port to configure and click Configure. SBS assigns only 5 ports by default. Answer A. Using GPOs and setting a specific time will actually compound this problem because you are now narrowing down the time window when agents can connect to the network, as well as changing current practices by dictating the log on time. Answer C. Ahem, this is a Microsoft exam. Answer D. Upgrading bandwidth would not be a solution.

Question #45: Answer: B

Automatic redirection is for 32-bit terminal services clients, enabling automatic printer redirection and will allow the user to print from the Terminal Service session to the local printer on his computer. This setting can be set on the user account properties in Active Directory on the Environment tab by selecting "connect client printers at logon." Answer A. The user is already logged on and working in the application, so this is not the problem. Answer C. The manual redirection is for 16-bit clients and local printers that require drivers other than those shipped with Windows Server 2003. Answer D. Bidirectional printing is not supported.

Question #46: Answer: B

Using the Remote Web Workplace lets you securely connect to all available member servers running terminal services. Answer A. This option will not work because the member servers are sitting behind a firewall with private (internal) IP addresses not accessible from the internet. Answer C. Same as B. Answer D. Same as B, only this is the old client used for NT 4.0

Question #47: Answer: C

The most cost-effective solution will be to install SBS 2003 Standard for the e-mail, fax and collaboration solution, and install Windows Server 2003 Standard with a separate SQL installation on it for the dedicated use of SQL server. Answer A. SBS 2003 Premium is more expensive then the SBS 2003 Standard edition. We can't use the SQL software that comes with this package since the software being developed needs a dedicated SQL server and needs to be installed on a separate server. Purchasing SBS 2003 Premium would not be cost effective. Answer B. This would not work since this would not achieve the objective. Answer D. This does not take into account the e-mail, faxing and collaboration solution.

Question #48: Answer: A

Remote Desktop uses RDP 5.2 with a 128 bit encryption. It allows you to be connected to several domain controllers simultaneously by opening a new remote desktop session for each, switching between the remote desktop sessions. Answer B. Remote Assistance requires a user to be logged on locally to give you control of the desktop. That would not be a solution. Answer C. SMS would not be cost effective. Answer D. Telnet is limited and would not be a "least administrative effort".

Question #49: Answer: A, C, F, G, H

After you install the new hard drive, you would first load a new copy of Windows Server 2003 and then reboot, hit the F8 key and select Directory Services Restore mode. You get another boot screen, press enter, and the server gets booted into a special safe mode that will not start Active Directory. Perform the non-authoritative restore of the full Friday backup including the system state. Then restore the Tuesday differential including the system state non-authoritatively. When you reboot and bring the server online, it will replicate the most current

Active Directory data from the other DCs that has changed since it was disconnected from the network.

Answer B. You must use DSRM (Directory Service Restore mode) regular safe mode will not support the restore functions as needed. Answer D. Using the F2 key is an ASR restore function. Answer E. If you were to perform an authoritative restore, it would increment the USN (update sequence number) by 10,000 and would therefore replicate the older data from Server2 back to Server3 and SBS1 because of the higher USN. That is not wanted. We want the latest AD objects to be replicated to Server2 from Server3 and SBS1.

Question #50: Answer: E

Adding the RemoteSales group to the Remote Desktop User local group on TS1 will provide proper permissions to log on to the terminal server and run the application. This gives the right to logon through terminal services which is assigned to the Remote Desktop Users group. Answer A. Adding ALL users to the Power User group would allow all users to log on remotely. Only the RemoteSales group is to have permissions. Answer B. Adding all users to the domain admins group would be a bad thing. Answer C. The Power User group has the right to log on remotely to the server, but this would mean they could also logon remotely to the SBS server. Permissions are too lenient. Answer D. Granting the log on locally right would also allow users in the RemoteSales group to log on interactively to the server when in the office. Permissions are too lenient. Answer F. Adding the Mobile Users group to the Remote Operators group will allow the wrong group to log on remotely with terminal services.

Question #51: Answer: 3

To allow B-Node broadcasts to be resolved across the network, a WINS proxy agent must be configured. The WINS proxy listens for B-Node broadcasts and contacts the WINS servers on the other subnets to resolve the name resolution request on behalf of the non-WINS client.

Question #52: Answer: 1

To allow hosts on other subnets to resolve the NetBIOS names of the UNIX server, a static mapping must be configured because the UNIX server is unable to register its NetBIOS record dynamically.

Question #53: Answer: 1

Clearly the most efficient answer is to make a DHCP database backup in the virtual environment and then restore it in the production environment. The DHCP backup and restore function allows this type of transfer between computers. There is no "reconcile" strategy with DHCP in this scenario. The copy and paste alternatives in (3) and (4) would take too long.

Question #54: Answer: 2

Changing the DHCP in RAS to static scope will insure that all client computers can connect to the Internet without restrictions to access.

Question #55: Answer: 4

DHCP servers must be authorized in Active Directory to be fully integrated into the network. Arp –a is used to review MAC addresses. No additional scope configuration was necessary.

Question #56: Answer: B

The most efficient way to set up new user accounts that have the same security groups and disk quotas is by creating a template and then using the Add User wizard to create the account.

Answer A will work but is not as efficient to set up. Answer D would not work because distribution groups do not have the right to log on to the domain, only to receive e-mail.

Question #57: Answer: D

When TS is installed, unlicensed clients can access the server for a 120-day evaluation period. Then TS will deny client access until it finds a TS license server to issue licenses. The TS server license service should not be installed on the TS server itself, but can be installed on the SBS server.

Question #58: Answer: C, D, F, G

In order to have fault tolerance for NetBIOS and FQDNs, you have to configure WINS and DNS (DNS resolves FQDN queries and WINS resolves NetBIOS queries) on the SBS 2003 server and the member server. In this case, if one is taken down for maintenance, the other server will continue to provide name resolution for both types of requests. Configuring clients as proxy clients would not create any type of fault tolerance. Configuring the DHCP scope does not provide fault tolerance.

Question #59: Answer: C, D, E

In order to prepare the server for an upgrade, you should remove discontinued Exchange Server components (Microsoft Exchange MSMail Connector, Connector for Lotus cc:Mail, Instant Messaging Service, Chat Service and the Key Management Service.) You should disconnect the external NIC and uninstall ISA2000.

The M:/ drive contains the Exchange database and should not be antivirus scanned. Installing ISA SP1 would not apply; this application must be removed because you are upgrading to SBS 2003 Standard Edition which does not include ISA. Since SBS is a bundled package, ISA 2000 should be removed. Reformating the system drive will turn this upgrade into a clean install.

Question #60: Answer: D

Shadow copies are enabled by default on SBS 2003. Running the "Configure My Documents Redirection" located on the server under Users AND Backup Links will change the target folder on all clients to point to a share on the server. Shadow copy will take two snapshots daily, one at 7 a.m. and one at 12 p.m.. Shadow copy is only enabled by default on the system drive; if you choose to use it on other drives, you must manually enable shadow copies there.

Question #61: Answer: D

You must install Dsclient.exe on the Windows 98 and NT4.0 workstations. The dsclient.exe is a f ree download from Microsoft. There is one dsclient.exe for each operating system respectively, in order for the clients to communicate with AD. All of the other answers are nonsense in this case.

Question #62: Answer: B, D

To add a member server to an SBS 2003 network, you must run the Server Computer Wizard and add the server name and IP address, and then run: http://SBSservercomputername/connectcomputer on the member server. You cannot add a server through the client computer wizard. Running dcpromo and creating a child domain will fail because you cannot have child domains on an SBS 2003 network. Running dcpromo on the SBS server would only give the option to demote the DC and cannot be used to add an additional server to the network.

Question #63: Answer: B

SBS 2003 Standard Edition will be the least expensive ($599) operating system and still support e-mail and faxing. Answer A. Windows XP could not manage e-mail. Answer C. SBS 2003 Premium is more expensive ($1499 retail). Answer D. Windows Server 2003 would require purchasing Exchange server as well as being more expensive.

Question #64: Answer: B, E, F, G

Upgrading from SBS 2000 to SBS 2003 Standard Edition requires you to uninstall ISA Server 2000 (that is a Premium Edition component), uninstall Terminal Services, which is no longer supported in SBS 2003 (requires separate server) and uninstall all incompatible Exchange Server components (MS Mail connector, connector for Lotus mail, Instant Messaging Service, Exchange Chat Service and Exchange Key Management Service). You must have Windows SBS 2000 SP1 installed before performing the upgrade. Answer A. Exmerging mailboxes does not contribute to a successful upgrade, but it would be a good measure in case the upgrade fails (but that is not the objective in this scenario). Answers C and D. There is no need to uninstall IIS or stop DNS or DHCP service.

Question #65: Answer: B, F, H

You would first convert two disks to dynamic disks and then create a RAID 1 volume (mirrored disks). In a RAID 1 volume, one disk is duplicated to the second disk, which will slow down write performance. But the trade off is that if one disk fails, the other disk will not be affected and the system will keep functioning at the same speed. You should configure the third disk for Volume Shadow Copy repository so users can restore documents on the fly. Answer A. Raid 0 does not provide redundancy. Answer C. RAID 1 cannot be created with three disks. Answer D. RAID 5 cannot be created with two disks. Answer E. This would be an option, but not the desired option in our scenario since we do not want to experience any slow down. When a RAID array loses one drive, it slows down while recreating the missing data from the two other disks, while it is rebuilding the third disk. Answer G. An extended partition would not meet any of the objectives.

Question #66: Answer: 1, 3

SBS 2003 will not tolerate another DHCP service provider on its subnet (network). Several alternatives exist to solve this problem. For example, change the subnet for the WifFi Hotspot (recommended). The DNS response doesn't figure into this solution set and moving the laptop to the WifFi network is not acceptable.

Question #67 : Answer: 2

UNIX will use the BOOTP service to assign IP addresses. Note this type of service has known to be referenced in story problems dealing with printers (in addition to the infrastructure example given above).

Question #68: Answer: 1, 2

These are the best answers to consider when troubleshooting this type of scenario. Cable companies have been known to block port traffic and port forward would be essential for the traffic flow.

Question #69: Answer: 2

This is the proper Class B Subnet Mask for this scenario.

Question #70: Answer: 3, 4, 5

It is important to understand this question has multiple responses and actions to arrive at the optimal answer. Active Directory is fully exploited in arriving at the solution (one domain, sites, OUs)

Question #71: Answer: C, D

You can install the GPMC only on Windows Server 2003 and Windows XP Professional with Service Pack 1 (or later) For installation on an XP machine with SP1, you need to also apply the hotfix Q326469 which is included with the GPMC. You cannot install the GPMC on any other operating systems.

Question #72: Answer: C, D

To enable Windows 95 clients to communicate with the SBS server, you need to either disable SMB signing on the server or install the Active Directory client extensions.

SBS 2003 server requires SMB signing and encryption to secure traffic on the network, and because Windows 95 computers do not support SMB signing you have to implement one of the two choices. None of this has anything to do with DHCP which assigns IP addresses. Theoretically Answer A could be right, but this will take more effort creating the scope and assigning static addresses (and for what reason?) Answer B. Active Directory server extensions do not exist.

Question #73: Answer: C

To get a quick look at domain controller issues, including DNS in general, use the dcdiag.exe tool. Dcdiag.exe will check for LDAP/ RPC connectivity, perform a basic DNS test, check DNS forwarders, DNS delegation, DNS dynamic updates and a record registration test and many more. (Check Technet for dcdiag.exe for a full list of tests performed.) The DNS console can be used as a monitoring tool for iterative and recursive tests for external DNS server verification. NSLookup.exe will retrieve zone information. The Health Monitor will give you overall server status health, not DNS issues.

Question #74: Answer: C

You can run the Monitor Configuration wizard from the Server Management console and select to e-mail a daily Performance Report and a bi-weekly usage report to specific user accounts or distribution groups. You can attach log files for application events, IIS, SBS Backup, security events and system events to the performance and usage reports in the Server Status Report Properties in the Change Server Status Report Settings tool. Answer A. That would be the opposite of the least amount of adminstrative effort. Answer B. Same as A; and you can't create custom alert thresholds in the Monitoring Configuration wizard. Answer D. Nonsense, there is no Usage report wizard and you can't attach system event log files in the Monitoring Configuration wizard.

Question #75: Answer: D

First you would restore the full database backup from 9:00 p.m. and then restore the differential backup and all transaction logs since the differential database backup. This will bring back the committed transaction 315 from the differential database backup. Since disk 1 failed, with the database, Transaction 315 will be committed when the transaction log is restored, which is located on disk 2 and completed successfully.

Question #76: Answer: B

You can use Remote Web Workplace or the TS client to remote into the SBS Server. In the Server Management Console, under the Users link, you have a link to Offer Remote Assistance. Answer A. Even though this would work, the employee is having e-mail trouble and couldn't send you an invitation. Answer C. The "Download Connection Manager" sets up client workstations with VPN connections and would not help in this situation. Answer D. Get real, this is a Microsoft Exam and third-party tools don't exist.

Question #77: Answer: C

Only the Wednesday information is lost, the server can be restored with last Friday's full backup and Tuesday's differential backup. Okay, here is the refresher on differential vs. incremental. Or better yet, go to TechNet and search for: "How Backup Works – Core

Operating Systems – Windows Server 2003." This will give you the low-down on the NTBackup Utility and prep you with all there is to know for the 70-282 Exam.

Question #78: Answer: C

Configuring to receive the fax in SharePoint would be the answer. That would be the most convenient and efficient way, and no paper would be used in the future and the report can't get lost. The fax will display with caller ID, number of pages, time received and size of the message file. Answer A. Viewing the fax over a mapped drive is just not as pretty as in SharePoint. Answer B. That would create tons of paper and why aren't they using a network printer? Answer D. That is not an option.

Question #79: Answer: C, D

You should run the My Document redirect wizard which can be found in the Server Management console under the "Backup" and under "Users" links. You then must enable VSS manually on that volume because SBS will only enable shadow copies on the volume where the Users Shared folders are located. In our case, they are part of the default installation and located on Volume one, whereas the Data folder resides on Volume three. Answer A. You can only set VSS on a Volume, not a folder. Answer B. This GPO setting will not give the option to select a folder or share to point to.

Question #80: Answer: B

Selecting the connection speed at the Remote Web Workplace logon screen will make the most efficient use of the connection. Answer A. This just places you at the logon portal and does not affect connection speed. Answer C. The Download Connection Manager downloads a shortcut VPN connection to the client desktop. Answer D. This will allow the SBS server to place a session cookie on the computer, which has nothing to do with the connection speed.

Question #81: Answer: 2, 3, 4

Answer 1 is not correct because Active Directory-integrated zones are read/write and pose security risks in screened subnets.

Question #82: Answer: 2, 4

The IT organization is centralized. All IT administration and resources are centrally located.

Question #83: Answer: 1

L2TP is a tunneling protocol, not an authorizing or authenticating mechanism. Only Answer #1 includes all the features that will allow authorization and authentication.

Question #84: Answer: 1,2,3,4

Group Policy Objects can be used to richly configure a user's environment including selectively assigning and publishing applications to desktops, managing security settings to define a security configuration, folder redirection and assigning scripts to run when the computer starts or shuts down or the user logs on or off.

Question #85: Answer: 1, 2

Active Directory uses the most efficient network connections by occasionally re-evaluating which connections are used, and by using multiple routes to replicate changes, it provides fault tolerance. Replications costs are minimized by only replicating changed information and not replicating all information on each DC.

Question #86: Answer: C

The ASR backup wizard only backs up Windows file-protected files (WFP), system state and system services, and minimal system files. When you do an ASR restore, ASR will reformat the C drive in the process. It will restore the system files, system state and WFP files, but if you had any other files on the C:\ drive, they will not be restored. Therefore, it is important to do additional backups and only ASR as part of your disaster recovery plan. Answer A. The ASR floppy point to the location where the backup media is located. If the ASR floppy would have been corrupt, the restore would have failed. Answer B. The ASR wizard works with external tape drives, some USB drives and over a network share. Answer D. You must hit the F2 key during the text mode installation process in order to initiate the ASR restore. If you do not hit the F2 key, it would have never restored the domain controller.

Question #87: Answer: D

You must use the SUS administration page (http://localhost/susadmin) to approve updates by selecting the updates and then clicking Approve. You can set up internal distribution points (in this case SERV2) for the downloaded updates. But even if all clients to SERV3, which is SERV2 and all client computers, are set to receive automatic updates, updates first must be approved before SERV2 will make them available to the clients.

Question #88: Answer: B

You should use the RSoP MMC snap-in (Resultant Set of Policies) to view how the GPO will affect the OUs. RSoP is a new feature in Windows domain controller 2003. You can run RSoP in two modes, either logging or planning. In this case you would use the planning mode to see the effects of a GPO before deployment. The logging mode enables you to view current GPO settings on a specific object in Active Directory. Answer A. The gpresult command line utility will give the same results as RSoP in logging mode. Answer C. This command is used to check for replication link failure between replication partners. Answer D. The replmon command line utility is used to manage replication between domain controllers.

Question #89: Answer: D

To delegate a zone, you must run the New Delegation wizard in the DNS console by right-clicking on the zone to be delegated. The zone corp. sbs.gadgets.com is a delegated zone of gadgets.com. Answer A. Setting forwarders to point to DNS3 will achieve the same result except that delegation takes precedence over forwarding and then it wouldn't be delegation, now would it? Answer B and C. The A and NS record will automatically be created by the New delegation wizard, again requiring less administrative effort.

Question #90: Answer: C

Encrypted File System (EFS) can be used to secure data on NTFS. After you encrypt a file, you can go to the files property sheet, General tab and click Advanced, Details and then Add and add the users that should have access to the file. Answer A and B. NTFS and share permissions do not provide this level of security. Even if the NTFS permissions were set to Full Control for Everyone, EFS will still protect the data. Answer D. IPSec is used for encrypting data that is sent over network connections.

Question #91: Answer: A

System Monitor would be the best way to identify the cause. There are about 60 DNS-related counters (too many to list here), including TCP and UDP, WINS, Zone transfers, Queries, Dynamic updates and memory counters. You can get to the Performance monitor by going to Start, Run and typing *perfmon.msc*. Right-click in the graph windows and click Add Counters. None of the other tools, even though very useful for troubleshooting, will allow for this granularity of monitoring.

Question #92: Answer: D

First you would want to do a non-authoritative restore of the last full backup; this way, you will not lose the new user accounts added on Wednesday. When a restore is non-authoritative, it will be overwritten when replication occurs. Because we don't want this to happen, you use the Ntdsutil and mark the deleted OU and its contents as authoritative. When you start the domain controller and replication occurs, the OU being marked as authoritative (has a higher USN) will replicate and overwrite the information on other domain controllers. All other objects that were not marked as authoritative will be overwritten by the synchronization information from the other servers (because the USN is lower) during normal replication. The new user accounts will remain in Active Directory this way. In order to undertake this entire operation, you will have to boot one domain controller into Directory Services restore mode (Active directory will not be initialized and the server will act as a stand-alone server). You restore the system state and use Ntdsutil.exe, configure what is authoritative and what is not, and then reboot the server, which will then go about its synchronization business. Answer A. Nah, don't do that. You will just end up working somewhere else and doing the same thing. So you may as well just grin and bear it. Answer B. A deleted OU cannot be marked authoritative unless it was first restored in a non-authoritative system state restore Answer C. That only gets us halfway there—the OU would not be restored. Answer E. This way you would get the OU back and lose the new user accounts.

Question #93: Answer: C

The host disk must be formatted with NTFS. The new volume must be empty. Answer A. Diskpart is used to create or delete partitions on a hard drive. Answer B and D. It doesn't matter if the new disk is a basic or dynamic NTFS volume.

Question #94: Answer: B

The GC is required for authentication. Only members of the Domain Administrators group are allowed to log on to the domain if the GC failed. An exception to this rule is that if a user has logged on previously, the logon will be successful because of the user's cached credentials. If this would be the first time a user logs on, the user would not be able to log on to the domain.

Question #95: Answer: B, C

L2TP and IPSec will give you the highest level of authentication and encryption. L2TP provides tunneling between the remote laptop and the server. IPSec uses Transport and Tunnel mode, encrypting the payload of the IP packet in transport mode and encrypts the header and payload of the IP packet in tunnel mode. Answer A. PPTP does not provide the security that L2TP provides. Answer D. PEAP (Protected Extensible Authentication Protocol) is currently used for securing wireless LANS and will not be available for VPN until the release of Longhorn.

Question #96: Answer: 1, 3, 4

GPOs are per domain and cannot be inherited across domains. Multiple GPOs can be associated with a single site, domain, and organizational unit, and vice-versa.

Question #97: Answer: 1, 3, 6

Only alphabet letters, A-Z, a-z, numbers 0-9, and the hyphen are allowed characters in a domain name.

Question #98: Answer: 2

Microsoft CRM SBE 3.0 requires the most robust database offered by Microsoft: SQL Server 2005.

Question #99: Answer: 3

As a rule of thumb, ISA Server 2004 should be backed up every time there is a firewall policy change, administrative rights are delegated or delegation is removed, a system rule changes or the cache size or location changes.

Question #100: Answer: 1,2,4

All three ISA Server 2004 client types support user-level authentication, the ISA Server 2004 clients are the Secure NAT client, Firewall client and Web Proxy client.

Question #101: Answer: B, C

You want to create a distribution group since this is just for the purpose of distributing e-mail to the members of the group. The two new hire user accounts belong in this group since they are the only ones to receive faxes. Then run the Configure Fax Services wizard and select "Use the Route through e-mail routing method" and add the distribution group name as the recipient (Faxpersonnel@ mycompany.com). Answer A. A security group is not needed since this requires a group for distribution only and user accounts have already been created so the new hires can log on to the domain. Answer D. There is no such option.

Question #102: Answer: B,E

The CEICW will automatically configure the ports on the UPnP firewall device for you. Any additional services should be added in under the Services Configuration screen in the CEICW, and the CEICW will configure SBS and your UPnP device appropriately. Answer A. Would work but also opens additional unused ports and would create more of an administrative burden. Answer C. That would not work. Answer D. That adds a certificate, will not configure the router. Answer F. The server itself would still block port 4008, so use the CEICW.

Question #103: Answer: C

Select the GPO to "set a time limit for disconnected sessions" in Computer Configuration\Administrative Templates\Windows Component\Terminal Services\Sessions to automatically log off a disconnected session after the time of your choice. SBS Remote Desktop allows only two sessions at a time. If users disconnect, the session continues to run indefinitely. Answer A. You cannot install Terminal Services on an SBS server. Answer B. Adding additional user accounts will not fix the disconnect issue. Answer D. Setting "Allow Automatic Reconnection" will reconnect a disconnected session, but not fix the issue.

Question #104: Answer: C

The Import File Wizard allows importing files and folders into a document library from a network drive. Answer A. That would be a mess and would take a huge administrative effort to fix. Answer B. There is no SharePoint migration tool. Answer D. The stsmigrate.exe tool is a command line tool used to migrate existing SharePoint sites to a different server and could not be used in this scenario.

Question #105: Answer: C

You can install up to four modems into the SBS server that will support simultaneous faxing. Since the one modem currently is not handling the load, and the load will double in a short period of time, you should install at least two additional modems and may end up adding a third modem to a total of four, based on the volume later on. Answer A. Purchasing a stand-alone Fax machine could be more expensive and would change the way users manage faxes, which they now send and receive from their desktop. Answer B. This could also be more costly in the long-term and would require users to be trained on the Internet faxing software. Answer D. One additional fax modem (bringing the total to two) would not be able to manage the anticipated fax load.

Question #106: Answer: C, E

Being a member of the Contributor Group allows users to discuss, edit, add and delete items in the list and view document libraries. The appropriate SBS way to change permissions on existing user accounts is by using the Change Permission Wizard. Answer A. The distribution list is an Exchange group that would not affect SharePoint access. Answer B. Readers can view the list and document libraries, but not discuss, add, edit or delete items. Answer D. Power users will automatically be added to the Administrator site group and would be able to create and modify lists, which is an option that should not be available to contractors in this scenario. Answer F and G. You cannot manage site group membership in Active Directory; you can manage site groups either in the HTML Administration pages or the command line administration tool.

Question #107: Answer: C

This answer does it all, with the least amount of effort. Also, by placing the office files in the client apps folder and adding those to assigned applications will make this install available for future use without any additional steps required. Answer A. This answer works, but requires more administrative effort. Answer B. Only shares, but does not install the application. Answer D. Again, would require more administrative effort.

Question #108: Answer: A

What a beautiful thing! A no-brainer. Set the PocketPC in its cradle, and sync with Exchange. This will transfer the certificate AND configure the server settings on the PocketPC. Remove from cradle and move on with your life. Answer B. Do not set it to sync with the local computer; it must sync with the Exchange server. Answer C. No. Answer D. No.

Question #109: Answer: C

It only requires one POP3 connector in SBS, and it will handle the distribution of all downloaded e-mail to all mail box-enabled user accounts. By default it downloads e-mail once every hour but you can set it to 15 minutes increments. Answer A. The POP3 connector; is installed during the SBS Installation Setup. POP3 is an e-mail retrieval method and can not push mail out. Answer B. There is only ONE POP3 connector, it will distribute all POP3 mail to the appropriate Exchange mail boxes. Answer D. This doesn't work; the POP3 connector needs to have Exchange to distribute e-mail into mail boxes. Also, this would not allow for calendar sharing or Outlook Web Access.

Question #110: Answer: B, F

You can select to create a self-signed SSL certificate in the Web Server Certificate screen in the CEICW. This will require you to type in the full Internet name of the server. The certificate, SBScert.cer will be placed in the Clientapps\SBSCert folder so it can be deployed to client computers by the Client Setup Wizard. You must also run the CEICW and select Outlook Mobile Access to configure the server. Answer A. This would not be the most cost-efficient manner since you can create your own certificate in the CEICW. Answer C and D. This would not fit the "least amount of effort" objective of the SBS methodology. Answer E. That again would have required purchasing a commercial certificate, which is not cost effective. Answer G. When will you learn to just do things using the wizard?

Index

A-126

Microsoft Small Business Specialist Primer
& 70-282 Exam Preparation Guide!

SMTP (Simple Mail Transfer Protocol)
5-23, 5-25, 6-6, 6-45, 6-46, 6-48, 7-6,
7-9, 7-26, 7-30, 7-38, 7-39, 7-41, 8-46,
8-58, 9-9, 10-18
SNMP (Simple Network Management
Protocol) 6-30, 6-45, 6-48, 7-18, 7-19,
7-38, 7-41, 7-43, 10-61, 15-25
Software Assurance 7-25, 15-15
SP2 (Service Pack 2) 4-8, 9-18, 9-19,
14-8, 14-10, 14-13
Spam 8-45, 15-9, 15-21
Split-DNS 11-2, 11-3
SQL Server 2000 4-8, 5-11, 7-22, 9-12,
9-13, 9-41, 9-46, 11-19, 11-33
SSL (Secure Socket Layer) 1-5, 6-2, 7-8,
7-28, 8-50, 9-43, 9-44, 11-16, 11-17,
11-32, 13-11, 13-12, 13-32
Standalone 3-12, 3-20, 11-1, 11-20, 11-
29, 11-31, 11-33, 15-9
STSADMIN 12-9, 13-12
SUS (Software Update Services) 6-28,
6-31, 6-32, 6-33, 6-34, 8-11, 8-30, 8-31

T

TCP/IP 3-13, 6-10, 6-30, 6-37, 6-40, 7-
17, 8-33, 9-5, 9-22, 9-39, 9-40, 9-44,
9-45, 10-18, 10-29, 10-30, 10-31, 10-
33, 10-37, 11-4, 11-5
TelNet 7-6
Terminal services (TS) 6-20, 6-45, 6-50,
7-38, 7-41, 7-42, 9-23, 9-37, 9-38, 9-
41, 9-43, 9-44, 9-47
Threshold 8-46, 10-60, 12-23, 12-28,
12-34
Timer 11-23, 12-7, 12-12, 12-29
Topology 1-5, 4-17, 10-17, 10-18, 11-31,
12-5, 12-8
Total cost of ownership 3-7

Total cost of ownership 3-8, 5-1
Trace 8-51, 10-60, 12-23, 12-24
Tri-homed 11-27
Trigger 10-45, 10-61, 12-31, 12-32
TSCC (Terminal Services Connection
Configuration) 9-26

U

UDP (User Datagram Protocol) 6-37,
6-45, 7-38, 9-29, 10-33
UNC (Universal Naming Code) 5-24, 8-
21, 12-12, 12-13
UPnP 4-7, 6-45, 7-4, 7-16, 7-33, 7-38
UPS (Uninterruptable Power Supply) 5-7,
5-8, 5-22, 6-45, 7-38, 10-4, 10-28
USB 4-13, 6-30, 8-6, 8-9, 8-47, 8-48,
10-74
User Templates 6-4, 6-15, 6-16, 6-17,
6-18, 7-20, 8-7

V

Value Added Reseller (VAR) 2-14
Virtual PC 4-8, 6-14, 10-10, 14-15
Virtual Private Network *see also VPN*
3-11, 11-31
Virus protection 5-27
VoIP 6-1
VPN *see also Virtual Private Network*
3-11, 4-4, 6-17, 7-6, 7-12, 8-24, 8-26,
8-27, 8-45, 8-60, 9-9, 9-36, 9-37, 9-43,
10-40, 10-41, 10-42, 10-43, 11-4, 11-27
VSS (Volume Shadow Service) 4-8, 4-
25, 8-6, 8-37, 8-54, 8-59

W

WAN (Wide Area Network) 6-43, 7-12,
7-36, 9-11

X

Z